Praise for *A First Look at SQL Se*

C000148614

"If you want to be the best at developin
2005, you need to read this book. This book is the Rosetta Stone of
SQL Server programming."

—Eric Brown
SQL Server Program Manager
Microsoft Corporation

"I'm glad to see that users will have a great book on SQL Server 2005
with great ADO.NET 2.0 coverage available right when the product
hits the streets."

—Pablo Castro
Program Manager, ADO.NET Team
Microsoft Corporation

"An excellent book for people who want to delve deep into the newest
features of SQL Server and understand the vision behind the
design. Being close to the development process from early stages,
the authors were able to obtain unique knowledge about the product
and they are passing it on to you."

—Alexander Vaschillo
Microsoft Product Manager
Father of the three-part data model mapping
Microsoft Corporation

"This book clearly explains the complex semantics behind Object
Spaces API in an intuitive way."

—Dinesh Kulkarni
Microsoft Product Manager, ObjectSpaces
Microsoft Corporation

A First Look at
SQL Server 2005
for Developers

Microsoft .NET Development Series

John Montgomery, *Series Advisor*
Don Box, *Series Advisor*
Martin Heller, *Series Editor*

The **Microsoft .NET Development Series** is supported and developed by the leaders and experts of Microsoft development technologies including Microsoft architects and DevelopMentor instructors. The books in this series provide a core resource of information and understanding every developer needs in order to write effective applications and managed code. Learn from the leaders how to maximize your use of the .NET Framework and its programming languages.

Titles in the Series

Brad Abrams, *.NET Framework Standard Library Annotated Reference, Volume 1*, 0-321-15489-4

Keith Ballinger, *.NET Web Services: Architecture and Implementation*, 0-321-11359-4

Bob Beauchemin, Niels Berglund, Dan Sullivan, *A First Look at SQL Server 2005 for Developers*, 0-321-18059-3

Don Box with Chris Sells, *Essential .NET, Volume 1: The Common Language Runtime*, 0-201-73411-7

Mahesh Chand, *Graphics Programming with GDI+*, 0-321-16077-0

Anders Hejlsberg, Scott Wiltamuth, Peter Golde, *The C# Programming Language*, 0-321-15491-6

Alex Homer, Dave Sussman, Mark Fussell, *A First Look at ADO.NET and System.Xml v. 2.0*, 0-321-22839-1

Alex Homer, Dave Sussman, Rob Howard, *A First Look at ASP.NET v. 2.0*, 0-321-22896-0

James S. Miller and Susann Ragsdale, *The Common Language Infrastructure Annotated Standard*, 0-321-15493-2

Fritz Onion, *Essential ASP.NET with Examples in C#*, 0-201-76040-1

Fritz Onion, *Essential ASP.NET with Examples in Visual Basic .NET*, 0-201-76039-8

Ted Pattison and Dr. Joe Hummel, *Building Applications and Components with Visual Basic .NET*, 0-201-73495-8

Chris Sells, *Windows Forms Programming in C#*, 0-321-11620-8

Chris Sells and Justin Gehtland, *Windows Forms Programming in Visual Basic .NET*, 0-321-12519-3

Paul Vick, *The Visual Basic .NET Programming Language*, 0-321-16951-4

Damien Watkins, Mark Hammond, Brad Abrams, *Programming in the .NET Environment*, 0-201-77018-0

Shawn Wildermuth, *Pragmatic ADO.NET: Data Access for the Internet World*, 0-201-74568-2

Paul Yao and David Durant, *.NET Compact Framework Programming with C#*, 0-321-17403-8

Paul Yao and David Durant, *.NET Compact Framework Programming with Visual Basic .NET*, 0-321-17404-6

For more information go to www.awprofessional.com/msdotnetseries/

A First Look at SQL Server 2005 for Developers

Bob Beauchemin
Niels Berglund
Dan Sullivan

✦✦Addison-Wesley

Boston • San Francisco • New York • Toronto • Montreal

London • Munich • Paris • Madrid

Capetown • Sydney • Tokyo • Singapore • Mexico City

Library of Congress Control Number:
2004107765

Copyright © 2004 by Pearson Education, Inc.

Pearson Education, Inc.
Rights and Contracts Department
75 Arlington Street, Suite 300
Boston, MA 02116
Fax: (617) 848-7047

ISBN: 0-321-18059-3
Text printed on recycled paper
2 3 4 5 6 7 8 9 10 11—CRS—0807060504
Second printing, September 2004

Contents

2005 development team mobilized around the idea of embracing and extending .NET in powerful ways. As a result, SQL Server 2005 is going to bring .NET into the grasp of the database developer. Middle-tier programmers are going crazy over powerful new features like cache invalidation and ObjectSpaces.

In short, the boundaries between database and middle tier have blurred, and these fiefdoms are being invaded. Developers are wearing lots of hats these days. They need to understand core relational database fundamentals, but they need to know how to write managed code and how to deal with things like XML and Web Services. So when we were trying to decide who we should partner with to get developers up to speed, the choice was clear.

Bob, Dan, and Niels wound their way through the maze of developers and program managers known as the SQL Server development team. Through trial and error and sheer determination, they explored some of the most esoteric aspects of SQL Server 2005 and figured out how to apply these capabilities in practical ways. After all of this painstaking R&D, they took the show on the road for us, delivering a rock-solid DevelopMentor class known as "Essential SQL Server 2005 for Developers" to a worldwide audience.

We used this class to train the Microsoft field technical personnel and many of our top customers and partners in Yukon Ascend. It's been a long time since I've heard the kind of positive feedback we received from this class, and I know that it's due to the deep knowledge, experience, and understanding that Bob, Dan, and Niels bring to the table. I know that you will find this book an enlightening and worthwhile read.

Roger Doherty
SQL Server Technical Evangelist, Platform Strategy and Partner Group
Microsoft Corporation

Foreword

Roger Wolter

MY FIRST JOB with Microsoft was in the COM+ group. One day I was having a problem getting an OLE DB sample program I was writing to work, and I asked someone who I should talk to about OLE DB. They said Bob Beauchemin. I asked, "Isn't there someone on the MDAC team I should talk to first?" and they replied, "The MDAC guys know about parts of OLE DB, but Bob knows it all." I think that after reading the book that Bob, Dan, and Niels have put together, you'll agree—Bob still knows it all.

SQL Server 2005 is the biggest release from a feature content point of view that the SQL Server team has ever done. Some may argue that the major rewrite in SQL Server 7 was more significant, but the feature content in SQL Server 2005 is larger than in any previous release. Given this, it may seem like hubris to write a book about all of SQL Server 2005, but I think this book is clear evidence that it's possible. This book doesn't cover every new feature in SQL Server 2005, but it describes the most significant ones in enough detail to be useful to anyone who needs to get up to speed on what SQL Server 2005 has to offer.

This book is also extremely well researched. The Service Broker chapter, for example, started with a two-hour conversation with me in a Starbucks in downtown Seattle, extended through many long e-mail threads, and went through a half-dozen different reviews before it ended up in the book. In addition to the research, the material in this book was used in an "Introduction to Yukon" class that has been presented to hundreds of students all over the world, so only the topics these students found most relevant have survived.

The first major section of the book deals with the most significant new feature in SQL Server 2005—the new programming model provided by the CLR engine deeply embedded into the SQL Server engine. This feature means stored procedures, triggers, and so on can be written in most .NET languages. I can't wait to see the first COBOL stored procedure running in SQL Server. As we have come to expect from DevelopMentor authors, these chapters are replete with well-documented code samples. Although this section was written with the database developer in mind, it will also be very useful to the DBA who has to deploy and manage CLR code in the database. After the CLR chapters, there is a chapter on the new security features that make SQL Server 2005 more secure and easier to configure with the exact permissions each user needs. The final chapter in this section covers the feature enhancements designed to make the T-SQL programmer's life easier and more productive. The highlights here are the RANK and PIVOT commands, recursive query support, and snapshot isolation. All these features have been near the top of the SQL Server wish list for several years.

The next section covers the improvements to XML integration into the database that are included in SQL Server 2005. The evolution from the XML-relational mapping technology introduced in SQL Server 2000 to the native XML data type functionality in SQL Server 2005 is presented clearly, and includes an explanation of the strengths and weaknesses of each approach and when to use each technology. The XQuery chapter is an excellent tutorial on the powerful new query language for XML data introduced in SQL Server 2005. This section concludes with coverage of the new HTTP/SOAP interface that makes it easy to expose your SQL Server 2005 stored procedures and functions as SOAP methods directly from the database without requiring a Web server.

The third part of the book moves from the server features to the new client-side features included in the Visual Studio release that accompanies SQL Server 2005. The first chapter emphasizes the client changes necessary to expose the new server features, like the XML data type and CLR user-defined types. There is also a good presentation of how to decide when to implement a function as a CLR stored procedure and when to implement it as client or middle-tier logic. This decision is much less clear-cut now that CLR code can run equally well in the server and in the client, and this section gives you the information you need to make that decision. There is also excellent coverage of the new client-side XML features available in this release. Many of the most requested features from SQLXML users are included.

Last but certainly not least, from my point of view, is excellent coverage of the SQL Server Service Broker. I spent quite a bit of time with Bob, Niels, and Dan indoctrinating them into the "Zen of Service Broker," and they put together an excellent explanation of how the Service Broker revolutionizes the way users will write database applications in the future. The power of queues as first-class database objects is presented very effectively.

This brief summary doesn't do justice to the broad coverage of all the new features included in this book. If you plan to design, implement, deploy, or support applications on SQL Server 2005, this is the book for you to start with. The clear explanations and examples will help you quickly master the most comprehensive SQL Server release ever.

Roger Wolter
Program Manager, SQL Server
Microsoft Corporation

Foreword
Andy Gammuto

AROUND THE TIME Microsoft SQL Server Yukon went into alpha, I was asked to take on the responsibility of program manager for Yukon evangelism. Among the many decisions to make and challenges to overcome, perhaps the greatest was finding a credible way to prove to developers that this newest release of SQL Server was worthy of their time and interest. After ten years at Microsoft, I knew that the key to achieving this lofty goal was to assemble the right team. I was fortunate to be joined by Don Petersen and Roger Doherty, both capable Microsoft veterans I had worked with before.

Microsoft SQL Server 2005 represents a major evolution of the product. The range of new capabilities makes it a very compelling and feature-rich release. While offering world-class capabilities in terms of management, performance, and reliability, it helps developers and database administrators simplify and reduce the effort involved in creating, managing, and deploying database applications. At the same time, it delivers economy without sacrificing anything. The tough part was figuring out how to prove this to the developer community.

As a former code slinger, I know that developers are skeptical by nature—particularly about claims about new and improved products. More importantly, they thrive on their curiosity—diving into products and technologies that interest them. They live to figure out how products like SQL Server work, and develop expertise that often rivals the people who wrote it.

We decided to reach out to developers early and build a program that delivered a hard-core drill-down on SQL Server Yukon beta 1 to prove how good it is. The experience had to be something worthy of their valuable time and worthy of taking them from their demanding schedules. We wanted to deliver five-day instructor-led training workshops and follow-on labs that were so content-rich they would make your head hurt. It was an ambitious plan. Our predicament was that outside of the SQL Server development teams who were working on the product, only a handful of experts at this early stage of Yukon's development were capable of creating and delivering this sort of training worldwide. Our search ended with DevelopMentor, and this is how I came to know Bob Beauchemin, Dan Sullivan, and Niels Berglund.

I admit to being cynical at first about our ability to accomplish the very high goals we set for our program. Developer training was one of the building blocks of our plan. If it wasn't high quality, we were doomed to mediocrity at best. We put our own reputations on the line and in many ways our faith in the skills of Bob, Dan, and Niels. The results from the first phase of our SQL Server Yukon evangelism program, which we called "Ascend," were remarkable. After observing the training workshops firsthand, I can honestly say these three guys are among the best I've seen. They are eerily consistent not only in their deep technical knowledge but also in their skill as trainers. It is almost as if some kind of mind meld has occurred between them. There was an astonishing energy in our Ascend training workshops. This is what happens when you combine smart developers with plugged-in trainers, working together to explore the inner workings of a cool new product.

Bob was the first to tell me that he and his colleagues were writing a book about SQL Server 2005. Naturally, I was thrilled with the idea, but it wasn't until after I met and spent some time with Dan and Niels that I realized how much of their combined knowledge and experience could be packed into this book. By virtue of what they do, trainers gain insight into product behaviors and experientially figure out what is happening. They get the most puzzling questions from their students and learn how to explain things clearly. There is no substitute for that kind of experience, and drawing from that makes for a great book.

It is evident that Microsoft SQL Server is a labor of love for the authors of this book. There is much to discover in SQL Server 2005, and I feel certain you will find value in this book as your introduction to exploring the product and as a useful guide for developers who are architecting and building their next-generation .NET applications.

Andy Gammuto
Program Manager, Yukon Evangelism
Microsoft Corporation

Foreword
Roger Doherty

I BET MY CAREER on SQL Server many years ago, when I joined Microsoft from Sybase in 1991. Over the years, I've watched SQL Server grow and change from a "departmental client/server database" running on OS/2 written by a small team of developers, to the rich enterprise database and development platform that it is today. In June 2003, I joined a team responsible for driving Microsoft's global developer evangelism initiative for SQL Server 2005, known as "Yukon Ascend."

Back in 1991, there was a small group of people at Microsoft who could speak that bizarre foreign tongue known as "SQL." It was always fun seeing e-mails come across the wire, where someone asked for technical help on "Sequel Server," or asking, "When will SQL Server incorporate FoxPro's Rushmore technology?" I took pleasure in seeing C++ programmers being confounded by simple join syntax. Databases in general were a mystery, a black art.

Things couldn't be more different today. It's been fun watching Microsoft try to figure out where this technology fits and how to integrate it with our operating systems, development tools, and applications. The development team is enormous, with literally thousands of developers and testers solving incredibly hard problems. The product is big; it's not just a relational database anymore. There are so many powerful integrated capabilities that it's difficult to keep track of them sometimes.

It's hard to overstate the impact of .NET on the SQL Server landscape. All things new and exciting seemed to be the domain of .NET, and poor old SQL Server was relegated to being "just a database." The SQL Server

2005 development team mobilized around the idea of embracing and extending .NET in powerful ways. As a result, SQL Server 2005 is going to bring .NET into the grasp of the database developer. Middle-tier programmers are going crazy over powerful new features like cache invalidation and ObjectSpaces.

In short, the boundaries between database and middle tier have blurred, and these fiefdoms are being invaded. Developers are wearing lots of hats these days. They need to understand core relational database fundamentals, but they need to know how to write managed code and how to deal with things like XML and Web Services. So when we were trying to decide who we should partner with to get developers up to speed, the choice was clear.

Bob, Dan, and Niels wound their way through the maze of developers and program managers known as the SQL Server development team. Through trial and error and sheer determination, they explored some of the most esoteric aspects of SQL Server 2005 and figured out how to apply these capabilities in practical ways. After all of this painstaking R&D, they took the show on the road for us, delivering a rock-solid DevelopMentor class known as "Essential SQL Server 2005 for Developers" to a worldwide audience.

We used this class to train the Microsoft field technical personnel and many of our top customers and partners in Yukon Ascend. It's been a long time since I've heard the kind of positive feedback we received from this class, and I know that it's due to the deep knowledge, experience, and understanding that Bob, Dan, and Niels bring to the table. I know that you will find this book an enlightening and worthwhile read.

Roger Doherty
SQL Server Technical Evangelist, Platform Strategy and Partner Group
Microsoft Corporation

About the Authors

BOB BEAUCHEMIN is an instructor, course author, and database curriculum course liaison for DevelopMentor. He has over 25 years' experience as an architect, programmer, and administrator for data-centric distributed systems. He's written articles on ADO.NET, OLE DB, and SQL Server for *Microsoft Systems Journal, SQL Server Magazine,* and others, and is the author of the book *Essential ADO.NET.*

NIELS BERGLUND is a member of DevelopMentor's technical research, curriculum development, and teaching staff in the UK. He specializes in the .NET system software and database areas and is co-author of several of DevelopMentor's database courses. Niels speaks regularly about .NET and database technologies at various industry conferences worldwide.

DAN SULLIVAN'S work in the computer industry has stretched from hardware development, such as design of audio processing systems and Digital Equipment's PDP-11 computers, to software development for manufacturing automation and image processing products driven by databases. Dan has worked with many operating systems, including first versions of DOS, Windows, and NT. He has worked with SQL Server since it was first distributed by Microsoft and ran on OS2. Dan has been a speaker at .NET user groups and WinDev. His articles have appeared in *MSDN Magazine* and *SQL Server Magazine.* He has written courses used by DevelopMentor and also does instruction for them. His present interests include .NET, SQL Server, XML, and Web Services. Dan has his own consulting company and can be reached at dsullivan@danal.com.

Preface

AFTER MY LAST BOOK, *Essential ADO.NET*, was handed in to the publisher ten days before .NET 1.0 shipped, I swore I'd never write another. To keep up with a technology while it was developing and the product features were being refined on an almost daily basis was too big an energy sink. Then, less than a year later, I caught wind of a new version of SQL Server, code-named Yukon. As with each version of SQL Server before it, since Microsoft's original 4.21 offering, there were lots of features for DBAs—high-availability features, tuning features, scalability features, and so on. A new, fast-growing field called *business intelligence* was being developed, and SQL Server was on the cusp of this. The features in this business intelligence area of Yukon were truly astounding. But the biggest changes that caught my eye were those in the developer area. I was hooked.

Transact-SQL has served us developers well all these years and continues to work quite well, thank you. This book lists the enhancements to this procedural dialect of SQL, and that chapter ended up to be much longer (because of the number of enhancements) than I originally thought. In the last few years, I'd been spending a lot of time in the XML space and done a lot of thinking about the differences and similarities between the XML and relational models. I liked the formal W3C standardization process for XML, slow as it seems at times. I started to investigate the ANSI SQL standards in earnest, though I'd read them before, and realized that SQL has a rich and deep foundation, starting with SQL-86 and up to the last mainstream standard, SQL-92, and past that to SQL:1999. But in 2002 there were specifications in progress to define how XML would be integrated into a relational database. There was a synergy with the XML work I'd been doing lately. I heard there would be XML functionality in Yukon, including an XML data type, XML schema validation, and an implementation of the emerging standard query language for XML, XQuery.

In addition, beginning with the object-oriented graphical user interface on the NeXT computer, I'd spent a lot of the last ten years using object-oriented techniques. And Yukon promised to integrate the .NET runtime into the database engine itself. Not that SQL Server internals were to be written in .NET, but that .NET would be directly accessible as a language for stored procedures and user-defined functions. I could use object-oriented programming techniques with my database programming as well. This might be a big assist to the procedural programming in T-SQL I was already doing, in those cases where I needed it. I'd read about using object-oriented languages in the ANSI SQL specifications. Finally, there was the rumor that .NET classes might be available in SQL Server as types that the server knew about. I'd read the ANSI spec for that too. I just *had* to see this product.

So we had been working on writing this book since late 2002 when I met with Eric Brown in Redmond, Washington, and we got the OK and the software. Since 2002 we'd badgered the SQL Server and Webdata teams with copious questions about not only how the software worked but why it was designed that way. They were very understanding about our persistence, but sometimes I felt that I was being a bit of a pest. When we started to teach the class in earnest, we tried to pay them back with information about how software vendors and others thought the features would be useful. At that time, Niels and I were writing, and Dan was reviewing and making suggestions; however, Dan got hooked too. We almost published in the beta 1 time frame, but held back. There were too many major enhancements to the way things actually worked, and we'd written about how things worked too early. Readers would think things worked the old way instead of the improved way. And there were more enhancements coming in beta 2. We held off writing and went for another revision. We were permitted, however, to write and teach a class to early adopters, based on the current state of our work and of the product. I think we've taught about 400 to 500 students as of this writing. The product evolved. More revisions. I'd told Mary that I was "almost done" so many times that she shook her head and laughed when I mentioned I might really be done again five minutes ago. It's certainly possible that some of the features or the implementation of them could change between now and when SQL Server 2005 ships. We'll try to keep you up to date with all the changes, update the book's code examples, and post some additional samples on the book's Web site. Look for pointers to the code and updates at the following locations:

- http://staff.develop.com/bobb
- http://www.danal.com
- http://staff.develop.com/nielsb

Yukon has all the stuff that I'd read about and more. At a SQL*PASS conference, I ran into Roger Wolter, a friend from the SQL Server team. We'd originally met when I was speaking at a Web Services conference on SQLXML Web Services in SQL Server 2000 Web Release 3. Little did I know that Roger, the "owner" of this feature, was in the audience. He said he liked the talk; I was relieved. When we met again at SQL*PASS, I asked Roger about Web Services in Yukon, and he told me about his latest project, called SQL Server Service Broker. It sounded to me like an implementation of a Web Service–like concept built over the robustness of a queuing system, built on top of the robustness of a database. Otherwise, his recollection of the meeting is about the same as mine. I was further intrigued.

So far I've mentioned Service Broker, Transact-SQL enhancements, security, .NET-based procedures, functions and user-defined types, built-in XML data type and queries, and Web Services. What else could there possibly be for developers? Most developers spend the greatest percentage of their time not in SQL Server Management Studio, but in Visual Studio 2005, writing the client front end. Many developers know the database engine and how to get the most out of it as well as race car drivers know how to get that last bit of speed out of their cars. Developers and application designers, as well as DBAs, must know how the new features work. In the case of snapshot isolation (versioning) or the XML data type, it could drastically affect how they design and write the application. With Service Broker, it opens a whole new raft of scalability choices that simply weren't there before. The last part of this book talks about client and application server features enabled either inside or outside SQL Server itself. The enabling technologies outside the database are ADO.NET's SqlClient and the client-side XML stack featuring its own XQuery engine. Client-side XQuery works against XML documents on the file system, against SQL Server, or both at the same time.

Finally, there are those developers who would rather not know that the database exists at all. They deal in objects and would just like to call "Load" and "Save" on their object model and have it taken care of. They're more interested in their business or application domain than in how to create a distributed partitioned view to spread the Customer table over multiple SQL Server instances. They see only Customer instances and collections. For these folks, ObjectSpaces and Microsoft Business Framework are what float their boat in this release. In addition to being able to persist their instances, they want "Load" and "Save" to take nanoseconds. ObjectSpaces was designed with optimization in mind.

In conclusion, I think there's quite a bit in Yukon for just about every developer, DBA, application designer, business analyst, and data miner. I've read in some trade publications that the new features just aren't that interesting; they're more like a recitation of glitzy acronyms than substance. This may be the initial perception, but let's rewind to mid-1981. I'm working for an insurance company in Seattle, and we're planning to convert our indexed file data, which we'd just converted from ISAM (indexed sequential access method) to VSAM (virtual storage access method), to a better, more robust database engine. The one we had in mind was IMS (IBM's Information Management System product). The salesperson, however, wants us to look at some new-fangled database they call SQL/DS (which eventually became DB2). After designing some tables and playing around with some queries, we asked some tough questions like "Why does it matter that a database engine is built on a mathematical theory?" and "Why would you want to learn a foreign query language called SQL rather than using nice, fast assembly language or COBOL programs?" and "Why did you just decompose our 2 nice, understandable records into 30 little tables just to join them back together again?" and "Why does it go so slow?" It was the beginning of the relational era. Relational engines weren't all that optimized yet, and smart programmers with fast disks could beat the engine every time. In 1981 we sent the product back, and I didn't learn SQL until 1987. By then I was a bit behind on the learning curve, but relational engines were a heck of a lot faster, and programmers wrote a little SQL and *much* less procedural code. And they got much more work done. So I smile when I see folks shake their head about the XML data models or the XQuery Formal Semantics. I saw the same raised eyebrows when mixing object-oriented concepts and data first came on the scene. Maybe the head-shakers are right, but I'm not waiting until 2010 to learn XQuery. It doesn't matter whether you choose to wait, however, or use relational exclusively. Yukon and .NET 2.0 have the enabling engines for all these data storage and query technologies—and more.

Bob Beauchemin
Portland, Oregon, March 2004

Acknowledgments

WE'D LIKE TO ACKNOWLEDGE our reviewers because without them this book would not exist or contain the level of depth that it does. Most of our reviewers are also program managers in one of the feature areas that the book covers. They took time from their busy schedules to provide information and answer our interminable questions not only about how the features work, but about why they work that way. Thanks.

* Roger Wolter
* Pablo Castro
* Peter Carlin
* Michael Rys
* Shankar Pal
* Joe Xavier
* Alex Laskos
* Richard Waymire
* Alazel Acheson
* Dan Winn
* Lubor Kollar
* Dinesh Kulkarni
* Eric Brown
* Paolo Tenti
* Rebecca Laszlo
* Claudio Mauad

- Tete Mensa-Annan
- Alex Vaschillo
- Ramachandran Venkatesh
- Srik Raghavan
- Bob Willer
- Greg Hinkle
- Jose Blakeley
- Wei Xiao
- Steven Pratschner
- Balaji Rathakrishnan
- Clifford Dibble
- Dirk Myers

▌1▪

Introduction

S QL SERVER 2005 CONTAINS features that constitute the biggest
change since the internal server rewrite of SQL Server 7. This is true
from both programmability and data model viewpoints. This chapter
describes SQL Server 2005 in terms of .NET programmability, SQL:1999
compliance, user-defined types (UDTs), and XML integration to present a
picture of holistic data storage, manipulation, and access.

The .NET Runtime and the Microsoft Platform

.NET is Microsoft's latest environment for running program code. The
concept of managed code, running under control of an execution engine,
has quickly permeated all major operating systems, including those from
Microsoft. .NET is one of the core technologies in Windows Server 2003,
Microsoft's latest collection of server platforms. Handheld devices and
computer-based mobile phones have quickly acquired .NET-based development environments. .NET is an integral part of both Internet Information Server (IIS) and Internet Explorer (IE). ASP.NET runs on the Windows
2000 version and up of IIS 5.0; IE 5.5 and up can load and run .NET code
referenced by <object> tags embedded in Web pages. Rich .NET-based
Windows applications, based on the WinForms library that comes with
.NET, may be deployed directly from the Internet and run on Windows-
based desktops. So what is it about .NET that has caused it to catch on?

Managed code has made .NET so compelling. Development tools produce managed code from .NET classes. Managed code is so named because it runs in an environment produced by `mscoree.dll`, the Microsoft common object runtime execution engine, which manages all facets of code execution. These include memory allocation and disposal, and class loading, which in traditional execution environments are a major source of programming errors. .NET also manages error recovery, and because it has complete information about the runtime environment, it need not always terminate an entire application in the face of an error such as an out-of-memory condition, but can instead just terminate a part of an application without affecting the rest of it.

.NET code makes use of code access security that applies a security policy based on the principal running the code, the code itself, and the location from which the code was loaded. The policy determines the permissions the code has. In .NET, by default, code that is loaded from the machine on which it runs is given full access to the machine. But code loaded from anywhere else, even if run by an administrator, is run in a sandbox that can access almost nothing on the machine. Prior to .NET, code run by an administrator would generally be given access to the entire machine regardless of its source. The application of policies is controlled by a system administrator and can be very fine grained.

Multiple versions of .NET, based on different versions of user-written classes or different versions of the .NET base class libraries (BCL), can execute side by side on the same machine. This makes versioning and deployment of revised and fixed classes easier. The .NET "kernel" or execution engine and the base class libraries can be written to work with different hardware. A common .NET programming model is usable in x86-based 32-bit processors, like those that currently run versions of Windows 9x, Windows NT, Windows 2000, and Windows XP, as well as mobile computers like the iPaq running on radically different processors. The development libraries are independent of chipset. Because .NET classes can be Just-In-Time compiled (JIT compiled), optimization based on processor type can be deferred until runtime. This allows .NET to integrate more easily with the new versions of 64-bit processors.

.NET tools compile code into an intermediate language (IL) that is the same regardless of the programming language used to author the program. Microsoft provides C#, Visual Basic .NET, Managed C++, JavaScript, and J#, a variant of the Java language that emits IL. Non-Microsoft languages such as COBOL.NET and Eiffel.NET are also first-class citizens. Code written in different languages can completely interoperate if written to the Common Language Specification (CLS). Even though language features might be radically different—as in Managed C++, where managed and unmanaged code can be mixed in the same program—the feature sets are similar enough that an organization can choose the language that makes the most sense without losing features. In addition, .NET code can interoperate with existing COM code (via COM-callable wrappers and runtime-callable wrappers) and arbitrary Windows Dynamic Link Libraries (DLLs) through a mechanism known as Platform Invoke (`PInvoke`).

So .NET with managed code is so compelling because it improves developer productivity and the reliability and security of applications, provides interoperability between a wide variety of languages, and supports use of legacy Windows code not written using .NET.

.NET's Effects on SQL Server

What does this mean with respect to SQL Server, Microsoft's flagship database management system (DBMS)? Originally, SQL Server shared a common ancestry with the Sybase database. SQL Server version 7 was split off from this common ancestry and rewritten using component-based programming. This makes adding new features at any level of functionality easier. Prior to version 7, SQL Server was a monolithic application. SQL Server version 7 factored code into layers, with communication between the relational and storage engines accessible through OLE DB. The SQL Server 7 component-based architecture is shown in Figure 1-1. In addition to easing accommodation of new features in future versions, such as SQL Server 2005, the new component-based model offered a variety of form factors, from the SQL Server Enterprise Edition, which provides a data store for an entire enterprise, to Microsoft Data Engine (MSDE), which provides a data store for a single application. Separation of the relational engine from the storage engine in SQL Server 7 made it easier to accommodate other data sources, such as Exchange or WebDav, which are traditionally not thought of as databases. SQL Server's relational engine can load OLE DB Rowsets from an Exchange or WebDav store just as though it were processing data managed by the storage engine.

In versions of SQL Server prior to SQL Server 2005, there were two ways to write programs that ran in SQL Server: Transact-SQL (T-SQL) and extended stored procedures. T-SQL is Microsoft's proprietary implementation of Persistent Stored Modules (SQL-PSM) as defined in SQL standards.

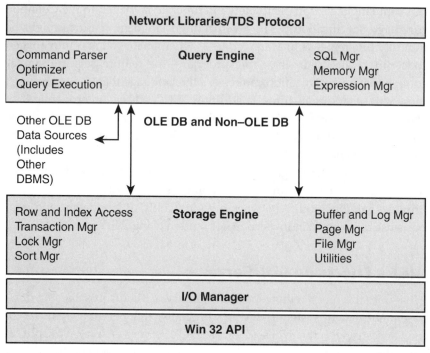

Network Libraries/TDS Protocol		
Command Parser Optimizer Query Execution	**Query Engine**	SQL Mgr Memory Mgr Expression Mgr

Other OLE DB Data Sources (Includes Other DBMS)   **OLE DB and Non–OLE DB**

Row and Index Access Transaction Mgr Lock Mgr Sort Mgr	**Storage Engine**	Buffer and Log Mgr Page Mgr File Mgr Utilities
I/O Manager		
Win 32 API		

FIGURE 1-1: SQL Server Architecture, Version 7 and Above

T-SQL code is highly integrated into SQL Server and uses data types that have the same representation in the storage engine as they do in T-SQL. Instances of these data types are passed between T-SQL and the storage engine without marshaling or conversion between representations. This makes T-SQL code as efficient in its use of type as the compiled code that runs in the storage engine.

On the other hand, SQL Server interprets T-SQL code—it does not compile it prior to use. This is not as efficient an execution technique as is used by the compiled code in the storage engine, but typically does not affect the performance of data access operations. It does affect, however, the performance of numeric and string-oriented operations. Prior to SQL Server version 7, T-SQL code was preparsed and precompiled into a tree format to alleviate some of this effect. Starting with SQL Server version 7, this is no longer done. An example of a simple T-SQL stored procedure is shown in Listing 1-1. Note that even though procedural code is interspersed with

SQL statements, T-SQL variables passed between T-SQL and the storage engine are not converted.

LISTING 1-1: A Simple Stored Procedure

```
CREATE PROCEDURE find_expensive (
  @category
  @price    MONEY,
  @verdict VARCHAR(20) OUTPUT
)
AS
IF (SELECT AVG(cost)
      FROM PRODUCTS WHERE cat = @category) > @price
  SET @verdict = 'Expensive'
ELSE
  SET @verdict = 'GoodBuy'
```

Extended stored procedures are an alternative to interpreted T-SQL code and prior to SQL Server 2005 were the only alternative to T-SQL. Extended stored procedures written in a compiled language, such as C++, do numeric and string operations more efficiently than T-SQL. They also have access to system resources such as files, the Internet, and timers that T-SQL does not. Extended stored procedures integrate with SQL Server through the Open Data Services API. Writing extended stored procedures requires a detailed understanding of the underlying operating system that is not required when writing T-SQL. Typically, the reliability of an extended stored procedure is more suspect than that of T-SQL.

In addition, data access operations by an extended stored procedure are not as efficient as T-SQL. Data accessed using ODBC or OLE DB requires data type conversion that T-SQL does not. An extended stored procedure that does data access also requires a connection to the database even though it runs inside of SQL Server itself. T-SQL directly accesses data in the storage engine and does not require a connection. Listing 1-2 shows a simple extended stored procedure written in C++.

LISTING 1-2: A Simple Extended Stored Procedure

```
ULONG __GetXpVersion()
{ return ODS_VERSION; }
SRVRETCODE xp_sayhello(SRV_PROC* pSrvProc)
{
    char szText[15] = "Hello World!";

    // error handling elided for clarity
    // describe the output column
```

```
srv_describe(pSrvProc, 1, "Column 1",
            SRV_NULLTERM, SRVVARCHAR,
            strlen(szText), SRVVARCHAR, 0, NULL);

// set column length and data
srv_setcollen(pSrvProc, 1, strlen(szText));
srv_setcoldata(pSrvProc, 1, szText);

// send row
srv_sendrow(pSrvProc);

// send done message
srv_senddone(pSrvProc,
            (SRV_DONE_COUNT | SRV_DONE_MORE),
            0, 1);
    return (XP_NOERROR);
}
```

SQL Server uses structured exception handling to wrap all calls to extended stored procedures. This prevents unhandled exceptions from damaging or shutting down SQL Server. There is, however, no way for SQL Server to prevent an extended stored procedure from misusing system resources. A rogue extended stored procedure could call the exit() function in the Windows runtime library and shut down SQL Server. Likewise, SQL Server cannot prevent a poorly coded extended stored procedure from writing over the memory SQL Server is using. This direct access to system resources is the reason that extended stored procedures are more efficient than T-SQL for non–data access operations, but is also the reason that a stored procedure must undergo much more scrutiny before it is added to SQL Server.

Under SQL Server 2005, T-SQL code continues to operate mostly as before. In addition to providing complete compatibility with existing code, this enables the millions of current T-SQL programmers to continue to write high-performance data access code for the SQL Server relational engine. For these programmers, T-SQL is still their language of choice.

SQL Server 2005 adds the ability to write stored procedures, user-defined functions, and triggers in any .NET-compatible language. This enables .NET programmers to use their language of choice, such as C# or VB.NET, to write SQL Server procedural code.

The .NET code that SQL Server runs is completely isolated from SQL Server itself. SQL Server uses a construct in .NET called an AppDomain. It completely isolates all resources that the .NET code uses from the resources that SQL Server uses, even though both SQL Server and the

AppDomain are part of the same process. Unlike the technique used to isolate stored procedures, the AppDomain protects SQL Server from all misuse or malicious use of system resources.

.NET code shares the advantage of compilation with extended stored procedures. .NET code is Just-In-Time compiled into machine instructions at execution time. .NET classes are objects to enable usage of object-oriented programming techniques. The execution engine controls storage allocation and memory management. This ensures that, short of a bug in the engine itself, .NET procedural code will never step on random memory buffers. In case of severe programmer error, the execution engine can always dispose of the offending thread or even an AppDomain without interfering while SQL Server continues to run without interruption. This is shown in Figure 1-2. Writing SQL Server procedural code is examined in detail in Chapters 3 and 4.

SQL Server 2005 ships with an in-memory .NET data provider to optimize data access from managed procedural code. When using this provider, programmers have a choice of using .NET types or SQL types. Some .NET types, like `System.Int32`, require no conversion or marshaling, but some, such as `System.Decimal`, are not exact matches. The .NET classes in `System.Data.SqlTypes` correspond exactly to the corresponding SQL Server types. Using these types in .NET procedures means no type

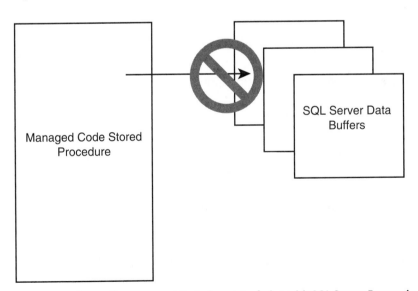

SQL Server Data Buffers

Managed Code Stored Procedure

FIGURE 1-2: Preventing Managed Code from Interfering with SQL Server Processing or Writing over Buffers

conversion or marshaling is required, and that means faster execution. SQL Server 2005's internal ADO.NET provider, known as `System.Data.SqlServer`, also contains optimizations such as the `SqlExecution Context class`, which allows .NET procedural code to share an execution environment (including `Connection` and `Transaction`) with its caller. .NET procedures can run in the security context of the user that cataloged the procedure or of the current user. The SQL Server internal managed provider is discussed in Chapter 4.

The SQL:1999 Standard — Extending the Relational Model

Many of the interesting changes to the programmability and data type extensions in SQL Server 2005 are related to ongoing changes to the SQL standard, so it is instructive here to take a look at that standard. SQL:1999 is the latest version of ANSI standard SQL, although at this writing a newer version yet, known as SQL:2003, is in progress. Some of the features added to standard SQL in SQL:1999 have always been part of SQL Server, such as triggers. The more interesting features of SQL:1999 have to do with extending the type system to support extended scalar types, distinct types, and even complex types. In SQL Server 2005, you can add a new scalar type to the relational type system yourself, without waiting for Microsoft to implement it in the engine. The most common use case for SQL Server 2005 user-defined types will be to add new scalar types.

A distinct type extends simple data types (such as INTEGER or VARCHAR) with special semantics. For example, a JPEG data type may be defined. This type is stored as an IMAGE data type in SQL Server, but the IMAGE type is extended with user-defined functions such as get_background_color and get_foreground_color. Extending a simple type by adding "behaviors" was inspired by object-relational databases of the mid-1990s. Adding functions to the simple IMAGE type enables SQL queries that accomplish a task, such as "select all the rows in the database where the JPEG column x has a background color of red." Without the user-defined functions to extend the type, the IMAGE would have to be decomposed into one or more relational tables for storage. As an alternative, the background color could be stored separately from the IMAGE, but this could introduce update anomalies if the IMAGE was updated but the background color was not. SQL:1999 codified the definition of the distinct type and defined some rules for its use. As an example, if the JPEG type and the GIF type are both distinct types that use an underlying storage type of IMAGE, JPEG types and

OrderID	OrderDate	Customer						
		Name	Address					Phone
			Street	City	State	Postcode		

FIGURE 1-3: Complex Types in Otherwise Relational Tables

GIF types cannot be compared (or otherwise operated on) without using the SQL CAST operator. CAST indicates that the programmer is aware that two distinct types are being compared. Using the JPEG type's get_background_color is likely to get incorrect results against a GIF column.

Complex types contain multiple data values, also called attributes. Including these data types in the SQL standard was inspired by the popularity of object-oriented databases in the early and mid-1990s. An example of a complex type is a "person" type that consists of a name, an address, and a phone number. Although these data types violate the first normal form of the relational data model and can be easily represented as a discrete table in a properly normalized database, these types have a few unique features. A diagram representing the data structures involved is shown in Figure 1-3.

The person type could be used in multiple tables while maintaining its "personness"—that is, the same attributes and functions are usable against the person type even when the person column is used in three unrelated tables. In addition to allowing complex types, SQL:1999 defined types that could be references to complex types. For example, a person type could contain a reference (similar to a pointer) to an address type in a different table, as shown in the following code.

```
CREATE TYPE PERSON (
    pers_first_name        VARCHAR(30),
    pers_last_name         VARCHAR(30),
    - other fields omitted
    pers_base_currency     REF(ADDRESS) SCOPE ADDR_TAB)
)

CREATE TYPE ADDRESS (
    addr_street            VARCHAR(20),
    addr_city              VARCHAR(30),
    addr_state_province    VARCHAR(10),
    addr_postal_code       VARCHAR(10)
)

CREATE TABLE ADDR_TAB (
    addr_oid               BIGINT,
    addr_address           ADDRESS
)
```

TABLE 1-1: New Data Types in SQL:1999

Data Type	Description
BOOLEAN	Bit switch
BLOB	Binary large object
CLOB	Character large object
Structured types	Distinct types and user-defined types
REF	Pointer to a persisted structured type
Array	Array
LOCATORs	Pointers to types inside the DBMS
DATALINK	Reference to an external data source

In addition, complex type–specific methods could be defined, and the SQL language was extended to support using attributes of a complex type in queries. An example of a complex type and a SELECT statement that uses it would look like the following.

```
SELECT ADDRESS FROM ADDR_TAB
    WHERE ADDR.addr_city like 'Sea%'
```

SQL:1999 expanded the type system to add some less revolutionary types, such as the BOOLEAN data type (which can contain TRUE, FALSE, or NULL) and the LOCATOR and DATALINK data types, which point to other storage inside or outside the database. A complete list of the new types is shown in Table 1-1.

User-Defined Types and SQL Server

SQL Server has always supported its own concept of a user-defined data type. These data types are known as "alias types" and are defined by using the system stored procedure sp_addtype. These data types share some functionality with SQL distinct types. They must be derived from a SQL Server built-in data type. You can add integrity constraints by using SQL Server RULES. You create a SQL Server RULE using CREATE RULE and associate a rule with a SQL Server user-defined type by using sp_bindrule. A single user-defined data type can be used in multiple tables, and a single

SQL Server rule can be bound to more than one user-defined type. Creating two SQL Server data types, creating rules, and binding the rules to the types is shown in Listing 1-3.

LISTING 1-3: Creating Types and Binding Them to Rules

```
- define two user-defined types
EXEC sp_addtype iq, 'FLOAT', 'NULL'
EXEC sp_addtype shoesize, 'FLOAT', 'NULL'


- specify constraints
CREATE RULE iq_range AS @range between 1 and 200
CREATE RULE shoesize_range AS @range between 1 and 20

- bind constraint to type
EXEC sp_bindrule 'iq_range', 'iq'
EXEC sp_bindrule 'shoesize_range', 'shoesize'
```

SQL Server user-defined types have some things in common with SQL distinct types. Like distinct types, they extend the SQL types by adding user-defined behaviors, in that a rule can be considered a behavior. Unlike SQL distinct types, they may not have associated user-defined functions that are scoped to the type. For example, although we defined the shoesize type and limited its values to floating point numbers from 1 to 20, we cannot associate a function named derive_suit_size_from_ shoesize with the type. This would be possible if shoesize were a SQL standard derived type. In addition, SQL Server user-defined types are comparable based on where the underlying built-in type is comparable, without using the SQL CAST operator. The SQL specification mandates that a user-defined type must be cast to a built-in or user-defined type before it can be used in a comparison operation, but attempting to apply the CAST operator to a user-defined type in SQL Server causes an error. Listing 1-4 shows this difference in behavior.

LISTING 1-4: Comparing Unlike User-Defined Types

```
- use the type
CREATE TABLE people (
  personid    INTEGER,
  iq          iq,
  shoe        shoesize,
  spouse_shoe shoesize
)

- SQL Server syntax
```

```
SELECT * from people WHERE iq < shoe

-- SQL:1999 syntax
-- invalid in SQL Server
-- SELECT * FROM people
   WHERE CAST(iq AS shoesize) < shoe
```

SQL Server 2005 goes beyond previous versions in support of SQL:1999 distinct and complex user-defined types. Extended data types must be defined as .NET classes and cannot be defined in Transact-SQL, although they are accessible in T-SQL stored procedures, user-defined functions, and other procedural code. These classes (types) may have member functions that are accessible in T-SQL à la SQL distinct types, and in addition they may have mutator functions that are usable in T-SQL UPDATE statements.

In addition to enabling users to define distinct types based on a single built-in data type, SQL Server 2005 allows user-defined types to have multiple storage items (attributes). Such a user-defined data type is considered a complex type in SQL:1999. Once defined to the SQL Server catalog, the new type may be used as a column in a table. Variables of the type may be used in stored procedures, and the type's attributes and methods may be used in computed types and user-defined functions. Although we'll see how to define user-defined distinct and complex types in Chapter 5, Listing 1-5 shows an example of defining a user-defined complex type, ComplexNumber, and using it as a column in a table.

LISTING 1-5: Defining a User-Defined Type and Using It in a Table

```
CREATE TYPE ComplexNumber
EXTERNAL NAME SomeTypes:ComplexNumber
GO

CREATE TABLE Transforms(
   transform_id      BIGINT,
   transform_input, ComplexNumber,
   transform_result ComplexNumber)
GO
```

After even a fundamental description, we should immediately point out that SQL Server complex types extend relational data types. The most common usage will not be to define "object" data types that might be defined in an object-oriented database, but to define new scalar types that extend the relational type system, such as the ComplexNumber type shown in Listing 1-5. In SQL Server 2005, the server is unaware of the inheritance relationships among types (although inheritance may be used in the implementation) or polymorphic methods, however, as in traditional object-oriented systems. That is, although we can define a complex user-defined type called `Person` that contains multiple data values (member variables) and instance methods, and define a complex type called `Author` that inherits from `Person`, we cannot invoke methods of the `Person` type when using an `Author` type or cast `Author` to `Person`. A domain-specific scalar type like `ComplexNumber` will be a more likely implementation.

In addition to supporting user-defined types, SQL Server 2005 supports user-defined aggregate functions. These types extend the concept of user-defined functions that return a single value, and can be written in any .NET language, but not T-SQL. The SQL specification defines five aggregates that databases must support (`MAX`, `MIN`, `AVG`, `SUM`, and `COUNT`). SQL Server implements a superset of the specification, including such aggregates as standard deviation and variance. By using SQL Server 2005 support for .NET languages, users need not wait for the database engine to implement their particular domain-specific aggregate. User-defined aggregates can even be defined over user-defined types, as in the case of an aggregate that would perform aggregates over the `ComplexNumber` data type described earlier.

Support of user-defined types and aggregates moves SQL Server closer to SQL:1999 compliance, and it extends SQL:1999 in that SQL:1999 does not mention user-defined aggregates in the specification.

XML—Data and Document Storage

XML is a platform-independent data representation format based originally on SGML. Since its popularization, it is becoming used as a data storage format. It has its own type system, based on the XML Schema Definition language (XSD). Both XML and XSD are W3C standards at the Recommendation level.[1] An XML schema defines the format of an XML document as a SQL Server schema defines the layout of a SQL Server database.

The XML type system is quite rigorous, enabling definition in XML Schema Definition language of almost all of the constructs available in a

---

[1] The W3C defines seven levels of specification. These are (in order of importance): Recommendation, Proposed Recommendation, Candidate Recommendation, Working Draft In Last Call, Working Draft in Development, Requirements, and Note. This means that a W3C "Recommendation" is an agreed-upon standard.

relational database. Because it was originally designed as a system that could represent documents with markup as well as what is traditionally thought of as "data," the XML type system is somewhat bifurcated into attributes and elements. Attributes are represented in the XML serialization format as HTML attributes are, using the `name='value'` syntax. Attributes can hold only simple data types, like traditional relational attributes. Elements can represent simple or complex types. An element can have multiple levels of nested subelements, as in the following example.

```
<table>
<row>
    <id>1</id>
    <name>Tom</name>
</row>
<row>
    <id>2</id>
    <name>Maureen</name>
</row>
</table>
```

This means that an element can be used to represent a table in a relational database. Each tuple (row) would be represented as a child element, with relational attributes (columns) represented as either attributes or subelements. The two ways of representing relational column data in XML are known as "element-centric mapping" (where each column is a nested subelement) and "attribute-centric mapping" (where each column is an attribute on an element tuple). These are illustrated in Listing 1-6.

LISTING 1-6: Element-Centric Mapping and Attribute-Centric Mapping

```
<! - element-centric mapping -->
<! - all data values are element content -->

<table>
<row>
    <id>1</id>
    <name>Tom</name>
</row>
<row>
    <id>2</id>
    <name>Maureen</name>
</row>
</table>

<! - same document in attribute-centric mapping -->
<! - id and name are represented as attributes -->
```

```
<! - and cannot themselves be complex types  ->
<table>
<row id="1" name="Tom" />
<row id="2" name="Maureen" />
</table>
```

Since subelements can be nested in XML documents, a document more closely corresponds to a hierarchical form of data than a relational form. This is reinforced by the fact that, by definition, an XML document must have a single root element. Sets of elements that do not have a single root element are called document fragments. Although document fragments are not well-formed XML documents, multiple fragments can be composed together and wrapped with a root element, producing a well-formed document.

In addition to being able to represent relational and hierarchical data, XML Schema Definition language can represent complex type relationships. XSD supports the notion of type derivation, including derivation by both restriction and extension. This means that XML can directly represent types in an object hierarchy.

A single XML schema document (which itself is defined in an XML form specified by the XML Schema Definition language) represents data types that scope a single XML namespace, although you can use XML namespaces in documents without having the corresponding XML schema. An XML namespace is a convenient grouping of types, similar to a user-schema in SQL Server. This is illustrated in Listing 1-7.

LISTING 1-7: An XML Namespace Defining a Set of Types

```
<schema targetNamespace="http://www.develop.com/order.xsd"
    xmlns:po="http://www.develop.com/order.xsd"
    xmlns="http://www.w3.org/2001/XMLSchema"
    elementFormDefault="qualified">

    <! - define a new type  ->
    <complexType name="PurchaseOrderType">
        <sequence>
            <element name="PONum" type="decimal"/>
            <element name="Company" type="string"/>
            <element name="Item" maxOccurs="1000">
                <! - a nested anonymous type  ->
                <complexType>
                    <sequence>
                        <element name="Part" type="string"/>
                        <element name="Price" type="float"/>
                    </sequence>
                </complexType>
```

```
      </element>
    </sequence>
  </complexType>

  <! - global element definition using type above  ->
  <element name="PurchaseOrder" type="po:PurchaseOrderType"/>
</schema>
```

An XML schema defines the namespace that its types belong to by specifying the `targetNamespace` attribute on the schema element. An XML document that uses types from a namespace can indicate this by using a default namespace or explicitly using a namespace prefix on each element or attribute of a particular type. Namespace prefixes are arbitrary; the `xmlns` attribute established the correspondence between namespace prefix and namespace. This is illustrated in Listing 1-8. This is analogous to using SQL Server two-part or three-part names in SQL statements.

LISTING 1-8: Referring to a Type via Namespace and Namespace Prefixes

```
<pre:PurchaseOrder
   xmlns:pre="http://www.develop.com/order.xsd"
   xmlns:xsi="http://www.w3.org/2001/XMLSchema-instance"
   xsi:schemaLocation="http://www.develop.com/order.xsd
                  http://www.develop.com/schemas/order.xsd">
   <pre:PONum>1001</pre:PONum>
   <pre:Company>DM Traders</pre:Company>
   <pre:Item>
     <pre:Part>Dons Boxers</pre:Part>
     <pre:Price>11.95</pre:Price>
   </pre:Item>
   <pre:Item>
     <pre:Part>Essential ADO.NET</pre:Part>
     <pre:Price>49.95</pre:Price>
   </pre:Item>
</ pre:PurchaseOrder>
```

Only when an XML document contains types defined by XML schemas is it possible to determine the exact data types of elements or attributes. XML elements and attributes are data type `string` by definition. A predecessor to XML schemas, known as Document Type Definition (DTD), was primarily concerned with defining document structure and allowed only limited information about data types. XSD is a superset of the aforementioned type systems, including all the DTD structure types. Using an XSD schema or schemas to determine if a document is "correct" is known as schema validation. Schema validation can be thought of as applying type constraints and declarative integrity constraints to ensure that an XML document is correct. A nonvalidated XML schema still must conform to XML "well-formedness" rules, and a single XML document adheres to a set of rules known as the XML Information Set (Infoset), consisting of structure and some content information. Validating an XML document against schemas produces what is called a Post-Schema-Validation InfoSet (PSVI). The PSVI information makes it possible to determine a strong, well-defined type for each XML element and attribute.

SQL Server 2005 introduces an XML data type. This data type can be used in table definitions to type a column, as a variable type in Transact-SQL procedural code, and as procedure parameters. A definition of a simple table containing an XML type would look like a "normal" CREATE TABLE statement.

```
CREATE TABLE xml_tab(
   id        INT primary key,
   xml_col   XML)
```

In addition, columns, variables, and parameters of the XML data type can be constrained by an XML schema. XML schemas are defined in the SQL Server catalog.

XML, like relational databases, has its own query language optimized for the data format. Since XML data is hierarchical, it's reminiscent of a hierarchical file system. The archetypical query language for XML documents is known as XPath. Queries in XPath reflect the hierarchical nature of XML, since nodesets are selected by using syntax similar to that used to specify files in the UNIX file system. As an example, when a typical XML document is queried using a hierarchical XPath query, the result is a node-set containing all the nodes at that level of hierarchy. Listing 1-9 shows an example of an XPath query that, when run against the purchase order document in Listing 1-8, produces a nodeset result containing all the item elements. Think of an XPath query as analogous to a SQL query.

LISTING 1-9: Simple XPath Query

```
<! - this query  ->
//pre:Item

<! - produces this nodeset  ->
<! - two Item nodes  ->
  <pre:Item>
    <pre:Part>Dons Boxers</pre:Part>
    <pre:Price>11.95</pre:Price>
```

```
</pre:Item>
<pre:Item>
  <pre:Part>Essential ADO.NET</pre:Part>
  <pre:Price>49.95</pre:Price>
</pre:Item>
```

Like a SQL query, an XPath query simply produces a resultset consisting of possibly multiple instances of items; unlike in SQL, these results are not always rectangular in shape. XPath results can consist of nodesets of any shape or even scalar values. In SQL, database vendors can implement a variation of SQL-PSM (persistent stored modules) that composes possibly multiple SQL queries and some procedural code to produce a more complex result. SQL Server's variation of SQL-PSM is known as Transact-SQL. XML processing libraries implement an analogous concept by using an XML-based nonprocedural language called XSLT. Originally meant to produce nice looking HTML pages from XML input, XSLT has evolved into an almost full-fledged programming language. Vendors have even added proprietary extensions to XSLT to allow it to execute code routines in procedural programming languages like Visual Basic or C#.

Since XPath and XSLT were not originally developed to process large amounts of data or data from multiple sources, a new programming language for XML, known as XQuery, has been developed. XQuery implements many of the best features of XPath and XSLT, and is developed from the ground up to allow queries that include multiple documents. It is also designed specifically to be optimizable. In addition, it adds some of the syntax features of SQL. XQuery's data can be strongly typed; this also assists in query optimization. XQuery includes a query language, the equivalent of SQL Server SELECT, but does not define a standard implementation of DML, SQL Server's INSERT, UPDATE, and DELETE statements.

SQL Server 2000 allowed users to define mapping schemas (normal XML schemas with extra annotations that mapped XML items and concepts to SQL items and concepts) that represented all or a portion of the database as a virtual XML document, and issue XPath queries against the resulting data structure. In addition, SQL Server 2000 extended Transact-SQL to enable relational resultsets to be returned as XML. This consists of support for a FOR XML clause; three different subcategories of FOR XML are supported. The SQL Server 2000 support allowed XML document composition from relational data and XML document decomposition into multiple relational tables; this will be discussed further in Chapter 8.

SQL Server 2005 extends this support by adding direct support for XQuery. The XQuery engine runs directly inside SQL Server, as opposed to

XPath support in SQL Server 2000. XPath support in SQL Server 2000 is accomplished by a portion of the SQL Server OLE DB provider (SQLOLEDB) that took a mapping schema and an XPath query, produced a SELECT... FOR XML query and sent that to SQL Server. Native support for XQuery, combined with XQuery's design for optimization, and support for multiple documents (a series of XML columns) should improve on the already good support for querying XML data.

Web Services—XML as a Marshaling Format

Marshaling data to unlike platforms has always been a problem. In the past vendors could not even agree on a marshaling format, let alone a common type system. Microsoft used COM (the component object model) for their distributed object model and marshaling format; they did not support CORBA, the common object request broker architecture. Processor differences such as endianness (byte ordering), floating point representation, and character set were considered in both these models; marshaling between systems required a "reader–make right" approach—that is, the receiver of a message had to determine the format and convert it to something understandable to their processor. In addition, the distributed programming models were plagued by the requirement to have a specific naming model or security system. As an example, porting COM to the Solaris platform required installing the equivalent of a Windows registry and an NTLM security service. But the biggest problem was network protocol and access to specific ports on network servers. COM not only used a proprietary protocol and network ports when run over TCP/IP, but required opening port 135 for the naming service to operate correctly, something that few system administrators would permit. By contrast, most system administrators gladly opened port 80 and allowed the HTTP protocol, even setting up special proxy servers rather than denying internal users access to the World Wide Web. Systems such as DCOM over HTTP and Java RMI over HTTP were the first steps away from a proprietary distributed programming system.

Vendors such as Microsoft, IBM, Oracle, and Sun are moving toward supporting distributed computing over HTTP using a framing protocol known as SOAP and using XML as a marshaling format. SOAP itself uses XML to frame XML-based payloads; elements and attributes used in SOAP are defined in two XSD schemas. SOAP also defined a portable way of representing parameters to remote procedure calls (RPCs), but since the completion and adaptation of XML schemas, a schema-centric format is now used. Using XML as a marshaling format, framed by SOAP, possibly over HTTP, is known as Web Services.

The popularity of XML and Web Services, like the popularity of SQL, is fairly easy to explain. Managers of computer systems have learned over time to shy away from proprietary solutions, mostly because companies often change hardware and operating system (and other) software over time. In addition, a company may have to communicate with other companies that use an unlike architecture. Therefore, protocols like HTTP, formats like XML and CSV (comma-separated value) files, and languages like SQL, XPath, XSLT, and XQuery tend to be used for a single reason—they are available on every hardware and software platform.

Consider as an example the RDS (remote data services) architecture used by Microsoft to marshal resultsets (known as `recordsets`) over HTTP in a compact binary format, as opposed to XML, a rather verbose text-based format. Because Microsoft invented the RDS marshaling format (known as Advanced Data Tablegrams, or ADTG), other vendors (such as Netscape) refused to support it. This is known as the NIH (not invented here) syndrome. On the other hand, visit any large software or hardware manufacturer on the planet and ask, "Who invented XML?" The answer is always the same: "We did." Since XML (or SQL, to expand the analogy) could not possibly be perceived as "a Microsoft thing" or "an Oracle thing," support is almost universal.

SQL Server as an XML Repository and Web Service Server

SQL Server 2005 supports creating Web Services and storing data to be used in Web Services at a few different levels. The `XML` data type and XQuery support mentioned previously is a good start. Data can be stored in XML format inside SQL Server and used directly with XQuery to produce or consume Web Services. With the addition of direct support in SQL Server for HTTP, we could think of SQL Server 2005 as a "Web Service server." This reduces the three-tier architecture usually required to support Web Services (database, middle tier, and client) to a two-tier architecture, with stored procedures or XQuery/XSLT programs being used as a middle tier.

Client Access—And Then There Are Clients

Client-Side Database APIs and SQL Server 2005

Database programmers, especially those who specialize in procedural dialects of SQL, tend to forget that without client access libraries, a database is just a place to keep data. Although the SQL language itself was supposed to ensure that ordinary clients could access the data, performance issues and the complexity of SQL queries (and XPath and XQuery queries, for that matter) ensure that very few (if any) users actually go right to Query Analyzer for the data they need, and no enterprise applications that we know of use Query Analyzer as a front end to the database. Applications, both rich Windows applications and Web applications, are written using high-level programming languages like C++, Visual Basic, and the .NET family of languages.

With all the new features in SQL Server 2005, client libraries such as OLE DB have quite a lot of work to do just to keep up. Although the designers of OLE DB and ADO designed support for user-defined types into the model, the intricacies of supporting them weren't made clear until support for these types was added to popular mainstream databases like SQL Server 2005. OLE DB and ADO are very `Rowset/Recordset`-centric and have limited support for user-defined types, invoking methods on database types and extending the type system. The next version of these libraries adds support for fetching complex types in a couple of different ways: as a data type `Object`, or as a nested resultset (`Rowset` or `Recordset`). Most of the support in OLE DB and ADO leverages existing objects and methods, and extends them to support the new types. Support for the SQL:1999 information schema `Rowsets` is another new feature in data access.

The client-side .NET data provider for SQL Server, known as `SqlClient`, has an easier time of it. Since user-defined types are .NET types, code to process these types might be downloaded to a client from a SQL Server or stored on a network share. It's possible to coerce a column in a `DataReader` from type `Object` to type `Person` and use it directly in a .NET program. Techniques such as network-based code make this work. Handling complex data in place or storing complex types in a .NET `DataSet` presents a different set of problems. The first book of one of the authors (Bob Beauchemin), *Essential ADO.NET* (Addison-Wesley, 2002), describes many of these problems and theoretical solutions to them based on the existing .NET libraries. Now that SQL Server supports columns that are classes or columns that are XML, this becomes an interesting area.

One limitation of SQL Server clients was that only a single `Rowset` or `Recordset` could be active at a time in the default cursorless mode of SQL Server data access. Different APIs solved this problem in different ways, and we'll talk about the repercussions of this in Chapter 11. SQL Server 2005 breaks through the one-active-rowset barrier by allowing the user APIs to multiplex active results on a single connection. This empowering feature is known as MARS (multiple active resultsets).

Client-Side XML-Based APIs and SQL Server 2005 Integration

XML is ubiquitous in the SQL Server 2005-era client APIs. User-defined types use .NET XML Serialization to be able to be marshaled or persisted as XML directly. The `FOR XML` syntax has been extended to allow a user to fetch data in an XML type. In addition, SQL Server Analysis Services can directly consume queries in XML format and produce XML results. This is called XML for Analysis and has been around for a while; in SQL Server 2005 it becomes a first-class API directly supported and on a par with OLE DB for Analysis. If you've gotten used to OLE DB for Analysis (or its automation equivalent, ADOMD), don't fret—XML for Analysis uses an OLE DB–style syntax, for both queries and properties.

The `XML` data type and the XQuery engine inside SQL Server 2005 are complemented by a rich middle-tier or client-side model for XML. This model exposes XML data outside the server using a variety of data models. These models include the XML Document Object Model (DOM) and abstract `XmlNavigator` model, in addition to streaming models known as `XmlReader` and `XmlWriter`. The standard XML query and transformation models, XPath and XSLT, have been part of the .NET platform since its inception and are being extended to support client-side XQuery and XPath 2.0. The `XmlReader` and `XmlWriter` classes are being enhanced to enable support of the XQuery 1.0 and XPath 2.0 XML data model. This is necessary because the new XML data model differs from the XML 1.0 and namespaces model. The XQuery 1.0 and XPath 2.0 data model extends the weakly typed nodeset model to include strongly typed sequences consisting of nodes, atomic values, or a combination of both. In addition, this data model is a closed data model, meaning that running an XQuery against an instance of the data model is guaranteed to produce an instance of the data model. In addition, enhancements to the `XPathDocument` class will enable it to support in-place editing and change tracking, and marshaling of sets of changes. This makes the in-memory client-side XML model on a par with the client-side relational `DataSet` class.

In a revolutionary approach to querying XML data from the client, a generalized client-side parsing and execution engine, known as the common query abstraction, will allow XPath, XSLT, and XQuery syntax to be compiled into an intermediate query format, in a method analogous to high-level languages being compiled into IL code. This allows programmers to use the query language that is most suitable for the job or the one that they are most familiar with. The query abstraction is extensible so that

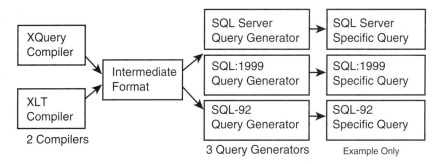

Compilers and Generators Added Independently

FIGURE 1-4: Using the Common Query Abstraction to Support Multiple Interoperable Query Languages

additional query languages and data sources other than native XML can be plugged in. This is pictured in Figure 1-4.

The most common scenario for the common query abstraction will be to pass the resulting intermediate format through an IL generator to generate .NET IL code, which would then be executed against .NET XML classes (like the XPathDocument) on the client to provide native support for XML query and transformation languages like XQuery, XPath, and XSLT.

The common query abstraction will be combined with a mapping technology that can map between relational data, XML data, and objects. One use of this will be to enable XQuery syntax over XML views of relational data, the natural successor to XML mapping schemas mentioned previously. The common query runtime will be able to compile an XQuery against an XML mapping (view) of data in SQL Server, and the resulting intermediate format will run through a SQL generator (rather than an IL generator), to generate Transact-SQL code for execution on SQL Server. The common query abstraction and mapping technologies will also be used to provide object-to-relational mappings and an object query language (OPath) in a technology known as ObjectSpaces.

ObjectSpaces—Objects on the Middle Tier or Client

Some object-oriented techniques are enabled by the use of complex user-defined types in SQL Server as discussed previously, but object-oriented design is used to a much greater degree on the client and middle tier. Most graphic user interface systems, large client-side applications, and even the .NET base class libraries themselves are based on an object-oriented implementation. After Booch, Jacobson, and Rumbaugh popularized decomposition of any computing problem with a set of well-known modeling techniques, the saying in the computing world became "Programmers just like to program with objects. It makes their job easier because it makes the problem domain easier to visualize." Techniques such as top-down design and structured programming have taken a backseat ever since. But data in a relational database such as SQL Server is decomposed into tuples and relations, not into object graphs. Therein lies the famous object-relational "impedance mismatch."

ObjectSpaces is a client-side object-relational integration technology that will be delivered as part of ADO.NET. This technology solves the problem of every programmer writing different code to coerce multiple rectangular `Rowsets` into object graphs that make up their programming object model. Since most client applications are built around object models, a standard set of APIs to ease the interaction between relational data and objects will be a welcome addition.

In the past few years, the concept of "entity objects" was popularized, but this concept has suffered, in general, from poor performance. In addition, entity objects usually were implemented in such as way as to produce far too many database round-trips and/or database locks held for too long to be useful. ObjectSpaces employs optimization techniques such as partial and lazy loading of object graphs, including programmer specification of graph loading depth and smart updates and deletions of database rows corresponding to graph instances, to increase performance. ObjectSpaces' graph accessor queries and mutators can be specified as stored procedures, to take advantage of SQL Server's processing power. In addition, you can query object graphs on the client side through an `ObjectQuery` class and a simple but powerful predicate language known as OPath. Using OPath is reminiscent of using XPath to select a subset of nodes in an XML document or using a `WHERE` clause in a SQL query.

Chapter 14 rounds out the discussion of relational data, object data, and XML with a discussion of Microsoft's object solution for the client or middle tier and its integration with SQL Server.

Extending SQL Server into the Platform — Service Broker and Notification Services

Finally, SQL Server 2005 adds two more pieces of data access and application programming functionality that bear mention. SQL Server Service Broker allows you to use T-SQL to send asynchronous messages. These messages must be sent to another SQL Server, but the messages can be sent to the same database, between databases in the same instance, or to a different instance on the same machine or different machines. The asynchronous messages work similarly to a message queuing system (they even use queues), but because SQL Server is controlling both the database data and the messages, messages can participate in a local database transaction. The Transact-SQL language is being extended to support the handling of queued messages that can be retrieved asynchronously.

SQL Server Service Broker uses dialogs to achieve coordinated messaging with multimessage correlation semantics. A dialog is a bidirectional series of messages between two endpoints, in which each message contains a conversation ID to enable the other side to correlate messages, as shown in Figure 1-5.

One of the main advantages of a dialog is that it maintains message order across transactions, threads, applications, and database restarts, something no other messaging system does. A dialog also allows guaranteed delivery of messages to a number of different subscribers. Multiple dialogs can be grouped into a single "application" known as a Conversation Group. A Conversation Group can maintain its state and share state between multiple dialogs. This goes beyond the concept of simple correlation ID message queuing systems, and it's handled automatically by Service Broker, rather than manually by the application programmer.

Using asynchronous messaging inside the database enables building scalable systems, because work that had to be handled serially in the past can now be multiplexed in the same transaction. In addition, Service Broker guarantees that the messages will arrive in order, even across transactions, and guarantees once-only delivery.

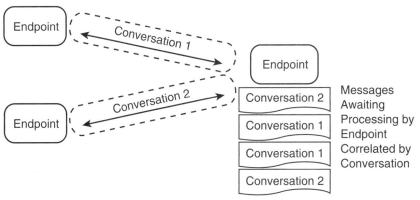

FIGURE 1-5: Messages and Dialogs

SQL Server Notification Services is an easy-to-use but powerful framework around which you can build scalable "notification applications" that can notify millions of users about millions of interesting events, using standard notification protocols like SMS (Simple Message Service) and programs like MSN Messenger. The unique pieces, such as an application, are defined using XML and integrate with the framework (which runs as a series of stored procedures over a mostly system-defined schema).

We'll discuss Service Broker and Notification Services in Chapters 15 and 16. In addition, SQL Server 2005 adds a Report Server to further extend the data-related platform, but this feature is outside the scope of this book.

Where Are We?

In this chapter, we've had a whirlwind tour of the plethora of new technologies in SQL Server 2005, the problems they are intended to solve, and, in some cases, the entirely new data models they represent. SQL Server 2005 supports .NET programming, user-defined data types and aggregates, and an XML data type. The support for these alternate data types extends from the server out to the client, with System.Xml and an object-oriented API known as ObjectSpaces.

In the rest of the book, we're going to explore the implementation and best practices when using these new data models, and see that SQL Server 2005 and improvements to the client libraries truly represent the integration of relational data, object-oriented data and concepts, and XML data.

2

Hosting the Runtime: SQL Server as a Runtime Host

THIS CHAPTER DISCUSSES what it means to be a .NET runtime host. Topics include how SQL Server differs from other runtime hosts such as Internet Information Server (IIS) or Internet Explorer (IE) and how it is similar with respect to loading and running code. Finally, we'll show how you would catalog a user assembly to be stored in SQL Server.

Why Care How Hosting Works?

If you are a SQL Server developer or database administrator, you might just be inclined to use the new Common Language Runtime (CLR) hosting feature to write stored procedures in C# or VB.NET without knowing how it works. But you should care. SQL Server is an enterprise application, perhaps one of the most important in your organization. When the CLR was added to SQL Server, there were three goals in the implementation, considered in this order:

1. Security
2. Reliability
3. Performance

The reasons for this order are obvious. Without a secure system, you have a system that runs reliably run code, including code introduced by hackers, very quickly. It's not what you'd want for an enterprise application. Reliability comes next. Critical applications, like a database management system, are expected to be available 99.999% of the time. You don't want to wait in a long line at the airport or the bank while the database restarts itself. Reliability is therefore considered over performance when the two clash; a decision might be whether to allow stack overflows to potentially bring down the main application, or slow down processing to make sure they don't. Since applications that perform transactional processing use SQL Server, SQL Server must ensure data integrity and its transactional correctness, which is another facet of reliability.

Performance is extremely important in an enterprise application as well. Database management systems can be judged on benchmarks, such as the TPC-C (Transaction Processing Performance Council benchmark C) benchmark, as well as programmer-friendly features. So although having stored procedures and user-defined types written in high-level languages is a nice feature, it has to be implemented in such a way as to maximize performance.

Since SQL Server 2005 is going to introduce fundamental changes such as loading .NET runtime engines and XML parsers, we'll first consider how SQL Server 2005 works as a .NET runtime host, how it compares with other .NET runtime hosts, and what special features of the runtime are used to ensure security, reliability, and performance. You may already know that an updated version of the .NET runtime, .NET 2.0, will be required for use with SQL Server. In this chapter, we'll explain why.

What Is a .NET Runtime Host?

A runtime host is defined as any process that loads the .NET runtime and runs code in a managed environment. The most common scenario is that a runtime host is simply a bootstrap program that executes from the Windows shell, loads the runtime into memory, and then loads one or more managed assemblies. An assembly is the unit of deployment in .NET roughly analogous to an executable program or DLL in prior versions of Windows.

A runtime host loads the runtime by using the `ICorRuntimeHost` or `CorBindToRuntimeEx`, prior to Whidbey. These APIs call a shim DLL, `MSCOREE.DLL`, whose only job is to load the runtime. Only a single copy of the runtime (also known as the CLR) engine can ever be loaded into a process during the process's lifetime; it is not possible to run multiple versions of the CLR within the same host. In pre-Whidbey versions of .NET, a host could specify only a limited number of parameters to `ICorRuntime Host` or `CorBindToRuntimeEx`, namely the following:

- Server or workstation behavior
- Version of the CLR (for example, version 1.0.3705.0)
- Garbage collection behavior
- Whether or not to share Just-In-Time compiled code across AppDomains (an AppDomain is a subdivision of the CLR runtime space)

Two examples of specialized runtime hosts are the ASP.NET worker process and Internet Explorer. The ASP.NET worker process differs in code location and how the executable code, threads, and AppDomains are organized. (We'll discuss AppDomains in the next section.) The ASP.NET worker process divides code into separate "applications," application being a term that is borrowed from Internet Information Server to denote code running in a virtual directory. Code is located in virtual directories, which are mapped to physical directories in the IIS metabase. Internet Explorer is another runtime host with behaviors that differ from the ASP.NET worker or SQL Server 2005. IE loads code when it encounters a specific type of <object> tag in a Web page. The location of the code is obtained from an HTML attribute of the tag. SQL Server 2005 is an example of a specialized runtime host that goes far beyond ASP.NET in specialization and control of CLR semantics.

SQL Server as a Runtime Host

SQL Server's special requirements of utmost security, reliability, and performance, in addition to the way that SQL Server works internally, have necessitated an overhaul in how the managed hosting APIs work as well as in how the CLR works internally. Although early versions of SQL Server 2005 did run on .NET version 1.0, the changes in the CLR are important in ensuring enterprise quality.

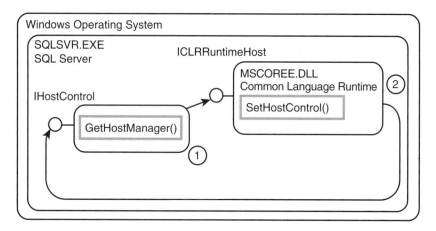

① SQL Server passes IHostControl to CLR via SetHostControl

② CLR delegates thread management, etc. to SQL Server via GetHostManager

FIGURE 2-1: Hosting the CLR

SQL Server is a specialized host like ASP.NET and IE, rather than a simple bootstrap mechanism. The runtime is lazy loaded; if you never use a managed stored procedure or user-defined type, the runtime is never loaded. This is useful because loading the runtime takes a one-time memory allocation of approximately 10–15MB in addition to SQL Server's buffers and unmanaged executable code, although this certainly will not be the exact number in SQL Server 2005. How SQL Server manages its resources and locates the code to load is unique as well.

To accommodate hosts that want to have hooks into the CLR's resource allocation and management, .NET 2.0 hosts can use ICLRRuntimeHost instead of ICorRuntimeHost. The host can then call ICLRRuntimeHost::SetHostControl, which takes a pointer to an interface (IHostControl) that contains a method that the CLR can call (GetHostManager) to delegate things like thread management to the host. SQL Server uses this interface to take control of some functions that the CLR usually calls down to the operating system for directly. Figure 2-1 shows how SQL Server 2005 hosts the CLR.

Resource Management

SQL Server manages its own thread scheduling, synchronization and locking, and memory allocation. In .NET runtime hosts, these are usually managed by the CLR itself. In SQL Server 2005 this conflict is resolved by layering the CLR's mechanisms on top of SQL Server's mechanisms. SQL Server uses its own memory allocation scheme, managing real memory rather than using virtual memory. It attempts to optimize memory, balancing between data and index buffers, query caches, and other internal data structures. SQL Server can do a better job if it manages all of the memory in its process. As an example, prior to SQL Server 2000, it was possible to specify that the TEMPDB database should be allocated in memory. In SQL Server 2000 that option was removed, based on the fact that SQL Server can manage this better than the programmer or DBA. SQL Server manages its memory directly by, in effect, controlling paging of memory to disk itself rather than letting the operating system do it. Because SQL Server attempts to use as much memory as is allocated to the process, this has some repercussions in exceptional condition handling, which we'll discuss next.

SQL Server also uses its own thread management algorithm, putting threads "to sleep" until it wants them to run. This facility is known as UMS (user-mode scheduler). Optionally, SQL Server can use fibers rather than threads through a configuration option, though this option is rarely used. The CLR also maintains thread pools and allows programmers to create new threads. The key point is that SQL Server uses cooperative thread scheduling; the CLR uses preemptive thread scheduling. Cooperative thread scheduling means that a thread must voluntarily yield control of the processor; in preemptive thread scheduling the processor takes control back from the thread after its time slice has expired. SQL Server uses cooperative thread scheduling to minimize thread context switches. With threading come considerations of thread synchronization and locking. SQL Server manages locking of its own resources, such as database rows and internal data structures. Allowing programmers to spin up a thread is not to be taken lightly. SQL Server 2005 CLR code executes under different permission levels with respect to CLR activities; we'll talk about how these relate to threading and locking later in this chapter.

The hosting APIs in .NET 2.0 are enhanced to enable the runtime host to either control or "have a say in" resource allocation. The APIs manage units of work called Tasks, which can be assigned to a thread or a fiber. The SQL scheduler manages blocking points, and hooks PInvoke and interop calls out of the runtime to control switching the scheduling mode. The new control points allow SQL Server to supply a host memory allocator, to be notified of low memory conditions at the OS level, and to fail memory allocations if desired. SQL Server can also use the hosting API to control I/O completion ports usually managed by the CLR. Although this may slow things down a little in the case of an allocation callback, it is of great benefit in allowing SQL Server to manage all of its resources, as it does today.

Exceptional Condition Handling

In .NET 1.0 certain exceptional conditions, such as an out-of-memory condition or a stack overflow, could bring down a running process (or App Domain). This cannot be allowed to happen in SQL Server. Although transactional semantics might be preserved, reliability and performance would suffer dramatically. In addition, unconditionally stopping a thread (using `Thread.Abort` or other API calls) can conceivably leave some system resources in an indeterminate state and, though using garbage collection minimizes memory leakage, leak memory.

Different runtime hosts deal with these hard-to-handle conditions in different ways. In the ASP.NET worker process, for example, recycling both the AppDomain and the process itself is considered acceptable since disconnected, short-running Web requests would hardly notice. With SQL Server, rolling back all the in-flight transactions might take a few minutes. Process recycling would ruin long-running batch jobs in progress. Therefore, changes to the hosting APIs and the CLR exceptional condition handling needed to be made.

Out-of-memory conditions are particularly difficult to handle correctly, even when you leave a safety buffer of memory to respond to them. In SQL Server the situation is exacerbated because SQL Server manages its own memory and attempts to use all memory available to it to maximize throughput. This leaves us between a rock and a hard place. As we increase the size of the "safety net" to handle out-of-memory conditions, we also increase the occurrence of out-of-memory conditions. The Whidbey runtime handles these conditions more robustly; that is, it guarantees availability and reliability after out-of-memory conditions without requiring SQL Server to allocate a safety net, letting SQL Server tune memory usage to the amount of physical memory. The CLR will notify SQL Server about the repercussions of failing each memory request. Low-memory conditions may be handled by permitting the garbage collector to run more frequently, waiting for other procedural code to finish before invoking additional procedures, or aborting running threads if needed.

There is also a failure escalation policy at the CLR level that will allow SQL Server to determine how to deal with exceptions. SQL Server can decide to abort the thread that causes an exception and, if necessary, unload the AppDomain. On resource failures, the CLR will unwind the entire managed stack of the session that takes the resource failure. If that session has any locks, the entire AppDomain that session is in is unloaded. This is because having locks indicates there is some shared state to synchronize, and thus that shared state is not likely to be consistent if just the session was aborted. In certain cases this might mean that finally blocks in CLR code may not run. In addition, finalizers, hooks that programmers can use to do necessary but not time-critical resource cleanup, might not get run. Except in UNSAFE mode (discussed later in the chapter), finalizers are not permitted in CLR code that runs in SQL Server.

Stack overflow conditions cannot be entirely prevented, and are usually handled by implementing exceptional condition handling in the program. If the program does not handle this condition, the CLR will catch these exceptions, unwind the stack, and abort the thread if needed. In exceptional circumstances, such as when memory allocation during a stack overflow causes an out-of-memory condition, recycling the App Domain may be necessary.

In all the cases just mentioned, SQL Server will maintain transactional semantics. In the case of AppDomain recycling, this is needed to assert that the principal concern is reliability, if needed, at the expense of performance. In addition, all the Framework class libraries (FX libraries) that SQL Server will load have gone through a careful review and testing to ensure that they clean up all memory and other resources after a thread abort or an AppDomain unload. We'll discuss AppDomains shortly.

Code Loading

Since in SQL Server users are not allowed to run arbitrary programs for reliability reasons, code (an assembly) is loaded a little differently than in other runtime hosts. The user or DBA must preload the code into the database and define which portions are invocable from Transact-SQL. Preloading and defining code uses ordinary SQL Server Data Definition Language (DDL). Loading code as a stream of bytes from the database rather than from the file system makes SQL Server's class loader unique. Later in this chapter, we'll look at the exact DDL that is used to "create" an assembly in SQL Server (that is, load or refresh the bytes of code in the database) and manage the behavior of the assemblies.

The class libraries that make up the .NET Framework are treated differently from ordinary user code in that they are loaded from the global assembly cache and are not defined to SQL Server or stored in SQL Server.

Some portions of the base class libraries may have no usefulness in a SQL Server environment (for example, System.Windows.Forms); some may be dangerous to the health of the service process when used incorrectly (System.Threading) or may be a security risk (portions of System.Security). The architects of SQL Server 2005 have reviewed the class libraries that make up the .NET Framework, and only those deemed relevant will be enabled for loading. This is accomplished by providing the CLR with a list of libraries that are OK to load.

SQL Server will take the responsibility for validating all user libraries, to determine that they don't contain non-read-only static variables, for example. SQL Server does not allow sharing state between user libraries and registers through the new CLR hosting APIs for notification of all interassembly calls. In addition, user libraries are divided into three categories by degree of danger; assemblies can be assigned to a category and use only the appropriate libraries for that category. We'll discuss this further after we've looked at the syntax involved in assembly definition.

Because code in SQL Server must be reliable, SQL Server will only load the exact version of the Framework class libraries it supports. This is analogous to shipping a particular tested version of ADO with SQL Server. Multiple versions of your code will be able to run side by side (though this was not enabled in beta 1), but the assemblies must be defined with different SQL Server object names.

Security

You may have noticed that we started this chapter by asserting that security was the most important consideration in an enterprise application but, in this discussion, we have saved it for last. This is because there is an entire chapter devoted to the subject of .NET code access security (CAS), assembly security, user security, and other security enhancements in SQL Server 2005 (see Chapter 6). We'll talk about XML namespace security in Chapter 8, which discusses the XML data type.

At this point, suffice it to say that there are three categories of access security for managed code. These are SAFE, EXTERNAL_ACCESS, and UNSAFE, which we mentioned previously with respect to class loading. This allows the DBA to determine if an assembly should be permitted certain privileges while knowing the risks. These categories equate to SQL Server–specific permission sets using code access security concepts. Having stated this, there is no specific enhancement to the CLR past the normal stack walk that intercepts all privileged operations as defined by the CLR permissions model and enforces user permissions.[1] For ensuring the integrity of user-permissions defined in the database, we depend on the principal execution context of the stored procedure or user-defined function in combination with database roles. See Chapter 6 for the specifics of security enhancements.

Loading the Runtime—
Processes and AppDomains

We've spoken of AppDomains quite a bit in previous paragraphs. It's time to describe exactly what they are and how SQL Server uses them. In .NET, processes can be subdivided into pieces known as application domains, or AppDomains. Loading the runtime loads a default AppDomain; user or system code can create other AppDomains. AppDomains are like lightweight processes themselves with respect to code isolation and marshaling. This means that object instances in one AppDomain are not directly available to other AppDomains by means of memory references; the parameters must be "marshaled up" and shipped across. In .NET, the default is marshal-by-value; a copy of the instance data is made and shipped to the caller. Another choice is marshal-by-reference, in which the caller gets a locator or "logical pointer" to the data in the callee's AppDomain, and subsequent use of that instance involves a cross AppDomain trip. This isolates one AppDomain's state from others.

Each process that loads the .NET Framework creates a default App Domain. From this AppDomain, you can create additional AppDomains programmatically, like this.

```
public static int Main(string[] argv) {

// create domain
AppDomain child = AppDomain.CreateDomain("dom2");

// execute yourapp.exe
int r = child.ExecuteAssembly("yourapp.exe",null,argv);

// unload domain
AppDomain.Unload(child);

return r;
}
```

----

[1] For more information on the stack walk process, see Keith Brown's article "Security in .NET: Enforce Code Access Rights with the Common Language Runtime" in the February 2001 issue of *MSDN Magazine*.

Although there may be many AppDomains in a process, AppDomains cannot share class instances without marshaling. The relationship between a process and its AppDomains is shown in Figure 2-2.

SQL Server does not use the default AppDomain for database processing, although it is used to load the runtime. Exactly how AppDomains are allocated in SQL Server 2005 is opaque to and not controllable by the user or DBA; however, by observation, in the beta version of SQL Server 2005, it can be determined that a separate AppDomain will be created for each database for running that database's code. Executing the system function `master.sys.fn_appdomains()` shows the AppDomains in the SQL Server process when more than one combination is in use. In the beta 1 version, the AppDomains were named "databasename.number"—for example, "AdventureWorks.2." This effectively isolates each database's user code from the others, albeit at the cost of more virtual memory. In beta 2, App Domains may be allocated based on the identity of the user owning the assembly, possibly resulting in more AppDomains, but isolating each assembly owner's code. This effectively prevents using reflection to circumvent SQL Server permissions without the overhead of intercepting each call.

The runtime-hosting APIs also support the concept of domain-neutral code. Domain-neutral code means that one copy of the Just-In-Time compiled code is shared across multiple AppDomains. Although this reduces the working set of the process because only one copy of the code and supported structures exists in memory, it is a bit slower to access static

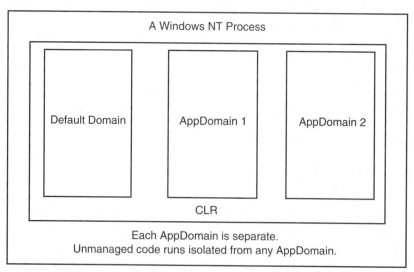

FIGURE 2-2: AppDomains in a .NET Process

variables, because each AppDomain must have its own copy of static variables and this requires the runtime to add a level of indirection. There are four domain-neutral code settings.

1. No assemblies are domain neutral.
2. All assemblies are domain neutral.
3. Only strongly named assemblies are domain neutral.
4. The host can specify a list of assemblies that are domain neutral.

SQL Server 2005 uses the fourth option—it will only share a set of Framework assemblies. It doesn't share strongly named user assemblies, because it means user assemblies that happen to be strongly named can never be unloaded.

AppDomains do not have a concept of thread affinity; that is, all App Domains share the common CLR thread pool. This means that although object instances must be marshaled across AppDomains, the marshaling is more lightweight than COM marshaling, for example, because not every marshal requires a thread switch. This also means it is possible to delegate the management of all threads to SQL Server while retaining the existing marshaling behavior with respect to threads.

Safe Code—How the Runtime Makes It Safer to Run "Foreign" Code

If you've used SQL Server for a while, you might be thinking at this point, "We've always been able to run code other than Transact-SQL inside the SQL Server process. OLE DB providers can be defined to load into memory. Extended stored procedures are written in C++ and other languages. What makes this scenario different?" The difference is that managed code is safe code. Except in the special UNSAFE mode, code is verified by the runtime to ensure that it is type-safe and validated to ensure that it contains no code that accesses memory locations directly. This all but eliminates buffer overruns, pointers that point to the wrong storage location, and so on.

The unmanaged extended stored procedure code does run under structured exception handling. You cannot bring down a SQL Server process by branching to location zero, for example. However, since an extended stored procedure runs directly in memory shared with SQL Server, it is possible for the procedure to access or change memory that it does not own. This has the capability to cause memory corruption and violate security, which is potentially more insidious.

Since code runs in its own AppDomain and is prevented from accessing memory except through the runtime, managed code is an order of magnitude safer than the extended stored procedures of the past. Note that it is possible to run unsafe .NET code inside SQL Server, but this code must be defined using the UNSAFE option in the CREATE ASSEMBLY DDL statement, with no constraints on it. It is worth noting that UNSAFE assemblies may only be cataloged by SQL Server administrators. .NET code in the Managed C++ compiler without the /safe compile switch and C# code that uses the unsafe keyword must use the UNSAFE declaration in the DDL. In addition to analyzing your code when it is cataloged to SQL Server, there are also runtime safety checks.

Host Protection Attributes

In an attempt to make .NET code more reliable to run inside hosts like SQL Server, the Host Protection Attribute was invented. The System. Security.Permissions.HostProtectionAttribute class can be applied to classes or methods to indicate that the class or method contains functionality that could cause instability in the host when invoked by user code. HostProtectionAttribute has a series of properties that can be set to indicate different potentially dangerous functionality types. The current set of properties is as follows:

- ExternalProcessMgmt
- ExternalThreading
- SelfAffectingProcessMgmt
- SelfAffectingThreading
- MayLeakOnAbort
- Resources
- SecurityInfrastructure
- SharedState
- Synchronization
- UI

Applying the HostProtectionAttribute to a class or method creates a LinkDemand—that is, a demand that the immediate caller have the permission required to execute the method. The LinkDemand is checked against the permission set of the assembly and/or the procedural code.

Setting permission sets on assemblies is shown in the section on CREATE ASSEMBLY later in the chapter. A HostProtectionAttribute differs from a normal security LinkDemand in that it is applied at the discretion of the host—in this case, SQL Server. Some hosts, like Internet Explorer, can choose to ignore the attribute, while others, like SQL Server, can choose to enforce it. If the host chooses to ignore the HostProtectionAttribute, the LinkDemand evaporates—that is, it's not executed at all.

All the Framework class libraries permitted to load in SQL Server have been decorated with HostProtectionAttributes. In conjunction with code access security (discussed in Chapter 6), HostProtectionAttributes produce a SQL Server-specific "sandbox" based on permission set that ensures the code running with any permission set other than UNSAFE cannot cause instability or lack of scalability in SQL Server.

Where the Code Lives—Storing .NET Assemblies (CREATE ASSEMBLY)

A .NET assembly is cataloged in a SQL Server database by using the CREATE ASSEMBLY statement. The following lines of code define an assembly to SQL Server and assign it the symbolic name SomeTypes.

```
CREATE ASSEMBLY SomeTypes
   FROM '\\zmv43\types\SomeTypes.dll'
```

This not only loads the code from the file, but assigns a symbolic name to it—in this case, SomeTypes. The code can be loaded from a network share or from a local file system directory, and it must be a library (DLL) rather than directly executable from the command line (EXE). No special processing of the code is needed beyond normal compilation; SomeTypes. dll is a normal .NET assembly. SomeTypes.dll must contain an assembly manifest, and although a .NET assembly can contain multiple physical files, SQL Server does not currently support multifile assemblies. The complete syntax for CREATE ASSEMBLY follows.

```
CREATE ASSEMBLY assembly_name
[ AUTHORIZATION owner_name ]

FROM { < client_assembly_specifier > | < assembly_bits > [,...n] }

[ WITH PERMISSION_SET = { SAFE | EXTERNAL_ACCESS | UNSAFE } ]

< client_assembly_specifier > :: =
    '\\machine_name\share_name\[path\]manifest_file_name'
< assembly_bits > :: =
    { varbinary_literal | varbinary_expression }
```

where:

- `assembly_name`—Is the name of the assembly; the name should be a valid SQL Server identifier.

- `client_assembly_specifier`—Specifies the local path or the network location (as UNC Path) of the assembly being loaded including the file-name of the assembly.

- `manifest_file_name`—Specifies the name of the file that contains the manifest of the assembly. SQL Server will also look for the dependent assemblies of this assembly, if any, in the same location—that is, the directory specified by `client_assembly_specifier`.

- `PERMISSION_SET = { SAFE | EXTERNAL_ACCESS | UNSAFE }`— Changes the .NET Code Access Permission Set property granted to the assembly. We'll have more to say about this later in the chapter and in Chapter 6.

- `assembly_bits`—Supplies the list of binary values that constitute the assembly and its dependent assemblies. If `assembly_bits` is specified, the first value in the list should correspond to the root-level assembly; that is, the name of the assembly as recorded in its manifest should match the `assembly_name`. The values corresponding to the dependent assemblies can be supplied in any order.

- `varbinary_literal`—Is a `varbinary` literal of the form 0x.

- `varbinary_expression`—Is an expression of type `varbinary`.

When you catalog an assembly using CREATE ASSEMBLY, the symbolic name you assign to the assembly need not agree with the name in the assembly manifest. This allows you to catalog multiple versions of the assembly or the same assembly that differ in version number or culture specifier.

The current NT user's identity is used to read the assembly file from the appropriate directory. Therefore, the user must have permission to access the directory where the assembly is located. You must be logged in to SQL Server using a SQL Server account defined with integrated security to create an assembly; attempting to use CREATE ASSEMBLY while you are logged in as a SQL Server security account will fail. Note that using CREATE ASSEMBLY copies the assembly's bits into the database and stores them physically in a system table (`sys.assembly_files`). There is no need for SQL Server to have access to the file system directory to load the bits the next time SQL Server is started; once the CREATE ASSEMBLY statement completes, SQL Server never accesses the location it loaded the assembly from again.

If the file or bits that CREATE ASSEMBLY points to does not contain an assembly manifest, or if the manifest indicates that this is a multifile assembly, CREATE ASSEMBLY will fail.

SQL Server will both verify that the assembly code is type-safe (except if PERMISSION_SET = UNSAFE) and validate the code when it is cataloged. This not only saves time, since this is usually done by the runtime during the JIT process (at first load), but also ensures that only verifiable code is cataloged into SQL Server. Unverifiable code will cause CREATE ASSEMBLY to fail. What happens during validation depends on the value of the PERMISSION_SET specified. The default PERMISSION_SET is SAFE. The permission sets control code access security permissions when the code executes, but also are meant to enforce semantics with respect to what kind of calls can be made. CREATE ASSEMBLY uses reflection to ensure that you are following the rules.

There are three distinct PERMISSION_SETs.

SAFE—This is the default permission set. An assembly cataloged with the SAFE permission set cannot compromise the security, reliability, or performance of SQL Server. SAFE code cannot access external system resources such as the registry, network, file system, or environment variables; the only CLR permission that SAFE code has is execution permission. SAFE code also cannot access unmanaged code through runtime-callable wrappers or use PInvoke to invoke a native Windows DLL. SAFE code can make data access calls using the current context but cannot access data through the SqlClient or other data providers. SAFE code cannot create threads or otherwise do any thread or process management. Attempting to use forbidden methods within a SAFE assembly will result in a security exception. The following example shows the security exception produced when a method in a SAFE assembly tries to connect to the Web using System.Net.WebRequest.

```
Msg 6522, Level 16, State 1, Line 2
A CLR error occurred during execution of 'GetFromWeb':
  System.Security.SecurityException:
  Request for the permission of type
     System.Net.WebPermission,
     System, Version=1.0.3300.0,
     Culture=neutral,
     PublicKeyToken=b77a5c561934e089 failed.
at System.Security.CodeAccessSecurityEngine.CheckHelper
   (PermissionSet grantedSet, PermissionSet deniedSet,
   CodeAccessPermission demand, PermissionToken permT...
```

EXTERNAL_ACCESS—Specifying EXTERNAL_ACCESS gives code the ability to access external system resources. Like SAFE, an assembly cataloged with the EXTERNAL_ACCESS permission set cannot compromise the security, reliability, or performance of SQL Server. The registry, network file system, external databases, and environment variables are available through the managed code APIs, but EXTERNAL_ACCESS code cannot use COM-callable wrappers or PInvoke, or create threads.

UNSAFE—UNSAFE code is not restricted in any way, including using reflection and unmanaged code. Since using UNSAFE could compromise SQL Server, only users that are members of the sql_admins role can even permit UNSAFE code. Usage permissions are described in Chapter 6, Security. Although it seems unwise to even permit UNSAFE code to execute, UNSAFE code is really no more unsafe than an extended stored procedure.

In addition to CAS permission sets, which will be discussed in Chapter 6, there is a series of .NET code requirements and coding constructs that can be used or not based on safety level. Table 2-1 shows a list of .NET constructs and their permitted usage in the three safety levels.

Assembly Dependencies—When Your Assemblies Use Other Assemblies

One very important point that we've only touched on so far is that assemblies are scoped at a database level. Since each database is its own App Domain, as mentioned previously, and assemblies may not be shared among AppDomain, they must be loadable in each AppDomain. However, you often might want to share an assembly within a single database. Examples would be statistical packages or spatial data types that are referenced by many user-defined assemblies in multiple databases. System utilities, such as collection classes, and user-defined class libraries can be used.

To ensure that a library that's being referenced by multiple assemblies is not dropped when a single library that references it is dropped, SQL Server will reflect on the assembly when CREATE ASSEMBLY is executed, to determine the dependencies. It automatically catalogs these dependencies in the SQL metadata tables. As an example, let's assume that both the Payroll department and the HR department reference a common set of formulas to calculate an employee's years of service. This library is called EmployeeRoutines.

TABLE 2-1: Code Requirements and Constructs and SQL Server Safety Levels

Feature or Construct	SAFE	EXTERNAL_ACCESS	UNSAFE
Shared state	N	N	Y
Synchronization	N	N	Y
`Thread.Create`	N	N	Y
Class constructors	Y	Y	Y
Register for static events	N	N	Y
Finalizers	N	N	Y
`Debug.Break`	N	N	N
`ThreadException.EventHandler`	N	N	N
`AppDomain.DomainUnloadEvent`	N	N	N
`PInvoke`	N	N	Y
IJW (note: `/clr:pure` and `/clr` are supported)	N	N	N
PE Verification	Y	Y	Y
Metadata Verification	Y	Y	Y
IL Verification	Y	Y	Y
Non-read-only static fields/properties	N	N	Y
Code must be type-safe	Y	Y	N
HPA `ExternalProcessMgmt`	N	N	Y
HPA `ExternalThreading`	N	N	Y
HPA `Synchronization`	N	N	Y
HPA `SharedState`	N	N	Y
HPA `SelfAffectedProcessMgmt`	N	N	Y
HPA `SelfAffectedThreading`	N	N	Y

When Payroll routines and HR routines are declared (in assemblies of analogous names), they each reference `EmployeeRoutines` as follows.

```
-- SQL Server reflection determines
-- that PayrollRoutines references EmployeeRoutines
-- EmployeeRoutines is cataloged too
CREATE ASSEMBLY PayrollRoutines FROM
     '\\zmv43\types\PayrollRoutines.DLL'
GO


-- SQL Server reflection determines
-- that HRRoutines references EmployeeRoutines
-- this sets up another reference to EmployeeRoutines
CREATE ASSEMBLY HRRoutines FROM
     '\\zmv43\types\HRRoutines.DLL'
GO
```

With the previous declarations, neither the Payroll programmers nor the HR programmers can change or drop the `EmployeeRoutines` without the consent of the other. We'll look at how you'd set up the permissions for this in Chapter 6, the security chapter.

Assemblies and SQL Schemas—Who Owns Assemblies (Information Schema)

Assemblies, like other SQL Server database objects, are the property of the user that catalogs them using CREATE ASSEMBLY, the schema owner. This has security repercussions for the users that wish to use the procedures, triggers, and types within an assembly. Though we'll go over all the security details in Chapter 6, we'd like to discuss execution context here. In addition, we'll see where exactly in the system tables (and the SQL:1999 INFORMATION_SCHEMA) information about assemblies is stored.

System Metadata Tables and INFORMATION_SCHEMA

Information about assemblies as well as the assembly code itself and the dependencies is stored in the system metadata tables, which, in general, store information about SQL Server database objects, such as tables and indexes. Some metadata tables store information for the entire database instance and exist only in the MASTER database; some are replicated in every database, user databases as well as MASTER. The names of the tables and the information they contain are proprietary. System metadata tables are performant, however, because they reflect the internal data structures of SQL Server. In the big rewrite that took place in SQL Server 7, the system metadata tables remained intact. In SQL Server 2005, the metadata tables have been overhauled, revising the layout of the metadata information and adding metadata for new database objects. In addition, programmers and DBAs can no longer write to the system metadata. It is really a read-only view.

The SQL INFORMATION_SCHEMA, on the other hand, is a series of metadata views defined by the ANSI SQL specification as a standard way to expose metadata. The views evolve with the ANSI SQL specification; SQL:1999 standard INFORMATION_SCHEMA views are a superset of the SQL-92 views. SQL Server 2000 supports the INFORMATION_SCHEMA views at the SQL-92 standard level; some of the SQL:1999 views may be added in SQL Server 2005. SQL Server is, so far, the only major database to support the INFORMATION_SCHEMA views. Listing 2-1 shows code that can be used to retrieve the list of tables in a specific database. The sample uses the system metadata tables, followed by analogous code using the INFORMATION_SCHEMA views. Note that neither query (in SQL Server, the SQL:1999 spec seems to indicate otherwise) includes the system tables in the list of tables.

LISTING 2-1: Getting Metadata from SQL Server

```
- this uses the system metadata tables
SELECT * FROM sysobjects
   WHERE type = 'U'

- this uses the INFORMATION_SCHEMA
SELECT * FROM INFORMATION_SCHEMA.TABLE
   WHERE TABLE_TYPE = 'BASE TABLE'
```

SQL Server 2005 includes a reorganization of the system metadata tables. This includes renaming the tables to use an arbitrary schema (named SYS) as well as table renames and reorganization of some of the information. The goal, once again, is speed and naming consistency. The equivalent query to the previous two using the new system metadata tables would be as follows:

```
SELECT * FROM SYS.TABLES
```

Note that the information returned by all three queries differs both in the number of columns returned, the column names used, and the information in the resultset. Although a complete description of all the new metadata tables is beyond the scope of this book, it helps to introduce the metadata information that is stored when CREATE ASSEMBLY is executed and to explain assembly properties.

Assembly Metadata

Information about assemblies and the assembly code itself is stored in three metadata tables. These tables exist on per database, since assemblies are scoped to the database and schema.

Sys.assemblies stores information about the assembly itself as well as schema_id, assembly_id, and the .NET version number. The complete list of columns in sys.assemblies is shown in Table 2-2.

TABLE 2-2: Contents of sys.assemblies

Column Name	Data Type	Description
name	sysname	Name of assembly, unique within schema.
principal_id	int	ID of the principal that owns this schema.
assembly_id	int	Assembly identification number, unique within a database.
clr_name	nvarchar(4000)	Canonical string that encodes the simple name, version number, culture, and public key of the assembly. It uniquely identifies the assembly on the CLR side.
permission_set	tinyint	Permission set/security level for assembly, one of: 1 = Safe Access only 2 = External Access allowed 3 = Unsafe Access allowed
permission_set_desc	nvarchar(60)	Description of permission set/security level for assembly, one of: SAFE_ACCESS EXTERNAL_ACCESS UNSAFE_ACCESS

TABLE 2-2: Contents of sys.assemblies *(continued)*

Column Name	Data Type	Description
is_visible	bit	1 if the assembly is visible to register T-SQL entry points (functions/procs/triggers/types/aggregates); 0 if it is intended only for managed callers (that is, provides internal implementation for other assemblies in the database).
create_date	datetime	Date assembly was created or registered.

The assembly dependencies are stored in sys.assembly_references, one row per assembly-reference pair. Table 2-3 shows the columns in sys.assembly_references. Note that this table does not contain information about which base class libraries an assembly references.

Finally, the assembly code itself is cataloged in sys.assembly_files. In all cases, this table contains the actual code rather than the name of the file where the code resided when it was cataloged. The original file location is not even kept as metadata. In addition, if you have added a debugger file, using the ALTER ASSEMBLY ADD FILE DDL statement, the debug information will appear as an additional entry in the sys.assembly_files table. Table 2-4 shows the contents of the sys.assembly_files table.

We'll discuss more about declaring routines and types in the CREATE ASSEMBLY DDL statement in Chapters 3 and 4. Notice that you can define an assembly that is "invisible" with respect to defining routines and types to the runtime. Lack of visibility is the default when SQL Server loads dependent assemblies of an assembly defined using CREATE ASSEMBLY. You might do this, for example, to define a set of utility routines to be

TABLE 2-3: Contents of sys.assembly_references

Column Name	Data Type	Description
assembly_id	int	ID of assembly to which this reference belongs
referenced_assembly_id	int	ID of assembly being referenced

TABLE 2-4: Contents of sys.assembly_files

Column Name	Data Type	Description
assembly_id	int	ID of assembly to which this file belongs
name	nvarchar (260)	Name of assembly file
file_id	int	ID of file, unique within an assembly
content	image	Bytes of assembly or debug symbols

invoked internally only. If you specify `IsVisible=true` (the default) this means that methods and types in this assembly can be declared as SQL Server methods and types, either through the "list" properties or directly through DDL.

Maintaining User Assemblies (ALTER ASSEMBLY, DROP ASSEMBLY)

Although we stated earlier in this chapter that SQL Server loads only a single version of the .NET runtime and base class libraries, assemblies may be versioned, their code reloaded, and properties (including the set of dependent assemblies) altered via DDL. Assemblies may also be dropped via DDL, subject to whether or not they are currently used by other system objects. An example of dropping the `SomeTypes` assembly defined earlier follows.

```
DROP ASSEMBLY SomeTypes
```

The complete syntax for dropping a defined assembly follows.

```
DROP ASSEMBLY assembly_name
[WITH drop_option [,..]]

drop_option::=
        CASCADE | DEPENDENT ASSEMBLIES
```

Note that unless the `CASCADE` option is specified, the `DROP ASSEMBLY` statement will fail if any existing routines, user-defined types, or user-defined aggregates exist that refer to the assembly. We'll get back to dependent assemblies in a moment.

You may change the properties of an assembly or even modify the assembly code in place using the `ALTER ASSEMBLY` statement. For example, let's assume that we'd decided that the `SomeTypes` assembly mentioned earlier needs to be present in SQL Server, but it need not be visible (for example, it is accessed only by other assemblies and not "from the outside"). To prevent routines in this assembly from inadvertently being declared publicly via DDL, we can alter its visibility like this.

```
ALTER ASSEMBLY SomeTypes
  VISIBILITY=OFF
```

To reload the `SomeTypes` assembly, as long as it is not currently being referenced, we can use the following syntax.

```
ALTER ASSEMBLY SomeTypes
  FROM '\\zmv43\types\SomeTypes.dll'
```

The complete syntax for ALTER ASSEMBLY follows. We'll discuss some of the more esoteric options in Chapters 4 and 5, and the security options in Chapter 6.

```
ALTER ASSEMBLY assembly_name
  [ FROM { < client_assembly_specifier > |
          < assembly_bits > [ ,...n ] ]
  [ WITH < assembly_option > [ ,...n ] ]
  [ DROP FILE { file_name [ ,...n ] | ALL } ]
  [ ADD FILE FROM { client_file_specifier
    [ AS file_name ] | file_bits AS file_name } [,...n ]

< client_assembly_specifier > :: =
    '\\computer_name\share-name\[path\]manifest_file_name'

< assembly_bits > :: =
    { varbinary_literal | varbinary_expression }

< assembly_option > :: =
      [ PERMISSION_SET { SAFE | EXTERNAL_ACCESS | UNSAFE } ]
      [ VISIBILITY { ON | OFF } ]
      UNCHECKED DATA
```

In order to change the permission set with ALTER ASSEMBLY, you must have analogous permissions as with CREATE ASSEMBLY—that is, you need EXTERNAL_ACCESS privilege to alter an assembly to the EXTERNAL_ACCESS safety level, and you must be sysadmin to alter an assembly to UNSAFE. You also must have analogous file access permissions as with CREATE ASSEMBLY if you are going to load any new code from a file.

You can use ALTER ASSEMBLY not only to change individual metadata properties, but to version or reload the code as well. Reloading the code (by using the FROM clause) not only reloads, but revalidates code as well.

Your new code can differ from the original only by the fourth part of the version number. Of course, this code must be built against the same version of the runtime and the base class libraries as the original.

If there are references to the assembly, any of the method signatures of the methods defined as stored procedures, triggers, and user-defined functions are not allowed to change. If your new version contains user-defined types, ALTER ASSEMBLY not only checks all the methods' signatures, but if the serialization format is Native, all the data members must be the same so that the user-defined type instances that have been persisted (as column values in tables) will still be usable. Other types of persisted data will be checked too, if your assembly contains the following:

- Persisted computed columns that reference assembly methods
- Indexes on computed columns that reference assembly methods
- Columns with check constraints that reference assembly user-defined functions (UDFs)

You can bypass checking persisted data by specifying the UNCHECKED DATA option; you must be DBO or db_ddlowner to use this option. The metadata will indicate that the data is unchecked until you use the command DBCC CHECKTABLE to manually check the data in each table. You must be sure that the formulas (content) of user-defined functions have not changed before you use the UNCHECKED DATA option, or else corrupted data could result.

When you use ALTER ASSEMBLY, there may be user sessions using the old version of the assembly. In order not to disrupt those sessions, SQL Server will create a new AppDomain to load your new code. Existing sessions continue to use the old code in the original AppDomain until logoff; new sessions will be routed to the new AppDomain. When all the existing sessions finish, the old AppDomain is shut down. This is the only (transient) case where two different versions of your code can be running at the same time, but is not the same as side-by-side execution.

One common usage for programmers will probably be to add debugging information to use during development. A .NET assembly can be debugged inside SQL Server with any of the usual .NET debuggers—for example, Visual Studio 2005. You may have noticed that one of the metadata tables (sys.assembly_files) will contain an additional entry if you have added the .NET debugging symbols for the assembly. This file usually has a .pdb extension when it is produced by the compiler. To add a debug symbols file for the assembly that we just defined earlier, you can execute the following statement.

```
ALTER ASSEMBLY SomeTypes
ADD FILE FROM '\\zmv43\types\SomeTypes.pdb'
go
```

The SQL Server project in Visual Studio 2005 will perform this step automatically when you use the Deploy menu entry.

Specification Compliance

The ANSI SQL specification attempts to standardize all issues related to relational databases, not just the SQL language. Although some databases allow external code to run inside the database (SQL Server permits this through extended stored procedures), this was not part of the SQL specification until recently. Two specifications appeared at the end of the SQL:1999 standardization process that relate to some of the concepts we're going to be covering in the SQL Server–.NET integration portion of this book. These specifications are related to the concept of managed code running inside the database and the interoperation of managed types and unmanaged types, and are called SQL/J part 1 and SQL/J part 2. There are two interesting features of these specs.

- They were added as addenda to SQL:1999 after the specification was submitted. SQL/J part 1 became SQL:1999 part 12, and SQL/J part 2 became SQL:1999 part 13. This specification was consolidated as part 13 of SQL:200x, and is there known as SQL-Part 13: Java Routines and Types (SQL/JRT).
- Although the specs are part of the ANSI SQL specification, the only managed language they address is Java, which is itself not a standard. Java was withdrawn from the ECMA standardization process. On the other hand, the .NET CLR is an ECMA standard.

Nevertheless it is interesting to at least draw parallels.

The closest equivalents to SQL Server 2005's CREATE ASSEMBLY/ALTER ASSEMBLY/DROP ASSEMBLY are SQL/J's SQLJ.INSTALL_JAR, SQLJ.REMOVE_JAR, SQLJ.REPLACE_JAR procedures. These procedures are not implemented by all the implementers of the standard. Because the SQL/J standard does not state that the actual code needs to be stored in the database, you can also change the defined path where the jar file resides with SQLJ.ALTER_JAR_PATH. Because SQL Server assemblies are stored inside the database, an equivalent function would be unnecessary.

Some of the ancillary concepts are analogous with respect to deploying the items that an assembly or `jar` file contains. The specification includes a bit to indicate whether a deployment descriptor included in the `jar` file should be read; an analogous concept would be the list of publicly declared methods and types in the CREATE ASSEMBLY or ALTER ASSEMBLY statement. Visibility of classes and methods is defined by using the public or private keywords, as it is in SQL Server 2005, but no notion of visibility at the `jar` level exists in the SQL specification to correspond to the SQL Server 2005 notion of assembly visibility. References are defined in the ANSI specification only with respect to path names; there is no concept of keeping references in the schema. The ANSI specification contains no notion of code access security level and execution context. Database permissions for managed code within an assembly are part of SQL Server 2005 and, to an extent, the code within a SQL/JRT file as well. We'll discuss this in Chapter 6 on security.

Conclusions

If your assembly is SAFE or EXTERNAL_ACCESS, nothing you can do will affect SQL security, reliability, or performance. You'll have to work hard to make your app itself unreliable and nonscalable at these safety levels. SAFE or EXTERNAL_ACCESS levels enforce the general principles of no-shared-state and no multithreaded programming. Writing secure, reliable, and performant code that doesn't follow these tenets is harder and is only possible for assemblies cataloged as UNSAFE.

Where Are We?

We've seen how SQL Server 2005 is a full-fledged runtime host and can run your managed code. SQL Server's choices as a runtime host are geared toward security and reliability, with an eye toward performance.

We've seen how to define an assembly (managed DLL) to SQL Server for storage inside the server and how to specify the execution context (identity) and degree of safety with which the code runs. The CLR's Framework class libraries are even categorized by degree of safety; this should ameliorate some of the DBA's concerns.

In the next chapter, we'll look at some of the specific code you'd write as managed–stored procedures, user-defined functions, and triggers—and see how this code is defined to SQL Server so that it's indistinguishable from T-SQL procedures to the caller.

■ 3 ■

Procedures and Functions in .NET Languages

T-SQL IS A SQL SERVER–SPECIFIC LANGUAGE used to extend the
functionality of SQL Server. Any language capable of creating a DLL
or a COM component can be used to extend the functionality of SQL
Server; but extended stored procedures and COM components lack the
reliability, security, and, in many cases, the performance that T-SQL provides. With SQL Server 2005, any .NET language can be used to extend the
functionality of SQL Server with the same level of reliability, security, and
performance that T-SQL provides.

Extending SQL Server

SQL Server's functionality can be extended by using T-SQL. It encapsulates common tasks and makes it easier to maintain and perform them. It,
in effect, allows you to write SQL batches that perform common tasks and
store those batches for later reuse directly in SQL Server.

Much of the functionality associated with SQL Server does not come
from the SQL programming language; it comes from extensions that
Microsoft has added to SQL Server using T-SQL, its proprietary language
for writing imperative code. For example, there is a Microsoft-written
stored procedure to add a new user to a database called `sp_adduser`. This
stored procedure inserts the parameters you pass in, login name and user

name, into appropriate database tables. You always use `sp_adduser` to add a user to the database, and do not need to know the details of what happens inside the database. In fact, Microsoft could completely change how SQL Server maintains users in a database, and it would not affect the way you add users to a database.

Prior to SQL Server 2005, except for T-SQL the only ways to extend SQL Server were to write an extended stored procedure or a COM component. T-SQL required you to know the T-SQL language. For many this meant learning an alternate programming language used much less than their primary one. For a VB.NET programmer, this might mean stumbling through something like "Dim id. Whoops, no, Declare id. Whoops, no, Declare @id as new int. Whoops, no, Declare @id int." Similar relearn-by-syntax-error journeys await programmers from other languages whenever they attempt to write a T-SQL-based stored procedure too.

Extended stored procedures require a rather tedious DLL to be created. However C++ programmers can use a wizard in Visual Studio to create this DLL and just fill in the functionality they choose. Likewise, VB6 programmers can create a COM component and add it in SQL Server using the `sp_OACreate` stored procedure. This allows C++ or VB6 programmers to use a familiar programming environment to extend SQL code. Extended stored procedures and COM components are also more flexible than T-SQL because they can access system services that are outside SQL Server. For example, the extension to SQL Server that allows it to send e-mail is an extended stored procedure. It could not have been written in T-SQL. Extended stored procedures have their own issues. Although it is possible to write extended stored procedures that are secure and reliable, the languages used to create them make this very difficult to do. In general, an extended stored procedure or a COM component must stand a much higher level of scrutiny than a T-SQL-based stored procedure and in some cases cannot match its performance.

SQL Server 2005 changes all this. Any .NET language can extend SQL Server. .NET languages run in the Common Language Runtime, the CLR. Extensions running in the CLR can be as safe and reliable as T-SQL and as flexible as an extended stored procedure or a COM component. This means that developers can use a familiar development environment to extend the functionality of SQL Server.

In addition, there are some tasks for which the CLR is just better suited. Typically, the CLR is a better choice for operations that involve numeric computations or string manipulation.

The CLR is not better suited for doing set operations. SQL is the clear winner here. However, the CLR can execute SQL expressions, just as T-SQL can and with the same efficiency. Being able to write code in a CLR language will not be a substitute for knowing how write SELECT A.au_fname, A.au_lname FROM authors A JOIN titleauthors T ON A.au_id = T.au_id when you need to find all the authors that have publications.

The previous chapter, Chapter 2, explained how assemblies are loaded into SQL Server. This chapter focuses on the basic mechanics of using the methods in those assemblies as stored procedures, scalar-valued functions, and triggers. The chapter that follows this, Chapter 4, explains how these methods can access SQL Server directly, in a performant way.

CLR Methods in SQL Server

A public static method of a public class can, with some restrictions, be used as a stored procedure, user-defined function, or trigger in SQL Server. We will cover the specific restrictions, but, in general, they limit the method parameters to those that make sense when used inside SQL Server.

To illustrate the use of CLR methods in SQL Server, we will look at a database for a company that makes pulley/belt drives. A pulley/belt drive is a kind of transmission; it has two round pulleys with a belt wrapped around them. Lots of kinds of equipment, from lawnmowers to drill presses, use the pulley/belt transmissions. Figure 3-1 shows an example of a pulley/belt drive.

A belt, whose length is L, wraps around pulley 1 and pulley 2. D1 is the diameter of pulley 1, and D2 is the diameter of pulley 2. C is the distance from the center of pulley 1 to pulley 2.

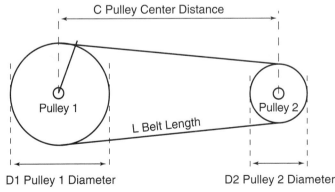

FIGURE 3-1: Pulley/Belt Drive

Our pulley/belt company uses a database to keep track of the kinds of pulleys and belts they stock. The database has a pulley table that lists each pulley by part number and diameter. It has a belt table that lists each belt by part number and length. Any combination of two pulleys and a belt can be used to make a transmission if the pulleys can be placed far enough part to not touch each other and still allow the belt to go around them.

This company wants a view that will show them all the possible transmissions that they can make from the parts that they stock. The transmission view should show the part numbers for the pulleys and belt, and it must also show the distance between the centers of the pulleys.

The distance between the pulleys requires a geometric calculation. Listing 3-1 shows a function that calculates the approximate distance between the two pulleys of a pulley/belt transmission, given the pulley sizes and belt length.

LISTING 3-1: PulleyDistance Function

```
public class CPulley
{
    public static double PulleyDistance(
    double Pulley1Diameter,
    double Pulley2Diameter,
    double BeltLength)
    {
    double length = 0;
    double a = 2.0;
    double b = BeltLength - 1.57 * (Pulley1Diameter + Pulley2Diameter);
    double c = System.Math.Pow(Pulley1Diameter - Pulley2Diameter, 2.0);
    // if this is not positive no chance the pulleys will fit
    double b1 = Math.Pow(b, 2.0) - (4 * a * c);
    if(b1 > 0)
    {
        length = (b + Math.Sqrt(b1)) / (2 * a);
        // check that pulleys fit
        if (length < ((Pulley1Diameter + Pulley2Diameter) / 2))
        {
            // return 0 if pulleys don't fit
            length = 0;
        }
    }
    // one decimal point is enough
    return System.Math.Round(length, 1);
    }
}
```

There are a number of formulas that govern the use and operation of pulley/belt transmissions. The formula the `PulleyDistance` function comes from the *McGraw-Hill Machining and Metalworking Handbook,* by Ronald Walsh (McGraw-Hill, 1994). Listing 3-2 shows a SQL batch that builds a sample database and the `Transmissions` view.

LISTING 3-2: Pulley/Belt Database

```
CREATE TABLE Pulley
(
model CHAR(10),
diameter FLOAT
)
CREATE TABLE Belt
(
model CHAR(10),
length CHAR
)
GO
 - generate pulley data
DECLARE @i INT
SET @i = 40
WHILE (@i > 0)
  BEGIN
  INSERT INTO Pulley VALUES ('P' + CONVERT(VARCHAR, @i), @i)
  SET @i = @i - 1
END
GO
- generate belt data
DECLARE @i INT
SET @i = 30
WHILE (@i > 0)
  BEGIN
  INSERT INTO Belt VALUES ('M' + CONVERT(varchar, @i), @i * 4)
  SET @i = @i - 5
END
GO


CREATE VIEW Transmissions
AS SELECT B.model AS Belt,
P1.model AS P1,
P2.model AS P2,
dbo.PulleyDistance(P1.diameter, P2.diameter, B.length) AS C
FROM
Belt B, Pulley P1, Pulley P2
WHERE dbo.PulleyDistance(P1.diameter, P2.diameter,
   B.length) > 0
AND P1.Diameter < P2.Diameter
GO
SELECT * FROM Transmissions
```

Belt	P1	P2	C
M30	P12	P29	20.9
M30	P11	P29	20.8
M30	P10	P29	20.6
...			

The SQL batch in Listing 3-2 first creates the Pulley and Belt tables and then fills the tables with test data. Next it creates a view called `Transmissions`. It uses the `PulleyDistance` function to determine the pulley center distance. If the distance is zero, it does not include that row in the view.

This function can be written in T-SQL. In a field like mechanical engineering, it is more likely that the experts in the field of pulley/belt transmission would be more familiar with C# or VB.NET than T-SQL. It is also likely that this function might be part of an existing, verified-by-usage code module. Using functions written in a CLR language is a powerful enhancement to SQL Server because it allows experts in a field to use a familiar programming environment and existing code without compromising reliability or security.

In order for the function in Listing 3-1 to be used, it must be added to the database that will call it. First, the assembly, which contains the function, must be added to the database, as was shown in Chapter 2. After the assembly as been added, the function itself must be added using the CREATE FUNCTION command, as would be done for any user-defined function added to a database. Listing 3-3 shows the `PulleyDistance` function being added to a database.

LISTING 3-3: Adding Functions to a Database

```
CREATE ASSEMBLY Pulleys FROM 'c:\bin\Pulleys.dll'
CREATE FUNCTION PulleyDistance(@P1 FLOAT, @P2 FLOAT, @Belt FLOAT)
   RETURNS FLOAT
   -- format is assembly.class.function
   EXTERNAL NAME Pulleys.CPully.PulleyDistance
```

Note that the case is significant in the EXTERNAL NAME even if the .NET language used to create the function is not case sensitive (for example, VB.NET). The case of the names of the class and function must match those in the source code.

Some notes on terminology for this chapter: Both SQL Server and the CLR can be thought of as having functions and procedures. To distinguish between code in SQL Server and code in the CLR, the remainder of this chapter uses the terms "procedure" and "function" refer to SQL Server stored procedures and functions. The term "method" refers to a function or procedure in a CLR type. In addition, this chapter will talk about the System.Data.SqlTypes namespace. This namespace contains a number of type definitions, such as SqlInt32. The term SqlType is a generic reference for one of these types.

The CLR allows methods to be overloaded—that is, two methods in the same class with the same name but different parameter types or count. Overloaded methods may not be used to implement a SQL procedure, function, or index. The following code fragment shows an example of overloaded methods.

```
// class is public
public class Arithmetic
{
        // method is static and public
        // but this method and the one that follows it
        // have the same name so neither can be used for
        // the implementation of a procedure, function, or index
        public static int AddTheseNumbers(int a1, int a2)
        {
                return a1 + a2;
        }
        // method is static and public
        public static int AddTheseNumbers(int a1, int a2, int a3)
        {
                return a1 + a2 + a3;
        }
}
```

The CLR allows type definitions to be nested—that is, a type definition that is within the scope of another type definition. Methods from nested type definitions may not be used to implement a SQL procedure, function, or trigger. The method named Invert in the following code fragment is an example of this.

```
// class is public
public class Arithmetic
{
        public class Numeric
        {
                // Invert may not be used to implement
                // a procedure, function, or trigger
                // because it is a member of a nested type
                public static int Invert(int a1)
```

```
        {
            Return -a1;
        }
    }
}
```

Methods used to implement procedures, functions, or triggers may access anything methods in the CLR may access, including files, network connects, and the wide range of capabilities provided by the .NET Framework. They are, however, limited by the permission set given the assembly containing them when it was cataloged, as shown in Chapter 2 and as will be discussed in detail in Chapter 5.

Only simple static, public methods from public classes that are not nested can be used to implement procedures, functions, and triggers. There are further restrictions on the parameters these methods can use, which are covered in the next section.

System.Data.SqlTypes

The `PulleyDistance` function in the previous section, though useful, does not have all the capabilities of a T-SQL function. For example, when the SQL batch in Listing 3-4 is run, it produces an error.

LISTING 3-4: PulleyDistance with a Null Argument

```
PRINT dbo.PulleyDistance(40, 20, NULL)
.Net SqlClient Data Provider: Msg 6569, Level 16, State 1, Line 1
'PulleyDistance' failed because input parameter 3 is not allowed
    to be null.
```

As the `PulleyDistance` method is written, there is nothing that can be done to prevent this error, because there is no way for it to check to see if an input parameter is NULL. A T-SQL function can, however, always check an argument for NULL, as is shown in Listing 3-5.

LISTING 3-5: Function That Tests for NULL

```
CREATE FUNCTION Width(@Size int)
RETURNS int
AS
IF (@Size IS NULL)
    RETURN NULL
RETURN -@Size
```

The problem that the `PulleyDistance` method has is that there is no way for the CLR data type double to represent a null. The `System.Data.` `SqlTypes` namespace contains data type definitions that more closely mimic the behavior of SQL data type. For example, the `PulleyDistance` method could be rewritten as shown in Listing 3-6 and handle null parameters in the same way a typical T-SQL function would.

LISTING 3-6: PulleyDistance Function Using SqlType

```
public class CPulley
{
    public static SqlDouble PulleyDistance(
    SqlDouble Pulley1Diameter,
    SqlDouble Pulley2Diameter,
    SqlDouble BeltLength)
  {
    if(Pulley1Diameter.IsNull ||
    Pulley2Diameter.IsNull ||
    BeltLength.IsNull)
    return SqlDouble.Null
...
```

The use of `System.Data.SqlTypes` in methods that implement T-SQL stored procedures, functions, or triggers is best practice. This section discusses `System.Data.SqlTypes`.

One of the restrictions on methods is that they must use data types for parameters and return values with which SQL Server is familiar. For example, SQL Server could not use a method that had a `System.Collections.` `Hashtable` as a parameter. The types used must be a `SqlType`, a type in the CLR that corresponds to a `SqlType`, or a user-defined type. (User-defined types will be discussed in Chapter 5.) Table 3-1 shows CLR types that correspond to the types in the `System.Data.SqlTypes` namespace. User-defined types, discussed in Chapter 5, are an exception to this table.

The first column shows types from the `System.Data.SqlTypes` namespace. The second column shows the corresponding CLR type. The type of a parameter or return value for a method must appear in either the `SqlType` or CLR Type columns of this table. Note that some programming languages use synonyms for CLR type names. In particular, C# and VB.NET refer to `Int32` as `int`, and `Int64` as `long`.

The third column shows the SQL native type that corresponds to the `SqlType`. You will need to know this when you add your code to SQL Server, which will be discussed later. The last column shows the `SqlDbType` that

TABLE 3-1: SqlType Correspondence to Other Types

SqlType	CLR	SQL Native	SQLDB
SqlBinary	Byte[]	BINARY	Binary
		VARBINARY	VarBinary
		TIMESTAMP	TimeStamp
		IMAGE	Image
SqlInt64	Int64	BIGINT	BigInt
SqlInt32	Int32	INT	Int
SqlInt16	Int16	SMALLINT	SmallInt
SqlByte	Byte	TINYINT	Byte
SqlString	String	CHAR	Char
		VARCHAR	VarChar
		NCHAR	NChar
		NVARCHAR	NVarChar
		TEXT	Text
		NTEXT	NText
		SYSNAME	VarChar
SqlDateTime	Datetime	DATETIME	DateTime
		SMALLDATETIME	SmallDateTime
SqlDecimal	Decimal	DECIMAL	Decimal
		NUMERIC	Numeric
SqlDouble	Double	FLOAT	Float
SqlSingle	Single	REAL	Real
SqlMoney	Decimal	MONEY	Money
		SMALLMONEY	SmallMoney
SqlGuid	Guid	UNIQUEIDENTIFIER	UniqueId
SqlBoolean	Boolean	BIT	Boolean

corresponds to the `SqlType`. You will need to know this when creating parameters for SQL commands. Chapter 4 discusses using OLE DB and ODBC providers, some of which use `SqlDbType`.

Note that this example and others that follow on the usage of a `SqlType` work independently of SQL Server. You can use this code in an ordinary console or Windows application to try it out without loading the code into SQL Server. All the examples reference `System.dll` and `System.Data.dll`, and should include the following `using` statements.

```
using System;
using System.Data;
using System.Data.Sql;
using System.Data.SqlTypes;
```

A `SqlType` has a property named `Value`. This property contains the value of the `SqlType` in terms of its corresponding CLR native type. The following code fragment is part of the C# type definition for `SqlInt32`, showing the definition of its `Value` property.

```
public struct SqlInt32 : ...
{
    ...
    // Value returns the CLR type corresponding to the SqlType,
    // in this case an int is returned for the SqlInt32 SqlType
        public int Value {get;}
}
```

Every `SqlType` has this property; the only difference among them is the type returned by `Value`. In some cases, you will need the CLR type to process the `SqlType`—for example, when you pass it as a parameter to a method that requires a CLR type. The following lines of C# code show a method that extracts a CLR type from a `SqlType`.

```
public class Limits
{
    // SqlDouble and SqlInt32 used as parameters
    public static int Edge(SqlDouble d1, SqlInt32 i2)
    {
        // gets SqlDouble value as CLR double
        // so its square root can be calculated
        if(System.Math.Sqrt(d1.Value) > 3.0)
        {
            return 7;
        }
        // gets SqlInt32 value as CLR int
```

```
        // so it can be returned as an int
        int i = i2.Value;
        return i;
    }
}
```

In the preceding example, the function `Edge` must get the value of d1 as a double in order to pass it to the `Sqrt` method. It must also get the value of i2 as an `int` in order to return it. Note that best practice says that this method should return some kind of `SqlInt`. It is returning an `int` so that it can illustrate the use of the `Value` property that all the data types in the `System.Data.SqlTypes` have.

An alternate way to get the value of a `SqlType` as a CLR type is to cast it to it. A cast is more flexible than using the `Value` property in that it can not only get the value of the `SqlType` as a CLR type, it can also coerce to a different type. The following code is an example of using a cast to get the value of a `SqlType` and coerce it to a CLR type that is different from the one that corresponds to the `SqlType`.

```
namespace Math
{
    public class Arithmetic
    {
        public static int SameAs1(SqlInt64 i)
        {
            // this compiles and works as expected
            // it coerces the SqlInt64 to a Int32
            // instead of long, which corresponds to SqlInt64
            return (int)i;
        }
        public static int SameAs2(SqlInt64 i)
        {
            // this produces a compile-time error
            // because Value is a long
            return i.Value;
        }
    }
}
```

A `SqlType` can be explicitly coerced to its corresponding CLR type and to any type that is compatible with that CLR type. Also, each `SqlType` can be explicitly coerced to another `SqlType`. Table 3-2 shows coercions allowed from one `SqlType` to another. The first column on the left lists the types to be coerced. The rest of the columns note the types to which it can be explicitly coerced by marking an X in it. For example, it shows that a `SqlGuid` can be explicitly coerced to a `SqlGuid`, a `SqlBinary`, and a `SqlString`.

TABLE 3-2: Explicit SqlType Coercions

	SqlBinary	SqlBoolean	SqlByte	SqlDate	SqlDateTime	SqlDecimal	SqlDouble	SqlGuid	SqlInt16	SqlInt32	SqlInt64	SqlMoney	SqlSingle	SqlString	SqlTime	SqlXMLReader
SqlBinary	X							X								
SqlBoolean		X	X			X	X		X	X	X	X	X	X		
SqlByte		X	X											X		
SqlDate				X												
SqlDateTime					X										X	
SqlDecimal		X	X			X			X	X	X	X		X		
SqlDouble		X	X			X	X		X	X	X	X	X	X		
SqlGuid	X							X						X		
SqlInt16		X	X						X					X		
SqlInt32		X	X						X	X				X		
SqlInt64		X	X						X	X	X			X		
SqlMoney		X	X						X	X	X	X		X		
SqlSingle		X	X			X			X	X	X	X	X	X		
SqlString		X	X	X	X	X	X	X	X	X	X	X	X			
SqlTime															X	
SqlXmlReader																X

It is interesting to note that SqlString can be explicitly coerced to almost any other SqlType. This mimics the behavior of strings within SQL Server itself. The following code fragment shows how explicit coercions can be used to coerce a SqlString to some other SqlType.

```
SqlString s = new SqlString("1.01");
SqlMoney m = (SqlMoney)s;
// this line prints out 1.01
Console.WriteLine(m);
```

```
SqlString s2 = "{90110409-6000-11D3-8CFE-0150048383C9}";
SqlGuid g = (SqlGuid)s2;
// this line prints out 90110409-6000-11D3-8CFE-0150048383C9
Console.WriteLine(g);
```

In addition to explicit coercions, implicit ones are supported. An implicit coercion means the type will automatically be coerced when required. For example, a method that is defined as returning a SqlInt64 can return a SqlInt32, because there is an implicit coercion from SqlInt32 to SqlInt64. An example of this follows.

```
public class Math
{
        public static SqlInt64 Same3(SqlInt32 i)
        {
                // i is implicitly cast to SqlInt64
                // because that is what is required
                // for the return value
                return i;
        }
}
```

Another example of implicit coercions follows.

```
SqlDecimal sdecimal = new SqlDecimal(1.0);
SqlDouble sdouble = 1.0;
// the following line does an explicit conversion
sdecimal = (SqlDecimal)sdouble;
// the following line does an implicit conversion
// not that it does not require (SqlDecimal)
Sdecimal = sdouble;
// the following attempts an implicit conversion but will
// not work because there is no implicit conversion
// from SqlDouble to SqlDecimal
sdecimal = sdouble; // compile-time error
```

In addition, a CLR type that corresponds to a SqlType can be implicitly coerced to that SqlType. The CLR type that corresponds to a SqlType is the type of the Value property of the SqlType. For example, the CLR type of the Value property of SqlDouble is System.Double. This means that no explicit conversion is required to set the value of a SqlDouble with a CLR double. The example that follows shows this.

```
SqlDouble sdouble = new SqlDouble(1.0);
// no explicit conversion is required because 3.0
// is a double and the type of the Value property
// of SqlDouble is double
sdouble = 3.0;
```

So implicit coercion makes code easier to read and requires less typing, but implicit coercion should never lose precision, and not all SqlTypes can be implicitly coerced from one to another. Table 3-3 shows the implicit coercions between SqlTypes that are available. The left column and first row lists each SqlType. An X in a column indicates that the SqlType named in the first column can be implicitly coerced to the SqlType listed at the top of the column. For example, it shows that a SqlDecimal can be implicitly coerced to a SqlDecimal, a SqlDouble, and a SqlSingle.

TABLE 3-3: Implicit SqlType Coercions

	SqlBinary	SqlBoolean	SqlDate	SqlDateTime	SqlDecimal	SqlDouble	SqlGuid	SqlByte	SqlInt16	SqlInt32	SqlInt64	SqlMoney	SqlSingle	SqlString	SqlTime	SqlXML Reader
SqlBinary	X															
SqlBoolean		X														
SqlDate			X													
SqlDateTime				X												
SqlDecimal					X	X							X			
SqlDouble						X										
SqlGuid							X									
SqlByte					X	X		X	X	X	X	X	X			
SqlInt16					X	X			X	X	X	X	X			
SqlInt32					X	X				X	X	X	X			
SqlInt64					X	X					X	X	X			
SqlMoney					X	X						X	X			
SqlSingle						X							X			
SqlString														X		
SqlTime															X	
SqlmlReader																X

Implicit coercion can be used to easily set the value of a `SqlType`. Also note that a `SqlType` cannot be implicitly coerced to its corresponding CLR type. Some examples of this are shown in the following code fragment.

```
// sets the Value of si to 12
SqlInt32 si = 12;
// this will produce a compile-time error
// because there is no implicit coercion from
// SqlInt32 to int
int i = si;
// you must use explicit coercion
int i1 = (int)si;
```

`SqlDouble` and `SqlSingle` behave a bit differently from their CLR counterparts. `SqlDouble` and `SqlSingle` cannot represent NaN or infinity. An attempt to set a `SqlDouble` or `SqlSingle` to either of these will result in a runtime error. The following code fragment shows this.

```
double d = double.Nan;
// this will cause a runtime error
SqlDouble sd = d;
d = 4.7;
// this will work as expected
SqlDouble sd2 = d;
```

The CLR defines several special names for methods that are used to implement binary and unary operators, such as `op_Addition` or `op_LogicalNot`. Most languages use these special names when a class implements them for operations like addition. Although the CLR doesn't prohibit it, some languages, including VB.NET and C#, do not allow you to use these names for methods in your classes or to call these methods. Instead, they have symbols that are used in their place—for example "+" and "!". The methods for these special names, if a class has them, are implemented as static methods taking up to two instances of the class's type as parameters and returning an instance of the class's type. The following code fragment shows how `SqlInt32` implements `op_Addition`.

```
public static SqlInt32 op_Addition(SqlInt32 x, SqlInt32 y);
```

Because of this, you can add one `SqlInt32` to another using the "+" operator. The following code fragment shows this.

```
public SqlInt32 A = new SqlInt32(3);
public SqlInt32 B = new SqlInt32(5);
// this uses op_Addition to add A and B
public SqlInt32 Sum = A + B;
```

Most of the `SqlTypes` implement many of the specially named opera-tors. Most of the operators are also implemented by CLR numeric types. The numeric operations that are implemented by a `SqlType` are just as perfor-mant as the ones on its corresponding CLR type in most cases, so typically there is no performance to be gained by coercing a `SqlType` to its corre-sponding CLR type to do a calculation.

The one exception to this is `SqlDecimal`. The numeric operations that are part of `SqlDecimal` may not be as fast as those on the CLR `decimal` type, but they cover a much wider range of numbers. `SqlDecimal` can rep-resent any number that the SQL Server decimal can, which is not the case for the CLR `decimal` type. For example, the largest number that `SqlDecimal` can represent is 99999999999999999999999999999999999999, but the largest number that the CLR `decimal` type can represent is only 79228162514264337593543950335. This property of `SqlDecimal` may cause a runtime error if it is coerced to the CLR `decimal` type and the value of the `SqlDecimal` is out of the range of values that the CLR `decimal` can represent.

```
SqlDecimal sd = SqlDecimal.MaxValue;
// this causes a conversion and produces a runtime error
decimal d = sd.Value;
```

The semantics of the operation invoked depends on the type. For arith-metic types like `SqlInt32`, the operands are added by the `op_Addition` method. For the `SqlBinary` type, the operands are concatenated. In gen-eral, the semantics will be intuitive. For specific details, consult the MSDN documentation.

Table 3-4 shows the operations that each `SqlType` can perform. The first column on the left lists the `SqlType`. The columns are marked with an X to indicate that the operation listed at the head of the column is available for the `SqlType` in the same row on the left. The operation includes the symbol used by C# and the name of the operation. Other languages may use different symbols for these operations. For example, this shows that `SqlBinary` supports the = =, +, >, >=, !=, <, and <= operations.

Note that for `SqlBoolean`, the Ones Complement operator means Log-ical Not.

Every `SqlType` implements the `IComparable` interface. This interface has one method, `CompareTo`. Its signature follows.

```
int CompareTo(object obj)
```

This signature is a bit deceptive. Even though it implies any object can be passed in, in fact only objects that are of the same type as the `SqlType`

TABLE 3-4: SqlType Operations

	== Equality	+ Add	− Sub	* Mul	/ Div	& Bitwise And		Bitwise Or	^ Bitwise XOR	> Greater Than	>= Greater Than Equal	!= Not Equal	< Less Than	<= Less Than Equal	% Modules	− Unary Negate	! Ones Complement
SqlBinary	X	X							X	X	X	X	X			
SqlBoolean	X					X	X	X			X					X
SqlByte	X	X	X	X	X	X	X	X	X	X	X	X	X	X	X	X
SqlDate	X								X	X	X	X	X			
SqlDateTime	X	X	X						X	X	X	X	X			
SqlDecimal	X	X	X	X	X				X	X	X	X	X	X		
SqlDouble	X	X	X	X	X				X	X	X	X	X	X		
SqlGuid	X								X	X	X	X	X			
SqlInt16	X	X	X	X	X	X	X	X	X	X	X	X	X	X	X	X
SqlInt32	X	X	X	X	X	X	X	X	X	X	X	X	X	X	X	X
SqlInt64	X	X	X	X	X	X	X	X	X	X	X	X	X	X	X	X
SqlMoney	X	X	X	X	X				X	X	X	X	X	X		
SqlSingle	X	X	X	X	X				X	X	X	X	X	X		
SqlString	X	X							X	X	X	X	X			
SqlTime	X								X	X	X	X	X			
SqlXmlReader																

involved can be passed in. If any other type is used, a runtime error will occur, even if there is an implicit coercion to the SqlType involved. The following code fragment illustrates a number of these errors.

```
SqlSingle s = 4.5F;
SqlDouble d = 4.5F;
```

```
// the following lines will compile without error
// but will cause a runtime error
Console.WriteLine(d.CompareTo("asdfasdf"));
// this will cause a runtime error too
Console.WriteLine(d.CompareTo(4.5));
// and so will thisConsole.WriteLine(d.CompareTo(s));
// this will work as expected
Console.WriteLine(d.CompareTo((SqlDouble)s));
```

The purpose of `CompareTo` is to determine the relative value of the instance of a `SqlType` to the `obj`. It is meant to be used to order objects. A 0 return value from `CompareTo` means `obj` is equal in value to the instance of `SqlType`. A positive return value means `obj` is greater in value than the instance of `SqlType`, and negative means the opposite.

Each `SqlType` is a value type and has all the behaviors of any other value type. The CLR uses value types to represent primitive types like `ints` and `floats`. The memory for each is allocated in place, not on the heap, unless it is a member of reference type. The important thing about value types for methods used to implement stored procedures, functions, or triggers is that they do not have a null representation. See Appendix A for a discussion of value types.

A `SqlType` also has the ability to represent a null value, which none of value types in the base class library of the CLR can do. It is important to understand how a `SqlType` represents a null because this behavior is probably quite different from what you are used to with value types. Every `SqlType` implements `INullable`, which has a single property named `IsNull`.

In addition, a `SqlType` has a public static field named `Null`. The value of this field is an instance of the `SqlType` that is null. The signature of `Null` for `SqlInt32` follows.

```
public static readonly SqlInt32 Null;
```

Note that though a `SqlType` can represent null, it itself cannot be null, because it is a value type. This means it cannot be compared to `null`; doing this will always produce a compile-time error. The following code fragment illustrates this.

```
SqlBoolean b = new SqlBoolean(false);
// this will produce a compile-time error
if(b == null)
{
    Console.WriteLine("b is null");
}
```

The `IsNull` property has to be used to check whether an instance of a `SqlType` is representing a null. The following code fragment illustrates the proper way to check a `SqlType` for null.

```
SqlBoolean b = new SqlBoolean(false);
// this will check to see if b is null
if(b.IsNull)
{
    Console.WriteLine("b is null");
}
```

Just as a `SqlType` cannot be compared to `null`, it cannot be set to `null` either. Again, this is because it is a value type. In fact there is no way to change the value of a `SqlType` to null if it is not null. You can make a variable of a `SqlType` null by assigning it a `SqlType.Null`, but you cannot change an existing value of a `SqlType` to null. The following code fragment shows assigning to a variable an instance of a `SqlType` that is representing null.

```
// the variable b is not null
SqlBoolean b = new SqlBoolean(false);
// this will check to see if b is null
if(b.IsNull)
{
    This code will not execute
    Console.WriteLine("b is null");
}
// this assigns a null to b
b = SqlBoolean.Null;
if(b.IsNull)
{
    This code will execute
    Console.WriteLine("b is null");
}
```

The comparison of one `SqlType` to another will always produce a `SqlBoolean`, not the CLR type `Boolean`. The assignment of a `SqlType` comparison to a `bool` will, therefore, produce a compile-time error. The following code fragment shows this.

```
SqlInt32 i1 = new SqlInt32(3);
SqlInt32 i2 = new SqlInt32(3);
// this will produce a compile-time error
bool b = i2 == i2;
```

Many languages provide a number of flow control expressions, such as `if` and `while`. These expressions evaluate a CLR type `Boolean` and use it to decide which branch of the flow to follow. However, the result of a `SqlType` comparison is a `SqlBoolean`, not a CLR `Boolean`. Some languages, including VB.NET and C#, extend this capability to types that are not CLR `Boolean`, if that type implements the CLR special named method `op_True`. `SqlBoolean` implements `op_True`, so a `SqlType` comparison may be the argument of a flow control expression in VB.NET or C#. The following C# code fragment shows this.

```
SqlInt32 i1 = new SqlInt32(3);
SqlInt32 i2 = new SqlInt32(3);
// this will compile and behave as expected even
// though the result of the comparison is SqlBoolean
if(i1 == i2)
{
        // this will be executed
        Console.WriteLine("i1 == i2")
}
```

Another factor that has to be considered when comparing one `SqlType` to another is that one or both may be representing a `null`. Any comparison of a `SqlType` representing null to another `SqlType` always results in `SqlBoolean.False`. This can result in two variables being neither equal nor not equal at the same time. The following code fragment shows an example of this.

```
SqlInt32 i1 = new SqlInt32.Null;
SqlInt32 i2 = new SqlInt32.Null;
if(i1 == i2)
{
        // this will be never executed
        Console.WriteLine("i1 == i2")
}
if(i1 != i2)
{
        // this will be never executed
        Console.WriteLine("i1 != i2")
}
```

There are other equality operations besides comparison, and these behave differently with respect to a `SqlType` representing null. The `Equals` method, which all types have, and the `CompareTo` method will show the comparison of two `SqlTypes` both of which are representing a null as being equal. The following code example shows this.

```
SqlInt32 i1 = new SqlInt32.Null;
SqlInt32 i2 = new SqlInt32.Null;
if(i1.Equals(i2))
```

```
{
    // this will be executed
    Console.WriteLine("i1 Equals i2")
}
if(i1.ComparesTo(i2) == 0)
{
    // this will be executed
    Console.WriteLine("i1 Compares To i2")
}
```

There is one more behavior of a `SqlType`, which is due to its inability to represent a null. Reference types, such as a `string`, can produce a runtime error because of a null reference. This typically happens because of a coding error. The following code fragment shows a simple way this can happen.

```
string str = null;
// this will cause a runtime error
// because of a null reference
Console.WriteLine(str.Length);
```

An instance of a `SqlType` that is representing a null can produce a similar sort of error. A runtime error will occur when an attempt is made to get the `Value` property of the `SqlType` or cast it to a CLR type, if that `SqlType` is representing a null. The following code fragment shows where this will happen.

```
SqlInt64 i64 = SqlInt64.Null;
// this will cause a runtime error
long l1 = i64.Value;
// this will cause a runtime error too
l1 = (long) i64;
```

Even though casting an instance of a `SqlType` that is representing a null to a CLR type will cause a runtime error, casting it to another `SqlType` will not, assuming that cast is allowed. For example, the following code fragment will not cause a runtime error.

```
Int32 i32 = SqlInt32.Null;
// this will compile and work as expected
SqlInt64 i64       = i32;
I64 = SqlInt64.Null;
// this will compile and work as expected
i32 = (SqlInt32)i64;
```

To summarize what we have covered on `SqlType`, we can say that a `SqlType` is a value type that can represent a null but otherwise behaves much like the CLR type that corresponds to it. A `SqlType` is used when it is desirable to copy the behavior of a SQL Server type. A `SqlType` has a `Value` property, which has its value in terms of its corresponding CLR type. A `SqlType` can be cast to another `SqlType` and to a CLR type, and some CLR types can be cast to `SqlTypes`.

So far we have covered the types typically used for parameters and return values in methods that will be used for procedures and functions. Now we will look at how to use a CLR method as a SQL Server procedure, function, or trigger.

Procedures

A SQL Server procedure has parameters and a return code. The parameters themselves may be passed by value or by reference. The return code from a procedure is, by convention, meant to indicate the error status that results when the procedure is executed. Typically, a return code of 0 indicates that the procedure executed with out any error. A nonzero result code is used to indicate what part of the procedure failed.

A SQL Server procedure is created using the CREATE PROCEDURE command. Before we look at the all the details of implementing a SQL Server procedure with the CLR, let's first look at a procedure implemented using T-SQL and then implement an equivalent procedure using a method.

Note that this example violates the convention of using a return code only for an error status just to make the example compact and show the construction of a stored procedure. Stored procedures typically manipulate a database by, for example, inserting something into a table. Chapter 4 will discuss how to write functions that manipulate the database; this example is just to illustrate the construction of a function that implements a stored procedure.

```
CREATE PROCEDURE PassCharsTSql (@c nvarchar(100))
AS
BEGIN
RETURN LEN(@c)
END
```

When this procedure is run, the return code will indicate the number of characters in @c. A short SQL batch that shows this follows.

```
DECLARE @i INT
EXEC @i = PassCharsTSql 'bcd'
PRINT @i
GO
3
```

In order to create a CLR method that can duplicate the functionality of this procedure, we must first decide what types should be used for the parameters of the method. This is done by using Table 3-1, shown earlier in this chapter. Look down the third column of this table until you find the SQL native type you want to use in the procedure when it is called from T-SQL. In this case, you would look for the nchar type. The SqlType you should use for this parameter is in the first column of the row—in this case, SqlString. Now you have enough information to write a method that will be the equivalent of the T-SQL PassCharsTSql procedure. It follows.

```
namespace Procedures
{
    public class Parameters
    {
        // SqlString is used as the type for str
        // because it is a SQLType for nchar
        // in Table 3-1
        public static int PassChars(SqlString str)
        {
            // the T-SQL LEN function trims trailing
            // spaces in the string, so you must too
            return str.Value.TrimEnd().Length;
        }
    }
}
```

The PassChars method almost duplicates the functionality of the PassCharTSql procedure, but it actually contains a bug. The bug is that it is not testing to see if str is representing a null. In T-SQL, nulls are often transparently handled. The following example SQL batch using PassCharTSql shows this.

```
DECLARE @i INT
EXEC @i = PassCharsTSql null
PRINT @i
GO
0
```

Notice that PassCharsTSql had a return code of 0. If a null were passed to the PassChars implementation shown earlier, the implementation would throw an exception and raise a T-SQL error, as follows.

```
DECLARE @i INT
EXEC @i = PassCharsTSql null
.Net SqlClient Data Provider: Msg 6522, Level 16, State 1, Procedure
PassChars, Line 0
A CLR error occurred during execution of 'PassChars'...
```

So, in general, when you are writing methods to be used to implement procedures and functions, it is important to always check whether an instance of `SqlType` you are using is representing a null. The following code is a corrected version of the `PassChars` method that does this.

```
namespace Procedures
{
    public class Parameters
    {
        // SqlString is used as the type for str
        // because it matches the nchar type
        // listed in Table 3-1
        public static int PassChars(SqlString str)
        {
            // test for null
            if(str.IsNull)
            {
                // return a 0 just like the PassCharsTSql does
                return 0;
            }
            // the T-SQL LEN function trims trailing
            // spaces in the string, so you must too
            return str.Value.TrimEnd().Length;
        }
    }
}
```

The return value of the method used to implement the procedure will be the return code for that procedure. The return type for the method may be `void`, `SqlInt32`, `SqlInt16`, `Int32`, or `Int16`. If `void` is used, the procedure will always have a return code of 0.

Once you have written a CLR method for a procedure, you must compile it and catalog its assembly, as was shown in Chapter 2. The following script can be run on the command line to compile and catalog the assembly shown earlier, which we will assume is in a file named `procedures.cs`. It will add this to a local database named `Chapter3`. Note that `sqlcmd` is a utility included with SQL Server 2005 that allows a SQL expression to be executed from the command line.

```
csc /target:library procedures.cs
sqlcmd -d Chapter3 -Q "CREATE ASSEMBLY procedures FROM
%CD%\procedures.dll with PERMISSION_SET = SAFE"
```

The `sqlcmd` line has been wrapped to fit onto the page. Also note that `%CD%` will be expanded by the command shell to the current directory, which is where the assembly produced by `csc` will be.

Once the assembly has been cataloged, the procedure that uses the `PassChars` method must be created, just as it must for a T-SQL-based procedure. The beginning of the command is the same as for a T-SQL procedure. The difference is that the end of the command has an EXTERNAL NAME instead of an implementation. The EXTERNAL NAME is used to refer to the assembly, namespace, class, and name of the method that implements the procedure. We have designed our procedure to have the same signature as `PassCharsTSql` does; the command that creates it follows.

```
CREATE PROC PassChars(@str char(100)) as EXTERNAL NAME
procedures.[Procedures.Parameters].PassChar
```

The syntax of an EXTERNAL NAME is broken into three parts. The first part is the name of the assembly, which must have already been cataloged in the database. The second part is separated from the first by a "." and is the class name, including the namespace if there is one. Note that when a namespace is used, the namespace and class must be enclosed in "[]". If the class is not part of a namespace, the "[]" are not required. The third part is separated from the second by a "." and is the name of the method that implements the procedure. Figure 3-2 shows the structure of an EXTERNAL NAME.

Parameters in a method for a procedure are passed by value for an INPUT and by reference for an OUTPUT argument in a T-SQL stored procedure. If they are passed by value, changes to the parameter inside the procedure are not reflected back to the caller. If they are passed by reference, changes to the parameter are passed back to the caller. In a C# method, the `ref` keyword is used to indicate that a parameter is a passed by reference. In a VB.NET program, the `ByRef` keyword is used. A value passed by reference can be used as a return value. A method may have more than one parameter that is passed by reference, so it is possible for a method to have multiple return values. The following method has one parameter passed

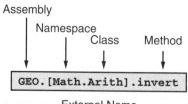

Assembly
Namespace
Class   Method

```
GEO.[Math.Arith].invert
```

External Name

FIGURE 3-2: Format of EXTERNAL NAME

by value and another passed by reference. Note that this method does not check whether any of the parameters are representing null, just to keep the example short.

```
public static void PassBack(SqlInt32 valueIn, ref SqlInt32
valueRef)
{
    // pass in + out to out
    valueRef += valueIn;
}
```

The T-SQL signature uses the OUTPUT keyword to indicate a parameter passed by reference. If no OUTPUT keyword is used, the parameter is passed by value. If we assume the preceding method was added to the previous assembly, the CREATE PROCEDURE command to create it follows.

```
CREATE PROCEDURE PassBack(@valueIn INT, @valueOut INT OUTPUT) as
EXTERNAL NAME procedures.[Procedures.Parameters].PassBack
```

Once this procedure has been added to the database, it can be used as is shown in the following SQL batch.

```
DECLARE @i INT
SET @i = 4
EXEC PassBack 3, @i OUTPUT
PRINT @i
GO
7
```

Note that a `ref` parameter in a method can be used to either pass a value in or get a value back or both. In this case, @i was initialized to 4, 3 was added to it and passed back, resulting in 7.

Procedures implemented with the CLR work the same as T-SQL procedures. For example, in a T-SQL procedure, parameters can be passed by position, as is shown in the preceding SQL batch, or passed by name. The following code is the preceding batch rewritten to pass parameters by name.

```
DECLARE @i INT
SET @i = 4
EXEC PassBack @valueRef = @i OUTPUT, @valueIn = 3
PRINT @i
GO
7
```

Parameters passed by name must use the name used in the CREATE PROCEDURE statement, not the names used in the CLR method.

T-SQL procedures may have default values for parameters, and this is true for procedures implemented with methods. In addition, a single method may be used to implement more than one procedure. This makes it possible to have several procedures, each with a different default value for a parameter, all implemented by the same CLR method. The following SQL script creates the `PassBack3` and `PassBack4` procedures, both implemented with the `PassBack` method, using a default value for `valueIn`.

```
CREATE PROC PassBack3(@valueIn INT = 5, @valueOut INT OUTPUT) as
EXTERNAL NAME procedures.[Procedures.Parameters].PassBack
CREATE PROC PassBack4(@valueIn INT = 7, @valueOut INT OUTPUT) as
EXTERNAL NAME procedures.[Procedures.Parameters].PassBack
```

The following SQL script executes the `PassBack3` procedure, using a default parameter.

```
DECLARE @i int
SET @i = 4
EXEC PassBack3 DEFAULT, @i OUTPUT
PRINT @i
GO
9
```

CLR types that correspond to a `SqlType` (see Table 3-1) can also be used as types for parameters in a stored procedure. The following code is a different version of the `PassBack` method, rewritten to make use of `int` instead of `SqlInt32`.

```
    public static void PassBack2(int valueIn, ref int valueRef)
    {
        // pass in + out to out
        valueRef += valueIn;
    }
```

In summary, procedures implemented using a CLR language can be used in the same way as procedures implemented using T-SQL. They can have parameters passed by value or reference and passed by position or name. A parameter can have a default value, and the same CLR implementation can be used for more than one procedure, each having different default values. CLR implementations that use `SqlType` parameters must be sure to check for parameters values that are representing null.

Scalar-Valued Functions

A scalar-valued function in SQL Server has input parameters, just as a procedure does, but those parameters can only be passed in by value. In addition, it returns a scalar value, not a return code. The return value can be of any of the types that input parameters can use. The following code is an example of a simple function written in T-SQL.

```
CREATE FUNCTION RepeatSql (@repeat INT, @str NCHAR(1))
RETURNS NCHAR(30)
AS
BEGIN
RETURN Replicate(@str, @repeat)
END
```

Repeat takes as input parameters an int and a character, and returns a string with the character repeated. The following SQL batch uses it.

```
PRINT dbo.RepeatSql(5, 'A')
GO
AAAAA
```

Using Table 3-1 as a guide, as we did for building the PassChars procedure, we can write a method that duplicates the RepeatSql function, which is shown in the following code fragment.

```
static public SqlString Repeat(SqlInt32 i, SqlString c)
{
    return new String(c.Value[0], i.Value);
}
```

The Repeat method is not doing the error checking it should just for the sake of keeping the example small. The syntax for adding a function is similar to that for adding a procedure except that it requires an additional piece of information, the return type. The following code is a SQL batch for creating a function from the Repeat method.

```
CREATE FUNCTION Repeat(@i INT, @c NCHAR(1)) RETURNS NCHAR(100)
EXTERNAL NAME functions.[Chapter3.Functions].Repeat
```

In spirit, the difference between procedures and functions is that a function returns a value that can be used as part of a query, a computed column, or an index. There is no way to use a procedure directly in a query or a computed column. The following SQL batch shows and uses a table that includes a computed column that uses the Repeat function.

```
CREATE TABLE R1
(
        Id CHAR(1),
    Other AS dbo.Repeat(3, Id)
)
INSERT INTO R1 VALUES ('A')
SELECT * FROM R1
GO
A   AAA
```

The value of the Other column is just the character in the first column, repeated three times. Although this is not a very useful use of a computed column, it does illustrate how they work.

Because a function can be used in a query or a column definition, SQL Server needs to know a few extra things about it. What would happen if the Repeat function were modified so that it repeated the character a random number of times, but not more than three? Each time you did a select from the R1 table, you could potentially see a different number of characters in the Other column. There is nothing intrinsically wrong with this behavior; some built-in functions in SQL Server give different results each time you call them.

Suppose further that an index was built on the Other column, with the random Repeat function. Would that make any sense? The index wouldn't be very useful, because it would only have a snapshot of what was in the column when it read it, so selects using it wouldn't work.

By default, SQL Server assumes that a function based on a CLR method cannot be used to build an index, and will produce an error if you try to make one. Every function in SQL Server has two properties that are associated with it that SQL Server uses to decide if that function can be used in an index: IsDeterministic and IsPrecise. By default, a function based on a CLR method has both of these properties as false.

Besides using a computed column as in index, you can also make it PERSISTED. When you make a computed column PERSISTED, it is calculated only once, and the resulting value is stored and then retrieved whenever it is needed. A PERSISTED computed column takes more space than one that isn't, but makes selects run faster. Obviously, a computed column that returned a different value every time you read it would not be any more useful as a PERSISTED column than as an index. Table 3-5 shows how SQL Server decides whether or not to allow a computed column to be PERSISTED or used in an index.

The Y* indicates the computed column involved must be PERSISTED or the index will not be allowed. An indexed view is special kind of view that

TABLE 3-5: Index and Persisted Column Usage of Function

IsDeterministic	IsPrecise	Peristed Column OK?	Index OK?	Indexed View OK?
T	T	Y	Y	Y*
T	F	Y	Y*	Y*
F	T	N	N	N
F	F	N	Y	N

stores the data for the view so that it does not have to run a query when it is selected.

The `IsDeterministic` and `IsPrecise` properties of a function must be properly set. For a function written exclusively in T-SQL, this is not a problem, because SQL Server will calculate what these settings should be. Methods that are used to implement functions must be decorated with the `SqlFunctionAttribute`, or both `IsDeterministic` and `IsPrecise` will be `false`. Two of the properties of `SqlFunctionAttribute` are `IsDeterministic` and `IsPrecise`. For example, the `Repeat` function we used at the beginning of this chapter can be rewritten as follows.

```
[SqlFunction(IsDeterministic = true, IsPrecise = true)]
static public SqlString Repeat(SqlInt32 i, SqlString c)
{
    return new String(c.Value[0], i.Value);
}
```

A method is considered deterministic if for a given set of inputs it always returns the same value. A method that meets this criterion should set `IsDeterministic=true`; otherwise, it should be false. Obviously, the `Repeat` method meets this criterion. The following code is an example of a method that is not deterministic.

```
[SqlFunction(IsDeterministic = false, IsPrecise = true)]
static public SqlGuid NewId()
{
    return new SqlGuid(Guid.NewGuid());
}
```

The `NewId` function is not deterministic, because each time the static method `Guid.NewGuid()` is called, it produces a different GUID.

A method is considered precise if its return value does not depend on any calculations that involve System.Single (FLOAT in SQL) or System.Double (REAL in SQL). A method that meets this criterion should set IsPrecise=true; otherwise, it should be false. The reason for this criterion is that typically the hardware in the processor implements arithmetic calculations involving System.Single or System.Double types. Different processors may produce slightly different results for the same calculations. This is not true for calculations involving SqlDecimal or System.Decimal. The Repeat function does not use System.Single or System.Double, so it is precise. The following code is an example of a method that is not precise.

```
[SqlFunction(IsDeterministic = true, IsPrecise = false)]
static public SqlInt32 Add3(SqlInt32 i)
{
    double d = 3.0;
    return i + (int)d;
}
```

Scalar-valued functions may be implemented by methods. They are similar to procedures, but they can return any scalar value or a user-defined type. Scalar-valued functions can be used in queries, computed columns, and indexes. For these indexes to work properly, the method that implements the function must be properly decorated with the Sql FunctionAttribute attribute.

Functions that return SqlTypes and some others sometimes must specify some extra information that is specific to the type. For example, a SqlDecimal has a precision and scale associated with it. Although an instance of a SqlDecimal has a MaxPrecision and a MaxScale field, the type definition does not. The SqlFacetAttribute is used to add information about the SQL characteristics of the return value of a function. The SqlFacetAttribute has five properties: IsFixedLength, MaxSize, Precision, Scale, and IsNullable. Methods should use the appropriate properties, as shown in the following example.

```
public SqlDecimal Value()
[return: SqlFacet(Precision=9, Scale=12)]
{
    // implementation
}
```

The SqlFacetAttribute is meant to be used only for return values. Table 3-6 shows the appropriate properties to use for the various SqlTypes.

Table 3-6: Usage of SqlFacetAttribute

Type	IsFixedLength	MaxSize	Precision	Scale	IsNullable
SqlBoolean	N	N	N	N	Y
SqlByte	N	N	N	N	Y
SqlInt16	N	N	N	N	Y
SqlInt32	N	N	N	N	Y
SqlInt64	N	N	N	N	Y
SqlSingle	N	N	N	N	Y
SqlDouble	N	N	N	N	Y
SqlDateTime	N	N	N	N	Y
SqlMoney	N	N	N	N	Y
SqlGuid	N	N	N	N	Y
SqlDecimal	N	N	Y	Y	Y
SqlString	Y	Y	N	N	Y
SqlBinary	Y	Y	N	N	Y
SqlXml	N	N	N	N	Y
SqlBytes	Y	Y	N	N	Y
SqlChars	Y	Y	N	N	Y
Embedded UDTs	N	N	N	N	Y
string	Y	Y	N	N	Y
Byte[]	Y	Y	N	N	Y
Char[]	Y	Y	N	N	Y
decimal	N	N	Y	Y	N

Table-Valued Functions

A user-defined function implemented with a CLR language can return a table, just as any user-defined function in T-SQL can. These are called table-valued user-defined functions, or TVFs. A TVF must return an `ISql Reader` or `ISqlRecord` interface. These interfaces are implemented by the `SqlDataReader`, discussed in Chapter 4, which is used to return the results of a tabular query.

Complete coverage of the implementation of `ISqlReader` and `ISql Record` are beyond the scope of this book, but we will cover the key points. A TVF acts like a cursor on a set of records. Each time you call `Read`, you advance the cursor to the next record. While the cursor is on a record, it allows you to access the fields in that record. The implementation of `ISqlReader` implements the cursor that moves over a set of records, and `ISqlRecord` provides access to the fields in each record.

For `ISqlReader`, the principal elements you must implement are the `Read()` method and the `HasRows` and `FieldCount` properties. `Read()` advances the cursor and returns true if the resulting cursor has not gone beyond the last row. `HasRows` returns a `boolean` that indicates that there is at least one row. And `FieldCount` returns an `int` that indicates the number of fields in a row.

To illustrate how to implement a table-valued function, we will implement one that produces a sequence of numbers called a Fibonacci sequence. The sequence starts with two numbers, and each number after the second one is the sum of the previous two. Here is an example.

```
1   2   3    5    8    13   21
    1+2 2+3  5+3  8+5  13+8
```

The TVF we will create is a function called `Fibonacci` that will return two columns, one called `next` and one called `previous`. It will take as input the first two numbers we want in our sequence and the length of the sequence. The following SQL script runs our function and produces a table with six rows.

```
select next, previous from dbo.Fibonacci(1,2,6)

next          previous
-- - - - - -  - - - - - - --
2             1
3             2
5             3
```

```
next        previous
-- -- -- --  -- -- -- --
8           5
13          8
21          13
```

The `next` column shows a number in the sequence, and the `previous` column shows the number that comes before it.

The implementation of the function itself is straightforward. It creates an object that has an `ISqlReader` and an `ISqlRecord` interface. It is shown next.

```
public class CBernoulli
{
    [SqlFunction(DataAccess = DataAccessKind.None,
            SystemDataAccess = SystemDataAccessKind.None,
            IsDeterministic = true,
            IsPrecise = true)]
    public static ISqlReader Bernoulli
    (int preStart, int start, int count)
    {
            // create object that implements both
            // ISqlReader and ISqlRecord
            BData b = new BData(preStart,
                            start,
                            count);
            ISqlReader dr = b;
            //return the ISqlReader
            return dr;
    }
}
```

The `BData` object is the more difficult part. In order to work properly, it will have to maintain some state that it updates with each call to `ISqlReader.Read()`. The constructor must pass in the first two values of the sequence and how long the sequence should be. Each call will change the state to the next value in a Bernoulli sequence.

SQL Server also has to be able to find the type of each column in the table produced by the TVF. The `BData` object has to implement the `GetSqlMetaData` method. This method is passed in an `int` and must return the `SqlDbType` of the column through an instance of a `SqlMetaData` class. There are also numerous other methods, mostly based on `SqlTypes` that also have to be implemented.

The following code shows the BData class and its constructor and Read() implementation.

```
class BData: ISqlReader, ISqlRecord
{
    // the previous number in the sequence
    int previous_;
    // the current number in the sequence
    int current_;
    // position in sequence
    int count_ ;
    // length of sequence
    int maxCount_;

    internal BData(int preStart, int start, int count)
    {
        previous_ = preStart;
        current_ = start;
        maxCount_ = count;
        this.count_ = 0;
    }
    public bool Read()
    {
        // just leave things as they are
        // for the first time through
        if (count_ != 0)
        {
        // calculate next number in
        // sequence and remember last
            int p = current_;
            current_ += previous_;
            previous_ = p;
        }
        // move to next number in sequence
        count_ = count_ + 1;
        if (count_ > maxCount_)
        {
            // done with sequence
            return false;
        }
        return true;
    }
}
```

The constructor just saves the first and second numbers in the sequence and the length of the sequence. Each time Read() is called, it just calculates the next number in the sequence. Note that the first time Read() is called, it does not do a calculation; it just leaves the initial values in place. SQL Server will keep on calling Read() to get a row until Read() returns false.

Once SQL Server has called Read(), it will then want to get the values for the fields read. It does this by using one of the accessors that are part of the ISqlRecord interface. There is an accessor for each type supported by SQL Server. Both of the columns the TVF returns are SqlInt32s, so it will call the GetSqlInt32 method and pass in the column that it wants. This is shown next, along with a helper accessor to get the column values.

```
int this[int pos]
{
        get
        {
                if (pos == 0)
                {
                        return current_;
                }
                return previous_;
        }
}
public SqlInt32 GetSqlInt32(int i)
{
        return new SqlInt32(this[i]);
}
```

There are quite a few details in the implementation of ISqlReader and ISqlRecord, but the basic implementation of the BData class is shown next.

```
class BData: ISqlReader, ISqlRecord
{
        // the previous number in the sequence
        int previous_;
        // the current number in the sequence
        int current_;
        int count_ ;
        int maxCount_;

        internal BData(int preStart, int start, int count)
        {
                previous_ = preStart;
                current_ = start;
                maxCount_ = count;
                this.count_ = 0;
        }
        int this[int pos]
        {
                get
                {
                        if (pos == 0)
                        {
                                return current_;
```

```csharp
                    }
                    return previous_;
            }
    }
    public bool NextResult()
    {
            // TODO:  Add BData.NextResult implementation
            throw new NotImplementedException();
    }
// many methods removed for clarity.
// see full example on Web site
    public bool HasRows
    {
            get
            {
                    if (maxCount_ > 0)
                    {
                            return true;
                    }
                    return false;
            }
    }
    public bool Read()
    {
            // just leave things as they are
            // for the first time through
            if (count_ != 0)
            {
                    int p = current_;
                    current_ += previous_;
                    previous_ = p;
            }
            // move to next number in sequence
            count_ = count_ + 1;
            if (count_ > maxCount_)
            {
                    // done with sequence
                    return false;
            }

            return true;
    }
    object System.Data.Sql.ISqlRecord.this[int i]
    {
            get
            {
                    if (i == 0)
                    {
                            return current_;
                    }
                    if (i == 1)
```

```
                      {
                              return previous_;
                      }
                      return null;
              }
      }
      public int FieldCount
      {
              get
              {
                      return 2;
              }
      }
      public string GetName(int i)
      {
              if (i == 0)
              {
                      return "next";
              }
              if (i == 1)
              {
                      return "previous";
              }

              return null;
      }
public SqlMetaData GetSqlMetaData(int i)
      {
              SqlMetaData md =  new SqlMetaData("Data", SqlDbType.Int);
              return md;
      }
      public int GetInt32(int i)
      {
              return this[i];
      }
}
```

Assuming that both the Bernoulli and the BData classes are in an assembly named TVFunc.dll, the script that follows catalogs them into SQL Server.

```
CREATE ASSEMBLY TVFunc FROM 'D:\ Samples\TVFunc\TVFunc\bin\TVFunc.dll'

CREATE FUNCTION Bernoulli(@preStart INT, @start INT, @count INT)
RETURNS TABLE (next INT, previous INT)
AS
EXTERNAL NAME TVFunc.CBernoulli.Bernoulli
```

Note that the CREATE FUNCTION command specifies the schema of the table returned by the Bernoulli method.

In summary, to create a TVF, you make a class that implements both `ISqlReader` and `ISqlRecord`. You also create a static function that creates an instance of this class and returns it through the `ISqlReader` or `ISql Record` interface. Then you catalog the function as you would any other CLR function in SQL Server, noting that it returns a `TABLE`. The `ISql Record` interface must return the appropriate data types for the columns you specify in this table.

Triggers

Triggers in SQL Server may be implemented by a CLR method. Methods that implement a trigger must return a void and have no parameters. The following code is an example of a C# method that can be used as a trigger.

```
public class Triggers
{
    public static void OnMyUpdate()
    {
            ... code that checks/modifies database
    }
}
```

Since a method that implements a trigger has no inputs or outputs, the only thing of consequence it can do, just as it is for a T-SQL trigger, is check what the operation that caused the trigger did to the database and possibly prevent it, change it, or roll it back. To do these operations, the CLR code must use SQL commands. Chapter 4 discusses using SQL commands as part of stored procedures, functions, and triggers implemented using a CLR language.

The CLR function that implements a trigger does so in a context called the `SqlTriggerContext`. The `SqlTriggerContext` is discussed in Chapter 4. It makes available to the method the `INSERTED` and `DELETED` logical tables that triggers use to determine what operation was done.

Triggers implemented using a CLR method are added to a database using a syntax similar to the one used for adding T-SQL triggers. The following code is an example of adding a trigger to a database.

```
CREATE TRIGGER OnMyUpdate
ON Invoices

AS EXTERNAL NAME Triggers.CInvoices.OnMyUpdate
```

The behavior and operation of CLR triggers is the same as for T-SQL triggers.

Where Are We?

This chapter shows that CLR functions can be used to implement T-SQL stored procedures, functions, and triggers. CLR languages will typically be better suited to doing numeric computations and also offer a familiar programming environment for problem space experts that typically don't write T-SQL applications. The `System.Data.SqlTypes` namespace provides data types that can be used in the CLR but have the properties of the corresponding data types in SQL Server.

◼4◼
The In-Process Data Provider

As a complement to the ability to run .NET code inside SQL Server 2005, SQL Server 2005 includes a new kind of data provider that runs inside the database itself. This gives .NET code that runs inside the database, such as user-defined functions and stored procedures, access to the database, just as ADO.NET gives client-side applications access to the database. In the past, extensions to SQL Server written as extended stored procedures had this capability, but only by making an inefficient connection to the database, just as client applications did. The new provider is different in this respect; it gives .NET code running inside the database access to the database that is almost on a par with the efficiency of T-SQL, without the overhead of a connection.

The SQL Server Programming Model

Accessing data from your applications normally involves using a provider to connect to the data source and subsequently to retrieve, insert, update, or delete data in the database. You have probably used ODBC drivers, OLE DB providers, or ADO.NET in your applications in the past. Your application, even if written in .NET, ran outside the database, and that access technology you used made a connection to the database to pass commands to it and retrieve results.

Now you can write .NET code that runs inside the database in the form of a stored procedure, user-defined function or any of the other .NET features of SQL Server 2005 mentioned in previous chapters. This code is as secure, reliable and scalable as T-SQL itself, as we have seen in previous chapters, so it makes no sense to require it to build a connection to the database as required of extended stored procedures. A connection requires significant resources in SQL Server 2005 itself and, probably more importantly, serializes all commands and results into a bit stream. When T-SQL accesses the database, it just uses the context in which it is running to access the database directly.

.NET code running inside the database can use the same interfaces as SqLCient code; this is called the SQL Server Programming Model (SPM). Code inside the database does not depend on making connections to the database; it accesses SQL Server 2005 directly through the context in which it runs in a way very similar to T-SQL itself. This capability is exposed using the ADO.NET data provider model. It is accessed through classes in the namespace `System.Data.SqlServer` and a few others.

With the first release of .NET, two different providers were available, located in the `System.Data.OleDb` and the `System.Data.SqlClient` namespaces, respectively. Because the `SqlClient` provider is optimized for SQL Server, you can use it to access only SQL Server, whereas you can use the `OleDb` provider to access data from any data source with a compliant OLE DB provider. Note that this architecture differs somewhat from the previous provider architectures—ODBC, OLE DB, ADO, and so on—in that with .NET you have different providers, depending on the data source. This gives provider writers the ability to add data store–specific functionality to the provider on the class level without breaking the model.

In OLE DB, provider writers had to add functionality through interfaces that in most cases ADO wouldn't see. This led to a trend where most providers implemented the same functionality and the ADO developer merely changed a property (or the connection string) in order to determine the data source to which to connect. The positive implication of this was that, as an ADO developer, you could code very generically, as Listing 4-1 shows. Notice that the equivalent code in ADO.NET, shown in Listing 4-2, is not as generic as in ADO.

LISTING 4-1: Connections in ADO

```
' Connections in ADO - Visual Basic.NET
Dim oConn as ADODB.Connection
Dim strConn As String
Dim oCmd As New ADODB.Command
```

```
' connection string for SQL Server
strConn = "Provider=SQLOLEDB;Data Source=myServer;" + _
          "Initial Catalog=pubs;User Id=uid;Password=pwd;"


'connection string for Oracle
strConn = "Provider=MSDAORA;Data Source=ora;User Id=scott;" + _
          "Password=tiger;"


'open the connection
'Provider is specified in connection string
oConn.Open strConn


oCmd.Connection = oConn
```

LISTING 4-2: Connections in ADO.NET

```
//connection to SQL Server
//data provider is not specified in connection string
string sqlConn = "server=localhost;database=pubs;uid=sa;pwd=6#B5p;";

//create an instance of SqlClient
IDbConnection conn = new SqlConnection(sqlConn);

conn.Open();

IDbCommand cmd = conn.CreateCommand();

//connection to Oracle using managed OLE DB provider
string oraConn = "Provider=MSDAORA;Data Source=ora;
                 User Id=scott; "Password=tiger;"

IDbConnection conn = new OleDbConnection(oraConn);

IDbCommand oCmd = conn.CreateCommand();

conn.Open();
```

In .NET, then, how do we achieve generic data access, given that we have different providers? The actual data provider portion is factored into common interfaces—IDbConnection, IDbCommand, IDataReader, and so on—which are being implemented by the providers and exposed by a series of provider-specific classes: SqlConnection, OleDbConnection, SqlCommand, OleDbReader, and so on. You code against the interfaces rather than the data-source-specific classes, and the only time you need to specify a database-specific class is when you open the connection. Factory classes and common base classes are added in .NET 2.0. This programming model for data access in .NET is called the General Programming Model for Managed Providers (GPM).

As already mentioned, until now the managed providers have lived in the managed code space and have existed outside the database process space. The SQL Server 2005 release needs a provider that runs in the same process space, because SQL Server 2005 hosts the .NET Common Language Runtime (CLR) inside SQL Server, allowing stored procedures, functions, and triggers to be written in any of the CLR-compliant languages. This provider is exposed in the `System.Data.SqlServer` namespace, although the exact namespace may change before the release of SQL Server 2005.

The `SqlServer` provider contains a common set of classes and interfaces that implement and extend those that the GPM defines, but the `SqlServer` provider is not the only provider that uses these new classes and interfaces. The `SqlClient` provider also uses some of the new classes and interfaces (refer to Chapter 12 for changes in the `SqlClient` provider). Microsoft adds a new, extended programming model, called the SQL Server Programming Model, to complement the GPM. These are the results.

- *Consistent programming model*—Regardless of what extensions or enhancements a specific provider implements, you obtain consistency by coding to the GPM. In other words, you have consistent APIs.

- *Consistency between mid-tier and in-process providers*—You can transparently migrate your code (and also optimize performance) between the tiers because both the `SqlClient` and the `SqlServer` providers implement the SPM. You can move code between the mid-tier and in-process providers just by changing the code you use to obtain a connection, as the following code shows.

```
//code to insert data from mid-tier
string connStr = GetConnectionStringFromConfigFile();
SqlConnection conn = new SqlConnection(connStr);
conn.Open();
SqlCommand cmd = conn.CreateCommand();
cmd.CommandText = "insert into yukontest values ('midtier1')";
cmd.ExecuteNonQuery();

//code to insert data in-proc
SqlConnection conn = SqlContext.GetConnection();
```

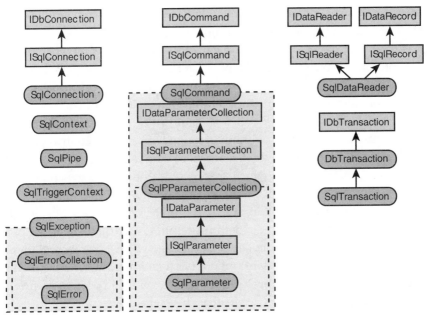

FIGURE 4-1: The SqlServer Provider Object Model

```
SqlCommand cmd = conn.CreateCommand();
cmd.CommandText = "insert into yukontest values ('inproc1')";
cmd.ExecuteNonQuery();
```

Figure 4-1 shows the object model for the `SqlServer` provider. Some of the classes and interfaces will be familiar to you if you have coded ADO.NET; others are part of the SPM (and therefore shared between the `SqlClient` and `SqlServer` providers); and yet others are extensions to the SPM and available only in the `SqlServer` provider.

It is worth noticing that Microsoft has changed the interface hierarchy and, in the COM spirit, added new interfaces with new functionality specific for SQL Server: `ISqlXXX` and friends, which implement the `IDataXXX` and `IDbXXX` interfaces from the GPM. Most of the classes in the diagram are likely to be familiar to you, but there are also a couple of new classes that didn't exist in the previous versions of ADO.NET.

Context—The SqlContext Class

The `SqlContext` class is one of the new classes, one of the extensions of the SPM; it is only part of the `SqlServer` provider, not the `SqlClient` provider. When you write data access code from the mid-tier, you always create and open a connection, precisely as in the preceding code listings. However, as seen from the server side, when a procedure or function is executed, it is executed as part of the user's connection. Whether that connection comes from ODBC, ADO.NET, or T-SQL doesn't really matter. You are in a connection, which has specific properties, environment variables, and so on, and you are executing within that connection; you are in the context of the user's connection.

A command is executed within the context of the connection, but it also has an execution context, which consists of data related to the command. The same goes for triggers, which are executed within a trigger context.

Prior to SQL Server 2005, the closest we came to being able to write code in another language that executed within the process space of SQL Server was to write extended stored procedures. An extended stored procedure is a C or C++ DLL that has been cataloged in SQL Server and therefore can be executed in the same manner as a "normal" SQL Server stored procedure. The extended stored procedure is executed in process with SQL Server and on the same Win32 thread as the user's connection.

Note, however, that if you need to do any kind of database access, even within the database to which the user is connected, from the extended stored procedure you still need to connect to the database explicitly either through DBLib, ODBC, or OLE DB, exactly as you would do from a client, as Figure 4-2 illustrates. Furthermore, once you have created the connection from the procedure, you may want to share a common transaction lock space with the client. Because you now have a separate connection, you need to explicitly ensure that you share the transaction lock space by using the `srv_getbindtoken` call and the stored procedure `sp_bindsession`.

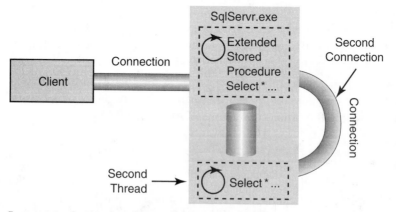

FIGURE 4-2: Connections from Extended Stored Procedures

In SQL Server 2005 when you use .NET to write procedures, functions, and triggers, you no longer need to explicitly create the connections, as was necessary when writing extended stored procedures. SQL Server 2005 and the CLR do this by introducing a class called SqlContext. So how does this work?

Remember that we mentioned contexts in the beginning of this section—namely, that we have contexts when connecting, executing, and doing other things in the database? You can see the SqlContext as a helper class—first retrieve the particular context the caller runs under and from there the managed representations of SQL Server objects: connections, commands, and so on. The managed representations of the different contexts are exposed as classes, and they are based on the caller's context, which has been abstracted into SqlContext. To get the different classes, you use static factory methods in SqlContext. Table 4-1 lists these methods and the respective classes. Some of the classes are probably familiar to you, whereas others are new.

You can instantiate some of the classes in Table 4-1—SqlCommand, for example—by using a constructor (New in VB.NET), but normally you would use the methods listed in the table, and we will cover those later in this chapter. You can create the other classes that are part of the SqlServer provider in the same way that you normally would create them if used from ADO.NET.

By now you may be wondering: If some of the managed classes are calling into SQL Server, does that mean that the internals of SQL Server are managed as well, and if not, are interoperability calls between managed and native code space happening? The answers are no and yes. No, the internals of SQL Server are not managed—Microsoft did not rewrite the

TABLE 4-1: SqlContext Methods

Method	Component	Class
GetConnection()	Connection	SqlConnection
GetCommand()	Command	SqlCommand
GetTransaction()	Transaction	SqlTransaction
GetPipe()	Pipe	SqlPipe
GetTriggerContext()	TriggerContext	SqlTriggerContext

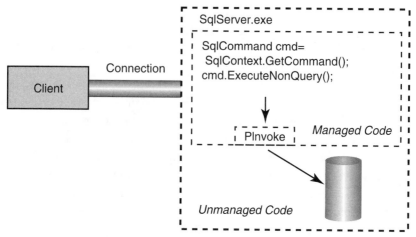

FIGURE 4-3: Interop to Retrieve the SQL Context

whole of SQL Server in managed code. And yes, interoperability calls happen. The managed classes are making PInvoke calls against the executable of SQL Server, `sqlservr.exe`, as shown in Figure 4-3, which exposes a couple of dozen methods for the CLR to call into.

When you read about interop, you may become concerned about performance. Theoretically, a performance hit is possible, but because SQL Server hosts the CLR (as discussed in Chapter 2) and the `SqlServer` provider runs in process with SQL Server, the hit is minimal. In the last sentence, notice that we said *theoretically:* Remember that when you execute CLR code, you will run machine-compiled code, which is not the case when you run T-SQL. Therefore, for some code executing in the CLR, the end result may be a performance improvement, compared with pure T-SQL code.

Now, that we have discussed the `SqlContext` class, let's see how we go about using it.

Connections

As already mentioned, when you are at server side and a client executes, you are part of that client's connection context, which in the SQL Server 2005 release is exposed through the static `GetConnection` method in the `SqlContext` class. So rather than creating a new connection (as is necessary with a connection from within extended stored procedures), you call `SqlContext.GetConnection`, as shown in the following code snippet.

```
public void static MyProc() {

    //retrieve the connection from the context
    SqlConnection conn = SqlContext.GetConnection();

    //do something useful with the connection

}
```

GetConnection returns a SqlConnection object that implements the ISqlConnection interface and exposes the public methods, properties, and events listed in Table 4-2. (Note that the table doesn't show members inherited from System.Object.)

If you compare the content of Table 4-2 with the members of the Sql Connection object in the SqlClient provider, the two will look more or less the same, and you can use the SqlConnection class in the SqlServer provider in much the same way you would use it in the SqlClient provider. There are, however, some differences.

- There is no constructor for the SqlConnection class. You cannot create a SqlConnection directly and must use the connection provided by SqlContext.GetConnection(). This makes sense since you are already executing with an open connection.
- There is a new method, CreateExecutionContext, which returns a SqlExecutionContext object. The SqlExecutionContext and associated interfaces and classes are covered later in this chapter.
- Because SqlConnection does not implement IDisposable, you have no Dispose method. This is good, because you do not want to dispose of an open connection under the "feet" of the client. Remember that you are in the context of the caller's connection. Along the same lines, if you try to call Close, you will get an application exception: "Cannot call close on context connection."
- There is an Open method, but at this time (March 2004), neither it nor the ChangeDatabase method has been implemented.

Another difference is transactions. When you use ADO.NET and the SqlClient provider, you have to explicitly attach a transaction to the command you execute, which is not the case if you code T-SQL. Listing 4-3 gives an example of transactions in ADO.NET compared with transactions in T-SQL.

TABLE 4-2: Public Members of SqlConnection

Name	Return Value/Type	Member Type
BeginTransaction()	SqlTransaction	Method
BeginTransaction (IsolationLevel)	SqlTransaction	Method
BeginTransaction (IsolationLevel, String)	SqlTransaction	Method
BeginTransaction(String)	SqlTransaction	Method
ChangeDatabase(String)	void	Method
Close()	void	Method
CreateCommand()	SqlCommand	Method
CreateCommand(String)	SqlCommand	Method
CreateExecutionContext (SqlDefinition)	SqlExecutionContext	Method
CreateRecord(SqlMetaData)	SqlDataRecord	Method
Open()	void	Method
ConnectionString	String	Property
ConnectionTimeout	Int32	Property
Database	String	Property
DataSource	String	Property
ServerVersion	String	Property
State	String	Property

LISTING 4-3: Transactions in ADO.NET versus T-SQL

```
//transactions using the SqlClient provider
SqlConnection conn = new SqlConnection(connString);
conn.Open();
SqlTransaction tx = conn.BeginTransaction();
SqlCommand cmd = new SqlCommand(someInsertStmt);
```

```
cmd.Connection = conn;
cmd.Transaction = tx;
cmd.ExecuteNonQuery();
tx.Rollback();


-transactions in T-SQL
BEGIN TRAN
 -do database edits/inserts/deletes in one or several
 - statements

 - roll back the transaction
ROLLBACK TRAN
```

In the SqlServer provider, you do have to associate a transaction with a command, although SqlCommands retrieved via the SqlContext are automatically associated with the context transaction, if one exists. Sql Command instances created with the new operator or SqlConnection. CreateCommand must be manually associated, as the following code snippet shows. We'll discuss transactions in detail later in the chapter.

```
//get the connection object
SqlConnection conn = SqlContext.GetConnection();

//get a transaction
SqlTransaction tx = conn.BeginTransaction();

//create the command
SqlCommand cmd = conn.CreateCommand();

cmd.CommandText = someStmt;
cmd.Transaction = tx;
cmd.ExecuteNonQuery();
//roll back the transaction
tx.Rollback();
```

A final thing to understand about SqlConnection is how commands are created. In ADO.NET you are probably accustomed to creating your command explicitly through the new keyword or through the Create Command method on the SqlConnection object. This is also available to you in the SqlServer provider, but you may have noticed in Table 4-1 a method on the SqlContext object called GetCommand. Regardless of the method you use, you will get a SqlCommand object back. The next section of this chapter looks at the SqlCommand object.

Commands—Making Things Happen

The `SqlServer` provider implements the `SqlCommand` class in order to execute action statements and submit queries to the database. The command class implements the `ISqlCommand` interface, and you can obtain the command object in a number of different ways.

When you already have retrieved your connection, you can get the command object from the `CreateCommand` method on your connection the same way you can in the `SqlClient` provider. One difference, if you compare this with previous versions of the `SqlClient` provider in ADO.NET, is that the `CreateCommand` is overloaded; and in the `SqlServer` provider, it can now take a command string as a constructor parameter, as the code in Listing 4-4 shows, in addition to the parameterless constructor.

LISTING 4-4: Create a Command from the Connection Object

```
//get a command through CreateCommand
SqlConnection conn = SqlContext.GetConnection();
SqlCommand cmd = conn.CreateCommand(cmdStatement);
```

Another way of getting to the command is to use the `SqlContext` object and call `GetCommand`, which you can do without first having retrieved the connection object, which Listing 4-5 shows.

LISTING 4-5: Use GetCommand from SqlContext

```
//use SqlContext and get command
SqlCommand cmd = SqlContext.GetCommand();
cmd.CommandText = cmdStatement;
```

Keep in mind that the `SqlCommand` in Listing 4-5 will automatically be enlisted as part of the transaction in the `SqlContext` if the caller started a transaction. The `SqlCommand` obtained in the example in Listing 4-4 must be manually enlisted.

An interesting thing to note is that the "context command" shown earlier is *not* the currently executing command. That is, the command's `CommandText` is *not* the name of the stored procedure or UDF that is currently being executed; the parameters collection does *not* give you access to the parameters used to call *your* procedure. It's simply an empty (but instantiated) `SqlCommand`, with the `SqlConnection` (and if applicable, the `SqlTransaction`) properties set to the context connection and the context transaction. You can use it like a `SqlCommand` obtained in any of the other ways shown earlier. In addition, you can call `SqlContext.GetCommand` multiple times, and a new `SqlCommand` instance will be retrieved each time. Each `SqlCommand` is associated with the context connection and context transaction (if one exists).

You can also call `new` on the `SqlCommand` as you can with the `Sql Command` in the `SqlClient` provider and then associate the instance you have created with an existing connection by setting the connection property of the command instance.

Having seen these different ways of creating a command object, you may wonder what the differences are between these various methods. It turns out that there are only subtle differences between calling `Create Command` on the connection object versus `SqlContext.GetCommand`; these have to do with enlisting the transaction. We'll discuss this in the section on transactions. However, the end result of both methods is that a constructor on the command object is being called with the instance of the connection as a parameter. In order to instantiate the command, `SqlContext.GetCommand` first retrieves the context and the connection object. A rule of thumb from a pure performance point of view is that if you already have your connection object (you have called `SqlContext.GetConnection`), you should call `CreateCommand` on the connection object instead of calling `GetCommand` on the `SqlContext` object. `GetCommand` is checking for existing context and connection, to see if it needs to create it, and because we know we already have those, we can call `CreateCommand` directly.

We have seen how a command is created; let's now look at what we can do with the command. Table 4-3 lists the public methods, properties, and events (the table doesn't show public members inherited from `System. Object`).

For those of you who are used to the `SqlClient` provider, most of the members are recognizable, but as with the connection object, there are some differences.

- There is a new method, `ExecuteRow`, that returns a single row. This method is equivalent to `SqlCommand.ExecuteReader (CommandBehavior.SingleRow)` in previous versions of the `SqlClient` provider. You should be sure that the SELECT statement is guaranteed to return only one row; if the result contains more than one row, you will be able to "see" only one row.

- There is a `Dispose` method on `SqlCommand`. Calling it makes the `SqlCommand` release unmanaged resources and is used to clean up the state of the instance.

TABLE 4-3: Public Members of SqlCommand

Name	Return Value/Type	Member Type
.ctor()	void	Constructor
Cancel()	void	Method
CreateParameter()	SqlParameter	Method
Dispose()	void	Method
ExecuteNonQuery()	int	Method
ExecuteReader()	SqlDataReader	Method
ExecuteReader (CommandBehavior)	SqlDataReader	Method
ExecuteRow()	SqlDataRecord	Method
ExecuteScalar()	Object	Method
ExecuteSqlScalar()	Object	Method
ExecuteXmlReader()	XmlReader	Method
Prepare()	void	Method
CommandText	String	Property
CommandTimeout	int	Property
CommandType	CommandType	Property
Connection	SqlConnection	Property
Parameters	SqlParameterCollection	Property
Notification	SqlNotificationRequest	Property
Transaction	SqlTransaction	Property
UpdatedRowSource	UpdateRowSource	Property

When you execute parameterized queries or stored procedures, you specify the parameter values through the `Parameters` property of the `SqlCommand` class. This property can contain a `SqlParameterCollection` that is a collection of `SqlParameter` instances. The `SqlParameter` instance contains a description of the parameter and also the parameter value. Properties of the `SqlParameter` class include parameter name, data type (including precision and scale for decimal parameters), parameter length, and parameter direction. Like the `SqlClient` provider, the `SqlServer` provider uses named parameters rather than positional parameters. Use of named parameters means the following.

- The parameter name is significant; the correct name must be specified.
- The parameter name is used as a parameter marker in parameter-ized SELECT statements, rather than the ODBC/OLE DB question mark parameter marker.
- The order of the parameters in the collection is not significant (with the exception of the `ReturnCode`, which, if specified, must be the zeroth parameter in the collection.
- Stored procedure parameters with default values may be omitted from the collection; if they are omitted, the default value will be used.

Parameter direction must be specified as a value of the `Parameter Direction` enumeration. This enumeration contains the values `Input`, `Output`, `InputOutput`, and `ReturnCode`. Although Chapter 3 mentioned that in T-SQL all parameters defined as OUTPUT can also be used for input, the `SqlServer` provider (and ADO.NET is general) is more precise. Attempting to use the wrong parameter direction will cause an error, and if you specify `ParameterDirection.Output`, input values will be ignored. If you need to pass in a value to a T-SQL procedure that declares it as OUTPUT, you must use `ParameterDirection.InputOutput`. An example of executing a parameterized T-SQL statement follows.

```
SqlCommand cmd = SqlContext.GetCommand();

// set the command text
// use names as parameter markers
cmd.CommandText =
    "insert into jobs values(@job_desc, @min_lvl, @max_lvl)";
```

```
// names must agree with markers
cmd.Parameters.Add("@job_desc", SqlDbType.VarChar);
cmd.Parameters.Add("@min_lvl", SqlDbType.TinyInt);
cmd.Parameters.Add("@max_lvl", SqlDbType.TinyInt);

// set values
cmd.Parameters[0].Value = "A new job description";
cmd.Parameters[1].Value = 10;
cmd.Parameters[2].Value = 20;

// execute the command
// should return 1 row affected
int RowsAffected = cmd.ExecuteNonQuery();
```

SqlExecutionContext and SqlDefinition

So far, what we've seen of coding data access through the SqlServer provider looks like dynamic SQL or, at best, parameterized SQL. Because we are actually in the database, however, we can gain additional speed by dividing the SqlCommand into the static portion (SqlDefinition) and the dynamic portion (SqlExecutionContext). This is because .NET object creation is fairly expensive; creating the same command instance, adding the parameters collection, and populating it with parameters can be optimized if we're going to execute the same command many times with different parameter values. In addition, it might be possible for the provider to access SQL Server's data buffers directly in some cases, adding further optimization. The SqlDefinition can also be saved across multiple invocations of the same .NET stored procedure or user-defined function. To accomplish this, you need to construct it in a static constructor and store it in a read-only static variable for later use.

SqlDefinition encapsulates the static portions of the SqlCommand and the shape of the SqlParametersCollection. SqlExecutionContext contains methods to set and get the parameter values and execute the command. The sequence of coding events to use these two classes is as follows.

1. Instantiate a SqlCommand.

2. Set the SqlCommand's Text property.

3. Instantiate a SqlParametersCollection and add SqlParameters.

4. Use the SqlCommand to extract a SqlDefinition and save it.

To use the SqlDefinition instance in .NET procedural code, follow these steps.

1. Obtain the `ISqlExecutionContext` interface from the current connection and the `SqlDefinition`.
2. Set the parameter values using `ISqlExecutionContext`.
3. Execute the command using `ISqlExecutionContext`.
4. Repeat steps 2–3 to taste.

This technique is illustrated in the following code example.

```
public class PubsProc
{

    // SqlDefinition in a read-only static variable
    static readonly SqlDefinition sd = null;

    // read-only static initialized in a static constructor
    static PubsProc()
    {
        SqlCommand cmd = SqlContext.GetCommand();
        cmd.CommandText = "select * from authors where au_id=@auid";
        cmd.Parameters.Add("@auid", SqlDbType.VarChar);
        cmd.Parameters[0].Size = 11;
        sd = new SqlDefinition(cmd);
        cmd.Dispose();
    }


    [SqlProcedure]
    public static void GetAuthorById (SqlString s)
    {
        // create the ExecutionContext
        // using the definition as a lookup key
        ISqlExecutionContext sc =
          SqlContext.GetConnection().CreateExecutionContext(sd);

        // set the parameter using ordinals
        sc.SetSqlString(0, s);

        ISqlReader rdr = sc.ExecuteReader();
        SqlContext.GetPipe().Send(rdr);
        rdr.Close();
    }
}
```

There are a couple of interesting implementation details to note about this example. Because using `SqlExecutionContext`/`SqlDefinition` uses SQL Server's buffers directly, you must take special precautions when using VARCHAR or CHAR parameters. The .NET `System.String` class is a

Unicode string; the only way to inform the provider that you mean to use single-byte characters is to set the length of the parameter directly. This is not necessary when you are using `SqlCommand` with either the `Sql Client` or `SqlServer` data providers, but is required with the optimized `SqlExecutionContext` class. In addition, the methods of `SqlExecution Context` use zero-based ordinals rather than names. Using ordinals avoids the overhead of an index lookup each time you use the procedure, at the possible expense of code readability. Although you can derive a parameter ordinal from a parameter name when using a `SqlParameters` collection using `SqlCommand.Parameters.IndexOf("parmname")`, there is currently no way to do this using `SqlExecutionContext` and `SqlDefinition`.

Obtaining Results

Execution of SQL commands can return the following:

- A numeric return code
- A count of rows affected by the command
- A single scalar value
- A single row
- One or more multirow results using SQL Server's "default (cursor-less) behavior"
- A stream of XML

Some commands, such as a command that executes a stored procedure, can return more than one of these items—for example, a return code, a count of rows affected, and many multirow results. You tell the `SqlServer` provider which of these output items you want by using the appropriate method of `SqlCommand`, as shown in Table 4-4.

When you return data from a SELECT statement, it is always best to use the "lowest overhead" choice. Because of the amount of internal processing and the number of object allocations needed, `ExecuteScalar` will be faster than `ExecuteRow`, which will be faster than `ExecuteReader`. Of course, you need to consider the shape of the data that is returned. As an example, using the command SELECT au_id, au_lname, au_fname FROM authors, `ExecuteScalar` will return only the first column of the first row, and `ExecuteRow` will return only the first row; therefore, you always want to use `ExecuteReader`. Using `ExecuteReader` to return a forward-only, read-only cursorless set of results is always preferred over using a

TABLE 4-4: How to Obtain Different Result Types

Result Desired	Mechanism to Obtain It
Return code	Parameter with `ParameterDirection` of `ReturnCode`
Count of rows affected	Returned value from `SqlCommand.ExecuteNonQuery;` or use `SqlCommand.ExecuteReader` and `SqlDataReader.RecordsAffected`
Scalar value	Use `SqlCommand.ExecuteScalar`
Single row	Use `SqlCommand.ExecuteRow`
Cursorless mode results	Use `SqlCommand.ExecuteReader`
XML stream	Use `SqlCommand.ExecuteXmlReader`

server cursor. An example of when to use each results-returning method follows.

```
SqlCommand cmd = SqlContext.GetCommand();

// 1. this is a user-defined function
// returning a single value (authorname) as VARCHAR
cmd.CommandText = "GetFullAuthorNameById";
// required from procedure or UDF
cmd.CommandType = CommandType.StoredProcedure;
cmd.Parameters.AddWithValue("@id", "111-11-1111");

SqlString fullname = (SqlString)cmd.ExecuteScalar();
// use fullname

// 2. returns one row
cmd.CommandText = "GetAuthorInfoById";
// required from procedure or UDF
cmd.CommandType = CommandType.StoredProcedure;
cmd.Parameters.AddWithValue("@id", "111-11-1111");

SqlDataRecord rec = cmd.ExecuteRow();
// use fields in SqlDataRecord

// 3. returns multiple rows
cmd.CommandText = "select * from authors";
cmd.CommandType = CommandType.Text;
cmd.Parameters.Clear();
```

```
SqlDataReader rdr = cmd.ExecuteReader();
while (rdr.Read() == true)
  // process rows in SqlDataReader}
```

SqlDataReader encapsulates multiple rows that can be read in a forward-only manner. You move to the next row in the set by using the SqlDataReader.Read() method, as shown in the preceding example. After you call ExecuteReader, the resultant SqlDataReader is positioned before the first row in the set, and an initial Read positions it at the first row. The Read method returns false when there are no more rows in the set. If more than one rowset is available, you move to the next rowset by calling SqlDataReader.NextResult. While you are positioned on a row, the IDataRecord interface can be used to read data. You can use loosely typed ordinals or names to read the data in single columns. Using ordinals or names is a syntactic shortcut to using IDataRecord.GetValue. This returns the value as a .NET System.Object, which must be cast to the correct type.

If you know the data type of the value, you can use more strongly typed column accessors. Both SQL Server providers have two kinds of strongly typed accessors. IDataReader.GetDecimal(0) is an example; this returns the value of the first column of the current row as a .NET System.Decimal data type. It is better to use ISqlRecord's SQL Server–specific accessors; these return instances of structures from the System.Data.SqlTypes namespace. These types are isomorphic with SQL Server data types; examples of their use and reasons they are preferable to the .NET data types were covered in Chapter 3. An example of using each type follows.

```
SqlCommand cmd = SqlContext.GetCommand();
cmd.CommandText = "select * from authors";
cmd.CommandType = CommandType.Text;
cmd.Parameters = null;

SqlDataReader rdr = cmd.ExecuteReader()
while (rdr.Read() == true)
{
  String s;
  // 1. Use ordinals or names
  //    must cast from object to desired type
  s = (string)rdr[0];
  s = (string)rdr["au_id"];

  // 2. Use GetValue (must cast)
  s = (string)GetValue(0);

  // 3. Strong typed accessors
  s = GetString(0);
```

```
// 4. Accessors for SqlTypes
SqlString s2 = GetSqlString(0);

}
```

Although you can process results obtained inside .NET procedural code, you can also pass these items back to the client. This is accomplished through the `SqlPipe` class, which is described later in the chapter. Note that each of the classes returns rows, which must be processed sequentially; these result cannot be updated in place.

Transactions

Multiple SQL operations within a stored procedure or user-defined function can be executed individually or composed within a single transaction. Composing multistatement procedural code inside a transaction ensures that a set of operations has "ACID" properties. ACID is an acronym for the following:

- Atomicity—Either all the statements in a transaction will succeed or none of them will.
- Consistency—None of the statements in a transaction are allowed to violate database rules such as constraints or even business rules that reside in a trigger.
- Isolation—Each transaction has its own view of the database state.
- Durability—These behaviors are guaranteed even if the database or host operating system fails—for example, because of a power failure.

You can use transactions in two general ways within the `SqlServer` managed provider—use T-SQL statements as `Command.Text`, or start a transaction by using the `SqlConnection.BeginTransaction` method. An example of each follows.

```
// Example 1: start transaction using T-SQL
SqlCommand cmd = SqlContext.GetCommand();
cmd.CommandText = "BEGIN TRANSACTION";
cmd.ExecuteNonQuery();

// Example 2: start transaction using the API
SqlTransaction tx = null;
tx = SqlContext.GetConnection().BeginTransaction();
```

It's also possible that a transaction existed for the current session before the .NET procedural code was invoked. You can get a handle to this transaction by using the `SqlContext.GetTransaction` method. The semantics of each type of transaction handling and the interaction between the transaction and the command (exposed as the `SqlCommand`'s `Transaction` property) are subtly different for each case.

When There Is No Transaction in the Context

This is the case when the .NET procedural code has been called in standalone mode (also called autocommit mode, because although each SQL statement is transactional, the database automatically "commits" after each statement. You can deduce this because `SqlContext.GetTransaction()` returns a null `SqlTransaction` instance. When you have no transaction in context, you can state one by using the `SqlConnection`'s `BeginTransaction` method, as shown in the following example. You can use this transaction with multiple SQL statements through a `SqlCommand` instance, or you can compose multiple `SqlCommand` instances in the same transaction. Once you have started a transaction, you must enlist each new `SqlCommand` (that you might create, for example, with `SqlConnection.CreateCommand` or a new `SqlCommand` instance) in this transaction. SQL Server 2005 does not support multiple transaction contexts on the same connection or support the behavior in which some `SqlCommand`s within the same connection are transactional and some are autocommit. The following code shows an example of composing multiple `SqlCommand`s within the same API transaction.

```
SqlTransaction tx = SqlContext.GetTransaction();

// this will fail if there's already a transaction
if (tx == null)
   tx = SqlContext.GetConnection().BeginTransaction();

// hook up the context command
SqlCommand ctxcmd = SqlContext.GetCommand();
ctxcmd.Transaction = tx;
ctxcmd.CommandText = "insert into t1 values('sometext')";
ctxcmd.ExecuteNonQuery();

// hook up another command
SqlCommand cmd = new SqlCommand();
cmd.Connection = SqlContext.GetConnection();
cmd.Transaction = tx;
cmd.CommandText = "insert into t1 values('moretext')";
cmd.ExecuteNonQuery();
```

```
// now commit the transaction
// this transaction must be committed
// or rolled back before you leave the procedure
tx.Commit();
```

The following example shows that attempting to use multiple transactions within a context will cause an error.

```
SqlTransaction tx = null;

// this will fail if there's already a transaction
if (SqlContext.GetTransaction() == null)
  tx = SqlContext.GetConnection().BeginTransaction();

// hook up the context command
SqlCommand ctxcmd = SqlContext().GetCommand();
ctxcmd.Transaction = tx;
ctxcmd.CommandText = "insert into t1 values('sometext')";
ctxcmd.ExecuteNonQuery();

// this fails
ctxconn = SqlContext.GetConnection();
SqlTransaction tx2 = ctxconn.BeginTransaction();

// start a new transaction with this command
SqlCommand cmd = new SqlCommand();
cmd.Connection = SqlContext.GetConnection();
cmd.CommandText = "BEGIN TRANSACTION";

// this fails too
// can't have more than one transaction
cmd.ExecuteNonQuery();
```

When you create an API transaction via `BeginTransaction`, you may not call `BeginTransaction` again in the same connection until either `Transaction.Commit` or `Transaction.Rollback` is called. Although SQL Server supports nesting transactions with multiple T-SQL BEGIN TRAN calls, the `SqlServer` provider does not. If you use the `BeginTransaction` method in your .NET procedural code, you must call either `Commit` or `Rollback` before you exit the procedure. Failing to do so will result in an error.

Using a Transaction in the Context

If your .NET procedural code is called from code (either T-SQL or .NET code) that has already begun a transaction, there will be a transaction in the context. That is, `SqlContext.GetTransaction` will return an active

SqlTransaction instance. Your context SqlCommand is already "enlisted" in this transaction—that is, SqlContext.GetCommand().Transaction will return the context transaction. SQL statements issued through this command become part of the transaction. An example .NET stored procedure body that uses a T-SQL statement follows. The T-SQL insert statement will be part of the transaction.

```
SqlTransaction tx = SqlContext.GetTransaction();
if (tx != null)
{
    // this is already part of the transaction
    SqlCommand ctxcmd = SqlContext.GetCommand();
    ctxcmd.CommandText = "insert into t1 values('sometext')";
    ctxcmd.ExecuteNonQuery();
}
```

Note that you cannot roll back the context transaction; this produces an error. You cannot commit the context transaction either; in this case, an error is produced when your stored procedure returns to the caller. This is shown in the following example and is the same error produced when you try to do this inside a called stored procedure using T-SQL code.

```
SqlTransaction tx = SqlContext.GetTransaction();

bool error_occured = false;
// ... do some SQL operations here

// either of these fail
if (error_occurred)
    tx.Rollback();
else
    tx.Commit();
```

Only the context command is implicitly enlisted in the transaction. If you instantiate a new SqlCommand either directly or with SqlContext.GetConnection().CreateCommand(), you must set its Transaction property to the context transaction yourself. Failure to set the transaction if one exists will cause an error when you call one of the command's set of Execute methods.

```
SqlTransaction tx = SqlContext.GetTransaction();
if (tx != null)
{
    // this is already part of the transaction
    SqlCommand ctxcmd = SqlContext().GetCommand();
    ctxcmd.CommandText = "insert into t1 values('sometext')";
    ctxcmd.ExecuteNonQuery();
```

```
// this one must be enlisted
SqlCommand cmd1   = new SqlCommand();
cmd1.Connection   = SqlContext.GetConnection();
cmd1.Transaction = tx;

// this one must be enlisted too
SqlConnection conn = SqlContext.GetConnection();
SqlCommand cmd2 = conn.CreateCommand();
cmd2.Transaction = tx;
}
```

Starting a Transaction with T-SQL Command.Text

The last way to start a transaction is to use T-SQL's BEGIN TRANSACTION as the command's Text property and use Command.ExecuteNonQuery to begin the transaction. This was shown at the beginning of the Transactions section. Interestingly, transactions started in this way behave differently from transactions started through the API. You can start a T-SQL transaction whether or not there is already a transaction in context, as in "ordinary" T-SQL; this just increases the @@trancount variable by one. You must commit or roll back the transaction through T-SQL using Command.Execute NonQuery with the appropriate Command.Text before exiting the procedure. In addition, calling ROLLBACK using Command.ExecuteNonQuery results in a SQL error on exit, just as in nested transactional T-SQL procedures.

Best Practice for Using Transactions in SQLCLR Stored Procedures

With so many choices and different transactional combinations, which one is best? We'd like to write a SQLCLR stored procedure with a few SQL statements that runs correctly standalone, but also works when the caller has already started a transaction. For ease of use, here are a few hints.

- Check for a context transaction first. If there is already a context transaction, use it. If one of the commands fails, return an error to the caller, rather than trying to call SqlTransaction.Rollback.
- If the context transaction does not exist, start one. Remember to call either SqlTransaction.Commit or SqlTransaction.Rollback before exiting the procedure.
- Use only the context command, unless you have a good reason to do otherwise. SqlContext.GetCommand always returns a new instance of a SqlCommand each time, enlisted in the current connection and transaction (if there is one).

Here's an example that illustrates these practices.

```
public static void InsertSomeJobs()
{
    // if we have no context transaction
    // we can start one
    // if we have one, we can use it and compose with it

    bool got_context_tx = false;
    bool error_occurred = false;
    SqlTransaction tx = SqlContext.GetTransaction();
    if (tx == null)
        tx = SqlContext.GetConnection().BeginTransaction();
    else
        got_context_tx = true;

    SqlCommand cmd = SqlContext.GetCommand();

    try
    {
        cmd.Transaction = tx;
        cmd.CommandText =
            "insert jobs values('row1', 10, 10)";
        cmd.ExecuteNonQuery();
        cmd.CommandText =
            "insert jobs values('row2', 10, 10)";
        cmd.ExecuteNonQuery();
    }
    catch (SqlException ex)
    {
        error_occurred = true;
        if (!got_context_tx)
            tx.Rollback();
        // or rethrow the exception
        throw ex;
    }

    // else commit the transaction
    // only if we started it
    if (!error_occurred && !got_context_tx)
        tx.Commit();
}
```

Transaction Exotica

In the following example, we've stuck strictly to local transactions at the default transaction isolation level. The `SqlServer` provider also supports other transaction isolation levels through the API. This is accomplished through an override of `SqlConnection.BeginTransaction`, just as with the `SqlClient` provider. It's also possible to use named savepoints in the

`SqlServer` provider. A named savepoint provides the ability for a "partial rollback" scenario, but as of this writing they don't work, because you can't start another transaction through the API if there is already one in the context.

```
// this should work whether there is a context tx or not
SqlTransaction tx =
    SqlContext.GetConnection().BeginTransaction("named");
SqlCommand cmd = SqlContext.GetCommand();

cmd.Transaction = tx;
cmd.CommandText = "insert jobs values('row1', 10, 10)";
cmd.ExecuteNonQuery();
cmd.CommandText = "insert jobs values('row2', 10, 10)";
cmd.ExecuteNonQuery();

tx.Commit();
```

Distributed transactions—that is, transactions that encompass more than one instance of SQL Server—are supported implicitly by using the `"BEGIN TRAN"` SQL command as `Command.Text` and then accessing data in another SQL Server using four-part names. You can also start them explicitly by setting the `Command.Text` to `"BEGIN DISTRIBUTED TRANSACTION"`. The `SqlServer` provider does not support the method on the `SqlConnection` to enlist in an existing distributed transaction manually as `SqlClient` does.

Pipe

In the section on results, we mentioned that you had a choice of processing results in your procedural code as part of its logic or returning the results to the caller. Consuming `SqlDataReaders` or the stream of XML in procedural code makes them unavailable to the caller; you cannot process a cursorless mode result more than once. The code for in-process consumption of a `SqlDataReader` is identical to `SqlClient`; you call `Read()` until no more rows remain. To pass a `SqlDataReader` (or any result) back to the client, you need to use a special class, `SqlPipe`.

The `SqlPipe` class represents a TDS (tabular data stream) output stream. You obtain a `SqlPipe` by using `SqlContext.GetPipe()`. Results, errors, and messages can be written to the pipe. A simple example of a stored procedure that returns a `SqlDataReader` to the client follows.

```
public static void getAuthorsByState(SqlString state)
{
    SqlCommand cmd = SqlContext.GetCommand();
```

```
cmd.CommandText = "select * from authors where state = @state";
cmd.Parameters.Add("@state", SqlDbType.VarChar);
cmd.Parameters[0].Value = state;
SqlDataReader rdr = cmd.ExecuteReader();
SqlPipe pipe = SqlContext.GetPipe();
pipe.Send(rdr);
}
```

In addition to returning an entire set of results through the pipe, `SqlPipe`'s `Send` method lets you send an instance of any class that implements `IDataRecord`. You can also batch the send operations however you'd like. An interesting feature of using `SqlPipe` is that the result is streamed to the caller immediately as fast as you are able to send it. This may improve performance at the client because you can process rows as fast as they are sent out the pipe. Note that you can combine executing a command and sending the results back through `SqlPipe` in a single operation with the `Execute` convenience methods, using either a `SqlCommand` or `SqlExecutionContext` as a method input parameter.

`SqlPipe` also contains methods for sending scalar values as messages and sending errors. We'll talk about error handling practices next. The entire set of methods exposed by `SqlPipe` is shown in Table 4-5.

TABLE 4-5: Methods of the SqlPipe Class

Method	What It Does
`Execute(SqlCommand)`	Execute command, return results through `SqlPipe`.
`Execute(SqlExecutionContext)`	Execute command through `SqlExecutionContext`, return results through `SqlPipe`.
`Send(string)`	Send a message as a string.
`Send(ISqlReader)`	Send results through `ISqlReader`.
`Send(ISqlRecord)`	Send results through `ISqlRecord`.
`SendResultsStart(ISqlRecord, bool)`	Start sending results.
`SendResultsRow(ISqlRecord)`	Send a single row after calling `SendResultsStart`.
`SendResultsEnd()`	Indicate finished sending rows.

Exception Handling

One of the reasons .NET procedures are appealing is that .NET has real structured exception handling. SQL Server 2005 includes improvements in error handling (see BEGIN-END TRY, BEGIN-END CATCH in Chapter 7, T-SQL Enhancements), but this isn't true structured exception handling. Any error that is caught in T-SQL's try/catch mechanism results in a doomed transaction; this isn't true for .NET procedures, as shown in the following example.

```
public static void EatException()
{
   try
   {
      // either one of these works
      // divide-by-zero exception
      int i = 42;
      int j = 0;
      j = i / j;

      // or SqlException (comment out previous exception)
      // cannot commit context transaction
      SqlContext.GetTransaction().Commit();
   }
   catch (Exception e)
   {
      SqlContext.GetPipe().Send("Ate the exception");
      SqlContext.GetPipe().Send(e.Message);
   }
}

-- Run this T-SQL code to test it
-- In each case the transaction commits
-- And the row is inserted

BEGIN TRANSACTION
INSERT INTO jobs VALUES('before exception', 10, 10)
EXECUTE EatException
COMMIT
```

You can even catch an error in .NET code and rethrow it. However, there is a catch (pun intended). Any unhandled exceptions that make their way out of your CLR procedure result in the same error at the client, whether the client is SQL Workbench or a user application. However, if you are called from a try/catch block inside another .NET stored procedure, that procedure can catch your exception without causing an underlying T-SQL exception. The following code in illustrates this.

```
public static void ExceptionThrower()
{
  try
  {
    int i = 42;
    int j = 0;
    j = i / j;
  }
  catch (Exception e)
  {
    SqlContext.GetPipe().Send("In exception thrower");
    SqlContext.GetPipe().Send(e.Message);
    throw (e);
  }
}

public static void ExceptionCatcher()
{
  try
  {
    SqlCommand cmd = SqlContext.GetCommand();
    cmd.CommandText = "ExceptionThrower";
    cmd.CommandType = CommandType.StoredProcedure;
    cmd.ExecuteNonQuery();
    SqlContext.GetPipe().Send("Shouldn't get here");
  }
  catch (Exception e)
  {
    // but it doesn't get here either
    SqlContext.GetPipe().Send("In exception catcher");
    SqlContext.GetPipe().Send(e.Message);
  }
}
```

The results of using the `ExceptionThrower` procedure, both stand-alone and from the `ExceptionCatcher`, are shown in the following code.

```
-- exception thrower standalone
begin tran
insert into jobs values('thrower', 10, 10)
exec ExceptionThrower
commit

-- results in the messages window
In exception thrower
Attempted to divide by zero.
.Net SqlClient Data Provider: Msg 6522,
    Level 16, State 1, Procedure ExceptionThrower, Line 3
```

```
A .NET Framework error occurred during execution of user defined
routine or aggregate 'ExceptionThrower': System.DivideByZeroException:
Attempted to divide by zero.
   at Except1.Class1.ExceptionThrower().

 - exception catcher calls exception thrower
begin tran
insert into jobs values('catcher', 10, 10)
exec ExceptionCatcher
commit

In exception catcher
A .NET Framework error occurred during execution of user defined
routine or aggregate 'ExceptionThrower': System.DivideByZeroException:
Attempted to divide by zero.
   at Except1.Class1.ExceptionThrower().
```

Note that, in each case, the transaction will commit. The only thing that would cause the transaction to roll back would be if the call to the standalone ExceptionThrower was called from a T-SQL try/catch block. If the case of ExceptionCatcher, it catches and discards the exception raised by the ExceptionThrower (the error message comes from Exception Catcher's write of e.Message to the SqlPipe. The only unusual thing is that we don't see the messages sent by the ExceptionThrower.

For procedure writers looking to expose custom errors through the API, SqlPipe.Send(SqlError) looks promising. However, SqlError doesn't have a constructor; the only errors that can be sent through this call are already existing T-SQL errors. To return a custom error, the tried-and-true method is best.

- Define your error to the SQL Server error catalog with sp_addmessage.
- Use the T-SQL RAISERROR command in SqlCommand.Text.
- Use SqlCommand.ExecuteNonQuery to return the error.

This method follows.

```
public static SqlInt32 getAuthorWithErrors(
  SqlString au_id, out SqlString au_info)
{
  //  - In SQL Workbench add custom message to be used
  //  - when an author cannot be found
  // sp_addmessage 50005, 16,
  //  'author with ssn: %s, not found in the database'
  //  go
```

```
// build a command
SqlCommand cmd = SqlContext.GetCommand();
// build command text
cmd.CommandText =
  "select address, city, state, zip" +
  " from authors where au_id = @au_id";

// make a parameter to hold the author id
cmd.Parameters.Add("@au_id", SqlDbType.VarChar);
// put in the value of the author id
cmd.Parameters[0].Value = au_id;

// use ExecuteRow because you know only
// a single row will come back
SqlDataRecord rec = cmd.ExecuteRow();

// make SqlString to hold result
// note that if you do not give this
// string a value it will be null
au_info = new SqlString();

// check to see if lookup was successful
if (rec == null)
{
  // lookup was not successful, raise an error
  cmd.CommandText = "Raiserror (50005, 16, 1, '" +
    au_id.ToString() + "') with seterror";
  cmd.ExecuteNonQuery();
  return -50005;
}
else
{
  // lookup was successful, set au_info to information string
  au_info = String.Format("{0} {1} {2} {3}",
    rec["address"], rec["city"], rec["state"], rec["zip"]);
}
// nothing to return, either success returned author info in au_info
// or error was raised
return 0;
}
```

SqlTriggerContext

SQL triggers have an execution context (represented by SqlContext) just as stored procedures and UDFs do. The environment settings, temporary tables in scope and so on, are available to a trigger. But triggers have additional context information; in T-SQL this information consists of logical tables for DML statements as well as information about which columns were updated, in the case of an update statement. In CLR triggers, this information is made available through the SqlTriggerContext class. You obtain the SqlTriggerContext through the SqlContext, as shown in the following example. SqlTriggerContext has a property to tell you whether the triggering action was an INSERT, an UPDATE, or a DELETE. This is handy if your trigger handles more than one action. The Columns Updated method returns a bitmask of columns by position, just like the T-SQL function of the same name. Finally, because SQL Server 2005 adds DDL and Event triggers to the mix, a property that exposes the EVENTDATA XML structure provides detailed information.

The INSERTED and DELETED logical tables work the same way that they do in T-SQL triggers; an interesting behavior is that they are visible from any SqlCommand that you create inside your trigger, not only the context SqlCommand. Because individual SQL statements are always transactional, any SqlCommand other than the context command must get the transaction property from the context and fill it in, as we showed earlier. This is shown in the following code.

```
public static void AddToObsolete()
{
    // get the trigger context so you can tell what is
    // going on
    SqlTriggerContext tc = SqlContext.GetTriggerContext();

    // this trigger is for deletes
    if (tc.TriggerAction == TriggerAction.Delete)
    {
        // Make a command. This can access the
        // "deleted" and "inserted" logical tables
        SqlCommand cmd = SqlContext.GetCommand();

        // so can this one, if it picks up the context transaction
        // SqlConnection conn = SqlContext.GetConnection();
        // SqlCommand cmd = conn.CreateCommand();
        // cmd.Transaction = SqlContext.GetTransaction();

        // so can this one, if it picks up the context transaction
        // SqlCommand cmd = new SqlCommand();
        // cmd.Connection = SqlContext.GetConnection();
        // cmd.Transaction = SqlContext.GetTransaction();

        // make a command that inserts the deleted row into
        // the obsoletejobs table
```

```
  cmd.CommandText = "insert into obsoletejobs select * from
deleted";

    // move the rows
    int rowsAffected = (int)cmd.ExecuteNonQuery();
  }
}
```

Because individual SQL statements (including triggers) are transactional, triggers in T-SQL use the ROLLBACK statement if the logic in the trigger determines that a business rule has been violated, for instance. Although inside a trigger the context transaction is visible, rolling it back produces an error just as in other CLR procedural code. The way to roll back the statement inside a trigger is to issue a ROLLBACK statement as Command.Text through Command.ExecuteNonQuery. An example of this follows.

```
public static void AddToObsolete()
{
  // get the trigger context so you can tell what is
  // going on
  SqlTriggerContext tc = SqlContext.GetTriggerContext();

  // this trigger is for deletes
  if (tc.TriggerAction == TriggerAction.Delete)
  {
    // Make a command
    SqlCommand cmd = SqlContext.GetCommand();

    // make a command that inserts the deleted row into
    // the obsoletejobs table
    cmd.CommandText = "insert into obsoletejobs select * from
deleted";

    // move the rows
    int rowsAffected = (int)cmd.ExecuteNonQuery();

    if (rowsAffected == 0)
    {
      // something bad happened, roll back
      cmd.CommandText = "rollback transaction";
      cmd.ExecuteNonQuery();
    }
  }
}
```

Where Are We?

This chapter looked at the `SqlServer` managed provider in depth. However, in the previous chapter, we stated that T-SQL is almost always best for data-centric code. When, then, is the best time to use the in-process provider? These cases include when it's appropriate to mix .NET-specific logic with data access code. Another case might be where structured exception handling is desired. In addition, because the SQL Server programming model is similar enough (though not identical) between `Sql Client` and `SqlServer` providers, some existing .NET code might be moved into the server for locality-of-reference benefits.

5

User-Defined Types and Aggregates

S QL SERVER PROVIDES types for scalars like FLOAT and CHAR. These can be represented by a single value such as a number or a string. Some scalars, such as a date, require more than one value to be represented. A date has a month, day, and year value in its representation. SQL Server provides the DATETIME scalar type for dates. There are other scalars that require more than one value to represent them for which SQL server does not provide a scalar type—for example, a dimension, like "12 in," which has a value and a unit. SQL Server 2005 allows a CLR language to be used to add scalar types and aggregates to SQL Server that can be used in the same way as any built-in scalar type or aggregate is.

Why Do We Need User-Defined Types?

User-defined types in SQL Server 2005 are used to extend its scalar type system. A column in a table is meant to hold a scalar. If you were given a sample set of data that looked like "12 4 9, 13 5 2, 9 14 11," you would say, "Those are triples of numbers, so each must be a vector, and I will need three columns to represent each one." You would know from experience and the first normal form that trying to squeeze each triple into a single column would be a false economy.

But not all triples are vectors. Consider this set of data: 10 13 1966, 6 15 1915, 7 4 1776. Writing them as follows might make it clearer that these are dates: 10/13/1966, 6/15/1915, 7/4/1776. Again, from experience, you would know that storing a date in three columns would make it difficult to work with. The triple, in this case, would use a single column. The reason you would want to use a single column is that storing a date in three columns makes no more sense or utility than storing the number 123 in three single-digit columns. The reason you can do this is that the SQL-92 specification realized how important it was to have a scalar type for a date, so it included DATETIME, which SQL Server implements.

There are other multifield values that are scalars. Angles, such as latitude and longitude, are written as having four fields: degrees, minutes, seconds, and direction. Geographic Information Systems (GIS) often have values that look like 34°6'12"N, 61° 35' 19"W. Unfortunately, the SQL Server scalar type system is missing the Latitude and Longitude data types. User-defined types allow you to make your own Latitude and Longitude types and use them in the same, convenient way you use the DATETIME type.

Scalars often have type-specific functions associated with them. For example, there are numerous functions, such as ASIN or CEILING, that are associated with numerical scalars. A user-defined type may also implement functions specifically associated with it. In some cases it may be useful to implement a user-defined type that is based on a built-in scalar type so that you may encapsulate some functionality with it.

Alias Types

You may be already familiar with the sp_addtype command, which SQL Server has had since well before SQL Server 2005. sp_addtype, along with CREATE RULE and sp_bindrule, is used to create an alias type. Alias types do not have the same capabilities as user-defined types and cannot be used in place of them. For example, there is no way to create an alias type for Latitude.

An alias type is used to constrain the value in a scalar type such as INT. The same constraints can be obtained by using CHECK constraints, and that is the recommended practice today. Information on CHECK constraints and alias types can be found in Books Online (BOL), which is included with SQL Server. Alias types are deprecated, and the ability to use them to enforce constraints may be removed from a future version of

SQL Server. In any case, even though user-defined types are scalar types, there is no way to use CREATE RULE and sp_bindrule to constrain them.

Overview of User-Defined Types

A user-defined type is implemented by a public CLR class that meets a set of requirements that are discussed later in this chapter. There is no way to implement a user-defined type using T-SQL. This class must implement the three key features of a user-defined type: a string representation, a binary representation, and a null representation. The string representation is the form of the user-defined type that a user will see; for example, the string representation of a Date is "2/5/1988". The binary representation is the form of the user-defined type that SQL Server will use to persist its value on disk. And lastly, a scalar in SQL Server must be able to have a null value, so the user-defined type must implement this.

The class that implements the user-defined type must be in an assembly that has been cataloged, as described in Chapter 2, into any database that uses it. The CREATE TYPE command is used to add the user-defined type in the class to the scalar type system for a database, much as CREATE PROCEDURE and CREATE FUNCTION are used to add procedures and functions based on CLR methods to a database.

User-defined types are similar to DATETIME types in that they are inserted into a column as a string but stored as a stream of bytes. That is, they are entered using their string representation but stored using their binary representation. The following example shows a date being stored as a stream of bytes.

```
CREATE TABLE Dates
(
    Date DATETIME
)
INSERT INTO Dates VALUES ('10/1/1900')
SELECT Date, CONVERT(VARBINARY(20), Date) FROM Dates
GO
10/1/1900 12:00:00 AM
0x0000000000000000000000000000000000000000000000000011100000000
```

This gives us the best of both worlds. We can write and read dates in a familiar notation and conveniently write predicates like (WHEN '1/1/1997' < InstallDate). User-defined types can also support this convenient comparison feature if their binary representation is appropriately designed, though they are not required to.

SQL Server provides a number of aggregate functions, such as MAX and AVG, for many of its scalar types. Likewise, in SQL Server 2005 you can create user-defined aggregates for the user-defined types that you create.

To illustrate a user-defined type, we will implement one that supports a simple linear dimension. It is called LDim. An instance of this type will contain a numeric value and units. The units can be any of "in", "ft", or "yd". A typical LDim we might write would look like "1 ft" or "7 yd". We want to be able to treat LDim as we would any other scalar variable, so we will also implement the aggregate functions LDimAvg and LDimMax for it. Listing 5-1 shows a SQL batch that uses LDim.

LISTING 5-1: Adding and Using a User-Defined Type

```
-- First we catalog an assembly we have previously
-- built that contains the implementation of LDim
-- This chapter is about how to make this assembly
CREATE ASSEMBLY LDim FROM 'c:\userTypes\bin\LDim.dll'
GO
-- Next we add LDim to the scalar type system
CREATE TYPE LDim EXTERNAL NAME LDim.[UDT.LDim]
GO
-- Now we can use LDim just like any other scalar type
-- Create a table that contains rectangular tiles,
-- using LDim for the dimensions of the tile
CREATE TABLE Tiles
(
  Id IDENTITY PRIMARY KEY,
  Length LDim,
  Width LDim
)
GO
-- add some tiles to the table
INSERT INTO Tiles VALUES (N'1 ft', N'6 in')
INSERT INTO Tiles VALUES (N'2 yd', N'2 in')
INSERT INTO Tiles VALUES (N'7 in', N'1 in')
INSERT INTO Tiles VALUES (N'2 ft', N'3 in')
INSERT INTO Tiles VALUES (NULL, NULL)
-- find all the tiles that are greater than 18 in long
SELECT Id FROM Tiles WHERE Length > N'18 in'
GO
2
-- order tiles by their width
SELECT Id from Tiles ORDER BY Width
go
3
2
4
1
5
```

```
- Find the average length and the sum of
- the widths of all of the tiles
SELECT CONVERT(CHAR, dbo.LDimAvg(Length)) as Avg, CONVERT(CHAR,
dbo.LDimMax(Length)) as Sum FROM Tiles
GO
30.2 in    36 in
```

CREATE ASSEMBLY, as explained in Chapter 2, adds the assembly that contains the user-defined type.

CREATE TYPE is used to add a user-defined type to a database. CREATE TYPE is followed by the name that you will use to refer to the user-defined type in SQL Server. In this case, we will refer to the type as LDim.

CREATE TYPE also has an EXTERNAL NAME that is used to reference the actual implementation of the user-defined type. The EXTERNAL NAME is broken into two parts separated by a period. The first part is the name of the assembly that contains the implementation. LDim is the name of the assembly that was previously loaded into the database using the CREATE ASSEMBLY command.

The second part of the EXTERNAL NAME is the name of the class, in the assembly, that actually implements the user-defined type. In this case, the class is UDT.LDim, because our LDim implementation is in namespace UDT. Note that the namespace name and the class name are enclosed in square brackets. This is required to distinguish the "." that separates the namespace from the class name, from the "." that separates the assembly name from the class name. If no namespace was involved, the square brackets would not be required.

Note the casing of the namespace and class names. These must match those used in the implementation. For case-sensitive languages like C#, this is not an issue. For case-insensitive languages like VB.NET, the casing must match that used in the definition of the class.

So, you can see that LDim acts the same way as any other scalar variable. It can be sorted, compared, and, with the help of LDim-specific aggregation functions, aggregated.

Creating a User-Defined Type

We will now look at how to create a user-defined type. We will create a type meant to represent a linear dimension. It has two parts: value and units. The value is a double. The units can be one of "in" for inches, "ft" for feet, and "yd" for yard.

There are two steps in creating a user-defined type. The first is to create an assembly that contains the implementation of the user-defined type. This can be done using any language that the CLR supports.

The second step is to add the assembly and the user-defined type to a database. The assembly is added to the database using the CREATE ASSEMBLY command, as was shown in Chapter 2. The user-defined type can then be added to the database by the CREATE TYPE command, as shown in Listing 5-1.

Note that user-defined types, unlike the built-in scalar types that SQL Server provides, must be specifically added to every database that requires them.

Implementing a User-Defined Type

The implementation of a user-defined type is a CLR class. The CLR classes are divided between reference types and value types. The principle difference between these two kinds of classes is how memory for instances of them is managed. The memory allocated for a reference type is always a pointer to a sequence of bits—that is, a pointer to an object. The memory allocated for a value type is a sequence of bits—that is, the object itself. There is no difference between these kinds of classes in the treatment of methods. Operationally, the semantics of parameter passing is different between them, and depending on usage, one may have a greater impact on performance or resource usage. Both the MSDN documentation and the Common Language Infrastructure Partition I discuss the differences between these. Either can be used to implement a user-defined type.

Both C# and VB.NET use the class keyword to define a CLR reference type class. C# uses the struct keyword, and VB.NET uses the Structure keyword to define the CLR value type class. We will use a struct to implement LDim. The following code is a skeleton of the CLR class that we will use to implement LDim. This skeleton meets the basic requirement that a user-defined type be a CLR class.

```
namespace UDT
{
    // struct is used to define a CLR value type class
    public struct LDim ...
    {
    // implementation
    ...
    }
}
```

Instances of user-defined types, just like any other scalar type, are saved to and read from disk as a stream of bytes. For all user-defined types, this stream of bytes can be no larger than 8,000 bytes. SQL Server needs to know how much space is required on disk for an instance of a user-defined type and what code to use to read and write the byte stream that is saved on the disk. SQL Server also needs to know whether or not it can be ordered according to the byte stream that is stored on disk for it. The `SqlUserDefinedTypeAttribute` used on a CLR class definition for a user-defined type provides this information. This is shown in the following code fragment.

```
namespace UDT
{
        // properties of SqlUserDefinedType describe to SQL Server
        // how to save and order an LDim
        [SqlUserDefinedType(...)]
        public struct LDim ...
        {
        // implementation
        ...
        }
}
```

The `SqlUserDefinedTypeAttribute` has a property named `Format`. When the `Format` property is set to `System.Data.Sql.Format.Native`, SQL Server provides the code that is used to read and write the byte stream. There are a number of requirements of a class that uses the `Native` setting of the `Format` attribute—the class must use the `StructLayout Attribute` with its `Value` property set to `LayoutKind.Sequential`; all fields in the CLR class must be blittable; and the class must have a `SerializableAttribute` attribute. For example, a class that has a field of type string may not have the `Format` property of the `SqlUserDefined TypeAttribute` set to `Native`.

The MSDN documentation enumerates the CLR classes that are blittable. In essence, only value types that have the same physical representation in the CLR as they do in the native operating system are blittable. The MSDN documentation specifically lists `System.Byte`, `System.SByte`, `System.Int16`, `System.UInt16`, `System.Int32`, `System.UInt32`, `System.Int64`, `System.UInt64`, `System.IntPtr`, `System.UIntPtr`, and any one-dimensional array of the types previously listed as being blittable. In addition to these, a `Format.Native` user-defined type may also use `System.Float`, `System.Double`, `SqlSingle`, `SqlDouble`, `SqlByte`, `SqlInt16`,

SqUInt16, SqlInt32, SqlUInt32, SqlInt64, SqlUInt64, and SqlDate Time, even though the MSDN documentation does not list them as being blittable. Note that System.Char, SqlDate, SqlBytes, SqlDecimal, and SqlBinary cannot be used as a field of a user-defined type that uses Format=Format.Native. Note that both the documentation and the run-time are beta implementations, so the types useable by Format.Native may be different by the time the final version ships. A code fragment of a CLR class definition that could use Format=Format.Native follows.

```
namespace UDT
{       [Serializable]
        [StructLayout[LayoutKind.Sequential)]
        public struct Position
        {
                public int X;
                public int Y;
        }
        [SqlUserDefinedType(
        Format=Format.Native, // SQL Server provides serialization code
        IsByteOrdered = true)] // Sorts and compares may be used
        [Serializable] // required for Native
        [StructLayout(LayoutKind.Sequential)] // required for Native
        public struct Contract ...
        {
                Position Location;
                SqlDateTime created;
                float Price;
                int LineCount;
                // implementation
                ...
        }
}
```

A user-defined type, whether it uses Format.Native or Format. UserDefined, can be sorted, used in an index, or used in a magnitude comparison only if the IsByteOrdered property of the SqlUserDefined TypeAttribute is set to true. This has implications on its implementation, which will be discussed later.

Sorting and magnitude comparisons of user-defined types are always done directly using the byte stream that is stored on disk, regardless of whether SqlUserDefinedTypeAttribute uses Format.Native or Format. UserDefined. In the case of Format.Native, the sort order will be determined by the order in which the fields of the CLR class definition are defined. The first field defined will be, in effect, the first sort key, the second field defined the second, and so on. The following code fragment of a user-defined type could be used to represent a nail that will be sorted first on its `Size` field and second on its `Price` field.

```
namespace UDT
{
      [SqlUserDefinedType(
      Format=Format.Native, // SQL Server provides serialization code
      IsByteOrdered = true)] // Sorts and compares may be used
      [Serializable] // required for Native
      [StructLayout(LayoutKind.Sequential)] // required for Native
      public struct Nail ...
      {
      int Size; // sort on Size first
      float Price // sort on Price second
      // implementation
      ...
      }
}
```

`Format = Format.Native` is best practice when it can be used. There are two simple cases when it cannot be used. One is when the class requires a field of a type that is not allowed for `Format.Native`. The other is that you cannot achieve the sort order that you wish by just ordering the fields in the CLR class.

A class that can't meet the requirements to use `Native` must use `System.Data.Sql.Format.UserDefined`. When `Format` is set to `User Defined`, the class implementing the user-defined type must provide the code to read and write the byte stream by implementing the `IBinary Serialize` interface. In addition, the `UserDefined` setting requires two other properties of `SqlUserDefinedTypeAttribute` to be set appropriately: the `IsFixedLength` and `MaxByteSize` properties.

The `MaxByteSize` property is used only when `Format = Format. UserDefined` and indicates the maximum size of the byte stream, in bytes, used to save the user-defined type. It is desirable to keep this as small as possible. You will have to accurately determine this when you implement the `IBinarySerialize` interface, which will be covered later.

The `IsFixedLength` property is used only when `Format = Format. UserDefined` and is set to `true` if the size of the byte stream is always the same size as indicated by `MaxByteSize`; otherwise, it is set to `false`. SQL Server needs to know this because the way it allocates space on the disk differs depending on whether its size is fixed or not. In general, SQL Server can more efficiently manage a fixed size type better than one whose size varies.

TABLE 5-1: Requirements for User-Defined Type Implementation

Form at	INullable	IBinarySerializable	MaxBytes	IsFixedLength	IsByteOrdered	Null Property	Parse Method	Reference Types	ToString Method	[Serializable]	[StructLayout]
UserDefined	Y	Y	Y	Y	Y	Y	Y	Y	Y	Y	N
Native	Y	N	N	N	Y	Y	Y	Y	Y	Y	Y

All classes that implement a user-defined type must be marked with the [Serializable] attribute. Regardless of the setting of the Format property, the maximum size of the byte stream used to save an instance of a user-defined type is 8,000 bytes.

Any class used to implement a user-defined type must also implement the INullable interface, override the System.Object.ToString method, and implement a static read-only property named Null and a static method named Parse.

Table 5-1 summarizes the requirements for classes used to implement a user-defined type. The requirements vary depending on whether Format.UserDefined or Format.Native is used. You can use this as a checklist when implementing a user-defined type. The first column on the left lists the two possible values for the Format property of the SqlUser DefinedTypeAttribute. The remaining columns show whether or not a particular feature is required for the implementation. For example, the IsFixedLength property of the SqlUserDefinedTypeAttribute attribute is required when Format.UserDefined is used, but is not required when Format.Native is used.

Listing 5-2 shows the skeleton implementation for the user-defined type we wish to create, LDim.

LISTING 5-2: Skeleton Implementation of LDim

```
[Serializable]
[SqlUserDefinedType(
    Format = Format.UserDefined,
    IsByteOrdered = true,
    IsFixedLength = true,
    MaxByteSize = 17
    )]
```

```
public struct LDim: INullable, IBinarySerialize
{
      double value;
      string units;
      public override string ToString()
      {
      }
      public bool IsNull
      {
      }
      public static LDim Null
      {
      }
      public static LDim Parse(SqlString s)
      {
      }
      public void Write(System.IO.BinaryWriter w)
      {
      }
      public void Read(System.IO.BinaryReader r)
      {
      }
}
```

Note that `LDim` sets the `Format` property of `SqlUserDefinedType` to `UserDefined`. Also note that the `LDim` field `units` is a string. Because of this, `LDim` must be implemented with `UserDefined`. Note that best practice in this case would be to use an `int` as the type for `units`, but the purpose of this example is to cover as many of the implantation details of a user-defined type as possible.

Listing 5-3 shows a skeleton implementation of a user-defined type for `Longitude`. This user-defined type sets the `Format` property of `SqlUserDefinedType` to `Native`. Note that implementation of this type will be similar to that for `LDim`, except that the `Write` and `Read` methods are not required.

LISTING 5-3: Skeleton Implementation of Longitude

```
[Serializable]
[SqlUserDefinedType(
    Format = Format.Native,
    IsByteOrdered = true
    )]
public struct LDim: INullable
{
      double degrees; // first sort key
      double minutes; // second sort key
```

```
double seconds; // third sort key
byte direction; // 0 for E, 1 for W, fourth sort key
public override string ToString()
{
}
public bool IsNull
{
}
public static LDim Null
{
}
public static LDim Parse(SqlString s)
{
}
}
```

Implementing LDim

We will now look at implementing the LDim user-defined type, shown in Listing 5-4. It will illustrate most, though not all, of the issues involved in implementing user-defined types.

LDim is a user-defined type that is used to represent a linear dimension. It has two properties associated with it: value and units. The units are used to scale the value so that, for example, "1 ft" is the same value as "12 in". This sort of data type is widely used in various engineering, architecture, and other disciplines. The basic implementation of LDim is shown in Listing 5-4.

LISTING 5-4: Basic Implementation of LDim

```
public struct LDim
{
        private double value;
        private string units;
        // rest of implementation
}
```

It is a requirement that a public CLR class must be used to implement a user-defined type. Note that in C# and VB.NET, a `struct` is a CLR class that is derived from `System.ValueType`. There are number of trade-offs to be made in choosing a class that derives from `System.ValueType` and one that doesn't. These are discussed in MSDN and other places. This basic implementation of LDim can maintain the state of a dimension.

Implementing INullable

INullable is an interface defined in the System.Data.Sql namespace. Implementing it is straightforward; it has a single, read-only property named IsNull that returns a System.Boolean (bool in C# or Boolean in VB.NET). Some thought has to be put into how a user-defined type will internally represent a null value. A simple way to do this is to add a field that stores a flag to indicate whether or not the value is null. This is shown in Listing 5-5.

LISTING 5-5: Simple Implementation of INullable

```
public struct LDim : INullable
{
    private double value;
    private string units;
    private bool valueNotNull;
    // read-only property
    public bool IsNull
    {
        get { return !valueNotNull;}
    }
    // rest of implementation
}
```

This implementation of IsNull is taking advantage of the fact that the fields of a struct are always initialized to zero. This means that the parameterless constructor for LDim will be initialized to be a null value. That is the reason for the double negative that appears in the IsNull property implementation.

This way of implementing IsNull has costs in space. One cost is in the memory taken up by the valueNotNull field, but in many cases this may be of no significance. The other cost is in the space taken up on the disk to store an instance of an LDim type, which will be multiplied by the number of rows in a database that contain LDim columns. There are two ways to mitigate this. If the class implements IBinarySerialize, it can choose a more compact way to save a null instance.

For convenience, this implementation ensures that when a new LDim is created using new LDim(), it will in fact be a null representation. Because of this, the test for null requires a double negative.

The other way is to encode the null representation in the existing fields of LDim. This will make it easier to implement IBinarySerialize, which we will see later. In addition, classes that do not implement IBinary Serialize—that is, those that set Format to Native in the SqlUser DefinedTypeAttribute—can also take advantage of the smaller byte stream on disk.

Since the units field can hold either a null or a reference to a string, an LDim class can put a null in the units field to indicate that it is representing a null. Note that encoding a representation like this has been used many times before. For example, a floating point number that is infinity or NaN just uses an encoding that can never occur when it is representing an actual number. Listing 5-6 shows the LDim implementation of INullable that uses this encoding technique.

LISTING 5-6: Encoded Implementation of INullable

```
public struct LDim : INullable
{
        private double value;
        private string units;
        // read only property
        public bool IsNull
        {
                get { return units == null;}
        }
        // rest of implementation
}
```

Implementing the Null Property

LDim must implement a public, static property named Null that returns an instance of LDim that represents a null. To do this, LDim can just return a new instance of the LDim class. Listing 5-7 shows the LDim implementation of the Null property.

LISTING 5-7: Implementation of the Null Property

```
public struct LDim : INullable
{
        public static LDim Null
        {
                get{ return new LDim();}
        }
        // rest of implementation
}
```

This implementation is simple because LDim is a struct—that is, it derives from System.ValueType. A new instance of a ValueType is guaranteed to have all its fields initialized to zeros. This produces an instance of LDim where units contain all zeros—that is, a null reference—which is just what we want.

In order to ensure that nulls sort properly, it is important that all instances of LDim that are representing null have identical values. However, because LDim is a struct, we are also guaranteed that value will be all zeros too.

A class that implements a user-defined type as a reference type—that is, a class in C# or VB.NET—should use a different technique for implementing Null. The implementation shown for LDim would not work well for a class that is a reference type, because each time the Null property was used, a different instance of the class would be allocated on the heap. This would not impair the functionality of Null, but it would make a lot of extra work for the garbage collector because it has to clean up things allocated on the heap. This is not an issue for LDim, because structs are not allocated on the heap.

Listing 5-8 shows an implementation of Null for a class that is a reference type.

LISTING 5-8: Implementation of the Null Property for a C# Class

```
public class PartNumber : INullable
{
        static readonly PartNumber nullPart = new PartNumber();
        public LDim Null
        {
                get{ return nullPart; }
        }
        // rest of implementation
}
```

This implementation of Null always returns the same instance of PartNumber, so there is no cleanup work for the garbage collector to do. Also, as noted in Chapter 2, static members of a class must be marked as read-only to be loaded as SAFE or EXTERNAL_ACCESS.

Implementing ToString

SQL Server will call the ToString method on a class whenever it needs a string representation of it. Listing 5-9 shows a query that uses the T-SQL CONVERT function on an LDim type column to convert it to a CHAR. The CONVERT function will call ToString on the class that implements LDim.

LISTING 5-9: SQL Server Calling ToString

```
-- create a Table that uses LDim
CREATE TABLE Lengths
(
      Length LDim
)
-- select something from that table
-- the CONVERT function will call ToString
-- on the implementation of LDim
SELECT CONVERT(CHAR, Length) FROM Lengths
```

ToString is a virtual function in the System.Object class. Every CLR class inherits System.Object whether or not it is explicitly specified. An implementation of a user-defined type must override this method. ToString returns a string that is considered the lexical representation of the value. Listing 5-10 shows the LDim implementation of ToString.

LISTING 5-10: Implementation of ToString

```
public struct LDim : INullable
{
      private double value;
      private string units;

      public override string ToString()
      {
            // check to see if units is null
            // if it is this instance is
            // representing a null
            if(null == units)
      {
                  return "null";
      }
            return String.Format("{0:d} {s}", value, units);
      }
      // rest of implementation
}
```

Note that when LDim is representing a null, it returns the string "null". Otherwise, it formats a string that consists of a number, whitespace, and the units string.

Implementing Parse

Parse is the functional complement of ToString. It must be a public static method. It takes a string as input and converts it into an instance of the user-defined type. Whenever SQL Server needs to convert a string to an LDim, it will call the `Parse` method. The following is some T-SQL code that will call the `Parse` method of LDim.

```
CREATE TABLE Lengths
{
    Length LDim
}
-- 3 ft must be converted to an LDIM to be inserted
-- SQL Server will call the Parse method on LDim to do this
INSERT INTO Lengths VALUES (N'3 ft')
```

Before it converts the string, the `Parse` method must first check to be sure that the string is formatted validly. If it is not, `Parse` must produce an error that indicates this.

Manually writing code that will completely check the format of a string and parse it typically is a very tedious task. The .NET Framework, however, has the `RegEx` class, which supports regular expressions as used in the Perl language. Taking advantage of this capability greatly reduces the effort to implement `Parse`.

The `RegEx` class has the ability to match a string to a regular expression. When used this way, the regular expression is, in effect, a set of rules that define the format of a string. When a string matches the regular expression, it is validly formatted according to those rules.

The same regular expression that is used to check the format of a string can be used to parse the string. A full discussion of regular expressions is beyond the scope of this chapter, but they are documented in MSDN. Listing 5-11 shows the implementation of `Parse` for LDim.

LISTING 5-11: Implementation of Parse

```
// regular expression to test and parse
static readonly string fp = @"-?([0-9]+(\.[0-9]*)?|\.[0-9]+)";
static readonly Regex vu =
  new Regex(@"(?<v>" + fp + @")(?<u>in|ft|yd)");
public static LDim Parse(SqlString s)
{
    // null in, null out
    if (s.IsNull || s.Value.ToLower() == "null")
        return Null;
    // check to make sure input is
    // properly formatted
    if (!vu.IsMatch(s.Value))
    {
        throw new ApplicationException("Bad format", null);
```

```
        }
        // parse the input
        Match m = vu.Match(s.Value);
        LDim d = new LDim();
        // get the units
        // the string for units will have the proper
        // value because it was checked by the regex
        d.units = m.Result("${u}");
        // get the value. Again it will be a
        // floating point number, the regex
        // checked it
        d.value = double.Parse(m.Result("${v}"));
        return d;
    }
```

Notice that the regular expression used to test and parse the input is held in a static read-only member of LDim. There is a cost in constructing a regular expression, and putting it into a static member of the class means it need be constructed only once and can then be reused every time Parse is called.

Once the input string has been validated as having the proper format, the regular expression is used again to crack out the value and the units. Notice that the double.Parse at the end of the implementation can never fail, because its input has already been validated as being a floating point number.

Implementing IBinarySerialize

Implementing IBinarySerialize is the most difficult part of creating a user-defined type. The implementation not only determines how an instance of a user-defined type will be saved on disk, it also determines how it will be sorted. IBinarySerialize is not implemented for user-defined types that set the SqlUserDefinedTypeAttribute Format property to Format.Native, which is the prime reason to use Native when it is possible.

The IBinarySerialize interface has two methods: Read, which passes in a System.IO.BinaryReader, and Write, which passes in a System. IO.BinaryWriter.

When SQL Server needs to read the data it has stored on disk for a user-defined type, it calls the Read method. The implementation of the Read method reads the stream, passes it through the BinaryReader, and reconstructs the state of the user-defined type.

When SQL Server needs to write a user-defined type to disk, it calls the Write method, and the implementation of the Write method writes into the BinaryWriter the state of the user-defined type.

The format used by SQL Server for the byte stream that it saves on disk is determined by the implementation of IBinarySerialize. The value field of LDim is a double. A detailed explanation of the representation of floating point numbers is beyond the scope of this chapter, but suffice it to say that the sort order of the representation in memory of a floating point number is not the same as the sort order of the numbers they represent. Listing 5-12 shows a SQL batch file that demonstrates this.

LISTING 5-12: Order of Floating Point Numbers

```
create table Numbers
(
    F float
)
go
Insert into S values (1)
Insert into S values (0)
Insert into S values (-1)
go
select * from Numbers order by F
go
F
 - - - - - - - - - -
-1
0
1
select * from Numbers order by Convert(binary, F)
go
F
 - - - - - - - - - -
0
1
-1
```

When the rows in the Numbers table are sorted by the F column, the rows are ordered as we would expect them to be. However, if the rows are ordered according to their binary representation, 0 comes before 1 and 1 comes before –1—not what you would expect. Listing 5-13 shows the implementation of Write.

LISTING 5-13: Implementation of Write

```
public void Write(System.IO.BinaryWriter w)
{
  if (IsNull)
  {
    for (int index = 0; index <= 9; index++)
    {
```

```
      w.Write((byte)0xFF);
  }
}
else
{
  Dim v;
  v.value = value;
  v.units = units;
  // normalize to inches
  if (v.units == "ft")
  {
    v.value *= 12;
  }
  if (v.units == "yd")
  {
    v.value *= 36;
  }
  v.units = "in";
  // serialize the approx log10 of value first
  // so you can squeeze it into a long
  // note that this order is only approximate
  UInt64 l10 = UInt64.MaxValue  >> 1;
  // there is a bit of a dance here
  // to make sure that the negative and
  // small number come out in the
  // right order
  if (v.value != 0.0)
  {
    if (v.value > 0.0)
    {
      Int64 l = (Int64)(Math.Log10(v.value) * 29921268260570000.0);
      if (l >= 0)
      {
        // divide by 4
        l10 = (UInt64)l >> 2;
        // add half of max
        l10 += (UInt64.MaxValue >>2) + (UInt64.MaxValue >>1);
        // result is in upper quarter of positive numbers
      }
      else
      {
        // divide by 2
        l10 = (UInt64)(-l >> 2);
        l10 += (UInt64.MaxValue >>2);
      // result is in lower quarter of upper half of positive numbers
      }
    }
    else
    {
      Int64 l = (Int64)(Math.Log10(-v.value) * 29921268260570000.0);
      if (l >= 0)
```

```
{
   l10 = (UInt64.MaxValue >>1) - (UInt64)1 >> 2;
   // result is in upper quarter of lower half of positive
      numbers
}
else
{
   l10 = ( UInt64.MaxValue >>1) -
   ( UInt64.MaxValue >>2) -
   (UInt64)(-1 >> 2);
   // result is in lower quarter of lower half of positive numbers
}
   }
}
// serialize out the high byte first
// ordering and sorting starts with the
// first byte output
for (int index = 7; index >= 0; index -)
{
   w.Write((byte)(l10 >> (8 * index)));
}
w.Write(value);
if (units == "in")
{
   w.Write((byte)1);
}
if (units == "ft")
{
   w.Write((byte)2);
}
if (units == "yd")
{
   w.Write((byte)3);
}
if (units == null)
{
   w.Write((byte)0);
}
}
```

The implementations of `Write` and `Read` determine the `MaxByteSize`. It is the number of bytes written by `Write`. `Write` first outputs 8 bytes, which are used to sort `LDim` values. Next it writes out the actual value, which is a double—another 8 bytes. This is followed by a single byte used to represent the units. `MaxByteSize` = 8 + 8 + 1, which is 17.

The implementations of `Write` and `Read` are tedious and complicated. They must take into account the physical representation of values in memory. Most of this is due to the fact that the binary representation of floating point numbers does not sort as we would want. There is no need to understand these implementations. The reason for showing them is twofold. One is to show a complete implementation of `Format.UserDefined`. The other is to emphasize that using `Format.Native` is always preferable whenever possible. `Write` and `Read` are not implemented when `Format.Native` is used.

The major part of the code in `BinaryWriter` is converting the `value` field to a `UInt64`. This is done by creating a `UInt64` that is proportional to the log of the `value` field. This not used to store the value of the field; it is just used as a value to sort the field.

The actual serialization is done at the end of the Write method, where `BinaryWriter` that was passed in as a parameter was used. The first thing that it serialized is the logarithmic value that will be used to order `LDims`. When SQL server attempts to sort an `LDim` column, it will do so by sorting its binary representation, starting with the first byte that was passed to the stream into the `Write` method.

After the logarithmic value is written, the value of the `value` field is written using the native format for a double.

After that has been done, the `units` field is serialized. The technique used here is to tokenize the `units` field by saving a 1 for inches, 2 for feet, 3 for yards, and 0 for `null` values.

The `Read` implementation is shown in Listing 5-14. It is much easier than the `Write` implementation because it can just throw away the part of the implementation used for sorting.

LISTING 5-14: Implementation of Read

```
public void Read(System.IO.BinaryReader r)
{
        // skip over order marker
        r.BaseStream.Seek(8L, SeekOrigin.Current);
        value = r.ReadDouble();

        byte c = r.ReadByte();

        switch (c)
        {
                case 0:
                        SetNull();
                        break;
                case 1 :
                        units = "in";
                        break;
```

```
              case 2 :
              units = "ft";
              break;
              case 3 :
              units = "yd";
              break;
        }
}
```

Read starts by just skipping over the part of the stream that is used for sorting. Next it reads in the value of the value field. Lastly it reads the token for the units field and fills it accordingly.

User-Defined Type Properties and Fields

Public fields and properties in the class that implements a user-defined type are exposed in SQL Server. The fields and properties are exposed by name. A variable or column can access a public field or property of a user-defined type by adding a suffix that consists of a "." followed by the name of the field or property. The field or property can then be referenced in the same way as any other variable or column. Listing 5-15 shows this syntax in a SQL batch.

LISTING 5-15: Field/Property Access Syntax

```
DECLARE @L as Longitude
SET @L = CONVERT(Longitude, '50 3" 32'' W')
PRINT @L.degrees
50
PRINT @L.minutes
3
PRINT @L.seconds
32
PRINT @L.direction
'W'
SET @L.direction='E'
```

Longitude is a user-defined type that has degrees, minutes, seconds, and direction as public fields in its implementation. The SQL batch in Listing 5-15 prints each of these fields and then changes the direction to "E".

Listing 5-16 shows a modified implementation of LDim that makes units a public field.

LISTING 5-16: Exposing the units Field of LDim

```
public struct LDim : INullable
{
    // public field can be accessed by SQL Server
    public string units;
    // rest of implementation
}
```

Listing 5-17 shows how the `units` field can be accessed in a SQL batch.

LISTING 5-17: Accessing a Field of a User-Defined Type

```
DECLARE @d AS LDim
SET @d = CONVERT(LDim, '1 ft')
PRINT @d.units
'ft'
SET @d.units='miles'
```

The example shown in Listing 5-17 declares an `LDim` variable, sets its value to "1 ft", and then prints out the unit "ft". It then sets the `units` field to "miles". Does this make sense? Miles is not one of the units that `LDim` supports. This implementation of `LDim` shows one of the traps into which it is easy to fall when exposing fields of the implementation of a user-defined type; this implementation is guaranteed to lead to corrupted data.

The best practice is to never directly expose the fields of the implementation of a user-defined type, but to instead wrap those fields in a property so that you can validate any change made to that field. Listing 5-18 shows a best practice implementation of exposing the `units` field of an `LDim`.

LISTING 5-18: Exposing units of LDim as a Property

```
// used to recalculate value when units change
private static double Factor(string units)
{
    if (units == "in")
        return 1.0;
    if (units == "ft")
        return 12.0;
    if (units == "yd")
        return 36.0;
    return 1.0;
}
// property that wraps units in a SqlString
public SqlString Units
{
    // return is simple
```

```
get { return units; }
// set must validate
set
{
        // if null is passed in make it null
        if (value.IsNull)
        {
                SetNull();
                return;
        }
        // if valid unit is passed in then change
        // unit and adjust value to match
        if (value == "in" || value == "ft" || value == "yd")
        {
                double curFactor = Factor(units);
                double newFactor = Factor(value.Value);
                units = value.Value;
                this.value *= curFactor / newFactor;
                return;
        }
        // if you get to here an
        // invalid unit was passed in so throw an exception
        throw new ApplicationException(value.Value +
                " Is not valid unit", null);
        }
    }
}
```

This code has a `Unit` property that wraps the `units` field in `LDim`. The `set` portion of the property validates any change to the `units` field and throws an exception when an attempt is made to set units to an unsupported value.

Note that this code is much more complex than just exposing a field. However, any code you add to SQL Server 2005 must protect the integrity of the database no matter what. The `get` part of the property is straightforward; it just returns the current value of `units`. The `set` part of the property must do two things. One is to check that a valid unit string is being used. The other is to convert the current value of the `LDim` to the value in the new units. This ensures that if the value of an `LDim` is "1 ft" and the units are changed to "in", the value is changed to 12.

User-Defined Type Validation

It is possible to insert a user-defined type value into a column without using the `Parse` method implemented in the user-defined type. This is done by just inserting a binary number directly into the column. Doing this could result in an invalid representation. For example, look at the following SQL batch that inserts a binary number into an LDim column. Note that binary numbers are implicitly converted to a user-defined type.

```
CREATE TABLE Dims
(data LDim)

INSERT INTO Dims VALUES
(0xBFFFFFFFFFFFFFFFE000000000000F03F01)

SELECT data FROM Dims

1 in
```

The binary number, 0xBFF . . . 3F01, is the binary representation of "1 in". The very last byte, the 01 on the right, enumerates the units of the dimension. "1" indicates inches, "2" feet, and "3" yards. What happens if that last number is a 4, so that 0xBFFF...3F04 is inserted? Nothing in the representation expects a 4 to be there, and there is no way for the LDim user-defined type to detect that the binary number was inserted. What happened is that a very subtle error was injected into the data, which may be detected at some later time or may just go on to corrupt other data.

The SqlUserDefinedTypeAttribute has a property that allows you to specify a method that SQL Server will use to validate an instance of a user-defined type no matter how that value was set. The ValidationMethod Name property takes a string as a parameter and specifies a method in the implementation of the user-defined type that SQL Server can call to validate the binary representation of an instance of the user-defined type. For example, we can extend the implementation of LDim as follows.

```
[Serializable]
[SqlUserDefinedType(
    Format = Format.Native,
    IsByteOrdered = true,
    IsFixedLength = true,
    MaxByteSize = 17,
    ValidationMethodName="CheckRep"
    )]
public struct LDim: INullable, IBinarySerialize
{
    // rest of implementation
      bool CheckRep()
      {
            if(double.IsInfinity(value) || double.IsNaN(value)
            {
            return false;
```

```
    }
    if(((units == null)
        or (units == ""))
        && (value != 0))
    {
        return false;
    }
    return true;
|}
```

The `CheckRep` function checks to make sure that `value` is an actual number. SQL Server does not have a representation for either NaN or infinity, so `value` could never be either of these. It also checks to see that the value is 0 if there are no units. So if somehow, by directly inserting binary into an `LDim`, `LDim` had an invalid binary representation, SQL Server could detect it.

Note that the `CheckRep` function is private. The only requirements of the method indicated by the `ValidationMethodName` are that it return a `bool` and take no arguments. Its scope can be private, internal, or public.

User-Defined Type Methods

Public methods in a class that implements a user-defined type can be exposed to SQL Server. The method must be marked with the `SqlMethod` `Attribute`, and its parameters and return value must be compatible with the types that SQL Server supports. Listing 5-19 shows an example of a method in the `LDim` implementation that can be used to set it.

LISTING 5-19: Method That Sets the Value of an LDim

```
namespace UDT
{
    public class LDim
    {
        // marks method to be exposed to SQL Server
        [SqlMethod(IsMutator=true, OnNullCall=false)]
        // method to set the value of an LDIM
        public void SetValue(SqlDouble value, SqlString units)
        {
            if (units == "in" || units == "ft" || units == "yd")
            {
                this.units = units.Value;
                this.value = value.Value;
            }
        }
    }
}
```

The `SqlMethodAttribute` provides SQL Server with information about how the method will interact with SQL Server. Some methods marked with `SqlMethod` will change the value of the object on which they are called. This is true for the `SetValue` method. Since the `SetValue` changes an `LDim` object, it must be used with a `set` syntax, as shown in the SQL batch in Listing 5-20.

LISTING 5-20: Using the LDim SetValue Method

```
DECLARE @d AS LDim
SET @d.SetValue(2.3, 'ft')
PRINT CONVERT(CHAR, @d)
2.3 ft
```

If the `IsMutator` property of the `SqlMethod` had been set to `false`, the SQL batch shown in Listing 5-20 would have produced an error when executed. Methods that have `IsMutator = false` can be used in `VIEWS` and `SELECT` statements but not in `UPDATE` statements.

The `SqlMethod` has another property, named `OnNullCall`, which affects its behavior when a `null` parameter is passed in. You can think of `OnNullCall=true` as meaning "Call this method even if a `null` is passed as a parameter." If `OnNullCall=false`, the method will not be called, and the instance of the user-defined type will be set to `null`. This property is set to `false` on the `SetValue` method. This means that when a `null` is passed to it, the `LDim` will be set to `null`. That is why the implementation of the `SetValue` method does not have to check whether any of the input parameters are `null`. The SQL batch in Listing 5-21 shows that `SetValue` is not called when a `null` is passed in.

LISTING 5-21: Passing a Null to SetValue

```
DECLARE @d AS LDim
SET @d.SetValue(2.3, 'ft')
PRINT CONVERT(CHAR, @d)
2.3 ft
SET @d.SetValue(null, 'ft')
PRINT CONVERT(CHAR, @d)
null
```

The beginning of the SQL batch in Listing 5-21 sets @d to "2.3 ft" and then prints it out. It then attempts to set it to `null` ft. It then prints out @d and shows that it has, in fact, been set to `null`. In addition, because `SqlMethodAttribute` derives from `SqlFunctionAttribute`, any of the

`SqlFunctionAttribute` properties (such as `DataAccessKind`) can be used to declare the behavior of UDT methods.

Chapter 3 discusses how to create stored procedures, functions, and triggers using a CLR language such as C#. It is sometime useful to create convenience functions for use with user-defined types. This is can be problematic when parametric values must be used to insert an instance of a user-defined type. This is shown in the SQL batch in Listing 5-22.

LISTING 5-22: Parametric Insertion of an LDim

```
DECLARE @d AS LDim
CREATE TABLE Dimensions
(
    dim LDim
)
GO
- parametric value
DECLARE @v AS FLOAT
DECLARE @u AS VARCHAR(2)
SET @v = 1
SET @u = 'yd'
INSERT INTO VALUES (Convert(varchar, @v) + ' ' + @u)
```

The SQL batch in Listing 5-22 inserts "1 yd" into the Dimensions table. To do this, it had to construct a string that could be inserted into an `LDim` column. This is an example of a case where a convenience function that can produce an instance of a user-defined type would be very useful.

Note that a convenience function is not an instance member of the class that implements the user-defined type and does not use the `SqlMethod` `Attribute` attribute; it is a static member of it. In fact, it is only for keeping it together with the user-defined type definition; it could be part of a completely different class. Listing 5-23 shows the implementation of the `Make` `LDimString` method. Note also that this method will have to be added to the database that uses it by using the `CREATE FUNCTION` command, as described in Chapter 3.

LISTING 5-23: Implementation of the MakeLDimString Method

```
public static LDim MakeLDim(SqlDouble value, SqlString units)
{
    if (value.IsNull || units.IsNull)
    {
        return new LDim();
    }
```

```
    return Parse(value.Value.ToString() + " " +
        units.Value.ToString());
    }
}
```

The `MakeLDim` function takes a double and a string as input. If either is null, it returns a `null` instance of an `LDim`. Otherwise, it builds a string and passes it to the `Parse` method. This will check the units passed into `MakeLDim`, and, if they are correct, create an instance of an `LDim` with the appropriate value. This convenience function makes the parametric insertion of an `LDim` much easier, as is shown in the SQL batch in Listing 5-24.

LISTING 5-24: Parametric Insertion Using MakeLDim

```
DECLARE @d AS LDim
CREATE TABLE Dimensions
(
    dim LDim
)
go
 - parametric value
DECLARE @v AS FLOAT
DECLARE @u as VARCHAR(2)
SET @v = 1
SET @u = 'yd'
INSERT INTO Dimensions VALUES (dbo.MakeLDim(@v, @u))
```

As a result of having the `MakeLDim` function, the code that inserts a new `LDim` with parameters for its value is much easier to both write and read.

Unsupported Functions in User-Defined Types

There are a few types of functionality that, while currently specified in SQL:1999, are unsupported in SQL Server SQL Server 2005's implementation of UDTs. It's possible that the SQL Server team will add some of these over time as the utility of UDTs becomes more apparent. These functions include the following:

- Overloaded methods.
- Inheritance exposed at the Transact-SQL level.
- Exposing SQL properties such as numeric precision and scale in a UDT.
- Support of ordering. SQL:1999 specifies that UDTs can support ordering based on state values, implementation of a specific

interface, or a `Map` function (a function that takes a UDT instance and returns an orderable scalar value). SQL Server UDTs only support ordering by state values. Note that this is done, as explained previously, only if the `SqlUserDefinedAttribute` property `ByteOrdered` is `true` for the class that implements the user-defined type.

XML Serialization

The `FOR XML` clause of a `SELECT` statement that includes a user-defined type and `DataSets` that include user-defined types depend on those types being XML serializable. Though a user-defined type is not required to be XML serializable, if it is not, it may produce errors or corrupt data when used with `FOR XML` and `DataSets`. It is best practice to ensure that the class you implement is XML serializable.

An explanation of the requirements for XML serializability is beyond the scope of this book. Typically, it is accomplished by having the class that implements the user-defined type also implement the `IXmlSerializable` interface. Refer to the `XmlSerializer` class in MSDN for details of XML serialization.

Maintaining User-Defined Type Definitions

There are two ways to replace a user-defined type. One is to use `DROP TYPE` followed by `CREATE TYPE`. The other is to use the `ALTER ASSEMBLY` command to replace the assembly that contains the implementation of the user-defined type.

Changing a user-defined type is a fundamental change to a database. Think about how you would feel if Microsoft said they were going to change how the `SQL DECIMAL` data type worked, even if they said it would just "improve the accuracy of decimal." The fact that calculations you had done in the past might produce different, albeit more accurate, results could easily have an overwhelming impact on your database because things that compared as equal in the past might not do so after the change. You must keep this level of impact in mind whenever you make a change to a user-defined type.

The safest way to change user-defined type is to export tables that refer to the type to a text file using SQL Server Data Transformation Services (DTS), drop and re-create the type and everything that references it, and then reload the tables. You will not miss anything that refers to the user-defined type, because you cannot drop a type if any table, stored procedure, and so on references it. All UDTs, by definition, support conversion to and from a string, so DTS will work with any UDT.

This is safest because it guarantees that any changes to the semantics of the type and how it is represented will be propagated to the entire database. Note that it may not be possible to reimport some of the data because the new type definition may not allow it. It will, however, guarantee the integrity of the database, which is paramount in any change.

In many cases, you will not be changing something as fundamental as the semantics of the type or how it is represented. In these cases, you can use the ALTER ASSEMBLY command, described in Chapter 2. The ALTER ASSEMBLY can replace an existing assembly with user-defined types in it without dropping objects such as tables and stored procedures that reference those types.

ALTER ASSEMBLY is meant to be used to make bug changes or improve implementations, not semantic or operational changes. For instance, you cannot use ALTER ASSEMBLY to replace an assembly with one whose assembly name is different in anything other than the revision of the assembly. Note that the revision is the fourth of the dotted list of numbers that specifies an assembly version. In the assembly version "1.2.3.4," "4" is the revision of the assembly.

It is your responsibility, however, when changing an assembly this way, to ensure that the meaning, sorting, and so on of any data persisted by user-defined types is not changed by replacing the assembly. The ALTER ASSEMBLY can check for some of these issues, but not all. Keep this in mind when deciding between drop and re-create, and ALTER ASSEMBLY. Maintaining integrity of data should always be the most important factor when you are making this decision.

Should Objects Be Represented by User-Defined Types?

If the object represents a scalar and requires more than one field to be described, a user-defined type should be used to represent it; otherwise, it should not. By definition, a column in a row of a relational table holds a scalar, so it can hold any object that is a scalar. This definition is crucial to features we associate with a relational database—such as the ability to have efficient declarative referential integrity via foreign keys and to order rows when they are used rather than when they are inserted.

A scalar is a value that can be represented in a single dimension. A value that requires more than one dimension to be represented is not a scalar. Note that the number of fields required to represent a value does not determine whether or not it is a scalar; we saw the date example at the beginning of this chapter that had three fields but was still a scalar.

Is a geometric point a scalar? No, because its representation requires two dimensions, not just two numbers. But why is a date that has three numbers a scalar but a point that has only two numbers associated with it not a scalar? You can ask of any date something like "Is date d2 between date d1 and date d3?" and get a consistent answer. But there is no way in general to consistently answer the question "Is point p2 between point p1 and point p3?" The reason you can't get a consistent answer to this question for points is that each answer to a "between" question makes a commitment to the next. For example, consider the following questions and answers.

"Is date d2 between date d1 and date d3?" "Yes."

"Is date d4 between date d1 and date d2?" "Yes."

If someone then asks, "Is date d4 between date d1 and date d3?" the answer must be "yes." This is because dates have an order—they in effect map onto the real number line. In fact, internally SQL Server can use floating point numbers to represent dates because of this.

This is not true for points, because they are not scalars. One of the problems with asking a "between" question of points is that our conventional notion of "between" would require all three of the points involved to be on the same line. If we use this kind of definition of "between" for points, there are many points for which we cannot answer the "between" question, because it makes no sense.

But if we can just come up with an alternate definition of "between" that works consistently, we can still consider points to be scalars. Let's try to make up something that is similar to the way "between" works for dates. For dates, we can say that d2 is between d1 and d3 if both abs(d2 - d1) < abs(d1 - d3) and abs(d2 - d3) < abs(d1 - d3) are true. The abs() function means absolute value, which we can think of as a distance or a number with any associated minus sign removed. Figure 5-1 illustrates this test.

The date d3 is between the dates d2 and d4 because both the distance between d3 and d2 and the distance between d3 and d4 are less than the distance between d2 and d4. Likewise, d1 is not between d2 and d4, because the distance between d1 and d4 is greater than the distance between d2 and d4.

We can try to apply a similar rule for points. Figure 5-2 shows four points and their relationships to each other in terms of distance.

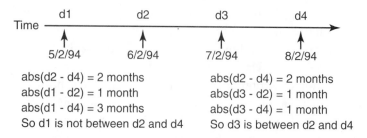

abs(d2 - d4) = 2 months   abs(d2 - d4) = 2 months
abs(d1 - d2) = 1 month   abs(d3 - d2) = 1 month
abs(d1 - d4) = 3 months   abs(d3 - d4) = 1 month
So d1 is not between d2 and d4   So d3 is between d2 and d4

FIGURE 5-1: Answering the "Between" Question for Dates

Because the distance between p1 and p2 and between p2 and p3 is less than the distance between p1 and p3, p2 is between p1 and p3. Also, the distance between p4 and p1 and between p4 and p2 is less than the distance between p1 and p2, so p4 is between p1 and p2. But it is obvious that the distance between p4 and p3 is greater than the distance between p1 and p3, so p4 could not be considered to be between p1 and p3, even though it is between p1 and p2. So it is not behaving like a scalar.

If you could find a set of rules for answering the "between" question consistently for points, you could consider a point to be a scalar. However, no such set of rules exists, so a point is not a scalar, even though it has fewer fields than a date does.

User-defined types should be used only for objects that represent scalars, even though it is physically possible to use user-defined types to represent any object whose state is less than 8,000 bytes, just by implementing IBinarySerialize.

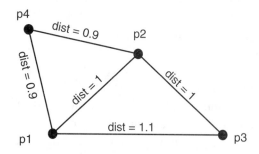

p2 is between p1 and p3
p4 is between p1 and p2
So p4 is between p1 and p3??

FIGURE 5-2: Answering the "Between" Question for Points

Just because an application uses objects to represent things that are not scalars does not mean that the database has to. Chapter 8 covers the XML data type, and Chapter 14 covers ObjectSpaces. SQL Server 2005 also still supports SQLXML. All these technologies are much more efficient for persisting objects in a relational database than user-defined types are, and best practice is to use these technologies for persisting nonscalar objects into SQL Server.

User-Defined Aggregates

An aggregate function operates on a set of rows and produces a scalar. The SUM function in SQL Server is an example of an aggregate. A SELECT statement is used to produce a set of rows, and the SUM function produces the arithmetic sum of some column in the rows produced by the SELECT statement. Listing 5-25 shows an example of a SQL batch using the SUM function.

LISTING 5-25: Using the SUM Aggregate Function

```
CREATE TABLE Items
(
  size int,
  price float
)
GO
INSERT INTO Items VALUES (3, 12.0)
INSERT INTO Items VALUES (5, 10.0)
INSERT INTO Items VALUES (3, 1.0)
INSERT INTO Items VALUES (3, 2.0)
GO
SELECT SUM(price) FROM ITEMS WHERE size = 3
GO
- - - - - - - - - - - --
15
```

The SELECT statement made a set of all the rows from the Items table where the size=3, and then the SUM function added up each of the price columns from those rows to produce 15.

This ability to do operations that produce a scalar result on sets of data is a key feature of a relational database. In fact, the SQL-92 specification requires that a database implement the COUNT, SUM, AVG, MAX, and MIN aggregate functions for compliance. SQL Server includes these aggregate functions and a number of others—for example, COUNT and COUNT_BIG, plus a number of statistical aggregates such as STDEV and VAR for standard deviation and variance.

You can create your own user-defined aggregates with SQL Server 2005. One reason you might want to do this is that you have created your own user-defined type and need to be able to aggregate it. None of the built-in aggregates in SQL Server will work with a user-defined type, so you will have to create your own in this case.

A second reason is performance. You do not need the SUM aggregate to calculate the sum of a column. Listing 5-26 shows a SQL batch that calculates the sum of prices that the example in Listing 5-25 did, but it does not use the SUM aggregate.

LISTING 5-26: Calculating a Sum without an Aggregate

```
DECLARE sumCursor CURSOR
     FOR SELECT price FROM ITEMS WHERE size = 3
OPEN sumCursor
DECLARE @sum float
SET @sum = 0
DECLARE @price float
FETCH NEXT FROM sumCursor INTO @price
WHILE @@FETCH_STATUS = 0
BEGIN
     SET @sum = @sum + @price
     FETCH NEXT FROM sumCursor INTO @price
END
CLOSE sumCursor
DEALLOCATE sumCursor
PRINT @sum
```

The sum technique shown in Listing 5-26 uses a CURSOR to iterate through the results of a query and add up the prices. It is at least an order of magnitude slower than using the built-in SUM aggregate and uses a lot more resources on the server because of the CURSOR. Prior to SQL Server 2005, if you needed an aggregate other than one of the built-in ones provided by SQL Server, you would have used this technique to create your own aggregation. In SQL Server 2005, you can write your own aggregate, and its performance will be on the order of the built-in aggregates.

In this section, we will look at creating a user-defined aggregate that is the equivalent of SUM for the LDim user-defined type. We will call this aggregate LDimSum, and it will produce an LDim that represents the arithmetic sum of the LDims that it processes. Listing 5-27 shows a SQL batch that makes use of the LDimSum aggregate function.

LISTING 5-27: Using the LDimSum Aggregate

```
CREATE TABLE Boards
(
  weight INT,
  length LDim
)
GO
INSERT INTO Boards VALUES (3, N'1 in')
INSERT INTO Boards VALUES (2, N'1 in')
INSERT INTO Boards VALUES (3, N'1 ft')
INSERT INTO Boards VALUES (3, N'2 in'))
GO
SELECT CONVERT(CHAR, LDimSum(length)) FROM Boards WHERE weight = 3
go
- - - - - - - - - - - - - - - - -
'14 in'
```

A user-defined aggregate is a public class that implements the four functions shown in the skeleton implementation of LDimSum in Listing 5-28.

LISTING 5-28: Skeleton of an LDimSum User-Defined Aggregate

```
public class LDimSum
{
        public void Accumulate(LDim dim)
        {
        }
        public LDim Terminate()
        {
        }
        public void Init()
        {
        }
        public void Merge(LDimSum)
        {
        }
}
```

SQL Server will use one or more instances of a user-defined aggregate class to calculate an aggregate. In some cases, it may create new instances when calculating an aggregate, in others it may reuse instances from a previous calculation, and in some cases a combination of both. Your implementation of the aggregate may not depend on SQL Server using any particular one of these behaviors.

The first method SQL Server will call on a user-defined aggregate is Init, when it uses it for an aggregate calculation. Init is used to initialize the aggregator in much the same way as a constructor is. However, it cannot depend on the fields of aggregator being set by an initializer as a conventional constructor can. Note that `Init` may be called more than once, but your implementation should always assume that each time it is called, it is for a new aggregate calculation. Listing 5-29 shows how the `Init` method must be used.

LISTING 5-29: Implementation of the LDim Init Method

```
public class LDimSum
{
        double length = 0.0;
        public void Init()
        {
                // Init does not depend on initializer
                // in class definition
                length = 0.0;
        }
        . . .
}
```

The `Terminate` method is the last method called on an aggregate object during an aggregate calculation; however, in some cases it may not be called at all. The `Terminate` method returns an instance of a scalar that is the result of the aggregate calculation. In the case of `LDimSum`, it returns an `LDim`.

For a given instance of an aggregator—for example, an `LDim` object—there is an order in which the methods in its implementation will be called. Note that in some cases SQL Server will use multiple instances of an aggregator in the process of calculating the aggregate. Also note that SQL Server may not always create a new instance of an aggregator class to do an aggregate calculation, but may reuse an instance of an aggregator from a previous calculation.

The `Accumulate` method is called once for each row being aggregated. The input parameter type determines the type of the aggregate function. In the case of `LDimSum`, the input parameter is of type `LDim`, meaning that this is an `LDim` aggregator. Note that although `Accumulate` is called once for each row being aggregated, these calls may be spread over multiple aggregator objects. The purpose of the `Accumulate` method is to collect, one row at a time, the information that will be required to calculate the result of the aggregation. For `LDimSum` this means maintaining a running sum. For other aggregates other information may be collected—for example, a count that will be used later to calculate an average. Listing 5-30 shows the implementation of `Accumulate` for `LDimSum`.

The `Terminate` function returns the aggregate value. The return type can be any scalar; it need not be the type being aggregated. In this case, because it is part of an aggregate that sums `LDims`, it does return an `LDim`.

LISTING 5-30: Implementation of the LDimSum Accumulate Method

```
public class LDimSum
{
        // running total of aggregate in inches
        double length = 0.0;
        public void Accumulate(LDim dim)
        {
                // normalize value to inches
                if (dim.units == "ft")
                {
                        dim.value *= 12;
                }

                if (dim.units == "yd")
                {
                        dim.value *= 36;
                }
                // added current value to running total
                length += dim.value;
        }
        ...
}
```

The `Accumulate` method for `LDim` first normalizes the value of the dimension to inches, and then adds it to the running total that it keeps in the `length` field.

The `Terminate` method, if it is called at all, is the last method called on an aggregator object. Its purpose is to return the scalar that is the result of the aggregation. In the case of `LDimSum`, the result of the aggregation is just the current running total in the `length` field. Listing 5-31 shows the implementation of `Terminate` for `LDimSum`.

LISTING 5-31: Implementation of the LDimSum Terminate Method

```
public class LDimSum
{
        // running total of aggregate in inches
        double length = 0.0;
        public LDim Terminate()
```

```
    {
        LDim d = new LDim;
        d.Value = length;
        d.Units = "in";
        return d;
    }
    ...
}
```

The `Terminate` method creates a new `LDim` object and sets its value and units. Note that this implementation of `Terminate` requires that the `value` and `units` fields of `LDim` have internal scope and that `LDim` and `LDimSum` are part of the same assembly.

The `Merge` method is used to combine an aggregate object with the aggregate object on which `Merge` is called. To understand what `Merge` must do and why it exists, we need to understand how SQL Server calls the methods in aggregator objects. In the beginning, we said that SQL Server may, in some cases, use more than one aggregate object to calculate an aggregate. Figure 5-3 shows two aggregator objects being used to calculate an aggregate function of the Price column in a table named Invoice.

Note that there are two aggregator objects: Price Aggregator 1 and Price Aggregator 2. The numbers in circles indicate the steps in which the aggregate is calculated. In step 1 `Init` is called on Price Aggregator 1. Steps 2, 3, and 4 call the `Accumulate` method on Price Aggregator 1 to process three rows from the Invoice table. Note that the rows are not processed in the order in which they exist in the table.

Step 5 calls the `Init` method on Price Aggregator 2, followed by step 6, which calls `Merge`. When `Merge` is called on Price Aggregator 2, Price Aggregator 1 is passed in as a parameter. The `Merge` function implementation

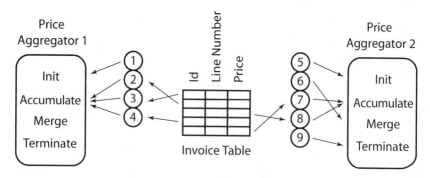

FIGURE 5-3: Method Order Using Two Aggregates

copies the data it needs from Price Aggregator 1 so that it can continue with the aggregate calculations.

Steps 7 and 8 call the `Accumulate` method on Price Aggregator 2 in order to process the last two rows needing processing in the Invoice table. Step 9 calls the `Terminate` method on Price Aggregator 2 to complete the calculation of the aggregate. Note that neither `Terminate` nor `Merge` is called on Price Aggregator 1. This example is just one possible way in which SQL Server might use multiple aggregator objects to calculate an aggregate.

Listing 5-32 shows the implementation of `Merge` for `LDim`.

LISTING 5-32: Implementation of the LDim Merge Method

```
public class LDimSum
{
        // running total of aggregate in inches
        double length = 0.0;
        public void Merge (LDimSum Group)
        {
                // add the running total of Group
                // to current running total of
                // this aggregator object
                length += Group.length;
        }
        . . .
}
```

The `Merge` implementation for `LDimSum` just adds the running length total for the aggregator that is passed in to its own. Note that even though the example in Figure 5-3 showed `Merge` being called immediately after `Init`, this may not always be the case. This is why the `Merge` method for `LDimSum` adds the length to its current running total rather than replacing it.

There are a few other things SQL Server needs to know about a user-defined aggregate. A `SqlUserDefinedAggregateAttribute` is added to the class that implements the user-defined aggregate to provide this information, much as the `SqlUserDefinedTypeAttribute` is used for a similar purpose on user-defined types.

SQL Server may have to serialize an instance of a user-defined aggregate. The `Format` property of `SqlUserDefinedAggregateAttribute` is required and serves the same purpose the `Format` property of the `SqlUserDefinedTypeAttribute` does. Its value may be `Format.Native` or `Format.UserDefined`.

The class that implements the user-defined aggregate must be marked as [Serializable] and, if Format.Native is used, must also be marked as [StructLayout(LayoutKind.Sequential)]. Listing 5-33 shows the usage of the SqlUserDefinedAggregateAttribute by LDimSum.

LISTING 5-33: SqlUserDefinedAggregateAttribute for LDimSum

```
[Serializable]
[StructLayout(LayoutKind.Sequential, InvariantToOrder=true)]
[SqlUserDefinedAggregate(Format.Native)]
public class LDimSum
{
    . . .

}
```

There are other properties of SqlUserDefinedAggregateAttribute that you may add to further define the behavior of a user-defined aggregate. This attribute do not affect the functional operation of the aggregate but can provide hints to the optimizer, which can improve the performance of the aggregate. For example, an aggregate is invariant to null— that is, its final value is not dependent on null values—and the optimizer knows that it has the option of not passing nulls to the aggregate.

If the value of a user-defined aggregate will be the same, whether or not some of the values it aggregates are null, it should set the IsInvariantToNulls property of the SqlUserDefinedAggregateAttribute to true. Its default value is false, so it can be left out if in fact the aggregate value will change when nulls are aggregated. If this property is set to true, the query optimizer has the option of not calling the Accumulate method for null values. However, you cannot assume that it will not call the Accumulate method in this case.

If the value of a user-defined aggregate will be the same if duplicate values are passed into it, it should set the IsInVariantToDuplicates property of the SqlUserDefinedAggregateAttribute to true. The default value of the property is false, so it can be left out if this is not the case. If this property is set to true, the query optimizer has the option of not calling the Accumulate method for duplicate values. However, you cannot assume it will not call the Accumulate method in this case.

If the value of a user-defined aggregate will be the same no matter in what order it processes rows, the IsInvariantToOrder property should be set to true. The default value for this property is false, so it can be left out if this is not the case. Note that for most simple aggregates, like

`LDim`, that just make a running total or count, this property should be set to `true`.

If the return value of the user-defined aggregate should be `null` if no rows are processed for the aggregate, the `IsNullIfEmpty` attribute should be set to `true`. If this attribute is set to `true`, the query optimizer has the option of not even creating an aggregate object if there are no rows to be processed. However, even if this attribute is set to `true`, SQL Server may still create an instance of the aggregate object, even if there are no rows to process. The default value for this attribute is `false`, so it may be left out if this is not the case.

Where Are We?

User-defined types are extensions to the SQL Server built-in scalar types. They are used in the same way and for the same purpose. They allow us to use an application-specific format for the string representation of a value—for example "1 ft"—in much the same way we use a string representation of a date—such as "12/1/1998"—for a `DATETIME` built-in data type.

User-defined types implement a number of well-known methods and use the `SqlUserDefinedTypeAttribute` attributes. These can be accessed from within SQL Server once their assembly has been added to a database and `CREATE TYPE` has been used to add them.

The user-defined type can be used in the definition of a column type for a table, a variable type, or a parameter type in a stored procedure or function. It is often useful to add user-defined-type-specific methods that can manipulate or extract information from an instance of that type. It is also often useful to add utility functions that can create initialized instances of a user-defined type.

User-defined types can also expose their properties and fields. This is useful when one of the fields of a user-defined type must be accessed or manipulated.

User-defined aggregates allow an aggregate function to be created using a CLR language. There is no way to create an aggregate function using T-SQL. Aggregate functions are often created for use with user-defined types. They may also be created for built-in types, and order variant aggregates may be created to calculate aggregate values that depend on the processing of rows in a particular order.

Both user-defined types and user-defined aggregate implementation must always be aware that they are manipulating data in SQL Server at a very low level and will often require extra code beyond the function they are implementing, to ensure that the data is not corrupted.

We've covered most of the new features of SQL Server 2005 that directly relate to .NET, finishing up with user-defined types and user-defined aggregates. Chapter 2 pointed out that no matter how flexible or powerful a database is, a database without security is less than useful. The next chapter talks about how security has been considered at every level when the new functionality was designed. In addition, we'll see how permissions work with the .NET features.

6

Security

C HANGES IN SQL SERVER 2005 help make SQL Server more secure
and security more approachable for the developer and the administrator. An entire new set of security requirements when hosting .NET code
inside SQL Server are addressed by using traditional role-based security
combined with .NET hosting API and attribute-based security. Classic SQL
security is improved by separating users from schemas and integrating
password management with Windows 2003 Server. And the security of
SQL Server in general is enhanced by having options turned off by default.

New Security Features in SQL Server 2005

SQL Server 2005 adds new security features, not only to make SQL Server
more secure, but to make security more understandable and easier to
administer. Some of these features will permit programmers to develop
database applications while running with the exact privileges that they
need. This is known as "the principle of least privilege." No longer does
every programmer need to run as database administrator or "sa." The
major new features include the following.

- Security for .NET executable code—Administration and execution
  of .NET code is managed through a combination of SQL Server permissions, Windows permissions, and .NET code security. What

the code can or cannot do inside and outside SQL Server is defined with three distinct levels.

- Password policies for SQL server users—If you run SQL Server 2005 on a Windows 2003 Server, SQL users can go by the same policies as integrated security users.

- Mapping SQL Server users to Windows credentials—SQL Server users can use Windows credentials when accessing external resources like files and network shares.

- Separation of users and schemas—SQL Server 2005 schemas are first-class objects that can be owned by a user, role, group, or application roles. The capability to define synonyms makes this easier to administer.

- Granting permissions—No longer do users or logins have to be in special roles to have certain permissions; they are all grantable with the GRANT, DENY, and REVOKE verbs.

- New security on SQL Server metadata—New metadata views are not directly updatable, and users can only list metadata about objects to which they have permission. There is also a new grantable VIEW DEFINITION permission.

- Execution context for procedural code—You can set the execution context for stored procedures and user-defined functions. You can also use the EXECUTE AS syntax to change the current user.

- Support of certificates and encryption keys—SQL Server 2005 can manage certificates and encryption keys for use with Service Broker, with Web Services SSL, for code authentication, and for new data encryption functions.

Some of the new security features are outside the scope of this book, and some were still in development at the time of this writing. But we'll look at most of them in detail in this chapter. Running non-T-SQL code in a secure and reliable fashion inside SQL Server is a new concept, and we will spend a lot of this chapter examining how SQL Server's new security features combine with the latest .NET runtime to make this possible. We include a review of how security currently works in SQL Server in general to establish a baseline of knowledge.

We will start by looking at a change in the general policy of how SQL Server is configured. Though having optional features turned off by default is technically not a feature as such, most will consider it an important step forward in securing SQL Server.

Optional Features Are Turned Off by Default

The SQL Server product has always been known for being feature-rich. A multitude of new features are added with each release, too many for many DBAs to keep track of. Although it's a treat to see new features (that's what this book is about, after all), in previous releases they usually arrive with the product, installed and enabled by default. And enabled features that you don't know exist can hurt you, by increasing the "surface area" exposed to attackers. These "bad guys" probe for any weakness in existing and new features, which in past releases included goodies such as command-line program invocation (xp_cmdshell), sending mail messages (xp_sendmail), and invocation of COM classes (sp_OACreate). Most of these features will run as the user that runs the SQL Server service process. Most times, for ease of installation, this is set to LocalSystem, a Windows superuser account. And if you are running in mixed security mode and you've set your "sa" password to null (that is, no password), you're wide open, although it must be pointed out that neither mixed security nor a blank password is the default, and a blank password is strongly discouraged throughout the product and all utilities.

In the SQL Server 2005 release, care has been taken to reduce the "attack surface area," especially with regard to SQL Server passwords and auto-enablement of new features. You'll read later in this chapter about improvements when using SQL Server logins and passwords. With regard to feature enabling, two good examples of the new policy are ENDPOINTs used for HTTP (discussed in Chapter 10) and SQLCLR features (discussed in Chapters 2–5).

HTTP ENDPOINTs (endpoints that allow SQL Server to expose stored procedures as Web services) are not enabled by default. Someone with an extended privilege must explicitly invoke CREATE ENDPOINT; there are no "default endpoints" set up on install. ENDPOINT definition prohibits using any security style but Windows integrated choices (Windows integrated security never sends passwords over the network, even in encrypted form) unless you are using the secure socket layer (SSL). SSL, though not as robust as Windows integrated (NTLM or Kerberos) authentication, does at least encrypt all network traffic for the connection. It's the same encryption you use to send credit card numbers over the Internet when you purchase products on the Web. When an ENDPOINT is defined, it's not ON by default; you must create it as ENABLED or explicitly enable it with an ALTER ENDPOINT command. No Web Services or batch access (available separately) is enabled by default within an ENDPOINT, either.

SQLCLR (the ability to run .NET code in SQL Server 2005) is enabled or disabled through a server configuration option. You can turn it on with the following code:

```
sp_configure 'clr enabled', 1
```

Although it has been enabled by default through much of the beta process, it will most likely be disabled by default when SQL Server 2005 ships.

Security and Metadata

One of the ways to gain information about a SQL Server database is to rummage through the system metadata views. In previous versions of SQL Server, you could retrieve metadata information on other users' database objects that you did not own or have access to. SQL Server 2005 remedies this situation.

One of the new permissions added to SQL Server 2005 is the VIEW DEFINITION permission. Not only are the new system metadata views (that start with the identifier sys.) read-only, but you can use the VIEW DEFINITION privilege to permit or prohibit access to metadata. This privilege is exposed on individual database objects; it's also very useful at the schema level. If you do not have VIEW DEFINITION permission, system views and stored procedures will not list object information (for example, through sp_helptext) or metadata.

Error messages have been changed as well, so as not to provide information that would indicate the existence of objects you don't have access to. For example, attempting to drop a procedure that you don't "know about" produces the following error message: "Cannot drop the procedure 'foo,' because it does not exist or you do not have permission." This makes SQL Server metadata less subject to random browsing.

A Quick Review of SQL Server Security Concepts with Enhancements

SQL Server 2005 extends the SQL Server security system to handle .NET assemblies and the calls that these assemblies might make. With a .NET assembly, we are concerned with both internal calls (calls to other assemblies, or "ordinary" stored procedure and table access) and external calls (calls from a .NET assembly to the world outside the SQL Server process) in SQL Server 2005. Because the new security is based on the original SQL

Server security system, and there have been many enhancements to SQL Server security in SQL Server 2005, it helps to start with a quick review of how SQL Server security works in general.

Authentication and Authorization—Principals and Permissions

Any security system is concerned with two main concepts: authentication and authorization. Authentication is the process of identifying a principal; authorization is determining what operations a principal can perform. In SQL Server a login is a principal, and authorization is done by SQL Server when a user logs in to it. For example, once a user—let's call him Bob—has identified himself to the SQL Server by logging in (that is, SQL Server is aware the user session "5" is actually "bob"), he can do whatever operations, such as add records to tables or query tables, he has authorization to do.

A SQL Server process is called an instance, as in "an instance of the service process sqlservr.exe." One or more SQL Server instances can run on one machine running Windows. Authentication is done per instance of SQL Server. Principals—that is, *logins*—that can log in to an instance, are originally identified to SQL Server by using DDL and stored in a system table, syslogins. In SQL Server 2005 this information is exposed through sys.server_principals and sys.sql_logins.

SQL Server supports Windows users and SQL Server users as logins, but it may be configured to support only Windows users as logins, which is recommended practice. Windows users may be local to the machine running SQL Server or users in the Active Directory for the enterprise to which SQL Server belongs. SQL Server no longer supports permitting only SQL Server users.

In SQL Server 2000, the DBA defines Windows logins to SQL Server using the sp_grantlogin system stored procedure. SQL Server–defined users are assigned their login name, password, and (optionally) language and default database using the sp_addlogin system stored procedure. These system stored procedures still exist in SQL Server 2005 but should be considered deprecated; the equivalent functionality is exposed in the CREATE LOGIN DDL statement in SQL Server 2005, which should be used instead.

Authenticated logins of a particular SQL Server instance can be mapped to principals called *users* in a particular database. Each login can have a default database; logging in will drop the user into this database. Logins may also be allowed to access databases other than their default database, as defined by the administrator. In SQL Server, the term "user" refers to a "login's" identity in a particular database. Depending on how users are mapped to logins by the administrator, the user ID for a particular user in a particular database may not be the same as the login ID. However, a login can have only a single user in a given database.

```
CREATE LOGIN bob WITH PASSWORD='m8b#5pL'
GO

USE PUBS
GO

CREATE USER pubsbob FOR LOGIN bob
GO

-the following will fail, login bob
- may only have a single user in a database
CREATE USER otherPubsBob FOR LOGIN bob
```

Figure 6-1 shows the relationship between logins and users.

Figure 6-1 shows an instance of SQL Server with two logins: bob and niels. The login bob is mapped to the user bob in the pubs database. The login bob has a default database of pubs, so when bob logs in, he will, by default, be referencing the pubs database as user bob. The login niels is

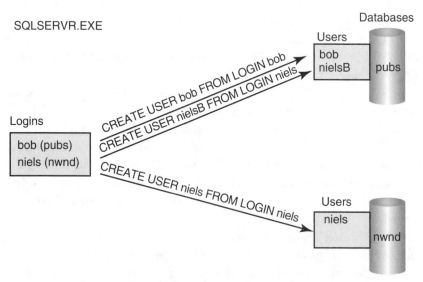

FIGURE 6-1: Defining Database Users for SQL Server Logins

mapped to the user `nielsB` on the database `pubs`, but the default database for this login is `nwnd`. The login `niels` will have to use a three-part name to reference `pubs`, and when he does, he will be referencing it as the user `nielsB`. The login `niels` is also mapped to the `nwnd` database as user `niels`, which is the default database for that login. When `niels` logs in, he will, by default, reference the `nwnd` database and do so as the user `niels`. Note that login `niels` has a different user name on `pubs` than on `nwnd`.

If a user is granted permission to access a database, but not assigned a user identity for the database, he accesses the database as a user called "guest."

A SQL Server user in a particular database can be permitted to perform DDL and DML operations; therefore, a database in SQL Server (rather than an instance) is usually the authorization domain. Users are granted permissions using the GRANT DDL statement, such as the following:

```
GRANT SELECT ON SOMESCHEMA.SOMETABLE TO SOMEUSER
```

In SQL Server 2005, permissions can also be granted on instance-level objects like ENDPOINTs and even commands like SHUTDOWN.

Permissions on a database table, view, or stored procedure, as well as other database object permissions, are granted to a user by the object's owner. A permission can be granted to each user, but this would be cumbersome and unwieldy as many users are added to the database. Therefore, SQL Server users can be grouped into *roles.* In addition to custom roles—which can be defined, for example, for users of a specific application—a few special, system-defined roles exist. The only two special roles we'll mention here are DBO, the database owner role, and public, the general public. Multiple users can be assigned to the DBO role for a particular database, and this role gives the user unlimited privilege inside that database. The role "public" refers to anyone who has access to a particular database. In addition to roles, SQL Server authorization is aware of *Windows groups,* if database users were derived from Windows-based logins.

In addition to user-based security, SQL Server also has the notion of application-based security. Some administrators might wish to permit or deny access based on the current application, rather than the user. For this purpose, SQL Server permits definition of *application roles.* Application roles are different from roles in that they contain no users. In fact, when a SQL Server user assumes an application role, because code in an application (for example, an inventory control application) issues a statement such as the following:

```
sp_setapprole @role='inventoryrole',
              @password= {Encrypt N 'inventorypassword'}, 'Odbc'
```

the user gives up all the permissions granted him. The user can only access those database objects that the role has permission to access.

The following object-level permissions can be granted to a user, a role, an application role, or a Windows group in SQL Server 2000:

* SELECT
* UPDATE
* DELETE
* INSERT
* EXECUTE
* REFERENCES

In SQL Server 2000, SELECT, INSERT, UPDATE, and DELETE are permissions that can be granted on SQL Server tables and views. EXECUTE permission can be granted on a stored procedure or user-defined function. REFERENCES permission means that a user who is the owner of table A can define a foreign key on table B, which she does not own, if she has REFERENCES permission on table B. REFERENCES permission is also used to allow a user to define a VIEW or UDF using the SQL WITH SCHEMABINDING option if the VIEW or UDF uses a table or view that is owned by a different owner. You can also use GRANT to grant a permission and give the user permission to grant access to others; this is called GRANT WITH GRANT OPTION.

SQL Server 2005 adds the following new object-level permissions:

* ALTER
* CONTROL
* RECEIVE (service broker queues)
* TAKE OWNERSHIP
* VIEW DEFINITION

If a user is permitted to create objects like tables, views, or stored procedures, when the user issues the CREATE statement, she becomes the owner of the object. Object owners have unlimited permissions on objects they create, including the permission to grant other users permissions. One special case is that if the user is a member of the DBO role, objects created by that user are considered owned by DBO. Because different users can define objects having the same name—that is, BOB.SOMETABLE and MARY. SOMETABLE—many SQL Server installations prefer to have all database objects defined and owned by DBO, although this can be done differently in SQL Server 2005 with the introduction of schemas (discussed later in the chapter). This simplifies determining permissions, which can become quite complicated, as we'll see later in this chapter.

As an aside, when a Windows system administrator or the SQL Server system administrator account, known as "sa," logs on to a SQL Server instance, she is automatically granted the DBO role in every database by default. Programmers should always test their programs by running the program when logged on to Windows as nonadministrators, to prevent surprises at deployment time. Obviously, security makes SQL DML statements act differently depending on the user that executes them. In addition, because changing databases inside a SQL Server instance using the USE SOMEOTHERDATABASE statement is an expensive operation, a best practice when using SQL Server from an application server (where like sessions will be pooled using connection pooling) is to define a special user for each distinct application in the application server, and give that user a default database that is appropriate for that application. Of course, when users must be distinctly identified inside SQL Server—for example, for auditing—this is not possible, although each user should have a default database that corresponds to the database he will be working in most often.

Execution Context and Ownership Chaining

When you execute a stored procedure or user-defined function or use a view prior to SQL Server 2005, access to objects inside the stored procedure occurs using the identity of the caller of the stored procedure. Many people don't recognize this at first glance, because permissions are only checked when the owner of the stored procedure is different from the owner of the object the stored procedure is accessing. This permits giving users access to database tables only through sanctioned stored procedures, while denying them access to the underlying tables directly.

In the following example, let's say the same user, FRED, owns both the employee table and the update_salary stored procedure. FRED does not grant BOB permission to access the employee table but does grant BOB permission to execute the `update_salary` stored procedure. BOB can now update the `employee` table, but only through the stored procedure.

```
-Logged in as FRED
CREATE TABLE employee (
  - other fields elided for clarity
  emp_id  INT,
  name    VARCHAR(20),
  address VARCHAR(50),
  phone   VARCHAR(15),
  salary_grade INT,
  salary  MONEY
)
go

- procedure for update
CREATE PROCEDURE update_salary(
 @EMP_ID INT,
 @NEW_SALARY MONEY)
AS
UPDATE employee SET salary = @NEW_SALARY
  WHERE emp_id = @EMP_ID
go

-- BOB can only execute the procedure
GRANT EXECUTE ON update_salary to BOB
go
```

If the same user (FRED) owns both the stored procedure and the table, permissions are never checked when the stored procedure accesses the table. Because BOB has EXECUTE permission on the stored procedure, the stored procedure works.

However, if FRED alters the store procedure to also access another table, owned by a different user (say, ALICE), inside the stored procedure, the ability of BOB (not FRED) to access the `salary_audit` table is checked.

```
- procedure for update
-- FRED owns the PROCEDURE
ALTER PROCEDURE update_salary(
 @EMP_ID INT,
 @NEW_SALARY MONEY)
AS
-- FRED owns the employee table
UPDATE employee SET salary = @NEW_SALARY
  WHERE emp_id = @EMP_ID

-- But ALICE owns the salary_audit table
INSERT INTO alice.salary_audit values(@EMP_ID, @NEW_SALARY)
go
```

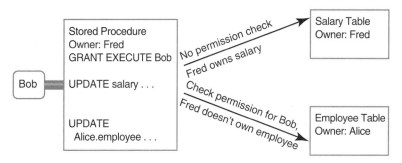

FIGURE 6-2: Checking Permissions with Different Owners

Figure 6-2 illustrates ownership chaining.
Notice two things about this diagram.

* Because BOB is invoking a stored procedure owned by FRED, BOB must have EXECUTE permission on the stored procedure. He need not have access to the underlying tables as long as FRED also owns the tables.

* Because FRED is the owner of the stored procedure but does not own the alice.employee table, permission of the caller (BOB) on the alice.employee_table is checked.

In general, SQL Server checks permissions only when an object accesses an object that is not owned by the same accessor. If the same user owns two objects and one object accesses the other, permissions are not checked at all, at any level. This is known as an *ownership chain*. If, at any level, an object accesses another object that is not owned by the accessor, permissions are checked because the ownership chain has been broken.

Until SQL Server 2000 SP3, ownership chains were permitted across databases. After SP3, this is no longer the default, but you can enable cross-database ownership chains on a per-database basis as an option, using the following statements.

```
USE master
EXEC sp_dboption MyDatabase, 'db chaining', 'true'
GO
```

In addition, permissions are always checked when you are using dynamic SQL inside a stored procedure. A different implementation of the update_salary stored procedure is shown in the following code.

```
- procedure for update
- FRED owns the PROCEDURE
ALTER PROCEDURE update_salary(
@EMP_ID INT,
@NEW_SALARY MONEY)
AS
- FRED owns the employee table
- table is accessed through dynamic SQL
execute ('UPDATE employee SET salary = @NEW_SALARY
  WHERE emp_id = @EMP_ID')
go
```

In this version, access is always checked when dynamic SQL is invoked, regardless of the owner of the object that the dynamic SQL statement accesses. Because we're using dynamic SQL, when BOB executes the stored procedure, BOB's access to the employee table is checked. Because BOB does not have access to the table, the stored procedure fails.

SQL Server 2005 refines the concept of ownership chaining to deal with the concept of schemas and introduces the notion of execution context other than "current user." Setting execution context can solve the dynamic SQL problem just described but must be managed carefully. We'll discuss it later in this chapter.

SQL Server Password Policies and Credentials

In addition to new security features related to .NET managed code, other security features are intended to tighten authentication through SQL Server logins when SQL Server runs under Windows Server 2003. As we mentioned at the beginning of this chapter, users can use Windows authentication or SQL Server authentication to log in to SQL Server. Windows authentication is secure. A user's password is never sent across the network, and the system administrator can enforce password policy. The password policy can require that users change their password at the first login to the NT domain or machine. The policy can require users to use strong passwords—for example, at least eight characters including at least one number, letter, and special character. The policy can also require users to change their password every so often. The policy can specify that a login will be locked out after a certain number of bad password attempts. When a database administrator switches all SQL Server logins to Windows authentication, SQL Server inherits this level of enforceable security. Until SQL Server 2005, SQL Server logins had none of these necessary security characteristics. And weak passwords are acknowledged to be the weakest link in most security systems.

With the new SQL Server 2005 security features, SQL Server logins will have all the same security policy features available. Both SQL Server users and application roles will use the policy. With Windows Server 2003 or later, the policy will be implemented via an OS-level call, Net ValidatePasswordPolicy, so that the administrator can use the same policy for both Windows integrated and SQL Server logins. To give companies that convert to SQL Server 2005 time to analyze how the policy will affect existing applications, the policy can be turned off on a per-login basis. Obviously, this is not recommended. As Windows provides users with the ability to change their password at login time (or while logged on to Windows), so SQL Server users will have the ability to change their password during login. Both the client APIs, like OLE DB and ADO.NET, and the client tools, like SQL Server Management Studio, will support this.

Password policy is set by using the Active Directory Users and Computers tool if you're using Active Directory, or by using the Local Security Settings administrator tool if you're administering a nondomain computer. Table 6-1 shows the settings that are exposed using Local Security Settings.

Note that Account Lockout Duration (the amount of time accounts are locked out when you reach the Account Lockout Threshold) and Reset

TABLE 6-1: Security Policies for Windows and SQL Server 2005 Logins

Policy Category	Policy Name	Default (Local Server)
Password Policy	Enforce Password History	0 passwords remembered
	Maximum Password Age	42 days
	Minimum Password Age	0 days
	Minimum Password Length	0 characters
	Password Must Meet Complexity Requirements	Disabled
	Store Passwords Using Reversible Encryption	Disabled
Account Lockout Policy	Account Lockout Duration	Not applicable
	Account Lockout Threshold	0 invalid login attempts
	Reset Lockout Counter After	Not applicable

Lockout Counter After (the amount of time after which the invalid login attempts revert to zero, if you haven't exceeded them) are not applicable until you set Account Lockout Threshold to something other than zero.

There are two password options for SQL Server logins: CHECK_EXPIRATION and CHECK_POLICY. CHECK_EXPIRATION encompasses minimum and maximum password age, and CHECK_POLICY encompasses all the other policies. When you run afoul of either policy, the SQL Server login must be unlocked by the DBA, as shown shortly in an example.

An administrator can add a new login through SQL Server Management Studio or by using the Transact-SQL statement CREATE LOGIN. The legacy stored procedure sp_addlogin will be supported for backward compatibility but will not expose the new features. As shown in the following example, you can create a new SQL Server login that requires the password to be changed on the user's first login attempt by using the MUST_CHANGE keyword. Attempting to access the SQL Server instance without changing the password will result in an error.

```
CREATE LOGIN fred WITH PASSWORD = 'hy!at54Cq' MUST_CHANGE,
   DEFAULT_DATABASE = pubs,
   CHECK_EXPIRATION = ON,
   CHECK_POLICY = ON
go
```

If a user has been locked out, the database administrator can unlock the login by using the following code.

```
ALTER LOGIN fred WITH PASSWORD = 'hy!at54Cq' UNLOCK
go
```

In those rare cases where the database administrator wants to turn off the password expiration enforcement or security policy enforcement, ALTER LOGIN can accomplish this. Neither of these statements will work when the MUST_CHANGE flag is set and the user has not yet changed his password.

```
ALTER LOGIN fred WITH CHECK_EXPIRATION = OFF
go
```

```
ALTER LOGIN fred WITH CHECK_POLICY = OFF
go
```

Credentials

SQL Server 2005 introduces .NET procedural code that makes it easier to access resources outside SQL Server. This access is controlled by security levels on assemblies, as will be discussed later in the chapter. When accessing resources outside the database, SQL Server logins have no specific privileges—only Windows principals defined to SQL Server are "known" to the underlying operating system. In previous versions of SQL Server, there were two choices for using external resources and SQL Server logins: Use the service account (the account of the service that runs `sqlserver.exe`) or use the guest account. The guest account is almost always disabled on Windows operating systems when hosting SQL Server.

In SQL Server 2005, you can assign Windows credentials to SQL Server logins by first cataloging them with SQL Server. The same credentials can be assigned to multiple SQL Server logins. It looks something like this.

```
CREATE CREDENTIAL sqlusers
  WITH IDENTITY = 'machine\sqlusers', SECRET = '*Y6fy)'
go
CREATE LOGIN mary WITH PASSWORD = 'mary'
GO

ALTER LOGIN mary WITH CREDENTIAL = sqlusers
GO
```

Note that the Windows principal (`machine\sqlusers`, in this case) must already be defined to the Windows security system.

Separation of Users and Schemas

SQL-99 defines the concept of a database schema as a named group of data that is owned by a particular authorization ID. Schemas are scoped to the database (called "catalog" in SQL:1999), and one database can contain one or more schemas. Schema objects, such tables, views, and stored procedures, live in a schema, and the two-part name of a database object is actually `schemaname.objectname`.

Prior to SQL Server 2005, the concept of a schema was tied to a particular user. Any objects created by a user were owned by that user, and SQL Server really defined the two-part name of a database object as `ownername.objectname` rather than `schemaname.objectname`. There was a CREATE SCHEMA DDL statement, but you did not have the option of naming your schema, only its owner.

```
- SQL Server 2000 create schema, no schema name
CREATE SCHEMA AUTHORIZATION fred
    GRANT SELECT ON v1 TO public
    CREATE VIEW v1 AS SELECT au_id, au_lname FROM authors
GO


- SQL Server 2005 create schema with name
CREATE SCHEMA fredstuff AUTHORIZATION fred
```

This pre–SQL Server 2005 CREATE SCHEMA statement actually was a convenient way to create objects that belonged to a specific user (like fred, in this case) and grant permissions to them in a single DDL statement batch. The problem of having database objects tied to a particular user was that in order to drop the user, the database administrator had to reassign or drop and re-create all of that user's database objects.

SQL Server 2005 introduces the concept of named schemas as separate from users. When you use the new CREATE USER DDL to statement to create a user, you can assign a default schema for that user. If a default schema is not assigned, the DBO (database owner) schema is the default.

```
- user's default schema is uschema
CREATE USER u1 FOR USER u1WITH, DEFAULT_SCHEMA = 'uschema'
go


- user's default schema is dbo
CREATE USER u2 FOR LOGIN u2
go
```

A schema can be owned not only by a specific user (created with a SQL Server login or Windows login), but also by a Windows group, a database role, or an application role defined in that database. The new CREATE APPLICATION ROLE DDL statement permits assignment of a default schema, but because many users can be assigned to a role (an ordinary role, not an application role), CREATE ROLE does not assign a default schema for the role. Note that the legacy procedures sp_adduser and sp_addapprole have been changed to first create a schema with the same name of the user or application role and then call the appropriate CREATE statement, specifying that schema as the default schema. Use of the new CREATE statements is preferred; the behavior of the stored procedures is kept only for backward compatibility.

The owner of a schema (a single user or multiple users) can create database objects within that schema and also grant schema-level privileges to others. The schema owner does have to be granted permission to create the database objects, but the grant permission exists on a database level, not on a schema level. Here's an example of a user that has an associated schema and is also the owner of that schema.

```
USE demo1
GO

CREATE LOGIN alogin1 WITH password = 'password1',
 DEFAULT_DATABASE = demo1
GO

- default named schema
CREATE USER auser1 FOR LOGIN alogin1
 WITH DEFAULT_SCHEMA = aschema1
GO

CREATE SCHEMA aschema1 AUTHORIZATION auser1
GO

GRANT CREATE TABLE TO auser1
GO

SETUSER 'auser1'
GO

- this works and creates aschema1.table1
CREATE TABLE table1 (theid INTEGER)
go
```

In this case, if we did not set a default schema for the `auser1` user, his default schema would be `dbo`. Because `auser1` is not a member of the `dbo` database role, the `CREATE TABLE` statement would fail.

What this means to the database administrator is that because schemas (and the objects they contain) can be owned by a role, an application role, or a Windows group, when a user is dropped from the database, the database objects she has have created do not have to be reassigned or dropped and re-created. Here's an example using a SQL Server role for a payroll system. We'll assume that a role called `payroll` has already been created.

```
USE payrolldb
GO

CREATE LOGIN janet WITH PASSWORD = 'temppwd',
 DEFAULT_DATABASE = payrolldb
GO
```

```
- default named schema
CREATE USER janet FOR LOGIN janet
  WITH DEFAULT_SCHEMA = prschema
GO

CREATE ROLE payroll -- if it does not exist GO

sp_addrolemember 'payroll', 'janet'

CREATE SCHEMA prschema AUTHORIZATION payroll
GO

GRANT CREATE TABLE TO janet
GO
```

Now, user `janet` can create tables, and they will be contained within the `prschema` schema. If Janet is reassigned, the user `janet` can be dropped from the database without affecting any of the tables she has created.

Having named schemas affects the way database object names are resolved. If Janet issues the SQL statement `SELECT * FROM benefits`, SQL Server will attempt to resolve the table name `benefits` in this order:

1. `prschema.benefits` (using the default schema)
2. `dbo.benefits`
3. `sys.benefits`

One further special case needs to be mentioned. It is possible that a database user will have a default schema that she does not own (such as `dbo`), but will have the ability to create database objects in a different schema. In that case, the database object in the `CREATE` DDL statement must explicitly use the two-part name. For example, if user `janet` was defined without a default schema keyword, her default schema would be `dbo`, since she is not a member of the `dbo` role.

```
- this statement would fail
CREATE TABLE benefits2003 (empid INT)  - other columns elided

- this statement would succeed
CREATE TABLE prschema.benefits2003 (empid INT)
```

Schemas have their own sets of permissions. You can grant or deny permissions like `SELECT`, `EXECUTE`, or `VIEW DEFINITION` on a schema-wide basis. The following SQL statement prohibits the group `public` from seeing any database objects in the `bob` schema using the system views.

```
DENY VIEW DEFINITION ON schema::bob TO public
```

Synonyms

SQL Server 2005 introduces support for a database object known as a *synonym*. A synonym is just an alternate name for an existing database object that keeps a database user (more likely, a database programmer) from having to use a multipart name for an object. Synonyms can be defined on a two-part, three-part, or four-part SQL Server object name. A synonym can be defined by the following database objects:

- Table
- View
- Stored procedure
- User-defined function
- Extended stored procedure
- Replication filter procedure

Although synonyms can be created on a multipart object name, they are scoped to the database that they are created in. Here are some examples of creating and using synonyms.

```
USE pubs
GO

CREATE SYNONYM customers_east FOR eastserver.northwind.dbo.customers
GO

CREATE SYNONYM employees FOR payroll.employees
GO

-- these work
SELECT * FROM customers_east
SELECT * FROM employees
GO

USE northwind
GO

-- so does this
SELECT * FROM pubs..customers_east
```

Specifying Execution Context for Procedural Code

In previous versions of SQL Server, cataloged procedural code always ran within the security context of the caller, as explained earlier in the section on ownership chaining. This is a good strategy for the most common case—for example, when you want to allow users access to tables through stored procedures without giving them access to the base tables. However, it is not always what you want. Take, for example, a stored procedure that executes dynamic SQL composed by concatenating strings. This does a type of indirect parameterization of the table name. This is necessary because you may want to build a query with a table name as a parameter.

```
- this won't work
CREATE PROCEDURE count_rows(@name NVARCHAR(50))
AS
SELECT COUNT(*) FROM @name
GO


- this will
- the dynamic SQL executes in the caller's context
CREATE PROCEDURE count_rows(@name NVARCHAR(50))
AS
EXECUTE('SELECT COUNT(*) FROM ' + @name)
GO
```

SQL Server 2005 now allows you to specify that procedural code execute in a different execution context. There are three reasons you might want to do this.

- You want dynamic SQL to execute in the context of the creator of the stored procedure, as static T-SQL would.
- Since data access code in CLR procedures (through the `SqlServer` data provider discussed in Chapter 4) is effectively dynamic SQL, you might want this code to execute in the context of the creator of the stored procedure as well.
- You want to evaluate ownership chains in the context of the creator of the stored procedure rather than the caller of the procedure.

You choose the execution context on a per-procedure basis when you create the procedure, using the EXECUTE AS parameter. Execution context can also be set on user-defined functions, except for inline table-valued user-defined functions. Examples are shown in the following code.

```
- pre-SQL Server 2005 execution context
- this will execute as the direct caller
CREATE PROCEDURE count_rows(@name NVARCHAR(50)
 WITH EXECUTE AS CALLER
AS
EXECUTE('SELECT COUNT(*) FROM ' + @name)
GO

- this will execute as the stored procedure creator
CREATE PROCEDURE count_rows_as_me(@name NVARCHAR(50))
  WITH EXECUTE AS SELF
AS
EXECUTE('SELECT COUNT(*) FROM ' + @name)
GO

- this will execute as a specific user
CREATE PROCEDURE count_rows_as_fred(@name NVARCHAR(50))
WITH EXECUTE AS 'FRED'
AS
EXECUTE('SELECT COUNT(*) FROM ' + @name)
GO
```

Note that the third option is just a convenience for a DBA running a CREATE script. It saves the DBA from having to do a SETUSER FRED (change the current user to FRED) before executing the CREATE statement.

The second option shows how ownership chaining affects stored procedures that make use of dynamic SQL. Prior to SQL Server 2005, permission was always checked against the identity of the caller of a stored procedure when it referenced a database object using dynamic SQL. That is still the default behavior in SQL Server 2005. EXECUTE AS SELF can be used in the definition of the stored procedure so that even though permission will be checked when dynamic SQL is used, the behavior will be the same as static SQL. Figure 6-3 shows using EXECUTE AS SELF to make dynamic SQL behave the same as static SQL.

Special care must be taken to guard against SQL injection (that is, piggybacking of dangerous code after "normal" parameters) when EXECUTE AS SELF is used. Although counting the rows in a table is pretty mundane code, the fact is that any dynamically constructed code in a stored procedure can be potentially dangerous. Given the count_rows_as_me stored procedure in the previous example, if the procedure was cataloged by the DBO role, the following code will execute as DBO, regardless of the user who calls it.

```
DECLARE @s VARCHAR(50)
SET @s = 'authors;drop table customers'
 - count the rows and drop the table!
count_rows_as_me @s
```

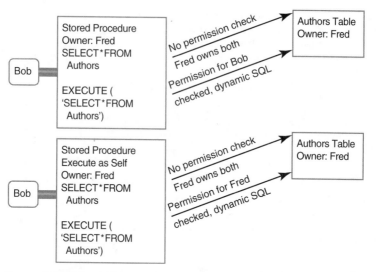

FIGURE 6-3: Using EXECUTE AS SELF with Dynamic SQL

This probably wasn't the desired result.

Although EXECUTE AS SELF looks interesting, it should be used with care because it can make ownership chains more complex. When the stored procedure count_rows_as_me accesses any table that the current owner does not own, an ownership chain will be broken and permissions on the underlying object will be checked. In addition, when a different stored procedure uses this stored procedure, it is possible that ownership chains could be broken at two levels, as shown in the script that follows.

```
- table FOO_TABLE is owned by DBO.
- using the count_rows_as_me procedure from the previous example
SETUSER JAY
GO
- this checks permissions if JAY is not DBO
count_rows_as_me 'foo_table'
-
-
SETUSER FRED
GO

CREATE PROCEDURE select_and_count
AS
SELECT * FROM customers
count_rows_as_me 'foo_table'
GO
```

```
- this does two ownership checks
- even if FRED is DBO
select_and_count
GO
```

By default, procedural code that uses a nondefault execution context can only access resources in the current database—that is, you may not use three-part names at all. This is to guard against a user with DBO privilege in one database gaining access to data in another database. If you need to access resources in another database or system-level resources, you must grant appropriate permissions to the executor of the code. Another option is to sign the code with a certificate, map the certificate to a login, and grant permissions to the certificate. This option is in development at the time of this writing.

SQL Server Permissions and the New Objects

We have six new kinds of SQL Server objects in the managed world of SQL Server 2005. Three of these objects are managed code variations on SQL Server objects:

- Stored procedures
- User-defined functions
- Triggers

Three of the objects are new with SQL Server 2005:

- Assemblies
- User-defined types
- User-defined aggregates

The reason that all these objects are new is that they all run executable code, rather than having SQL Server run the code. In previous versions of SQL Server, extended stored procedures or COM objects using COM automation to run code always ran that code in the context of the Windows user account that was running the SQL Server service process. With the introduction of a managed environment that can control aspects of code loading (through the assembly loading policy mentioned in Chapter 2) and code execution through Host Protection Attributes (HPAs) that work through code access security, execution of .NET assembly code is safer than extended stored procedures and as safe as running Transact-SQL code from inside SQL Server.

When SQL Server is used as a host for the .NET runtime:

- Managed user-code does not gain unauthorized access to user data or other user code in the database.
- There are controls for restricting managed user-code from accessing any resources outside the server and using it strictly for local data access and computation.
- Managed user-code does not have unauthorized access to system resources such as files or networks by virtue of running in the SQL Server process.
- CLR procedures and functions are a way to provide security wrappers similarly to the way T-SQL procedures and functions do, by using ownership chaining.

We'll first look at the extension of the traditional SQL Server object security to the new objects and then go on to describe .NET-specific considerations.

Assembly Permissions— Who Can Catalog and Use an Assembly?

In order to catalog assembly code to SQL Server, a user must have the ability to execute the CREATE ASSEMBLY DDL statement. ALTER ASSEMBLY and DROP ASSEMBLY are related DDL statements. By default, only members of the sysadmin server role and the db_owner and ddl_admin database roles have the permission to execute the assembly-related DDL statements. The permission can be granted to other users. The user or role executing the statement becomes the owner of the assembly. In addition, it is possible to assign an assembly to another role using the AUTHORIZATION parameter of CREATE ASSEMBLY or ALTER ASSEMBLY, as shown in Listing 6-1.

LISTING 6-1: Using ASSEMBLY DDL

```
--
-- create an assembly while logged on as sysadmin
-- owned by sysadmin
--
CREATE ASSEMBLY SomeTypes
  FROM '\\mysvr\types\SomeTypes.dll'
GO
```

```
- create an assembly owned by DBO
- while logged on as sysadmin
CREATE ASSEMBLY SomeMoreTypes
  AUTHORIZATION dbo
  FROM '\\mysvr\types\SomeMoreTypes.dll'

- alter the first assembly to be owned by DBO
ALTER ASSEMBLY SomeTypes
  AUTHORIZATION dbo
```

In the most common scenario, CREATE ASSEMBLY reads bytes from the Windows file system; although if you specify CREATE ASSEMBLY, specifying the hexadecimal bytes that make up the assembly as part of the CREATE ASSEMBLY DDL statement, no file system access of any kind is required. The preceding example reads bytes from a network share. ALTER ASSEMBLY may also read bytes from the file system if the options of ALTER ASSEMBLY that reload code or load debugging symbols are used. Some Windows security principal must have the permission to read the required files. But what security principal is used? This depends on the privilege of the user running the SQL Server service process and whether the SQL Server user is using Windows integrated security or SQL Server security to log in to the server.

If the user is logged in using a SQL Server security login, the access to the remote file system will fail. SQL Server logins can, however access the remote file system, using the credentials of the service process (if "sa") or other credentials if defined to SQL Server users as shown earlier. When a Windows security login is used, access to the bits is obtained through impersonation. That mean file system access will fail if the user running the SQL Server service process does not have the (Windows) right to perform impersonation—that is, to change the currently executing thread so it executes as a different user. If the user running the SQL Server service process has impersonation authority and the user is logged in to SQL Server as an NT user, the request to read bytes executes using an impersonation token of the currently logged-on user.

One final piece of the puzzle is needed for CREATE ASSEMBLY and ALTER ASSEMBLY. We can define three different levels of code access security for a specific assembly—SAFE, EXTERNAL_ACCESS, and UNSAFE, listed in order of decreasing code safety. Although these levels relate to code access security, additional permissions are required to execute CREATE and ALTER ASSEMBLY and give the resulting assembly any permission set other than SAFE. The executing user should have CREATE ASSEMBLY permission or be a member of the ddl_admin, dbowner, or sysadmin roles, and if the

EXTERNAL_ACCESS permission set is specified, should also have the EXTERNAL_ACCESS permission. The user should be a member of the sys admin role if the UNSAFE permission set is specified. In addition, if you use the UNSAFE permission set, you must sign your assembly using either a certificate or a strong named key. The certificate or strong named key must then be cataloged to the database, so that it is known to SQL Server.

Permissions and Assemblies

Some of the permissions that relate to an assembly are based on the user's identity—that is, normal SQL Server authorization. In general, access to all the .NET-based SQL Server objects is predicated on the checking of three different types of interobject links. These are known as invocation links, schema-bound links, and table-access links. Invocation links refer to invocation of code and are enabled by the EXECUTE permissions. The code may be managed or Transact-SQL code, such as a stored procedure.

Examples of this could be a user calling a database object (for example, a user calling a stored procedure) or one piece of code calling into another piece of code (for example, an assembly calling another assembly, or a procedure accessing a UDT column).

Schema-bound links are always between two database objects and are enabled by the REFERENCES permission. The presence of the schema-bound link causes a metadata dependency in SQL Server that prevents the underlying object from being modified or dropped as long as the object that references it is present. For example, you cannot drop an assembly if it contains a user-defined type that has been cataloged, and you cannot drop a user-defined type that is in use as a column in a table.

Table-access links correspond to retrieving or modifying values in a table, a view, or a table-valued function. They are similar to invocation links except they have a finer-grained access control. You can define separate SELECT, INSERT, UPDATE, and DELETE permissions on a table or view.

REFERENCES permission gives a user the ability to reference CLR stored procedures and user-defined functions, when using a VIEW that is created with the WITH SCHEMABINDING option. With respect to triggers, user-defined types, and assemblies, REFERENCES permission gives a user the ability the create objects that reference these; for example, REFERENCES on a UDT gives a user permission to create tables that use the UDT as a column. REFERENCES permission allows the grantee to define schema-bound links to that object.

EXECUTE permission on an assembly allows a user to catalog additional assemblies that invoke methods or instantiate public classes within that assembly. These allow interassembly invocation links. Granting a user EXECUTE permission on an assembly does not automatically give him access to the stored procedures, user-defined functions, and UDTs that are defined within an assembly as SQL Server objects. Permissions to the specific object to be accessed must also be granted.

Shared Assemblies and Security

As we discussed in Chapter 2, when you execute the CREATE ASSEMBLY DDL, SQL Server uses .NET reflection to determine which other assemblies your assembly depends on. It catalogs all of these as well. This means that there are two types of user assemblies that SQL Server 2005 will load: "visible" and "invisible." By visible, we mean those assemblies that have a SQL Server object name associated with them.

Users can only obtain permissions on visible assemblies, because the GRANT DDL statement requires a name. This makes invisible assemblies private to the assembly that references them. To share assemblies, make them visible and grant REFERENCES permission to others. This is shown in Listing 6-2.

LISTING 6-2: Visible and Invisible Assemblies

```
-
- if assembly SomeTypes.dll uses assembly SomeCommonTypes.dll
- this will catalog SomeCommonTypes as well
-
CREATE ASSEMBLY SomeTypes
  FROM '\\mysvr\types\SomeTypes.dll'
GO

- Let Fred access SomeTypes
GRANT EXECUTE ON SomeTypes To FRED
GO

- Fred will need direct access to SomeCommonTypes
- error: SomeCommonTypes does not exist in the SQL Server catalog
GRANT EXECUTE ON SomeCommonTypes TO FRED
GO

- this makes it visible
ALTER ASSEMBLY SomeCommonTypes
  FROM '\\mysvr\types\SomeCommonTypes.dll'
  SET VISIBILITY = ON
```

```
- this gives FRED access
GRANT EXECUTE ON SomeCommonTypes TO FRED
GO
```

Permissions, Visibility, UDTs, and User-Defined Aggregates

A user-defined type must be defined in the SQL Server catalog to be visible to SQL Server stored procedures and other T-SQL procedural code, just as an assembly is. Once a UDT is defined in the SQL Server catalog, users need the appropriate permission to invoke it, just as they do for any other database object.

Classes in an assembly are not directly accessible to T-SQL but may be used by other assemblies if they are public. For example, a CLR-based user-defined function may want to make use of a class from an assembly other than the one in which it is defined. This will only be allowed if the identity used to access the user-defined function, or other CLR-based procedural code, has EXECUTE rights to that assembly.

A UDT that is cataloged to SQL Server with CREATE TYPE is secured through permissions like any other SQL Server object. As with assemblies, you can grant REFERENCES and EXECUTE permissions on a UDT; with a UDT, however, the meaning is slightly different. Schema-bound links, in the context of a UDT, consist of:

- Creating a table with the UDT as a column
- Defining a stored procedure, UDF, or trigger on the static method of a UDT
- Defining a view using the WITH SCHEMABINDING option that references the UDT

EXECUTE permission on a UDT is defined at the class level, not at the method level. Granting EXECUTE permission on a UDT does not automatically grant permission on every stored procedure or user-defined function in the UDT. This must be granted by granting permission to the stored procedure or UDF SQL Server object directly. EXECUTE permission is also required to fetch a UDT or execute its methods from code inside the SqlServer data provider.

User-defined aggregates follow the same rules. A schema-bound link to a user-defined aggregate would consist of:

- Creating a table with the user-defined aggregates used in a constraint
- Defining a stored procedure, UDF, or trigger that uses the user-defined aggregate
- Defining a view using the WITH SCHEMABINDING option that uses the user-defined aggregate

REFERENCES permission would be required to create any of the database objects listed earlier.

Ownership chains apply when using user permissions with SQL Server objects, just as they do when using other SQL objects, like tables and views. Here are a few examples that will illustrate the concepts.

- User bob attempts to execute CREATE ASSEMBLY for bobsprocs. The bobsprocs assembly has a method that references another assembly, timsprocs, that is already cataloged in the database. Bob needs to have REFERENCES permission to the timsprocs assembly, because a schema-bound link will be set up between the two assemblies.
- If user bob creates a procedure, bobproc1, that is based on a method in the bobsprocs assembly, no permissions are checked. However, if user fred creates the bobproc1 procedure, this will set up a schema-bound link. User fred needs to have REFERENCES permission to the bobsprocs assembly.
- The procedure bobproc1 in bobsprocs is specified as execution_context = caller. When user alice attempts to execute bobproc1, she must have EXECUTE permissions on the procedure, but the code runs as bob. (We'll discuss execution context shortly.)
- User alice then defines a table, atable, using the UDT bobtype, which is part of the assembly bobsprocs. To do this, she needs REFERENCES permission on the bobsprocs assembly and on the bobtype UDT.
- User joe attempts to execute a SELECT statement that contains the UDT bobtype in the table atable. To do this, he needs SELECT permission on atable and EXECUTE permission on bobtype.

What Can .NET Code Do from within SQL Server: Safety Levels

SQL Server permissions take care of dealing with security from a SQL Server–centric point of view. But if a .NET stored procedure can load arbitrary assemblies from the file system or the Internet, the security of the SQL Server process could be compromised. The first concern is taken care of by the new .NET hosting APIs. Aside from a specific subset of the .NET base class libraries, SQL Server handles all assembly loading requests. You cannot instruct SQL Server to load arbitrary assemblies from the local file system or the Internet. In addition, the IL code in each .NET assembly is checked for validity when CREATE ASSEMBLY is run. On a more granular level, .NET not only uses SQL Server user-based permissions, but also .NET code access security.

Introduction to Code Access Security

.NET code access security is meant to check the permissions of code before executing it, rather than checking the permissions of the user principal that executes the code. Code access security determines how trustworthy code is by mapping pieces of evidence—such as where the code was loaded from, whether the code was signed with a digital signature, and even which company wrote the code—to permissions. This evidence is collected and inspected when the code is loaded. Code access security matches evidence against the security policy, to produce a set of permissions. Security policy is a combination of enterprise security policy, machine policy, user-specific policy, and AppDomain security policy. The general concept of determining permissions from evidence and security policy is discussed in the .NET documentation.

In most ordinary .NET programs, code access security is used when code is loaded, to determine the location (most likely, the file system or network) of the code. .NET assemblies loaded from SQL Server, however, can only be loaded from two places:

- The SQL Server database itself (user code must be cataloged and stored in the database)
- The global assembly cache (Framework class libraries, FX, only)

When CREATE ASSEMBLY is run, the code is analyzed and any outside code that it calls (dependent assemblies) is also cataloged and stored inside

SQL Server. Code location evidence means very little for SQL Server assemblies, because .NET code is never loaded from the Internet or the local file system. SQL Server enforces a stronger security policy, using HPAs as well as three levels of security that are declared when the assembly is cataloged. If SQL Server determines that the assembly contains code it shouldn't be allowed to execute, CREATE ASSEMBLY simply fails. The .NET Framework class libraries are the only code loaded from the global assembly cache, and they are subject to strong constraints, which we will discuss shortly.

Code access security enforces permission-based security through HPAs at execution time as well. With each access to any resource that requires a permission (such as a file or DNS resolver), the CAS access security inspects the call stack to ensure that every piece of code, up to the original caller, has the appropriate permission. This is known as the stack walk.

Between code analysis at create assembly time and the execution-time stack walk, the .NET code access security system and SQL Server's extensions to strengthen it ensure that no code is called that could compromise the stability and security of the system in unforeseen ways. This is a big improvement over pre–SQL Server 2005 compiled code, which consisted of extended stored procedures and COM-based components.

Code Access Security and .NET Assemblies

Because SQL Server controls assembly loading, as well as facets of .NET code execution, it can also assign a custom "safety level" to an assembly. Safety levels determine what non–SQL Server resources .NET assemblies can access. There are three safety levels: SAFE, EXTERNAL_ACCESS, and UNSAFE. These are specified on CREATE ASSEMBLY and changed by using ALTER ASSEMBLY under the control of the database administrator. The different safety levels approximately correspond to the following.

- SAFE—Can access computational .NET classes. Safety is equivalent to a T-SQL procedure.

- EXTERNAL_ACCESS—Can access all code that SAFE mode can and, in addition, items like the file system and other databases through ADO.NET. Approximately equivalent to a T-SQL procedure that can access some of the system extended stored procedures.

- UNSAFE—Can access most (but not all) code in a subset of the FX assemblies. Approximately equivalent to a user-written extended stored procedure without the bad pointer and memory buffer overflow problems.

What these different levels can do is enforced by a permission set. Each assembly author indicates which classes and methods might threaten the stability of SQL Server by decorating classes and methods with Host Protection Attributes. These Host Protection Attributes are enforced at execution time (or possibly at JIT-compile time), based on the code's security level. Because SQL Server HPAs and permission sets are documented, third-party library writers are free to instrument their libraries to be sensitive to SQL Server's permissions. Table 6-2 shows a summary of the general behavior of each of the named permission sets.

In addition, SQL Server 2005 will load only a certain subset of the Framework class libraries at runtime. The list consists of the following:

- mscorlib
- System
- System.Data
- System.Data.SqlXml
- System.Xml
- System.Security
- System.Web.Services
- Microsoft.VisualBasic
- Microsoft.VisualC
- CustomMarshalers
- System.Runtime.Remoting
- System.Runtime.Serialization.Formatters.Soap

TABLE 6-2: General Behavior of SQL Server Permission Sets

Permission Set	Guarantees against Information Leakage	Guarantees against Elevation Attack (against Malicious Code)	Guarantees for Reliability (for Nonmalicious Code)
SAFE	Yes	Yes	Yes
EXTERNAL_ACCESS	No	No	Yes
UNSAFE	No	No	No

In addition to these libraries, SQL Server 2005 may load libraries that are referenced by these libraries. For example, `System.Data.dll` may have a reference to `System.Drawing.dll`, which may be loaded, but `System.Data.dll` will be coded not to reference certain entry points in `System.Drawing.dll`. The static list of Framework class libraries is enforced at runtime rather than "catalog time;" attempting to load a library not on the list will not throw an exception at runtime.

Let's go through an example of how safety levels would work in practice. The following short program accesses a search service on the Web. This code uses `System.Web`.

```
public static String WebSearch(String subject) {
String url =
 "http://www.websearch.com/search?subject=";

//Submit Web request and get response
url = String.Concat(url, subject);
WebRequest req = WebRequest.Create(url);
WebResponse result = req.GetResponse();

Stream ReceiveStream = result.GetResponseStream();
String outstring = "";

//Load response stream into string
Byte[] read = new Byte[1024];
int bytes = ReceiveStream.Read(read, 0, 1023);

while (bytes > 0)
  {
  outstring = String.Concat(outstring,
    System.Text.Encoding.ASCII.GetString(read, 0, bytes));
  bytes = ReceiveStream.Read(read, 0, 512);
  }
return outstring;
}
```

We'll use it as part of a class that is compiled into an assembly. Now, we define the assembly to SQL Server, using two CREATE ASSEMBLY statements and two symbolic names with different safety levels.

```
-Register the unrestricted access privileged assembly
- Create assembly with external access
create assembly searchEA
from 'c:\types\searchEA.dll'
with permission_set = external_access
go
```

```
-- Create assembly without external access
create assembly searchSafe
from 'c:\types\searchSafe.dll'
with permission_set = safe
go
```

Then, use the symbolic names to define two versions of the same user-defined function.

```
-- Create function on assembly with external access
create function WebSearchEA(@sym nvarchar(10))
returns real
external name searchEA:SearchEngine::WebSearch
go
```

```
-- Create function on assembly with no external access
create function WebSearchSafe(@sym nvarchar(10))
returns real
external name searchSafe.SearchEngine.WebSearch
go
```

```
-- now, attempt to use them
declare @a REAL
```

```
-- this will work properly
SET @a = dbo.GoogleSearchEA('SQL+Server+Yukon')
PRINT @a
```

```
-- this fails with a code access security violation
SET @a = dbo.WebSearchSafe('SQL+Server+Yukon')
PRINT @a
```

What happens when a stored procedure that has limited access (SAFE) attempts to call a stored procedure that is declared as UNSAFE? Because of the way the stack walk works, this enforces security in a way that is even more restrictive than SQL Server ownership chains. Remember that an ownership chain is only checked when it is broken—that is, when the caller is not the owner of the object she attempts to access. The stack walk checks permissions all the way up the stack; failing permission at any level will cause the call to fail. Because System.Security.dll is not allowed, there is no way for an assembly to do an Assert and subvert the stack walk. This may also have some performance impact since it implies that every stack walk goes all the way up to the top. Code access security provides an additional level of security, regardless of the user principal that executes the code.

Where Are We?

In Chapter 2, we started out by declaring that the most important aspect of any database's execution was security. SQL Server 2005, as with every new version of SQL Server, includes features that make the system more secure. SQL Server 2005 mandates password policy enforcement for SQL Server–based logins, providing equivalent safety with Windows integrated logins. SQL Server 2005 metadata uses access control like the rest of SQL Server, to prohibit arbitrary access without permission. SQL Server 2005 permits procedural code to specify its execution context, making properly written dynamic SQL safer. And finally, it improves on extended stored procedures with verifiable custom hosted .NET code.

Because .NET code can not only access SQL Server objects but also call out to the .NET base class libraries, .NET code inside SQL Server is subject to three levels of checking. The base class libraries are classified to determine which are safe to use, and SQL Server will refuse to load any library deemed to be inapplicable or unsafe. .NET procedural code, including assemblies and user-defined types and aggregates, is subject to normal SQL Server user authorization checks. Finally, SQL Server defines three different security levels for .NET code that can be specified at CREATE ASSEMBLY time. Each of the base class libraries was outfitted with custom permissions that mandate what the assembly will be able to do at each level. This is enforced via .NET code access security.

▪ 7 ▪

T-SQL Enhancements

SQL SERVER 2005 includes new Transact-SQL (T-SQL) functionality. The enhancements span the range from an alternative mechanism for transaction isolation to declarative support for hierarchical queries. And statement-level recompilation even improves existing T-SQL applications that were written before 2005.

Improvements to Transact-SQL

Microsoft has continually improved the Transact SQL language and the infrastructure of SQL Server itself. In brief, the improvements include the following:

- SNAPSHOT isolation—Additional isolation level that does not use write locks
- Statement-level recompile—More efficient recompilation of stored procedures
- Event notifications—Integration of Data Definition Language (DDL) and DML operations with Service Broker
- Large data types—New data types that deprecate TEXT and IMAGE
- DDL triggers—Triggers that fire on DDL operations
- Common Table Expressions—Declarative syntax that makes a reusable expression part of a query

- Hierarchical queries—Declarative syntax for tree-based queries
- PIVOT—Declarative syntax aggregations across columns and converting columns to rows
- APPLY—New JOIN syntax made for use with user-defined functions and XML
- TOP—Row count based on an expression
- Transaction abort—TRY/CATCH syntax for handling errors

SNAPSHOT Isolation

SQL Server changes the state of a database by performing a transaction on it. Each transaction is a unit of work consisting of one or more steps. A "perfect" transaction is ACID, meaning it is atomic, consistent, isolated, and durable. In short, this means that the result of performing two transactions on a database, even if they are performed simultaneously by interleaving some of the steps that make them up, will not corrupt the database.

Atomic means that a transaction will perform all of its steps or fail and perform none of its steps. Consistent means that the transaction must not leave the results of a partial calculation in the database; for example, if a transaction is to move money from one account to another, it must not terminate after having subtracted money from one account but not having added it to another. Isolated means that none of the changes a transaction makes to a database become visible to other transactions until the transaction making the changes completes, and then they all appear simultaneously. Durable means that changes made to the database by a transaction that completes are permanent, typically by being written to a medium like a disk.

A transaction need not always be perfect. The isolation level of a transaction determines how close to perfect it is. Prior to SQL Server 2005, SQL Server provided four levels of isolation: READ UNCOMMITTED, REPEATABLE READ, READ COMMITTED, and SERIALIZABLE.

A SERIALIZABLE transaction is a perfect transaction. Functionally, a database could always use SERIALIZABLE—that is, perfect transactions, but doing so would typically adversely affect performance. Judicious use of isolation levels other than SERIALIZABLE, when analysis of an application shows that it does not require perfect transactions, will improve performance in these cases.

SQL Server uses the isolation level of a transaction to control concurrent access to data through a set of read and write locks. It applies these locks pessimistically; that is, they physically prevent any access to data that might compromise the required isolation level. In some cases, this will delay a transaction as it waits for a lock to be freed, or may even cause it to fail because of a timeout waiting for the lock.

SQL Server 2005 adds SNAPSHOT isolation that, in effect, provides alternate implementations of SERIALIZABLE and READ COMMITTED levels of isolation that use optimistic locking to control concurrent access rather than pessimistic locking. For some applications, SNAPSHOT isolation may provide better performance than pre–SQL Server 2005 implementations did. In addition, SNAPSHOT isolation makes it much easier to port database applications to SQL Server from database engines that make extensive use of SNAPSHOT isolation.

SQL Server 2005 has two kinds of SNAPSHOT isolation: transaction-level and statement level. Transaction-level SNAPSHOT isolation makes transactions perfect, the same as SERIALIZABLE does. Statement-level SNAPSHOT isolation makes transactions that have the same degree of isolation as READ COMMITTED does.

The transaction-level SNAPSHOT isolation optimistically assumes that if a transaction operates on an image of that database's committed data when the transaction started, the result will be the same as a transaction run at the SERIALIZABLE isolation level. Some time before the transaction completes, the optimistic assumption is tested, and if it proves not to be true, the transaction is rolled back.

Transaction-level SNAPSHOT isolation works by, in effect, making a version of the database by taking a snapshot of it when a transaction starts. Figure 7-1 shows this.

There are three transactions in Figure 7-1: transaction 1, transaction 2, and transaction 3. When transaction 1 starts, it is given a snapshot of the initial database. Transaction 2 starts before transaction 1 finishes, so it is also given a snapshot of the initial database. Transaction 3 starts after transaction 1 finishes but before transaction 2 does. Transaction 3 is given a snapshot of the initial database plus all the changes committed by transaction 1.

The result of using SERIALIZABLE or transaction-level SNAPSHOT isolation is the same; some transactions will fail and have to be retried, and may fail again, but the integrity of the database is always guaranteed.

Of course, SQL Server can't actually make a snapshot of the entire database, but it gets that effect by keeping track of each change to the database until all transactions that were started before the change was made are completed. This technique is called *row versioning*.

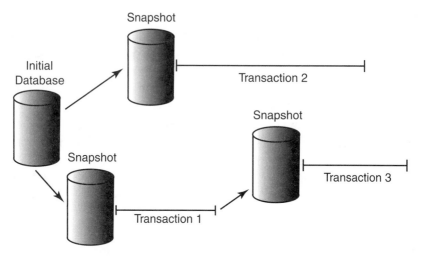

FIGURE 7-1: Snapshot Versioning

The row versioning model is built upon having multiple copies of the data. When reading data, the read happens against the copy, and no locks are held. When writing the data, the write happens against the "real" data, and it is protected with a write lock. For example, in a system implementing row versioning, user A starts a transaction and updates a column in a row. Before the transaction is committed, user B wants to read the same column in the same row. He is allowed to do the read but will read an older value. This is not the value that A is in the process of updating to, but the value A is updating from.

In statement-level SNAPSHOT isolation, the reader always reads the last committed value of a given row, just as READ COMMITTED does in a versioning database. Let's say we have a single-row table (called tab) with two columns: ID and name. Table 7-1 shows a versioning database at READ COMMITTED isolation.

The other transaction isolation level in a versioning database, SERIALIZABLE, is always implemented by the behavior that the reader always reads the row as of the beginning of the transaction, regardless of whether other users' changes are committed during the duration of the transaction or not. This was shown qualitatively in Figure 7-1. Table 7-2 shows a specific example of how two transactions interoperate when the SERIALIZABLE level of SNAPSHOT isolation is used.

The difference between this table and Table 7-1 occurs at step 5. Even though user 2 has updated a row and committed the update, user 1, using the SERIALIZABLE transaction isolation level, does not "see" the

TABLE 7-1: Versioning Database at READ COMMITTED Isolation

Step	User 1	User 2
1	BEGIN TRAN SELECT name FROM tab WHERE id = 1 **value is 'Name'	
2		BEGIN TRAN UPDATE tab SET name = 'Newname' WHERE id = 1
3	SELECT name FROM tab WHERE id = 1 **value is 'Name'	
4		COMMIT
5	SELECT name FROM tab WHERE id = 1 **value is 'NewName'	
6	COMMIT	
7	SELECT name FROM tab WHERE id = 1 **value is 'NewName'	

next value until user 1 commits his transaction. He sees the new value only in step 7. In SQL Server this is called "transaction-level SNAPSHOT isolation."

Both statement- and transaction-level SNAPSHOT isolation require that SNAPSHOT be enabled by using the SNAPSHOT isolation option of the ALTER DATABASE command. The following SQL batch does this for the pubs database.

```
ALTER DATABASE pubs
SET ALLOW_SNAPSHOT_ISOLATION ON
```

SNAPSHOT isolation can be turned on or off as needed.

Once SNAPSHOT isolation has been enabled, transaction-level isolation is used by specifically setting the transaction isolation level to SNAPSHOT. The following SQL batch does this.

TABLE 7-2: Versioning Database at SERIALIZABLE Isolation

Step	User 1	User 2
1	BEGIN TRAN SELECT name FROM tab WHERE id = 1 **value is 'Name'	
2		BEGIN TRAN UPDATE tab SET name = 'Newname' WHERE id = 1
3	SELECT name FROM tab WHERE id = 1 **value is 'Name'	
4		COMMIT
5	SELECT name FROM tab WHERE id = 1 **value is 'Name'	
6	COMMIT	
7	SELECT name FROM tab WHERE id = 1 **value is 'NewName'	

```
ALTER DATABASE pubs
SET ALLOW_SNAPSHOT_ISOLATION ON
GO
USE pubs
GO
SET TRANSACTION ISOLATION LEVEL SNAPSHOT
BEGIN TRANS
 - SQL Expressions
COMMIT TRANS
```

The SQL expression in the preceding batch will be executed, in effect, against a snapshot of the database that was taken when BEGIN TRANS was executed.

Statement-level SNAPSHOT isolation requires the use of an additional database option, READ_COMMITTED_SNAPSHOT. If this database option and ALLOW_SNAPSHOT_ISOLATION are ON, all transactions done at the READ UNCOMMITTED or READ COMMITTED levels will be executed as READ COMMITTED–level transactions using versioning instead of locking. Both transactions shown in the SQL batch that follows will be executed as READ COMMITTED using versioning.

```
- alter the database
ALTER DATABASE pubs
SET ALLOW_SNAPSHOT_ISOLATION ON
SET READ_COMMITTED_SNAPSHOT ON
GO
USE pubs
GO
SET TRANSACTION ISOLATION LEVEL READ UNCOMMITTED
BEGIN TRAN
- SQL expression will be executed as READ COMMITTED using versioning
END TRAN
SET TRANSACTION ISOLATION LEVEL READ COMMITTED
BEGIN TRAN
- SQL expression will be executed as READ COMMITTED using versioning
END TRAN
```

Whether ALLOW_SNAPSHOT_ISOLATION is ON or not can be checked for a particular database by the DATABASEPROPERTYEX command. This command returns the current database option or setting for a particular database. The setting to check is the SnapshotIsolationFramework setting, as in following code for the pubs database:

```
SELECT DATABASEPROPERTYEX ('pubs', 'SnapshotIsolationFramework')
```

As stated earlier, SQL Server does not actually make a copy of a database when a SNAPSHOT transaction is started. Whenever a record is updated, SQL Server stores in TEMPDB a copy (version) of the previously committed value and maintains these changes. All the versions of a record are marked with a timestamp of the transactions that made the change, and the versions are chained in TEMPDB using a linked list. The newest record value is stored in a database page and linked to the version store in TEMPDB. For read access in a SNAPSHOT isolation transaction, SQL Server first accesses from the data page the last committed record. It then retrieves the record value from the version store by traversing the chain of pointers to the specific record version of the data.

The code in Table 7-3 shows an example of how SNAPSHOT isolation works. The example uses a table, snapTest, looking like this.

```
-it is necessary to run
-SET ALLOW_SNAPSHOT_ISOLATION ON
-if that's not done already
```

```
CREATE TABLE snapTest ([id] INT IDENTITY,
                       col1 VARCHAR(15))

--insert some data
INSERT INTO snapTest VALUES(1,'Niels')
```

TABLE 7-3: Example of SNAPSHOT Isolation

Step	User 1	User 2
1	SET TRANSACTION ISOLATION LEVEL SNAPSHOT BEGIN TRAN UPDATE snapTest SET col1 = 'NewNiels' WHERE id = 1	
2		SET TRANSACTION ISOLATION LEVEL SNAPSHOT BEGIN TRAN SELECT col1 FROM snapTest WHERE id = 1 ** receives value 'Niels'
3	COMMIT TRAN	
4		SELECT col1 FROM snapTest WHERE id = 1 ** receives value 'Niels'
5		COMMIT TRAN
6		SELECT col1 FROM snapTest WHERE id = 1 ** receives value 'NewNiels'

The steps in Table 7-3 do the following:

1. We start a transaction under SNAPSHOT isolation and update one column in one row. This causes SQL Server to store a copy of the original value in TEMPDB. Notice that we do not commit or roll back at this stage, so locks are held. If we were to run sp_lock, we would see an exclusive lock on the primary key.

2. We start a new transaction under a new session and try to read from the same row that is being updated at the moment. This is the row with an exclusive lock. If this had been previous versions of SQL Server (running under at least READ COMMITTED), we would be locked out. However, running in SNAPSHOT mode, SQL Server looks in the version store in TEMPDB to retrieve the latest committed value and returns "Niels".

3. We commit the transaction, so the value is updated in the database and another version is put into the version store.

4. User 2 does a new SELECT (from within his original transaction) and will now receive the original value, "Niels".

5. User 2 finally commits the transaction.

6. User 2 does a new SELECT (after his transaction commits) and will now receive the new value, "NewNiels".

SNAPSHOT isolation is useful for converting an application written for a versioning database to SQL Server. When an application is developed for a versioning database, the developer does not need to be concerned with locking. Converting such an application to SQL Server may result in diminished performance because more locking is done than is required. Prior to SQL Server 2005, this sort of conversion may have required rewriting the application. In version 2005, in many cases the only thing that will have to be done is to enable SNAPSHOT isolation and READ_COMMITTED_SNAPSHOT.

SNAPSHOT isolation is also beneficial for applications that mostly read and do few updates. It is also interesting to note that when SQL Server 2005 is installed, versioning is enabled in the MASTER and MSDB databases by default.

Drawbacks of Versioning

Versioning has the capability to increase concurrency but does come with a few drawbacks of its own. Before you write new applications to use versioning, you should be aware of these drawbacks. You can then assess the value of locking against the convenience of versioning.

It can be costly because record versions need to be maintained even if no read operations are executing. This has the capability of filling up TEMPDB. If a database is set up for versioning, versions are kept in TEMPDB whether or not anyone is running a SNAPSHOT isolation–level transaction. Although a "garbage collector" algorithm will analyze the older versioning transaction and clean up TEMPDB eventually, you have no control over how often that cleanup in done. Plan the size of TEMPDB accordingly; it is used to keep versions for all databases with SNAPSHOT enabled. If you run out of space in TEMPDB, long-running transactions may fail.

In addition, reading data will sometimes cost more because of the need to traverse the version list. If you are doing versioning at the READ COMMITTED isolation level, the database may have to start at the beginning of the version list and read through it to attempt to read the last committed version.

There is also the possibility of update concurrency problems. Let's suppose that in Table 7-1 user 1 decides to update the row also. Table 7-4 shows how this would look.

In this scenario, user 1 reads the value "Name" and may base his update on that value. If user 2 commits his transaction before user 1 commits his, and user 1 tries to update, he bases his update on possibly bad data (the old value he read in step 1). Rather than allowing this to happen, versioning databases produce an error. The error message in this case is as follows:

```
Msg 3960, Level 16, State 1, Line 1. Cannot use snapshot isolation
to access table 'tab' in database 'pubs'. Snapshot transaction aborted
due to update conflict. Retry transaction.
```

Obviously, retrying transactions often enough will slow down the overall throughput of the application. In addition, the window of time for a concurrency violation to occur increases the longer a transaction reads old values. Because, at the SERIALIZABLE isolation level, the user always reads the old value until he commits the transaction, the window is much bigger—that is, concurrency violations are statistically much more likely to occur. In fact, vendors of versioning databases recommend against

SNAPSHOT ISOLATION ■ 221

TABLE 7-4: Versioning Database at SERIALIZABLE Isolation—Concurrent Updates

Step	User 1	User 2
1	BEGIN TRAN SELECT name FROM tab WHERE id = 1 **value is 'Name'	
2		BEGIN TRAN UPDATE tab SET name = 'Newname' WHERE id = 1
3		COMMIT
4	UPDATE tab SET name = 'Another name' WHERE id = 1 ** produces concurrency violation	
5	ROLLBACK (and try update again?)	

using SERIALIZABLE isolation (SQL Server ISOLATION LEVEL SNAPSHOT) in most cases. READ COMMITTED is a better choice with versioning.

Finally, as we said before, in versioning databases reads don't lock writes, which might be what we want. Is this possible with a versioning database? Locking-database programmers, when using versioning, tend to lock too little, introducing subtle concurrency problems. In a versioning database, there must be a way to do insist on a lock on read. Ordinarily this is done by doing a SQL SELECT FOR UPDATE. But SQL Server does not support SELECT FOR UPDATE with the appropriate semantic. There is, however, a solution. Even when READ_COMMITTED_SNAPSHOT is on, you can ensure a read lock by using SQL Server's REPEATABLE READ isolation level, which never does versioning. The SQL Server equivalent of ANSI's SELECT FOR UPDATE is SELECT with (REPEATABLEREAD). Note that this is different from the SQL Server UPDLOCK (update lock), which is a special lock that has similar semantics but only works if all participants in all transactions are using UPDLOCK. This is one place where programs written for versioning databases may have to change their code in porting to SQL Server 2005.

Monitoring Versioning

Allowing versioning to achieve concurrency is a major change. We've already seen how it can affect monitoring and capacity planning for TEMPDB. Therefore, all the tools and techniques that we've used in the past must be updated to account for this new concurrency style. Here are some of the enhancements that make this possible.

There are the following new T-SQL properties and metadata views:

- DATABASEPROPERTYEX—Tells us if SNAPSHOT is on
- sys.fn_top_version_generators()—Tables with most versions
- sys.fn_transaction_snapshot()—Transaction active when a SNAPSHOT transaction starts
- sys.fn_transactions()—Includes information about SNAPSHOT transaction (or not), if SNAPSHOT includes information about version chains and SNAPSHOT timestamps

There are new performance monitor counters for the following:

- Average version store data-generation rate (kilobytes per minute)
- Size of current version store (kilobytes)
- Free space in TEMPDB (kilobytes)
- Space used in the version store for each database (kilobytes)
- Longest running time in any SNAPSHOT transaction (seconds)

SNAPSHOT isolation information is also available during event tracing. Because a SNAPSHOT transaction has to be aware of any updates committed by other users, other users' updates appear in SQL Profiler while tracing a SNAPSHOT isolation transaction. Beware, since this can significantly increase the amount of data collected by Profiler.

Statement-Level Recompilation

The next thing we'll look at is a performance enhancement that is part of the infrastructural improvements in T-SQL: statement recompilation. In SQL Server 2000, the query plan architecture differs from previous versions, and it is divided into two structures: a compiled plan and an executable plan.

- Compiled plan (a.k.a. query plan)—A read-only data structure used by any number of users. The plan is reentrant, which implies that all users share the plan and no user context information (such as data variable values) is stored in the compiled plan. There are never more than one or two copies of the query plan in memory—one copy for all serial executions and another for all parallel executions.

- Executable plan—A data structure for each user that concurrently executes the query. This data structure, which is called the executable plan or execution context, holds the data specific to each user's execution, such as parameter values.

This architecture, paired with the fact that the execution context is reused, has very much improved the execution of not only stored procedures but functions, batches, dynamic queries, and so on. However, there is a common problem with executing stored procedures, and that is recompilation. Examples of things that cause recompilation to occur are as follows:

- Schema changes
- Threshold changes in rows
- Certain SET options

A recompilation can incur a huge cost especially if the procedure, function, or batch is large, because SQL Server 2000 does module-level recompilation. In other words, the whole procedure is recompiled even if the cause of the recompilation affects only a small portion of the procedure. In addition, if the recompilation happens because a SET option changes, the executable plan will be invalidated and not cached. The code in Listing 7-1 is extremely simple, but it can be used to illustrate the problem.

Listing 7-1 is a stored procedure which in the middle of the procedure changes the CONCAT_NULL_YIELDS_NULL option. When this runs against SQL Server 2000, a recompilation happens for each execution of the procedure.

LISTING 7-1: Procedure That Causes Recompilation

```
CREATE PROCEDURE test2
AS

SELECT 'before set option'
```

```
-//change a set option
SET CONCAT_NULL_YIELDS_NULL OFF

SELECT 'after set option'
```

To verify that recompilation happens on SQL Server 2000, do the following:

1. Catalog the procedure in Listing 7-1.
2. Open the SQL Server Profiler and from the File menu, select New | Trace.
3. When the Trace Properties dialog comes up, choose the Events tab.
4. In the Stored Procedures event group, choose the SP:Recompile event, click the Add button, as shown in Figure 7-2, and then click Run.

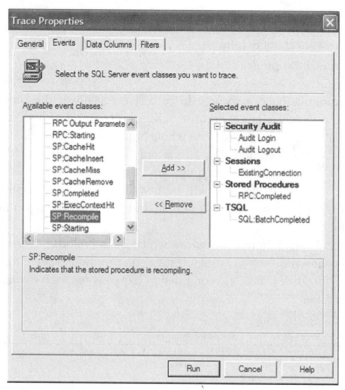

FIGURE 7-2: Trace Properties Dialog for SQL Profiler

5. Execute the procedure a couple of times from Query Analyzer and view the trace output.

6. The output from the trace will show a couple of entries in the Event Class column with the value of SP:Recompile, as in Figure 7-3. This indicates that the procedure has been recompiled.

As mentioned before, the cost of recompilation can be very high for large procedures, and in the SQL Server 2005 release, Microsoft has changed the model to statement-level re-compilation. At this stage you may worry that performance will suffer if each statement in a procedure is individually recompiled. Rest assured that the initial compilation is still on the module level, so only if a recompile is needed is it done per statement.

Another performance benefit in SQL Server 2005 is the fact that when statement recompilation is done, the execution context will not be invalidated. The procedure in Listing 7-1 can be used in SQL Server 2005 to compare the differences between SQL Server 2000 and 2005. In SQL Server 2005, follow the steps listed earlier and notice in the trace how a recompile happens only the first time; for each subsequent execution, there is no recompile. This is due to the fact that an execution plan will be created after the initial recompile. Run the following code after you have executed the procedure a couple of times, and notice that the result you get consists of both a compiled plan and an executable plan.

```
SELECT * FROM syscacheobjects
WHERE dbid = db_id('pubs')
AND objid = object_id('test2')
```

FIGURE 7-3: Trace Output

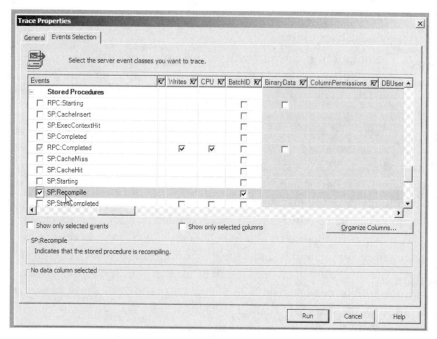

FIGURE 7-4: Trace Properties Dialog in SQL Server 2005

To be certain that you get the correct result, you can clean out the cache before you execute the procedure by executing dbcc freeproccache.

When setting up the trace, you will see how the SQL Profiler allows you to trace more events than in SQL Server 2000. Figure 7-4 shows the Events Selection tab from the Trace Properties dialog.

As mentioned in the beginning of this chapter, the statement-level recompilation can be seen as a purely infrastructural enhancement. As a developer or DBA, you will not explicitly use it even though you implicitly benefit from it, and it may change the way you develop stored procedures. No longer do recompiles have as much of a negative impact on performance.

DDL Triggers

A trigger is a block of SQL statements that are executed based on the fact that there has been an alteration (INSERT, UPDATE, or DELETE) to a table or on a view. In previous versions of SQL Server, the statements had to be written in T-SQL, but in version 2005, as we saw in Chapter 3, they can also be written using .NET languages. As we mentioned, the triggers are fired based on action statements (DML) in the database.

What about changes based on Data Definition Language statements, changes to the schema of a database or database server? It has not been possible to use triggers for that purpose—that is, until SQL Server 2005. In SQL Server 2005 you can create triggers for DDL statements as well as DML.

The syntax for creating a trigger for a DDL statement is shown in Listing 7-2, and as with a DML trigger, DDL triggers can be written using .NET languages as well.

LISTING 7-2: Syntax for a DDL Trigger

```
CREATE TRIGGER trigger_name
ON { ALL SERVER | DATABASE }
[ WITH ENCRYPTION ]
{ FOR | AFTER } { event_type [ ,...n ] | DDL_DATABASE_LEVEL_EVENTS }
    [ WITH APPEND ]
    [ NOT FOR REPLICATION ]
{ AS
    { sql_statement [ ...n ] | EXTERNAL NAME < method specifier > }
}
< method_specifier > ::=
    assembly_name:class_name[::method_name]
```

The syntax for a DML trigger is almost identical to that for a DDL trigger. There are, however, some differences.

* The ON clause in a DDL trigger refers to either the scope of the whole database server (ALL SERVER) or the current database (DATABASE).
* A DDL trigger cannot be an INSTEAD OF trigger.
* The event for which the trigger fires is defined in the event_type argument, which for several events is a comma-delimited list. Alternatively, you can use the blanket argument DDL_DATABASE_LEVEL_EVENTS.

The SQL Server Books Online has the full list of DDL statements, which can be used in the event_type argument and also by default are included in the DDL_DATABASE_LEVEL_EVENTS. A typical use of DDL triggers is for auditing and logging. The following code shows a simple example where we create a trigger that writes to a log table.

```
-first create a table to log to
CREATE TABLE ddlLog (id INT PRIMARY KEY IDENTITY,
    logTxt VARCHAR(MAX))
GO
```

```
-create our test table
CREATE TABLE triTest (id INT PRIMARY KEY)
GO

- create the trigger
CREATE TRIGGER ddlTri
ON DATABASE
AFTER DROP_TABLE
AS
INSERT INTO ddlLog VALUES('table dropped')
```

You may wonder what the VARCHAR(MAX) is all about in creating the first table—we'll cover that later in this chapter. The trigger is created with a scope of the local database (ON DATABASE), and it fires as soon as a table is dropped in that database (ON DROP_TABLE). Run following code to see the trigger in action.

```
DROP TABLE triTest
SELECT * FROM ddlLog
```

The DROP TABLE command fires the trigger and inserts one record in the ddlLog table, which is retrieved by the SELECT command.

As mentioned previously, DDL triggers can be very useful for logging and auditing. However, we do not get very much information from the trigger we just created. In DML triggers, we have the inserted and deleted tables, which allow us to get information about the data affected by the trigger. So, clearly, we need a way to get more information about events when a DDL trigger fires. The way to do that is through the event data function.

Eventdata

The eventdata() function returns information about what event fired a specific DDL trigger. The return value of the function is XML, and the XML is typed to a particular schema (XSD). Depending on the event type, the XSD includes different information. The following four items, however, are included for any event type:

- The time of the event
- The SPID of the connection that caused the trigger to fire
- The login name and user name of the user who executed the statement
- The type of the event

The additional information included in the result from `eventdata` is covered in SQL Server Books Online, so we will not go through each item here. However, for our trigger, which fires on the `DROP TABLE` command, the additional information items are as follows:

- Database
- Schema
- Object
- ObjectType
- TSQLCommand

In Listing 7-3 we change the trigger to insert the information from the `eventdata` function into the `ddlLog` table. Additionally, we change the trigger to fire on all DDL events.

LISTING 7-3: Alter Trigger to Use eventdata

```
- alter the trigger
ALTER TRIGGER ddlTri
ON DATABASE
AFTER DDL_DATABASE_LEVEL_EVENTS
AS
INSERT INTO ddlLog VALUES CONVERT(VARCHAR(max)eventdata())
```

From the following code, we get the output in Listing 7-4.

```
-delete all entries in ddlLog
DELETE ddlLog

-create a new table
CREATE TABLE evtTest (id INT PRIMARY KEY)

-select the logTxt column with the XML
SELECT logTxt
FROM ddlLog
```

LISTING 7-4: Output from eventdata

```
<EVENT_INSTANCE>
  <PostTime>2004-01-30T11:58:47.217</PostTime>
  <SPID>57</SPID>
  <EventType>CREATE_TABLE</EventType>
  <ServerName>ZMV44</ServerName>
  <LoginName>ZMV44\Administrator</LoginName>
  <UserName>ZMV44\Administrator</UserName>
```

```
<DatabaseName>pubs</DatabaseName>
<SchemaName>dbo</SchemaName>
<ObjectName>foo</ObjectName>
<ObjectType>TABLE</ObjectType>
<TSQLCommand>
  <SetOptions ANSI_NULLS="ON" ANSI_NULL_DEFAULT="ON"
   ANSI_PADDING="ON" QUOTED_IDENTIFIER="ON"
   ENCRYPTED="FALSE" />
  <CommandText>
    CREATE TABLE evtTest (id int primary key)
  </CommandText>
</TSQLCommand>
</EVENT_INSTANCE>
```

Because the data returned from the function is XML, we can use XQuery queries to retrieve specific item information. This can be done both in the trigger and from the table where we store the data. The following code illustrates how to retrieve information about the EventType, Object, and CommandText items in the eventdata information stored in the table ddlLog. Notice that we first store it into an XML data type variable, before we execute the XQuery statement against it.

```
DECLARE @data XML
SELECT @data = logTxt FROM ddlLog
WHERE id = 11

SELECT
CONVERT(NVARCHAR(100),
@data.query('data(//EventType)')) EventType,
CONVERT(NVARCHAR(100),
@data.query('data(//Object)')) Object,
CONVERT(NVARCHAR(100),
@data.query('data(//TSQLCommand/CommandText)')) Command
```

If the syntax in the previous code snippet seems strange, that's because it is XML and XQuery; read Chapters 8 and 9, where the XML data type and XQuery are covered in detail.

The programming model for both DML and DDL triggers is a synchronous model, which serves well when the processing that the trigger does is relatively short-running. This is necessary because DDL and DML triggers can be used to enforce rules and can roll back transactions if these rules are violated. If the trigger needs to do longer-running processing tasks, the scalability inevitably suffers. Bearing this in mind, we can see that for certain tasks, it would be beneficial to have an asynchronous event model. Therefore, in SQL Server 2005 Microsoft has included a new event notification model that works asynchronously: *event notifications*.

Event Notifications

Event notifications differ from triggers by the fact that the actual notification does not execute any code. Instead, information about the event is posted to a SQL Server Service Broker (SSB) service and is placed on a message queue from where it can be read by some other process.[1] Another difference between triggers and event notifications is that the event notifications execute in response to not only DDL and DML statements but also some trace events.

The syntax for creating an event notification is as follows.

```
CREATE EVENT NOTIFICATION event_notification_name
ON { SERVER | DATABASE |
[ ENABLED | DISABLED ]
{ FOR { event_type |
    DDL_DATABASE_LEVEL_EVENTS } [ ,...n ]
TO broker_service
```

The syntax looks a little like the syntax for creating a DDL trigger, and the arguments are as follows.

- `event_notification_name`—This is the name of the event notification.
- `SERVER`—The scope of the event notification is the current server.
- `DATABASE`—The scope of the event notification is the current database.
- `ENABLED`—This specifies that the event notification is active when the `CREATE` statement has executed.
- `DISABLED`—This specifies that the event notification is inactive until the notification is activated by executing an `ALTER EVENT NOTIFICATION` statement.

---

[1] SQL Server Service Broker is a new technology in SQL Server 2005 that facilitates sending messages in a secure and reliable way. It is covered in Chapter 15.

- event_type—This is the name of an event that, after execution, causes the event notification to execute. SQL Server Books Online has the full list of events included in event_type.

- DDL_DATABASE_LEVEL_EVENTS—The event notification fires after any of the CREATE, ALTER, or DROP statements that can be indicated in event_type execute.

- broker_service—This is the SSB service to which SQL Server posts the data about an event.

The event notification contains the same information received from the eventdata function mentioned previously. When the event notification fires, the notification mechanism executes the eventdata function and posts the information to the Service Broker. For an event notification to be created, an existing SQL Server Service Broker instance needs to be located either locally or remotely. The steps to create the SQL Server Service Broker are shown in Listing 7-5. Chapter 15 covers SSB in detail and also covers how to create queues, services, and so on.

LISTING 7-5: Steps to Create a Service Broker Instance

```
--first we need a queue
CREATE QUEUE queue evtDdlNotif
WITH STATUS = ON

--then we can create the service
CREATE SERVICE evtDdlService
ON QUEUE evtDdlNotif
 --this is a MS supplied contract
 --which uses an existing message type
 -{http://schemas.microsoft.com/SQL/Notifications}EventNotification
(http://schemas.microsoft.com/SQL/Notifications/PostEventNotification)
```

First, the message queue that will hold the eventdata information is created. Typically, another process listens for incoming messages on this queue, or another process will kick off when a message arrives. A service is then built on the queue. When a SQL Server Service Broker service is created, there needs to be a contract to indicate what types of messages this service understands. In a SQL Server Service Broker application, the developer usually defines message types and contracts based on the application's requirements. For event notifications, however, Microsoft has a predefined message type, {http://schemas.microsoft.com/SQL/Notifications}EventNotification, and a contract, http://schemas.microsoft.com/SQL/Notifications/PostEventNotification.

The following code shows how to create an event notification for DDL events scoped to the local database, sending the notifications to the evt DdlService.

```
CREATE EVENT NOTIFICATION ddlEvents
ON DATABASE
FOR DDL_DATABASE_LEVEL_EVENTS
TO SERVICE evtDdlService
```

With both the event notification and the service in place, a new process can now be started in SQL Server Management Studio, using the WAITFOR and RECEIVE statements (more about this in Chapter 15) as in the following code.

```
WAITFOR(
RECEIVE * FROM evtDdlNotif
)
```

You can now execute a DDL statement, and then switch to the process with the WAITFOR statement and view the result. Running CREATE TABLE evtNotifTbl (id INT) shows in the WAITFOR process a two-row resultset, where one of the rows has a message_type_id of 20. This is the {http://schemas.microsoft.com/SQL/Notifications}EventNotification message type. The eventdata information is stored as a binary value in the message_body column. To see the actual data, we need to change the WAITFOR statement a little bit.

```
DECLARE @msgtypeid INT
DECLARE @msg VARBINARY(MAX)

WAITFOR(
RECEIVE TOP(1)
@msgtypeid = message_type_id,
@msg = message_body
FROM evtDdlNotif
)
 -check if this is the correct message type
IF @msgtypeid = 20
```

```
BEGIN
 -do something useful WITH the message
 -here we just select it as a result
 SELECT CONVERT(NVARCHAR(MAX), @msg)
 END
```

Running this code against the CREATE TABLE statement shown earlier produces the same output as in Listing 7-4. An additional benefit with event notifications is that they can be used for both system level and trace events in addition to DDL events. The following code shows how to create an event notification for SQL Server logins.

```
CREATE EVENT NOTIFICATION loginEvents ON SERVER
FOR audit_login TO SERVICE evtLoginService
```

For system-level event notifications, the ON SERVER keyword needs to be explicitly specified; it cannot be used at the database level. Listing 7-6 shows the eventdata information received after executing a login.

LISTING 7-6: eventdata Output from Login

```
<EVENT_INSTANCE>
 <PostTime>2003-06-29T09:46:23.623</PostTime>
 <SPID>51</SPID>
 <EventType>AUDIT_LOGIN</EventType>
 <ServerName>ZMV44</ServerName>
 <LoginName>ZMV44\Administrator</LoginName>
 <UserName>ZMV44\Administrator</UserName>
 <Database>eventstest</Database>
 <! - additional information elided  ->
</EVENT_INSTANCE>
```

You may wonder what happens if the transaction that caused the notification is rolled back. In that case, the posting of the notification is rolled back as well. If for some reason the delivery of a notification fails, the original transaction is not affected.

Some of the previous code examples have used VARCHAR(MAX) as the data type for a column. Let's look at what that is all about.

Large Value Data Types

In SQL Server 2000 (and 7) the maximum size for VARCHAR and VARBINARY was 8,000 and for NVARCHAR 4,000. If you had data that potentially exceeded that size, you needed to use the TEXT, NTEXT, or IMAGE data types (known as Large Object data types, or LOBs). This was always a hassle because they were hard to work with, in both retrieval and action statements.

This situation changes in SQL Server 2005 with the introduction of the MAX specifier. This specifier allows storage of up to 2^{31} bytes of data, and for Unicode it is 2^{30} characters. When you use the VARCHAR(MAX) or NVARCHAR(MAX) data type, the data is stored as character strings, whereas for VARBINARY(MAX) it is stored as bytes. These three data types are commonly known as Large Value data types. The following code shows the use of these data types in action.

```
CREATE TABLE largeValues (
   lVarchar VARCHAR(MAX),
   lnVarchar NVARCHAR(MAX),
   lVarbinary VARBINARY(MAX)
)
```

We mentioned earlier that LOBs are hard to work with. Additionally, they cannot, for example, be used as variables in a procedure or a function. The Large Value data types do not have these restrictions, as we can see in the following code snippet, which shows a Large Value data type being a parameter in a function. It also shows how the data type can be concatenated.

```
CREATE FUNCTION dovmax(@in VARCHAR(MAX))
RETURNS VARCHAR(MAX)
AS
BEGIN
 - supports concatenation
RETURN @in + '12345'
END
```

SQL Server's string handling functions can be used on VARCHAR(MAX) and NVARCHAR(MAX) columns. So instead of having to read in the whole amount of data, SUBSTRING can be used. By storing the data as character strings (or bytes), the Large Value data types are similar in behavior to their smaller counterparts VARCHAR, NVARCHAR, and VARBINARY, and offer a consistent programming model. Using the Large Value data types instead of LOBs is recommended; in fact, the LOBs are being deprecated.

When we first came across the enhanced size of the VARCHAR data type in SQL Server 7 (from 256 to 8,000), we thought, "Great, we can now have a table with several VARCHAR columns with the size of 8,000 instead of a text column." You probably know that this doesn't work, because in SQL Server 7 and 2000, you cannot have a row exceeding 8,060 bytes, the size of a page. In SQL Server 2005 this has changed as well, and a row can now span several pages.

T-SQL Language Enhancements

Even though this book is much about the CLR and outside access to SQL Server, let's not forget that Microsoft has enhanced the T-SQL language a lot in SQL Server 2005. In this section, we will look at some of the improvements.

TOP

TOP was introduced in SQL Server 7. Until SQL Server 2005, the TOP clause allowed the user to specify the number or percent of rows to be returned in a SELECT statement. In SQL Server 2005, the TOP clause can be used also for INSERT, UPDATE, and DELETE (in addition to SELECT), and the syntax is as follows: TOP (expression) [PERCENT]. Notice the parentheses around the expression; this is required when TOP is used for UPDATE, INSERT, and DELETE.

The following code shows some examples of using TOP.

```
--create a table and insert some data
CREATE TABLE toptest (col1 VARCHAR(150))
INSERT INTO toptest VALUES('Niels1')
INSERT INTO toptest VALUES('Niels2')
INSERT INTO toptest VALUES('Niels3')
INSERT INTO toptest VALUES('Niels4')
INSERT INTO toptest VALUES('Niels5')

--this returns 'Niels1' and 'Niels2'
SELECT TOP(2) * FROM toptest

--this sets 'Niels1' and 'Niels2' to 'hi'
UPDATE TOP(2) toptest SET col1 = 'hi'
SELECT * FROM toptest

--the two rows with 'hi' are deleted
DELETE TOP(2) toptest
SELECT * FROM toptest

--create a new table and insert some data
CREATE TABLE toptest2 (col1 VARCHAR(150))
```

```
INSERT INTO toptest2 VALUES('Niels1')
INSERT INTO toptest2 VALUES('Niels2')
INSERT INTO toptest2 VALUES('Niels3')
INSERT INTO toptest2 VALUES('Niels4')
INSERT INTO toptest2 VALUES('Niels5')

-'Niels1' and 'Niels2' are inserted
INSERT top(2) toptest
SELECT * FROM toptest2

SELECT * FROM toptest
```

An additional difference between the TOP clause in previous versions of SQL Server and in SQL Server 2005 is that we now can use expressions for number definition. The following code shows a couple of examples of that (it uses the tables from the preceding example).

```
-declare 3 variables
DECLARE @a INT
DECLARE @b INT
DECLARE @c INT

-set values
SET @a = 10
SET @b = 5
SELECT @c = @a/@b

-use the calculated expression
SELECT TOP(@c)* FROM toptest

-insert some more data in toptest
INSERT INTO toptest VALUES('Niels6')
INSERT INTO toptest VALUES('Niels7')
INSERT INTO toptest VALUES('Niels8')

-use a SELECT statement as expression
-this should return 5 rows
SELECT TOP(SELECT COUNT(*) FROM toptest2) *
FROM toptest
```

The next T-SQL enhancement we'll look at is something completely new in SQL Server: the OUTPUT clause.

OUTPUT

The execution of a DML statement such as INSERT, UPDATE, or DELETE does not produce any results that indicate what was changed. Prior to SQL Server 2005, an extra round trip to the database was required to determine the changes. In SQL Server 2005 the INSERT, UPDATE, and DELETE statements have been enhanced to support an OUTPUT clause so that a single round trip is all that is required to modify the database and determine what changed. You use the OUTPUT clause together with the inserted and deleted virtual tables, much as in a trigger. The OUTPUT clause must be used with an INTO expression to fill a table. Typically, this will be a table variable. The following example creates a table, inserts some data, and finally deletes some records.

```
--create table and insert data
CREATE TABLE outputtbl
(id INT IDENTITY, col1 VARCHAR(15))
go

INSERT INTO outputtbl VALUES('row1')
INSERT INTO outputtbl VALUES ('row2')
INSERT INTO outputtbl VALUES ('row5')
INSERT INTO outputtbl VALUES ('row6')
INSERT INTO outputtbl VALUES ('row7')
INSERT INTO outputtbl VALUES ('row8')
INSERT INTO outputtbl VALUES ('row9')
INSERT INTO outputtbl VALUES ('row10')

- make a table variable to hold the results of the OUTPUT clause
DECLARE @del AS TABLE (deletedId INT, deletedValue VARCHAR(15))
--delete two rows and return through
--the output clause
DELETE outputtbl
OUTPUT DELETED.id, DELETED.col1 INTO @del
WHERE id < 3
SELECT * FROM @del
GO
deletedId    deletedValue
- - - - -- - - - - - - - --
1            row1
2            row2

(2 row(s) affected)
```

The previous example inserted the id and col1 values of the rows that were deleted into the table variable @del.

When used with an UPDATE command, OUTPUT produces both a DELETED and an INSERTED table. The DELETED table contains the values before the UPDATE command, and the DELETED table has the values after the UPDATE command. An example follows that shows OUTPUT being used to capture the result of an UPDATE.

```
-update records, this populates
-both the inserted and deleted tables
DECLARE @changes TABLE
(id INT, oldValue VARCHAR(15), newValue VARCHAR(15))
UPDATE outputtbl
SET col1 = 'updated'
OUTPUT inserted.id, deleted.col1, inserted.col1
INTO @changes
WHERE id < 5
SELECT * FROM @changes
GO
id            oldValue        newValue
- - - - --    - - - - - - --  - - - - - - --

3             row5            updated
4             row6            updated

(2 row(s) affected)
```

Common Table Expressions and Recursive Queries

A Common Table Expression, or CTE, is an expression that produces a table that is referred to by name within the context of a single query. The general syntax for a CTE follows.

```
[WITH <common_table_expression> [,...n] ]
<common_table_expression>::=
    expression_name
    [(column_name [,...n])]
    AS
    (<CTE_query_expression>)
```

The following SQL batch shows a trivial usage of a CTE just to give you a feeling for its syntax.

```
WITH MathConst(PI, Avogadro)
AS
(SELECT 3.14159, 6.022e23)
SELECT * FROM MathConst
GO
PI                           Avogadro
- - - - - - - - - - - - - -  - - - - - - - - - - -

3.14159                      6.022E+23
(1 row(s) affected)
```

The WITH clause, in effect, defines a table and its columns. This example says that a table named MathConst has two columns named PI and Avogadro. This is followed by a SELECT statement enclosed in parentheses after an AS keyword. And finally, all this is followed by a SELECT statement that references the `MathConst` table. Note that the syntax of the `WITH` clause is very similar to that of a `VIEW`. One way to think of a CTE is as a `VIEW` that lasts only for the life of the query expression at the end of the CTE. In the example, `MathConst` acts like a `VIEW` that is referenced in the query expression at the end of the CTE.

It is possible to define multiple tables in a CTE. A SQL batch follows that shows another trivial usage of a CTE that defines two tables, again shown just to make the syntax clear.

```
WITH MathConst(PI, Avogadro)
AS
(SELECT 3.14159, 6.022e23),
-- second table
Package(Length, Width)
AS (SELECT 2, 5)
SELECT * FROM MathConst, Package
PI                         Avogadro            Length
Width
- - - - - - - - - - - - - - -  - - - - - - - - - - - - - -  - - - - - - - -
3.14159                    6.022E+23           2             5

(1 row(s) affected)
```

In this example, the CTE produced two tables, and the query expression merely joined them.

Both of the previous examples could have been done without using CTEs and, in fact, would have been easier to do without them. So what good are they?

In once sense, a CTE is just an alternate syntax for creating a `VIEW` that exists for one SQL expression, or it can be thought of as a more convenient way to use a derived table—that is, a subquery. However, CTEs are part of the SQL-92 standard, so adding them to SQL Server increases its standards compliance. In addition, CTEs are implemented in other databases, so ports from those databases may be easier with the addition of CTEs.

In some cases, CTEs can save a significant amount of typing and may provide extra information that can be used when the query plan is optimized. Let's look at an example where this is the case.

For this example, we will use three tables from the `AdventureWorks` database, a sample database that is distributed with SQL Server. We will use the `SalesPerson`, `SalesHeader`, and `SalesDetail` tables. The `Sales Person` table lists each salesperson that works for `AdventureWorks`. For each sale made at `AdventureWorks`, a `SalesHeader` is entered along with a `SalesDetail` for each item that that was sold in that sale. Each `Sales Header` lists the ID of the salesperson who made the sale. Each `Sales Detail` entry lists a part number, its unit price, and the quantity of the part sold.

The stock room has just called the Big Boss and told him that they are out of part number 90. The Big Boss calls you and wants you to make a report that lists the ID of each salesperson. Along with the ID, the Big Boss wants the text "MakeCall" listed if a salesperson made a sale that depends on part number 90 to be complete. Otherwise, he wants the text "Relax" printed. Just to ensure that the report lights a fire under the salespeople, the Big Boss also wants each line to list the value of the sale and the salesperson's sales quota.

Before we actually make use of the CTE, let's first write a query that finds all the IDs of salespeople who have sales that depend on part number 90.

```
SELECT DISTINCT SH.SalesPersonId FROM SalesOrderHeader SH JOIN
SalesOrderDetail SD ON SH.SalesOrderId = SD.SalesOrderId
AND SD.ProductID = 90
SalesPersonId
GO
SalesPersonId
- - - - - - --
14
21
22
more rows
(14 row(s) affected)
```

But the Big Boss has asked for a report with lines that look like this.

```
Action    SalesPersonID SalesQuota              Value
- - - -   -- - - - - --  - - - - - - - - - - - - - -  - - - - -
MakeCall 22            250000.0000              2332.7784
... more lines
Relax    35            250000.0000              0
```

Each line number has the ID of a salesperson. If that salesperson has an order that depends on part number 90, the first column says "MakeCall" and the last column has the value involved in the order. Otherwise, the first column says "Relax" and the last column has 0 in it.

Without CTEs, we could use a subquery to find the salespeople with orders that depend on the missing part to make the report the Big Boss wants, as in the SQL batch that follows.

```
SELECT  'MakeCall' AS Action, S.SalesPersonID,  S.SalesQuota,
(SELECT SUM(SD.UnitPrice * SD.OrderQty) FROM SalesOrderHeader SH
JOIN SalesOrderDetail SD ON
SH.SalesOrderId = SD.SalesOrderId
AND SD.ProductID=90 AND SH.SalesPersonID=S.SalesPersonID
)
FROM SalesPerson S
WHERE EXISTS
(
SELECT * FROM SalesOrderHeader SH JOIN SalesOrderDetail SD ON
SH.SalesOrderID = SD.SalesOrderID AND SD.ProductID = 90
AND SH.SalesPersonID = S.SalesPersonID
)
UNION
SELECT  'Relax' AS Action, S.SalesPersonID,  S.SalesQuota, 0
FROM SalesPerson S
WHERE NOT EXISTS
(
SELECT * FROM SalesOrderHeader SH JOIN SalesOrderDetail SD ON
SH.SalesOrderID = SD.SalesOrderID AND SD.ProductID = 90
AND SH.SalesPersonID = S.SalesPersonID
)
```

Notice that the subquery is reused in a number of places—once in the calculation of the value of the sales involved in the missing part and then again, twice more, in finding the salespeople involved in sales with and without the missing part.

Now let's produce the same report using a CTE.

```
WITH Missing(SP, AMT)
AS(
SELECT SH.SalesPersonID, SUM(SD.UnitPrice * SD.OrderQty) FROM
SalesOrderHeader SH
JOIN SalesOrderDetail SD ON SH.SalesOrderId = SD.SalesOrderId
AND SD.ProductID=90 GROUP BY SH.SalesPersonID
)
SELECT  'MakeCall' AS Action, S.SalesPersonID,  S.SalesQuota,
Missing.AMT
FROM Missing JOIN SalesPerson S ON Missing.SP = S.SalesPersonID
UNION
SELECT  'Relax' AS Action, S.SalesPersonID,  S.SalesQuota, 0
FROM SalesPerson S WHERE S.SalesPersonID NOT IN (SELECT SP FROM
  Missing)
```

The Missing CTE is a table that has a row for each salesperson who has an order that depends on the missing part, and the value of what is missing. Notice that the Missing table is used in one part of the query to find the value of the missing parts and in another to determine whether a sales person should "MakeCall" or "Relax".

Although your opinion may differ, the CTE syntax is a bit clear and more encapsulated; that is, there is only one place that defines what orders are missing part number 90. Also, in theory, the CTE is giving the optimizer a bit more information in that it is telling the optimizer it plans on using `Missing` more than once.

The CTE is also part of another feature of SQL Server 2005 that is also part of the SQL:1999 standard. It is called a recursive query. This is especially useful for a chart of accounts in an accounting system or a parts explosion in a bill of materials. Both of these involve tree-structured data. In general, a recursive query is useful anytime tree-structured data is involved. We will look at an example of a chart of accounts to see how recursive queries work.

Figure 7-5 shows a simple chart of accounts containing two kinds of accounts: detail accounts and rollup accounts. Detail accounts have an actual balance associated with them; when a posting is made to an accounting system, it is posted to detail accounts. In Figure 7-5, account 4001 is a detail account that has a balance of $12.

Rollup accounts are used to summarize the totals of other accounts, which may be detail accounts or other rollup accounts. Every account, except for the root account, has a parent. The total of a rollup account is the sum of the accounts that are its children. In Figure 7-5 account 3002 is a rollup account, and it represents the sum of its two children, accounts 4001 and 4002.

In practice, one of the ways to represent a chart of accounts is to have two tables: one for detail accounts and the other for rollup accounts. A detail account has an account number, a parent account number, and a balance for columns. A rollup account has an account number and a parent

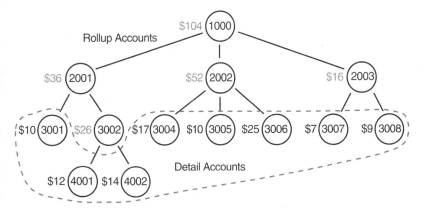

FIGURE 7-5: A Chart of Accounts

but no balance associated with it. The SQL batch that follows builds and populates these two tables for the accounts shown in Figure 7-5.

```
CREATE TABLE DetailAccount(id INT PRIMARY KEY,
parent INT, balance FLOAT)
CREATE TABLE RollupAccount(id INT PRIMARY KEY,
parent INT)
INSERT INTO DetailAccount VALUES (3001, 2001, 10)
INSERT INTO DetailAccount VALUES(4001, 3002, 12)
INSERT INTO DetailAccount VALUES(4002, 3002, 14)
INSERT INTO DetailAccount VALUES(3004, 2002, 17)
INSERT INTO DetailAccount VALUES(3005, 2002, 10)
INSERT INTO DetailAccount VALUES(3006, 2002, 25)
INSERT INTO DetailAccount VALUES(3007, 2003, 7)
INSERT INTO DetailAccount VALUES(3008, 2003, 9)

INSERT INTO RollupAccount VALUES(3002, 2001)
INSERT INTO RollupAccount VALUES(2001, 1000)
INSERT INTO RollupAccount VALUES(2002, 1000)
INSERT INTO RollupAccount VALUES(2003, 1000)
INSERT INTO RollupAccount VALUES(1000, 0)
```

Note that this example does not include any referential integrity constraints or other information to make it easier to follow.

A typical thing to do with a chart of accounts it to calculate the value of all the rollup accounts or, in some cases, the value of a particular rollup account. In Figure 7-5 (shown earlier) the value of the rollup accounts is shown in gray, next to the account itself. We would like to be able to write a SQL batch like the one that follows.

```
SELECT id, balance FROM Rollup   -- a handy view
id          balance
- - - -- --  - - - - - - -- -- - - -
1000        104
2001        36
2002        52
2003        16
3001        10
3002        26
3004        17
3005        10
3006        25
3007        7
3008        9
4001        12
4002        14


(13 row(s) affected)
```

```
SELECT id, balance FROM Rollup WHERE id = 2001
id          balance
- - - - --  - - - - - - - - - - -
2001        36

(1 row(s) affected)
```

This query shows a view name, `Rollup`, that we can query to find the values of all the accounts in the chart of accounts or an individual account. Let's look at how we can do this.

To start with, we will make a recursive query that just lists all the account numbers, starting with the top rollup account, 1000. The query that follows does this.

```
WITH Rollup(id, parent)
AS
(
   - anchor
   SELECT id, parent FROM RollupAccount WHERE id = 1000
   UNION ALL
  - recursive call
SELECT R1.id, R1.parent FROM
(
    SELECT id, parent FROM DetailAccount
    UNION ALL
    SELECT id, parent FROM RollupAccount
) R1
JOIN Rollup R2 ON R2.id = r1.parent
)
 - selecting results
SELECT id, parent FROM Rollup
GO
id          parent
- - - - --  - - - - --
1000        0
2001        1000
2002        1000
2003        1000
3007        2003
3008        2003
3004        2002
3005        2002
3006        2002
3001        2001
3002        2001
4001        3002
4002        3002

(13 row(s) affected)
```

Query	Result	
SELECT id, parent FROM RollupAccount WHERE id = 1000	1000 0	◄— Anchor
SELECT id, parent FROM DetailAccount . . . RollupAccount	2001 1000 2002 1000 2003 1000	◄—Recursive Call 1 Children of 1000

SELECT id, parent FROM DetailAccount . . . RollupAccount	3007 2003
	3008 2003
	3004 2002
	3005 2002
	3006 2002
	3001 2001
	3002 2001
		◄— Recursive Call 2
		    Children of 2001,
		    2002, and 2003

SELECT id, parent FROM DetailAccount . . . RollupAccount	4001 3002 4002 3002	◄— Recursive Call 3 Children of previous

SELECT id, parent FROM DetailAccount . . . RollupAccount		◄— Recursive Call 4
		    No results,
		    recursion stops

FIGURE 7-6: Recursive Query

The previous batch creates a CTE named Rollup. There are three parts to a CTE when it is used to do recursion. The anchor, which initializes the recursion, is first. It sets the initial values of Rollup. In this case, Rollup is initialized to a table that has a single row representing the rollup account with id = 1000. The anchor may not make reference to the CTE Rollup.

The recursive call follows a UNION ALL keyword. UNION ALL must be used in this case. It makes reference to the CTE Rollup. The recursive call will be executed repeatedly until it produces no results. Each time it is called, Rollup will be the results of the previous call. Figure 7-6 shows the results of the anchor and each recursive call.

First the anchor is run, and it produces a result set that includes only the account 1000. Next the recursive call is run and produces a resultset that consists of all the accounts that have as a parent account 1000. The recursive call runs repeatedly, each time joined with its own previous result to produce the children of the accounts selected in the previous recursion. Also note that the recursive call itself is a UNION ALL because the accounts are spread out between the DetailAccount table and the RollupAccount table.

After the body of the CTE, the SELECT statement just selects all the results in Rollup—that is, the UNION of all the results produced by calls in the CTE body.

Now that we can produce a list of all the accounts by walking through the hierarchy from top to bottom, we can use what we learned to calculate the value of each account.

To calculate the values of the accounts, we must work from the bottom up—that is from the detail accounts up to the rollup account 1000. This means that our anchor must select all the detail accounts, and the recursive calls must progressively walk up the hierarchy to account 1000. Note that there is no requirement that the anchor produce a single row; it is just a SELECT statement.

The query that follows produces the values of all the accounts, both detail and rollup.

```
WITH Rollup(id, parent, balance)
AS
(
 - anchor
SELECT id, parent, balance FROM DetailAccount
UNION ALL
 - recursive call
SELECT R1.id, R1.parent, R2.balance
FROM RollupAccount R1
JOIN Rollup R2 ON R1.id = R2.parent
)
SELECT id, SUM(balance) balance FROM Rollup GROUP BY id
GO
id              balance
- - - - --  - - - - - - - - - - -
1000            104
2001            36
2002            52
2003            16
3001            10
3002            26
3004            17
3005            10
3006            25
3007            7
3008            9
4001            12
4002            14

(13 row(s) affected)
```

This query starts by having the anchor select all the detail accounts. The recursive call selects all the accounts that are parents, along with any balance produced by the previous call. This results in a table in which accounts are listed more than once. In fact, the table has as many rows for an account as that account has descendant accounts that are detail accounts. For example, if you looked at the rows produced for account 2001, you would see the three rows shown in the following diagram.

```
id              balance
- - - - --      - - - - - - - - - - - - -
2001            14
2001            12
2001            10
```

The balances 14, 12, and 10 correspond to the balances in the detail accounts 3001, 4001, and 4002, which are all decedents of account 2001. The query that follows the body of the CTE then groups the rows that are produced by account ID and calculates the balance with the SUM function.

There are other ways to solve this problem without using CTEs. A batch that uses a stored procedure that calls itself or a cursor could produce the same result. However, the CTE is a query, and it can be used to define a view, something a stored procedure or a cursor-based batch cannot. The view definition that follows defines a view, which is the recursive query we used earlier, and then uses it to get the balance for a single account, account 2001.

```
CREATE VIEW Rollup
AS
WITH Rollup(id, parent, balance)
AS
(
SELECT id, parent, balance FROM DetailAccount
UNION ALL
SELECT R1.id, R1.parent, R2.balance
FROM RollupAccount R1
JOIN Rollup R2 ON R1.id = R2.parent
)
SELECT id, SUM(balance) balance FROM Rollup GROUP ID id
GO
-- get the balance for account 2001
SELECT balance FROM rollup WHERE id = 2001
GO
balance
- - - - - - - - - - - - -
36

(1 row(s) affected)
```

One of the strengths of a recursive query is the fact that it is a query and can be used to define a view. In addition, a single query in SQL Server is always a transaction, which means that a recursive query based on a CTE is a transaction.

Recursive queries, like any recursive algorithm, can go on forever. By default, if a recursive query attempts to do more than 100 recursions, it will be aborted. You can control this with an `OPTION (MAXRECURSION 10)`, for example, to limit recursion to a depth of 10. The example that follows shows its usage.

```
WITH Rollup(id, parent, balance)
AS
(
 - body of CTE removed for clarity
)
SELECT id, SUM(balance) balance FROM Rollup GROUP BY id
OPTION (MAXRECURSION 10)
GO
```

APPLY Operators

T-SQL adds two specialized join operators: `CROSS APPLY` and `OUTER APPLY`. Both act like a `JOIN` operator in that they produce the Cartesian product of two tables except that no `ON` clause is allowed. The following SQL batch is an example of a `CROSS APPLY` between two tables.

```
CREATE TABLE T1
(
    ID int
)
CREATE TABLE T2
(
  ID it
)
GO
INSERT INTO T1 VALUES (1)
INSERT INTO T1 VALUES (2)
INSERT INTO T2 VALUES (3)
INSERT INTO T2 VALUES (4)
GO
SELECT COUNT(*) FROM T1 CROSS APPLY T2
- - - - - - - - --
4
```

The `APPLY` operators have little utility with just tables or views; a `CROSS JOIN` could have been substituted in the preceding example and gotten the same results. It is intended that the `APPLY` operators be used with a table-valued function on their right, with the parameters for the table-valued function coming from the table on the left. The following SQL batch shows an example of this.

```
CREATE TABLE Belt
(
  model VARCHAR(20),
```

```
    length FLOAT
)
GO
 - fill table with some data
DECLARE @index INT
SET @index = 5
WHILE(@index > 0)
BEGIN
INSERT INTO BELT VALUES ('B' + CONVERT(VARCHAR, @index), 10 * @index)
SET @index = @index - 1
END
GO
 - make a table-valued function
CREATE FUNCTION Stretch (@length FLOAT)
RETURN @T TABLE
(
   MinLength FLOAT,
   MaxLength FLOAT
)
AS BEGIN
IF (@length > 20)
INSERT @T VALUES (@length - 4, @length + 5)
RETURN
END
GO
SELECT B.* S.MinLength, S.MaxLength FROM Belt AS B
CROSS APPLY Stretch(B.Length) AS S
GO
- - - - - - - - - - - - - -
B30, 26, 35
B40, 36, 45
B50, 46, 55
```

The rows in the Belt table are cross-applied to the Stretch function. This function produces a table with a single row in it if the @length parameter passed into it is greater than 20; otherwise, it produces a table with no rows in it. The CROSS APPLY operator produces output when each table involved in the CROSS APPLY has at least one row in it. It is similar to a CROSS JOIN in this respect.

OUTER APPLY is similar to OUTER JOIN in that it produces output for all rows involved in the OUTER APPLY. The following SQL batch shows the results of an OUTER APPLY involving the same Belt table and Stretch function as in the previous example.

```
SELECT B.* S.MinLength, S.MaxLength FROM Belt AS B
CROSS APPLY Stretch(B.Length) AS S
GO
- - - - - - - - - - - -
B10, 6, 15
B20, 16, 25
B30, 26, 35
B40, 36, 45
B50, 46, 55
```

The preceding example could have been done using CROSS and OUTER
JOIN. CROSS APPLY is required, however, when used in conjunction with XML
data types in certain XML operations that will be discussed in Chapter 9.

PIVOT Command

SQL Server 2005 adds the PIVOT command to T-SQL, so named because it
can create a new table by swapping the rows and columns of an existing
table. PIVOT is part of the OLAP section of the SQL:1999 standard. There
are two general uses for the PIVOT command. One it to create an analytical
view of some data, and the other is to implement an open schema.

A typical analytical use of the PIVOT command is to covert temporal
data into categorized data in order to make the data easier to analyze. Consider a table used to record each sale made as it occurs; each row represents
a single sale and includes the quarter that indicates when it occurred. This
sort of view makes sense for recording sales but is not easy to use if you
want to compare sales made in the same quarter, year over year.

Table 7-5 lists temporally recorded sales. You want to analyze same-
quarter sales year by year from the data in the table. Each row represents a
single sale. Note that this table might be a view of a more general table of
individual sales that includes a date rather than a quarterly enumeration.

The PIVOT command, which we will look at shortly, can convert this
temporal view of individual sales into a view that has years categorized by
sales in a quarter. Table 7-6 shows this.

Presenting the data this way makes it much easier to analyze same-
quarter sales. This table aggregates year rows for each given year in the previous table into a single row. However, the aggregated amounts are broken
out into quarters rather than being aggregated over the entire year.

The other use of the PIVOT command is to implement an open schema.
An open schema allows arbitrary attributes to be associated with an entity.
For example, consider a hardware store; its entities are the products that it
sells. Each product has a number of attributes used to describe it. One common attribute of all products it the name of the product.

TABLE 7-5: Individual Sales, Including Quarter of Sale

Year	Quarter	Amount
2001	Q1	100
2001	Q2	120
2001	Q2	70
2001	Q3	55
2001	Q3	110
2001	Q4	90
2002	Q1	200
2002	Q2	150
2002	Q2	40
2002	Q2	60
2002	Q3	120
2002	Q3	110
2002	Q4	180

The hardware store sells "Swish" brand paint that has attributes of quantity, color, and type. It also sells "AttachIt" fastener screws, and these have attributes of pitch and diameter. Over time, it expects to add many other products to its inventory. With this categorization "Swish, 1 qt, green, latex" would be one product or entity, and "Swish, 1qt, blue, oil" would be another.

A classic solution to designing the database the hardware store will use to maintain its inventory is to design a table per product. For example, a

TABLE 7-6: Yearly Sales Broken Down by Quarter

Year	Q1	Q2	Q3	Q4
2001	100	190	165	90
2002	200	250	230	180

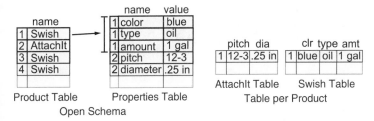

FIGURE 7-7: Tables for Hardware Store

table named Swish with columns for quantity, color, and type. This, of course, requires products and their attributes to be known and for those attributes to remain constant over time. What happens if the manufacturer of the Swish paint adds a new attribute, "Drying Time", but only to certain colors of paint?

An alternate solution is to have only two tables, regardless of the number of products involved or the attributes they have. In the case of the hardware store, there would be a Product table and a Properties table. The Product table would have an entry per product, and the Properties table would contain the arbitrary attributes of that product. The properties of a product are linked to it via a foreign key. This is called an open schema. Figure 7-7 shows the two ways of designing tables to represent the inventory of the hardware store.

The PIVOT operator can easily convert data that is stored using an open schema to a view that looks the same as the table-per-product solution. Next, we will look at the details of using PIVOT to analyze data and support open schemas, and then how to use PIVOT to work with open schemas. There is also an UNPIVOT operator, which can be used to produce the original open schema format from previously pivoted results.

Using PIVOT for Analysis

In this example, we are going to use PIVOT to analyze the sales data we showed in an earlier table. To do this, we build a SALES table and populate it with data, as is shown in the following SQL batch.

```
CREATE TABLE SALES
(
[Year] INT,
Quarter CHAR(2),
Amount FLOAT
)
GO
```

```
INSERT INTO SALES VALUES (2001, 'Q2', 70)
INSERT INTO SALES VALUES (2001, 'Q3', 55)
INSERT INTO SALES VALUES (2001, 'Q3', 110)
INSERT INTO SALES VALUES (2001, 'Q4', 90)
INSERT INTO SALES VALUES (2002, 'Q1', 200)
INSERT INTO SALES VALUES (2002, 'Q2', 150)
INSERT INTO SALES VALUES (2002, 'Q2', 40)
INSERT INTO SALES VALUES (2002, 'Q2', 60)
INSERT INTO SALES VALUES (2002, 'Q3', 120)
INSERT INTO SALES VALUES (2002, 'Q3', 110)
INSERT INTO SALES VALUES (2002, 'Q4', 180)
GO
```

To get a view that is useful for quarter-over-year comparisons, we want to pivot the table's Quarter column into a row heading and aggregate the sum of the values in each quarter for a year. The SQL batch that follows shows a PIVOT command that does this.

```
SELECT * FROM SALES
PIVOT
(SUM (Amount)  - Aggregate the Amount column using SUM
FOR [Quarter]  - Pivot the Quarter column into column headings
IN (Q1, Q2, Q3, Q4))  - use these quarters
AS  P
GO
Year    Q1              Q2              Q3              Q4
- - --  -- -- -- -- --  -- -- -- -- --  -- -- -- -- --  -- -- -- -- --
2001    100             190             165             90
2002    200             250             230             180
```

The SELECT statement selects all the rows from SALES. A PIVOT clause is added to the SELECT statement. It starts with the PIVOT keyword followed by its body enclosed in parentheses. The body contains two parts separated by the FOR keyword. The first part of the body specifies the kind of aggregation to be performed. The argument of the aggregate function must be a column name; it cannot be an expression as it is when an aggregate function is used outside a PIVOT. The second part specifies the pivot column—that is, the column to pivot into a row—and the values from that column to be used as column headings. The value for a particular column in a row is the aggregation of the column specified in the first part, over the rows that match the column heading.

Note that it is not required to use all the possible values of the pivot column. You only need to specify the Q2 column if you wish to analyze just the year-over-year Q2 results. The SQL batch that follows shows this.

```
SELECT * FROM SALES
PIVOT
(SUM (Amount)
FOR [Quarter]
IN (Q2))
AS P
GO


Year          Q2
- - - - --  - - - - - - - - - -
2001          190
2002          250
```

Note that the output produced by the PIVOT clause acts as though SELECT has a GROUP BY [Year] clause. A pivot, in effect, applies a GROUP BY to the SELECT that includes all the columns that are not either the aggregate or the pivot column. This can lead to undesired results, as shown in the SQL batch that follows. It uses essentially the same SALES table as the previous example, except that it has an additional column named Other.

```
CREATE TABLE SALES2
(
[Year] INT,
Quarter CHAR(2),
Amount FLOAT,
Other INT
)
INSERT INTO SALES2 VALUES (2001, 'Q2', 70, 1)
INSERT INTO SALES2 VALUES (2001, 'Q3', 55, 1)
INSERT INTO SALES2 VALUES (2001, 'Q3', 110, 2)
INSERT INTO SALES2 VALUES (2001, 'Q4', 90, 1)
INSERT INTO SALES2 VALUES (2002, 'Q1', 200, 1)
INSERT INTO SALES2 VALUES (2002, 'Q2', 150, 1)
INSERT INTO SALES2 VALUES (2002, 'Q2', 40, 1)
INSERT INTO SALES2 VALUES (2002, 'Q2', 60, 1)
INSERT INTO SALES2 VALUES (2002, 'Q3', 120, 1)
INSERT INTO SALES2 VALUES (2002, 'Q3', 110, 1)
INSERT INTO SALES2 VALUES (2002, 'Q4', 180, 1)

SELECT * FROM  Sales2
PIVOT
(SUM (Amount)
FOR Quarter
IN (Q3))
AS P
GO
```

```
Year          Other        Q3
- - - - - --  -- - - - --  - - - - - - - - - - - - - -
2001          1            55
2002          1            115
2001          2            110
```

Note that the year 2001 appears twice, once for each value of `Other`. The `SELECT` that precedes the `PIVOT` keyword cannot specify which columns to use in the `PIVOT` clause. However, a subquery can be used to eliminate the columns not desired in the pivot, as shown in the SQL batch that follows.

```
SELECT * FROM
(Select Amount, Quarter, Year from Sales2
) AS A
PIVOT
(SUM (Amount)
FOR Quarter
IN (Q3))
AS P
GO
Year        Q3
- - - - - --  - - - - - - - - - - - - -
2001        165
2002        230
```

A column named in the `FOR` part of the `PIVOT` clause may not correspond to any values in the pivot column of the table. The column will be output, but will have null values. The following SQL batch shows this.

```
SELECT * FROM SALES
PIVOT
(SUM (Amount)
FOR [Quarter]
IN (Q2, LastQ))
As P
GO
Year        Q2                           LastQ
- - - - - --  -- - - - - - - - - - --  - - - - - - - - - - - - - -
2001        190                          NULL
2002        250                          NULL
```

Note that the `Quarter` column of the `SALES` table has no value "`LastQ`", so the output of the `PIVOT` lists all the values in the `LastQ` column as `NULL`.

Using PIVOT for Open Schemas

Using `PIVOT` for an open schema is really no different from using `PIVOT` for analysis, except that we don't depend on `PIVOT`'s ability to aggregate a result. The open schema has two tables, a Product table and a Properties table, as was shown in Figure 7-7. What we want to do is to take selected rows from the Properties table and pivot them—that is, rotate them—and then add them as columns to the Product table. This is shown in Figure 7-8.

Figure 7-9 shows the PIVOT we will use to select the line from the Product table for "Swish" products and joint them with the corresponding pivoted lines from the Properties table.

This query selects row from the Properties table that have a string equal to "color", "type", or "amount" in the value column. They are selected from the value column because value is the argument of the MAX function that follows the PIVOT keyword. The strings "color", "type", and "amount" are used because they are specified as an argument of the IN clause after the FOR keyword. Note that the arguments of the IN clause must be literal; there is no way to calculate them—for example, by using a subquery.

The results of the pivot query in Figure 7-9 are shown in Figure 7-10.

Note that the columns that were selected from the Properties table now appear as rows in the output.

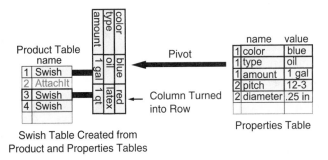

FIGURE 7-8: Rotating Properties

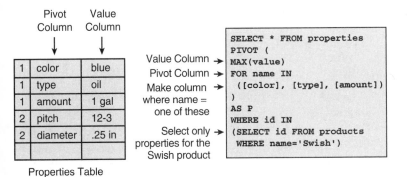

FIGURE 7-9: Basic PIVOT

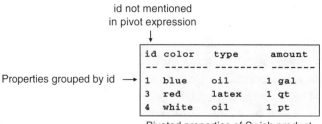

id not mentioned
in pivot expression

Properties grouped by id →

```
id color    type     amount
-- -------  -------- -------
1  blue     oil      1 gal
3  red      latex    1 qt
4  white    oil      1 pt
```

Pivoted properties of Swish product

FIGURE 7-10: Results of Open Schema Pivot

Ranking and Windowing Functions

SQL Server 2005 adds support for a group of functions known as ranking functions. At its simplest, ranking adds an extra value column to the resultset that is based on a ranking algorithm being applied to a column of the result. Four ranking functions are supported.

ROW_NUMBER() produces a column that contains a number that corresponds to the row's order in the set. The set must be ordered by using an OVER clause with an ORDER BY clause as a variable. The following is an example.

```
SELECT orderid, customerid,
       ROW_NUMBER() OVER(ORDER BY orderid) AS num
FROM orders
WHERE orderid < 10400
AND    customerid <= 'BN'
```

produces

```
orderid    customerid num
- - -- --  - - - - -  - - - - - - - - - - -
10248      VINET      1
10249      TOMSP      2
10250      HANAR      3
10251      VICTE      4
10252      SUPRD      5
10253      HANAR      6
10254      CHOPS      7
10255      RICSU      8
... more rows
```

Note that if you apply the ROW_NUMBER function to a nonunique column, such as customerid in the preceding example, the order of customers with the same customerid (ties) is not defined. In any case,

ROW_NUMBER produces a monotonically increasing number; that is, no rows will ever share a ROW_NUMBER.

```
SELECT orderid, customerid,
       ROW_NUMBER() OVER(ORDER BY customerid) AS num
FROM orders
WHERE orderid < 10400
AND    customerid <= 'BN'
```

produces

```
orderid     customerid num
- - - - --  - - - - -  - - - - - - - - - - -
10308       ANATR       1
10365       ANTON       2
10355       AROUT       3
10383       AROUT       4
10384       BERGS       5
10278       BERGS       6
10280       BERGS       7
10265       BLONP       8
10297       BLONP       9
10360       BLONP      10
```

RANK() applies a monotonically increasing number for each value in the set. The value of ties, however, is the same. If the columns in the OVER(ORDER BY) clause have unique values, the result produced by RANK() is identical to the result produced by ROW_NUMBER(). RANK() and ROW_NUMBER() differ only if there are ties. Here's the second earlier example using RANK().

```
SELECT orderid, customerid,
       RANK() OVER(ORDER BY customerid) AS [rank]
FROM orders
WHERE orderid < 10400
AND    customerid <= 'BN'
```

produces

```
orderid     customerid rank
- - - - --  - - - - -  - - - - - - - - - - -
10308       ANATR       1
10365       ANTON       2
10355       AROUT       3
10383       AROUT       3
10384       BERGS       5
10278       BERGS       5
10280       BERGS       5
10265       BLONP       8
```

```
10297       BLONP       8
10360       BLONP       8
... more rows
```

Note that multiple rows have the same rank if their customerid is the same. There are holes, however, in the rank column value to reflect the ties. Using the DENSE_RANK() function works the same way as RANK() but gets rid of the holes in the numbering. NTILE(n) divides the resultset into "n" approximately even pieces and assigns each piece the same number. NTILE(100) would be the well-known (to students) percentile. The following query shows the difference between ROW_NUMBER(), RANK(), DENSE_RANK(), and TILE(n).

```
SELECT orderid, customerid,
       ROW_NUMBER() OVER(ORDER BY customerid) AS num,
       RANK()       OVER(ORDER BY customerid) AS [rank],
       DENSE_RANK() OVER(ORDER BY customerid) AS [denserank],
       NTILE(5)     OVER(ORDER BY customerid) AS ntile5
FROM   orders
WHERE  orderid < 10400
AND    customerid <= 'BN'
```

produces

orderid	customerid	num	rank	denserank	ntile5
10308	ANATR	1	1	1	1
10365	ANTON	2	2	2	1
10355	AROUT	3	3	3	2
10383	AROUT	4	3	3	2
10278	BERGS	5	5	4	3
10280	BERGS	6	5	4	3
10384	BERGS	7	5	4	4
10265	BLONP	8	8	5	4
10297	BLONP	9	8	5	5
10360	BLONP	10	8	5	5

The ranking functions have additional functionality when combined with windowing functions. Windowing functions divide a resultset into partitions, based on the value of a PARTITION BY clause inside the OVER clause. The ranking functions are applied separately to each partition. Here's an example.

```
SELECT *,
   RANK() OVER(PARTITION BY COUNTRY ORDER BY age) AS [rank]
FROM
(
```

```
SELECT lastname, country,
   DATEDIFF(yy,birthdate,getdate())AS age
FROM employees
) AS a
```

produces

```
lastname              country         age          rank
- - - - - - - - - -   - - - - - - --  - - - - --   - - -
Dodsworth             UK              37           1
Suyama                UK              40           2
King                  UK              43           3
Buchanan              UK              48           4
Leverling             USA             40           1
Callahan              USA             45           2
Fuller                USA             51           3
Davolio               USA             55           4
Peacock               USA             66           5
```

There are separate rankings for each partition. An interesting thing to note about this example is that the subselect is required because any column used in a PARTITION BY or ORDER BY clause must be available from the columns in the FROM portion of the statement. In our case, the seemingly simpler statement that follows:

```
SELECT lastname, country,
   DATEDIFF(yy,birthdate,getdate())AS age,
   RANK() OVER(PARTITION BY COUNTRY ORDER BY age) AS [rank]
FROM employees
```

wouldn't work; instead, you'd get the error "Invalid column name 'age'". In addition, you can't use the ranking column in a WHERE clause, because it is evaluated after all the rows are selected, as shown next.

```
- 10 rows to a page, we want page 40

- this won't work
SELECT
  ROW_NUMBER() OVER (ORDER BY customerid, requireddate) AS num,
  customerid, requireddate, orderid
FROM orders
WHERE num BETWEEN 400 AND 410

- this will
SELECT * FROM
(
SELECT
  ROW_NUMBER() OVER (ORDER BY customerid, requireddate) AS num,
  customerid, requireddate, orderid
```

```
FROM orders
) AS a
WHERE num BETWEEN 400 AND 410
```

Although the preceding case looks similar to selecting the entire result-set into a temporary table, with num as a derived identity column, and doing a SELECT of the temporary table, in some cases the engine will be able to accomplish this without the complete set of rows. Besides being usable in a SELECT clause, the ranking and windowing functions are also usable in the ORDER BY clause. This gets employees partitioned by country and ranked by age, and then sorted by rank.

```
SELECT *,
  RANK() OVER(PARTITION BY COUNTRY ORDER BY age)) AS [rank]
FROM
(
 SELECT lastname, country,
   DATEDIFF(yy,birthdate,getdate())AS age
 FROM employees
) AS a
ORDER BY RANK() OVER(PARTITION BY COUNTRY ORDER BY age), COUNTRY
```

produces

lastname	country	age	rank
Dodsworth	UK	37	1
Leverling	USA	40	1
Suyama	UK	40	2
Callahan	USA	45	2
King	UK	43	3
Fuller	USA	51	3
Buchanan	UK	48	4
Davolio	USA	55	4
Peacock	USA	66	5

You can also use other aggregate functions (either system-defined aggregates or user-defined aggregates that you saw in Chapter 5) with the OVER clause. When it is used in concert with the partitioning functions, however, you get the same value for each partition. This is shown next.

```
-- there is one oldest employee age for  each country
SELECT *,
  RANK() OVER(PARTITION BY COUNTRY ORDER BY age) AS [rank],
  MAX(age) OVER(PARTITION BY COUNTRY) AS [oldest age in country]
FROM
(
 SELECT lastname, country,
```

```
    DATEDIFF(yy,birthdate,getdate())AS age
  FROM employees
) AS a
```

produces

lastname	country	age	rank	oldest age in country
Dodsworth	UK	37	1	48
Suyama	UK	40	2	48
King	UK	43	3	48
Buchanan	UK	48	4	48
Leverling	USA	40	1	66
Callahan	USA	45	2	66
Fuller	USA	51	3	66
Davolio	USA	55	4	66
Peacock	USA	66	5	66

Transaction Abort Handling

Error handling in previous versions of SQL Server has always been seen as somewhat arcane, compared with other procedural languages. You had to have error handling code after each statement, and to have centralized handling of errors, you need GOTO statements and labels. SQL Server 2005 introduces a modern error handling mechanism with TRY/CATCH blocks. The syntax follows.

```
BEGIN TRY
    { sql_statement | statement_block }
END TRY
BEGIN CATCH TRAN_ABORT
    { sql_statement | statement_block }
END CATCH
```

The code you want to execute is placed within a TRY block. The TRY block must be immediately followed by a CATCH block in which you place the error handling code. The CATCH block can only handle transaction abort errors, so the XACT_ABORT setting needs to be on in order for any errors with a severity level less than 21 to be handled as transaction abort errors. Errors with a severity level of 21 or higher are considered fatal and cause SQL Server to stop executing the code and sever the connection.

When a transaction abort error occurs within the scope of a TRY block, the execution of the code in the TRY block terminates and an exception is thrown. The control is shifted to the associated CATCH block. When the code in the CATCH block has executed, the control goes to the statement after the

CATCH block. TRY/CATCH constructs can be nested, so to handle exceptions within a CATCH block, write a TRY/CATCH block inside the CATCH. The following code shows a simple example of the TRY/CATCH block.

```
-make sure we catch all errors
SET XACT_ABORT ON
BEGIN TRY
   --start the tran
   BEGIN TRAN
   --do something here
   COMMIT TRAN
END TRY
BEGIN CATCH TRAN_ABORT
   ROLLBACK
   --cleanup code
END CATCH
```

Notice how the first statement in the CATCH block is the ROLLBACK. It is necessary to do the ROLLBACK before any other statements that require a transaction. This is because SQL Server 2005 has a new transactional state: "failed" or "doomed." The doomed transaction acts like a read-only transaction. Reads may be done, but any statement that would result in a write to the transaction log will fail with error 3930:

```
Transaction is doomed and cannot make forward progress. Rollback
Transaction.
```

However, work is not reversed and locks are not released until the transaction is rolled back.

We mentioned previously that errors had to be transactional abort errors in order to be caught. This raises the question: What about errors created through the RAISERROR syntax—in other words, errors that you raise yourself? In SQL Server 2005, RAISERROR has a new option called TRAN_ABORT, which tags the raised error as a transactional abort error, which therefore will be handled in the CATCH block.

Where Are We?

With the inclusion of the CLR in SQL Server 2005 and the ability to use .NET languages natively from within SQL Server, there has been speculation on the future of T-SQL. T-SQL continues to be advanced and remains the best (and in some cases the only) way to accomplish many things. We firmly believe that the enhancements to T-SQL in this release of SQL Server show the importance of T-SQL and its power and future.

8

XML in the Database: The XML Data Type

S QL SERVER 2005 introduces a new scalar data type, the XML data type. XML is a first-class data type in SQL Server now, and this has a wide-ranging impact on the use of XML.

The XML Data Type

A new type of data has gained popularity in recent years, XML. XML has evolved from a simple data transfer format to a data model that includes its own schema-definition vocabulary, XSD, as well as query languages. In this chapter, we'll look at the XML data type and see how it differs from conventional CLOB (TEXT field) storage of an XML document.

You can use the XML data type like any other data type in SQL Server. It can be used in the following ways:

- As a column in a table
- As a variable in Transact-SQL
- As a stored procedure or user-defined function parameter
- As a user-defined function return value

The XML type is quite similar, but not identical, to the distinct type defined by SQL:1999 and discussed in Chapter 1. It is similar in character to a CLOB (VARCHAR(MAX)), but you must convert it to and from a varchar type, rather than assign it. Like distinct types, the XML data type cannot be compared with other data types without being cast or converted, but unlike distinct types, two instances of an XML data type cannot be compared at all.

Like a SQL:1999 distinct type, the XML type has its own methods; these methods enable the use of an alternate query language, XQuery. The data in an XML type does not follow the relational data model, but is based on the XML Infoset model, which is used to model structured—that is, hierarchical data.

A column that is defined as being of type XML stores its data in the database itself. The column is not a pointer to an XML document on the file system. This means that XML data is included in the backup and restore process, is subject to ordinary SQL Server security (and some extensions to security, as we'll mention later), and participates in transactions, constraints, and logging. Having XML data inside a relational database may offend some relational purists, but it means that your data lives in a single repository for reasons of administration, reliability, and control.

Using the XML Data Type in Tables

Let's begin by using the XML data type to define a column in a table. The following DDL statement creates a table.

```
CREATE TABLE xml_tab (
   the_id INTEGER,
   xml_col XML)
```

Note that you can also have a table that consists of only a single XML data type column; however, the XML data type cannot be used itself as a primary key. The following code, which attempts to use the XML column as a primary key, fails.

```
CREATE TABLE xml_tab (
   xml_col XML PRIMARY KEY)
```

Interestingly, the following error message occurs when you try to make an XML data type the primary key:

```
Column 'xml_col' in table 'xml_tab' is of a type that is invalid for
use as a key column in an index.
```

Later we will see that you can create an XML-specific index on this column, but this index will not be used in SQL comparisons—it will be used to improve the performance of the functions associated with an XML data type. In addition to the previous example that created a single XML type column in a table, you can have tables that contain more than one XML data type column. You can create a table with an XML column in local or global temporary tables as well as ordinary tables. An XML data type column can be used in a VIEW as well.

XML data type columns have certain limitations when used in tables.

- They may not be declared as a PRIMARY KEY in a table.
- They may not be declared as a FOREIGN KEY in a table.
- They may not be declared with a UNIQUE constraint.
- They may not be declared with the COLLATE keyword.

These first three limitations exist because individual instances of the XML data type may not be compared with each other. Although it would not be difficult to perform a string comparison with XML data, it would be an order of magnitude more difficult to perform a comparison at the Infoset level. For example, the two XML documents in the following example are Infoset-equivalent, but not lexically equivalent.

```
<! - These two documents are equivalent  ->
<doc1>
    <row au_id="111-11-1111"/>
</doc1>

<doc1>
    <row au_id='111-11-1111'></row>
</doc1>
```

The XML data type cannot use the COLLATE keyword, because XML provides its own encoding via the encoding attribute on the XML document declaration. The following code is an example of using encoding. If the document uses an encoding that is unknown or unsupported, SQL Server will return an error. An error will also result if the content does not match the specified encoding; for example, the encoding specifies UTF-16 but contains characters encoded as ANSI. Although encoding specified in the XML document declaration is preserved, documents are always physically stored as UTF-16.

```
<! - This works correctly  ->
<?xml version="1.0" encoding="utf-8"?>
<doc1>
    <row au_id="111-11-1111"/>
</doc1>
```

```
<! - This fails with an unknown encoding error  ->
<?xml version="1.0" encoding="i-bogus"?>
<doc1>
   <row au_id='111-11-1111'></row>
</doc1>
```

XML data type columns can have NULL constraints (the default nullability is the current default of your SQL Server session). CHECK constraints based on the XML Infoset model are supported, using methods that are specific to the XML type. Although we'll talk about the methods in more detail in the next chapter, a typical check constraint on an XML type is shown next.

```
- pdoc must have a person element
- as a child of the people root
CREATE TABLE xmltab(
  id INTEGER PRIMARY KEY,
  pdoc XML CHECK (pdoc.exist('/people/person')=1)
)
```

Because XML data types follow the XML Infoset data model, they are constrained not by relational constraints, but by a collection of one or more XML schemas. SQL Server's XML data type supports schema validation. We will explore this in detail in the next section.

The XML data type supports an implicit conversion from any character or National character data type, but not from other SQL Server data types. This includes CHAR, VARCHAR, NCHAR, and NVARCHAR. You can use CAST or CONVERT to convert BINARY, VARBINARY, TEXT, NTEXT, and IMAGE data types to the XML data type for storage as well. Casting from TEXT and NTEXT is permitted to enable forward compatibility for users who have stored their XML data in these data types in previous versions of SQL Server. Casting from the BINARY data types is useful for features like SQL Server Service Broker that can communicate using binary or XML. In addition, you can store a SQL_VARIANT data type into an XML data type table after casting it to a character-based type. Listing 8-1 shows inserting rows into a table containing an XML data type.

LISTING 8-1: Inserting Rows into a Table with an XML Data Type

```
CREATE TABLE xml_tab(
  the_id INTEGER PRIMARY_KEY IDENTITY,
  xml_col XML)
GO
```

```
-- these work fine
INSERT INTO xml_tab VALUES('<doc1></doc1>')
INSERT INTO xml_tab VALUES(N'<doc1></doc1>')

-- so does this (if first cast to varchar/nvarchar)
DECLARE @v SQL_VARIANT
SET @v = N'<someotherdoc></someotherdoc>'
INSERT INTO xml_tab VALUES(CAST(@v AS varchar(max)))

-- this fails at the insert statement
DECLARE @SOMENUM FLOAT
SET @SOMENUM = 3.1416
INSERT INTO xml_tab VALUES(CAST(@SOMENUM as XML))
```

Although we've only stored well-formed XML documents in the XML data type column so far, we can also use this column to store document fragments or top-level text nodes. This is useful because we can store the results of a SELECT . . . FOR XML query or XQuery results, which may not be complete documents, in an XML data type column. However, the documents or fragments must abide by XML well-formedness rules. Listing 8-2 shows some examples.

LISTING 8-2: Inserting XML Data into a Table

```
CREATE TABLE xml_tab(
   the_id INTEGER PRIMARY_KEY IDENTITY,
   xml_col XML)
GO

-- ok, complete document
INSERT INTO xml_tab VALUES('<doc2></doc2>')

-- ok, document fragment
-- though it's not a single well-formed document
-- (two root elements)
INSERT INTO xml_tab VALUES('<doc1></doc1><doc2></doc2>')

-- ok, text element
INSERT INTO xml_tab VALUES('The Window and Shade Store')

-- error, not well-formed
INSERT INTO xml_tab VALUES('The Window & Shade Store')

-- error, not well-formed
INSERT INTO xml_tab VALUES('<doc1><doc2></doc1></doc2>')
```

There is no implicit conversion from the XML data type to any other data types, but the CAST or CONVERT operators do convert between any of the character or National character data types, as well as BINARY and VARBINARY. When you cast from BINARY and VARBINARY, you can either specify the encoding in the XML itself or include the beginning byte-order mark (0xFFFE) if the format is Unicode. When you cast to BINARY or VARBINARY, the XML will be cast to UTF-16 with the byte-order mark present. You can cast a TEXT or NTEXT data type instance to an instance of the XML type, but you cannot cast an instance of the XML type to TEXT or NTEXT. Using one of the special methods of the XML data type (the value method, discussed later in this chapter) can produce different SQL data types. Listing 8-3 shows retrieving data from an XML data type column.

LISTING 8-3: Returning Data from an XML Data Type Column

```
CREATE TABLE xml_tab(
  the_id INTEGER PRIMARY_KEY IDENTITY,
  xml_col XML)
GO

INSERT INTO xml_tab VALUES('<doc2></doc2>')
INSERT INTO xml_tab VALUES(N'<doc2></doc2>')
GO

 - both rows' values are cast to the same data type
SELECT CAST(xml_col as nchar(2000)) FROM xml_tab
SELECT CONVERT(nchar(2000), xml_col) FROM xml_tab
GO

 - illegal
SELECT CAST(xml_col as sql_variant) FROM xml_tab
SELECT CONVERT(sql_variant, xml_col) FROM xml_tab
GO
```

Since the values of two XML data type instances cannot be compared (except using IS NULL), you cannot use the XML data type in SQL predicates or SQL clauses that require comparison, such as GROUP BY and ORDER BY. The XML data type also cannot be used in any scalar function or aggregate where comparison is required. However, because the XML data type is castable to any character-based type, this functionality will work if CAST (or CONVERT) is used. This behavior is exactly the behavior specified for a distinct data type by the SQL:1999 specification. Although comparison of the XML document type as a string is risky, notice that in the preceding example, both '<doc2/>' and '<doc2></doc2>' are "converted" to the same lexical form, '<doc2/>', when the CAST or CONVERT functions are used. The XML data type does retain Infoset fidelity but does not guarantee lexical fidelity. Listing 8-4 illustrates what you can and cannot do with the XML data type in SQL statements.

LISTING 8-4: Using the XML Data Type in SQL Statements

```
- assume the same xml_tab as in previous examples

- comparison to NULL works
SELECT the_id FROM xml_tab
  WHERE xml_col IS NULL

- illegal
SELECT xml_col FROM xml_tab
  GROUP BY xml_col
SELECT xml_col FROM xml_tab
  ORDER BY xml_col
SELECT xml_col FROM xml_tab
  WHERE xml_col = '<doc2/>'
SELECT SUBSTRING(xml_col,1,2) FROM xml_tab

- casting to string allows this to work
SELECT xml_col from xml_tab
  WHERE CAST(xml_col AS VARCHAR) = '<doc2/>'
```

Using XML Data Variables and Parameters

SQL Server 2005 allows you to use the XML data type as a normal scalar variable in Transact-SQL. You can assign XML documents or fragments to the variable as you would any other variable. Usually, you will do this by casting or converting a character-based variable, as shown in this example.

```
- declare a variable of XML data type
DECLARE @x XML

- cast a string to it (must be a valid XML document or fragment)
SET @x = CAST('<doc1><name>Bob</name></doc1>' AS XML)

- use it
INSERT  xml_tab VALUES(@x)
```

Just as with an XML column, variables of the XML data type can be used as input to an assignment statement. Variables of the XML data type have the same processing limits as columns of the XML data type; they may not be used in place of a string in scalar functions such as SUBSTRING, in comparisons, or in ORDER BY or GROUP BY clauses in dynamic SQL, or as parameters, without first being cast or converted to a character data type. Stored procedures or user-defined function parameters and user-defined function return codes may be XML types. This allows you to return dynamic XML to the user based on logical operations, such as in the following example.

```
- create the user-defined function
CREATE FUNCTION my_business_logic(
  in_dept INTEGER
)
RETURNS XML
AS
DECLARE @x XML
 - do some business logic that produces an XML document
RETURN @x
GO

 - now call it, using dept 10
SELECT * FROM dbo.my_business_logic(10)
```

Note that the XML return code is a scalar type, rather than a TABLE type.

As with XML data type columns and variables, procedure parameters and return codes can be declared with a schema collection name and used to ensure schema validity. Although being able to schema-validate input parameters may obviate the requirement for a lot of domain-checking of input, we can still use the fact that we can do processing inside procedures to make the XML a lot more dynamic.

We'll see how using and producing XML based on dynamic rules and being able to pass in XML as just another data type can be used in conjunction with new extended features of the composition and decomposition functions, SELECT . . . FOR XML and OpenXML, in a few sections.

Typed and Untyped XML—
Cataloging and Using XML Schema Collections

In addition to storing untyped XML documents or fragments in an XML data type column, you can use SQL Server to validate your XML data type column, variable, or parameter by associating it with an XML schema collection. Therefore, you can think of XML data types as being either schema-validated (containing data types defined by a specific set of XML schemas) or untyped (containing any well-formed XML). Whether your XML type is typed or untyped, it can still contain documents or fragments, since fragments can also be schema-valid. In addition, when you define an XML type to be schema-validated, you can also specify that it can contain only XML documents, or XML documents or fragments (known as XML content).

XML schemas define a series of data types that exist in a particular namespace. Schemas are themselves well-formed schema-compliant XML documents, just as relational table definitions and other DDL are valid Transact-SQL. Although there can be more than one schema definition document for a particular namespace, a schema definition document defines types in only one namespace. The XML Schema Definition language (XSD) defines a standard set of base types that are supported as types in XML documents, just as the SQL:1999 standard defines a set of base types that relational databases must support. The XSD base data types are shown in Figure 8-1.

Schema documents may also import types from other namespaces, using the `import` element. There are also some special namespaces that are "imported" by default in SQL Server's XML type. Two of the most important ones are:

* The *http://www.w3.org/2001/XMLSchema* namespace. This namespace defines the constructs (elements and attributes) used in XML schema documents.
* The *http://www.w3.org/2001/XMLSchema-instance* namespace. This namespace defines the constructs to be used in XML documents that are not schemas.

These are usually assigned the namespace prefixes `xs` and `xsi`, respectively, although a lot of other schema-manipulating products will use the `xsd` prefix rather than `xs`. A complete explanation of the XML Schema specification is beyond the scope of this book, but Listing 8-5 illustrates the main concept.

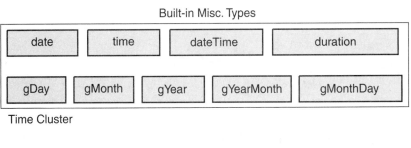

Built-in Misc. Types

date	time	dateTime	duration
gDay	gMonth	gYear	gYearMonth	gMonthDay

Time Cluster

boolean	base64Binary	hexBinary

Misc. Cluster

FIGURE 8-1: XSD Base Data Types

Built-in Numeric Types

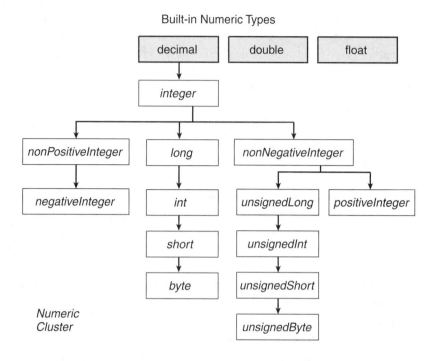

Numeric
Cluster

Built-in XML Types

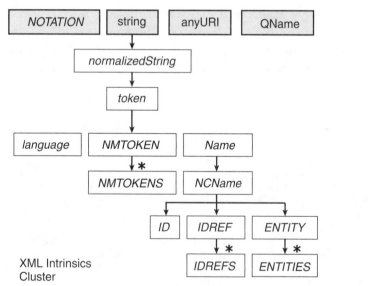

XML Intrinsics
Cluster

FIGURE 8-1: XSD Base Data Types (continued)

LISTING 8-5: A Simple XML Schema

```
<! -- defines types for the namespace 'http://example.org/People'
     This is known as the targetNamespace but does not indicate
     The location of the schema document  -->
<xsd:schema xmlns:xsd='http://www.w3.org/2001/XMLSchema'
            xmlns:tns='http://example.org/People'
            targetNamespace='http://example.org/People' >

  <xsd:simpleType name='personAge' >
    <xsd:restriction base='xsd:float' >
      <xsd:maxInclusive value='120' />
      <xsd:minExclusive value='0' />
    </xsd:restriction>
  </xsd:simpleType>

  <xsd:element name='age' type='tns:personAge' />

</xsd:schema>
```

Note that an XSD schema includes some schema elements, such as `maxInclusive` and `minExclusive`, that serve to constrain or restrict the base data types. This constraint process is known as *derivation by restriction*, and the schema elements and attributes that act as constraints are known as *facets*.

Although there is an `xsi:schemaLocation` attribute that can be helpful in locating arbitrary schema documents in an instance document, the XML schema specification does not mandate an algorithm by which an XML document locates its schema. SQL Server 2005 stores schema documents inside the database and keeps track of them based on the schema collection; it doesn't use `xsi:schemaLocation`.

SQL Server XML Schema Collections

Schema documents are cataloged in SQL Server as part of a named XML schema collection by using the CREATE XML SCHEMA COLLECTION DDL statement.

```
USE pubs
GO

CREATE XML SCHEMA COLLECTION peoplecoll AS
' <xsd:schema xmlns:xsd="http://www.w3.org/2001/XMLSchema">
   <! - other types omitted  -->
   <xsd:simpleType name="personAge" >
     <xsd:restriction base="xsd:float" >
       <xsd:maxInclusive value="120" />
```

```
            <xsd:minExclusive value="0" />
          </xsd:restriction>
      </xsd:simpleType>
      <xsd:element name="age" type="personAge" />
</xsd:schema>
<xsd:schema xmlns:xsd="http://www.w3.org/2001/XMLSchema"
            xmlns:tns="http://example.org/LogansRun"
            targetNamespace="http://example.org/LogansRun" >
    <!- other types omitted ->
    <xsd:simpleType name="personAge" >
      <xsd:restriction base="xsd:float" >
        <xsd:maxInclusive value="30" />
        <xsd:minExclusive value="0" />
      </xsd:restriction>
    </xsd:simpleType>
    <xsd:element name="age" type="tns:personAge" />
</xsd:schema>'
```

Note that an XML schema collection has a SQL Server object name
(dbo.peoplecoll, in this case) and consists of one or more schemas, defining the permitted types in one or more XML namespaces. It cannot be
referenced outside the database it is defined in or by using a three-part
object name, like pubs.dbo.peoplecoll. An XML schema that will be
used to validate XML content also can have no associated namespace,
like the first schema in the previous collection. This is known as the
"no-namespace schema" and is distinguished by the fact that its schema
element has no targetNamespace attribute. You are restricted to one no-
namespace schema per XML schema collection.

Typed XML

XML data type columns, parameters, and variables may be typed or untyped; that is, they may conform to a schema or not. To specify that you are
using a typed column, for example, in our XML column in the previous table,
you would specify the schema collection name in parentheses, like this.

```
CREATE TABLE xml_tab (
    the_id INTEGER,
    xml_col XML(peoplecoll)
)
```

By doing this, you've just defined a series of integrity constraints with
respect to what can appear in the XML that makes up that column! Typing
the XML data in a column by using an XML schema collection not only
serves as an integrity constraint, but is an optimization for SQL Server's

XQuery engine because you are using typed data in the query. It also allows the XQuery engine to know the data type of its intermediate and final results. If the XML data is not strongly typed, XQuery treats everything as a weakly typed "string" called `xdt:untypedAtomic`.

The integrity checking for a typed XML column happens each time a new value is set into it. This would occur when you are inserting or updating the column into a table. As an example, creating the following table and adding some rows to it will cause each instance of the XML data type to be schema-validated at insert time.

```
CREATE TABLE person_tab(
 id INT IDENTITY PRIMARY KEY,
  - the person column can only contain
  - infoset items that are defined in the schema collection
  - defined above
 person XML(peoplecoll))
GO

- this works, person between 0 and 30 years old
INSERT INTO person_tab VALUES(
'<age xmlns="http://example.org/LogansRun">11</age>')

- so does this, using the no-namespace schema
INSERT INTO person_tab VALUES(
'<age>75</age>')

- this insert fails
INSERT INTO person_tab VALUES(
'<age xmlns="http://example.org/LogansRun">31</age>')
```

You can precede your schema collection identifier with the keywords DOCUMENT or CONTENT. If you do not use one of these keywords, the default is equivalent to specifying CONTENT. If DOCUMENT is specified, the column can only contain XML documents (a document is defined as having a single root element), but if you specify CONTENT, the column can contain documents or fragments, as long as all the elements are schema-valid. Here's an example that illustrates the difference.

```
CREATE TABLE person_docs(
 id INT IDENTITY primary key,
 person XML(DOCUMENT peoplecoll))
GO

CREATE TABLE person_content(
 id INT IDENTITY PRIMARY KEY,
 person XML(CONTENT peoplecoll))
GO
```

```
-- this works with either table, a single root element
INSERT INTO person_docs VALUES(
'<age xmlns="http://example.org/LogansRun">11</age>')
INSERT INTO person_content VALUES(
'<age xmlns="http://example.org/LogansRun">11</age>')

-- this fails, more than one root element
INSERT INTO person_docs VALUES(
'<age xmlns="http://example.org/LogansRun">5</age>
 <age xmlns="http://example.org/LogansRun">5</age>
')
GO

-- this works because it's a valid fragment
INSERT INTO person_content VALUES(
'<age xmlns="http://example.org/LogansRun">5</age>
 <age xmlns="http://example.org/LogansRun">5</age>
')
GO
```

XML variables can also be schema-validated by declaring them with a name of an already-defined schema collection.

```
-- this document or fragment must correspond to this schema collection
DECLARE @x XML(accountingcoll)

-- input is validated here
SET @x =
'<po xmlns="urn:com-develop:purchaseorder">
  <orderid>4321</orderid>
  <customerid>10753</customerid>
  <items>
     <itemno>987-65</itemno>
     <qty>5</qty>
  </items>
</po>'
```

There are three ways to specify the type of an XML element in an XML document. You can define an XML namespace prefix for a particular namespace and use the prefix on the element in question, use a default XML namespace definition, or use xsi:type to specify the data type.

Management of XML Schemas and Schema Collections

When an XML schema collection is stored in SQL Server, its schemas are not stored directly as XML documents. Instead, they are shredded into a proprietary format that is useful for optimizing schema validation. Although you can reconstruct your XML schemas using the system function `xml_schema_namespace()`, as shown in the following example, comments and schema annotations are not recovered.

```
- this returns a single XML schema document
- for the 'http://invoice' namespace
- if it occurs in the XML schema collection 'mycoll'
DECLARE @s XML
SELECT @s = xml_schema_namespace(
    N'dbo', N'mycoll', N'http://invoice')
PRINT CONVERT(varchar(max), @s)
GO

- this returns all of the XML schema documents
- in the mycoll XML schema collection
- multiple schema documents are separated by a space
DECLARE @s2 XML
SELECT @s2 = xml_schema_namespace(N'dbo', N'mycoll')
PRINT CONVERT(varchar(max), @s2)
GO
```

The exact signature of `xml_schema_namespace` is:

```
XML_SCHEMA_NAMESPACE (relational_schema,
                      xml_schema_collection_name[,namespace])
```

where `relational_schema` is the relational schema that contains the collection. It returns a schema document (as an XML data type instance) representing the content of the XML schema namespaces associated with the SQL XML schema collection identifier.

If you need to keep track of an original schema in its exact text format, you should store it separately. A convenient way to keep track of your schemas is to insert them into a table with a NVARCHAR(max) column.

```
CREATE TABLE xml_schema_save_tab (
  the_id INTEGER PRIMARY KEY,
  xml_schema_col NVARCHAR(max))
go

INSERT INTO xml_schema_save_tab VALUES(1,
N'<xsd:schema xmlns:xsd="http://www.w3.org/2001/XMLSchema"
        xmlns:tns="http://example.org/LogansRun"
        targetNamespace="http://example.org/LogansRun" >
  <! - this schema defines a single data type, personAge,
      and I want to save this comment as well as the schema  -->
  <xsd:simpleType name="personAge" >
    <xsd:restriction base="xsd:float" >
      <xsd:maxInclusive value="30" />
      <xsd:minExclusive value="0" />
```

```
    </xsd:restriction>
   </xsd:simpleType>
   <xsd:element name="age" type="tns:personAge" />
</xsd:schema>')
GO
```

XML schema collections are tied to a specific SQL schema within a specific database; they are first-class SQL Server database objects that can be referenced by a one-, two-, or three-part name by users with the appropriate permission. Because many XML documents use types from multiple XML namespaces, an XML schema collection can contain multiple unrelated schemas. In addition, many XML schemas import types from other schemas; you can use the XML schema <import> statement to import another XML schema namespace that you use in a second schema definition for a different namespace. In addition to defining all the schemas in a collection by using the CREATE XML SCHEMA COLLECTION DDL statement, you can add more schemas to a collection after it's been created using ALTER XML SCHEMA COLLECTION. For example, if we first define the following XML schema collection:

```
CREATE XML SCHEMA COLLECTION mytrees AS
'<xsd:schema xmlns:xsd="http://www.w3.org/2001/XMLSchema"
            xmlns:tns="http://example.org/Trees"
            targetNamespace="http://example.org/Trees" >
   <xsd:simpleType name="treeAge" >
     <xsd:restriction base="xsd:float" >
       <xsd:maxInclusive value="1000" />
       <xsd:minExclusive value="0" />
     </xsd:restriction>
   </xsd:simpleType>
   <xsd:element name="treeage" type="tns:treeAge" />
</xsd:schema>'
```

it is permissible to import that schema definition into another schema definition for a different namespace, as the following code shows.

```
ALTER XML SCHEMA COLLECTION mytrees ADD
'<xsd:schema xmlns:xsd="http://www.w3.org/2001/XMLSchema"
            xmlns:tns="http://example.org/Trees2"
            targetNamespace="http://example.org/Trees2" >
 <xsd:import namespace="http://example.org/Trees"/>
   <xsd:simpleType name="treeAge2" >
     <xsd:restriction xmlns:t2="http://example.org/Trees"
                      base="t2:treeAge" >
       <xsd:maxInclusive value="500" />
       <xsd:minExclusive value="0" />
```

```
      </xsd:restriction>
    </xsd:simpleType>
    <xsd:element name="treeage2" type="tns:treeAge2" />
</xsd:schema>'
```

Notice that the `simpleType treeAge2` in the namespace `http://example.org/Trees2` is derived by restriction from the base type `t2:treeAge` in a different namespace. We could also have defined both schemas in the collection with a single `CREATE XML SCHEMA COLLECTION` DDL statement.

An XML schema collection is dropped from the database like any other SQL Server object and is subject to the same constraints; for example, you may not drop an XML schema collection if it is being used to type an XML data type column.

```
-- this would fail if the XML schema collection
-- was used to type an XML data type column
DROP XML SCHEMA COLLECTION mycoll
```

Security for Schema Collections and Strongly Typed Instances

Security for XML schema collections and strongly typed instances is applied on the database objects and is analogous to security on native SQL Server data. XML schema collections are scoped to the SQL schema within a database, so you can permit users or roles to define XML schemas.

```
GRANT CREATE XML SCHEMA COLLECTION TO public
```

Once a specific XML schema collection is cataloged, permissions must be granted to reference the schema or use strongly typed columns or parameters. The syntax looks somewhat like the syntax for a .NET procedure or UDT.

```
GRANT REFERENCES ON XML SCHEMA COLLECTION mycoll
   TO FRED
```

The permissions that can be granted on a specific schema collection are as follows:

* REFERENCES—Gives permission to define tables and views that reference a schema collection
* EXECUTE—Gives permission to use strongly typed columns, parameters, or variables that refer to a given schema collection

Creating an Index on an XML Column

You can create indexes on an XML column, using approximately the same syntax that you use for a SQL index. Four kinds of XML indexes can be created. In order to create any kind of XML index, the table must have an ordinary SQL data type primary key column. You must first create the "primary index" or node table. This index associates each node with the SQL key column and is useful for ad hoc queries. You can create an XML index over only the document structure, using the FOR PATH keyword. This is similar to the concept of creating a "key" in XSLT; this type of index helps in XQuery path statements. You can also create an index only over the values of the elements and attributes in the XML data type column with the FOR VALUE keyword. This type of index can help in XQuery content searches. The FOR PROPERTY keyword creates an index that is most usable when your XML consists of a shallow hierarchy with many elements or attributes that are really name/value pairs. Additional XML index types may be defined in the future. If you create an XML index on the entire document or column, you cannot index subsets of the document. The syntax is shown in Listing 8-6.

LISTING 8-6: Creating XML Indexes

```
CREATE TABLE xml_tab(
  the_id INTEGER PRIMARY_KEY IDENTITY,
  xml_col XML)
GO


CREATE PRIMARY XML INDEX xmlidx1 ON xml_tab(xml_col)
GO

 - structural index
CREATE XML INDEX xmls1 ON xml_tab(xml_col)
 USING XML INDEX xmlidx1 FOR PATH
GO

 - property index
CREATE XML INDEX xmlp1 ON xml_tab(xml_col)
 USING XML INDEX xmlidx1 FOR PROPERTY
GO


 - value index
CREATE XML INDEX xmlv1 ON xml_tab(xml_col)
 USING XML INDEX xmlidx1 FOR VALUE
GO
```

Although this similar to a "normal" SQL primary key and index creation statement with an extra XML keyword, the actual effect of the statement is much different from creating a SQL Server index. What you are creating in the case of an XML column is an index over the internal representation or structure of the column whose purpose is to optimize XQuery queries rather than SQL queries. Remember that the SQL comparison operators cannot be used on an XML column. However, because the index contains the (SQL) primary key of the table, it can assist in queries that use XQuery criteria and a primary key value in a SQL WHERE clause. Though the internal representation of the XML index is an internal implementation detail, suffice it to say that creating such an index will not help optimize queries that cast or convert the XML data to character types first.

Because the XML index is not a "normal" SQL index, some limitations apply to these indexes.

- You cannot create an XML composite index—that is, an index on more than one XML column or an XML column and a non-XML column.
- You cannot create an XML index as a clustered index or use it as a partitioning criterion.

In addition, because all XML indexes and SQL indexes share the same value space in a database, you cannot create an XML index (of any kind) and a SQL index with the same index name, or two different kinds of XML index with the same name. Although an XML type can also be used with full-text search, this is outside of the scope of this book.

XML Type Functions

In addition to being used as a table or view column, variable, or parameter in its entirety, the XML data type contains a variety of type-specific methods. These are invoked by using `variable.method` syntax, similar to methods of .NET user-defined types. Although the syntax is the same, it should be pointed out that the XML data type is not implemented as a .NET user-defined type. The implementation of the XML type is proprietary, private, and not open to programmers to extend or refine.

The XML type functions encompass a few different groups of functionality.

- Determining if a node or nodes exist that satisfy a given XQuery expression (`exist`)

- Selecting a single value using XQuery and returning it as a SQL data type (`value`)
- Querying the value of the XML type via XQuery (`query`)
- Modifying the value of the XML type via XQuery DML (`modify`)
- Partitioning a set of nodes into a row per node to be used as context nodes with the other XQuery functions (`nodes`)

Because all the current functions on an XML data type are built around using XQuery to query an instance of the type, we'll defer these until the next chapter. Other functions—for example, validating an instance of an XML type on demand that have nothing to do with XQuery—may be added to the XML data type in the future.

SELECT . . . FOR XML Enhancements

SQL Server 2000 provides an enhancement to Transact-SQL permitting composition of XML document fragments using SQL queries against relational tables. This is the SELECT . . . FOR XML syntax. This syntax can produce fragments in element or attribute normal form XML and even produce a combination of elements and attributes. There are three "dialects" of FOR XML queries.

- FOR XML RAW—Produces one XML element for each row in the result, no matter how many tables participate in the query. There is an attribute for each column, and the names of attributes reflect the column names or aliases. FOR XML RAW has been enhanced in SQL Server 2005 to allow element normal form XML.

- FOR XML AUTO—Produces one XML element by row in the result, but produces nested XML elements if there is more than one table in the query. The order of nesting is defined by the order of the columns in the SELECT statement.

- FOR XML EXPLICIT—Produces XML by means of SQL UNION queries. Each arm of the UNION query produces a different level of XML. This is by far the most flexible dialect and can produce element or attribute normal form and nesting XML exactly as you like. This is also by far the most complex dialect to program.

Listings 8-7, 8-8, and 8-9 show the results of FOR XML SELECT statements against the pubs database.

LISTING 8-7: FOR XML RAW Syntax and Results

```
- this query:
SELECT Customers.CustomerID, Orders.OrderID
FROM Customers, Orders
WHERE Customers.CustomerID = Orders.CustomerID
ORDER BY Customers.CustomerID
FOR XML RAW

- produces this XML output document fragment
  <row CustomerID="ALFKI" OrderID="10643" />
  <row CustomerID="ALFKI" OrderID="10692" />
  <row CustomerID="ALFKI" OrderID="10703" />
  <row CustomerID="ALFKI" OrderID="10835" />
  <row CustomerID="ANATR" OrderID="10308" />
```

LISTING 8-8: FOR XML AUTO Syntax and Results

```
- this query:
SELECT Customers.CustomerID, Orders.OrderID
FROM Customers, Orders
WHERE Customers.CustomerID = Orders.CustomerID
ORDER BY Customers.CustomerID
FOR XML AUTO

- produces the following XML document fragment
  <Customers CustomerID="ALFKI">
    <Orders OrderID="10643" />
    <Orders OrderID="10692" />
    <Orders OrderID="10702" />
    <Orders OrderID="10835" />
  </Customers>
  <Customers CustomerID="ANATR">
    <Orders OrderID="10308" />
  </Customers>
```

LISTING 8-9: FOR XML EXPLICIT Syntax and Results

```
- this query:
SELECT      1 as Tag, NULL as Parent,
            Customers.CustomerID as [Customer!1!CustomerID],
            NULL as [Order!2!OrderID]
FROM        Customers
UNION ALL
SELECT      2, 1,
            Customers.CustomerID,
            Orders.OrderID
FROM        Customers, Orders
WHERE       Customers.CustomerID = Orders.CustomerID
```

```
ORDER BY [Customer!1!CustomerID]
FOR XML EXPLICIT

- produces this output document fragment
<Customer CustomerID="ALFKI">
   <Order OrderID="10643"/>
   <Order OrderID="10692"/>
   <Order OrderID="10702"/>
</Customer>
```

In SQL Server 2005, there are quite a few refinements and enhancements to FOR XML queries.

- There is a new dialect of FOR XML query called FOR XML PATH.
- FOR XML can produce an instance of an XML type.
- FOR XML is able to prepend the XML result with an inline schema in XSD schema format. The previous version of FOR XML could only prepend an inline XDR (XML Data Reduced) schema.
- You can select the namespace for the inline XSD schema referred to earlier.
- You can nest FOR XML queries.
- You can produce element-centric XML using FOR XML RAW.
- You can choose to generate xsi:nil for NULL database values rather than leaving that element out of the XML result entirely.
- You can produce a root element for the XML fragment, making it an XML document.
- There is improved whitespace handling through entitization.
- There are subtle improvements to the algorithm for determining nesting in FOR XML AUTO.

Let's explore some of these features to see how they would be useful.

FOR XML PATH Mode

SQL Server 2000's choices of XML output are rich and varied. FOR XML RAW and FOR XML AUTO produce two well-known but "static" XML documents. There is a maximum of one level of nesting with FOR XML RAW; FOR XML AUTO requires that all columns selected from the same table occur at the same nesting level. With RAW and AUTO modes, you must choose either element normal form or attribute normal form. Mixing elements and attributes in the same document requires FOR XML EXPLICIT, which is quite a bit more complex to write. FOR XML PATH is a new mode that gives you more control over nesting levels and mixing attributes and elements. It combines the ease of coding of AUTO and RAW modes with the power of EXPLICIT mode. In fact, it should be possible to code almost all the document formats that require EXPLICIT mode (or post-query XML transformation) using FOR XML PATH mode.

With PATH mode you shape the XML document by using column aliases that contain XPath expressions. When PATH mode sees an alias that contains a forward slash, it creates another level of hierarchy in the output document. Listing 8-10 shows an example using the authors table that combines the first and last name into a single name element and makes au_id an attribute by using PATH mode.

LISTING 8-10: FOR XML PATH Syntax and Results

```
SELECT au_id AS @authorid,
       au_fname AS [name/firstname],
       au_lname AS [name/lastname]
  FROM authors
  WHERE au_id > '998'
  FOR XML PATH
GO

 - this produces the following document fragment:
<row au_id="999-99-9999">
  <name>
    <firstname>Somename</firstname>
    <lastname>Somelast</lastname>
  </name>
</row>
```

In addition to being able to mix elements and attributes and create new hierarchy levels, you can use the following XPath node test functions.

- node()—The content is inserted as a text node. If the content is a complex UDT, the entire tree is inserted. You can also use " * " as a shortcut for node().

- text()—The content is inserted as a text node, but this produces an error if the column's data type is UDT or XML.

- data()—The content is inserted as an atomic value followed by a single space. This allows you to produce lists of element and attribute values.

- `comment()`—This produces an XML comment using the value.
- `processing-instruction()`—This produces an XML processing instruction using the value.

Producing an XML Data Type

It is now possible to use the XML fragments or the documents produced by FOR XML to populate an XML data type column in a table or an XML variable or procedure parameter. This can be done using a few different methods. First, we can set the result of a SELECT...FOR XML query to a variable of the XML data type, like this.

```
-- declare a variable of type XML
DECLARE @x XML
-- now, write to it
SET @x = SELECT * FROM authors FOR XML AUTO, TYPE
```

You can also use FOR XML queries to produce input to a table using SELECT INTO syntax, like this.

```
-- create a table
CREATE TABLE xml_tab(id INT IDENTITY PRIMARY KEY, xml_col XML)
GO

-- populate it with a FOR XML query
INSERT INTO xml_tab
  SELECT * FROM pubs.dbo.authors FOR XML AUTO
GO
```

Finally, because the XML type is a distinct type, you may want to return it to the caller as a VARCHAR or NVARCHAR data type. You can use the result of a FOR XML query for this. Here's an example.

```
DECLARE @x NVARCHAR(max)
SET @x = (SELECT * FROM pubs.dbo.authors FOR XML RAW)
```

Using a VARCHAR or NVARCHAR data type differs from using the TYPE directive in that the TYPE directive will raise errors if invalid characters and non-well-formed fragments are created.

Producing an XML data type column drastically affects how the data is presented to clients. In OLE DB/ADO 2.6 clients with SQL Server 2000, FOR XML queries produced a single stream of data rather than a one-column, one-row rowset. The .NET library Microsoft.Data.SqlXml, introduced with the SQLXML 3.0 Web release, is a .NET wrapper around the unmanaged OLE DB code to enable .NET clients to use streaming mode XML output. Although this stream of data appeared in Query Analyzer as though it were a one-column rowset with a single column named with a specific GUID, this was only a limitation of Query Analyzer. The special GUID was an indication to the TDS libraries that the data was actually streamed.

When the TYPE specifier is used, a FOR XML query does produce a one-row, one-column rowset. This should reduce the confusion for client-side programmers who were never quite comfortable with a SQL statement that produced a stream of XML. OLE DB/ADO 2.8 clients can now produce an XML data type column that can be consumed with "ordinary" rowset-handling code, as shown in the following example. See Chapter 11 for examples of handling XML data type columns from the client.

Producing an Inline XSD Format Schema

FOR XML queries now can include an inline schema that describes the resultset in XML Schema Definition format. This only works with RAW and AUTO modes. At the time that SQL Server 2000 was released, the XSD schema was not yet a W3C standard. Rather than support an intermediate version of XSD, SQL Server 2000 was able to prepend an XML Data Reduced format schema. XDR is a Microsoft-specific precursor of the XSD schema specification designed around OLE DB; it was submitted to the W3C as a note prior to the standardization of XSD. XDR is still used by products like BizTalk and APIs like ADO classic. XDR is supported, though deprecated, in ADO.NET as well. Listing 8-11 shows how to prepend an XDR schema or XSD schema to a SELECT . . . FOR XML result.

LISTING 8-11: Prepending Schemas to FOR XML Results

```
- prepend an XDR schema
SELECT * FROM authors
  FOR XML AUTO, XMLDATA

- prepend an XSD schema (new in SQL Server 2005)
SELECT * FROM authors
  FOR XML AUTO, XMLSCHEMA
```

ADO classic supports XDR schemas when used inline with ADODB. Recordsets; however, ADO is very picky about the exact dialect of XDR supported, requires specific XDR annotations, and is not compatible with FOR XML, XMLDATA. BizTalk did support using FOR XML, XMLDATA queries to describe its data, although BizTalk 2000 can support XSD schemas in addition to XDR.

ADO.NET 1.0 exposes a method, `SqlCommand.GetXmlReader`, that returns a document fragment from a `SELECT...FOR XML` query. In version 1.0, using the `XMLDATA` option to generate an inline schema was a requirement in order to correctly use the returned `XmlReader` to populate a `System.Data.DataSet`. Using the new `FOR XML, XMLSCHEMA` version should provide much better results, since the XSD support in .NET (including ADO.NET) far outstrips XDR support. `FOR XML, XMLSCHEMA` queries should be able to be used in BizTalk and other Microsoft products as well. These can be wrapped in SOAP packets and used manually in a Web Service, although we'll discuss Web Service support in SQL Server 2005 in more detail in Chapter 10.

For producing interoperable XML in this manner, the picture is a little less rosy. The XML schema specification does not mandate the way in which an XML document locates its schema during validation. Although the XSD specification provides the attribute `xsi:schemaLocation` (in the XSI namespace described earlier), XML processors are not required to support even this mechanism, and the location of a schema is completely implementation defined. SQL Server uses a set of precataloged system and user schemas when doing its own validation.

What we're getting to is that very few non-Microsoft XML processors or tools recognize inline schemas and will use them to do schema validation. The XML editor XML Spy is a notable exception. So, although inline schemas are fine in an environment where they will be consumed by Microsoft tools, they are not interoperable. Although it would be inconvenient to use, a generic XSLT program could, however, be used to split out the inline schema.

NULL Database Values

The XML model, especially XML schemas, handles missing or unknown values differently from SQL. SQL specifies that both missing and unknown values are represented as `NULL`. In an XML schema, the definition for an attribute that could be missing is specified as `use="optional"`; therefore, in `FOR XML` queries, `NULL` attribute values are simply omitted. When `FOR XML AUTO, ELEMENTS` or `FOR XML RAW, ELEMENTS` is specified, though, there are two choices for the XML representation. By default, when the database contains a `NULL` value, the element in the `FOR XML` result is simply omitted. In an XML schema, this representation format would be defined in XML as an element with the `"maxOccurs=1"` and `"min Occurs=0"` facets.

With elements, in the SQL Server 2005 version of FOR XML, we have a different choice. Rather than leave an element corresponding to a NULL database value out entirely, we can also specify that the FOR XML query use `xsi:nil="1"` to indicate an XML nil value. An example should clarify the choices. We have created and populated a simple table as follows.

```
CREATE TABLE students (
   id INTEGER, name VARCHAR(50), major VARCHAR(20) NULL)

INSERT students VALUES(1, 'Bob Smith', 'Chemistry')
INSERT students VALUES(2, 'Fred Jones', NULL)
```

Using the query SELECT * FROM students for XML AUTO, ELEMENTS in SQL Server Management Studio yields the following result.

```
<wb:root
  xmlns:wb="http://schemas.microsoft.com/sqlserver/2003/sqlworkbench">
 <students>
  <id>1</id>
  <name>Bob Smith</name>
  <major>Chemistry</major>
 </students>
 <students>
  <id>2</id>
  <name>Fred Jones</name>
 </students>
</wb:root>
```

Note that Fred Jones's major element is simply missing. Using the query SELECT * FROM students FOR XML AUTO, ELEMENTS XSINIL yields the following results.

```
<wb:root
  xmlns:wb="http://schemas.microsoft.com/sqlserver/2003/sqlworkbench">
 <students xmlns:xsi="http://www.w3.org/2001/XMLSchema-instance">
  <id>1</id>
  <name>Bob Smith</name>
  <major>Chemistry</major>
 </students>
 <students xmlns:xsi="http://www.w3.org/2001/XMLSchema-instance">
  <id>2</id>
  <name>Fred Jones</name>
  <major xsi:nil="1" />
 </students>
</wb:root>
```

Using `xsi:nil="1"` indicates that the value of Fred Smith's major is nil. Because some Web Service toolkits use `xsi:nil` (and expect it in SOAP messages that are sent to them), this is a nice option to have when generating XML.

Producing a Root Element

By default, FOR XML queries produce XML fragments—that is, otherwise well-formed XML that lacks a root element. APIs that expect an XML document, such as `XmlDocument.Load`, will fail in attempting to load the fragment. The reason for this behavior is that output from multiple FOR XML queries can be composed into a single document; the client-side data access API (such as `Microsoft.Data.SqlXml` in SQLXML 3.0) is expected to add the root element. For users and libraries that do not expose a method to add the root element, you can now add it using the ROOT directive of a FOR XML query. You are allowed to name the root element anything you want; the syntax is shown here.

```
- this query:
SELECT Customers.CustomerID, Orders.OrderID
FROM Customers, Orders
WHERE Customers.CustomerID = Orders.CustomerID
ORDER BY Customers.CustomerID
FOR XML AUTO, ROOT('NorthwindCustomers')

- produces the following XML document (not a fragment)
<NorthwindCustomers>
  <Customers CustomerID="ALFKI">
    <Orders OrderID="10643" />
    <Orders OrderID="10692" />
    <Orders OrderID="10702" />
    <Orders OrderID="10835" />
  </Customers>
  <Customers CustomerID="ANATR">
    <Orders OrderID="10308" />
  </Customers>
</NorthwindCustomers>
```

Other Features

Two features that may need more explanation are whitespace entitization and nested XML queries. Whitespace entitization is an improvement on the way in which the SQL Server 2000 FOR XML generation algorithm treats carriage returns and line feeds in the output XML. SQL Server 2000 renders carriage returns and line feeds as their native hexadecimal characters, causing problems with parsers that expect these characters to be XML entities. In SQL Server 2005 the carriage return, for example, is encoded as

 this improves fidelity on the client side when the XML is processed, but is incompatible with your current FOR XML applications.

In SQL Server 2005's FOR XML processing, you can use nested queries to produce levels of nesting in your XML. These are similar to subqueries in SQL, except that the resultset is not flat but produces multiple nested levels of hierarchy. For example, using the stores and discounts tables in the pubs database, the following query:

```
SELECT stor_id, stor_name, state,
  (SELECT discounttype, discount FROM discounts d
    WHERE d.stor_id = s.stor_id
    FOR XML AUTO, ELEMENTS, TYPE)
FROM stores s
ORDER BY s.stor_id
FOR XML AUTO, ELEMENTS
```

will yield the following nested XML in SQL Server Management Studio.

```
<wb:root
  xmlns:wb="http://schemas.microsoft.com/sqlserver/2003/sqlworkbench">
  <s>
  <stor_id>6380</stor_id>
  <stor_name>Eric the Read Books</stor_name>
  <state>WA</state>
  </s>
  <! - some elements omitted here  ->
  <s>
  <stor_id>8042</stor_id>
  <stor_name>Bookbeat</stor_name>
  <state>OR</state>
  <d>
    <discounttype>Customer Discount</discounttype>
    <discount>5.00</discount>
  </d>
  </s>
</wb:root>
```

Note that in all the previous examples when SQL Server Management Studio is used, SQL Server Management Studio will wrap the actual result in a <wb:root> element. This is done in order to ensure that the XML will display using the Internet Explorer–specific stylesheet in SQL Server Management Studio, because the actual result may be an XML fragment. The actual result returned by the SQL SELECT . . . FOR XML statement does *not* contain the <wb:root> element.

Mapping SQL and XML Data Types

Throughout this chapter, we've been able, through the new XML data type, to mix XML and relational types at will, sometimes even in the same query. SQL types can be used in the production of XML data types, and XML data types and XML queries against these types can return output that is usable in T-SQL, perhaps even as input to complex .NET types. At this point, before we discuss the composition and decomposition functionality, it behooves us to realize that we are actually dealing with two different type systems. These are the SQL type system, as defined by SQL:1999, and the XML type system, as defined by the XML 1.0 and Namespaces, the XPath 2.0 and XQuery 1.0 data model, and XML Schema specifications. We are mostly concerned with the XML Schema specification, since this is the heart of the XML type system definitions.

XML Schema is a rich type system, encompassing simple types (similar to SQL types), XML types (from XML's SGML roots), and complex types using object-oriented type principles like the .NET type system and SQL:1999 user-defined types. Some of the constructs go beyond the bounds of the current SQL type system, even when SQL:1999 complex types are included. For example, an XML facet can indicate that an array of elements always consists of exactly five or six elements (minOccurs=5, maxOccurs=6); nothing in SQL:1999 is analogous. In this section, we go over the idiosyncrasies and edge cases in mappings, showing mappings from SQL types to XML types and vice versa. The exact mappings between SQL and XML are found in the SQL:2003 specification and, for SQL Server, the schemas discussed in Chapter 11. We'll also defer the subject of mapping XML data types to SQL types until the next chapter, since this is used in XQuery, although to a lesser extent in OpenXML.

Mapping SQL Types to XML Types

You can produce XML types from the underlying SQL types when using these features of SQL Server 2005:

- FOR XML queries
- sql:variable and sql:column in server-side XQuery functions on the XML data type (discussed in Chapter 9)
- Producing SOAP messages from SQL Server (discussed in Chapter 10)
- XML views of relational data (discussed in Chapter 13)

Microsoft defines a specific XML namespace to codify the mapping, http://schemas.microsoft.com/sqlserver/2004/sqltypes, and tries to align this mapping to the SQL/XML ANSI standard (more on the standard later). This schema provides a direct mapping of SQL Server types to XML types, and, therefore, it refers to SQL Server data types that are not explicitly mentioned in the spec, and leaves out types that SQL Server does not support. In general, this schema defines an XML SimpleType named after the corresponding SQL Server type, but derived by restriction in XML. For example, the SQL Server CHAR data type is represented as follows.

```
<xsd:simpleType name="char">
     <xsd:restriction base="xsd:string"/>
</xsd:simpleType>
```

String, Binary, and Decimal Types

Character-based data types in SQL Server are mapped to the xsd:string data type. Because each column in a SQL Server table or SELECT statement can have character strings of a different length (CHAR(x)) or maximum length (VARCHAR(x)), the mapping is divided into mapping the general case (the data type VARCHAR, for example) and the specific case, the usage of a specific length of VARCHAR in a T-SQL variable or a column. In the general case, the types are mapped to an xsd:string with no xsd:maxLength facet.

```
<! - other character data types elided for clarity  ->
<xsd:simpleType name="varchar">
          <xsd:restriction base="xsd:string"/>
</xsd:simpleType>
<xsd:simpleType name="nvarchar">
          <xsd:restriction base="xsd:string"/>
</xsd:simpleType>
```

In specific resultsets or columns, you would add the maxLength facet, or, in the case of CHAR, the maxLength and minLength facets, just as you would in SQL Server.

```
<! - a column that is defined as NVARCHAR(40)  ->
<xsd:element name="first_name" minOccurs="0">
          <xsd:simpleType>
                <xsd:restriction base="sqltypes:nvarchar">
                       <xsd:maxLength="40"/>
                </xsd:restriction>
          </xsd:simpleType>
</xsd:element>
```

It seems odd at first glance to group binary and decimal data types with the character data types. The reason for doing this is that binary data types can have a maximum length but can be variable. Decimal data types can have a variable precision and scale. In mapping to SQL Server, these are approached the same way character data types are. In general, the binary data types (`binary`, `varbinary`, and `image` in SQL Server) are defined as `xsd:base64Binary`. The decimal data type maps to `xsd:decimal`. When specific instances are referred to in resultset schemas, the correct `maxLength`, precision, and scale facets are added.

Other General Data Types

The integral data types, bit data type, and float data types have almost exact mappings to XSD data types. In the case of integral types, they will have restrictions based on the value space; for example, the SQL Server data type `INT` has a value space that is slightly different than `xsd:integer`. Another case is the SQL Server `MONEY` and `SMALLMONEY` data types, which map to decimal types with specific `maxInclusive` and `minInclusive` facets.

```
<xsd:simpleType name="smallmoney">
    <xsd:restriction base="xsd:decimal">
        <xsd:totalDigits value="10"/>
        <xsd:fractionDigits value="4"/>
        <xsd:maxInclusive value="214748.3647"/>
        <xsd:minInclusive value="-214748.3648"/>
    </xsd:restriction>
</xsd:simpleType>
```

Pattern-Based Data Types

Some SQL Server data types do not have an exact, or even an approximate, value-space-based relationship to any corresponding XSD data type. Examples of this include SQL Server's GUID data type and SQL Server's date-based data types, which are not based at all on the ISO8601 standard date used by XSD. These types are mapped to XSD by using the XSD pattern facet and considered a derivation by restriction of either `xsd:string` (in the case of GUID) or `xsd:dateTime`. As an example, here is the mapping of a GUID.

```
<xsd:simpleType name="uniqueidentifier">
  <xsd:restriction base="xsd:string">
      <xsd:pattern value="([0-9a-fA-F]{8}-[0-9a-fA-F]{4}-[0-9a-fA-F]{4}-
[0-9a-fA-F]{4}-[0-9a-fA-F]{12})|(\{[0-9a-fA-F]{8}-[0-9a-fA-F]{4}-[0-9a-
fA-F]{4}-[0-9a-fA-F]{4}-[0-9a-fA-F]{12}\})"/>
```

```
            </xsd:restriction>
        </xsd:simpleType>
</xsd:simpleType>
```

Wildcard Data Types

The two SQL Server types that must be represented as wildcards are SQL_VARIANT and the SQL Server XML type. SQL_VARIANT must map to xsd:any because there is no simple combination of restrictions that would cover all the different possibilities. SQL Server's XML type would map to xsd:any with a possible wildcard schema region—that is, any in a specific namespace. This is even more straightforward in the case of typed XML instances.

Nullability

SQL Server type instances, when defined as columns in tables, can be defined as NULL or NOT NULL. NOT NULL is the default in XSD schemas, as represented by the default facets maxOccurs=1 and minOccurs=1. Data types that are declared NULL in SQL Server tables must be represented as max Occurs=0. NULL values in XML can be represented by simply omitting the element or by specifying an empty element with the attribute xsi: type=nil. When using SQL Server's FOR XML, you can choose either option using the new ELEMENTS XSINIL directive discussed previously. Note that there is also a new column directive, !xsinil, for the EXPLICIT mode.

OpenXML Enhancements

SQL Server 2000 provides a system-defined function, OpenXML, that creates Rowsets from XML documents. This allows an XML document to be decomposed into possibly multiple Rowsets. These Rowsets can be exposed as resultsets or used with the SELECT . . . INSERT INTO statement to insert rows into one or more relational tables. This is also known as "shredding" an XML document. OpenXML requires an XML document handle as input; this handle is produced by using a system stored procedure, sp_xml_preparedocument. OpenXML uses a subset of XPath 1.0 to indicate which nodes to select as rows and also to indicate which elements and attributes correspond to columns in the Rowset. An example of using OpenXML is shown in Listing 8-12.

LISTING 8-12: Using OpenXML to Insert Rows

```
DECLARE @h int
DECLARE @xmldoc VARCHAR(1000)

SET @xmldoc =
'<root>
<stores stor_id="8888" stor_name="Bob''s Books"
    stor_address="111 Somewhere" city="Portland"
    state="OR" zip="97225">
</stores>
<stores stor_id="8889"
    stor_name="Powell''s City Of Books"
    stor_address="1005 W Burnside" city="Portland"
    state="OR" zip="97209">
</stores>
</root>'

EXEC sp_xml_preparedocument @h OUTPUT, @xmldoc

INSERT INTO stores
SELECT * FROM OpenXML(@h,'/root/stores')
WITH stores

EXEC sp_xml_removedocument @h
```

There are two changes to OpenXML going forward.

- The XML data type is also supported as an output column or an overflow column in the OpenXML WITH clause.
- You can pass an XML data type variable directly into sp_xml_preparedocument as long as it contains an XML document (not a fragment).

Another improvement in SQL Server 2005 that should assist in OpenXML processing is the introduction of the VARCHAR(MAX) and XML data types. In SQL Server 2000, although you could pass in TEXT fields as procedure parameters, you could not operate on them or generate them inside the procedure. Because, in SQL Server 2005 you can have parameters of VARCHAR(MAX) and XML data type, you can preprocess these types prior to using them in OpenXML processing. In addition, because SELECT...FOR XML now produces variables of the XML data type with a root element, you can generate the input to OpenXML from a FOR XML query.

You must take care when using OpenXML, because it produces Rowsets from an XML DOM (document object model). The integer returned from `sp_xml_preparedocument` is actually a pointer to an instance of an XML DOM. This object (a COM object in the current implementation) is very memory intensive. SQL Server will produce errors if a server-wide memory limit for XML processing is exceeded. Using the XML data type as input to `sp_xml_preparedocument` produces a DOM even though the XML data type may already be parsed.

SQL Server 2005 provides an alternate, preferred way to produce a rowset from XML: the `xml.nodes` function. We'll talk about the `xml.nodes` function in the next chapter.

Using XML Bulk Load inside the Database

For loading large XML documents into the database, parsing the documents into a DOM just to use `OpenXML` is very memory intensive. Users are encouraged to use the XML Bulk Load facility on the client side. This Bulk Load facility works by reading the XML and producing SQL statements on the client side, which are sent to SQL Server as a batch. In SQL Server 2005, the XML Bulk Load facility has been enhanced to be usable from either client or server, and to insert XML data stored in flat files directly into XML data type columns. This saves on network traffic because you specify the exact SQL statement to be used rather than having the client Bulk Load shred an XML document into relational tables by using a mapping schema.

Using the new XML Bulk Load is accomplished by using the system rowset provider function `OPENROWSET` and specifying the `BULK` provider. The `BULK` provider can also deal with parsing XML data into XML columns. Given a file that looks like this:

```
1,<Root><Invoice InvoiceID="12345" /></Root>
2,<Root><Invoice InvoiceID="13579" /></Root>
```

and a two-column table defined in SQL Server as follows:

```
CREATE TABLE invoices (rowid INTEGER PRIMARY KEY, invoicedoc XML)
```

this SQL Server statement uses the `BULK` provider to quickly populate the `invoices` table.

```
INSERT invoices
  SELECT *
  FROM  OPENROWSET
    (Bulk 'c:\myinvoices.txt') AS X
go
```

If your table contains only a single XML column to be inserted—for example, if the rowid in the previous invoices table is an identity column, you can use the bulk copy SINGLE_CLOB or SINGLE_BLOB option, like this.

```
INSERT invoices
 SELECT *
 FROM OPENROWSET
  (Bulk 'c:\myinvoices.txt', SINGLE_CLOB) AS X
go
```

Usage of SINGLE_BLOB is actually better, since it does not have conflicting codepage encoding issues. Once your flat file, which might be obtained from a customer using BizTalk, is loaded into a SQL Server data type column, it can be parsed into relational tables by using OpenXML. A temporary table with an XML column might be used as a way to load large documents for later processing.

ANSI SQL Standard Compliance

In addition to the prolific specifications for everything XML guided by the W3C, the ANSI SQL committee has gotten into the act with an effort to standardize the integration of XML and relational databases. This series of specifications was started under the auspices of the SQLX committee of database vendors but has been subsumed as part 14 of the ANSI SQL 2003 specification. A committee that includes representatives from Microsoft, Oracle, and IBM, among others, is working on this part of the SQL spec. This specification touches on a number of subjects that we've discussed in this chapter, and it's interesting to look at how Microsoft's attempts to integrate SQL and XML relate to the specification.

XML Data Type

The XML data type in SQL Server 2005 conforms to the ANSI SQL specification. In fact, one of the architects on the SQL Server XML team is a member of the ANSI SQL standardization committee. The XML type is defined as a new scalar data type that can be used in variables, procedure parameters, and columns in tables. The limitations of SQL Server's XML data type (for example, two instances of the XML data type cannot be compared for equality) are specification compliant. Casting and converting to and from other data types differs from the spec, which mandates the XMLPARSE and XMLSERIALIZE methods.

The data model of the XML data type defined by ANSI SQL part 14 is based on a slightly extended XML information set model, where the document information item is replaced by a root information item that roughly corresponds to the document node in the XPath 2.0/XQuery 1.0 data model. This data model permits an XML data type to contain XML documents, document fragments, and top-level text elements. The SQL Server XML data type adheres to this standard. Because both the XPath and XQuery data model and ANSI SQL part 14 are specifications in progress, the specs may be out of sync at various points in the standardization process. The XPath and XQuery data model permits "lax" validation of its instances. That is, for an instance of the XML, if you can find the schema definition for an element, you do strict validation and throw an error if it doesn't validate correctly; but if you can't find the definition, you "skip" validate. When using schema validation, SQL Server does not permit "lax" validation and allows only "strict" or "skip" validation. The ANSI SQL spec distinguishes two variations of the XML data type: XML document with prolog and XML content. The difference between the two is used in defining how concatenating two XML types should behave. SQL Server allows you to make a similar distinction (document versus content) between schema-validated XML data types, but does not allow concatenation of two XML data type instances directly, though you can cast each one to a character data type, concatenate the character types, and cast the result to the XML data type.

```
DECLARE @x1 XML, @x2 XML, @x3 XML

SELECT @x1 = '<doc1></doc1><doc2></doc2>'
SELECT @x2 = '<doc3/>'

 - this is permitted by the spec
 - but produces an error in SQL Server
@SELECT @x3 = @x1 + @x2

 - this works
DECLARE @v1 VARCHAR(max)
SET @v1 = (CAST(@x1 AS VARCHAR(max))) + (CAST(@x2 AS VARCHAR(max)))
SET @x3 = @v1
```

The ANSI SQL spec indicates that XML data type values will probably be stored in either UTF-8 or UTF-16, although alternate encodings will be permitted. The spec also defines that XML data type columns cannot use the SQL COLLATION keyword or functions; this is consistent with SQL Server 2005 behavior.

Finally, the ANSI SQL specification defines a series of XML data type constructor functions, such as XmlForest and XmlElement. SQL Server 2005 does not currently support these functions. However, SQL Server's

FOR XML TYPE keyword syntax can be used to construct an XML data type; this syntax in SQL Server predates the specification and is easier to use. In addition, in SQL Server 2005, XQuery constructor functions can be used to create an instance of an XML data type.

Mapping SQL Catalogs and Tables to XML

The ANSI SQL spec defines canonical mappings of SQL catalogs, schemas, and tables to a virtual XML document, which can then be used to produce instances of an XML data type. The ANSI standard provides for both a table-as-document and a table-as-forest mapping. The ANSI standard mapping to a document is roughly equivalent to SQL Server's SELECT * FROM table FOR XML RAW, ELEMENTS, ROOT('table'). Mapping as a forest is roughly equivalent to SQL Server's SELECT * FROM table FOR XML AUTO, ELEMENTS. SQL Server's FOR XML capability provides a rich superset of the ANSI standard for in-the-database XML generation. The following example shows the table-as-document and table-as-forest documents that result when the standard is applied with a simple SQL table.

```
<!-- Canonical mapping of a table in the ANSI spec -->
<!-- Also, it's the result of -->
<!-- "SELECT * FROM EMPLOYEE
        FOR XML RAW,ELEMENTS ROOT('EMPLOYEE')" -->
<!-- in SQL Server -->

<EMPLOYEE>
 <ROW>
  <EMPNO>000010</EMPNO>
  <FIRSTNAME>CHRISTINE</FIRSTNAME>
  <LASTNAME>HAAS</LASTNAME>
  <BIRTHDATE>1933-08-24</BIRTHDATE>
  <SALARY>52750.00</SALARY>
 </ROW>
 <ROW>
  <EMPNO>000020</EMPNO>
  <FIRSTNAME>MICHAEL</FIRSTNAME>
  <LASTNAME>THOMPSON</LASTNAME>
  <BIRTHDATE>1948-02-02</BIRTHDATE>
  <SALARY>41250.00</SALARY>
 </ROW>
 .
 .
 .

</EMPLOYEE>

<!-- ANSI mapping as an XmlForest -->
```

```
<!-- Also the result of -->
<!-- "SELECT * FROM EMPLOYEE FOR XML AUTO,ELEMENTS -->
<!-- in SQL Server -->

<EMPLOYEE>
  <EMPNO>000010</EMPNO>
  <FIRSTNAME>CHRISTINE</FIRSTNAME>
  <LASTNAME>HAAS</LASTNAME>
  <BIRTHDATE>1933-08-24T00:00:00</BIRTHDATE> <!-- ISO 8606 -->
  <SALARY>52750.00</SALARY>
</EMPLOYEE>
<EMPLOYEE>
  <EMPNO>000020</EMPNO>
  <FIRSTNAME>MICHAEL</FIRSTNAME>
  <LASTNAME>THOMPSON</LASTNAME>
  <BIRTHDATE>1948-02-02T00:00:00</BIRTHDATE>
  <SALARY>41250.00</SALARY>
</EMPLOYEE>
```

SQL Server also addresses mapping SQL Server data to XML data in the middle tier using a set of managed classes known as SQLXML, augmented by annotated XML schemas known as mapping schemas. In the SQL Server 2005 timeframe, this middle-tier or client functionality will be known as XML/SQL and its mapping capability greatly increased. We'll discuss Microsoft's XML/SQL equivalent (known as client-side SQLXML) and mapping in Chapter 13.

In addition, the ANSI spec provides a method to convert SQL names to XML names. Many names that are valid (for tables and columns) in SQL are not valid XML names. For example, the XML specification forbids certain constructs in names (such as names that begin with "XML" or contain spaces) that are valid SQL names. The specification mandates replacing characters that are illegal in XML with "_xHHHH_," where "HHHH" are the hexadecimal characters that make up the Unicode code point. For example, "hire date" in SQL becomes "hire_x0020_date" in XML. In addition, any SQL name that begins with "XML" is prefixed by "_xFFFF_"; for example, "xmlcol" becomes "_xFFFF_xmlcol". SQL Server 2005's FOR XML extension completely complies with the specification.

Mapping SQL Data Types to XML Data Types

The ANSI SQL standard also establishes a mapping of ANSI SQL types, which do not have a one-to-one correspondence to SQL Server data types. This has a namespace (whose name itself is under discussion) of http:// www.iso-standards.org/9075/2003/sqlxml. Other than the set of types covered, there are a few big differences between the ANSI specification and SQL Server's implementation.

The ANSI SQL spec permits both `xsd:base64Binary` and `xsd:hexBinary` as choices for representing a `VARBINARY` type. SQL Server chose `xsd:base64Binary`. The spec also allows representing nullable data as `xsd:nillible=true` and using `xsi:nil` on the empty element. SQL Server 2005 supports either type.

Finally, the ANSI SQL spec suggests the use of `xsd:annotations` (XSD comments) to indicate SQL constructs that cannot be described (such as data-specific types) or have no meaning in XSD. For example:

```
<! - annotation for database-specific SMALLINT data type in ANSI SQL -->
<xsd:annotation>
  <xsd:appinfo>
    <sqlxml:sqltype kind="PREDEFINED" name="SMALLINT"/>
  </xsd:appinfo>
</xsd:annotation>
```

The SQL Server `sqltypes` schema does not use these annotations and instead makes the SQL Server data type name the XSD data type name. Perhaps in future releases, the SQL Server XML types might be defined as a specialization of the ANSI standard types, or there might be an option to produce schema definitions in SQL Server that are ANSI compliant.

Where Are We?

In this chapter, we looked closely at the new `XML` data type, which provides integration of relational and XML functionality in addition to permitting XML data to be stored in the database. This XML data can be security protected, can be XSD schema–validated, can take part in transactions, can be operated on by SQL utilities, and, in general, is a great step forward from storing XML in files on the file system. On the other hand, the next version of Windows will include a SQL Server–based file system.

We've also seen how SQL Server's XML functionality adheres closely to XML standards and is an implementation of the new SQL 2003 part 14 standard, for the most part. This allows interoperability among not only Microsoft products but also those from third-party and other large vendors.

In the next chapter, we'll investigate the newest XML query languages, XQuery 1.0 and XPath 2.0, and see how these work inside SQL Server.

9

XML Query Languages: XQuery and XPath

X ML BRINGS WITH IT some powerful query languages for dealing with the hierarchical format that is typical of an XML document. This chapter covers XQuery integration as well as the differences between native query language hosting and SQLXML support in SQL Server 2000.

What Is XQuery?

In the preceding chapter, we covered the XML native data type in SQL Server 2005. The XML data type is typically a complex type—that is, a type that almost always contains more than one data value. We can use XML data type columns in two distinct ways.

- Query the data and perform actions on it as though it were a simple data type. This is analogous to the way we would treat an XML file in the file system; we read the entire file or write the entire file.
- Run queries and actions on the XML data in the column, using the fact that the XML Infoset model allows the concrete data to be exposed as a sequence of data values or nodes. For this we need an XML query language.

Currently, the most used query language in XML is XPath. XPath 1.0 is a mature W3C recommendation. XPath uses a syntax for queries that is similar to the syntax you'd use to locate a file or files on the UNIX file system (that is, using forward slashes to indicate levels of hierarchy). XPath queries are used to select data from an XML document in XSLT, the XML stylesheet language. XSLT is also a mature W3C recommendation. XSLT operates on a data model defined in the XPath recommendation, which is a somewhat different view of XML than that provided by the Infoset. XPath 1.0 and XSLT are supported in the .NET base class libraries as part of the `System.Xml` namespace.[1]

XQuery 1.0, XPath 2.0, and XSLT 2.0 are in the midst of the W3C standardization process at the time of this writing; that is, they are "standards" in flux. Both XQuery 1.0 and XSLT 2.0 use XPath 2.0 to select subsets of data to operate on. XQuery is a query language designed to be SQL-like in its appearance and to be optimizable. A native XQuery 1.0 engine and XPath 2.0 parser will live inside the SQL Server 2005 "kernel," along with the relational engine. This will change the diagram of SQL Server internals presented in Chapter 1, to look like Figure 9-1.

Because you can load arbitrary .NET classes inside SQL Server 2005, it is also possible to use the client-side APIs inside the server. We'll defer the discussion of the client-side XML APIs until Chapter 13. The SQL Server 2005 internal implementation of XQuery implements the most-useful subset of the entire XQuery language for server-side processing. The client-side implementation of XQuery implements almost all of the specification. An XQuery query can encompass more than one source of data. In the most common implementations of XQuery, these might be multiple DOM (document object model for XML) instances or multiple files. In SQL Server's implementation, the query is tied to an instance of an `XML` data type or an XML type variable with the additional option of using other SQL columns or variables.

We'll start by describing XQuery from the latest W3C standards documents without making direct reference to the implementation inside SQL Server. Remember as we go that SQL Server implements a useful subset of the specification. We'll continue by comparing XQuery with SQL, the language used by every SQL Server developer. After you are comfortable with the XQuery language, we'll look at the implementation of XQuery in SQL

---

[1] Although XML and .NET use the concept of namespace for approximately the same thing—to disambiguate similarly named data (classes in .NET, attributes and elements in XML)—namespace is an overloaded term. We'll try to use "XML namespace" to refer to namespaces as defined by the XML Namespaces specification, and ".NET namespace" to refer to .NET namespaces, when the meaning could be unclear.

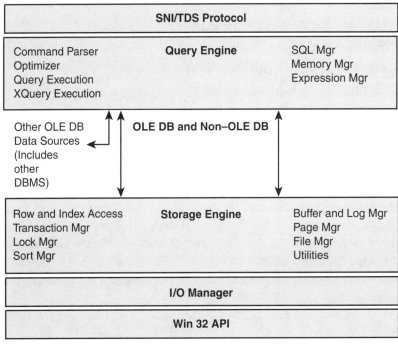

FIGURE 9-1: SQL Server 2005 Internals

Server 2005, pointing out differences from the spec whenever they are relevant. SQL Server implements some nice XQuery extension functions to allow integration of SQL and XML data inside the XQuery query itself.

An Introduction to XQuery

The XQuery specification consists of a series of specification documents and some related documents. The specification describes not only the query language semantics, but also the underlying data model, the XPath 2.0 path expression language used in XQuery expressions, a formal algebra, and a way to represent XQuery queries in an XML format. The names of the specifications follow. To see the most current versions of these specifications, browse to http://www.w3.org/XML/Query.

- XML Query Requirements
- XML Query Use Cases
- XQuery 1.0 and XPath 2.0 Data Model

- XSLT 2.0 and XQuery 1.0 Serialization
- XQuery 1.0 and XPath 2.0 Formal Semantics
- XQuery 1.0, an XML Query Language
- XQuery 1.0 and XPath 2.0 Functions and Operators
- XML Syntax for XQuery 1.0 (XQueryX)
- XPath Requirements Version 2.0
- XML Path Language (XPath) 2.0
- XML Query and XPath Full-Text Requirements
- XML Query and XPath Full-Text Use Cases

The documents that you may be going back to most often if you use them for reference will probably be "XQuery 1.0, an XML Query Language" and "XQuery 1.0 and XPath 2.0 Functions and Operators," but the key concept document is "XQuery 1.0 and XPath 2.0 Data Model" because you can't understand how to use XQuery if you don't understand the model of the data you are querying.

The main building block of the XQuery data model is the *sequence*. A sequence is an ordered collection of zero or more *items*. Items in a sequence are either *nodes* or *atomic values*. There are seven types of XML nodes: document, element, attribute, text, namespace, processing instruction, and comment. Atomic values are instances of the XPath 2.0/XQuery 1.0 data model. This model includes types defined in the XML Schema specification, Part 2, Datatypes, and some additional types (including xdt:untypedAtomic and xdt:anyAtomicType) that are specific to the XPath 2.0/XQuery 1.0 data model.

Another way to say this is that XQuery language uses the XML Schema type system; instances of XML Schema types are recognized as first-class items in XQuery sequences. XQuery sequences can consist of only items that are nodes, only items that are atomic values, or a combination of both. To quickly demonstrate, here is an XML fragment that consist of two element nodes, each with an attribute node, and a text node.

```
<hello color="green">world</hello>
<hello color="red">world</hello>
```

And here are a few atomic values.

```
42      (an instance of type xs:integer)
hello world (an instance of type xs:string)
2003-08-06 (an instance of type xs:date)
```

The thing to notice here is that "world" in the node example is a text node of type `string` and the "hello world" in the atomic value example is an atomic value, not a node. The difference is subtle. The XQuery data model is a closed data model, meaning that the value of every expression is guaranteed to be an instance of the data model. In other words, each expression will yield a sequence, even if it is a sequence containing no items or only a single item. A sequence cannot contain another sequence.

According to the specification, the data model, like XML itself, is a node-labeled, tree-structured graph, although sequences are flat. Two main concepts of the data model are *node identity* and *document order*. Nodes (but not atomic values or sequences) have a unique identity that is assigned when the node constructor is used to construct a node or when data containing nodes is parsed by the query. No two nodes share the same node identity. In the XQuery data model, order is significant, and an algorithm for determining the order of nodes in an XML document or fragment is defined in the specification. Here is the document order algorithm defined in the spec.

- The root node is the first node.
- The relative order of siblings is determined by their order in the XML representation of the tree. A node N1 occurs before a node N2 in document order if and only if the start tag node of N1 occurs before the start of N2 in the XML representation.
- Namespace nodes immediately follow the element node with which they are associated. The relative order of namespace nodes is stable but implementation-dependent.
- Attribute nodes immediately follow the namespace nodes of the element with which they are associated. The relative order of attribute nodes is stable but implementation-dependent.
- Element nodes occur before their children; children occur before following-siblings.

Finally, the XQuery data model is defined in terms of the XML Information Set (Infoset) after schema validation, known as the Post-Schema-Validation Infoset (PSVI). Some of the items defined in the Post-Schema-Validation Infoset definition are not used in the XQuery data model, however, and the XQuery language itself does not use all of the information yielded by schema validation either. The data model supports well-formed XML documents defined in terms of the XML 1.0 and Namespaces specification, as well as the following types of XML documents:

- Well-formed documents conforming to the Namespaces and XML spec
- DTD-valid documents conforming to the Namespaces and XML spec
- XML Schema validated documents

The data model goes beyond the XML Infoset to support data that does not conform to the Infoset as well. This data can consist of the following:

- Well-formed document fragments (XML with multiple top-level nodes)
- Sequences of document nodes
- Sequences of atomic values
- Top-level atomic values (top-level text, for example)
- Sequences mixing nodes and atomic values

Now that we know what we are querying, let's look at the structure of the query itself. XQuery, like XML itself, is case sensitive. Keywords are all lowercase. The query consists of two parts: an optional *query prolog*, followed by the *query body*. The query prolog sets up part of the "environment" in which to query. A simple example of this environment would be the default XML Namespace to which elements without a namespace prefix belong, as shown next.

```
(: This is an XQuery comment. Query Prolog begins here :)
declare default element namespace = "http://example.org"

(: XQuery body begins here :)
(: somelement is in namespace "http://example.org" :)
let $x := <somelement />
```

Items that can be declared in the XQuery prolog include the following:

- Default element namespace
- Default attribute namespace
- Default namespace for functions
- Namespace declarations with a corresponding namespace prefix

- XML Schema `import` statements
- `XMLSpace` declarative (that is, whether boundary whitespace is preserved)
- Default collation
- User-defined function definitions

Note also that if you do not define a default element, attribute, or function namespace, the default is "no namespace." In addition to the namespace prefixes that you define yourself, there are six namespace prefix/namespace pairs that are built in and never need to be declared in the query prolog.

- `xml = http://www.w3.org/XML/1998/namespace`
- `xs = http://www.w3.org/2001/XMLSchema`
- `xsi = http://www.w3.org/2001/XMLSchema-instance`
- `fn = http://www.w3.org/2003/11/xpath-functions`
- `xdt = http://www.w3.org/2003/11/xpath-datatypes`
- `local = http://www.w3.org/2003/11/xquery-local-functions`

SQL Server's implementation also includes:

- `sql = urn:schemas-microsoft-com:xml-sql`
- `sqltypes = http://schemas.microsoft.com/sqlserver/2004/sqltypes`

Finally, in addition to the user-defined functions that you can define yourself in the query prolog, XQuery has a rich set of built-in functions and operators, defined in the "XQuery 1.0 and XPath 2.0 Functions and Operators Version 1.0" document. We'll look at system-defined and user-defined functions in the context of SQL Server's implementation later in the chapter.

The XQuery Expression Body

Now, we'll move on to the query body, the part of the query that actually produces the output that we want. An XQuery query consists of expressions, variables, and data. There are many different types of expressions, the simplest being the literal expression, which is a simple string or numeric literal. For example, the expression `'Hello World'` is a valid (though fairly useless) XQuery query. The query result consists of that same string, "Hello World." XQuery variables are named by variable name. The `let` expression assigns a value to a variable. The following query declares a variable, $a, assigns the value of a string literal to it, and returns the variable's value as the result of the query.

```
let $a := 'Hello World'
return $a
```

Note that according to the latest W3C specification, you can also declare variables in the prolog.

Because you'll probably want to do something more with your query than emit "Hello World," you'll need to provide some XML input to the query. XQuery has the concept of an execution context for its queries, and part of the execution context is the input sequence. In general, the way that the input sequence is provided is implementation-defined, but XQuery defines some functions that can be used in conjunction with input: `fn:doc` and `fn:collection`. The `fn:doc` function, in its simplest form, can be used to return a document node, given a string URI that references an XML document. It also may be used to address multiple documents or document fragments. The `fn:collection` function returns a sequence of nodes pointed to by a collection that is named by a URI. Note that you can always implicitly set the context node or provide data via externally bound variables. Now we have input! The following query echoes the content of a file containing an XML document using the `fn:doc` function.

```
let $a := doc("data/test/items.xml")
return $a
```

Notice that this query illustrates two items that are implementation dependent. The parser that uses this query allows the use of the document function without the namespace prefix, because it is a built-in system function. Also, the parser allows the use of a relative path name rather than strictly requiring a URI; the current part used to resolve the relative path name is part of the environment. This is just an example of possible parser implementation-dependent behavior.

Two of the most important constructs of the XQuery language are path expressions and FLWOR expressions. Path expressions refer to XPath, the selection language portion of XQuery. XPath expressions consist of a series of evaluation steps, separated by forward slashes. Each evaluation step selects a sequence of nodes, each item of which is input to the next evaluation step. The result of the final evaluation step in the output is the final result of the XPath expression. If any location step returns an empty sequence, the XPath expression stops (because there are no items for the next step to process) and returns an empty sequence. XPath expressions can be used as standalone queries. In fact, if all you want to do is simply select a sequence of nodes in document order, this may be all you need. Let's assume we have a simple document that looks like the following.

```
<items>
  <itm status="sold">
    <itemno>1234</itemno>
    <seller>Fanning</seller>
    <description>Antique Lamp</description>
    <reserve-price>200</reserve-price>
    <end-date>12-31-2002</end-date>
  </itm>
  <itm status="sold">
    <itemno>1235</itemno>
    <seller>Smith</seller>
    <description>Rugs</description>
    <reserve-price>1000</reserve-price>
    <end-date>2-1-2002</end-date>
  </itm>
</items>
```

The following XQuery:

```
doc("data/test/items.xml")/items/itm/itemno
```

produces the following output, a sequence of nodes.

```
<itemno>1234</itemno>
<itemno>1235</itemno>
```

Because XML documents are hierarchical, XPath expression steps can operate on different axes of data. Although the XPath specification defines 13 different axes, an XQuery implementation has to support only 6 of them, though implementations may choose to support more.

- The child axis contains the children of the context node.
- The descendant axis contains the descendants of the context node; a descendant is a child or a child of a child and so on; thus the descendant axis never contains attribute or namespace nodes.
- The parent axis contains the parent of the context node, if there is one.

- The attribute axis contains the attributes of the context node; the axis will be empty unless the context node is an element.
- The self axis contains just the context node itself.
- The descendant-or-self axis contains the context node and the descendants of the context node.

Figure 9-2 shows the nodes that make up the main XPath axes for a particular document, given a particular context node.

The context node that we are referring to here is the starting point of the evaluation step. In our earlier simple XPath expression, the starting point of the first evaluation step was the document node, a concrete node. In the XQuery data model, this is the root node (that is, the root node returned by `fn:root()`). The root node is the `items` node in this example document. In the second evaluation step, the `items` node would be the context node; in the third evaluation step, each `itm` node would be the context node in turn; and so on. Each evaluation step can filter the resulting sequence using a *node test* that can filter by name or by node type. For example, in the last evaluation step, only children of `itm` named `itemno` will be selected. If we wanted to select all the children of `itm` nodes, include

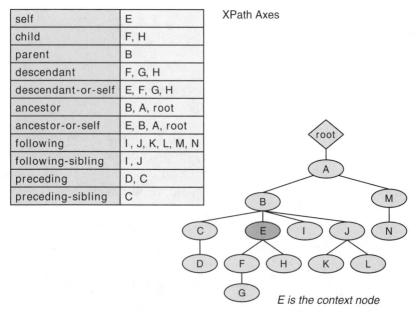

self	E
child	F, H
parent	B
descendant	F, G, H
descendant-or-self	E, F, G, H
ancestor	B, A, root
ancestor-or-self	E, B, A, root
following	I, J, K, L, M, N
following-sibling	I, J
preceding	D, C
preceding-sibling	C

XPath Axes

E is the context node

FIGURE 9-2: XPath Axes

seller nodes, description nodes, and all others, we could change the path expression to the following.

```
doc("data/test/items.xml")/items/itm/*
```

Each evaluation step has an axis; in our simple query, we have let the axis default to "child" by leaving it out. The same query could be expressed this way.

```
doc("data/test/items.xml")/child::items/child::itm/child::*
```

Any other valid axis could also be used. Another common abbreviation is to abbreviate the attribute axis to @. The evaluation step /attribute:: status in a query against the document above could be abbreviated to /@status.

Although XPath has much more functionality and a function library of its own (that can be used in path expressions in XQuery) in addition to being able to use the XPath and XQuery operators and functions, we'll finish by discussing XPath predicates. After you filter any evaluation step by using a node test, you can filter the results further by using a *query predicate*. Query predicates follow the node test in square brackets. For example, this predicate filters itm elements whose itemno subelement has a text subelement with a value less than 1000.

```
doc("data/test/items.xml")/items/itm[itemno/text() < 1000]
```

A predicate can be as simple or complex as you want, but it must evaluate to a boolean value. More exactly, it is evaluated using the Effective Boolean Value (essentially, the rules for fn:boolean)—for example, /a[1]. You can even have multiple predicates on the same evaluation step if you want.

The heart of XQuery expressions, what forms most of the "selection logic" in an XQuery query, is called the FLWOR expressions. FLWOR is an acronym for the five main expression keywords: for, let, where, order by, and return. We've already seen the let expression, to assign a value to a variable, and the return expression, for returning the value of a variable in the query.

```
let $a := doc("data/test/items.xml")
return $a
```

We'll briefly define the use of each expression.

The `for` and `let` keywords are used to set up a stream of tuples, each tuple containing one or more bound variables. The `for` keyword is used for iteration. In the following query:

```
for $p in doc("mydocument.xml")/people/person
let $a := $p/age
where $a > 50
return $p/name/firstName/text()
```

the `for` statement uses an XPath expression to select a sequence of items. The `for` statement iterates over all the items that match the XPath expression, assigning a different item to the variable `$p`, one value for each time around the loop. For example, if the sequence produced is (`<person name='joe'/> <person name='bob'/>, <person name='phil'/>`), the loop is executed three times, with `$p` assigned to one node for each iteration. The `let` keyword is used by assignment. The expression on the right side of the assignment is assigned to the variable in its entirety. The assignment takes place whether the value is a single item (as in the `let $a := $p/age` statement in the preceding query) or an entire sequence. To show the difference between iteration and assignment, consider the following two queries.

```
for $p in (1,2), $q in (3,4)
let $a := (7,8,9)
return ($p, $q, $a)
(: this returns (1,3,7,8,9),(1,4,7,8,9), (2,3,7,8,9), (2,4,7,8,9) :)

for $p in (1,2)
let $a := (7,8,9), $q := (3,4)
return ($p, $q, $a)
(: this returns (1,3,4,7,8,9),(2,3,4,7,8,9) :)
```

You can use the `where` keyword to filter the resulting tuples. You can filter based on the value based on any XQuery expression. Interestingly, in many situations you could use an XPath predicate in the `for` statement to achieve the same effect as using a `where` keyword. For example, the earlier query that looks for people could be just as easily expressed as this.

```
for $p in doc("mydocument.xml")/people/person[age > 50]
return $p/name/firstName/text()
```

The `order by` keyword changes the order of the returned tuples. Usually, tuples are returned in the order of the input, which often is the document order (which we defined previously in this chapter). The following query orders the returned items by the text of the `lastName` subelement of the name.

```
for $p in doc("mydocument.xml")/people/person[age > 50]
order by $p/name/lastName/text() descending
return $p/name/firstName/text()
```

The `return` keyword defines what the sequence that constitutes the return value will look like. In the last few queries, we have only been returning information derived from tuples as simple items. But items can be composed from scratch or using existing tuple information using node constructors. Node constructors can use simple literal strings with individual items separated by commas, but they can also use calculated values enclosed in curly braces. An example follows.

```
<descriptive-catalog>
  {
    for $i in doc("catalog.xml")//item,
        $p in doc("parts.xml")//part[partno = $i/partno],
        $s in doc("suppliers.xml")//supplier[suppno = $i/suppno]
    order by $p/description, $s/suppname
    return
      <item>
        {
        $p/description,
        $s/suppname,
        $i/price
        }
      </item>
  }
</descriptive-catalog>
```

Notice that this example uses construction twice. The `<descriptive-catalog>` element is constructed by simply using it as a literal. The `<item>`s in the return clause are constructed with a literal, but all `<item>` subelements are constructed by evaluation of the expressions between the curly braces.

Here's a list of some of the other types of expressions available in XQuery:

- Function calls
- Expressions combining sequences
- Arithmetic and logic expressions
- Comparisons—Content, identity, and order based

- Quantified expressions—Where one element satisfies a condition
- Expressions involving types—Cast, instance of, treat, and typeswitch

Finally, let's explore the question of what type of data models (XML can represent many different data models) should XQuery be used on? Some authors have attempted to make a distinction between XQuery and XSLT based on the premise that although XSLT and XQuery can be used for almost all the same functions (at least if you compare XSLT 2.0 and XQuery 1.0), XSLT with its template mechanism is better for data-driven transformations, while XQuery is better suited for queries. We find it instructive to look at the XQuery use cases document to see what the inventors of XQuery had in mind. The use cases mention many different kinds of data.

- Experiences and exemplars—General XML
- Tree—Queries that preserve hierarchy
- Sequence—Queries based on document ordering
- Relational—Relational data (representing tables as XML documents)
- SGML—Queries against SGML data
- String—String search (a.k.a. full-text search)
- Queries using namespaces
- Parts explosion—Object and Codasyl databases usually do this well
- Strong types—Queries that exploit strongly typed data
- Full-text use cases (separate specification)

So it appears that XQuery can be useful with all kinds of data; however, particular implementations may not implement certain features that their data types cannot take advantage of. We'll see this point when we look at the XQuery implementation inside SQL Server.

Comparing and Contrasting XQuery and SQL

SQL (specifically, Transact-SQL) is the native language of SQL Server. SQL Server programmers have used it exclusively, until the CLR language becomes available in SQL Server 2005. These same programmers are probably not familiar with XQuery, an XML-centric query language that is still a work in progress, and it is instructive to compare the two languages to make SQL programmers more at home.

SQL currently is a more complete language than XQuery with regard to its use. SQL can be used for data definition (DDL), data manipulation (INSERT, UPDATE, and DELETE), and queries (SELECT). XQuery delegates its DDL to XML Schema, and the rest of XQuery equates to the SQL SELECT statement, although Microsoft and others have proposed data manipulation extensions to XQuery, and data manipulation extensions are part of SQL Server 2005. So we'll compare SQL SELECT and XQuery's FLWOR expressions.

The clauses of a SQL SELECT statement have an almost one-for-one correspondence in function to the clauses of a FLWOR statement, as is shown in Figure 9-3.

Both SQL's SELECT and FLWOR's return statements enumerate data to be returned from the query. SELECT names columns in a resultset to be returned, whereas return can name a node or an atomic value to be returned. Fairly complex nodes can be returned using, for example, element constructors and nested elements, but items in a sequence are what is being returned nevertheless. Another similarity is that both return and SELECT can be nested in a single statement.

SQL's FROM clause lists the tables from which the data will be selected. Each row in each table is combined with each row in other tables to yield a Cartesian product of tuples, which make up the candidate rows in the resultset. XQuery's for works exactly the same way. Multiple clauses in a for statement, separated by commas produce a Cartesian product of candidate tuples as well. Because a for clause in XQuery can contain a selection using XPath, for also has some of the functionality of a SQL WHERE clause; this is especially noticeable when the XPath predicate is used. Both SQL and XQuery do support WHERE and ORDER BY; although the XQuery

SQL	FLWOR
SELECT a,b,c	RETURN a,b,c
FROM tablex,tabley	FOR $b in doc("x"), FOR $y in doc("y")
SET @z = 20	LET $z = 20
WHERE	WHERE
ORDER BY	ORDER BY

FIGURE 9-3: SQL SELECT and FLWOR

WHERE clause is based on existence (this is known as existential qualification), the SQL one is not.

Both XQuery `let` and SQL's `SET` can be used for assignment, though `let` can be used as an adjunct to `for` inside a FLWOR expression. `SET` in SQL is usually a clause in a SQL `UPDATE` statement or a standalone statement in a SQL batch or a stored procedure. In fact, in Transact-SQL, `SELECT` can also be used for assignment. Though some of the matches are not 100% exact, it should not be a big stretch for SQL users to learn XQuery. The ease of adoption by SQL programmers, rather than data models served, is probably the reason for relational database vendors (or for that matter, OODBMS vendors, since XQuery also resembles OQL) to embrace XQuery over the functionally equivalent XSLT language.

SQL and XQuery differ with respect to their data models. Attributes (column values) in SQL usually have two possible value spaces: an atomic value or `NULL`. Having `NULL` complicates some of the SQL operations; for example, `NULL`s are not included by default in aggregate operations. XQuery has the `NULL` sequence (a sequence with zero items), which has some of the same semantics (and complications) as the SQL `NULL`. In addition, XQuery has to deal with complications of nodes versus atomic values as well as the complications of possibly hierarchical nodes or multivalue sequences. This makes some of the rules for XQuery quite complex. As an example, value comparisons between unlike data types in SQL are not possible without casting (although SQL Server performs implicit casting in some cases). Comparing a value with `NULL` (including `NULL`) is always undefined. This rule could be stated in two sentences with two cases. Contrast this to the rules for value comparison in XQuery.

1. Atomization is applied to each operand. If the result is not an empty sequence or a single atomic value, a type error is raised.

2. If either operand is an empty sequence, the result is an empty sequence.

3. If either operand has the most specific type `xdt:untypedAtomic`, that operand is cast to a required type, which is determined as follows:

4. If the type of the other operand is numeric, the required type is `xs:double`.

5. If the most specific type of the other operand is `xdt:untypedAtomic`, the required type is `xs:string`.

6. Otherwise, the required type is the type of the other operand.

7. If the cast fails, a dynamic error is raised.

8. The result of the comparison is true if the value of the first operand is (equal, not equal, less than, less than or equal, greater than, greater than or equal) to the value of the second operand; otherwise, the result of the comparison is false. B.2 Operator Mapping describes which combinations of atomic types are comparable and how comparisons are performed on values of various types. If the value of the first operand is not comparable with the value of the second operand, a type error is raised.

Quite a bit more complex, don't you agree?

SQL is a more strongly typed language than XQuery. In XQuery, static typing is possible but optional, although SQL Server's implementation of XQuery implements static typing. In SQL, strong typing is required. When static typing is used, having schemas assists optimization. Both SQL and XQuery are declarative languages; however, Transact-SQL is more procedural, especially when combined with stored procedures that can contain procedural logic. Oracle's Transact-SQL equivalent, PL/SQL, actually stands for "Procedural Language extensions to SQL." While we're mentioning stored procedures, the XQuery equivalent to SQL's stored procedures and user-defined functions (Persistent Stored Modules, as they are called in ANSI SQL) is user-defined functions. XQuery allows for implementation-dependent extensions to store and access user-defined functions in libraries. XQuery's functions are supposed to be side effect free. All of SQL's PSMs are not guaranteed to be side effect free, although SQL user-defined functions can make this guarantee.

In conclusion, the SQL SELECT statement has a lot in common with the XQuery language, though XQuery is more complex because of the underlying data model. XQuery has some of the functionality of data manipulation through the use of constructors, but no way to affect the underlying data. It more reflects the querying and reporting functionality of SQL SELECT and stored procedures.

Using XQuery with the XML Data Type

SQL Server supports XQuery on the XML data type directly. It does this through four of the XML data type's methods.

- xml.query takes an XQuery query as input and returns an XML data type as a result.

- `xml.value` takes an XQuery query as input and returns a SQL type as a scalar value.

- `xml.exist` takes an XQuery query as input and returns 0, 1, or NULL, depending on whether the query returns an empty sequence (0), a sequence with at least one item (1), or the column is NULL.

- `xml.nodes` takes an XQuery query as input and returns a one-column rowset that contains references to XML documents with the XQuery context set at the matching node.

Currently, SQL Server 2005 XQuery is aligned to the November 2003 XQuery draft, with some implementation restrictions. As SQL Server 2005 approaches RTM (release to manufacturing), the dialect may be aligned to a later draft.

Although the XQuery language itself can be used to produce complex documents, as we've seen, this functionality is really only used to a great extent in SQL Server in the `xml.query` function. When using `xml.value` and `xml.exist`, we'll really be using simple XPath 2.0 expressions rather than complex XQuery with sequences, constructors, formatting information, and so on. Although we could use more complex XQuery, the reason for this is that `xml.value` can only return a sequence containing a single scalar value (it cannot return an XML data type), and `xml.exist` is used to check for existence. So let's cover them first.

xml.exist(string xquery-text)

The `xml.exist` function refers to a single column or variable of the XML data type. For example, if we define the following table:

```
CREATE TABLE xml_tab(
  the_id INTEGER PRIMARY KEY IDENTITY,
  xml_col XML)
```

and fill the table with some rows, the `xml.exist` function will search the XML column specified, looking for data that matches the given XQuery expression. For each row, if the row contains matching data in the specified column, the function returns true (1). For example, if the rows inserted look like this:

```
INSERT xml_tab VALUES('<people><person name="curly"/></people>')
INSERT xml_tab VALUES('<people><person name="larry"/></people>')
INSERT xml_tab VALUES('<people><person name="moe"/></people>')
GO
```

the XQuery `xml.exist` expression to see if any row in the table contains a person named `"moe"` would look like this:

```
SELECT xml_col.exist('/people/person[@name="moe"]') AS is_there_moe
  FROM xml_tab
```

The result will be a three-row rowset containing the value "True" (1), "False" (0), or NULL in the `is_there_moe` column. Notice that if we add just a single row containing a single XML document with multiple `<person>` elements:

```
- insert one row containing an XML document with 3 persons
- rather than 3 rows each containing an XML document with 1 person
INSERT xml_tab VALUES(
'<people>
   <person name="curly"/>
   <person name="larry"/>
   <person name="moe"/>
 </people>')
```

the result is a one-row rowset, not one row for each person in the XML document. The rows are the rows of a SQL rowset, rather than XML results.

The `xml.exist` function would most often be used as a predicate in a SQL statement—that is, in a SQL WHERE clause. This SQL statement would only select rows that had an XML document containing a person named `"moe"`.

```
SELECT the_id FROM xml_tab
  WHERE xml_col.exist('/people/person[@name="moe"]') = 1
```

A good use for `xml.exist` is in a selection predicate in a query that then produces complex XML for the same or another XML column by using the `xml.query` function. We'll come back to this when we discuss `xml.query`.

xml.value(string xquery-text, string SQLType)

The `xml.value` function takes a textual XQuery query as a string and returns a single scalar value. The SQL Server type of the value returned is specified as the second argument, and the value is cast to that data type. The data type can be any SQL Server type except the following:

- SQL Server XML data type
- A user-defined type
- SQL Server TIMESTAMP data type

The `xml.value` function must return a single scalar value, or else an error is thrown. You wouldn't need to have `xml.value` to return a single XML data type, because that's what `xml.query` does.

Using our overly simple document from the `xml.exist` section:

```
CREATE TABLE xml_tab(
  the_id INTEGER PRIMARY KEY IDENTITY,
  xml_col XML)
GO

INSERT xml_tab VALUES('<people><person name="curly"/></people>')
INSERT xml_tab VALUES('<people><person name="larry"/></people>')
INSERT xml_tab VALUES('<people><person name="moe"/></people>')
GO
```

the following SQL query using `xml.value`:

```
SELECT the_id,
  xml_col.value('/people[1]/person[1]/@name', 'varchar(50)') AS name
  FROM xml_tab
```

would produce a single row containing `the_id` and `name` columns for each row. The result would look like this:

the_id	name
1	curly
2	larry
3	moe

This function must only return a scalar value, however, so if the following row was added to the table:

```
INSERT xml_tab VALUES(
 '<people>
    <person name="laurel"/>
    <person name="hardy"/>
  </people>')
GO
```

the same SQL query would only use the first person, even though there are two `person` elements. Note that we've had to use the subscript `[1]` in every query to ensure that we're only getting the first person. This is because of SQL Server XQuery's static typing. If we didn't use the subscript, the engine would have to assume that the document permits multiple `person` elements, and would fail with the error "XQuery: Expression must return a singleton."

The `xml.value` function is good for mixing data extracted from the XML data type in the same query with columns returned from SQL Server, which, by definition contain a single value. In addition, it can also be used as a predicate in a SQL WHERE clause or a JOIN clause, as in the following query.

```
SELECT the_id
  FROM xml_tab
  WHERE xml_col.value(
    '/people[1]/person[1]/@name', 'VARCHAR(50)') = 'curly'
```

xml.query(string xquery-text)

Although all the functions of the XML data type do invoke the internal XQuery engine, the function that actually executes a complete XQuery query on an instance of the XML data type is `xml.query`. This function takes the XQuery text, which can be as simple or complex as you like, as an input string and returns an instance of the XML data type. The result is always an XQuery sequence as the specification indicates, except when your XQuery instance is NULL. If the input instance is NULL, the result is NULL. The resulting instance of the XML data type can be returned as a SQL variable, used as input to an INSERT statement that expects an XML type, or returned as an output parameter from a stored procedure.

XQuery usually gets its input from the XQuery functions `doc()` or `collection()` in dealing with documents from the file system or input from a stream. XQuery can also use a user-defined "context document." In SQL Server 2005, though, remember that the `xml.query` function refers to a specific column (or instance of the XML data type), and input will come from that column or instance's data; this is the context document. The simplest XQuery query might be one that consists only of an XPath 2.0 expression. This would return a sequence containing zero or more nodes or scalar values. Given our previous document, a simple XQuery query like this:

```
SELECT xml_col.query('/people/person') AS persons
  FROM xml_tab
```

would return a sequence containing a single node for each row.

```
persons
- - - - - - - - - - --
<person name="curly"/>
<person name="larry"/>
<person name="moe"/>
```

The query does not have to return a single node or a well-formed document, however. If the following row is added to the table, the results are different.

```
INSERT xml_tab VALUES(
 '<people>
    <person name="laurel"/>
    <person name="hardy"/>
  </people>')
GO

SELECT xml_col.query('/people/person') AS persons
  FROM xml_tab
```

These are the results.

```
persons
- - - - - - - - - - - - - - - - - - - - - - - - - - - - - - - - - - - - - - - - -
<person name="curly"/>
<person name="larry"/>
<person name="moe"/>
<person name="laurel"/>
<person name="hardy"/>
```

Note that the result from the last row is a multinode sequence, and though it is not a well-formed XML document, it does adhere to the XQuery 1.0 data model.

In addition to simple XQuery statements consisting of a simple XPath expression, you can use the FLWOR expressions that we saw at the beginning of this chapter. (Note that at this time, SQL Server's implementation of XQuery does not support the let FLWOR operator). This query uses FLWOR expressions and produces the same result as the previous query.

```
SELECT xml_col.query('
  for $b in /people/person
  return ($b)
 ')
 FROM xml_tab
```

You can subset the results with an XQuery predicate and the WHERE clause, as well as with an XPath predicate. For example, these two queries return the same results.

```
- XQuery WHERE clause
SELECT the_id, xml_col.query('
  for $b in /people/person
```

```
  where  $b/@name = "moe"
  return ($b)
') AS persons
FROM xml_tab

- XPath predicate
SELECT the_id, xml_col.query('/people/person[@name="moe"]') AS persons
  FROM xml_tab
```

Note that for the columns in which `"moe"` did not occur, the result is an empty sequence rather than an empty string or a NULL value.

```
the_id        persons
- - - - - - - - - - - - -

1
2
3             <person name="moe"/>
4
```

You can also return literal content interspersed with query data by using the standard curly brace notation. The following query returns a series of results surrounded by XHTML list tags (`<li>`). Note that this uses an element normal form version of the XML in the table, rather than the attribute normal form we've been using thus far.

```
CREATE TABLE xml_tab(
   the_id INTEGER PRIMARY KEY IDENTITY,
   xml_col XML)
GO

INSERT xml_tab
VALUES('<people><person><name>curly</name></person></people>')
INSERT xml_tab
VALUES('<people><person><name>larry</name></person></people>')
INSERT xml_tab
VALUES('<people><person><name>moe</name></person></people>')

INSERT xml_tab VALUES(
  '<people>
     <person><name>curly</name></person>
     <person><name>larry</name></person>
     <person><name>moe</name></person>
     <person><name>moe</name></person>
   </people>')
GO

- literal result element and
- constructor with curly braces
SELECT xml_col.query('
```

```
  for $b in //person
  where  $b/name="moe"
  return <li>{ string($b/name[1] }</li>
 ')
 FROM xml_tab
GO
-- returns
- <li>moe</li><li>moe</li>
```

This query also uses the XQuery string function, which leads us to talking
about XQuery standard functions. We'll talk about XQuery standard functions and operators shortly.

xml.nodes(string xquery-text)

The xml.nodes XML data type function produces a single column rowset
from the contents of an XML data type column. This function takes an
XQuery expression and produces zero or more rows that contain a single
column that is an opaque reference to a special type of XML document.
This reference is special because the context node for future XQuery functions is set at the node that matches the XQuery statement in the xml.
nodes clause. This document must be used with other XQuery functions,
like query or value, and can even be used as input to another nodes function. Because xml.nodes produces a context node other than the root node,
relative XQuery/XPath expressions can be used with the resultant document reference. The xml.nodes function must be used in conjunction with
the CROSS APPLY or OUTER APPLY clause of a SELECT statement, because the
table that contains the XML data type column must be part of the left-hand
side of the CROSS APPLY clause; the rowset cannot be returned directly.

Here's a simple example that shows its usage. Starting with the simple
XML data type table of people:

```
CREATE TABLE xml_tab(
  the_id INTEGER PRIMARY KEY IDENTITY,
  xml_col XML)
GO

INSERT xml_tab
VALUES('<people><person><name>curly</name></person></people>')
INSERT xml_tab
VALUES('<people><person><name>larry</name></person></people>')
INSERT xml_tab
VALUES('<people><person><name>moe</name></person></people>')
INSERT xml_tab values('
  <people>
```

```
    <person><name>laurel</name></person>
    <person><name>hardy</name></person>
  </people>')
GO
```

we can use the `xml.nodes` method to extract a series of rows, one for each person's name.

```
xml_col.nodes('/people/person[1]') AS result(a)
```

This produces a four-row, one-column rowset of abstract documents (most likely pointers) with each abstract document pointing at a different XML context node. We can then use the `xml.value` function to extract values.

```
SELECT the_id, a.value('text()[1]', 'VARCHAR(20)') AS name
  FROM xml_tab
  CROSS APPLY
    xml_col.nodes('/people/person/name') AS result(a)
```

This produces a rowset that looks like this.

```
the_id      name
- - - - - --   - - --
1           curly
2           larry
3           moe
4           laurel
4           hardy
```

Notice that we could not have produced the same result by using either the `xml.value` function or the `xml.query` function alone. The `xml.value` function would produce an error, because it needs to return a scalar value. The `xml.query` function would return only four rows, a single row for the "laurel and hardy" person.

There are a few interesting features to note about this syntax.

- The `xml.nodes` method produces a named resultset (rowset), which must be given an alias enclosed within the keyword `result`.
- The `xml.value` method on the left-hand side of the CROSS APPLY keyword refers to the a result column from the `xml.nodes` method.
- The `xml.nodes` statement on the right-hand side of the CROSS APPLY keyword refers to the `xml_col` column from the `xml_tab` table. The `xml_tab` table appears on the left-hand side of the CROSS APPLY keyword.

- The SELECT statement can also refer the other columns in the xml_tab table—in this case, the the_id column.

You could use OUTER APPLY instead of CROSS APPLY. In this case, because all the row values contain a matching <name> node, the result will be the same, but if we added a "nameless person" as follows:

```
INSERT xml_tab VALUES('<people><person></person></people>')
```

the CROSS APPLY version would produce five rows, and the OUTER APPLY version would produce six rows with the name as a NULL value. A similar condition doesn't distinguish between CROSS APPLY and OUTER APPLY, however. Say we look for a node in the xml.value portion (l_name) that doesn't exist in any of the noderefs.

```
SELECT the_id, a.value('l_name[1]/text()[1]', 'varchar(20)') AS l_name
  FROM xml_tab
  CROSS APPLY
    xml_col.nodes('/people/person/name') AS result(a)
```

Both CROSS APPLY and OUTER APPLY produce the same number of rows, all with NULL values for l_name.

Although the syntax for producing the rowset may seem strange at first, this equates to the second parameter in the OpenXML function, which also produces one row for each node selected by the expression in the second parameter. You use each reference node produced by the xml.nodes function as a starting node (context node) for the XML data type xml.query, xml.value, or xml.nodes functions. Using the reference node with xml.exist is technically possible but of limited value. These functions are used to produce additional columns in the rowset, analogous to the WITH clause in OpenXML. When used in conjunction with the XML data type functions, the xml.nodes function is a less memory-intensive version of OpenXML. It uses less memory because data in the XML data type column is already parsed; we get similar results to using OpenXML without the overhead of having a DOM in memory.

XQuery Standard Functions and Operators

The XQuery standard includes two companion specifications that describe the data model and its extension functions. These standards apply not only to XQuery, but also to XPath 2.0 and indirectly to XSLT 2.0, which uses XPath 2.0 as its query language. The first specification, "XQuery 1.0 and XPath 2.0 Data Model," lays the groundwork for both specifications and defines the data model as being based on the XML Information Set data model, with some extensions. It also describes functions that each XQuery processor should implement internally. Note that although these are described using functional notation, these are meant to be implemented inside the parser and should not be confused with the standard function library. We discussed the data model in the last chapter, along with its implementation in the SQL Server 2005 XML data type.

The second companion spec is more relevant to XQuery and XPath as query languages. It is called "XQuery 1.0 and XPath 2.0 Functions and Operators Version 1.0," and describes a standard function library and a standard set of operators for XQuery engine implementers. This would be similar to a standard function library in SQL:1999. The XQuery engine in SQL Server 2005 implements some of the standard functions, concentrating on the ones that make the most sense for a database or where the functionality is similar to a T-SQL function.

The functions and operators are grouped in the spec according to the data type that they operate on or their relationship to other functions and operators. The complete list of groups is as follows:

- Accessors
- Error function
- Trace function
- Constructors
- Functions and operators on numerics
- Functions on strings
- Functions and operators on boolean values
- Functions and operators on durations, dates, and times
- Functions related to QNames
- Functions and operators for anyURI
- Functions and operators on base64Binary and hexBinary
- Functions and operators on NOTATION
- Functions and operators on nodes
- Functions and operators on sequences
- Context functions
- Casting

Some of these categories require further explanation.

Accessors get information about a specific node. Examples include `fn:node-kind`, `fn:node-name`, and `fn:data`, which obtain the kind of node, the `QName`, and the data type.

The error function is called whenever a nonstatic error (that is, an error at query execution time) occurs. It can also be invoked from XQuery or XPath applications and is similar to a .NET exception.

Constructors are provided for every built-in data type in the XML Schema, Part 2, Datatypes, specification. These are similar to constructors in .NET classes and may be used to create nodes dynamically at runtime.

Context functions can get information about the current execution context—that is, the document, node, and number of items in the current sequence being processed. These are similar to environment variables in a program or the current environment (`SET` variables) in a SQL query.

Casting functions are used to cast between different data types, similar to casting in a programming language, the `CType` function in VB.NET, or the `CAST` function in SQL:1999. A specific casting function is defined for each legal cast among the XML Schema primitive types.

SQL Server XQuery Functions and Operators

The SQL Server engine's implementation of XQuery provides a rich subset of the XQuery and XPath functions and operators. Since both the SQL Server XQuery engine and the XQuery function specification are still in flux, the set of functions may change in the future or even before the time you read this. The functions that are implemented are listed in the box titled "XQuery Functions Supported by SQL Server."

XQuery Functions Supported by SQL Server

Data Accessor Functions

```
string

data
```

Functions on Numeric Values

```
floor

ceiling

round
```

XQuery Functions Supported by SQL Server (*continued*)

Functions on String Values

```
concat
contains
substring
string-length
```

Constructors and Functions on Booleans

```
not
```

Functions on Nodes

```
number
id
get-local-name-from-QName
get-namespace-from-QName
```

Context Functions

```
position
last
```

Functions on Sequences

```
empty
distinct-nodes
distinct-values
```

Aggregate Functions

```
count
avg
min
max
sum
```

Constructor Functions: to create instances of any of the XSD types (except `QName` and subtypes of `xs:duration`)

The box titled "XQuery Operators, Expressions, and Constructs Supported by SQL Server" lists all the operators and expressions supported by SQL Server 2005's implementation of XQuery. The list may change slightly by the time of release.

XQuery Operators, Expressions, and Constructs Supported by SQL Server

Supported Operators

    Numeric operators: `+, -, *, /`

    Value comparison operators: `eq, ne, lt, gt, le, ge`

    General comparison operators: `=, !=, <, >, <=, >=`

Supported Expressions and Constructs

    Prolog with namespace declarations and schema imports

    Node comparison

    Order comparison

    Path expressions

    Constructors with evaluation

        Element and attribute dynamic constructors

    `FWOR (no let)`

    Conditional (`if-then-else`)

    Quantified expressions

Note also that although the specification defined that each standard function live in a specific namespace, SQL Server's XQuery engine does not require the namespace prefix. This saves on required namespace declarations in every query.

SQL Server XQuery Extended Functions

Because the XQuery engine is executing in the context of a relational database, it is convenient to provide a standard way to use non-XML data (that is, relational data) inside the XQuery query itself. SQL Server provided two extension functions for exactly this purpose: `sql:column` and `sql:variable`. These keywords allow you to refer to relational columns in tables and Transact-SQL variables, respectively, from inside an XQuery query.

These functions can be used anywhere an XQuery query can be used, namely `xml.exist`, `xml.value`, `xml.query`, and `xml.modify`; `xml.modify` is discussed in the next section. The functions cannot be used to assign a value to SQL data; that means that they cannot be used on the left-hand side of an assignment statement in XQuery, as in `let sql:column := 'somevalue'`. The functions can refer to any SQL data type with the following exceptions:

- The `XML` data type
- User-defined data types
- `TIMESTAMP`
- `UNIQUEIDENTIFIER`
- `TEXT` and `NTEXT`
- `IMAGE`

sql:column

This function refers to a column in the current row of the current SQL query. The column can be in the same table as the `XML` data type column, or it can be included in the result as part of a join. The table must be in the same database and owned by the same schema owner, and is specified using a two-part name in the format "Tablename.Columnname" (without the quotes). Here's an example, using the table with name as a subelement that we've been using in the XQuery `xml.nodes` examples.

```
SELECT xml_col.query('
    for $b in //person
    where  $b/name="moe"
    return <li>{ $b/name/text() } in record number
           {sql:column("xml_tab.the_id")}</li>
 ')
 FROM xml_tab
```

This returns the following result (note: the first two rows in the result are empty).

```
<li>moe in record number 3</li>
<li>moe in record number 4</li>
```

sql:variable

The `sql:variable` function allows you to use any Transact-SQL variable that is in scope at the time the XQuery query is executed. This will be a single value for the entire query, as opposed to the `sql:column`, where the column value changes with every row of the result. This function is subject to the same data type limitations as `sql:column`. An example of using `sql:variable` in an XQuery query would look like this.

```
DECLARE @occupation VARCHAR(50)
SET @occupation = ' is a stooge'
SELECT xml_col.query('
   for $b in //person
   where  $b/name="moe"
   return <li>{ $b/name/text() } { sql:variable("@occupation") }</li>
')
FROM xml_tab
```

This statement uses the value of a T-SQL variable, `@occupation`, in the returned sequence in the XQuery query.

Multiple Document Query in SQL Server XQuery

As we saw in the XQuery specification discussion earlier in this chapter, queries can encompass more than one physical XML document, by using the `doc` or `collection` functions. However, in SQL Server's implementation of XQuery, the functions that allow input are not implemented. This is because the XQuery functions are implemented as instance functions that apply to a specific instance of the XML data type. Using the instance functions (`xml.query`, `xml.exist`, and `xml.value`), the XQuery query is single-document-only. So what if you want to combine more than one document, the XQuery equivalent of a SQL JOIN?

One way to combine multiple documents to produce a single XQuery sequence as a result is to perform the query over each document separately and concatenate the results. This can be easily accomplished using the `SELECT...FOR XML` syntax. This may not always be what you want, however. Some multidocument queries are based on using one document to "join" another in a nested `for` loop. These types of queries cannot be accomplished by using sequence concatenation. Another way to accomplish multidocument queries is to use the `xml.query` function on different types, combined with the SQL JOIN syntax. This doesn't deal with the nested tuple problem either.

Because .NET stored procedures and UDFs can use most of the .NET APIs, it is possible to use `System.Xml.Query` (the client-side implementation of XQuery) inside SQL Server. With the client-side implementation of XQuery, the input, document, and collection functions are supported, and multiple documents (or multiple instances of the XML data type) can be passed in as input parameters to a .NET stored procedure. We'll look at the .NET client XML APIs in Chapter 13.

XML DML—Updating XML Columns

One thing that was left out of the XQuery 1.0 specification was a definition of an XQuery syntax for mutating XML instances or documents in place. A data manipulation language (DML) is not planned for the first version of XQuery, but a working draft is under development. Because SQL Server 2005 will use XQuery as the native mechanism for querying the XML data type inside the server, it is required to have some sort of manipulation language. The alternative would be to only be able to replace the instance of the XML type as an entire entity. Since changes to XML data type instances should participate in the current transaction context, this would be equivalent to using SELECT and INSERT in SQL without having a corresponding UPDATE statement. Therefore, SQL Server 2005 introduces a heretofore nonstandard implementation of XML DML.

XML DML is implemented using XQuery-like syntax with SQL-like extensions. This emphasizes the fact that manipulating an XML instance inside SQL Server is equivalent to manipulating a complex type or, more accurately, a graph of complex types. You invoke XML DML by using the xml.modify function on a single XML data type column, variable, or procedure parameter. You use XML DML within the context of a SQL SET statement, using either UPDATE...SET on an XML data type column or using SET on an XML variable or parameter. As a general rule, it would look like this.

```
- change the value of XML data type column instance
UPDATE some_table
  SET xml_col.modify('some XML DML')
  WHERE id = 1

- change the value of an XML variable
DECLARE @x XML
- initialize it
SET @x = '<some>initial XML</some>'
- now, mutate it
SET @x = @x.modify('some XML DML')
```

Note that this syntax is used only to modify the XML nodes contained in an existing instance of an XML data type. To change a value to or from

NULL, you must use the normal XML data type construction syntax. With the xml.modify function, you can use XQuery syntax with the addition of three keywords: insert, delete, and replace value of. Only one of these keywords may be used in a single XML DML statement.

xml.modify('insert . . .')

You use the XML DML insert statement to insert a single node or an ordered sequence of nodes into the XML data type instance as children or siblings of another node. The node or sequence to be inserted can be an XML or XQuery expression, as can the "target node" that defines the position of the insert. The general format of the insert statement is as follows:

```
insert
    Expression1
       {as first | as last} into | after | before
    Expression2
```

where Expression1 is the node or sequence to be inserted and Expression2 is the insert target. Any of the seven node types and sequences of those types may be inserted as long as they do not result in an instance that is malformed XML. Remember that well-formed document fragments are permitted in XML data types.

The keywords as first, as last, or into are used to specify inserting child nodes. Using the into keyword inserts the node or sequence specified in Expression1 as a direct descendant, without regard for position. It is usually used to insert child nodes into an instance where no children currently exist. Using as first or as last ensures that the nodes will be inserted at the beginning or end of a sequence of siblings. These are usually used when you know that the node already contains child nodes. These keyword are ignored and do not cause an error when attribute nodes are being inserted. When processing instruction or comment nodes are being inserted, "child" refers to the position in the document rather than a real parent-child relationship.

Let's start with an instance of an XML invoice and mutate the invoice. Here's our starting point.

```
-- declare XML variable and set its initial value
DECLARE @x xml
SET @x =
'<Invoice>
    <InvoiceID>1000</InvoiceID>
    <CustomerName>Jane Smith</CustomerName>
```

```
    <LineItems>
        <LineItem>
            <Sku>134</Sku>
            <Quantity>10</Quantity>
            <Description>Chicken Patties</Description>
            <UnitPrice>9.95</UnitPrice>
        </LineItem>
        <LineItem>
            <Sku>153</Sku>
            <Quantity>5</Quantity>
            <Description>Vanilla Ice Cream</Description>
            <UnitPrice>1.50</UnitPrice>
        </LineItem>
    </LineItems>
</Invoice>'
GO
```

You could insert a new `InvoiceDate` element as a child of the `Invoice` element using the following statement.

```
SET @x.modify('insert <InvoiceDate>2002-06-15</InvoiceDate>
               into /Invoice[1]')
```

This statement would insert the `InvoiceDate` element as the last child of `Invoice`, after `LineItems`. To insert it as the first child of `Invoice`, simply change the statement to the following.

```
SET @x.modify('insert <InvoiceDate>2002-06-15</InvoiceDate>
               as first
               into /Invoice[1]')
```

Here's an example of inserting an attribute, `status="backorder"`, on the `Invoice` element.

```
SET @x.modify('insert attribute status{"backorder"}
               into /Invoice[1]')
```

Notice that this uses the constructor evaluation syntax (curly braces) to define the value of the attribute (`backorder`). You can also insert an entire series of elements using the `insert` statement. For example, if you wanted to add a new `LineItem`, you would do the following.

```
SET @x.modify('insert
    (
        <LineItem>
            <Sku>154</Sku>
            <Quantity>20</Quantity>
```

```
      <Description>Chocolate Ice Cream</Description>
      <UnitPrice>1.50</UnitPrice>
   </LineItem>
   )
   into /Invoice[1]/LineItems[1]')
```

The `after` and `before` keywords are used to insert siblings at the same level of hierarchy in the document. These keywords cannot be used in the same statement as `into`; this produces an error. It is also an error to use the `after` and `before` keywords when inserting attributes.

Following our earlier example, if you want to set the `InvoiceDate` at a specific position in the `Invoice` element's set of children, you need to use the `before` or `after` keywords and have an XPath expression that points to the appropriate sibling.

```
SET @x.modify('insert <InvoiceDate>2002-06-15</InvoiceDate>
   before /Invoice[1]/CustomerName[1]')

- this works too, and equates to the same position
SET @x.modify('insert <InvoiceDate>2002-06-15</InvoiceDate>
   after /Invoice[1]/InvoiceID[1]')
```

The key to understanding the `insert` statement is that although `Expression1` can be any of the seven node types and can contain multiple nodes in a sequence or even hierarchical XML, `Expression2` must evaluate to a single node. If `Expression2` evaluates to a sequence of nodes and no node, the `insert` statement will fail. In addition, `Expression2` cannot refer to a node that has been constructed earlier in the query; it must refer to a node in the original XML instance. This is what the variable looks like after all the previous modifications. Although `InvoiceDate` was used multiple times in multiple examples, we've chosen to show only the insert position from the last example (ignoring the first two examples, where `InvoiceDate` was inserted in a different position).

```
- value in the variable @x after modifications
'<Invoice status="backorder">
   <InvoiceID>1000</InvoiceID>
   <InvoiceDate>2002-06-15</InvoiceDate>
   <CustomerName>Jane Smith</CustomerName>
   <LineItems>
      <LineItem>
         <Sku>134</Sku>
         <Quantity>10</Quantity>
         <Description>Chicken Patties</Description>
         <UnitPrice>9.95</UnitPrice>
```

```
        </LineItem>
        <LineItem>
           <Sku>153</Sku>
           <Quantity>5</Quantity>
           <Description>Vanilla Ice Cream</Description>
           <UnitPrice>1.50</UnitPrice>
        </LineItem>
        <LineItem>
           <Sku>154</Sku>
           <Quantity>20</Quantity>
           <Description>Chocolate Ice Cream</Description>
           <UnitPrice>1.50</UnitPrice>
        </LineItem>
     </LineItems>
  </Invoice>'
  go
```

xml.modify('delete . . .')

The `delete` XML DML command, as input to the `modify` function, deletes zero or more nodes that are identified by the output sequence of the XQuery query following the keyword `delete`. As in SQL, you can qualify the `delete` statement with a `where` clause. The general syntax of `delete` is:

```
delete Expression
```

Each node returned by `Expression` is deleted. Returning a sequence of zero nodes just deletes zero nodes; it is not an error. As with the `insert` command, attempting to delete a constructed node (a node that was produced earlier in the query rather than a node in the original document) will cause an error. Attempting to delete a value rather than a node will result in an error. Also, attempting to delete a metadata attribute, such as a namespace declaration, will result in an error. To delete all the `LineItem` elements in our example, you could execute the following statement:

```
set @x.modify('delete /Invoice/LineItems/LineItem')
```

xml.modify('replace value of . . .')

Unlike a searched UPDATE in SQL and also unlike `xml.modify` (`'delete...'`), `xml.modify('replace value of...')` modifies the value of a single node. It is not a searched UPDATE that uses a WHERE clause to select a sequence of nodes. The general syntax for update follows.

```
replace value of
   Expression1
```

```
with
    Expression2
```

`Expression1` must return a single node; if a sequence of zero nodes or multiple nodes is returned, an error is produced. Note that, again, this is unlike a SQL searched UPDATE statement in SQL, where returning zero rows to update is not an error. It is more similar to UPDATE WHERE CURRENT OF in SQL when using a cursor. `Expression1` is used to find the current node.

`Expression2` must be a sequence of atomic values. If it returns nodes, they are atomized. The sequence in `Expression2` completely replaces the node in `Expression1`. Here's an example that updates the `CustomerName` element's `text` child element from "Jane Smith" to "John Smith".

```
SET @x.modify('update value of
    /Invoice[1]/CustomerName[1]/text()[1]
    to "John Smith"
    ')
```

General Conclusions and Best Practices

XML DML can be used to update portions of an XML data instance in place. The insert, update, and delete can be composed as part of a transaction. This is a unique ability for XML; although XML is often compared to databases and complex types, the usual pattern was to retrieve the XML, update the corresponding XML DOM (or in .NET, `XPathNavigator`), and then write the entire document back to the file system. XML DML treats XML more like a complex type or a database and as similar to functionality found in XML-specific databases.

There are a few general rules to remember when using XML DML.

- The nodes referenced by modify operations must be nodes in the original document.
- XML DML is not analogous to SQL DML. Although `insert` and `delete` are similar, position is all important. For SQL programmers, it is the equivalent of using an updateable cursor.
- The resulting XML document or fragment cannot be malformed, or the `xml.modify` operation will fail.
- If the XML instance is validated by an XML schema, the `xml.modify` operation cannot interfere with schema validation.

Special Considerations When Using XQuery inside SQL Server

Using Strongly Typed XML with XQuery

Unlike XPath 1.0, XPath 2.0 and XQuery 1.0 are strongly typed query languages. This is quite evident in the wide range of constructors and casting functions for different data types. The reasoning behind this is that XQuery is built to be optimized, and using strong types rather than using every element and attribute as type `string` allows the query engine to do a better job in optimizing and executing the query. Imagine that the Transact-SQL query parser had to deal with everything as a single data type!

Every `XML` data type column, XML variable, and XML procedure parameter can be strongly typed by reference to an XML schema or can be untyped. When typed XML is used in an XQuery, the query parser has more information to work with. If untyped XML is used, the query engine must start with the premise that every piece of data is type `string`; the `xf:data()` built-in function can be used with strongly typed data to return the exact data type.

XQuery supports static type analysis, meaning that if the types of items that are input to an expression are known, the output type of an expression can be inferred at "parse time." In addition, strong typing permits the XQuery language to syntax check the input based on types at "parse time," as Transact-SQL can, so fewer runtime errors occur. XQuery also allows the query processor to reorder the queries; although this is a performance optimization, this could on occasion lead to runtime errors.

You've seen a very noticeable example of SQL Server XQuery's strong typing in almost all the example queries in this chapter. In these queries, whenever a function or return value requires a singleton, we must use the `[1]` subscript to ensure it's really a singleton; otherwise, a parse-time error results. Almost all other XQuery processors (without strong typing) will execute the query and produce a runtime error if the value is not actually a singleton. If we had a strongly typed XML column instead, in which the schema defined the elements we're referring to as `maxOccurs=1` `minOccurs=1` (the default), a query without the subscript would succeed, because the parser "knows" that the element in question is a singleton. Having a schema-validated column permits you to do the type-checking at column insert/update time, rather than take the extra measure of requiring a subscript to enforce it at XQuery parse time.

Even though the XML instance that is input to an XML function can be typed or untyped, remember that the result of an `xml.query` function is always an untyped XML instance. Typed XML should always be used, if possible, to give the XQuery engine a chance to use its knowledge of the data type involved. This also makes the resulting query run faster as well as producing more accurate results and fewer runtime errors.

Optimization Decisions in the XQuery Engine

The XQuery engine's implementation provides some optimizations over the the XQuery standard. It does this by restricting the functionality defined by the spec. There are four main restrictions: query over constructed sequences, usage of filter expressions other than at the end of the path, usage of `order by` with multiple or out-of-scope iterators and heterogeneous sequences. Here are some short examples.

The following is a query over a constructed sequence.

```
"for $i in (for $j in //a return <row>{ $j }</row>)
 return $i"
```

Next is a filter expression with a filter in the middle of the path.

```
"/a/b/(some-expression(.))/d"
```

Here is an example of using `order by` with multiple iterators.

```
"for $x in //a
 for $y in //b
 order by $x > $y
 return $x, $y"
```

We'll discuss heterogeneous sequences in more detail here.

In XQuery, sequences are defined to be able to contain all nodes, or all scalar values, or a combination of nodes and scalar values. SQL Server 2005's XQuery engine restricts sequences to either all nodes or all scalar values; defining a heterogeneous sequence will result in an error. Permitting only homogeneous sequences allows the engine to optimize queries over sequences, because it will not try to determine the data type of each member of the sequence.

Early SQL parsers were unoptimized; this was one of the reasons that early relational databases ran slowly. The performance improvement in relational databases since their inception is due, in no small way, to the optimization of SQL query processors, including static type analysis as well as other, physical optimizations such as types of indexes. With an XML data type, the possibility of strong typing through XML Schemas, and a query language that allows optimizations based on strong typing, XQuery users will most likely experience the same improvements in performance as the data type and query language matures. Programmers (and especially data center managers) like the idea of the same code running faster as vendors improve their parser engines, with minimal changes to the query code itself.

Where Are We?

SQL Server 2005 not only introduces XML as a new scalar data type, it introduces a query language and a data manipulation language to operate on it. The query language selected for operation inside SQL Server is XQuery, a new query language that is still in standardization. (At the time of this writing, XQuery was a W3C Working Draft). The XQuery implementation inside the database makes some simplifications and optimizations when compared with the entire specification. The subsetting is done to allow the queries to be optimizable and fast. This is a goal of XQuery itself, although the specification does not define implementable subsets.

Because XQuery does not specify a data manipulation language, SQL Server provides a proprietary language that uses XQuery expressions to produce sequences to mutate, known as XML DML. The standardization of XML DML is being considered, because every implementation by relational or XML database vendors is different. This is reminiscent of the early days of SQL.

In addition to the SQL Server XML engine, Microsoft provides an abstraction of query languages in the client XML stack. This can consume a query in any XML-based query language and produce a standard representation of the query. This abstraction will be used to expose XML Views over SQL data using the query language of the programmer's choice.

Finally, because SQL Server 2005 can run .NET code, and SQL Server XML Views are based on .NET, it is feasible to run a normally "client-side" XML stack from within a stored procedure or user-defined function. This variation of XQuery, XPath, and XSLT is more likely to correspond more closely to the complete specification for these languages, but because it operates on documents in memory rather than directly accessing the database, it should be used sparingly in the server, based on document size. We'll explore XML Views and the client-side XML stack in Chapter 13.

■ 10 ■

SQL Server as a Platform for Web Services

S QLXML 3.0 INTRODUCED the concept of exposing SQL Server as a Web Service, through the use of a special Internet Services API (ISAPI) DLL running under Internet Information Server. SQL Server 2005 moves this capability into the server itself, removes the need for Internet Information Server, and expands dramatically on the functionality provided by SQLXML 3.0.

Mixing Databases and Web Services

Communication with SQL Server (or any database management system, for that matter), has always required using a special proprietary protocol. In the case of SQL Server, this protocol is called TDS (tabular data stream) and uses a special set of client network libraries. These libraries are the SQL Server network libraries and are only available on Windows operating systems. Originally, the TDS protocol was shared with the Sybase database since they shared a mostly common codebase. Since then, each database has improved the protocol in different ways. Although SQL Server supports a backward-compatibility mode for using old versions of the TDS protocol, and therefore supports using Sybase network libraries on other operating systems, today these libraries support only a subset of Microsoft TDS functionality. A Windows client and operating system is required for full functionality. Not only is TDS a proprietary protocol, but it needs some special firewall configuration to work over the Internet. A specific network port (port 1433 in the default case) needs to be open on any firewall in order to communicate through TDS over TCP/IP. In addition, later versions of SQL Server use integrated security using NTLM or Kerberos security systems. NTLM will not pass through firewalls, and Kerberos will only with great difficulty. Most firewall administrators, with good reason, won't open the ports needed for users to connect directly to SQL Server over the Internet.

Web Services expose a standard mechanism for communication that uses standard protocols and a common message format. The network protocol most often used is HTTP. The message format is known as SOAP. Web Services can be produced and consumed by any platform with an HTTP stack and an XML stack. It has become a popular means of communication among unlike systems and may displace proprietary protocols over time.

SQL Server 2000 allowed communication via HTTP by using Internet Information Server and an ISAPI DLL. This DLL allowed users to issue HTTP requests (subject to security, of course) to well-known endpoints exposed with XML-based files known as templates. The ISAPI application parses the template and uses TDS to talk to SQL Server. These templates could use SQL or XPath queries, embedded in SQL. The result of these queries was XML in a well-known format, and this XML could also be postprocessed with XSLT inside the ISAPI DLL. In addition, with the proper configuration of the ISAPI application, users could enter endpoints that corresponded to SQL or XPath queries via a URL parameter. Through a number of post–SQL Server 2000 Web releases, known as SQLXML, the functionality of the ISAPI application was expanded to support direct posting of updates in XML formats (known as DiffGrams and Update-Grams) and producing the XML output on the client side, allowing additional postprocessing capabilities.

SQLXML 3.0 expanded the capability of the ISAPI DLL to include the production of SOAP packets, therefore exposing SQL Server through IIS as a Web Service. Any stored procedure, user-defined function, or template query can be exposed as a SOAP endpoint. Output is available in a variety of formats, some optimized for the .NET consumer, but all using the SOAP protocol. The ISAPI application was also expanded to produce Web Service Description Language (WSDL), a standardized dialect of XML that describes the format and location of a Web Service. This allowed any program that could consume WSDL to know how to communicate with SQL Server.

All the SQLXML 3.0 capabilities are available to SQL Server 2005 and SQL Server 2000. But if you have installed SQL Server 2005 on the Windows 2003 Server operating system, additional SOAP functionality can also be exposed directly from the SQL Server engine itself. The reason you need Windows 2003 Server is that in Windows 2003 Server the HTTP stack has been moved into the operating system kernel (this implementation is called HTTP.SYS). SQL Server 2005 Web Services use HTTP.SYS and do not require IIS. This not only allows faster execution of HTTP requests, but allows HTTP to be served from multiple applications running under the operating system, including SQL Server and IIS. You can service HTTP requests from both of them at the same time.

Communication with SQL Server through SOAP makes the SOAP protocol an alternative to the TDS protocol. You can define which endpoints will be exposed through SOAP and what protocol these endpoints will use for SQL Server authorization, and use SSL to encrypt the data stream. In addition, you can configure the endpoint with the capability to accept batches of SQL directly. This makes SQL Server truly available to non-Windows clients and available directly over HTTP. No client network libraries are needed. The rest of this chapter will cover SQL Server 2005's internal "SOAP network libraries," although you might notice that most of the SOAP functionality is similar to that exposed in SQLXML 3.0's ISAPI DLL. The biggest enhancement is that you can produce XML output by running a stored procedure or user-defined function that produces an instance or instances of the XML type as output.

HTTP Endpoint Declaration

The way that we defined an HTTP endpoint with SQLXML 3.0 was to use either a COM object model that wrote to the IIS metabase and the Windows registry, or to use a graphic user interface that encapsulated this object model. The new functionality is built directly into SQL Server. The information is stored in SQL Server metadata, and the way to define it is to use Transact-SQL. The relevant DDL statements are CREATE ENDPOINT, ALTER ENDPOINT, and DROP ENDPOINT. You can use these DDL statements to define endpoints for protocols other than HTTP (for example, SQL Server Service Broker endpoints), but in this chapter we'll only cover using them to define HTTP endpoints. We'll discuss them here and in the same time correlate these DDL statements with the COM object model that you would be using if you use SQLXML 3.0.

The complete syntax for cataloging an HTTP endpoint definition in Transact-SQL follows.

```
CREATE ENDPOINT endPointName [AUTHORIZATION <login>]
[ STATE = { STARTED | STOPPED | DISABLED } ]
AS HTTP (
    [ SITE = {'*' | '+' | 'webSite' } ,]
    PATH = 'url'
    , PORTS = ({CLEAR | SSL} [,... n])
[, CLEAR_PORT = clearPort ]
[, SSL_PORT = SSLPort ]
    , AUTHENTICATION =({ANON | BASIC | DIGEST | INTEGRATED} [,...n])
[, AUTH_REALM = { 'realm' | NONE } ]
[, DEFAULT_LOGON_DOMAIN = {'domain' | NONE } ]
[, COMPRESSION = { ENABLED | DISABLED } ]
[, RESTRICT_IP = { NONE | ALL }
[, EXCEPT_IP = ({ <4-part-ip> | <4-part-ip>:<mask> } [,...n]) ]
)
[ FOR SOAP
    (
        [ { WEBMETHOD [ 'namespace' .] 'methodalias' (
    NAME = three.part.name
    [, SCHEMA = { NONE | STANDARD | DEFAULT }]
    [, FORMAT = { ALL_RESULTS | ROWSETS_ONLY }])
        } [,... n] ]
[    BATCHES = { ENABLED | DISABLED } ]
[ , WSDL = { NONE | DEFAULT | 'sp_name' } ]
[ , SESSIONS = { ENABLED | DISABLED } ]
[ , SESSION_TIMEOUT = {int | NEVER}]
[ , DATABASE = { 'database_name' | DEFAULT } ]
[ , NAMESPACE = { 'namespace' | DEFAULT } ]
[ , SCHEMA = { NONE | STANDARD } ]
[ , CHARACTER_SET = { SQL | XML }]
)
```

This syntax, seen in its entirety, may seem imposing at first. So to start with, let's break it down into its component pieces. Note that endpoints can be owned by a specific user by specifying the AUTHORIZATION keyword, just as with other SQL Server database objects.

The parameters in CREATE ENDPOINT that are used by HTTP endpoints are divided into these groups of functionality:

- Endpoint state
- Serving HTTP
- Authentication

- Defining whether you can invoke specific procedures, arbitrary batches, or both
- Defining the exact format of the SOAP message

Endpoint State

First, we'd like to point out that no HTTP endpoints are defined by default in SQL Server. When you install a fresh version of SQL Server on a .NET Server machine, you have no HTTP connectivity. Someone with administrative privileges has to define and enable HTTP endpoints before they are available; this behavior is for the sake of added security.

All endpoints can be defined with state parameters.

STATE—When SQL Server comes up, it tries to establish an HTTP listener on the sites, paths, and ports that you specify, if STARTED is selected. If STOPPED is selected, the endpoint does not automatically service requests at startup time, but an administrator can enable it by using ALTER ENDPOINT... STATE=STARTED. Note that STOPPED is the default. If you specify DISABLED, SQL Server must be stopped and restarted for the endpoint to be enabled.

Note that you can also enable or disable HTTP for the entire SQL Server instance by using the system stored procedure sp_configure. The entire T-SQL statement would look like this.

```
- option 0 turns it off
- option 1 turns it on
sp_configure 'enable http', {0 | 1}
```

Parameters That Relate to Serving HTTP

Let's talk about Web server information, deferring the security information until a later section. There are a few parameters to CREATE ENDPOINT that are usually specified in the IIS metabase if you are using the IIS Web server. Because SQL Server is acting as the "Web server" in this case, these parameters must be defined in the DDL statement. These were not needed in SQLXML 3.0 because you were using IIS as a Web server. The relevant parameters are as follows.

SITE—This is the name of the Web site ("Web server") that will be used by the client when connecting. If you specify '*' (asterisk), it means that you want to listen on all possible host names for the machines that are not otherwise explicitly reserved by other programs that serve HTTP (like IIS).

If you specify ' + ' (plus sign), it means that you want to listen on all possible host names for the machine. ' * ' is the default.

PATH—The path on the Web server that users connect to. You must specify this parameter, and there are special security requirements to be able to use any path that is not a subpath of /sql.

PORTS, CLEAR_PORT, and **SSL_PORT**—These define the TCP ports to use and whether you can use unencrypted (CLEAR_PORT) or encrypted (SSL_PORT) communication or both. By default, unencrypted HTTP uses port 80, and SSL encryption uses port 443. Note that in the beta release of SQL Server 2005, if you want to use SSL, you must have an IIS server running on the same machine with a server certificate installed on it.

COMPRESSION—This defines whether the endpoint uses HTTP compression. Because SOAP messages can be rather verbose but, being XML-based, are prone to size improvements when compression algorithms are used, that is usually a performance improvement. You must ensure that your clients can deal with the compressed message format, however.

As an example of the parameters we've defined so far, the following CREATE statement:

```
CREATE ENDPOINT myendpoint
STATE = STARTED
AS HTTP (
  SITE = '*',
  PATH = '/sql/mydatabase',
  PORTS = (CLEAR),
  COMPRESSION = ENABLED
)
GO
```

would partially define an endpoint with the symbolic name myendpoint that listens for requests at http://myservername/sql/mydatabase on port 80. Because security information is missing, the CREATE statement would not succeed; it's only for illustration. This endpoint is available at SQL Server startup. Note that myendpoint is only a symbolic name that identifies the endpoint in the SQL Server metadata and has no bearing on the physical HTTP endpoint. In this example, myservername is the DNS name of our machine that is running SQL Server. We specified this by using the SITE='*' parameter, or since SITE='*' is the default, we could have left it out all together.

As nice a definition as this is, we can reach SQL Server but have no permission to do anything yet. We need to address security and add the FOR SOAP portion of the definition for that.

SQLXML 3.0 Functionality

In SQLXML 3.0, the equivalent functionality would be defined by using the "IIS Virtual Directory Management for SQL Server" GUI tool and adding a new virtual directory. Because we are using native HTTP support rather than an ISAPI application, when we use CREATE ENDPOINT in SQL Server 2005, we are not adding a virtual directory to IIS.

Security Choices and XML Web Services

The same reasons that HTTP is conveniently usable as a transport also make it a security risk. Firewall administrators routinely leave port 80 open for HTTP traffic. Web spiders and other search engines scour arbitrary servers looking for content to index (or break into). Tools exist that make it easy to execute a denial of service attack on an arbitrary Web server. A server listens to TCP port 80 at its own risk. It is not the case that the HTTP protocol itself is less secure than, say, the TDS protocol; it is just more of a known quantity. The fact that the headers and verbs are text based (a feature shared by SOAP and XML) makes any message readable by default. Arbitrary TDS messages may be run through a binary decoding filter, but when you are using a text-based protocol, the "filter" is your eyes. Making security explicit and denying access the default behavior is crucial when using HTTP to talk directly to your corporate database.

As we mentioned before, SQL Server's HTTP support is turned off by default. Enabling HTTP is required. Endpoints are not started by default, and no endpoints are predefined. This is a big improvement over software that comes with Web servers preinstalled, autostarted, with security turned off. Because SQL Server endpoints are their own "Web servers," you use traditional HTTP security protocols for authentication. In addition to authentication, SQL Server's HTTP endpoints allow IP address filtering by using the RESTRICT_IP and EXCEPT_IP parameters on CREATE ENDPOINT. This is similar to the equivalent functionality found in most Web servers.

You can permit access to SQL Server endpoints using either SQL Server authentication or Windows integrated security logins on SQL Server. A variety of authentication protocols are supported, including WS-Security (the Web Service standard security authentication protocol), which will be added before SQL Server 2005 ships. Once authenticated, access to SQL Server resources (authorization) is handled by SQL Server permissions. In general, authentication is providing information, be it a user ID and password or a token containing a Kerberos ticket, to identify yourself to the application and prove that you are who you claim to be. Once you have been authenticated, SQL Server knows who you are, and your SQL Server roles and permissions authorize you to access various resources.

The parameters AUTHENTICATION, AUTH_REALM, and DEFAULT_LOGIN_DOMAIN determine what mechanism a user uses to identity herself to SQL Server. There are four AUTHENTICATION choices, analogous to the choices in IIS.

ANON—This allows anonymous access to the endpoint. The user does not have to identify herself to SQL Server at all. Anonymous access will not be permitted on CLEAR ports—in other words, unless SSL is also used. When a user contacts an endpoint using anonymous access, she actually connects to SQL Server through SQL Server's Windows integrated security option using the Windows "guest" account on the machine.

BASIC—This choice uses HTTP basic authentication as defined by RFC 2617. Basic authentication requires a user ID and password, which will be transmitted over the network, and therefore is not permitted on CLEAR ports. When basic authentication is used, a user can specify either SQL Server credentials or Windows credentials (user ID and password), and if these credentials have logon access (that is, a record in syslogins), these will be used to log on to SQL Server.

DIGEST—Using digest authentication consists of hashing the user name and password, using a one-way hashing algorithm and sending the hash output to the server. It is defined in RFC 2617. In Windows operating systems, this requires that the machine be a Windows Active Directory domain controller and is not used frequently. In digest authentication, the user logs in to SQL Server using Windows security (a native SQL Server login is not possible).

INTEGRATED—Integrated security in Windows operating systems uses a protocol to negotiate which authentication mechanism to use; this negotiation protocol is also the default when signing on to Windows 2000 and above operating systems. If an Active Directory is being used in a domain configuration, the Kerberos protocol is used; otherwise, NTLM protocol is used. Kerberos is an industry-standard security protocol; NTLM is proprietary to Windows operating systems. When integrated security is used, SQL Server must also be operating with Windows integrated security enabled.

AUTH_REALM and DEFAULT_LOGIN_DOMAIN determine which set of user accounts to use for authentication. AUTH_REALM can be used with digest authentication; DEFAULT_LOGIN_DOMAIN is used with Windows operating systems and basic authentication. Authentication realm is a term used by the RFC that defines digest authorization and can mean a Kerberos authentication realm in systems where MIT standard Kerberos is used. In SQL Server HTTP endpoints, the value of AUTH_REALM is sent with the original digest authentication challenge and is only used with the digest authentication protocol.

Once a user is authorized, the user can be routed to a specific database by using the DATABASE= parameter in CREATE ENDPOINT. If the SQL Server login representing the user's identity does not have permission to the specified database, it is not allowed access; if DATABASE=DEFAULT is specified, the user is logged on to her default database. Notice that when we define "SOAP Web methods" later on using the WEBMETHOD= parameter in CREATE ENDPOINT, three-part names are required. This means, regardless of which database the user actually logs in to, access to the endpoints is possible if the appropriate stored procedure or UDF permission is granted.

One last parameter that has security ramifications is WSDL=NONE/ STANDARD/stored procedure name. WSDL stands for Web Service Description Language and is a way to publish details of a Web Service to arbitrary users through HTTP. We'll go into detail about WSDL in the next section. If all the potential users are aware of how to communicate with your HTTP endpoint, WSDL support is not necessary. Rather than making the WSDL publicly available, you can send it to system users through out-of-band communication.

There is also security associated without endpoint creation and maintenance. In addition to defining endpoints with CREATE ENDPOINT, you can alter and delete endpoints with the ALTER ENDPOINT and DROP ENDPOINT statements. The complete syntax for these is:

```
ALTER ENDPOINT endPointName [AUTHORIZATION <login>]
[ STATE = { STARTED | STOPPED | DISABLED } ]

[ AS HTTP
[ SITE = {'*' | '+' | 'webSite' } ]
[, PATH = 'url'  ]
[, PORTS = ( { CLEAR | SSL } [,... n] ) ]
[, CLEAR_PORT = clearPort]
[, SSL_PORT = SSLPort ]
[, AUTHENTICATION = ({ANON | BASIC | DIGEST | INTEGRATED}[,...n] ) ]
[, AUTH_REALM = {'realm' | NONE } ]
[, DEFAULT_LOGON_DOMAIN = { 'domain' | NONE } ]
[, COMPRESSION = { ENABLED | DISABLED } ]
[, RESTRICT_IP = { NONE | ALL } ]
[, ADD EXCEPT_IP = ( { <4-part-ip> | <4-part-ip>:<mask> } [,...n] )
```

```
[, DROP  EXCEPT_IP = ( {<4-part-ip> | <4-part-ip>:<mask> } [,...n] )
      ]
[ FOR { SOAP
      (
[ { ADD WEBMETHOD [ 'namespace' .] 'methodalias'
   (
    NAME = three.part.name
    [, SCHEMA = {NONE | STANDARD | DEFAULT}]
    [, FORMAT = { ALL_RESULTS | ROWSETS_ONLY }])
   } [,... n] ]
[ { ALTER WEBMETHOD [ 'namespace' .] 'methodalias'
   (
    NAME = three.part.name
    [, SCHEMA = { NONE | STANDARD }]
    [, FORMAT = { ALL_RESULTS | ROWSETS_ONLY }])
   } [,... n] ]
[ { DROP WEBMETHOD [ 'namespace' .] 'methodalias' } [,...n] ]

     [ , BATCHES = { ENABLED | DISABLED } ]
  [ , WSDL = { NONE | DEFAULT | 'sp_name' } ]
  [ , SESSIONS = { ENABLED | DISABLED } ]
  [ , SESSION_TIMEOUT = {int | NEVER}]
  [ , DATABASE = { 'database_name' | DEFAULT }
  [ , NAMESPACE = { 'namespace' | DEFAULT } ]
  [ , SCHEMA = { NONE | STANDARD } ]
  [ , CHARACTER_SET = { SQL | XML }]
     )

DROP ENDPOINT endPointName
```

Although SQL Server permissions are used to define who can create HTTP endpoints, some additional considerations apply. CREATE/ALTER/ DROP ENDPOINT permission is required to be able to control access to SQL Server through HTTP. By default, this is granted only to members of the sysadmin role, though it can be granted to others. In addition, all SQL Server authenticated users have the additional restriction that they can only create endpoints in the default SQL Server URL namespace. This is /sql for SQL Server default instances and /sql/[instance name] for named instances. Even the SQL Server superuser "sa" cannot create endpoints outside this URL namespace. Users logging in with Windows integrated security can create endpoints outside the /sql namespace (for example, /mydatabase), but OS system administrator permission on the machine that is running SQL Server is also required for this function.

HTTP Endpoint Permissions

HTTP endpoints have a standard set of permissions. Although the CREATE permission works as in other database objects, there is a more granular ALTER permission and unique CONNECT, TAKE OWNERSHIP, and CONTROL permissions. You can grant permission to create ENDPOINTs (since HTTP endpoints are scoped to a SQL Server instance, any permission statements must be executed on the MASTER database) on a global basis by issuing the following command:

```
GRANT CREATE ENDPOINT to SomeLogin
```

Note that because endpoints are scoped to an instance, permission is granted to a database login rather than a database user. Logins can be permitted to alter a specific endpoint or all endpoints on a SQL Server instance. If you specify a specific endpoint, you must use the ENDPOINT:: endpointname syntax, which is similar to the syntax for XML schemas and namespaces. The following examples illustrate the syntax.

```
- all endpoints
GRANT ALTER ANY HTTP ENDPOINT TO SomeLogin

- a specific endpoint named 'querypubs'
GRANT ALTER ON HTTP ENDPOINT::querypubs TO SomeLogin
```

CONNECT permission allows you to execute any request on a specific endpoint. This includes SQL batches and queries for WSDL documents, if they are enabled, in addition to stored procedures and user-defined functions. To allow only access to stored procedures and user-defined functions, you can define a different endpoint that prohibits WSDL and/or SQL batches; there is no way to do this with permissions.

TAKE OWNERSHIP is a very granular permission that determines whether a specific login account can change the AUTHORIZATION clause of an ENDPOINT. It is best to grant this privilege to as few logins as possible, to prevent hackers logged in as a specific SQL Server account from granting themselves more database access.

CONTROL is a combination privilege. It allows a login to connect, take ownership, alter, or drop a specific endpoint.

Note that CONNECT, TAKE OWNERSHIP, and CONTROL can only be granted (or denied or revoked) on a specific ENDPOINT, not all ENDPOINTs. The syntax is similar to the GRANT ALTER statement on the querypubs ENDPOINT listed earlier.

Defining Access through HTTP

Defining access through HTTP consists of adding the appropriate FOR SOAP parameters to our CREATE ENDPOINT definition. We can define the following two types of access as well as some parameters that cover both access types:

- Access to specific "Web methods" (stored procedures and user-defined functions)
- Access to invoke arbitrary SQL

Access to invoke specific Web methods is defined by using the WEB METHOD parameter. You can specify that any user-defined stored procedure or UDF in any database be accessible as a Web method. You must specify a three-part name for the procedure, even though you can specify DATABASE = as part of the FOR SOAP clause, because you might want to execute a stored procedure in a database other than the default database. Normal SQL Server permissions also apply with respect to executing the stored procedure or UDF. You must define a new Web method for each procedure that you want to expose through HTTP, and Web methods may be deleted or added by using ALTER ENDPOINT.

Each Web method specifies a method alias, an optional (XML) namespace, and the format of the results. This is used when the client constructs a SOAP input request and when SQL Server constructs a SOAP response. For example, we define a WEBMETHOD like this.

```
CREATE ENDPOINT myendpoint
  STATE = STARTED
AS HTTP (
  SITE = '*',
  PATH = '/sql/mydatabase',
  PORTS = (CLEAR),
  AUTHENTICATION = (INTEGRATED)
)
FOR SOAP (
  WEBMETHOD 'urn:develop:procs'.'myproc' (NAME=
'mydb.dbo.mystoredproc')
)
GO
```

We would invoke the procedure by sending a SOAP message that looks like this:

```
<SOAP-ENV:Envelope
   xmlns:SOAP-ENV="http://schemas.xmlsoap.org/soap/envelope/"
   xmlns:myns="urn:develop:procs"
>
   <SOAP-ENV:Body>
     <myns:myproc>
     </myns:myproc>
   </SOAP-ENV:Body>
</SOAP-ENV:Envelope>
```

to the HTTP endpoint, and this would invoke the procedure `mydb.dbo.mystoredproc`. This is the equivalent of writing the following in ADO. NET client-side code.

```
SqlConnection conn = new SqlConnection("...connect string...");
SqlCommand cmd = new SqlCommand("mydb.dbo.mystoredproc", conn);
cmd.CommandType = CommandType.StoredProcedure;
conn.Open();
int i = cmd.ExecuteNonQuery();
```

The only difference is that one uses SOAP and HTTP and the other uses the SQL Server client libraries and TDS. This code only works if the stored procedure has no input parameters and no output parameters and returns no resultsets. We'll talk about using parameters and other features of the SOAP message in client code later in this chapter.

Access to arbitrary SQL is set up by using the BATCHES=ENABLED parameter in the FOR SOAP portion of the definition. You can use DATABASE= to put the user in a specific database by default. The user can execute arbitrary SQL commands, with or without parameters, and receive results. This is all subject to SQL Server database security, of course. The NAMESPACE= parameter defines an XML namespace for the SOAP message and also acts as the default namespace for WEBMETHODs defined without a namespace on a per-method basis. To show an example of arbitrary SQL, if we define the following endpoint:

```
CREATE ENDPOINT myendpoint
   STATE = STARTED
AS HTTP (
   SITE = '*',
   PATH = '/sql/mydatabase',
   PORTS = (CLEAR),
   AUTHENTICATION = (INTEGRATED)
)
FOR SOAP (
   BATCHES=ENABLED,
```

```
    DATABASE='pubs',
    NAMESPACE='http://www.myns.com'
)
GO
```

we could send the following SOAP message to it.

```
<SOAP-ENV:Envelope
  xmlns:SOAP-ENV="http://schemas.xmlsoap.org/soap/envelope/"
  xmlns:myns="http://www.nyns.com"
  xmlns:sql="http://schemas.microsoft.com/SQLServer/2004/SOAP"
>
  <SOAP-ENV:Body>
    <sql:sqlbatch>
      <sql:BatchCommands>
        select * from authors
      </sql:BatchCommands>
    </sql:sqlbatch>
  </SOAP-ENV:Body>
</SOAP-ENV:Envelope>
```

Notice that the `<sql:sqlbatch>` and `<sql:BatchCommand>` are both from the `http://schemas.microsoft.com/SQLServer/2004/SOAP` namespace. This is a special XML namespace that is used to define parameters that apply to SQL XML SOAP requests. It also defines various output formats. Think of an XML namespace in this case as analogous to an `include` directive in C++ or `Imports` in VB.NET; once we've specified the namespace and its prefix, we can refer to various types defined within. We'll go into more detail about exactly what gets sent in the SOAP message and what is returned to the caller later in this chapter.

SOAP Messages and SQL Batches in SQLXML 3.0

SQLXML 3.0 has similar functionality that could be defined within the SQLXML Configuration Tool or COM object model. Defining a SOAP endpoint is accomplished by adding a SOAP "virtual name" via the tool and configuring its Web methods. In SQLXML 3.0 you can expose SQLXML template files as well as stored procedures and user-defined functions. Template files are files in XML format that define SQL or XPath queries that are sent to SQL Server via the Web server and produce output. For more information on template files, see Chapter 7 of *Essential ADO.NET*, by Bob Beauchemin (Addison-Wesley, 2002). The template files give you a little more flexibility with respect to pre- and postprocessing of the results, but the same functionality can be programmed into stored procedures in SQL Server 2005.

SQLXML 3.0's equivalent of executing batches was accomplished by a setting to "Allow URL queries." This gave the user the ability to issue any query by specifying it as part of the URL. The equivalent to the SOAP packet shown earlier would be an HTTP request to `http://myserver/sql/mydatabase?SQL=select+*+from+authors+for+xml+auto` (spaces must be replaced by plus signs in the URL). Note that neither the request nor the response in is SOAP format when using URL queries.

HTTP Endpoint Metadata Views

HTTP endpoint information is stored in five metadata views in SQL Server 2005. These views exist in the resource database. HTTP endpoints can have an owner, but they exist in the `MASTER` database and are part of the `sys` schema. These are the five metadata views.

- `sys.endpoints`—This view stores general metadata about any type of endpoint, and includes the endpoint owner, the endpoint state, and other items.

- `sys.http_endpoints`—This view stores most of the general metadata about HTTP endpoints, including Web site information and authentication type. There is one row per endpoint.

- `sys.ip_exceptions`—This view stores one row per IP-Exception list member.

- `sys.soap_endpoints`—This view stores general information about whether an endpoint is SOAP-enabled or batch-enabled, the default database, or other parameters defined in the `FOR SOAP` clause. There is one row per endpoint that is SOAP-enabled.

- `sys.endpoint_webmethods`—This view stores one row of information per SOAP `WEBMETHOD` defined and contains information about the method definition.

XML Input and Output Types from SQL Server Web Services

So far, we've looked at the basics of HTTP and SOAP access, seen how to define endpoints and alter their definition, and seen the SOAP packets required to call a simple Web method. Now we'll look at how to pass input parameters with SOAP messages, the exact XML formats to expect output, error handling, and a meta-language for describing the format to arbitrary consumers. All of this falls in a domain called "XML Web Services," but there are actually two discreet audiences for this functionality.

- Arbitrary users on any platform that will consume our Web Services "on the fly" as part of a generalized application.
- Power users that have preexisting knowledge of the formats involved and can consume special hints in addition to basic metadata.

As an example of the second kind of usage, it should be theoretically possible to write a .NET data provider or a JDBC driver that accesses SQL Server using only HTTP endpoints and SOAP for communication, eschewing TDS entirely. A .NET consumer might achieve great performance benefit from the XML attribute hint `msdata:isDataSet='true'` because the `DataSet` is a native .NET class. These two types of users are not mutually exclusive, and SQL Server HTTP endpoints attempt to provide features for each type.

SQL Server HTTP endpoints use a set number of input and output message formats. These formats are defined in an XML schema with the namespace `http://schemas.microsoft.com/SQLServer/2004/SOAP`. In addition to this main schema, a number of other schemas are used for additional functionality. These are listed in Table 10-1 (note that the exact namespaces may change by SQL Server release).

The easiest way to see the exact definitions of these schemas is to use the URL http://yourhost/yourendpoint?wsdl if WSDL is enabled; these schemas may appear in the WSDL `<types>` section. Newer versions of SQL Server 2005 may move the schemas from the body of the WSDL file itself to the Internet, so if you don't see them in your WSDL file, check the location that is specified in the WSDL. The content of the schemas is similar to a definition of the (binary) formats used in TDS packets, with the difference that these messages are all exchanged in XML in text format, and wrapped by SOAP packets. In fact, on first glance, the types defined in the XML namespaces are exactly analogous to the types defined in the `System.Data.SqlClient` namespace. The main difference is that `Sql Client` defines the types using .NET types; the XML namespaces use XML schema-compliant types and definitions!

There are a few different types of result format, defined in the namespaces listed in Table 10-1. Each result is wrapped in a `SqlResultStream` element; it is the "parent" XML element for all the results from a particular query. The formats are as follows:

- `SqlRowSet`—The XML representation of a resultset from a SQL `SELECT` statement
- `SqlXml`—An XML fragment resulting from a `SELECT...FOR XML` query
- `SqlMessage`—A SQL Server warning or error message
- `SqlResultCode`—A return code from a stored procedure
- `Parameters, SqlParameter`—A parameter collection of SQL Parameters

Although some of the message formats are fixed, parameters on the `CREATE ENDPOINT` definition may affect which format is used and the details of the contents of the messages.

Here is an example of the simplest possible messages that might be produced from invocation of a SQL batch that returns no output and has successfully completed.

```
<SOAP-ENV:Envelope
    xmlns:SOAP-ENV="http://schemas.xmlsoap.org/soap/envelope/"
    xmlns:sql="http://schemas.microsoft.com/SQLServer/2004/SOAP"
```

TABLE 10-1: Namespaces Used in HTTP Endpoint Messages

Description	Namespace
Main schema for formats	`http://schemas.microsoft.com/SQLServer/2004/SOAP`
SQL output types	`http://schemas.microsoft.com/sqlserver/2004/sqltypes`
Transaction information	`http://schemas.microsoft.com/SQLServer/2004/SOAP/types/SqlTransaction`
Count of rows affected	`http://schemas.microsoft.com/SQLServer/2004/SOAP/SqlRowCount`
Error message from SQL Server	`http://schemas.microsoft.com/SQLServer/2004/SOAP/SqlMessage`
Wraps a series of result messages	`http://schemas.microsoft.com/SQLServer/2004/SOAP/SqlResultStream`
Parameters	`http://schemas.microsoft.com/SQLServer/2004/SOAP/SqlParameter`
Options	`http://schemas.microsoft.com/SQLServer/2004/SOAP/Options`

```
   xmlns:sqltypes="http://schemas.microsoft.com/SQLServer/2004/SOAP/
   types"
   xmlns:sqlmessage=

"http://schemas.microsoft.com/SQLServer/2004/SOAP/types/SqlMessage"
   xmlns:sqlresultstream=

"http://schemas.microsoft.com/SQLServer/2004/SOAP/types/
SqlResultStream"
   xmlns:s0="http://schemas.microsoft.com/SQLServer/2004/SOAP"
   xmlns:tns="http://endpointns.com"
>
   <SOAP-ENV:Body>
     <s0:sqlbatchResponse>
       <s0:sqlbatchResult xsi:type="sqlresultstream:SqlResultStream">
         <sqlresultstream:SqlXml xsi:type="sqltypes:SqlXml" />
         <sqlresultstream:SqlResultCode
                 xsi:type="sqltypes:SqlResultCode">
            0
         </sqlresultstream:SqlResultCode>
       </s0:sqlbatchResult>
     </s0:sqlbatchResponse>
   </SOAP-ENV:Body>
</SOAP-ENV:Envelope>
```

As you can see, including all the schema namespaces at the beginning of every message makes this format unambiguous but rather verbose. Now that you've seen an overview, let's go into some implementation-specific details, starting with the HTTP endpoint parameters.

Message Format Choices in CREATE ENDPOINT

Message format choices are defined in the FOR SOAP portion of CREATE ENDPOINT. Some choices are only applicable to HTTP WEBMETHODs, because batch queries produce a consistent output style.

NAMESPACE—This parameter specifies the namespace that is used in the body of the SOAP request. It can be defined at the endpoint level and overridden on a method-by-method basis. The default namespace is http://tempuri.org.

CHARACTER_SET—This is the value that determines what the endpoint will do if the result includes characters that are invalid in XML. If the value XML is specified, invalid characters will result in an error. If the value SQL is specified, invalid characters will be encoded as entity references and the operation will succeed. This can be specified at the endpoint level and cannot be overridden at the method level.

FORMAT—Stored procedures can consist of many SQL statements, and each SQL query or action statement (SELECT, INSERT, UPDATE, DELETE) may return Rowsets (resultsets) or counts of rows affected. Specifying ROWSETS_ONLY returns only SqlRowSet elements. This is very useful when using HTTP endpoints with .NET clients, since it permits the .NET client proxy generator to generate System.Data.DataSet as the return value. Specifying ALL_RESULTS returns Rowsets (SqlRowSet elements), row counts (SqlRowCount elements), and all other types (including errors) that can be returned from invocation of SQL.

SCHEMA—When SQL statements or stored procedures are executed, each resultset is unique. There is not only a different number in result columns (SELECT * FROM authors returns a different number of columns than SELECT * FROM jobs), but the columns are different data types depending on the query. This makes generating a generalized XML schema that would represent the result of any SQL resultset problematic. The only choice that correctly represents a generic SQL resultset is <xsd:any>, the XML Schema wildcard. For Web Service consumers seeking to use strong typing, returning an <xsd:any> tag to describe the resultset is similar to saying, "There's XML here, but we don't know what elements and attributes it contains, exactly."

On the other hand, although you can't define a generic schema for a resultset other than as <xsd:any>, each instance of a resultset does have a unique instance schema. SQL Server communicates this to you when you use TDS by prepending the results with TDS describe packets. These describe each column's data type, whether it's an identity column, and other properties that you also find in an XML schema. Why can't you generate a schema for each instance and prepend it to the resultset like TDS does?

The schema option SCHEMA=STANDARD, which can be used at the endpoint or method level, let's you do exactly that. Each resultset actually consists of an XML schema describing the instance followed by the instance resultset. This works fine for clients that understand this format, and since the SqlRowSet uses the same format as the .NET DataSet class, a SqlRowSet with a standard schema can be read right into a .NET DataSet when you use this in conjunction with the ROWSETS_ONLY option described earlier. This doesn't help things for non-.NET consumers and consumers who don't understand this out-of-band protocol, but it allows a .NET consumer to easily read the XML result in a newly created DataSet. SCHEMA=NONE tells SQL Server not to generate an inline schema. For communicating with SOAP toolkits that don't know what to do with an inline schema, this is the option you want. Almost none of the non-Microsoft SOAP toolkits can handle inline schemas.

Parameter Handling in HTTP/SOAP Calls

Parameterized queries allow query plans to be reused for generic SQL SELECT statements. A SELECT statement with a parameter can be reused with a different value for the parameter, allowing you to save the query processor the job of parsing your SQL and figuring out a query plan each time. In addition, almost all stored procedures and UDFs have parameters; these parameters are specified as part of the declaration. A couple of facts about SQL Server's parameters for procedural code are pertinent to our forthcoming discussion of how to represent them in SOAP calls.

- Parameters have a specific data type and can also be NULL.
- SQL Server parameters specified as OUTPUT parameters are really the equivalent of SQL:1999's IN OUT parameters. Although you do not need to pass an input value to a parameter declared as OUTPUT unless it is actually used, you can pass input values to any parameter declared in Transact-SQL as OUTPUT. Most database APIs will let you declare these parameters as OUTPUT only and not require an input value.
- Parameters can be declared in Transact-SQL to have default values. If you don't pass a value in, SQL Server assumes the default.
- Parameters have names in SQL Server stored procedures, and most database APIs will allow you to call them by using the names and leaving out parameters with defaults. Some APIs (like ODBC) require that you pass parameters in the order that they are declared; some (like ADO.NET, when you use the SqlClient data provider) will allow passing them in any order and will match by name.
- Some APIs will let you ignore output parameter values if you want to.
- Output parameters in SQL Server/TDS always follow any resultsets that are produced by a stored procedure.

Since there are so many different ways of using parameters and representing them in data APIs, there need to be some rules about how to represent them in SOAP calls. Because the SQL Server SOAP processor will do strict validation of the XML input, these rules must be followed exactly by both the caller and SQL Server. We'll look at the rules for encoding parameters by using an example stored procedure. Note that the same rules apply when parameters are used in SQL batches. Here's the stored procedure.

```
CREATE PROCEDURE some_proc(
  @in_parm1 varchar(20),
  @in_parm2 integer default 0,
  @out_parm output double)
AS
SELECT * FROM some_table
SET @out_parm = 99.99
```

We'll start with the input message. There are a few considerations here. We can pass in a value for the first parameter or the NULL value. We can pass in a value for the second parameter or let it default. And we can pass in a value for the third parameter or leave it out, seeing in the stored procedure implementation that the parameter is assigned to, but its input value is never used. In the simplest case, we'll specify all the values. The SqlParameters portion of the request would look like this.

```
<sql:Parameters>
  <sqlparameter:SqlParameter name="@in_parm1" maxLength="20" >
    <sqlparameter:Value xsi:type="xsd:string">
    myvalue
    </sqlparameter:Value>
  </sqlparameter:SqlParameter>
  <sqlparameter:SqlParameter name="@in_parm2">
    <sqlparameter:Value xsi:type="xsd:integer">
    0
    </sqlparameter:Value>
  </sqlparameter:SqlParameter>
  <sqlparameter:SqlParameter name="@out_parm1">
    <sqlparameter:Value xsi:type="xsd:double">
    0.00
    </sqlparameter:Value>
  </sqlparameter:SqlParameter>
</sql:Parameters>
```

The first thing to notice is that you must specify all the parameters using the correct parameter name and in the correct order. This is required in the SOAP calls even though order is not significant if you use named parameters in SQL Server.

Special attributes of the SqlParameter and Value elements make things more accurate as well as more flexible. For example, to specify a parameter value of NULL for the first parameter, you simply set the xsi:nil attribute on the value to true.

```
- specify a NULL value
<sqlparameter:SqlParameter name="@in_parm1" maxLength="20" >
  <sqlparameter:Value xsi:nil="true" />
</sqlparameter:SqlParameter>
```

To use a default value you can specify the following.

```
- specify a default value
<sqlparameter:SqlParameter name="@in_parm2">
  <sqlparameter:Value useDefaultValue="true" />
</sqlparameter:SqlParameter>
```

To indicate that you don't care about receiving the value of the output parameter, you can use this.

```
- don't send the output
<sqlparameter:SqlParameter name="@out_parm1">
  <sqlparameter:Value outputRequested="false" />
</sqlparameter:SqlParameter>
```

You can also use these attributes to specify exact precision and scale for a decimal parameter, the type name for a user-defined type and `LocaleID`, and comparison options for string types. For a list of all the attributes that affect parameters, see the SQL Server Books Online.

Error Handling

Errors are loosely separated into these three groups:

- HTTP transport errors
- SOAP faults
- SQL Server errors

The first two groups are defined by the SOAP protocol. An HTTP transport error might be caused by sending a bad HTTP request and will be returned as a bad HTTP return code. An example might be "400 Bad Request." SOAP faults are defined by the SOAP specification and can be caused by either the client sending in a bad request or the server receiving an unrecoverable error while processing the request. A SOAP fault is returned to the caller as an HTTP response code "500 Internal Server Error" and a response message consisting of an ordinary SOAP `Envelope` and a SOAP `Body` containing a SOAP `Fault` element. This element is a complex type and contains a `faultcode` (indicating whether the client or the server caused the error), a `faultstring`, and an optional `detail` element. A typical SOAP fault message would look like this.

```
<SOAP-ENV:Envelope
  xmlns:SOAP-ENV="http://schemas.xmlsoap.org/soap/envelope/"
  xmlns:sql="http://schemas.microsoft.com/SQLServer/2004/SOAP">
  <SOAP-ENV:Body>
        <SOAP-ENV:Fault>
              <faultcode>SOAP-ENV:Client</faultcode>
              <faultstring></faultstring>
              <detail></detail>
        </SOAP-ENV:Fault>
  </SOAP-ENV:Body>
</SOAP-ENV:Envelope>
```

SQL Server endpoints also support SOAP 1.2 format faults and add extra error information. A sample SOAP 1.2 fault with extended information would look like this.

```
<SOAP-ENV:Fault xmlns:sqlsoapfaultcode=
  "http://schemas.microsoft.com/sqlserver/2004/SOAP/SqlSoapFaultCode">
 <SOAP-1_2-ENV:Code>
  <SOAP-1_2-ENV:Value>SOAP-1_2-ENV:Sender</SOAP-1_2-ENV:Value>
  <SOAP-1_2-ENV:Subcode>
   <SOAP-1_2-ENV:Value>sqlsoapfaultcode:InvalidXml</SOAP-1_2-ENV:
Value>
  </SOAP-1_2-ENV:Subcode>
 </SOAP-1_2-ENV:Code>
 <SOAP-1_2-ENV:Reason>
  <SOAP-1_2-ENV:Text xml:lang="en-US">There was an error in the
incoming SOAP request packet:  Sender, InvalidXml
  </SOAP-1_2-ENV:Text>
 </SOAP-1_2-ENV:Reason>
 <SOAP-1_2-ENV:Node>http://mysvr:80/sql</SOAP-1_2-ENV:Node>
 <SOAP-1_2-ENV:Role>
    http://schemas.microsoft.com/SQLServer/2001/12/SOAP
 </SOAP-1_2-ENV:Role>
 <SOAP-1_2-ENV:Detail>
  <sqlresultstream:SqlMessage xsi:type="sqlmessage:SqlMessage">
  <sqlmessage:Class>16</sqlmessage:Class>
  <sqlmessage:LineNumber>0</sqlmessage:LineNumber>
  <sqlmessage:Message>
   XML parsing: line 3, character 0, incorrect document syntax
  </sqlmessage:Message>
  <sqlmessage:Number>9422</sqlmessage:Number>
  <sqlmessage:Source>Microsoft-SQL/9.0</sqlmessage:Source>
  <sqlmessage:State>1</sqlmessage:State>
  </sqlresultstream:SqlMessage>
 </SOAP-1_2-ENV:Detail>
</SOAP-ENV:Fault>
```

HTTP endpoints in SQL Server 2005 never return SOAP faults for SQL Server error conditions. SOAP faults would be returned under conditions such as the following:

- Attempting to send a message to a stored procedure that was not found
- Invalid SOAP Header or SOAP envelope
- An out-of-memory condition in the server

For SQL Server errors that might be returned from a stored procedure when an error is raised, SQL Server HTTP endpoints return a "200 OK" HTTP response with a `SqlMessage` element. `SqlMessage` elements contain all the information that might be returned to an API like ADO.NET: the SQL Server error code, stored procedure name, and other information. The schema definition for a `SqlMessage` is shown in Listing 10-1.

LISTING 10-1: SqlMessage Definition

```
<xsd:complexType name="SqlMessage">
 <xsd:attribute ref="sqltypes:IsNested" />
 <xsd:sequence minOccurs="1" maxOccurs="1">
  <xsd:element name="Class" type="sqltypes:nonNegativeInteger" />
  <xsd:element name="LineNumber" type="sqltypes:nonNegativeInteger" />
   <xsd:element name="Message" type="xsd:string" />
   <xsd:element name="Number" type="sqltypes:nonNegativeInteger" />
   <xsd:element name="Procedure" type="xsd:string" />
   <xsd:element name="Server" type="xsd:string" />
   <xsd:element name="Source" type="xsd:string" />
   <xsd:element name="State" type="sqltypes:nonNegativeInteger" />
 </xsd:sequence>
</xsd:complexType>
```

If a batch of SQL statements or a stored procedure produces multiple results, `SqlMessage` elements may be interspersed with other results if the error that produced the `SqlMessage` does not terminate the stored procedure.

HTTP Session Support in Endpoints

Two further parameters that can be specified in the FOR SOAP portion of an HTTP endpoint have to do with session management. When a SQL Server TDS client logs on to an application, it establishes a session with the database instance. This session controls resources like memory buffers, temporary tables, and SQL environment variable and language settings;

these remain in-scope for the lifetime of the session. Because HTTP is a stateless protocol (TDS is stateful), the concept of a SQL Server session must be grafted on by using the concept of an "HTTP Session." This is similar in concept to using HTTP cookies, but is accomplished in SQL Server 2005 Web Services by special HTTP headers. Although HTTP cookies are a standard for Web application state management (they're used by ASP.NET, ASP, and JSP), there is not yet a recognized standard for sessions in Web Services. The SQL Server 2005 implementation will most likely be able to switch to the standard, should one appear.

The main reason for using sessions is that without them you would have to log in to SQL Server with every SOAP request, which has a big performance cost. But there's another reason for session management. In a .NET client, it's possible for a programmer to forget to shutdown connections (sessions) to SQL Server. This not only wastes resources, but gives an arbitrary person who happens to walk up to such an application "after hours" a live connection to the corporate database. With Windows clients, the screen saver with a login screen provides protection against this. With an HTTP client that could conceivably be run over a "public" computer in an Internet cafe, we need even more protection. Therefore, we not only need the implementation of sessions, but the concept of a session timeout value.

You specify sessions and the session timeout value of parameters of the FOR SOAP section of the CREATE ENDPOINT DDL statement. Here's an example of its use.

```
CREATE ENDPOINT myendpoint
  STATE = STARTED
AS HTTP (
  SITE = '*',
  PATH = '/sql/mydatabase',
  PORTS = (CLEAR),
  AUTHENTICATION = (INTEGRATED)
)
FOR SOAP (
  BATCHES=ENABLED,
  DATABASE='pubs',
  SESSIONS = ENABLED,
  SESSION_TIMEOUT = 300,
  NAMESPACE='http://www.myns.com'
)
GO
```

This enables session management and sets the session timeout value to 300 seconds (5 minutes). Session timeout refers to the amount of idle time after the last batch executed before the session times out; it does not represent the total session time allocated. In this case, as long as the user executed a SQL statement using SOAP every 5 minutes, the session would remain active. To set the session timeout value to "infinite" (making it equivalent to the TDS behavior), you would specify SESSION_TIMEOUT=NEVER.

SQLXML 3.0

SQLXML 3.0's SOAP endpoints were implemented approximately the same way as HTTP endpoints. They have a few subtle differences.

In SQLXML 3.0 you can configure an endpoint to return a single .NET DataSet with multiple resultsets, multiple DataSets with a single resultset in each one, or a SqlXml element. You could also specify that FOR XML type processing be done on your resultset on the client side (that is, within the ISAPI application). When FOR XML processing was done on the client, only a SqlXml element could be produced as output. These options are not all available in the same specific form in HTTP endpoints, but similar results could be produced by writing a stored procedure in .NET code that would produce any output style that you wanted as an output parameter of the XML data type.

In SQLXML 3.0 you can also suppress SqlMessage elements and return any SQL Server errors as SOAP errors to the client. Although this is a useful tool when you are using SQLXML to build a Web site (you don't want the user to receive a SQL Server error message), its usefulness in a Web Service environment, where the consumer is expecting error information, is limited.

Using the XML Data Type and Web Services

We've just seen how HTTP endpoints can be used to expose SQL Server stored procedures and user-defined functions to any Web client. Stored procedures and functions in SQL Server 2005 can also consume and return instances of the XML data type. By using XML data type parameters that have an associated XML schema, we can expose more complex, XML-based messages through SQL Server. In addition, by using schema-valid types, we enable the system to know more exactly what XML our input and output messages should contain.

Here's an example of a stored procedure that returns an instance of an XML type, and the CREATE ENDPOINT definition that defines this stored procedure as an HTTP method.

```
CREATE PROCEDURE getxml (@x XML(peoplecoll) OUTPUT)
AS
BEGIN
 - trivially simple implementation
SET @x = '<age xmlns="http://example.org/People">11</age>'
END
GO

CREATE ENDPOINT xmldb_endpoint
        STATE = STARTED
AS HTTP (
        SITE = '*',
        PATH = '/xmldb/',
        AUTHENTICATION = (INTEGRATED),
        PORTS = (CLEAR)
)
FOR SOAP
(
  WEBMETHOD 'testns'.'getxml'
  (
    NAME='xmldb.dbo.getxml',
    SCHEMA = STANDARD
  ),
  BATCHES = ENABLED,
  WSDL = DEFAULT,
  DATABASE = 'xmldb'
)
go
```

This is interesting because of the schema portion of the WSDL that is produced. The purpose of WSDL is to make clear to users of the endpoint (Web Service) the exact XML format of the parameter they need to pass in or, in this case, should expect as output. Because the XML parameter value is associated with an XML schema, the set of possibilities is limited by the types that the schema exposes. The WSDL that some consumers will use to assist in processing the Web Service looks like this.

```
<! - remainder of the WSDL types section elided for clarity  ->
<xsd:import namespace="http://example.org/People" />

<xsd:element name="getxml">
  <xsd:complexType>
    <xsd:sequence>
      <xsd:element name="x" minOccurs="1" maxOccurs="1"
nillable="true">
      <xsd:complexType mixed="true">
        <xsd:sequence>
          <xsd:any minOccurs="0" maxOccurs="unbounded"
            processContents="strict"
```

```
            namespace="http://example.org/People" />
          </xsd:sequence>
        </xsd:complexType>
      </xsd:element>
      </xsd:sequence>
    </xsd:complexType>
  </xsd:element>
```

Note that the schema for strongly typed output parameters is mentioned in an XML schema `import` statement, but unless the client already possesses the schema, there is no way to locate it. The procedure parameter is represented as an `xsd:any` type, with the qualification that it must be an element in the namespace that is part of the XML schema collection (for example, `http://example.org/People`) and that this will be strictly checked (`processing="strict"`). Although some Web Service consumers may have problems processing the `xsd:any` type tag, this is an improvement over untyped XML, which would appear as an `xsd:any` type with no qualifications.

Accessing HTTP Endpoints with .NET Code

Most Web Services toolkits, including Microsoft's Web Service support, can generate programmer-friendly proxy classes, which allow an HTTP ENDPOINT's WEBMETHODs to appear as method calls on an object. You can make calls on the object and obtain results using the proxy class. Toolkits usually produce proxy classes by consuming WSDL exposed by the Web Service. A WSDL document contains all the information that a client would need to determine what messages to send to a SOAP endpoint, which endpoint to use, and information about the XML schema types produced and consumed by each message. A complete definition of WSDL is beyond the scope of this book. For more information, you can read the WSDL specification at W3C, or for a more understandable form, we'd recommend *Real World XML Web Services*, by Yasser Shohoud (Addison-Wesley, 2002). To use an analogy, we'd say that WSDL exposes information about a Web Service endpoint as Interface Definition Language (IDL), or a Type Library exposes information about a COM component as a database schema exposes database information. There are many tools that will read a database schema and build a proxy to it, such as the OLE DB and ODBC wizards in Visual Studio. WSDL is the schema for a Web method, and programming tools can use it to build the proxies.

SQL Server 2005 HTTP endpoints can automatically produce WSDL if WSDL=DEFAULT or WSDL='your stored procedure' is specified in the FOR

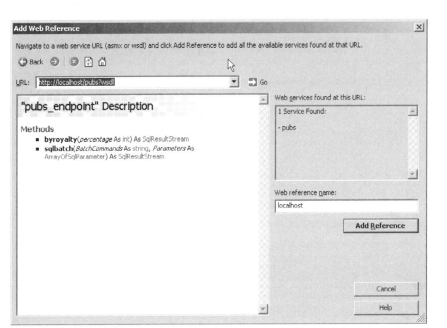

FIGURE 10-1: Consuming a SQL Server 2005 HTTP Endpoint in Visual Studio 2005

SOAP portion of the CREATE ENDPOINT statement. Enabling WSDL permits SQL Server to serve WSDL for a particular endpoint at http://myserver/ sql/myendpoint?WSDL, if /sql/myendpoint is specified in the PATH=. This WSDL can be consumed by the .NET SDK's WSDL.exe utility and Visual Studio 2005 with good fidelity, using the "Add Web Reference" item in a .NET project. Adding a reference to an HTTP endpoint with Visual Studio 2005 is shown in Figure 10-1.

The "Add Web Reference" functionality consumes the WSDL and produces a proxy class, allowing you to program the endpoint as if it were a set of object-oriented classes. The proxy class exposes properties that permit you to configure the URL if the server changes and it inherits from System.Web.Services.Protocols.SoapHttpClientProtocol, a class that encapsulates System.Web.WebRequest. This means that you can set the Credentials desired, as shown in Listing 10-2. Listing 10-2 show an extremely simple Web Service client using the WSDL-generated proxy.

LISTING 10-2: Client That Uses WSDL-Generated Proxy

```
static void Main(string[] args)
{
  ConsoleApplication1.zmv43.SqlParameter[] p = null;
  pubs_endpoint e = new pubs_endpoint();
```

```
  e.Credentials = System.Net.CredentialCache.DefaultCredentials;
  object[] o = e.sqlbatch(
    "select * from authors where au_lname = 'Ringer'", ref p);
  for (int i=0;i<o.Length;i++)
  {
   Type t = o[i].GetType();
   Console.WriteLine(t);
   switch (t.ToString())
   {
     case "ConsoleApplication1.zmv43.SqlMessage":
       Console.WriteLine(((SqlMessage)o[i]).Message);
       break;
     case "System.Data.DataSet":
       Console.WriteLine("DataSet contains {0} tables",
               ((DataSet)o[i]).Tables.Count);
       // process DataSet further...
       break;
     default:
       Console.WriteLine("unknown or unexpected type");
       break;
   }
  }
}
```

Because the endpoint can return multiple results, including `DataSets`, `SqlMessages`, and possibly other types, the return code from the call to `sqlbatch` must return an array of `Object` types and postprocess each result according to the type. If we define an endpoint that returns either a single `DataSet` or an exception using the `ROWSET_ONLY` option in our HTTP endpoint DDL, we can simplify the code to this.

```
try {
  pubs_endpoint e = new pubs_endpoint();
  e.Credentials = System.Net.CredentialCache.DefaultCredentials;
  DataSet ds = e.someMethodReturningDataSet();
}
catch (Exception e) {
  Console.WriteLine(e.Message);
}
```

This option was available in SQLXML 3.0, but the error message produced was not the rich SQL error, à la `SqlMessage`, but a generic SOAP error.

You can also write a more "manual" .NET client that uses the XML APIs to produce and consume the required SOAP packets, and `HttpWeb Request` and `HttpWebResponse` to communicate with the endpoint. The outline of such a program would look like Listing 10-3. This program reads the SOAP formatted request from a file.

LISTING 10-3: HTTP Endpoint Client Using HttpWebRequest/Response

```
// create request for URL
HttpWebRequest req = (HttpWebRequest)WebRequest.Create("url");
req.Method = "POST";
req.Credentials = CredentialCache.DefaultCredentials;

// copy file contents into array of bytes
FileStream fs = new FileStream(
  "somefile", FileMode.Open);

byte[] data = new byte[(int)fs.Length];
fs.Read(data, 0, (int)fs.Length);
fs.Close();

// get HTTP request message body
Stream s = req.GetRequestStream();

// copy bytes into HTTP request message
s.Write(data, 0, data.Length);
s.Close();

HttpWebResponse resp;
try {
  // send request message and wait for response
  resp = (HttpWebResponse)req.GetResponse();
}
catch (WebException we) {
  // if server returns an error, capture that response
  resp = (HttpWebResponse)we.Response;
}

// dump response body
StreamReader reader = new StreamReader(
  resp.GetResponseStream());
Console.WriteLine(reader.ReadToEnd());
reader.Close();
```

A lot of the benefit of Web Services, however, centers on interoperability. For non-.NET clients, building a rich application around a generic `Rowset` consumer like the `DataSet` is much more difficult. Web Service toolkits tend to want exact WSDL representation of XML schema, and the use of the `<xsd:any>` tag to represent the `DataSet` is problematic. Even a Visual Basic 6 Web Service client would have a problem processing this tag, although conceivably a conversion class could be written to transform the .NET `DataSet` into a series of ADO `Recordsets` or JDBC `RowSets`.

Although HTTP endpoints can return results that prepend an instance schema for each `DataSet` produced, few generic toolkits know how to process a response that includes an inline schema. Although the `SqlRowSet` type correctly indicates an XSD schema followed by an <xsd:any> tag, there is nothing in the XSD specification to indicate that "this schema describes the format of the <xsd:any> tag that follows."

For use of SQL Server HTTP endpoints with generic clients, one way to solve this problem is to remember that although SQL Server does not analyze every stored procedure to determine the shape of every possible resultset returned, if the programmer knows the shape of the DataSet that will be produced for a given procedure, it is a simple task to dump out the DataSet's XML Schema using the DataSet.WriteXmlSchema method, manually construct a WSDL file for a specific procedure by replacing the <xsd:any/> tag with the DataSet's schema, and publish the resulting WSDL on a separate WSDL endpoint. The HTTP endpoint definition facilitates this by letting you specify WSDL='your stored procedure' and writing a custom stored procedure that generates exactly the WSDL you want.

Writing a Stored Procedure That Generates WSDL

A stored procedure that generates WSDL can allow proxy class generators like those found in Visual Studio 2005, Microsoft's COM-based SOAP toolkit, or Java-based SOAP toolkits like the one found in Websphere, to generate strong "object" types using the type system of their choice rather than consuming the Web Service as arbitrary DataSets or XML documents. You can achieve the same effect by hand-coding the proxy based on out-of-band knowledge of the exact output format, or hand-coding the WSDL and feeding it to a proxy generator. The WSDL-generating stored procedure used with HTTP endpoints just makes the WSDL publicly available and stores the generation code in SQL Server along with the rest of the HTTP endpoint metadata.

Your goal is to replace the <xsd:any/> tag that represents arbitrary resultset output by the exact definition of the specific resultset that your stored procedure will return. Here's an example. Say that we are executing the stored procedure GetAuthorsAndTitles, which looks like this.

```
CREATE PROCEDURE GetAuthorsAndTitles
AS
SELECT authors.au_id, authors.au_lname, authors.au_fname,
       titles.title_id, titles.title
   FROM authors
     LEFT INNER JOIN titleauthor ON authors.au_id = titleauthor.au_id
     LEFT INNER JOIN titles ON titles.title_id = titleauthor.title_id
   ORDER BY authors.au_id
GO
```

With the WSDL=DEFAULT parameter, if you specify SCHEMA=NONE on the Web method, the resultset from the stored procedure will be represented as a SqlXml type, which amounts to this.

```
<xsd:complexType name="SqlXml" mixed="true">
 <xsd:sequence>
  <xsd:any />
 </xsd:sequence>
</xsd:complexType>
```

What you want to do, is to specify WSDL that replaces the <xsd:any/> by the complexType shown in Listing 10-4, which more accurately represents the resultset.

LISTING 10-4: The complexType Produced by the Resultset

```
<xs:complexType name="AuthorsAndTitlesResultset">
 <xs:sequence>
   <xs:element name="authors" minOccurs="0" maxOccurs="unbounded">
     <xs:complexType>
      <xs:sequence>
        <xs:element name="au_id" type="xs:string" minOccurs="0" />
        <xs:element name="au_lname" type="xs:string" minOccurs="0" />
        <xs:element name="au_fname" type="xs:string" minOccurs="0" />
        <xs:element name="title_id" type="xs:string" minOccurs="0" />
        <xs:element name="title" type="xs:string" minOccurs="0" />
      </xs:sequence>
     </xs:complexType>
   </xs:element>
 </xs:sequence>
</xs:complexType>
```

The stored procedure that exposes WSDL will produce a one-column, one-row rowset containing the WSDL as a VARCHAR or an NVARCHAR type. An example might look like this.

```
CREATE PROCEDURE wsdl_procedure (
  @EndpointID int = 65536,
  @IsSSL bit = 0,
  @Host nvarchar(256),
  @QueryString varchar(256)
)
AS BEGIN
 - set the body of the wsdl document here
 - as an example
 - this can be stored as an XML data type in a table
SELECT cast(wsdlcol as nvarchar(max))
  FROM xmldb..wsdl_table
```

```
    WHERE endpointid = @EndpointID
    AND isssl = @IsSSL
END
GO
```

This example assumes that you've hand-generated the WSDL and stored it as an XML data type column (wsdlcol) in a table (wsdl_table). The table can contain other columns (such as endpointid and isssl in the previous example) to serve as discriminators and make the procedure more general purpose.

SQLXML 3.0

A SQLXML 3.0 client would be almost identical to an HTTP endpoint client, with the additional ability to specify a DataSet return and a generic SOAP error, as described earlier. Although this does not provide rich error information, it does simplify the code quite a bit. You would specify the combination of DataSet and SOAP error using the Windows Administration tool, as shown in Figure 10-2.

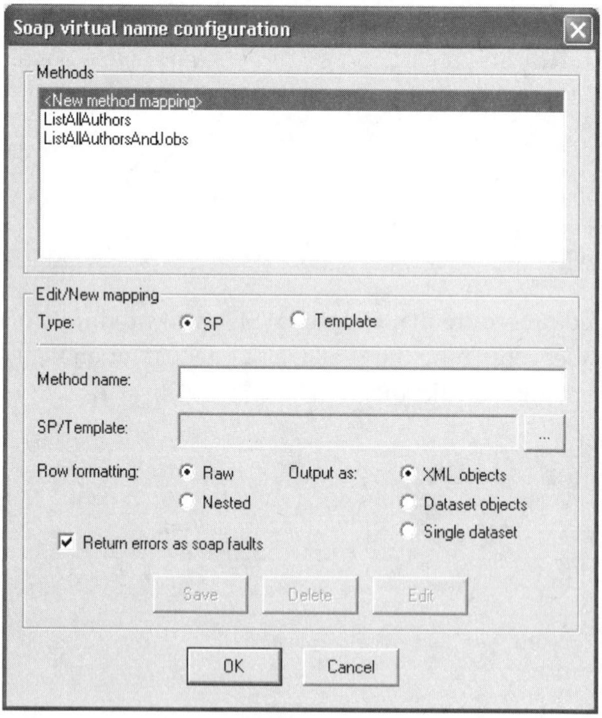

FIGURE 10-2: Configuration Choices to Produce Simplified Code

Where Are We?

SOAP and HTTP, combined with HTTP endpoints in SQL Server 2005 or using SQLXML 3.0 with non–.NET Server machines, can combine to provide an HTTP-based alternative for TDS. In addition, because SOAP uses XML as its marshaling format, it is possible for any platform that can speak HTTP and produce and consume XML to communicate with SQL Server without the installation of a specific network library or even a .NET runtime. HTTP endpoints introduce some optimizations that make it easier for a .NET consumer—at the possible expense of generic consumers that expect to use dynamic but exact WSDL—to provide a description of the endpoint. But if the few relatively simple types and rules are baked into a client, it is absolutely possible for any consumer on any platform to consume an HTTP endpoint and communicate with SQL Server 2005 as though it were a Web Service.

Having explored the new server features (and there are an amazing number of them), we'll move on from here to discuss "traditional" clients using ADO.NET, OLE DB, ADO, and ODBC. The major changes affect these clients from many different angles, from support of user-defined types in the ADO.NET `DataSet` to exposure of new features like notifications. We'll also look at an object-oriented framework for ADO.NET clients known as ObjectSpaces, and finish by looking at some new "generic application–like" features that allow straightforward integration of SQL Server into specific problem domains.

▛ 11 ▪

ADO and ADO.NET Enhancements

WITH THE ADVENT of CLR user-defined types, as well as improved Large Value data support and XML support, comes enhancement of the client APIs. This chapter will look at the enhancements to the ADO. NET client libraries as well as the classic data access APIs—OLE DB, ADO, and ODBC—to support new SQL Server 2005 data types.

User-Defined Types and Relational Data Access APIs

SQL Server 2005 offers inside-the-database support for some new data types. Although basic support of the new VARCHAR(MAX) data types is straightforward, the user-defined types and the XML data type are complex types. Because we'd like to deal with the user-defined types and XML in its native form on the client as well as on the server, the client APIs need to be enhanced as well. In the book *Essential ADO.NET*, by Bob Beauchemin (Addison-Wesley, 2002), Bob speculated on the challenges of adding UDT support to the .NET DataSet. We'll also discuss how this is supported.

Most client application programming interfaces designed for use with relational databases were not designed with complex-type features built in. The original database-independent library, ODBC, was tailored specifically around SQL-92-style database operations. It was not updated when extended types were introduced into the SQL standard in SQL:1999. Each ODBC column binding was supposed to refer to an ODBC-defined data type; user-defined types were not recognized as an ODBC type. The COM-based data access APIs, OLE DB and ADO, were designed with some thought given to UDTs; there is an OLE DB DBTYPE_UDT, and ADO maps this data type to its adUserDefined data type. However, DBTYPE_UDT was meant to be used to bind to data as COM objects using the COM interfaces IUnknown or IDispatch.

Though ADO.NET was not designed with user-defined types in mind either, this is the client-side library that programmers using SQL Server 2005 are most likely to use. ADO.NET does contain rich support for mixing relational and XML data, however. Combined with the fact that user-defined types are actually .NET types (classes and structures), this gives ADO.NET the tightest and richest integration with the new extended SQL Server type model.

Using .NET UDTs in ADO.NET

When we deal with UDTs from clients in ADO.NET, we'll usually be storing them in tables or retrieving them from tables. The "instance" of the UDT is actually stored in the database, and we manipulate it in place. We can do this all from the client by using conversion from strings or through carefully thought-out mutator functions, regardless of the API. Here's a simple example in ADO.NET. (Authors' note: Everywhere that we use a connection string in an example program, we obtain it through a pseudo-code method named GetConnectStringFromConfigFile. In general, it's not a good idea to hardcode connection strings in program code. You can either get them from a configuration file or, in ADO.NET 2.0, use the DbConnectionString class that's provided in System.Data.dll.)

```
/*
 assuming a UDT called Point that has m_x and m_y properties
 and a table point_tab defined like this:
  CREATE TABLE point_tab(
    oid integer,
    point_col POINT)
*/

string connect_string = GetConnectStringFromConfigFile();
SqlConnection conn = new SqlConnection(connect_string);
SqlCommand cmd = new SqlCommand();
cmd.Connection = conn;
```

```
conn.Open();
cmd.CommandText =
  "insert into point_tab values(1, convert(Point, '10:10'))";
int i;
i = cmd.ExecuteNonQuery();
cmd.CommandText =
  "update point_tab
    set point_col.SetXY(15,20)
    where oid = 1";
i = cmd.ExecuteNonQuery();
```

Note that in this example we're using the `Point` type only on the server, passing in string values to insert and integer values to update through the mutator. We don't have to have access to the `Point` type code at all on the client.

It is possible to manipulate user-defined types from client code by only using SQL statements, stored procedures, and user-defined functions. Instances of user-defined types will not ordinarily be held in the database past the end of a SQL batch, however. If we want to manipulate the same instance of the UDT over multiple batches, we could store it in a SQL Server temporary table, but this would incur the overhead of serializing and deserializing the instance (from the temporary table) each time we access it.

New functionality in ADO.NET permits the use of UDT code in client programs as well as server programs. You can deploy the UDT code to each client as part of a program's installation process. You can early bind to UDT code if you reference it in an application or use .NET reflection to use late binding. You can also use UDTs as stored procedure or user-defined function parameters. Let's see how this would look in code.

Fetching UDT Data from a DataReader

In the previous simple example, we did all the UDT manipulations in code on the server side. We didn't need the UDT on the client at all. But we could also change the statement to fetch the entire UDT over to the client via a `SqlDataReader`. The code would start by looking like this.

```
// Use the same point_tab as in the first example.

string connect_string = GetConnectStringFromConfigFile();
SqlConnection conn = new SqlConnection(connect_string);
SqlCommand cmd = new SqlCommand();
cmd.Connection = conn;
```

```
conn.Open();

// get the entire point column
cmd.CommandText = "select oid, point_col from point_tab";

SqlDataReader rdr = cmd.ExecuteReader();

while (rdr.Read())
  {
  // rdr[1] contains an instance of a Point class
  // easiest access, call ToString()
  Console.WriteLine("column 1 is {0}", rdr[1].ToString());
  }
rdr.Close();
cmd.Dispose();
conn.Dispose();
```

The `Point` class inside the `DataReader` can be used in a few different ways, but the bottom line is always the same. To manipulate the `Point`, including the simplest method, which consists of returning a string representation of it, the code for the `Point` class has to exist on the client. If you've not deployed it, the code exists only inside the SQL Server instance. When the attempt to load the `Point` class using normal assembly loader mechanisms fails, the ADO.NET client code will throw an exception. Although the information in the TDS data stream is sufficient to "fill in" an instance of the `Point` class that exists on the client, it is not sufficient to instantiate a `Point` if the assembly does not exist on the client. It's more like an opaque binary blob. There is additional information in the TDS stream to identify the class name and the assembly version, however.

The server's version of the UDT will be used as the "reference" version; the UDT on the client must exactly match the server's version. This is the case even if a different version of the UDT is directly referenced in the client assembly. Matching is stricter than even the usual .NET four-part assembly name matching; the module version ID (MVID) must also match for assemblies to be considered identical, although this requirement will probably be relaxed before RTM. The UDT assembly must be deployed into the global assembly cache (GAC) or available in the caller's current directory, or instantiating it on the client will fail.

In addition to retrieving the information from the `Point` class, you can directly create an instance of `Point` for every row read through the `DataReader` by getting the value of the column and casting it to the correct type, like this.

```
while (rdr.Read())
  {
```

```
// rdr[1] contains an instance of a Point class
// get a strongly typed instance
Point p = (Point)rdr[1];
}
```

Note that the big difference between using ToString and using the previous code is that you must have an assembly containing the Point class available at compile time. This method will probably be most often used, because it lets you deal with the SQL Server CLR classes as though they were "normal" client classes, with special data access methods based on the fact that they can be persisted.

There are a few slight performance optimizations based on either dealing with the instance as a stream of bytes or using your own object serialization code. If you just want to pass the stream of bytes around without deserializing it—for instance, to perform a kind of manual object replication—you can use GetBytes or GetSqlBytes to read the bytes as a binary stream. If you have implemented your own serialization using IBinary Serialize or want to hook the serialized form into a .NET technology like remoting, you can pass the bytes around and deserialize them manually. Here's an example that uses a Point class that implements an IBinary Serialize interface.

```
Point pt = new Point();
while (rdr.Read())
  {
  // rdr[1] contains an instance of a Point class
  // initialize copy with GetSqlBytes
      byte[] b = new byte[3200];
  long idx = 0; long numbytes = rdr.GetBytes(1,idx,b,0,3200);
      MemoryStream m = new MemoryStream(b);
      BinaryReader brdr = new BinaryReader(m);
      pt.Read(brdr);
      Console.WriteLine(pt.m_x + ":" + pt.m_y);
  }
```

The preceding code gets slightly better performance by allocating a single instance of Point outside the loop and calling Read (a method of IBinarySerialize) each time, although except in applications that need a very high degree of optimization, the small performance gain is not worth the increase in code complexity.

When you get an instance of a UDT through a DataReader using any of the methods shown earlier, it is not a reference to the data in the DataReader; you are making a copy. The instance data in the DataReader is read-only, but the data in the copy can be updated. When you update the data, accessing the data again from the `DataReader` will return the original data, not the changed data. Here's an illustrative example.

```
SqlDataReader rdr = cmd.ExecuteReader();

Point p1, p2;
rdr = cmd.ExecuteReader();
while (rdr.Read())
  {
    // rdr[1] contains an instance of a Point class
    // p1 is a copy of rdr[1]
    p1 = (Point)rdr[1];

    // attempting to update this will work
    p1.m_x = 1000;

    // retrieve the value in the DataReader again
    Point p2 = (Point)rdr[1];
    // now p1 != p2
  }
```

This covers almost every case in which we'd want to access a UDT from a `DataReader`. But what if we were writing a generic access layer, had a library of types loaded, and wanted to know the type so that we could instantiate the correct strongly typed class at runtime? Or we wanted to be able to specify a UDT as a parameter in a parameterized query, stored procedure, or user-defined function?

The way to get information about a `DataReader`'s columns at runtime in ADO.NET 1.0 is to use the method `SqlDataReader.GetSchemaTable`. `GetSchemaTable` returns a `DataTable` containing one row of information about each column in the resultset, and using it in our code would look like this.

```
SqlDataReader rdr = cmd.ExecuteReader();
DataTable t = rdr.GetSchemaTable();
```

A typical row in the `DataTable` of schema information would contain columns of information about the data. Although the `SqlDbType` is present, the SQL Server metadata that would completely describe the UDT is absent, and the `SqlDbType` would be `SqlDbType.SqlUdt`. We have a similar issue when we go to set the data type of a `SqlParameter`. Only `Sql DbType` is actually specified using the current implementation of `IDb Parameter`. We need to be able to read and to specify more metadata. Although you could read all the metadata by processing the results of

`GetSchemaTable` and calling `GetDataTypeName` and `GetFieldType` for the column value in question, it would be nice to have all that information wrapped in a particular class. Enter `SqlMetaData`.

Using the SqlMetaData Class

`SqlMetaData` is a class that is used to completely describe a single column of data. It can be used with columns of data returned through a `Sql DataReader` or with `SqlParameter` instances. You can access the instance of `SqlMetaData` for a column in the `SqlDataReader` by ordinal, like this.

```
SqlDataReader rdr = cmd.ExecuteReader();
// get metadata for column ordinal zero
SqlMetaData md = rdr.GetSqlMetaData(0);
```

`SqlMetaData` instances obtained from `SqlDataReader.GetSqlMeta Data` return the extended metadata from new format-extended TDS describe packets used by SQL Server 2005 as well as working with earlier versions of TDS. Listing 11-1 lists the properties exposed by the `SqlMeta Data` class; this is a superset of the information exposed by each column when `GetSchemaTable` is called.

LISTING 11-1: Properties of SqlMetaData

```
class SqlMetaData {

    //datatype info
    public SqlDbType sqlType;      // SqlDbType enum value
    public DbType dbType;          // DbType enum value
    public Type Type;             // .NET data type
    public string TypeName;       // .NET type name
    public string UdtTypeName;    // SQL Server 3-part type name

    //metadata info
    public bool IsPartialLength;
    public long Max;
    public long MaxLength;
    public byte Precision;
    public byte Scale;
    public string Name;           // column name
    public string SchemaName;     // relational schema
    public string DatabaseName;
    public SqlCompareOptions CompareOptions;
    public long LocaleId;

    // XML schema info for XML data type
    public string XmlSchemaCollectionDatabase;
```

```
public string XmlSchemaCollectionName;
public string XmlSchemaCollectionOwningSchema;
};
```

In addition to using this information to find out which assembly and class you're using in the case of a generic UDT access layer, you also need to specify the UdtTypeName when using UDT parameters in a parameterized query.

Let's look at calling a user-defined function that adds two Point instances together, returning another Point instance as the result. The UDF could be written like this in .NET.

```
public class Point
{
  // rest of the Point class deleted for clarity...
  // definition of the user-defined function
  public static Point AddPoint(Point a, Point b)
  {
    Point ret = new Point();
    ret.m_x = a.m_x + b.m_x;
    ret.m_y = a.m_y + b.m_y;
    return ret;
  }
}
```

The .NET implementation would be defined like this in T-SQL.

```
--
-- CREATE the POINT Assembly and load it into SQL Server
--
CREATE ASSEMBLY Point
FROM 'e:\types\point.dll'
GO


--
-- CREATE the POINT User-Defined Type
-- This assumes that we have a class named Point
-- in our assembly
--
CREATE TYPE Point
EXTERNAL NAME Point.Point
GO


--
-- CREATE UDF from the Point Assembly
--
create function AddPoint (@a Point, @b Point)
returns Point
```

```
external name Point.Point.AddPoint
go
```

Alternatively, the UDF could be defined in T-SQL, using only the .NET implementation of the POINT class.

```
-
- T-SQL implementation of AddPoint
-
CREATE FUNCTION AddPoint2 (@a Point, @b Point)
returns Point
as
begin
 declare @c Point
 set @c = convert(Point, '0:0')
 set @c.m_x = @a.m_x + @b.m_x
 set @c.m_y = @a.m_y + @b.m_y
 return @c
end
GO
```

Because no data access is done in adding two Points together, it might be best to implement this operation either completely on the server side (call the AddPoint UDF from another UDF or a SQL statement) or all on the client side (instantiate two Point objects and add them on the client) rather than calling from client to server, but we'll use this example to demonstrate calling a parameterized function from the client.

To invoke the UDF from the client, we'll need to instantiate a Sql Command and add the parameters to its ParametersCollection, the Parameters property of the SqlCommand. The code would look like this.

```
string connect_string = GetConnectStringFromConfigFile();
SqlConnection conn = new SqlConnection(connect_string);
SqlCommand cmd = new SqlCommand("dbo.AddPoint", conn);
cmd.CommandType = CommandType.StoredProcedure;

// define two Points to add
Point p1 = new Point(10, 10);
Point p2 = new Point(20, 20);

// now, define the Parameters
// use the overload that takes a parameter name and type for the input
parms
cmd.Parameters.Add("@a", SqlDbType.Udt);
cmd.Parameters[0].Value = p1;
cmd.Parameters.Add("@b", SqlDbType.Udt);
cmd.Parameters[1].Value = p2;
```

```
// define the output parameters. This parameter need not be
initialized
cmd.Parameters.Add("@c", SqlDbType.Udt);
cmd.Parameters[2].Direction = ParameterDirection.ReturnValue;
```

This code is incomplete because although the client is telling SQL Server that the parameter contains a user-defined type, there is no indication of which user-defined type we're passing in! We need to specify the correct metadata to SQL Server; this consists of the fully qualified SQL Server UdtTypeName. Once SQL Server has the correct name, it can check to see that we're passing in the correct parameter type and then invoke the UDF. We specify the type name using the SqlParameter or SqlMetaData class. Our finished code would look like this.

```
// now, define the Parameters
// use the overload that takes a parameter name and type for the input
parms
cmd.Parameters.Add("@a", SqlDbType.Udt);
cmd.Parameters[0].UdtTypeName = "pubs.dbo.Point";
cmd.Parameters[0].Value = p1;
cmd.Parameters.Add("@b", SqlDbType.Udt);
cmd.Parameters[1].Value = p2;
cmd.Parameters[1].UdtTypeName = "pubs.dbo.Point";

// define the output parameters. This parameter need not be
initialized
cmd.Parameters.Add("@c", SqlDbType.Udt);
cmd.Parameters[2].UdtTypeName = "pubs.dbo.Point";
cmd.Parameters[2].Direction = ParameterDirection.ReturnValue;
```

Using .NET UDTs in ODBC, OLE DB, and ADO Clients

Not all programmers who use SQL Server 2005 will be writing all of their client-side code in ADO.NET. Using ODBC never quite went out of style, and even though installations might take advantage of the new SQL Server 2005 features, including user-defined types that must be coded in a .NET Framework language, the legacy client might be maintained using ODBC. The ODBC API will not be specifically enhanced to use user-defined types. ODBC users will, however, be able to get a string representation of these types. You'd do this by using ToString in the SQL SELECT statement and retrieving the data as a SQL_VARCHAR or SQL_LONGVARCHAR data type. Alternatively, you can select the entire UDT column and get the binary representation as a SQL_VARBINARY or SQL_LONGVARBINARY type (note that this could also return the XML representation, if the UDT was converted to

XML format on the server). The SQL statements to accomplish this are pretty straightforward and are shown next.

```
-
- enable getting Point as a SQL_VARCHAR or SQL_LONGVARCHAR
-
SELECT oid, point_col.ToString() as point_str
  FROM point_tab
GO
-
- binary format
-
SELECT oid, point_col FROM point_tab
```

In all three of these cases, you are required to reformat and use the string or binary form manually; though because .NET types can be exposed as COM types, you may be able to instantiate the type and call Read or Parse in your ODBC program.

OLE DB and ADO

Because OLE DB and ADO are based on COM, and .NET types can be exposed as COM types and vice versa, the ability to use UDTs and the other new data types directly from within data access calls is richer. To accommodate legacy applications, .NET types can be exposed as COM types by running a utility called TLBEXP.exe (Type Library Exporter). This utility reads the type information in a .NET assembly and produces a COM type library that COM programmers can use in their programs. Because COM types must be cataloged in the registry to be usable, another utility, called REGASM, will catalog all the .NET class as COM classes. There is even an option in REGASM to create a type library at the same time, therefore obviating the need for programmers to run TLBEXP.exe at all. One thing to remember about REGASM is that if the .NET DLLs are not being registered in the .NET global assembly cache, the /codebase command-line switch must be used to tell the .NET runtime where to find the assembly at load time. Sample syntax for these command-line utilities follows.

```
' create a type library only (for the developer)
TLBEXP MyPoint.dll /out:MyPoint.tlb

' create a type library and register the .NET classes as COM classes
' (on the developers machine)
' assumes MyPoint.dll will be installed in the GAC
REGASM MyPoint.dll /tlb:MyPoint.tlb
```

```
' only register the .NET classes as COM classes (on the client)
' assumes MyPoint.dll will be installed in the GAC
REGASM MyPoint.dll

' register MyPoint.dll,
' the DLL will reside in the C:\myclasses directory
REGASM MyPoint.dll /codebase C:\myclasses
```

Note that although the .NET classes are registered as COM classes, the .NET runtime must be installed on each client for the classes to be usable. When .NET classes are instantiated through COM, the COM registry entry actually names `mscorlib.dll` as the library to load; `mscorlib.dll` then loads the appropriate .NET class into memory. Note that there is currently a problem doing this with members and methods that use `SqlTypes`, because `SqlTypes` are marked with the attribute `ComVisible = false`. This attribute is inherited by `SqlTypes`; it's specified at the assembly level for the `System.Data.dll` assembly.

Once we have everything registered, the choices for using SQL Server UDTs and ADO classic are very similar to the choices in ADO.NET. Let's look at some Visual Basic 6 examples of using UDTs in ADO code.

The OLE DB specification (used by OLE DB and ADO) already contained a constant in the `DBTYPES` enumeration for user-defined types. When a UDT column is fetched in an ADO `Recordset`, it is correctly identified as this data type. In addition, ADO 2.8 adds some extended properties to the `Field` object's `Properties` collection to identify the class name of the UDT.

```
Dim conn as New Connection
Dim rs as New Recordset
conn.Open
rs.Open "select oid, point_col from point_tab", conn

' this prints 132, which corresponds to adUserDefined
Debug.Print rs.Fields("point_col").Type

' this prints Point
Debug.Print rst.Fields("point_col").Properties("UDTNAME").Value

' this prints Point.Point (the full name)
Debug.Print _
    rst.Fields("point_col").Properties("UDTBOUNDCLASS").Value
```

ADO adds a new property on the ADO `Field` class that allows programmers to specify whether a field is to be bound as a `Variant` or as an

`Object`. Binding as an `Object` allows ADO to fetch the UDT as a (.NET) object instance, just as ADO.NET does.

```
Dim conn as New Connection
Dim rs as New Recordset
conn.Open
rs.Open "select oid, point_col from point_tab", conn

While not rs.EOF
  ' Define an instance of a .NET Point class
  Dim p as Point.Point

  'use the correct BindType
  rs("point_col").BindType = adBindObject

  ' make a copy of the Point
  Set p = rs("point_col").Value

  ' work with the copy
  Debug.Print p.m_x & " " & p.m_y
  p.m_x = 42

  ' move to the next record
  rs.MoveNext
Wend
```

The key point to notice here is that we're making a copy of the `Point` and assigning it to the variable p. Changing the value of p does not change the value of `rs("point_col")`.

As well as specifying that the `Point` UDT should be retrieved as a strongly typed class, in Visual Basic 6 you can use the weakly typed `Object` class to retrieve the `Point`.

Updating a UDT

Using ADO, you can update a UDT column by either using a direct SQL `UPDATE` statement in a `Command` containing a mutator function of the UDT, a parameterized update statement, or update-in-place through a server-side cursor. `Command` parameters and update-in-place work in a similar manner to using ADO.NET.

So that programmers can specify parameters of UDT types, additional extended metadata properties have been added to the ADO `Parameter` class. ADO `Parameters` also have a `BindType` property to enable binding the `Parameter` as an `Object`. A simple parameterized `UPDATE` is shown next.

```
Dim conn as Connection = new Connection
Dim Command cmd = new Command
```

```
Set cmd.ActiveConnection = conn
conn.Open
cmd.CommandText = "update point_tab set point_col = ? where oid = ?"

' set the parameters
Dim parm1 as Parameter, parm2 as Parameter

Set parm1 = cmd.CreateParameter("point_col", adUserDefined, _
                                 adParamInput)
Set parm2 = cmd.CreateParameter("oid", adInteger, adParamInput)
cmd.Parameters.Append parm1
cmd.Parameters.Append parm2

Dim p as New Point.Point
p.m_x = 10
p.m_y = 10

' add the additional metadata properties for the Point parameter
cmd.Parameters(0).BindType = adBindObject
cmd.Parameters(0).Properties("UDTCATALOGNAME") = "dbo"
cmd.Parameters(0).Properties("UDTSCHEMANAME") = "pubs"
cmd.Parameters(0).Properties("UDTNAME") = "point"

' move in the values
cmd.Parameters(0).Value = p
cmd.Parameters(1).Value = 1

' rows affected, should be 1
Dim rows as Integer
cmd.Execute rows
```

To update a UDT column in place, you need a server-side updateable cursor. You obtain one of these in ADO by using the appropriate cursor type, as shown next.

```
Dim conn as New Connection
Dim rs as New Recordset

conn.Open
rs.Open "select oid, point_col from point_tab", conn, _
  adOpenStatic, adLockOptimistic

While not rs.EOF
  'use the correct BindType
  rs("point_col").BindType = adBindObject


  ' using a server cursor, this gets a reference to the Point
  Set p = rs("point_col").Value
  p.m_x = 42
```

```
' update the UDT
rs.Update

' move to the next record
rs.MoveNext
Wend
```

OLE DB–Specific Coding Considerations

Although ADO is the API that most programmers will use, low-level programmers and software manufacturers may prefer to use the OLE DB API directly. Using OLE DB entails setting OLE DB properties in OLE DB property sets; these properties correspond directly to the ADO extended properties. The SQL Server OLE DB provider, SQLOLEDB, will expose an additional property set pertaining to Parameters.

The ADO Field properties do not come from an OLE DB property set but by using two OLE DB interfaces. The "basic" ADO Field properties come from invoking OLE DB's IColumnsInfo::GetColumnsInfo method; extended properties come from invoking OLE DB's IColumnsRowset:: GetColumnsRowset. The Rowset returned by GetColumnsRowset contains metadata about each column in a resultset. To accommodate additional UDT information, an additional interface, IColumnsInfo2, will be supported. The information in IColumnsRowset will be supplemented with additional UDT-specific information on a per-column basis.

OLE DB does not use object-oriented Fields and Parameters collections, but instead uses memory buffers and structures called accessors. An introduction to the OLE DB accessor is available at DevelopMentor's DevResources Web site. Rowset accessors use a DBBINDING structure to tell the provider how to bind to a specific column in a memory buffer; Parameter accessors using a DBPARAMINFO structure. To permit binding to a UDT column as an Object type with a Rowset accessor, the dwFlags field of the DBBINDING structure will support setting a bit flag to indicate "bind to Object." To permit binding to a UDT column as a Parameter, a new extended structure, DBPARAMINFO2, has been defined.

OLE DB accessors contain fields that indicate what data type (OLE DB DBTYPE) the data in the buffer should be exposed as. If the DBTYPE specified does not match the type of the column in the database, the OLE DB provider will convert the data. Although UDT types are exposed from the database as DBTYPE_UDT, the SQLOLEDB provider will permit accessor bindings to DBTYPE_BYTES, DBTYPE_VARIANT, and DBTYPE_IUNKNOWN. DBTYPE_ IUNKNOWN binds the data to a COM interface pointer (interface in the UDT).

DBTYPE_VARIANT will bind to a COM Variant type that actually contains the bytes.

OLE DB and ADO Standard Schema Tables

OLE DB exposes, as part of the OLE DB standard, a set of informational Rowsets that allow providers to expose database catalog information, such as the tables in a database or the columns in a table. These informational Rowsets are a superset of the information contained in the SQL-92 Information Schema. In OLE DB, you obtain this information by using the interface IDBSchemaRowset. They are also exposed via ADO as Schema Tables that return Recordsets, and, through the ADO.NET OleDb data provider, as DataTables of information obtained by calling OleDbConnection. GetSchemaTable.

To accommodate the new user-defined types, as well as to accommodate a new metadata catalog scheme in SQL Server 2005, some of the OLE DB information Rowsets are being expanded, and a new information Rowset is being added. The additional information available through OLE DB brings OLE DB closer to the SQL:1999 Information Schema standard. Note that the three new metadata Rowsets are SQL Server–specific, since the OLE DB specification permits OLE DB providers to defined data source–specific metadata information. Table 11-1 shows the new and extended metadata information.

TABLE 11-1: Schema Rowset Changes in OLE DB

Schema Rowset Name	Change from OLE DB 2.7
PROCEDURE_PARAMETERS	Three new UDT-related items added
COLUMNS	Three new UDT-related items added
SQL_ASSEMBLIES	Assembly information (SQL Server–specific)
SQL_DEPENDENT_ASSEMBLIES	Assembly dependencies (SQL Server–specific)
SQL_USER_TYPES	UDT information (SQL Server–specific)

Supporting the XML Data Type in ADO and ADO.NET Clients

SQL Server 2005 includes a new native XML data type, described in Chapter 8. Although this type can be manipulated on the server, and also using SQLXML mapping (described in Chapter 13), we'd like to manipulate it using the client-side data access APIs as well.

One method for using XML is to serialize it into a string of characters. The original specification for XML (Extensible Markup Language 1.0) is a description of "a class of data objects called XML documents" and is couched entirely in terms of this serialized form. In addition to being able to work with the serialized form as a string, you can simply consume XML by using XML APIs such as DOM (Document Object Model), SAX (Simple API for XML), or XmlReader. Both ADO (used in conjunction with MSXML) and ADO.NET provide a way to consume the XML database and use it in parameterized queries using both strings and XML APIs.

Using the XML Data Type in ADO.NET

In ADO.NET SqlDataReader, SqlTypes, and SqlParameter recognize XML as a SQL Server data type. Although the data type will always be reported in the metadata as SqlDbType.Xml, you can use it in the API as either a String or a System.Data.SqlTypes.SqlXml. SqlXml is a special .NET type that contains a CreateReader method that can be used to obtain a System.Xml.XmlReader. The difference between using String and SqlXml is that SqlXml can contain a SQL NULL value; that is, it implements INullable.

You can read XML as a SqlDataReader, as a String, or as an XmlReader on a per-column basis. You can use a weakly typed getter, GetObject, as well the strongly typed getter, GetSqlXml. Here's code to get an XML data type column as either a String or an XmlReader.

```
string connect_string = GetConnectStringFromConfigFile();
SqlConnection conn = new SqlConnection(connect_string);
SqlCommand cmd = new SqlCommand("select * from xml_tab1", conn);

conn.Open();

SqlDataReader rdr = cmd.ExecuteReader();
rdr.Read();

// it's an XML type column
Console.WriteLine(
  "Datatype of col1 is {0}", rdr.GetDataTypeName(1));
```

```
// get contents as string
Console.WriteLine(rdr[0]);

// get contents as XmlReader
SqlXml xrdr = rdr.GetSqlXml(1);
XmlReader xr = xrdr.CreateReader();

// a database NULL value produces a null XmlReader
if (xr == null)
  Console.WriteLine("[null]");
else
{
  xr.Read()
  Console.WriteLine(xr.ReadOuterXml());
}
```

In addition to these methods, SqlCommand supports a method, Execute XmlReader, that produces a single XmlReader directly. Because ExecuteXml Reader supports the return of only a single XmlReader, if the SELECT statement contains additional XML columns or other scalar-valued columns, only the first column's XML value will be returned. Additional data will be ignored. Here's an example.

```
string connect_string = GetConnectStringFromConfigFile();
SqlConnection conn = new SqlConnection(connect_string);
SqlCommand cmd = new SqlCommand("select * from xml_tab1", conn);

conn.Open();

// only one XML result,
// even if xml_tab1 contains multiple XML type columns
XmlReader xr = cmd.ExecuteXmlReader();

// a DbNull.Value produces a null XmlReader
if (xr == null)
  Console.WriteLine("it's null");
else
{
  xr.Read()
  Console.WriteLine(xr.ReadOuterXml());
}
```

Because SQL Server will implicitly coerce strings (VARCHAR or NVAR CHAR) to XML when using the value in a SQL INSERT statement, when you use XML as a SqlParameter, you can either use a VARCHAR/NVARCHAR for the parameter's data type or use SqlDbType.Xml. If you use SqlDbType. Xml, you wrap a concrete XmlReader subclass (like XmlTextReader or

XmlNodeReader) in a SqlXml before sending it to the server (by the time you read this, there may be a shortcut to pass in an XmlReader subclass directly, unless you want a NULL value). If you know your XML data type column is schema-constrained (see Chapter 8 for information on strongly typed XML data type columns), you could even use XmlValidatingReader, saving yourself a trip to the server if the XML would have been rejected because of schema constraints anyway. Here are two simple examples, using strings and XmlReaders.

```
// use string, coerce into XML value
string connect_string = GetConnectStringFromConfigFile();
SqlConnection conn = new SqlConnection(connect_string);
SqlCommand cmd = new SqlCommand(
  "INSERT INTO xml_tab1 (xml_col) VALUES (@v)", conn);

conn.Open();
cmd.Parameters.AddWithValue("@v",
  "<Person><Name>John Doe</Name><Age>30</Age></Person>");

cmd.ExecuteNonQuery();


// use SqlXml and XmlReader subclass
string connect_string = GetConnectStringFromConfigFile();
SqlConnection conn = new SqlConnection(connect_string);
SqlCommand cmd = new SqlCommand(
  "INSERT INTO xml_tab1 (xml_col) VALUES (@v)", conn);

conn.Open();
XmlTextReader rdr = new XmlTextReader("somexml.xml");
cmd.Parameters.Add("@v", SqlDbType.Xml);

cmd.Parameters[0].Value = new SqlXml(rdr);

cmd.ExecuteNonQuery();
```

Using the XML Data Type in ADO Classic

The easiest way to consume XML in ADO is to treat it as a string. This string can be used as input to either the DOM or the SAX APIs. When we bind an XML column in a Recordset as a string in ADO, we bind it using adBindVariant. Assuming that we have a table that contains an XML type column named xml_col, binding as a string looks like this.

```
Dim rs As New ADODB.Recordset

Dim connect_string as String
connect_string = GetConnectStringFromConfiguration
rs.Open "select xml_col from xml_tab1", connect_string
```

```
' Prints 141 - XML
Debug.Print rs(0).Type

' adBindVariant is the default
' Deserializes as a String
Debug.Print rs(0)

' Load it into a DOM
Dim dom As MSXML2.DOMDocument40
dom.loadXML rs(0)
```

We can also use a string as input to a SAX `Reader`. Assuming that we define a SAX `ContentHandler` and `ErrorHandler` elsewhere, the same `Recordset` could be used like this.

```
Dim rs As New ADODB.Recordset

Dim saxXMLReader As New SAXXMLReader40
Dim saxContentHandler As New clsSAXHandler
Dim saxErrorHandler As New clsSAXError

Dim connect_string as String
connect_string = GetConnectStringFromConfiguration
rs.Open "select xml_col from xml_tab1", connect_string

' default binding as string
rs.Fields("xml_col").BindType = adBindVariant

' Load SAX Reader, hook up handlers, parse
Set saxXMLReader.contentHandler = saxContentHandler
Set saxXMLReader.errorHandler = saxErrorHandler
saxXMLReader.parse (rs.Fields("xml_col").Value)
```

With SAX, we can also use object binding to bind the field directly as a `SAXXMLReader40`. Using object binding, the code would look like this.

```
Dim rs As New ADODB.Recordset

Dim saxXMLReader As New SAXXMLReader40
Dim saxContentHandler As New clsSAXHandler
Dim saxErrorHandler As New clsSAXError

Dim connect_string as String
connect_string = GetConnectStringFromConfiguration
rs.Open "select xml_col from xml_tab1", connect_string

' default binding as object
rs.Fields("xml_col").BindType = adBindObject
```

```
' Load SAX Reader, hook up handlers, parse
Set saxXMLReader = rs.Fields("xml_col").Value
Set saxXMLReader.contentHandler = saxContentHandler
Set saxXMLReader.errorHandler = saxErrorHandler
saxXMLReader.parse
```

You can use direct updating or parameterized updating through either strings or SAXXMLReader40. The code for updating through a Recordset and a SAXXMLReader40 would look like this.

```
Dim xmlStream as Stream
Dim saxXMLReader As New SAXXMLReader40

' populate the stream
Set saxXMLReader.InputStream = xmlStream

' Update the Recordset through the SAX Reader
' Remember that the BindType of the field is
'  adBindObject
Set rs.Fields("xml_col").Value = saxXMLReader
rs.Update
```

Using the New Types with the .NET DataSet and SqlDataAdapter

The way to get a set of data from SQL Server back to the client that supports client-side updates and flush updates back to the database is to use the ADO.NET DataSet. To review, the SqlDataAdapter class consists of four SqlCommand instances, one each to SELECT, INSERT, UPDATE, and DELETE rows from SQL Server. SqlDataAdapter.Fill uses the SqlData Adapter's SelectCommand to move rows from SQL Server to the DataSet. The data can be changed offline in the DataSet. SqlDataAdapter.Update uses the InsertCommand, UpdateCommand, and DeleteCommand Sql Command instances to push updated data back to the database. Insert/ Update/DeleteCommand can have a CommandText property that refers to textual parameterized update commands or stored procedures. Figure 11-1 shows a diagram of the SqlDataAdapter class. A short sample of code showing updating through a DataAdapter and a DataSet is shown in Listing 11-2. For more information on the DataAdapter, see Chapter 5 of *Essential ADO.NET*.

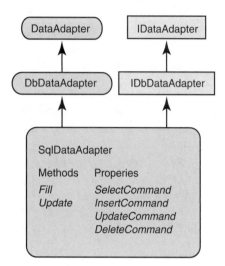

FIGURE 11-1: Layout of the SqlDataAdapter

LISTING 11-2: Updating through a SqlDataAdapter and DataSet

```
// Instantiate a SqlDataAdapter
string connect_string = GetConnectStringFromConfigFile();

SqlDataAdapter da = new SqlDataAdapter(
  "select * from authors", connect_string);

// command builder for default update commands
SqlCommandBuilder bld = new SqlCommandBuilder(da);
DataSet ds = new DataSet();
da.Fill(ds, "authors");

// update the fifth row, third column
ds.Tables[0].Rows[4][2] = "Bob";
// use the default update commands
da.Update(ds, "authors");
```

This is an example of a generalized update pattern involving Sql DataAdapter, DataSet, and SqlCommandBuilder. Note that, at this point, SqlCommandBuilder does not support generating commands that involve UDT or XML data type columns.

The DataSet is a disconnected cache. It consists of DataTables that contain DataRows and DataColumns, with semantics that mimic a relational database. DataTables, DataRows, and DataColumns are built over the .NET ArrayList type; ArrayList is a .NET collection class that

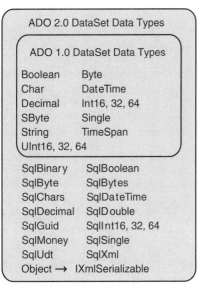

ADO 2.0 DataSet Data Types

ADO 1.0 DataSet Data Types

Boolean	Byte
Char	DateTime
Decimal	Int16, 32, 64
SByte	Single
String	TimeSpan
UInt16, 32, 64	

SqlBinary	SqlBoolean
SqlByte	SqlBytes
SqlChars	SqlDateTime
SqlDecimal	SqlDouble
SqlGuid	SqlInt16, 32, 64
SqlMoney	SqlSingle
SqlUdt	SqlXml
Object → IXmlSerializable	

FIGURE 11-2: Supported Types in the ADO.NET DataSet

implements a dynamic array. Rows can be selected in a DataTable using a SQL-like syntax known as data expression language. The DataSet can be marshaled as XML for use in Web Service scenarios.

In ADO.NET 1.0 and 1.1, DataColumns in the DataSet were limited to a discreet set of .NET types corresponding to the primitive types in a relational database. ADO.NET 2.0 extended this support to include the SqlTypes data types, including those added for SQL Server 2005. A list of the data types supported in version 2.0 of the DataSet is shown in Figure 11-2.

Moving data from a database to the DataSet generally meant mapping a database data type to the closest-fit .NET data type, mostly in the case of mapping SQL Server's DECIMAL type to .NET's System.Decimal. Although SQL Server's DECIMAL type can contain up to 38 digits of precision, .NET's System.Decimal can hold only 28. In addition, supporting any other type (such as a SQL Server 2005 UDT) inside a DataSet did not throw an error and mostly worked, but had some shortcomings.

- When the DataSet was serialized to XML, and the DataColumn's type was not in the supported list, serialization was accomplished by calling ToString() on the type. Most types' ToString() method did not render the object as XML.

- There was no obvious corollary to `ToString()` to deserialize the XML on the other side. The `Parse` method is not required, and so the `DataSet` couldn't rely on its being implemented by every class.

- Data expression language did not support column types other than the primitive, supported types.

These behaviors are described in detail in *Essential ADO.NET*, Chapters 6 and 7.

In the SQL Server 2005 version of ADO.NET, this would present major problems for users of the `DataSet`. The data types that would cause problems would be UDTs and XML.

The user-defined types would tend to be the most problem, because a single `DataColumn` could contain multiple attributes (properties). There is some new functionality in the `DataSet` that takes care of this. The problem with the new non-UDT data types is resolved by support of new types in `System.Data.SqlTypes` and support of the `SqlTypes` family of classes in the `DataSet`. In addition, all of the classes and structures that represent SQL Server data types in `System.Data.SqlTypes` are serializable. This means that they can be used in .NET remoting scenarios or other places where `System.Runtime.Serialization` is used.

As mentioned earlier, types other than the discrete set of types supported by the `DataSet` could always be pushed into a `DataSet`. There were a few problems with usability, however; most have been solved in ADO.NET 2.0. User-defined types are automatically serialized separately using `System.Xml.Serialization`, rather than calling `ToString`. That obviates the necessity of implementing an XML-emtting `ToString()` method and a constructor that takes a single `String` as an argument. In addition, the interface `System.Xml.Serialization.IXmlSerializable` has been surfaced (in versions of .NET, it was documented as "internal use only") as the way to implement custom serialization of an arbitrary class. `System.Data.SqlTypes.SqlDateTime` is one example of a class that implements `IXmlSerializable`. When the `DataSet` serializes itself into XML, if the classes contained in the underlying column implement `IXml Serializable`, this implementation will be called.

One final piece of client-side disconnected model support needs to be mentioned. Although the `DataSet` supported (somewhat) `SqlTypes` as column values—and this would be helpful for the SQL DECIMAL value, for example—very few programmer used `SqlTypes` inside even a local `DataSet`, because there was no way to tell the `SqlDataAdapter` to use `SqlTypes` rather than .NET types when `Fill` is called to fill the `DataSet`.

In the new version of `SqlDataAdapter`, you can use the `ReturnProvider SpecificTypes` property to accomplish this. .NET types inside the `DataSet` are still the default. In addition, a simplified but more ADO `Recordset`-like `DataSet`, the `SqlDbTable` class (this is not specific to `SqlClient`—all providers can implement a class that derives from `System.Data.DbTable`) can use strong types as well.

Comparing the Client and Server Model for Stored Procedures

With the advent of procedural code that can be written using either `System.Data.SqlClient` or `System.Data.SqlServer` using the Managed Data Access SQL Server programming model, the question has arisen of when to use a series of textual SQL commands and when to encapsulate these commands into a .NET procedure that can either be executed on the client or transparently moved to the server and declared as a .NET stored procedure. In addition, SQL Server 2005 adds UDTs into the mix and allows complex types with properties and methods to execute either on the server or on the client. With so much functionality at any tier, what are the best coding practices and deployment techniques? We'll discuss this more in the final chapter, but for now let's mention stored procedures invoked from the client versus procedural code invoked on the server.

The SQL Server engine works best fetching and operating on its own data, managing execution plans, memory buffers, and data buffers. If you could do the same on the client, you would have replicated the database functionality, à la XBase databases. If, however, you are going to perform operations that SQL Server doesn't support internally—say, processor-intensive operations—you could use the server to query and filter your data down to a small subset and then distribute processor-intensive operations to every client. These operations wouldn't necessarily need to involve traditional data management unless you are working with UDTs that need to be sorted and grouped and don't support binary ordering. So, in general, for data-intensive operations, stored procedures executed on the server with results returned to the client in a single round-trip are still best.

Where Are We?

In this chapter we've seen how the new SQL Server data types, especially UDTs and the `XML` type, affect the client libraries and cause us to rethink our coding models. Although ADO.NET has the richest support for the new nonrelational types, OLE DB and ADO (mostly because of COM interop and rich XML support) can take advantage of them as well. Because the authors of the SQL:1999 specification did not enhance SQL-CLI, the SQL Call-Level Interface implemented by Microsoft and others as ODBC, this API has only cursory support for the new complex types.

In the next chapter, we'll look at the plethora of other new features exposed though the ADO.NET APIs in the client tier. Some of these enhancements are directly related to enhancements in SQL Server 2005; others have been driven by customer demand and can be used with any version of SQL Server. After looking at the relational APIs in Chapter 12, we'll explore a library that allows us to map sets of relational columns in the database directly to objects on the client side, in Chapter 14. This object-relational library is known as ObjectSpaces, and it provides a big usability boost over using `SqlDataReaders` and `DataSets` directly.

12

SQL Client Enhancements

I N T H I S C H A P T E R, we round out the functionality enhancements for SQL Server clients. Some of the enhancements are available only when SQL Server 2005 is the database, and some are backward compatible—that is, they work with SQL Server 2000 and SQL Server 7 as well. We'll look at these enhancements using the ADO.NET `SqlClient` provider, though we'll point out where equivalent new functionality is available to other ADO.NET data providers or through other APIs.

ADO.NET 2.0 and the SqlClient Data Provider

The new version of `System.Data.SqlClient` reflects two major changes. As we mentioned in Chapter 4, the `SqlClient` data provider and the `SqlServer` data provider implement a common set of SQL Server–specific interfaces. Although database-neutral interface-based programming can be accomplished by using `IDbConnection`, `IDbCommand`, `IDataReader`, and `IDataRecord`, these are extended for SQL Server programming. Both `SqlClient` and `SqlServer` implement `ISqlConnection`, `ISqlCommand`, `ISqlReader`, and `ISqlRecord`. This factoring into common interfaces is known as the SQL Server Programming Model (SPM). Database-specific types are also factored into the model. In Chapters 3 and 4 we mentioned the advantages of using database-specific types instead of .NET types, for speed and precision. Therefore, both `SqlClient`'s and `SqlServer`'s `SqlDataReader`s implement a new `ISqlGetTypedData` interface. This interface inherits from

the generic `IGetTypedData`. As an example, `IGetTypedData` contains
a method, `GetDecimal`, that retrieves a .NET `System.Decimal` data type,
while `ISqlGetTypedData` contains an analogous method, `GetSqlDecimal`,
that returns a `System.Data.SqlTypes.SqlDecimal` data type. The picture
looks like Figure 12-1.

As we look toward the release, later versions of ADO.NET and SQL
Server may even merge the providers' code into a single DLL, in which
case the common interfaces may be removed.

The second major change was the refactoring of the entire client-side
provider model in .NET 2.0 to permit generic coding. Although OLE DB,
ODBC, and JDBC used connection string or DSN parameters to determine
which provider to load if you wanted to support multiple databases with
the same program, ADO.NET 1.0 and 1.1 did not have a method to use
generic factories to instantiate the correct provider at runtime. This made
database-independent coding more difficult than it needed to be, and a
number of factory libraries appeared in the community. ADO.NET 2.0
includes a `DbProviderFactories` class with static methods that can return
a provider-specific `ProviderFactory` class. Not only can a `Provider
Factory` be used to obtain a provider-independent `Connection`, `Command`,
or `DataAdapter`, but provider writers can implement data source enu-
merators that provide a list of data sources that the provider supports.

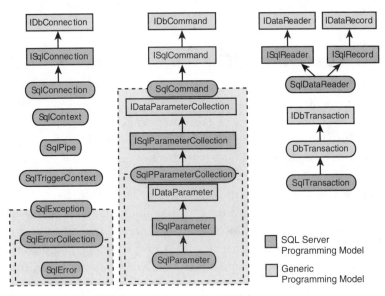

FIGURE 12-1: The SQL Server Programming Model

A simple example of using the factory, common base classes, and enumerator with `SqlClient` is shown later in Listing 12-1.

To permit richer generic coding and provide "starter" functionality for provider writers, ADO.NET 2.0 contains two new levels of base classes. In ADO.NET 1.0 and 1.1, `System.Data.Common` contained very few base classes. Only a base class for the `DataAdapter` class existed, although it was factored into two base classes. `System.Data.Common.DataAdapter` contained basic functionality, and `System.Data.Common.DbDataAdapter` contained additional methods for provider writers that wanted to implement a `CommandBuilder` class. `CommandBuilder` classes (like `SqlCommand Builder`) could be used to produce writeback functionality, used when you changed data in the disconnected `DataSet` class and wanted to build commands to synchronize the `DataSet` and the database.

In ADO.NET 2.0, more base classes were added to `System.Data. Common`. This namespace now contains a `DbConnection`, `DbCommand`, `DbParameter`, `DbParameterCollection`, `DbDataReader`, `DbDataRecord`, and `DbCommandBuilder`. There are also base classes to "genericize" the new functionality already contained in `SqlClient`, such as `DbAsync Result`. Using a combination of the factory classes and classes in `System. Data.Common`, you can now write completely provider-generic code using ADO.NET. A simple generic program that uses a provider string and connection string to determine which database to connect to is shown in Listing 12-1.

LISTING 12-1: Generic Coding with ADO.NET 2.0

```
static void Main(string[] args)
{
  // These provider string names are tied to factory classes
  // and provider classes for installed providers
  // in the global machine.config file

  GetAndOpenConnection("System.Data.SqlClient");
  GetDataSources("System.Data.SqlClient");
}

static void GetAndOpenConnection(String s)
{
  DbConnection conn = GenericGetConnection(s);
  conn.ConnectionString = ConfigurationSettings.AppSettings["conn"];
  conn.Open();
  conn.Dispose();
}
```

```
static DbConnection GenericGetConnection(string s)
{
  DbProviderFactory fact = DbProviderFactories.GetFactory(s);
  return fact.CreateConnection();
}

static void GetDataSources(strings)
{
  DbProviderFactory fact = DbProviderFactories.GetFactory(s);
  DbDataSourceEnumerator en = fact.CreateDataSourceEnumerator();
  DataTable t = en.GetDataSources();
  for (int i=0;i<t.Rows.Count;i++)
    for (int col=0;col<t.Columns.Count;col++)
      Console.WriteLine("{0} = {1}",
          t.Columns[col].ColumnName,
          t.Rows[i][col].ToString());
}
```

In case you were wondering, the provider factory is associated with the provider string based on a list of installed providers in .NET's machine.config file. Listing 12-2 shows a fragment of machine.config that configures the providers. In there you can see the registration of the SqlClient, Odbc, OleDb, and OracleClient providers.

LISTING 12-2: ADO.NET Provider Information in the machine.config Configuration File

```
<system.data>
 <DbProviderFactories>
     <add name="Odbc Data Provider" invariant="System.Data.Odbc"
support="1BF" description=".Net Framework Data Provider for Odbc"
type="System.Data.Odbc.OdbcFactory, System.Data, Version=1.2.3400.0,
Culture=neutral, PublicKeyToken=b77a5c561934e089"/>
     <add name="OleDb Data Provider" invariant="System.Data.OleDb"
support="1BF" description=".Net Framework Data Provider for OleDb"
type="System.Data.OleDb.OleDbFactory, System.Data, Version=1.2.3400.0,
Culture=neutral, PublicKeyToken=b77a5c561934e089"/>
     <add name="OracleClient Data Provider"
invariant="System.Data.OracleClient" support="1AF" description=".Net
Framework Data Provider for Oracle"
type="System.Data.OracleClient.OracleFactory,
System.Data.OracleClient, Version=1.2.3400.0, Culture=neutral,
PublicKeyToken=b77a5c561934e089"/>
     <add name="SqlClient Data Provider"
invariant="System.Data.SqlClient"    support="1FF" description=".Net
Framework Data Provider for SqlServer"
type="System.Data.SqlClient.SqlClientFactory, System.Data,
Version=1.2.3400.0, Culture=neutral,
PublicKeyToken=b77a5c561934e089"/>
   </DbProviderFactories>
</system.data>
```

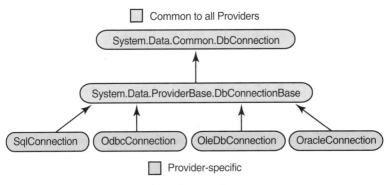

FIGURE 12-2: Class Hierarchy for SqlConnection

Finally, Microsoft released a second set of base classes that contained some common implementation code. These live in the System.Data. ProviderBase namespace. The four data providers that are included with .NET 2.0 (System.Data.SqlClient, System.Data.OleDb, System.Data. Odbc, and System.Data.OracleClient) all use the same base code. As an example, the class inheritance hierarchy for System.Data.SqlClient. SqlConnection is shown in Figure 12-2; other classes in SqlClient are implemented similarly.

Although the in-database SqlServer provider shares the SQL Server–specific interface hierarchies with SqlClient, it does not implement the common base classes.

As we mentioned in Chapter 4, functionality that can mostly be shared between SqlClient and SqlServer providers, as well as some SqlServer-specific classes, is combined in the System.Data.Sql namespace. Some of the new shared classes, like SqlMetaData, live in this namespace. Although there are abstract base classes for the SqlServer-specific classes, SqlPipe, SqlContext, and SqlTriggerContext also are part of System.Data.Sql. It goes without saying that you cannot use these abstract classes from a client-side program, and of course it is not possible to use any of the code in System.Data.SqlServer (or elsewhere in sqlaccess.dll, for that matter) anywhere outside SqlServer. You can, however, use the SqlClient data provider inside SQL Server.

Multiple Active Resultsets

SQL Server clients can fetch data from the server using two different semantics: server-side cursors and forward-only, read-only, "cursorless" mode. Although a single client connection can open multiple database cursors at the same time, and fetch data from any of them, before SQL Server 2005 only one cursorless mode resultset could be active at a time. Cursorless mode is the default behavior of all SQL Server database APIs when using resultsets, from DBLib to ADO.NET. Cursorless mode consumes fewer resources on the server, is the fastest mode for fetching data, and is the only mode to support processing multiple resultsets produced by a single batch of SQL statements. This mode reads rows in a forward-only, read-only fashion, however. Although multiple resultsets can be processed, the results must be read sequentially; you cannot interleave reads from the first and second resultset. This was due to the inner workings of the TDS protocol, the network protocol that SQL Server clients use.

In the SQL Server 2005 release, the SQL Server engine has been changed to permit multiple batches to be active simultaneously on a single connection. Because SQL Server batches can produce resultsets, this means that more than one cursorless mode resultset can be read at the same time using the same connection. This feature was nicknamed MARS, for "multiple active resultsets." Although this feature is enabled on the server, the TDS protocol and client libraries had to be updated to permit clients to access this functionality.

In the past, database APIs dealt with the single batch limitation in different ways. For example, in ADO (classic) the API made it appear that you could execute multiple simultaneous batches.

```
Dim conn as New ADODB.Connection
Dim rs1 as ADODB.Recordset
Dim rs2 as ADODB.Recordset

rs1.Open "select * from authors", conn
rs2.Open "select * from jobs", conn

' Note: This only reads as many rows
' as are in the shortest resultset
' rows from the longest resultset are dropped
While not rs1.EOF and not rs2.EOF
    Debug.Print rs1(0)
    Debug.Print rs2(0)
    rs1.MoveNext
    rs2.MoveNext
Wend

conn.Close
```

Although this gave the appearance of multiple active batches, it was accomplished by a little library sleight of hand. The ADO library simply opened additional connections under the covers to service the additional request. Although this prevented runtime errors, a well-meaning programmer could accidentally use up connections if he wasn't aware of the way things worked. The following code will open a separate connection for every row in the loop that processes `Recordset rs1`.

```
Dim conn as New ADODB.Connection
Dim rs1 as ADODB.Recordset
Dim rs2 as ADODB.Recordset

rs1.Open "select * from authors", conn
While not rs1.EOF
    rs2.Open "select * from titleauthor where au_id = " & _
        rs1("au_id"), conn
    rs1.MoveNext
Wend
```

Although it annoyed programmers who weren't aware of how the protocol worked, ADO.NET's way of dealing with the pre–SQL Server 2005 limitation was an improvement over ADO. When you attempted to open multiple batches containing results using `SqlCommand.ExecuteReader`, a runtime error occurred. The error message was verbose but exactly described the situation: "There is already an open DataReader associated with this Command which must be closed first." Programmers had to be careful to play by the rules.

ADO.NET and other SQL Server APIs can use an updated network library (`sni.dll`, the SQL Server Networking Interface) to achieve true multiplexing of result batches on a single connection. Because this functionality is actually implemented on the server, it only works with a SQL Server 2005 database, though OLE DB, ADO, and ODBC can take advantage of it as well as ADO.NET. We'll look at the implementation in ADO.NET.

MARS is enabled by connection string parameters when you are using the ADO.NET data provider in .NET 2.0 and a SQL Server 2005 client. The beta release uses the connection string parameter `MultipleActive Resultsets=true` to indicate MARS support. The default value is `true`, but you can set the value to `false` if you desire the legacy behavior.

Although you use the same `SqlConnection` instance with multiple resultsets, you must use different `SqlCommand` instances for each simultaneous resultset. The resultset is encapsulated by the `SqlDataReader` class, so you will have two `SqlDataReaders` as well. You can read from either

SqlDataReader, although the behavior of SqlDataReader is still forward-only and read-only. A simple example follows.

```
string connect_string = GetConnectStringFromConfigFile();
SqlConnection conn = new SqlConnection(connect_string);
conn.Open();

SqlCommand cmd1 = new SqlCommand(
  "select * from authors", conn);
SqlCommand cmd2 = new SqlCommand(
  "select * from jobs", conn);

SqlDataReader rdr1 = cmd1.ExecuteReader ();

// second resultset, same connection
SqlDataReader rdr2 = cmd2.ExecuteReader ();

while
  ((rdr1.Read() == true && rdr2.Read() == true))
{
  // write first column of each resultset
  Console.WriteLine (rdr1[0]);
  Console.WriteLine (rdr2[0]);
}

// clean everything up
rdr1.Close();
rdr2.Close();
cmd1.Dispose();
cmd2.Dispose();
conn.Dispose();
```

Note also that each command can contain an entire batch of statements and return more than one resultset. The basic functionality of the cursorless mode resultset has not changed, however, so these resultsets must be read in order. If, in the previous example, the CommandText for cmd1 was select * from authors; select * from titles, we would read all the authors rows first, followed by the titles rows. This also does not change the fact that the stored procedure output parameters are returned after all the resultsets, and the SqlDataReader must still be closed before the output parameters are available. See *Essential ADO.NET*, by Bob Beauchemin (Addison-Wesley, 2002), Chapter 3, for details.

Although you can execute multiple batches in parallel over the same connection, parallel transactions over the same connection are not supported. The following example shows that the transaction is still scoped to the connection.

```
string connect_string = GetConnectStringFromConfigFile();
SqlConnection conn = new SqlConnection(connect_string);
conn.Open();

// one transaction
SqlTransaction tx1 = conn.BeginTransaction();

// this would fail
//SqlTransaction tx2 = conn.BeginTransaction();

SqlCommand cmd1 = new SqlCommand
  ("update_authors_and_getresults", conn, tx1);

// both SqlCommands must be enlisted
SqlCommand cmd2 = new SqlCommand(
  "update_authors_and_getresults", conn, tx1);
cmd1.CommandType = CommandType.StoredProcedure;
cmd2.CommandType = CommandType.StoredProcedure;

SqlDataReader rdr1 = cmd1.ExecuteReader();

// second resultset, same connection
SqlDataReader rdr2 = cmd2.ExecuteReader();

while
  ((rdr1.Read() == true && rdr2.Read() == true))
{
  // write first column of each resultset
  Console.WriteLine (rdr1[0]);
  Console.WriteLine (rdr2[0]);
}

// commit one transaction (both authors & jobs)
tx1.Commit();

// but you cannot roll back just one or the other,
// attempt to build second transaction failed
// tx2.Rollback();

// clean everything up
rdr1.Close();
rdr2.Close();
cmd1.Dispose();
cmd2.Dispose();
conn.Dispose();
```

Besides making things easier for the programmer, if multiple simultaneous operations need to be performed in parallel, the MARS feature can be used in conjunction with asynchronous execution, which we'll describe later in this chapter. MARS can greatly simplify ASP.NET data binding code as well. Rather than using batches and being careful to bind the proper resultset to the proper ASP.NET WebControl, you can use multiple SqlCommands. Each SqlCommand binds to a separate control, but all Sql Commands use a single connection. This preserves connections and makes the data binding code less brittle.

Notification Support

One of the features that programmers have always wanted is the ability to notify the client or the middle tier when data that they are interested in has been changed in the database by another user. This type of "almost real-time" notification could be used to refresh a grid in a Windows Forms application with the latest data or refresh a middle-tier cache without having to retrieve the entire resultset on a schedule. SQL Server 2005 provides the underlying database feature to enable such notifications; database changes can invoke SQL Server Service Broker. The Broker has the ability to queue the notifications to one or many clients. This is more scalable and reliable than using triggers to change some external resource (for example, change a file in a directory being watched by a FileWatcher instance) because the file change happens synchronously.

Although the infrastructure for firing the notification exists on the server, catching the notification on the client is built into the SqlClient provider at two different levels. You can register for and process raw notifications by using the SqlNotificationRequest class directly, or use the built-in convenience class, SqlDependency.

In addition to having this functionality in the SqlClient data provider, the ASP.NET Cache class (System.Web.Caching.Cache) has been outfitted with methods to register for SQL Server notifications directly, by means of the SqlCacheDependencyAdmin and SqlCacheDependency classes. This ASP.NET functionality works with pre–SQL Server 2005 versions of SQL Server but is implemented differently, by polling the database.

To use notifications directly, you set up a SQL Server Service Broker QUEUE on the server (see Chapter 15 for more information on SQL Server Service Broker). The T-SQL DDL to accomplish this follows.

```
-- first, create the queue and the service
-- we're going to register the service
-- and read from the queue
CREATE QUEUE NWNotifQ
GO
```

```
- the trick to this is that
- the service must be registered to abide by the contact
- else it cannot be used as a target, only send messages
CREATE SERVICE NWNotifSvc
ON QUEUE NWNotifQ
([http://schemas.microsoft.com/SQL/Notifications/PostQueryNotification])
GO
```

Now that SQL Server is properly configured, you instantiate a `Sql NotificationRequest` object on the client. The `SqlNotificationRequest` requires two properties to be useful: the name of the queue that you want to "listen on" and an arbitrary ID to correlate listeners to queue messages. One you've initialized the `SqlNotificationRequest`, you use it to set the `SqlCommand`'s `Notification` property, and execute the command.

```
public SqlDataReader GetPrices(SqlConnection conn, int Category)
{
  SqlDataReader rdr = null;
  try
  {
    SqlCommand cmd = new SqlCommand(
      "Select ProductName, UnitPrice from Products " +
      "where CategoryID = @CatID", conn);
    cmd.Parameters.AddWithValue("@CatID",Category);

    // We've defined PriceQueue in SQL Server
    SqlNotificationRequest not = new SqlNotificationRequest();
    // identify this request
    not.Id = Guid.NewGuid().ToString();

      // Notice that this name is not the "short" service name
    // But contains the hostname, "sql/MSSQLSERVER"
    // and database name also
    not.Service = "//localhost/sql/MSSQLSERVER/northwind/NWNotifSvc";
    not.Timeout = 0;

    // associate notification with command
    cmd.Notification = not;

    // Execute the SELECT statement and
    // register to be notified
    SqlDataReader rdr = cmd.ExecuteReader();
  }
  catch (Exception ex)
  {
    Console.WriteLine(ex.Message);
  }

    return rdr;
}
```

When you execute a properly configured `SqlCommand` that returns a resultset, `SqlClient` automatically registers for notifications on subsequent changes made by other users that would affect the resultset's rows. After you've issued the `SqlCommand`, you must issue a SQL statement to wait for messages to arrive on the notification queue, or interact with SQL Server Service Broker in some other way to receive the notification. For example, you could have your own trigger in your own private notification queue to implement a custom version of the `SqlDependency` functionality.

```
// look for notifications and receive them from the queue
public void WaitForChanges(conn)
{
  // look for messages coming in on the queue
  SqlCommand cmd = new SqlCommand(
    "WAITFOR (RECEIVE message_body from NWNotifQueue)", conn);
  cmd.CommandTimeout = 10000;
  SqlDataReader = cmd.ExecuteReader();
  // process results here
  // now, refresh the original resultset!
}
```

Tying this all together, we:

1. Define the QUEUE and the SERVICE in the database.

2. Set up a `SqlNotificationRequest` instance.

3. Tie it to a `SqlCommand`.

4. Specify the correct SERVICE to listen to using a URI-like syntax, not the bare service name.

5. Execute the `SqlCommand`.

6. Listen to be notified of changes to the resultset.

7. Wander off to do other useful work.

```
void ReadAndWait()
{
string connect_string = GetConnectStringFromConfigFile();
SqlConnection conn = new SqlConnection(connect_string);
  conn.Open();
  SqlDataReader rdr = GetProducts(conn, 100);
  if (rdr != null)
  {
    //Process the resultset here!!
    rdr.Close();
    // DO OTHER USEFUL WORK HERE, then...
    WaitForChanges(conn);
  }
```

In order for this to be useful, we really must wait for messages to arrive on a separate thread and signal the main thread when changes have arrived. .NET exposes a paradigm for doing just such event handling through .NET delegates. We could manually set up a delegate with an asynchronous callback, but the SqlClient provider already includes the functionality. For this, we use the SqlDependency convenience class.

SqlDependency is a class that automatically hooks notifications on the current resultset and exposes a delegate that we can hook to our own event handler. Using SqlDependency to accomplish the same task is a lot simpler.

```
static void Main(string[] args)
{
string connect_string = GetConnectStringFromConfigFile();
SqlConnection conn = new SqlConnection(connect_string);
SqlCommand cmd = new SqlCommand("Select count(*) from jobs",conn);

try
{
  conn.Open ();

  // create dependency associated with cmd
  SqlDependency depend = new SqlDependency(cmd);

  // register handler
  depend.OnChanged += new OnChangedEventHandler(MyOnChanged);

  SqlDataReader rdr = cmd.ExecuteReader();

  while (rdr.Read())
    Console.WriteLine(rdr[0]);

  // Wait for invalidation to come through
  Console.WriteLine("Press Enter to continue");
  Console.ReadLine();
}
catch (Exception e)
{
  Console.WriteLine(e.Message);
  Console.WriteLine(e.StackTrace);
}
}

static void MyOnChanged(object caller, SqlNotificationEventArgs e)
{
  Console.WriteLine("an event arrived");
  Console.WriteLine(e.Source);
  Console.WriteLine(e.Type);
}
```

When using SqlDependency, you need only to create a new Sql Dependency instance, using a SqlCommand instance in the constructor. This automatically creates a SqlNotificationRequest for you; the only other work you have to do is to register your event handler routine with the SqlDependency's OnChanged event, execute the command, and do other work until a change notification arrives. This works the same way as an ordinary handler for a Button in a Windows Forms program. Note that the event could be fired in an arbitrary thread, so synchronization may be needed if accessing shared state. Also, in Windows Forms, controls cannot be manipulated from any thread.

Handling the Notification

The notification that arrives when you read from the queue is ordinarily a message that someone has deleted or changed a row in your resultset. This notification can arrive at any time after you've issued the command, but you only get one such invalidation request. When you write code to handle the notification, you must reregister (or use the SqlCommand that's already associated with the SqlDependency) in order to receive further notifications. The notification does not contain any information about the operation that invalidated your resultset; you usually refresh the entire resultset. If your SqlCommand is associated with a SqlDataAdapter that was used to fill a DataSet, you can simply call SqlDataAdapter.Fill again. One final piece of advice: When you use SqlDependency, you will get a callback immediately after you register the handler. You can check SqlNotificationEventArgs.Type, because you do not want to refresh the resultset because of this event.

You'll almost always be using SqlDependency instead of Sql NotificationRequest because setting up to receive the notification is automatic. You simply register the event handler. As a final convenience, the ASP.NET Cache object lets you associate a SqlDependency on objects in the cache, and will automatically invalidate the objects when a notification is received.

Asynchronous Support

The OLE DB specification contained interfaces that providers could implement to enable asynchronously opening a connection and asynchronously executing a command. If these operations took a long time, your program could do other work in the meantime, such as responding to events in the graphical user interface or showing a progress bar. Implementing these interfaces was optional, and the SQLOLEDB provider did not implement them in the protocol. With the advent of the new client network libraries, asynchronous operation can be achieved not only with SQL Server 2005, but also with SQL Server 7 and 2000. This support has been added to OLE DB, ADO, and ADO.NET; for exposition we'll look at the ADO.NET implementation.

SqlClient uses the standard .NET paradigm for asynchronous operations. In addition to the ordinary method for synchronous invocation—for example, SqlConnection.Open, there is a pair of related methods, Begin Open and EndOpen, for asynchronous invocation. BeginOpen starts the operation and returns immediately to the caller. When the operation completes, you use EndOpen to harvest the return code (or an error) and the results of the operation.

```
string connect_string = GetConnectStringFromConfigFile();
SqlConnection conn = new SqlConnection(connect_string);
SqlCommand cmd = new SqlCommand("Select count(*) from jobs",conn);

try {
  // begin the operation
  IAsyncResult ar = conn.BeginOpen();

  // busywait, check every 250 milliseconds
  while (!ar.IsCompleted)
  {
   // do something useful here
   Console.Write(".");
   Thread.Sleep(250);
  }

  // error thrown here if Open fails
  conn.EndOpen(ar);

  // remainder of processing elided
}
catch (Exception e) {
  Console.WriteLine(e.Message);
  Console.WriteLine(e.StackTrace);
}
finally {
conn.Close();
}
```

Notice in the case of SqlConnection.Open, there are no results to return. SqlConnection either returns or throws an error. Note also that the error occurs only when EndOpen is called. Although SqlConnection.Open does not return any result, you can also use an asynchronous SqlCommand.

Asynchronous methods around `SqlCommand.ExecuteReader`, `Execute XmlReader`, and `ExecuteNonQuery` (but not `ExecuteScalar`) are provided. Here's the equivalent code to execute a SQL UPDATE statement asynchronously and retrieve the number of rows affected by the UPDATE.

```
string connect_string = GetConnectStringFromConfigFile();
SqlConnection conn = new SqlConnection(connect_string);

SqlCommand cmd = new SqlCommand
("UPDATE authors set state='OR' where state='CA'", conn);
try
{

  // Synchronous Open
  conn.Open();

  // Asynch command execution
  IAsyncResult ar = cmd.BeginExecuteNonQuery();

  while (!ar.IsCompleted)
  {
    Console.Write(".");
    Thread.Sleep(250);
  }

  // retrieve the results (or error) here
  int i = cmd.EndExecuteNonQuery(ar);
  Console.WriteLine("done, {0} rows affected", i);
}
catch (Exception e) {
  Console.WriteLine(e.Message);
  Console.WriteLine(e.StackTrace);
}
finally {
  cmd.Dispose();
  conn.Dispose();
}
```

Executing an asynchronous operation using `Begin` and `End` uses non-blocking overlapped I/O against the network. A thread from the .NET AppDomain's thread pool is only used when the I/O completion notification is dispatched to the process.

A more useful paradigm than just busy-waiting in the code (which just adds complexity and thread switching to the program, slowing down overall execution) is to register an event handler to be called when the operation completes.

```
SqlCommand gcmd = new SqlCommand ("select * from authors");
public void UseEventHandler()
{
string connect_string = GetConnectStringFromConfigFile();
SqlConnection conn = new SqlConnection(connect_string);

gcmd.Connection = conn;
try
{

  // Synchronous Open
  conn.Open();

  // Asynch command execution
  gcmd.BeginExecuteReader(
    new AsyncCallback(GetResults,
    null,
    CommandBehavior.CloseConnection);
}
catch (Exception e) {
  Console.WriteLine(e.Message);
  Console.WriteLine(e.StackTrace);
}
finally {
  gcmd.Dispose();
  conn.Dispose();
}
}

public void GetResult(IAsyncResult result)
{
  // harvest results (or error) here
  SqlDataReader rdr = gcmd.EndExecuteReader(result);

  // use results to populate GUI
}
```

You can also use asynchronous execution to perform two or more operations at the same time. This is useful in two major scenarios. You might be
doing multiple data gathering operations in parallel over the same connection to fill up multiple sets of controls in a graphical user interface. This is
where the MARS feature we saw previously comes in handy. The other
scenario consists of doing multiple long-running operations against two
different databases, which may each be in a faraway location. In each case,
you want to synchronize at a point when all operations are complete, and
continue. Multiple WaitHandles (a .NET synchronization primitive) can
come in handy here. You start a few operations and call WaitHandle.
WaitAll to wait until they all complete. Here's an example that uses

MARS to wait for two different resultsets on the same connection, though the multiple database code would look similar.

```
public void UseWaitHandles()
{
string connect_string = GetConnectStringFromConfigFile();
SqlConnection conn = new SqlConnection(connect_string);

// execute these simultaneously
SqlCommand cmd1 = new SqlCommand("select * from authors", conn);
SqlCommand cmd2 = new SqlCommand("select * from titles", conn);

WaitHandle[2] handles = new WaitHandle[2];

try
{

  conn.Open();

IAsyncResult ar1 = cmd1.BeginExecuteReader(null, null);
IAsyncResult ar2 = cmd1.BeginExecuteReader(null, null);
handles[0] = ar1.AsyncWaitHandle;
handles[1] = ar2.AsyncWaitHandle;

  // wait for both commands to complete
  WaitHandle.WaitAll(handles);

  SqlDataReader rdr1 = cmd1.EndExecuteReader(ar1);
  SqlDataReader rdr2 = cmd2.EndExecuteReader(ar2);

  // process both readers
  // ...

  rdr1.Close(); rdr2.Close();
}
catch (Exception e) {
  Console.WriteLine(e.Message);
  Console.WriteLine(e.StackTrace);
}
finally {
  cmd1.Dispose();
  cmd2.Dispose();
  conn.Dispose();
}
}
```

You can also process multiple results when any one of the commands completes by using WaitAny instead of WaitAll. This might be used to make a graphical user interface more responsive.

Although executing each method call asynchronously may sound like a good idea at first mention, don't use the asynchronous calls unless:

- You have an operation that you know will take a long time.
- You have something useful to do with that time.

In the first two examples, we were simply spinning and wasting processor time. As noted earlier, excessive thread switching will slow down your application. In addition, be aware that when using the AppDomain's thread pool, you are guaranteed to get the completion (the end request) on a *different* thread than the one on which you issued the original call. Some .NET classes, such as GUI controls that wrap Window Handles, are usable only on the thread that the Window Handle is "stuck to." Finally, remember that when you read a resultset through a `DataReader`, SQL server queues (and locks) a buffer's worth of data at a time on the server, waiting for you to fetch it. Waiting around before reading the results can cause excessive memory utilization and locking on the server, and affect the throughput of your SQL Server instance. Use asynchronous operations wisely and correctly.

Snapshot Isolation

In Chapter 7, we discussed one of the biggest enhancements to the SQL Server engine in SQL Server 2005: the ability to use versioning rather than locking to achieve user isolation inside a SQL Server transaction. This capability is also exposed in the client in a way analogous to that on the server, as a database capability and a new transaction isolation level. The code to accomplish this using `SqlClient` is straightforward.

```
public void DoSnapshot(string connstr)
  {
    SqlConnection conn = new SqlConnection(connstr);
    conn.Open();

    SqlCommand myCommand = conn.CreateCommand();
    SqlTransaction tx = null;

    // Start a local transaction.
    tx = conn.BeginTransaction(IsolationLevel.Snapshot);

    // Associate Command with Transaction
    SqlCommand cmd = new SqlCommand(
       "insert into jobs values('new job', 100, 100)",
       conn, tx);

    try
    {
```

```
    // first insert
    cmd.ExecuteNonQuery();

    // second insert
    cmd.CommandText =
  "insert into jobs values('Grand Poobah', 200, 200)",
cmd.ExecuteNonQuery();
      tx.Commit();
    }
    catch(Exception e) {
      try {
        tx.Rollback();
      }
      catch (SqlException ex) {
        // no-op catch, tx already rolled back
      }
    }
    finally {
      cmd.Dispose();
      conn.Dispose();
    }
}
```

This is normal client-side local transaction code; the only thing that may look a little odd is that when you roll back a transaction from the client, you do so in a `try/catch` block and ignore the error that you catch. This is because the transaction may already have been rolled back inside the database; attempting to roll back a nonexistent transaction will cause an exception. You can safely catch and ignore the exception.

Promotable Transactions

Microsoft Transaction Server (MTS) and its successors, COM+ and `System. EnterpriseServices`, popularized the concept of distributed transactions, for better or worse. These server and object-based libraries permitted programmers to specify "automatic transactions" on a class or method level. Because the COM+ interceptor had no knowledge of which database the instance was going to use, or whether it was going to use a single database or multiple databases, COM+ always began a distributed transaction.

Distributed transactions are always slower than local transactions, sometimes much slower. The network traffic that is generated when the distributed transaction coordinator (MSDTC) is involved is substantial. For an in-depth description of how distributed transactions work and how MTS/COM+ works, refer to *Transactional COM+*, by Tim Ewald (Addison-Wesley, 2001).

Promotable transactions is a feature that will transparently promote an existing local transaction to a distributed transaction automatically if the `SqlConnection` attempts to access two different instances of SQL Server inside a transactional method. Promotion also works on a single SQL Server and any other transactional resource. This requires code both inside the SQL engine and in the client-side libraries, but does not require the programmer to write additional program logic, although it is designed for cases where the new `System.Transaction` library is used to manipulate distributed transactions. Simply starting a transaction and using a command to access multiple instances of SQL Server will cause the transaction to be promoted automatically.

Bulk Import in SqlClient

There are a number of different ways to import an array of rows into SQL Server. We just mentioned command batches and multiple parameter-set commands earlier in this chapter. In SQL Server 2005, there is a .NET API to Data Transformation Services (DTS), the utility that replaced SQL Import/Export in version 7.0 and provides a job scheduler and programmatic control over transformations in addition to simple importing and exporting of data. The fastest way to import data, as long as the data to import is in a local file, is to use the T-SQL BULK INSERT statement. This statement can be invoked from a .NET program using the `SqlCommand` class and the BULK INSERT statement as command text.

Each data access API has exposed the bulk insert functionality as an extension to the base API. You can use the SQL Server BCP utility programmatically through DBLib and through ODBC. BCP is the command-line utility that has been around since the early days of SQL. It is a favorite of database administrators and programmers alike, consuming and producing text files in a variety of formats, including comma-separated values and fixed-length text. OLE DB exposed similar programmatic functionality by means of a custom interface and property set on SQLOLEDB's Session cotype implementation. The custom interface, `IRowsetFastLoad`, has functionality reminiscent of SQL Server's built-in BULK INSERT.

In ADO.NET 2.0, `SqlClient` follows ODBC and DBLib and exposes a programmatic API with `IRowsetFastLoad`-like functionality called `Sql BulkCopy`. The class can use rows from a `DataTable` in memory or be hooked up to a `DataReader` over the set of data to be inserted into the database. In the simplest case, you need only instantiate a `SqlBulkCopy`

instance, set properties on it, and point the `DataReader` at it, using the
`WriteToServer` method. Here is a simple example that copies the `jobs`
table in the SQL Server database to a nearly identically structured table
named `newjobs`.

```
string connect_string = GetConnectStringFromConfigFile();
SqlConnection conn = new SqlConnection(connect_string);


SqlCommand createcmd = new SqlCommand (
@"create table newjobs(
job_id smallint primary key,
job_desc varchar(30),
min_lvl tinyint,
max_lvl tinyint)",
conn);

SqlCommand cmd = new SqlCommand(
"select * from jobs", conn);

conn.Open();
SqlDataReader rdr = cmd.ExecuteReader();

// Copy the Data to SqlServer
string connect_string = GetConnectStringFromConfigFile();
SqlBulkCopy bcp = new SqlBulkCopy(connect_string);

bcp.DestinationTableName = "newjobs";
bcp.WriteToServer(rdr);
```

Importing rows is rarely that simple, however. You usually need to map
fields in the source data to equivalent fields in the target table, perhaps
doing some data type coercion along the way. `SqlBulkCopyMapping` is the
class you use to map source to target.

```
// Retrieve data from the source server.

string src_connect_string = GetConnectStringFromConfigFile("src");
SqlConnection src = new SqlConnection(src_connect_string);
src.Open();
SqlCommand cmd = new SqlCommand("select * from orders", src);
IDataReader srcrdr = cmd.ExecuteReader();

// Connect to target server.
string dest_connect_string = GetConnectStringFromConfigFile("dest");
SqlConnection dest = new SqlConnection(dest_connect_string);
dest.Open();

// open a bulk copy using the destination connection
SqlBulkCopy bcp = new SqlBulkCopy(dest))
```

```
{
    bcp.DestinationTableName = "order_history";

    // map the columns
    bcp.ColumnMapping.Add("orderid", "order_hist_id");
    bcp.ColumnMapping.Add("description", "order_hist_desc");
    bcp.ColumnMapping.Add("date", "order_hist_date");
    bcp.WriteToServer(srcrdr);
}

dest.Dispose();
srcrdr.Close();
cmd.Dispose();
src.Dispose();
```

In addition to these simple examples that use `IDataReader`, `SqlBulk Copy` can use a `System.Data.DataTable` or an array of `DataRows` as input. `SqlBulkCopy` exposes properties that will look familiar to anyone who has used the BCP utility. `SqlBulkCopy` actually uses the new (`OPENROWSET`) form of the `BULK INSERT` statement and the `BULK` rowset provider. A list of the properties and their equivalents in `OPENROWSET`/`BULK INSERT` is shown in Table 12-1. As an example of its usefulness, one high-performance

TABLE 12-1: SqlBulkCopy and BCP Equivalents

SqlBulkCopy	OPENROWSET/BULK INSERT Option
`ColumnAssociators` collection	`FORMATFILE`
`BatchSize`	`ROWS_PER_BATCH`
`BulkCopyTimeout`	No equivalent
`NotifyAfter`	No equivalent
`OnRowsCopied` event	No equivalent
`SqlBulkCopyOptions.CheckConstraints`	`CHECK_CONSTRAINTS`
`SqlBulkCopyOptions.Default`	N/A
`SqlBulkCopyOptions.KeepIdentity`	`KEEPIDENTITY`
`SqlBulkCopyOptions.KeepNulls`	`KEEPNULLS`
`SqlBulkCopyOptions.TableLock`	`TABLOCK`

way of importing a large number of rows is to implement a custom `IDataReader` and have `SqlBulkCopy` pull rows and push them into the server.

Miscellaneous Features

Password Change Support

SQL Server 2005 will expire passwords on SQL Server security accounts, just as the Windows 2003 security authority expires passwords on Windows accounts used by SQL Server. Because you only use a SQL Server account to log on to SQL Server, the `SqlClient` libraries will provide a secure mechanism allowing a SQL Server account to change password during login.

When a SQL Server user with an expired password attempts to log in using ADO.NET, he receives an exception with a specific SQL Server state code. After catching the error, the program can prompt for a password (at the time of this writing, there was no standard "password expired" dialog) and obtain a new password and the old password from the user. After validating the old password against the password in the connection string, the program will use a static method on the `SqlConnection` class, `ChangePassword`, to change the password on SQL Server. Using the `ChangePassword` method looks something like this.

```
string connstring = GetConnectionString();
SqlConnection conn = new SqlConnection(connstring);
for(int i=0; i < 2; i++)
  {
  try
    {
    conn.Open();
    break;
    }
  catch(SqlException e)
    {
    if (e.State == State.PasswordExpired)
      {
      // prompt the user for the new password
      string newpw = PromptPassword();
      // change it on SQL Server
      SqlConnection.ChangePassword(connstring, newpw);

      // fix connection string in config and SqlConnection instance
      // to include the new password

      // reattempt the login
      }
```

```
    }
}
```

Note that you must define your own `PromptPassword` method and write program-specific code to change both the configuration file and the connection string currently being used to use the new password. It was a programmer inconvenience to hardcode connection strings containing passwords in programs in the past because the source code needed to be changed if the administrator changed the password. With the advent of SQL Server password expiration policies, connection strings containing passwords must be stored outside the program. Not only should they be stored in a configuration file, but the connection string should be encrypted to guard against unauthorized access through the configuration file.

Client Statistics

The SQL Server ODBC driver enabled collection and reading of statistics on a per-connection basis via API calls. This has been added to the .NET 2.0 version of `SqlClient`. Because collection of statistics adds overhead, statistics must be enabled on a per-connection basis. You enable statistics on a `SqlConnection` by setting its `StatisticsEnabled` property. In addition, the `SqlConnection` exposes methods to retrieve and reset statistics. Here's a simple example of statistics gathering, followed by the output statistics that are gathered (shown in Listing 12-3). Using the client statistics API should make profiling client-side data access much simpler.

```
static void Main(string[] args)
{
string connect_string = GetConnectStringFromConfigFile();
SqlConnection conn = new SqlConnection(connect_string);
conn.Open();

// Enable
conn.StatisticsEnabled = true;

// do some operations
//
SqlCommand cmd = new SqlCommand("select * from authors", conn);
SqlDataReader rdr = cmd.ExecuteReader();

Hashtable stats = (Hashtable)conn.RetrieveStatistics();

// process stats
IDictionaryEnumerator e = stats.GetEnumerator();
while (e.MoveNext())
Console.WriteLine("{0} : {1}", e.Key, e.Value);
```

```
conn.ResetStatistics();

}
```

LISTING 12-3: Statistics Output from the Previous Program

```
BytesReceived : 2207
SumResultSets : 0
ExecutionTime : 138
Transactions : 0
BuffersReceived : 1
CursorFetchTime : 0
IduRows : 0
CursorOpens : 0
PreparedExecs : 0
BytesSent : 72
SelectCount : 0
ServerRoundtrips : 1
CursorUsed : 0
CursorFetchCount : 0
ConnectionTime : 149
Prepares : 0
SelectRows : 0
UnpreparedExecs : 1
NetworkServerTime : 79
BuffersSent : 1
IduCount : 0
```

Where Are We?

We've covered a lot of new features of the SQL Server client libraries in this and the previous chapter. Some of the features are enabled by new server functionality and are only available when using SQL Server 2005 as the server. Table 12-2 shows where these features are available.

Support of the new data types, MARS, `SqlNotifications`, and `SNAPSHOT` isolation depend on SQL Server 2005. Some features also depend on the new SQL client network library. Asynchronous invocation is an example of a network library–dependent feature that works against any version of SQL Server (7 and above). The network library enhancements are built into the .NET 2.0 `SqlClient` provider, however. The rest of the features are enhancements to the ADO.NET API, including a tracing facility that was still in development as of this writing. We covered the ones that were SQL Server–specific, including `SqlMetaData`, `Sql Dependency`, and use of `System.Data.SqlTypes`. Automatic caching and

TABLE 12-2: SQL Server Version and Feature Availability

	SQL Server 7	SQL Server 2000	SQL Server 2005
`SqlClient`	X	X	X
MARS			X
`SqlNotificationRequest`			X
`SqlDependency`			X
`IsolationLevel.Snapshot`			X
`Async`	X	X	X
Bulk import	X	X	X
Password update			X
Statistics	X	X	X
Tracing	X	X	X

paging of results, and multiple parameter sets were examples of `SqlClient` enhancements. It is possible that other data provider vendors such as Data-Direct Technologies, IBM, and Oracle Corporation will follow suit and enhance their data providers to support the new features.

One part of the client-side access we didn't mention yet is the new `SqlXml` library. This library has been completely rewritten in managed code in .NET 2.0 and enhanced to support client-side XQuery. It's the subject of our next chapter.

13

Client-Side XML: SQLXML and Mapping

MICROSOFT STARTED INCLUDING XML functionality inside SQL Server with SQL Server 2000. The functionality included the FOR XML Transact-SQL extension and the OPENXML rowset provider to shred XML data into relational rowsets. In SQL Server 2005 this functionality is extended with the XML data type and server-side XQuery support.

As an adjunct to inside-the-server functionality, Microsoft supported client-side integration in the SQL Server 2000 version of the SQLOLEDB provider and extended SQL Server's XML support with a series of Web releases, collectively known as SQLXML. This provided SQL and XML integration functionality that lived on the client or, more commonly, on a middle-tier Web server. This functionality included XML Views of SQL Server data, achieved by mapping SQL data to an XML format. Queries and updates on these Views can be done on the Web server through HTTP, through the SQLOLEDB provider directly, and through a set of managed classes known as the SqlXml data classes. Although the existing SQLXML releases will continue to work with SQL Server 2005, a new XML query architecture and a new mapping format provide more extensible mapping schemas and allow query optimization.

The Common Query Abstraction

The key to providing generalizable queries and updates over XML data sources lies in optimizing the query engines, along with indexing the data. When relational databases were first introduced, performance was suboptimal as compared with other database systems of the time, like IBM's IMS and Cullinane's IDMS. SQL is, however, based on a query algebra that itself can be and is now, after approximately 20 years have passed, highly optimized by execution engines. To get a feeling for how effective this kind of optimization can be, just think of the simple high school algebra problem shown in Figure 13-1.

High school algebra, just like the query algebra for SQL, has a number of operations associated with it that can be used to simplify its symbolic form. In fact, the equation in Figure 13-1 can be reduced to that shown in Figure 13-2.

Optimizing the formula greatly reduces the calculation required, and the optimization itself can be reused whenever the same formula is submitted for calculation. The same technique can be applied to queries involving XML data or any other query that has a well-defined form.

The complication in XML systems is that many XML standards have their own different data models. The XSLT data model has rules slightly different from the DOM level 2.0 data model, which is slightly different from the XML Infoset model, and so forth. Quite a few XML APIs and object models are supported by Microsoft in .NET, and although they use approximately the same query capabilities, they each use their own parser and optimization method. Finally, none of the current models is strongly typed; although you can use the `XmlValidatingReader`, it does not add anything to the data model—it only exposes XML schema types as it is parsing. The document produced by `XmlDocument.Load` is the same whether `XmlValidatingReader` or `XmlReader` is used. The strong types are not stored, for example, in an `XmlDocument` if an `XmlValidating Reader` is used with `XmlDocument.Load`.

$a = 3$
$b = 6$
$c = 5$
$x = (abc^{-2} + ac^{-2})/(b^2c^{-2} + bc^{-2})$

What is x?

FIGURE 13-1: Simple High School Algebra Problem

$x = (abc^{-2}+ac^{-2})/(b^2c^{-2}+bc^{-2})$

$x = (ab+a)/(b^2+b)$

$x = a(b+1)/(b^2+b)$

$x = a(b+1)/((b+1)b)$

$x = a/b$ ◄─── this can be saved for future use

$x = 3/6$

$x = 0.5$

FIGURE 13-2: Optimized Solution

The Common Query Abstraction is a query execution engine architecture that abstracts query optimization away from the specifics of the front-
end and back-end query languages, the data models, and even the eventual
back-end data source that the query will execute against. At its lowest levels,
it consists of these two pieces:

- A set of query compilers that takes a query as input and
produces a query language–independent intermediate format
- A set of query generators (one per data source) that takes a
compiled query and input data source and generates code to
execute the query, that is customized for the query engine, data
model, and data source that is used

This architecture allows different query languages and different data
sources to plug in to the architecture at will. The optimization code for
queries is split between the compiler, the generator, and optimizing the
intermediate format itself. Any performance gains achieved in any of the
layers of the query architecture are enjoyed by any component that uses
that layer. In addition, any performance gains achieved by optimizing the
intermediate format itself are available to all participants.

For example, we might have an XQuery query that executes against an
XML file on the file system and/or executes against a mapping layer that
maps SQL Server to a virtual XML document. Because both queries use the
XQuery compiler and the intermediate format, any optimization provided
by these components affect both queries. On the other side, we could have
an XQuery query or an OPath (an object query language used in the
ObjectSpaces API; see Chapter 14) query that executes against the same
SQL mapping layer and that both wind up executing Transact-SQL commands against SQL Server. These two components share any intermediate

format optimizations as well as any intermediate format-to-SQL optimizations in the SQL generator component.

In addition, in this new architecture, only one SQL generator is needed, and it will be reused by XPath, XQuery, OPath, and other languages. Just one XQuery parser will suffice to execute XQuery queries against files, databases, and so on. In the other words, if you have N languages and M data sources, in the past you would have to implement $M*N$ different modules. Now, all that is needed is $M+N$. Furthermore, if anybody invents a new language, "ZQuery," he only needs to implement one compiler of "ZQuery" into the intermediate format, and he will be able to execute this new query language against all M back ends immediately.

The compilation of the query consists of two steps, both of which are encapsulated in the compiler's `Compile` method. Figure 13-3 shows a logical representation of this.

The query is first parsed into intermediate format nodes. Usually any query compiler (including the Transact-SQL compiler) will transform the query language into some type of intermediate form. The difference is that whether the query is XQuery, XPath, OPath, XSLT, or another query language, the intermediate form is always the same. At this time, the specifics of the intermediate format are undocumented, but the node types may be exposed in the future for enabling third-party query generators. Intermediate format nodes represent logical operations such as element construction, rather than physical operations like I/O optimization.

The second step in query compilation is normalizing and optimizing the query plan. This step would include a logical analysis of the query to determine if some operations (nodes) could be eliminated or combined, for example. It would reduce the intermediate language to a more simple, efficient form in the same way that the algebraic formula in Figure 13-1 was

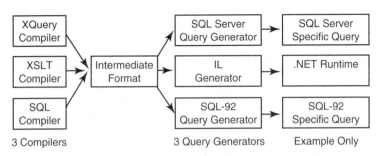

3 Compilers   3 Query Generators   Example Only

Compilers and generators added independently

FIGURE 13-3: Query Compilation Using the Common Query Abstraction

reduced to the one in Figure 13-2. This step is critical for XML Views that use mapping schemas, as we'll see shortly.

Next, we need to generate the final query. This step takes the intermediate format nodes and translates them into either MSIL code (meaning, calls to the input XML processor) or SQL statements for submission to SQL Server. The result is a prepared XQueryCommand or SqlXmlCommand instance. As with a prepared SQL query (SqlCommand, if we use the Sql Client provider), you could use this command over and over, skipping the parsing and command compilation steps.

All that is left to do now is to execute the query and produce the output. We need an input URI class to point at the input file and also need an "environment" for our query. The two parts of the environment are an XmlResolver and an optional XmlArgumentList. We'll have more to say about them later. If we are using an XQueryCommand, we can use an Xml DataSourceResolver to "resolve" our SQL Server connection to "virtual XML input." That is, we use XmlDataSourceResolver to inform XQuery Command where to go to run our SELECT...FOR XML query.

That's all there is to it. The results consist of a sequence because it is XQuery. As an example of where we could go from here, since we already have the precompiled query, we could execute it against the same data source with different parameters. Or we could execute it against a different input file without going through all the compilation steps. That's similar to using a stored procedure in SQL Server, except that the Command is not serialized and stored in the database; it is saved at a higher, abstract level so that optimizations of the query itself, access to the data, and the data repository itself can all be realized.

Mapping between Different Data Models

Before you can execute XML-based queries against a relational database, you must decide what sort of document you want the database to look like as XML. There are two general ways to accomplish this: You can declare a canonical representation of what a SQL table, schema, or database looks like as an XML document (see Chapter 8 for an example of this), or you can use mapping schemas to map relational to XML in any way that suits your application. The second style (mapping) is clearly a superset of the canonical approach, because you can always declare mappings for the canonical form in addition to other mappings. SQL Server's SQLXML Views take the mapping approach, as shown in Figure 13-4.

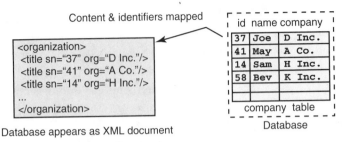

Content & identifiers mapped

```
<organization>
  <title sn="37" org="D Inc."/>
  <title sn="41" org="A Co."/>
  <title sn="14" org="H Inc."/>
  ...
</organization>
```

id	name	company
37	Joe	D Inc.
41	May	A Co.
14	Sam	H Inc.
58	Bev	K Inc.

company table

Database appears as XML document

Database

FIGURE 13-4: SQL Server XML Mappings

There are also two ways to accomplish mapping. The SQLXML 2.0 Web release required that you use annotated schemas—that is, traditional XML schemas with SQLXML-specific annotations. The mapping schema method of SQLXML in .NET 2.0 uses a different approach, which doesn't require you to annotate the schema, but puts annotations in a separate portion of the mapping schema. A .NET 2.0 mapping document would look like this in general.

```
<MappingSchema
   xmlns="http://schemas.microsoft.com/mapping/2003/06/msd">
      <DataSources>
        <DataSource Name="Northwind">
    <!-- relational schema represented as XML -->
    <!-- can be generated by a SQL schema-reading tool -->
    <Schema Location="Northwind.rsd"/>
   </DataSource>
        <DataTarget Type="XML">
    <!- XML schema (not annotated) -->
    <Schema Location="Northwind.xsd"/>
      </DataTarget>
   </DataSources>
   <Mappings>
     <!-- mappings between source and target -->
   </Mappings>
<MappingSchema>
```

Note that, currently, the only supported DataSource is SQL Server; either XML data or Object data is supported as a DataTarget. The architecture is extensible, and more DataSources may be added. Mapping documents have an underlying object model (known as MSOM, or mapping schema object model) that lives in the mapping libraries inside System. Data.SqlXml.dll.

Although you don't have to add any annotations to your XSD schemas, the format is wordier than in previous versions. The schema for each

`DataSource` or `DataTarget` is specified either by specifying the schema's location or including the schema inline. Note that the relational and object domains have specific XML format schemas, and you have to specify these separately. By convention (the schemas will be generated by a modeling tool in the common case) relational domain schemas have the suffix .RSD, and the object domain, .OSD. We'll even use the convention of using the suffix .MSD for the mapping schema documents themselves. Although these schemas are in XML format, they describe items that relational and object modelers are familiar with. For example, a vastly simplified schema for part of the Northwind database would look like this.

```xml
<! - this schema lives in the file Northwind.rsd  ->
<r:Databases Product="SqlServer" Version="2000"
xmlns:r="http://schemas.microsoft.com/mapping/2003/06/rsd-sql">
 <r:Database Name="NorthWind">
  <r:Schemas>
   <r:Schema Name="dbo">
    <r:Tables>
     <r:Table Name="Customers">
      <r:Columns>
        <r:Column Name="CustomerID">
         <r:StringType Name="nchar" Length="5"/>
        </r:Column>
        <r:Column Name="CompanyName">
         <r:StringType Name="nvarchar" Length="40"/>
        </r:Column>
        <r:Column Name="ContactName" AllowDbNull="true">
         <r:StringType Name="nvarchar" Length="30"/>
        </r:Column>
       </r:Columns>
      <r:Constraints>
        <r:PrimaryKey Name="PK_Customers">
         <r:Column Name="CustomerID" />
        </r:PrimaryKey>
      </r:Constraints>
     </r:Table>
     <r:Table Name="Orders">
      <r:Columns>
       <r:Column Name="OrderID" AutoIncrement="true">
        <r:NumericType Name="int"/>
       </r:Column>
       <r:Column Name="CustomerID">
        <r:StringType Name="nchar" Length="5"/>
       </r:Column>
        <r:Column Name="OrderDate">
         <r:DateType Name="datetime"/>
        </r:Column>
       </r:Columns>
```

```
    <r:Constraints>
     <r:PrimaryKey Name="PK_Orders">
      <r:Column Name="OrderID" />
     </r:PrimaryKey>
    </r:Constraints>
   </r:Tables>
  </r:Schema>
 </r:Schemas>
 <r:Relationships>
  <r:Relationship Name="FK_Cust_Order" Parent="Customers"
     Child="Orders" CascadeDelete="Server" CascadeUpdate="Server"
     IsLogical="true" Cardinality="OneToMany">
   <r:ColumnJoin ParentColumn="CustomerID" ChildColumn="CustomerID"/>
  </r:Relationship>
 </r:Relationships>
 </r:Database>
</r:Databases>
```

In addition to tables, you can define views, stored procedures, user-defined functions, user-defined types, and "custom tables" in the RSD schema; these are used as sources in the mapping section. Custom tables are a data source similar to an updateable database view, except that it is defined in terms of instances of the four basic SQL server statements: SELECT, INSERT, UPDATE, and DELETE. This can retrieve and/or persist data from arbitrary tables using any logic that you want. Most of the elements in the RSD format have XML attributes that specify properties of the element—for example, the Name and AllowDbNull attributes on the Column element. We'll discuss the OSD schema format in the next chapter. Note that using the appropriate namespace declaration is required; there are XML schemas for RSD and OSD files, so the mapping schema information can be validated at compile time and at runtime.

Relationships are used to define how one table is related to another table for restricting the set of objects used in the mapping. These can be primary key/foreign key relationships in the relational domain or subelement, or Key/Keyref relationships in the XML domain, although Key/Keyref is not directly used in mapping schemas. Object relationships such as Inheritance or Containment are specified in the OSD schema.

For the target data source, you specify what the XML schema should look like.

```
<!-- this schema lives in the file Northwind.xsd -->
<xsd:schema xmlns:xsd="http://www.w3.org/2001/XMLSchema">
  <xsd:element name="Customer" type="CustomerType"/>
  <xsd:complexType name="CustomerType" >
```

```
<xsd:sequence>
  <xsd:element name="Order">
   <xsd:complexType>
    <xsd:attribute name="OrderID" type="xsd:integer" />
    <xsd:attribute name="OrderDate" type="xsd:datetime" />
   </xsd:complexType>
  </xsd:element>
 </xsd:sequence>
 <xsd:attribute name="CustomerID" type="xsd:string" />
 <xsd:attribute name="CompanyName" type="xsd:string" />
 <xsd:attribute name="ContactName" type="xsd:string" />
 </xsd:complexType>
</xsd:schema>
```

This is an ordinary XSD format XML schema. No special annotations are needed, as they were in the SQLXML mapping format in SQL Server 2000. This makes maintenance easier because you don't have to keep track of a special version of your XSD schema just for mapping. Another common case is using one XSD schema and mapping it to two (or more) databases. In this case you only keep one XSD, and it is used by several map files. The XSD may be owned and maintained by another organization. Different databases may have different mappings for the same XSD elements/attributes. The mappings can change independently without the need to revise the XSD version.

In this initial implementation of mapping schemas, the relational data is always the `DataSource`; Object or XML data sources are always the `DataTarget`. This is true no matter which way the data actually flows. For example, even if you use mapping to populate a SQL Server table with `XmlBulkLoad` or write back to a relational database from a graph of objects, the relational schema is the source schema.

Bear in mind that you will not usually define the mapping files "by hand." The schemas might be derived from existing data sources with a GUI tool; you could select tables or stored procedures with the GUI and accomplish the mapping using drag and drop. The tool would extract explicitly defined primary key/foreign key relationships from the relational schema. If you have ever used the BizTalk mapper, you will find that some of the concepts in the mapping process are similar. The mapping tools are still under development as of this writing.

Now let's look at the mapping section. The mapping section begins and ends with a single `Mapping` element. Subelements of `<Mapping>` define corresponding `Source` and `Target` items and name the list of fields that each mapping supports. You can think of these `Mapping` subelements as "virtual tables" or "views" of one item in a different data model. Three types of Mapping subelements are used:

- Map—Simple source variable-to-target mapping
- FieldMap—Individual items to be mapped
- RelationshipMap—Indicator of which relationships are used to relate two previously defined Relationships

The Map elements contain sets of FieldMap subelements. These subelements correspond to individual fields (columns) in a relational database; attributes, simple-type elements, and text nodes in XML; and properties in Objects. For each FieldMap entry, you can specify Source Field or SourceConstant, TargetField or TargetConstant. You can only have one SourceField/Constant and one TargetField/Constant per FieldMap. Additional attributes on the FieldMap elements are used to define database NULL value handling and whether or not the field is used for concurrency checking in object-relational mapping updates. We'll talk more about concurrency checking in the chapter on ObjectSpaces.

Here is a simple set of Map elements underlying FieldMaps and a RelationshipMap.

```
<! - assumes underlying Source/Target schemas already defined  -->
<! - assumes underlying Variables and Relationships already defined  -->
<Map Source="Customers" Target="/Customer">
    <RelationshipMap Source="FK_Cust_Order" Target="Order"/>
    <FieldMap SourceField="CustomerID" TargetField="@CustomerID"/>
    <FieldMap SourceField="ContactName" TargetField="@CustomerName"/>
    <FieldMap SourceField="CompanyName" TargetField="@CompanyName"/>
</Map>
<Map Source="Orders" Target="/Customer/Order">
    <FieldMap SourceField="OrderID" TargetField="@OrderID"/>
    <FieldMap SourceField="OrderDate" TargetField="@OrderDate"/>
    <FieldMap SourceField="Policy" TargetConstant="1"/>
</Map>
```

Notice that in this relational-to-XML Map, TargetSelect is an XPath statement that defines where the element lives in the previous XSD schema. In mapping there is no field inference; that is, if a field is left out of the FieldMap, it won't appear in the virtual XML document or be used in XQuery output.

When we put this all together, a complete (but simplified) mapping schema would look like Listing 13-1. The RSD and XSD schemas for source and target are not shown for brevity.

LISTING 13-1: A Complete SQL-XML Mapping Schema

```
<m:MappingSchema
  xmlns:m="http://schemas.microsoft.com/mapping/2003/06/msd">
      <m:DataSources>
  <m:DataSource Name="Northwind">
   <m:Schema Location="Northwind.rsd"/>
  </m:DataSource>
  <m:DataTarget Type="Xml">
           <m:Schema Location="Northwind.xsd"/>
      </m:DataTarget>
 </m:DataSources>

 <m:Mappings>
  <m:Map>
   <m:RelationshipMap Source="FK_Cust_Order" Target="Order"/>
   <m:FieldMap SourceField="CustomerID" TargetField="@CustomerID"/>
   <m:FieldMap SourceField="ContactName" TargetField="@CustomerName"/>
   <m:FieldMap SourceField="CompanyName" TargetField="@CompanyName"/>
  </m:Map>
  <m:Map Source="Orders" Target="/Customer/Order">
   <m:FieldMap SourceField="OrderID" TargetField="@OrderID"/>
   <m:FieldMap SourceField="OrderDate" TargetField="@OrderDate"/>
   <m:FieldMap SourceField="Policy" TargetConstant="1"/>
  </m:Map>
 </m:Mappings>
<m:MappingSchema>
```

There are some additional domain-specific features, but we won't describe them in detail here. This mapping schema format supports all the functionality of the original SQLXML Web release XML Views mapping format and doesn't require that you annotate schemas. Some of the most important features for SQL-XML mapping are described briefly here. Additional object-relational mapping features specified in mapping schemas will be discussed in the ObjectSpaces chapter.

- MappingParameters/MappingParameter—An element used to specify parameter defaults for parameterized queries. The Parameters will be used in Condition elements, which will be transformed into queries.

- OverflowMap—A subelement of Map used with XML documents that contain open content models. All of the unmapped content is placed in this field.

- Extentions—Used with one or multiple XmlField elements to specify XML-specific features. The features currently supported are encoding (URL or Base64), Prefix, and UseCData (true or false).

XML Queries over XML Views of Relational Data

When we use relational to XML mappings with either the original mapping schemas or the improved .NET 2.0 mapping format, this is known as XML Views of SQL Server. Although you map SQL Server tables one to one to XML complex types with .NET 2.0 mappings, you can also create mappings that look nothing like the original SQL Server tables. Once you have the mappings in place, you can execute XML queries against XML Views of SQL Server tables the same way you would execute SQL statements against a SQL VIEW. Figure 13-5 shows the way the abstraction would handle this query.

XQuery is supported against ordinary XML documents or SQL Server FOR XML queries via System.Xml.XQueryCommand and is supported using mapping via System.Xml.SqlXmlCommand. You must add a reference to System.Data.SqlXml.dll to use this and related classes. Because XPath is effectively a subset of XQuery, simple XPath queries are supported using this class as well. Although the new System.Xml.Query.XsltProcessor uses the Common Query Abstraction as well, mapping is not supported in combination with XSLT directly.

There are two basic ways to use SQL Server data in combination with XQuery. If a single mapping schema/database connection is used, you can use the SqlXmlCommand to execute the query. This class is easy to use for programmers who are familiar with the SqlCommand class in ADO.NET.

```
SqlConnection conn = new SqlConnection (
  "server=.;integrated security=sspi;database=northwind");
StreamWriter w = new StreamWriter ("outView.xml");
string cmdText =  "/Customer";
XmlMapping map = new XmlMapping("c:\\schemas\\sqlx_mapping.msd");
SqlXmlCommand xcmd = new SqlXmlCommand(cmdText, map, conn);
```

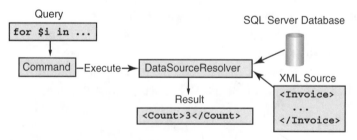

FIGURE 13-5: Query Executed through Mapping

```
try
{
  conn.Open ();
  xcmd.Execute(w);
}
catch (Exception ex)
{
  Console.WriteLine (ex.Message);
  if (ex.InnerException != null)
    Console.WriteLine (ex.InnerException.Message);
}
finally
{
  w.Close ();
  conn.Close ();
}
```

In this case, the `SqlXmlCommand` produces a compiled SQL command based on the combination of the XQuery and the mapping schema specified, and `Execute` passes in the SQL to whatever database the `Sql Connection` points to. The interesting thing about this mechanism is that the same compiled command can be used over again; for example, `Execute` could be reissued later on against the same database or even a different database. Note that because we only have a single data source, our data source is the XQuery "context document;" you don't even need to use the XQuery `doc()` function.

Because the XQuery query always executes against a SQL Server database, `SqlXmlCommand` exposes a `Transaction` property and a `Parameters` collection, which will be used in the underlying SQL Server processing. The parameters are specified using XQuery syntax inside the query string (that is, using the "$parmname" parameter marker) and without the "$" when specified in the `Parameters` property, as shown in the following code. The `Parameters` property is actually an `XmlArgumentList`.

```
// Same as the previous example, but using a Parameter
string cmdText =  "/Customer[State=$TheState]";
XmlMapping map = new XmlMapping("e:\\schemas\\sqlx_mapping.msd");
SqlXmlCommand xcmd = new SqlXmlCommand(cmdText, map, conn);
xcmd.Parameters.AddParameter("TheState", "WA");
```

The `SqlXmlCommand` is still in development at the time of this writing; some of the specific property and method names may change before release.

Using XQueryCommand with SQL Server or XML Documents

The XQueryCommand class allows you to issue XQuery queries against SQL Server (by using SQL Server FOR XML queries) or XML documents, and has separate methods to compile and execute the query. XQueryCommand allows you to use FOR XML queries through a special function. There is an overload of Execute that uses an XmlArgumentList so that you can use parameterized queries, and you can also use parameters in your SQL Server FOR XML queries.

When using Execute, we need input data and parameters for our query. These two parts of the environment are an XmlResolver and an XmlArgumentList. XmlResolver is an abstract class that is used to resolve entities, which are an XML construct that may exist inside or outside the main file that we are querying. Because XQuery is strongly typed, one of the items we might want to resolve is the XML schemas in validation to provide the strong data types. Other things that you might resolve with a resolver would be DTDs, entities, included XSLT files, and imported schemas. It we are using SQL Server or multiple inputs, we use an Xml DataSourceResolver instead to "resolve" our SQL Server connection to "XML input." Here's an example that puts this all together.

```
SqlConnection conn = new SqlConnection (
  "server=.;integrated security=sspi;database=northwind");
StreamWriter w = new StreamWriter ("outInline.xml");

try
{
  XQueryCommand xcmd = new XQueryCommand ();
  StringReader sr = new StringReader ("declare namespace
sql='http://schemas.microsoft.com/framework/2003/xml/sql'
sql:query('select * from customers for xml auto',
        'NorthwindDB')/Customer");

  // map a symbolic name to a connection
  XmlDataSourceResolver ds = new XmlDataSourceResolver ();
  ds.Add ("NorthwindDB", conn);

  xcmd.Compile (sr);

  conn.Open ();
  xcmd.Execute (ds, w);
}
catch (Exception ex)
{
  Console.WriteLine (ex.Message);
```

```
    if (ex.InnerException != null)
      Console.WriteLine (ex.InnerException.Message);
}
finally
{
  w.Close ();
  conn.Close ();
}
```

This is pretty straightforward, except for the `sql:query` function used in the query. The `sql:query` function is a client-side XQuery-defined extension function that causes the `SELECT...FOR XML` query to be executed against SQL Server. Its formal definition looks like this.

```
node* query(xs:string sqlQuery, xs:string connectionName
    (, xs:string+ parmNames, xs:untypedAtomic+ parmValues) ?)
```

Note that the `sqlQuery` parameter in this extension function must be a `SELECT...FOR XML` query; an "ordinary" SQL `SELECT` statement cannot be used. The `sql:query` function can also specify parameter name/value pairs. The "values" in this case are the XQuery parameter names, as this example shows.

```
string TheQuery =
  "declare namespace
    sql='http://schemas.microsoft.com/framework/2003/xml/sql'
    (: for exposition, actually set parm through XmlArgumentList :)
    (: let $statename := 'CA' :)
    sql:query(
    'select * from customers where state = @thestate for xml auto',
    'NorthwindDB', '@thestate', '$statename'
    )/Customer";
```

Optimizing Queries

Now that we've seen the examples, note that, using mapping and `SqlXml Command`, the query processor has quite a bit of information to work with at compile time. It has an XML query over an XML representation of the source. This is actually more information than the query processor would have in the case when it is used with an untyped XML document, when the source document format is not known until execution time. So the query processor can factor the document structure into the query, coming up with a final query plan. This is analogous to the case in which an XML query processor has an XML schema to work with, or a SQL parser with a database schema. There is a much better chance for optimization in this case.

In the `SqlXmlCommand` example, the XQuery query is compiled into a SQL query using the SQL query generator instead of the IL query generator. Because XML must be returned (and SQL queries return rectangular results), the generator will generate a `SELECT...FOR XML` query—specifically, a `SELECT...FOR XML EXPLICIT` query. This query is then executed, returning the results as a `StringWriter`.

In this part of the query, the query generator does not have as much information to work with as a normal SQL parser would. For example, there is no way for the (client-side) query generator to acquire SQL statistics to choose between different queries that could lead to optimized processing on the server. However, there is still a chance for optimization when the query is received at the server. The SQL parser will parse the query at execution time and produce an optimized query plan. This is a huge improvement over the alternative, however, where the entire, potentially large resultset is brought back to the client, turned into XML, and postprocessed in XML format on the client.

On the other hand, you use the `sql:query` function and the XQuery `Command` for specifying exactly what Transact-SQL statement is executed on the server and the nodelist that is being returned. However, just as in a native SQL Server query, queries that select all the columns, like "`SELECT` * from sometable for xml auto," should be used with care. If the underlying database changes (for example, a column is added), the shape of the XML result could change. This is less likely when you are using mapping.

In addition to using the `sql:query` function, the `XQueryCommand` can be used with ordinary XML documents or multiple documents, although it does not yet support XML document collections (that is, the XQuery `collection()` function). The client-side XQuery processor requires an `XmlResolver` to resolve input sources, whether those sources are XML documents or `SELECT...FOR XML`. For the simplest single document case, you can use the `XmlUrlResolver` or `XmlSecureResolver`. The `XmlUrl Resolver` simply resolves a URL to an input source (currently file:// and http:// URLs are supported). The `XmlSecureResolver` permits you to use a permission set calculated from the URI. Code illustrating the `XmlUrl Resolver` was shown in the low-level XQuery example earlier in this chapter.

In addition to the version of the `XmlDataSourceResolver`'s `Add` method, which you've already seen, that takes a `SqlConnection` as input, there are overloads that take the following:

- A URL string as a single document
- An XmlReader
- An XPathNavigator (actually any class implementing IXPathNavigable)

Client versus SQL Server XQuery Functionality

After looking at the base APIs for client-side XML and client-side XQuery, and the server-side XQuery functions, you might wonder when to use which APIs, because they appear to take the same input (XML data and XQuery statement) and produce the same output (a sequence conforming to the XPath 2.0 and XQuery 1.0 data model). Server-side XQuery and client-side XQuery are designed for completely different scenarios. Server-side XQuery is designed for scenarios in which the data you are storing is inherently XML—that is, the actual XML in the database. The client-side mapping or using SELECT. . . FOR XML is designed for a scenario in which you are storing relational data that has no idea that it is being viewed as an XML View. Client-side XQuery can take your regular legacy relational data that you entered 20 years ago and expose it as XML using an XML View. All your reports are still running on this relational data; they will probably not be converted to the new XML data type. The client- and server-side models also have some different functional characteristics, although they have a similar vocabulary and semantics; let's discuss them now.

Server-side XQuery is the equivalent of a function associated with an instance of a specific data type, the XML type. There is no way currently to use a SQL Server XQuery query over more than one instance of an XML column at the same time. You can accomplish this by running XQuery over many instances, casting all the results to strings (VARCHAR), and concatenating the results, but there is no way to use the doc() or collection() functions in server-side XQuery. Although you can access other SQL values using the sql:column() function on the server side, queries are centered around the XML data type. Client-side XQuery through the Common Query Abstraction fully supports multidocument queries and the XQuery doc() and (in future) collection() functions.

Both server-side and client-side XQuery supports strong typing when used against a strongly typed XML data type column instance or parameter. This allows the use of SQL Server as a schema repository, but also means that all schemas must be stored (that is, namespaces must be cataloged) and associated with the instance before you run the query. In fact, as of this writing, SQL Server XML schema validation does not support partial document validation; nodes from unknown namespaces will cause a validation error. This is stricter than the XQuery data model demands. Finally, SQL Server enforces user-level security through XML schema collections.

The client-side model permits a `SchemaCollection` or `Resolver` to be specified so that the XQuery might "look for" the schema in the absence of a central repository, but this is time-consuming (the schema may need to be loaded and parsed each time). The client-side model permits a different type of security based on .NET code access security (CAS). An interesting combination of these might be achieved by creating an `XmlResolver` class that resolves schemas by querying SQL Server. Previously retrieved schemas might be cached on the client side (on a per–SQL Server principal basis) for better performance.

Both client- and server-side XQuery parsers can perform optimizations based on strong typing on static syntax evaluation, but server-side XML columns can also contain XML indexes that can be used to further optimize the fetching, or sequences that result from common XPath expressions within XQuery programs. XML schemas and XML columns inside SQL Server are also stored in an optimized format (see Chapter 8), making schema validation faster.

As mentioned in Chapter 9, client- and server-side XQuery are aligned with the same version of the XQuery specification (November 2003 as of this writing) and will implement almost exactly the same set of functionality and functions and operators. A small difference is that the client-side implementation will work with heterogeneous sequences. Neither will be 100% compliant with the W3C specification, but each will have the same strong typing extensions.

SqlXml Bulk Load and the SqlXmlRowsetAdapter

SQLXML Web release 1 in SQL Server 2000 introduced the `XmlBulkLoad` facility. This is analogous functionality to the `XML` data type's `nodes` function (or `OpenXml`) of SQL Server or using the `BULK` provider to shred a document into many tables. The `nodes` function and the `BULK` provider were described in Chapters 8 and 9, which covered the `XML` data type and XQuery. One drawback of the `nodes` function and the `BULK` provider (although it is not as much of a problem in the `BULK` provider) is that the transformation of XML to relational rows takes place inside SQL Server itself. In order to free up resources inside the server, `XmlBulkLoad` was enhanced to use the new mapping schema format for the new version of the `SqlXml` client libraries. In addition, it was converted to use native .NET code; the original provider was written using COM components.

Here's an example of using the new `SqlXml` bulk loading class.

```
XmlBulkLoad b = new XmlBulkLoad ();

// behaviors
b.CheckConstraints = true;
b.ForceTableLock = false;
b.KeepIdentity = false;
b.KeepNulls = true;

b.ClientBufferSize = 10000;
b.ClientSideIDPropagation = true;
b.IgnoreDuplicateKeys = false;
b.UpdateOnExisting = true;
b.TransactionMode = TransactionMode.NonTransaction;

XmlMapping s = new XmlMapping(
    "file://e:/schemas/xmls_mapping1.msd");
b.Mapping = s;

string connstr =
    "server=.;integrated security=sspi;database=pubs";
SqlConnection conn = new SqlConnection (connstr);
conn.Open ();
b.Execute ("inputfile.xml", conn);
conn.Dispose();
```

The mapping schema used in this case looks similar to the mappings usually used by the `SqlXmlCommand`. As previously described, the relational schema is specified as the source and the XML schema is the target, but the actual direction of the data flow is XML input to SQL output.

A database is not the only relational store that might be filled with XML data. The `XmlRowsetAdapter` can fill a `DataSet` via mapping using the `Fill` method and an input XML file. Although the `DataSet` can load 90% of the XML directly through its `ReadXml` and `ReadXmlSchema` methods, there is some XML that the `DataSet` can't handle, because of its inference rules for mapping XML data to relational data. Because the `XmlRowset Adapter` uses mapping directly rather than inference rules, it can handle that last 10%. Here's an example of using `XmlRowsetAdapter` to fill a `DataSet`.

```
DataSet ds = new DataSet ();
XmlRowsetAdapter ra = new XmlRowsetAdapter ();
```

```
XmlMapping s = new XmlMapping(
  "file://e:/schemas/xmls_mapping1.msd");
ra.Mapping = s;
ra.Fill (ds, "somexml.xml");
```

SqlXml DBObject

One last piece of SQLXML completes the conversion of all client-side SQLXML functionality to use .NET classes rather than COM objects. Starting with SQLXML Web release 1, the Web server could serve a single column as XML, based on a one-column query. If the single column contained IMAGE data, this was rendered as BASE64 encoded binary; this was most often the reason for its use. This was known as DBObject; its main use was to render pictures stored in IMAGE columns in SQL Server into XML for incorporation into Web pages, because the resulting XML could be transformed with XSLT into HTML format. In the updated version of SQLXML, the DBObject is exposed as a class in the System.Data.SqlXml namespace. It does not automatically BASE64 encode IMAGE data, but it does permit you to retrieve the column through an XmlDataReader or Stream and update it through a Stream.

Using the DBObject class does not require an XML mapping schema; you simply use a SqlConnection to connect to the database of your choice, and use a simple XPath-like syntax. The grammar for the syntax is defined here.

```
dbobject       = "dbobject";
tableName      = dbobject + "/(?<tableName>^[/\\s]+)";
columnName     = "@(?<columnName>[^\\s]+)";
predicateName  = "@(?<predicateName>[^=\\s]+)";
predicateValue =
"(?<predicateValue>('[^']*('' [^']*)*')|(\"[^\"]*(\"\"[^\"]*)*\")|(\\$[^\
\s]+)|([0-9]+(.[0-9]+)?))";
straightPredicatePair = predicateName + "\\s*=\\s*" + predicateValue;
reversePredicatePair  = predicateValue + "\\s*=\\s*" + predicateName;
predicatePair         = "((" + straightPredicatePair + ")|
(" + reversePredicatePair + "))";
andString             = "[aA][nN][dD]";
predicate             = "(\\[\\s*" + predicatePair + "(\\s+" +
andString + "\\s+" + predicatePair + "\\s*)*" + "\\s*\\])";
grammar               = tableName + predicate + "?/" + columnName + "\\s*";
```

A more concrete example would be the query to read the Photo column in the Employees table in the Northwind database, passing in a variable,

$EmpID, as the number of the employee to use. This query would simply be as follows:

```
dbobject/Employees[@EmployeeID=$EmpID]/@Photo
```

You can then read the large object as a single stream of data. The following example shows how it's done.

```
// connection string
string connstr =
    "server=.;uid=bob;pw=bob;database=pubs";
SqlConnection conn = new SqlConnection (connstr);
SqlDataReader rdr = null;
MemoryStream stm = new MemoryStream (new byte[100000]);

XmlArgumentList args = new XmlArgumentList();
args.AddParameter("theid", "", "42");

DBObject dbo = new DBObject ();
dbo.Path = "/dbobject/mytable[myid=$theid]/mycol";
dbo.Retrieve (stm, args, conn);

// or retrieve into a DataReader
//rdr = dbo.Retrieve (ags, conn);

// do something with the stream
// change the object, then
dbo.Update (stm, conn);
```

The previous example also illustrates the new functionality in DBObject; you can update the IMAGE column by changing the underlying stream and calling DBObject.Update.

Where Are We?

SQL Server 2005 and .NET 2.0 each introduce a powerful new query language for XML data, XQuery. SQL Server supports the language by implementing methods on the SQL Server XML data type. The .NET client libraries in System.Xml also support XQuery, but at a level of compliance that is closer to the specification. In addition, XML queries against XML Views of SQL Server are supported by the client libraries, by mapping a representation of the database's relational data to XML using a mapping schema.

Along with the mapping schemas for SQL Server's XML Views, the rest of the System.Xml XML query and transformation stack is being updated to support the XQuery data model and allow more changes for optimization by using a Common Query Abstraction against native XML data and mapped data. This new stack even includes a disconnected cache of XML, the functionality-enhanced (from `System.Xml` version 1.0) `XPath Document`. With the enhanced `XPathDocument`, you can update pieces of the XML, examine the original and changed documents at the same time, and write the changes with full fidelity.

The Common Query Abstraction can be used not only with XML and relational data, but also with Object data. This is accomplished by using mappings between objects and relational data in SQL Server with the same mapping format we looked at in the chapter. In addition, an object query language can be compiled into intermediate language and used against the mapped data using the Common Query Abstraction. The implementation of object-relational mapping and Common Query Abstraction-based queries is known as ObjectSpaces. ObjectSpaces is the subject of the next chapter.

▌14▪

ObjectSpaces

S QL SERVER 2005 permits you to create user-defined types inside the
database to extend the scalar type system, but this is not meant to be a
vehicle for SQL Server to manage a traditional object model. It is better to
do this in the client or middle tier, and a set of APIs called ObjectSpaces
allows you to do this by creating a map between relational data in SQL
Server and object graphs in the client or middle tier. ObjectSpaces is
an integral part of the Microsoft Business Framework (MBF) offering and
is likely to be available for use outside MBF as well. Object-relational
mapping can introduce performance problems if not optimized properly.
ObjectSpaces has optimizations for lazy graph instantiation and on-
demand population. With ObjectSpaces you can issue queries against an
object model using a predicate language called OPath, in much the same
way queries are issued against relational data or XML data using SQL or
XQuery.

Introduction to Object-Relational Mapping

Object-oriented data—that is, classes that consist of state and behavior and
can use the object-oriented concepts of inheritance and polymorphism—
are not represented in the traditional relational database model. SQL
Server 2005 permits storage of user-defined types, but this is meant to
extend the scalar type system; the database does not recognize inheritance,
polymorphic behavior, or navigable/retrievable relationships in UDTs. To

complete the picture, it would be useful to be able to map relational tables that contain traditional simple data types or UDTs as columns to graphs of traditional objects on the client or middle tier. The impedance mismatch in traditional object-oriented systems that store their data in relational databases is usually addressed by an object-to-relational mapping layer.

Scott Ambler described some of the basic principles of object-relational mapping in his paper "Mapping Objects to Relational Databases" in 1998. His basic principles have been refined over the past years, and implementations of these concepts appear in commercial products. Another way to solve the impedance mismatch was to use object-oriented databases as an alternative to storing the data in relational form. Object-oriented databases (OODBMS) stored object instances and code directly in the database. This type of database model was standardized under the auspices of the Object Data Management Group (ODMG) in the early 1990s. Some of the more popular object-oriented databases include Object Design's ObjectStore, Versant, and Poet. This group also defined a standardized object query language for OODBMS, known as OQL, as an alternative to SQL.

The popularity of object-relational mapping and middle-tier application servers was codified as a concept in Microsoft Transaction Server (MTS) and subsequently made part of an application server standard in Enterprise Java Beans (EJB) entities. Entities have suffered historically from the fact that each set of relational rows is usually mapped to a collection of objects in a one-table-one-class mapping. EJB 1.0 also mandated that each field must be accessed with specific accessor and mutator methods; this made entities slow. In addition, the specification for transactional entities was implemented in both MTS and EJB using distributed transactions. Both systems originally mandated that these transactions run at the serializable transaction isolation level, which causes excessive database locking and unacceptable performance.

Microsoft has addressed the storage of nonrelational data in a few different ways. ADO.NET's `DataSet` class mapped relational tables and relationships to XML using a series of XML-relational mapping rules. These rules and their implementation in ADO.NET are described in the book *Essential ADO.NET*, by Bob Beauchemin (Addison-Wesley, 2002).

Microsoft's new client-side API, called ObjectSpaces, allows mapping relational database tables and relationships between the tables to object graphs on the client side. A variety of mapping definitions are supported through the same mapping schemas that support relational-to-XML mappings, seen in the previous chapter. Object-relational mappings include support for identity columns and for mapping private persistent fields to publicly accessible properties of .NET classes. In addition, ObjectSpaces implements some special semantics to solve some of the problems that made previous entity object implementations slow. Currently, the Object-Spaces API supports only SQL Server databases, and only SQL Server 2000 and above. Support for other databases may be added in future releases.

ObjectSpaces uses the same mapping schema format that we saw in SQLXML mapping to define object-relational mapping details. You can create these files with any XML editor or with Notepad, but a mapping tool to make it easy to define object-relational mapping files is in development as part of the Microsoft Business Framework. Figure 14-1 shows, at a high level, the files that ObjectSpaces uses to map object graphs to relational tables.

Three files are involved: an object schema definition, called an OSD file; a relational schema definition, called an RSD file; and a mapping schema definition, called an MSD file. This design allows the object mapping to be independent of the database mapping, and indeed allows the same object mapping to be used on different databases and vice versa.

There are two ways to use the ObjectSpaces API; they are designed for developers that want different levels of control. You can use the low-level API directly, through the ObjectEngine class, or use a façade class that encapsulates most of the common uses of the API, the ObjectSpace class. Developers wanting more control will use ObjectEngine, and we'll mention how to use it at the end of this chapter. For the vast majority of developers, writing a program centered on the ObjectSpace class will provide

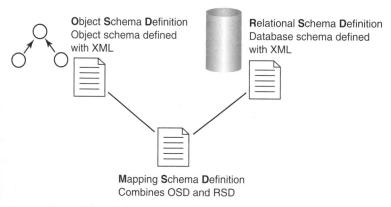

FIGURE 14-1: Object-Relational Mapping

more than enough functionality. In addition to mapping object schema to relational schema, some program semantics can be expressed in the mapping file, so it is an intrinsic portion of every ObjectSpaces application.

A Simple ObjectSpaces Application

Let's create a simple Console Application that uses ObjectSpaces to manipulate object instances and store them in a SQL Server database. Before writing the program, we must design the object model—that is, decide which .NET types (classes) we would like to represent the data we're working with, and which columns in which tables this would correspond to in the SQL Server database. There need not be a one-to-one mapping between .NET types and database tables, although we'll start with this type of mapping, using one simple class and one database table for simplicity. In addition, the .NET types need not expose all the nullable columns in a specific SQL Server table, although we'll do this in our simple example. We'll expose the Authors table in the pubs database. Figure 14-2 shows objects that are related to database objects.

There are some important features of the mapping that ObjectSpaces uses. Note that an object can be related one-to-one with a row in a database. An object might use just a few columns of a row or even be spread out in columns of multiple tables.

The ObjectSpace class is initialized with a mapping schema and an object that represents the physical source of the data. For the simplest one-data-source case, you can use an IDbConnection interface as a data source. ObjectSpaces also provides the ObjectSourceCollection class to enable you to use a collection of data sources. You instantiate an ObjectSource Collection instance and use the Add method to add data source–symbolic name pairs to the collection. The symbolic names are matched with the <DataSource> element names in the mapping schema to resolve where the data comes from. This extra level of indirection allows the resolution

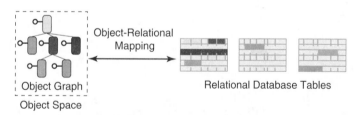

Object Graph
Object Space

Relational Database Tables

FIGURE 14-2: Objects and Their Relation to a Database

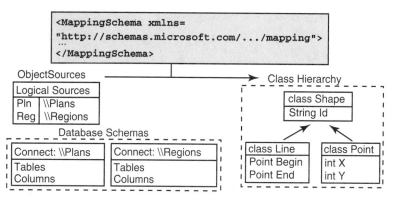

FIGURE 14-3: Object Source

of the physical locations of object sources to be deferred until runtime. Figure 14-3 shows this extra level of indirection.

The mapping schema file will usually be generated by MBF's object-relational mapping tool, but here we will write mapping files by hand. This file works to tie the classes in the program (in this example, the `Author` class) to the tables in the SQL Server database. Our mapping file contains an XML representation of the relational schema (RSD file or elements), an XML representation of our object model (OSD file or elements), and the definitions of the mappings between the two, from the MSD namespace. Here's our mapping schema file. We'll defer the intricacies of the RSD schema file and OSD schema file until later; at this point, just notice that the `TargetField` attributes represent fields in the `Author` class in the program, and the `SourceField` attributes represent column names in the relational table `Authors`.

```
<!-- Mapping schema file  -->
<m:MappingSchema
xmlns:m="http://schemas.microsoft.com/mapping/2003/06/msd">
<m:DataSources>
 <m:DataSource Name="PubsR">
  <m:Schema Location="Pubs.rsd"/>
 </m:DataSource>
 <m:DataTarget Type="Object">
  <m:Schema Location="Pubs.osd"/>
 </m:DataTarget>
</m:DataSources>
<m:Mappings>
   <m:Map Source="Authors" Target="Author">
    <m:FieldMap SourceField="au_id" TargetField="Id"/>
    <m:FieldMap SourceField="au_lname" TargetField="CustName"/>
```

```
  <m:FieldMap SourceField="au_fname" TargetField="Company"/>
  <m:FieldMap SourceField="phone" TargetField="Phone"/>
  <m:FieldMap SourceField="address" TargetField="Address"/>
  <m:FieldMap SourceField="city" TargetField="City"/>
  <m:FieldMap SourceField="state" TargetField="State"/>
  <m:FieldMap SourceField="zip" TargetField="Zip"/>
  <m:FieldMap SourceField="contract" TargetField="Contract"/>
 </m:Map>
</m:Mappings>
</m:MappingSchema>
```

In effect, what we have done here is to write our data access code. We, of course, didn't actually write the code; we wrote a description of what we wanted the code to do. At runtime ObjectSpaces will use this description to "write" the actual code. All we need to do now is write some procedural code that manipulates object instances. To start, create a new Console Application in Visual Studio and add a reference to `System.Data.ObjectSpaces.dll` in the `Add Reference` dialog. We'll also add a C# `using` statement for `System.Data.ObjectSpaces` so that we can access the classes by their non-namespace-qualified names.

We can define our classes in the main application file, or add a reference to classes in libraries defined in other assemblies. For simplicity, we'll define a class called `Author` that exposes the public members corresponding to the columns in the `Authors` table in the `pubs` database. You can also reverse engineer the database schema into an object model using Visual Studio or a similar tool to get started. You'll probably want to keep the class definitions in a separate file, but, for now, a single file solution will be used for simplicity. The source file should now look like Listing 14-1.

LISTING 14-1: File with Class Defined

```
using System;
using System.Data.ObjectSpaces;

//
// Author class.
//

public class Author
{
  public string Id;

  public string FirstName;
  public string LastName;
```

```
    public string Phone;
    public string Address;
    public string City;
    public string State;
    public string Zip;
    public bool   Contract;
}

public class Class1
{
    public static void Main()
    {
    }
}
```

Notice a few things about the `Author` class as it pertains to the Object Spaces API. The `Author` class is a public class and all its members are public. This need not be the case; you can hide the class members behind properties and refer to the property names as aliases in the mapping file. The `Author` class inherits directly from `System.Object`; no inheritance from a specific `ObjectSpace`-related class is required. This is good because you can easily use classes in an existing object model in ObjectSpaces. Finally, the `Author` class is a data-only type; it does not contain any methods. This is not a requirement of the ObjectSpaces API; you can use "normal" classes that contain methods as well as members and properties. You can also use `structs` inside a class in addition to primitive types.

Now that we've defined our mapping files and our classes, let's use them with ObjectSpaces. We'll define all of our code in `Main` and not repeat the entire source file with every step. First, we initialize the ObjectSpaces environment by creating an instance of the `ObjectSpace` class and initializing it with the information mapping schema file. Because there is a single data source, we can pass in a `SqlConnection` as the second parameter. The connection does not have to be open, but the `ConnectionString` property must be set.

We'll use normal get and set statements to manipulate our `Author` instances. Once we've created the instances, we need to make the `ObjectSpace` aware of their existence. We use the `StartTracking` method of the `ObjectSpace`, passing in the instance and an `ObjectState` of Inserted. This means that the `ObjectSpace` should note that the instance does not already exist in the database and should be inserted into the database when you use a persistence method. Finally, we persist our changes to the underlying database using the `PersistChanges` method. Notice that we inserted new rows into the database table just by creating instances and calling methods of the `ObjectSpace` class.

```
public static void Main()
{
  string connect_string = GetConnectStringFromConfigFile();
  SqlConnection conn = new SqlConnection(connect_string);

  // simplest case, one data source
  ObjectSpace os = new ObjectSpace("mappings.msd", conn);

  // create two Author instances and initialize
  Author a1 = new Author();
  a1.Id = "111-11-1111";
  a1.FirstName = "John";
  a1.LastName = "Doe";
  a1.Phone = "800-111-2222";
  a1.Address = "111 Any St";
  a1.City = "Portland";
  a1.State = "OR";
  a1.Zip = "97225";
  a1.Contract = false;

  Author a2 = new Author();
  a2.Id = "111-11-1112";
  a2.FirstName = "Meg";
  a2.LastName = "Jones";
  a2.Phone = "800-111-2222";
  a2.Address = "123 SomeOther St";
  a2.City = "Portland";
  a2.State = "OR";
  a2.Zip = "97225";
  a2.Contract = true;

  // Make the ObjectSpace "notice" the instances
  os.StartTracking(a1, ObjectState.Inserted);
  os.StartTracking(a2, ObjectState.Inserted);

  // Use them to update the database
  os.PersistChanges(a1);
  os.PersistChanges(a2);
}
```

Although it appears that we've just substituted `ObjectSpace` calls for database calls in a one-to-one manner, notice that we didn't have to deal with SQL INSERT statements, opening and closing connections, or issuing parameterized commands at all. The `ObjectSpace` class and mappings took care of this for us. We'll see later that it is possible to optimize the behavior of the `ObjectSpace` to issue multiple inserts in a single database round-trip, use stored procedures to accomplish the SQL operations, and control other database-specific optimizations in our data operations. Notice also that we didn't need to dispose the `ObjectSpace`. If you turn connection pooling off (add `pooling=false` to the connection string in the data source parameter file) and watch SQL Profiler while this program runs, you'll notice that the connection to the database is kept open for the shortest possible time while `os.PersistChanges` is being run. In this simple program, the fact that we called `os.PersistChanges` twice made our data access not optimal, but we'll take care of this shortly. Figure 14-4 shows objects and persisting their changes.

Getting a stream of objects out of the database and into the appropriate class instances is accomplished by using an `ObjectReader` class. `Object Reader` is related in functionality to a `SqlDataReader` in ADO.NET; it returns a collection of object instances as a `SqlDataReader` returns a collection of rows. Rather than using SQL to determine what instances to return, it uses an OPath expression. We'll go into OPath in more detail later; right now we'll use a very simple OPath expression. Here's a simple `Main` method that initializes an `ObjectSpace` as in the first program, issues an OPath command, and returns an `ObjectReader`.

```
public static void Main()
{
   string connect_string = GetConnectStringFromConfigFile();
   SqlConnection conn = new SqlConnection(connect_string);
   ObjectSpace os = new ObjectSpace("mappings.msd", conn);
   ObjectQuery<Author> query = new ObjectQuery<Author>("State = 'OR'");
   ObjectReader<Author> ordr =
     os.GetObjectReader<Author>(query);

   foreach (Author a in ordr)
     Console.WriteLine("author {0} found", a.Id);

   ordr.Close();
}
```

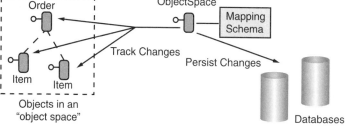

FIGURE 14-4: Objects Persistence

As with the `SqlDataReader`, the instances are read-only and only available while we are reading them in the `ObjectReader`. In this case, the database connection stays open until we close the `ObjectReader`. It's fairly obvious to see, if you are familiar with ADO.NET, that an `ObjectReader`, at least when used with this simple flat single class, is similar in behavior to a `SqlDataReader`. In our `ObjectQuery` and `ObjectReader`, we specify the .NET type that we want using .NET generics syntax. Generics are a new feature of .NET 2.0 that allow structures, classes, and interfaces to be parameterized by the types of data that they store and manipulate.

In the first example, we used only the methods of the `ObjectSpace` class to persist instances to a database and produce instances with a query. An `ObjectSpace` can be used to get collections of objects from database data through two different semantic mechanisms, with a corresponding class to encapsulate each one. `ObjectReader` represents a set of objects that can be used in a forward-only manner to populate object collections or bind to ASP.NET WebForms data controls. `ObjectSet` is a set of objects that have been fetched from the database and can be bound to Windows Forms or ASP.NET `WebForms` data controls. In addition, you can get an individual instance by using `GetObject`. If you are familiar with ADO. NET, `ObjectReader` has semantics similar to a `DataReader`, `ObjectSet` acts somewhat like a `DataSet`. `ObjectSet` can also be used to construct an empty set of instances or a cache of instances by using an `ObjectQuery`, allow them to be managed by the programmer or the Windows Forms `BindingContext` and `CurrencyManager`, and persist them to the database. Here's an example that does just that.

```
public class Form1 : System.Windows.Forms.Form
{
    // define the ObjectSpace and grid at form scope
    public ObjectSpace os = null;
    public ObjectSet<CCustomer> oset = null;
    public DataGrid dataGrid1;

    public void btnLoad_Click(object sender, System.EventArgs e)
    {
        string connect_string = GetConnectStringFromConfigFile();
        SqlConnection conn = new SqlConnection(connect_string);
        os = new ObjectSpace("mappings.msd", conn);

        ObjectQuery<CCustomer> oq = new ObjectQuery<CCustomer>("");
        oset = os.GetObjectSet<CCustomer>(oq);
        dataGrid1.DataSource = oset;
    }
```

```
private void btnSave_Click (object sender, System.EventArgs e)
{
            os.PersistChanges(oset);
}
}
```

In this series of simple examples, we've seen that the ObjectSpace class is the central type that provides interaction with instances of a single class and permits a couple of object fetching semantics: streaming and caching. The mapping model can provide for more complex object-oriented concepts, such as inheritance. The ObjectQuery can specify an abstract class as well as a concrete class and permits fetching heterogeneous collections with a common base class. The ObjectSpace can manage singletons, related collections, or entire graphs of objects through a variety of automatic and user-defined transaction models. We'll see this as we examine each ObjectSpaces API class and more complex mapping models in greater depth.

Data Manipulation Classes in the ObjectSpaces API

The ObjectSpaces API consists of very few data manipulation classes, if you are using the ObjectSpace façade class to manage your data. The ObjectSpace class is the central class through which you accomplish almost all of your data manipulation. The ObjectSpace class tracks each instance's state and identity through an internal class, ObjectManager. Objects are retrieved from the database through two main classes, Object Reader and ObjectSet, although there may be additional specializations of these that permit reporting and SQL customization in the future. Objects that are retrieved through GetObjectSet or GetObject are implicitly tracked by the ObjectSpace's default ObjectManager.

These retrievals are based on an ObjectQuery, which is a compilable set of instructions that tell the ObjectSpaces engine how to retrieve objects. You can precompile queries for reuse using the CompiledQuery class.

Accessing a Database with the ObjectSpace

ObjectSpace is the class that manages the interaction between the database and the instances of types (objects). The ObjectSpace correlates object types to SQL Server databases by using two subordinate classes: Object SourceCollection and ObjectMapping. The ObjectSpace has constructors that take an ObjectSourceCollection and an ObjectMapping instance, one that uses a configured database connection in lieu of `Object SourceCollection`, and two that take XML-format mapping files instead of an `ObjectMapping` instance. These files are the crux of the ObjectSpaces system, and we'll be looking at them in more detail in the next section.

You can use methods of the `ObjectSpace` instance to:

- Start, commit, and roll back a local transaction.
- Compile an `ObjectQuery`.
- Get an `ObjectReader`, `ObjectSet`, or single `Object` based on an `ObjectQuery`.
- Fetch related objects of a given instance by property name.
- Update the database with objects that have changed at different levels of granularity.
- Resynchronize objects with the current database data at different levels of granularity.

An `ObjectSpace` usually uses at most one connection to a data source at a time. The connection remains open for the least possible time, to assist in scalability. One of the things that will keep a connection to the database open is to start a local transaction. `BeginTransaction` starts a transaction. You can also specify a transaction isolation level for this transaction. The transaction applies only to objects in the implicit `ObjectManager` associated with the `ObjectSpace`. After you have made changes and called `PersistChanges`, you can use `Commit` and `Rollback` to affect the permanence of the database changes.

ObjectSpaces supports automatic enlistment in COM+ transactions as well. In order for COM+ transactions to be used, the `ObjectSpace` instance must be created within a .NET type that inherits from `Serviced Component`. For example, in the simple program that added two `Authors`, if the class that created the `ObjectSpace` instance (`Class1` in this case) had inherited from `ServicedComponent`, the two calls to add `Author` instances to the database would automatically have been enlisted in a COM+ distributed transaction, if the component were configured to be transactional. COM+ transactions have the requirement that components that use them (your `Class1` component) be registered as a COM+ component in a COM+ application package. You do this by using the utility program `REGSVCS. exe`. For more information about using COM+ transactions, refer to *Essential ADO.NET*, Chapter 3.

The `ObjectSpace` is a factory for `ObjectReaders` and `ObjectSets`. You can also get individual instances (or a graph with a single root) by using the `GetObject` method. The `ObjectSpace` includes `PersistChanges` and `Resync` methods. These methods synchronize the state of a set of objects with the state of the mapped data in the database using the state information stored in the `ObjectManager`. `PersistChanges` writes the changes that you've made to back to the database. `Resync` refetches the data from the database and refreshes the state of all the objects in the `ObjectManager`. This writes over the current state of the objects if the state has been changed after the objects were fetched.

Patterns and Mapping

Because the ObjectSpaces API is based on mapping object types to columns, tables, and views, and other items in databases, before we go any further, we must look at mapping different object-relational paradigms in detail. We'll do this in conjunction with looking at the mapping syntax. Although you won't be coding these maps by hand, it makes the similarities and differences between object relationships and table relationships stand out.

Type and Relationship in the Mapping File

The mapping file is just a variation of the mapping format we discussed in the previous chapter, with an "object schema" as a `DataTarget` and a relational database as a `DataSource`. ObjectSpaces uses an XML format to correlate relational data to .NET class definitions and to represent advanced constructs in the case where mapping is not one class per table. The object `DataTarget` information is defined in an XML format known as object schema definition. Because most of the object-oriented constructs are defined as part of the class hierarchy itself and you can obtain this information using reflection in .NET, the OSD format only defines the following:

- Information for defining the persistent subset of the class for the ObjectSpaces persistence engine
- Relationships between types—for example, a one-to-many relationship or an inheritance relationship
- Information that is used for advanced persistence features— for example, description of a database-defined primary key.

Here is a simple example of the OSD information generated for three related classes, the Customer, Order, and OrderDetail classes, where there is a one-to-many relationship between Customer and Order and between Order and OrderDetail.

```
// class definitions for one-to-many relationships
public class CCustomer
{
  public string CustId;
  public string CustName;
  public string Company;
  public string Phone;
  public List<COrder> Orders;
}

public class COrder
{
  public string OrderId;
  public DateTime OrderDate;
  public DateTime ShipDate;
  public double Freight;
  public CCustomer Customer;
  public List<COrderDetails> Details;
}

public class COrderDetail
{
  public string OrderId;
  public DateTime ProductId;
  public Decimal Price;
  public int Qty;
  public Decimal discount;
}


<osd:ExtendedObjectSchema Name="OpathDBOBJ"
 xmlns:osd=
 "http://schemas.microsoft.com/data/2002/09/20/persistenceschema">
 <osd:Classes>
  <osd:Class Name="CCustomer">
  <osd:Member Name="CustId" Key="true" />
  <osd:Member Name="CustName" />
  <osd:Member Name="Company" />
  <osd:Member Name="Phone" />
  <osd:Member Name="Orders" />
  </osd:Class>
  <osd:Class Name="COrder">
   <osd:Member Name="OrderId" Key="true" />
   <osd:Member Name="CustId" Hidden="true" />
   <osd:Member Name="OrderDate" />
```

```
    <osd:Member Name="ShipDate" />
    <osd:Member Name="Freight" />
    <osd:Member Name="Customer" />
    <osd:Member Name="OrderDetails" />
  </osd:Class>
  <osd:Class Name="COrderDetail">
    <osd:Member Name="OrderId" Key="true" />
    <osd:Member Name="ProductId" Key="true" />
    <osd:Member Name="Price" />
    <osd:Member Name="Qty" />
    <osd:Member Name="Discount" />
  </osd:Class>
 </osd:Classes>
 <osd:ObjectRelationships>
  <osd:ObjectRelationship Name="CustomerOrders"
     ParentClass="CCustomer" ParentMember="Orders"
     ChildClass="COrder" ChildMember="Customer"
     ParentCardinality="1" ChildCardinality="*" />
  <osd:ObjectRelationship Name="OrderDetails"
     ParentClass="COrder" ParentMember="OrderDetails"
     ChildClass="COrderDetail"
     ParentCardinality="1" ChildCardinality="*" />
 </osd:ObjectRelationships>
</osd:ExtendedObjectSchema>
```

There are a few interesting extensions defined by the OSD format for these classes. Note the use of the `Key="true"` attribute to define which fields in the class correspond to keys in the database. Multiple `Key="true"` attributes for items in the same class correspond to a composite primary key in the database. This has nothing to do with traditional object-oriented concepts, but is provided only to assist in managing instance state. Note that although there is a `CustomerID` member in the `COrder` class, there is also a field that is a reference to the corresponding `Customer` instance. Also, the `osd:Member` for `OrderId`, `ProductId`, and most of the other fields is a simple data type; `osd:Member` for `OrderDetails` in the `COrder` class is likely to correspond to a generic collection class like `List<T>` or even an "ordinary" collection class like `Array` or `ArrayList`. We indicate the direction and cardinality as attributes of the relationship in the `Object Relationship` element. Child and parent cardinality are specified separately. `ParentClass` and `ChildClass` indicate the relationship direction. The most interesting part of the `ObjectRelationship` element is the definition of `ParentMember` and `ChildMember`. `ParentMember` is the field in the parent class that is the collection of child instances; conversely, `Child Member` is the field in the child instance that represents the parent instance. This is in addition to defining the corresponding keys.

Mapping Elements and One-to-Many Relationships

Now that we've defined the object schema and relational schema in XML format, all that remains is to use the mapping elements to define the persistence behavior of the graph. You've already seen the `<DataSources>` section of the mapping file in the simple example. ObjectSpaces supports either an external schema location for mapping files; or using an inline schema.

ObjectSpaces supports the three most common relationships among classes based on designing classes around traditional relational design. Figure 14-5 shows these.

The mapping elements are from a different namespace than either the object elements or the relational data elements, although the namespace for MSD is used in the `<DataSources>` section and in a separate `<Mappings>` section. The persistence behavior usually has more to do with mapping tables to class members and mapping object relationships to relational keys and relationships than the inheritance or other object relationship concepts. As in SQLXML, we define one `<Map>` element for each unique mapping of source to destination variables. This includes class-to-"table" mappings, field mappings, and relationship mappings. We'll complete our example of a simple mapping file and move on to describing how the advanced mapping concepts would be used.

```
<!-- Mapping schema file -->
<m:MappingSchema
xmlns:m="http://schemas.microsoft.com/mapping/2003/06/msd">
<m:DataSources>
 <m:DataSource Name="NorthwindRSD">
  <m:Schema Location="Northwind.rsd"/>
 </m:DataSource>
 <m:DataTarget Type="Object">
  <m:Schema Location="Northwind.osd"/>
 </m:DataTarget>
 </m:DataSources>
<m:Mappings>
 <m:Map Source="Customer" Target="CCustomer">
  <m:FieldMap SourceField="customerID" TargetField="CustId" />
  <m:FieldMap SourceField="contactName" TargetField="ContactName" />
  <m:FieldMap SourceField="companyName" TargetField="CompanyName" />
  <m:RelationshipMap Source="FK_CustomerOrder" Target="Orders"/>
 </m:Map>
 <m:Map Source="Order" Target="COrder">
  <m:FieldMap SourceField="OrderID" TargetField="OrdId" />
  <m:FieldMap SourceField="OrderDate" TargetField="OrderDate" />
  <m:FieldMap SourceField="Freight" TargetField="Freight" />
  <m:RelationshipMap Source="FK_CustomerOrder" Target="Customer" />
```

```
  <m:RelationshipMap Source="FK_OrdersDetails" Target="OrderDetails"/>
  </m:Map>
  <m:Map Source="OrderDetail" Target="COrderDetail">
   <m:FieldMap SourceField="OrderID" TargetField="OrderId" />
   <m:FieldMap SourceField="ProductID" TargetField="ProductId" />
   <m:FieldMap SourceField="Price" TargetField="Price" />
   <m:FieldMap SourceField="Qty" TargetField="Qty" />
   <m:FieldMap SourceField="Discount" TargetField="Discount" />
  </m:Map>
  </m:Mappings>

  </Mapping Schema>
```

This portion of the mapping schema contains a simple one-to-one mapping of tables to classes, including a `<FieldMap>` for each variable that
maps columns of relational tables to fields in classes. Note that in the `<Map>`
element, there is also one `<RelationshipMap>` element for each field in the
class that comes from a relationship between the SQL tables. To map the
`Orders` field in the `CCustomer` class, you include a `<RelationshipMap>`,
naming the database relationship (`FK_CustomerOrder`) that is the source
of this field, and the field name as the target. To produce the `Customer` field
in the `Orders` table, you use the same `<RelationshipMap>` element in the
`Orders` `<Map>` with the `Target` pointing at the parent field. Also, the "parent reference" or "child reference" members of the class (the `Customer`
member in the `COrder` and the `Order` member in the `COrderDetail` class)
are not specified in the mappings. These come from the corresponding
attribute of the `<ObjectRelationship>` element in the OSD schema.

Although we've shown the intricate coding details of the mapping file
in this simple one-to-many example, as we describe other mappings, we
won't pay as much attention to the coding of the MSD file. The reason for
this is, with all but the most trivial examples, you'll actually be "writing"
these files with the graphic mapping tool.

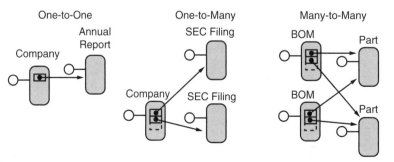

FIGURE 14-5: Common Object Relationships

Mapping Zero-or-One-to-One Relationships

Although the zero-or-one-to-one relationship might be considered a specialized case of a zero-or-one-to-many relationship, in the relational space this is not necessarily a simple primary key/foreign key relationship as with one-to-many. In addition, in the ObjectSpaces API, whether a relationship is one-to-one or one-to-many means using different collection classes if you want to enable lazy instantiation (using `IObjectHolder` or `IObject List`).

In the relational space, you could map one-to-one relationships as follows:

- A common primary key
- A single (one-way) foreign key relationship
- Two symmetric foreign key relationships

This affects the behavior and possible representations of the corresponding classes. Using a common primary key makes the relationship in the object domain read-only, because ObjectSpaces doesn't support updating primary key equivalents in objects. Deleting one side of the relationship (one instance) will cause the other instance to be specified, unless zero-or-one cardinality is specified. Cascading deletes and cascading updates are supported by ObjectSpaces and mapping, or they can happen on the server (through declarative integrity constraints) or as part of the SQL generated by ObjectSpaces. When a single foreign key relationship is used, if one side is inserted or updated, the other may be inserted or updated manually, or it will be set to null by default. Deleting one side of the relationship can result in a cascading delete, setting the other side to a default value (manually) or null. With a symmetric foreign key relationship, the ObjectSpaces engine and the `ObjectManager` have enough information to set the corresponding relation field automatically.

Mapping Many-to-Many Relationships

Many-to-many relationships are usually represented in relational databases by using a separate relationship (join) table. For example, if one author can write more than one book and any book title may have more than one author, there is bound to be a table named "titleauthor." In ObjectSpaces and mapping, this is accomplished by having a "logical" `<Relationship>` element in the RSD file that relates the two sides of the many-to-many. You do not even need to define the join table as part of the object model unless it contains fields that you are interested in. Each class in a many-to-many relationship has a corresponding List<T> (or other collection class, like ObjectList<T>) for members of the other class. You maintain these manually in the program, and ObjectSpaces flushes the correct updates back to the database.

Implementing Inheritance in a Relational Database Using Mappings

Inheritance relationships don't map naturally or easily to relational database relationships. In fact, this may be the salient point in the "object-relational mapping mismatch" argument. Ambler's original article discusses an abstract Person class and two concrete subclasses, Customer and Employee, and looks at the following three ways to map inheritance, and the possible strengths and drawbacks of each one:

- One table per class
- One table per concrete class
- One table per hierarchy with all the fields from the most derived class, using a discriminator column in the table to indicate which class is used

In all these cases, there are multiple <Map> elements, one for each abstract and concrete class. In each case, the object (OSD) portion of the schema uses the can inherit attribute to indicate inheritance, but the details of the inheritance hierarchy come from the classes themselves. Mapping tools will use reflection to extract this information. Mapping one table per concrete or abstract class requires no special elements or subelements. Using one table per hierarchy with a discriminator field to distinguish between the classes is accomplished by specifying multiple <Map> elements that point to the same table, with a LimitField attribute on the discriminator field. This is shown next.

```
<! - Mappings section  ->
   <m:Mappings>
      <! - abstract base class, no LimitValue  ->
      <m:Map Name="PersonMap" Source="Employees" Target="Person">
         <m:FieldMap SourceField="EmployeeID" TargetField="Id" />
         <m:FieldMap SourceField="LastName" TargetField="LastName" />
         <m:FieldMap SourceField="FirstName" TargetField="FirstName" />
```

```
            <m:FieldMap SourceField="BirthDate" TargetField="BirthDate" />
        </m:Map>
        <m:Map Ref="PersonMap" Target="Employee">
            <m:FieldMap SourceField="HireDate" TargetField="HireDate" />
            <m:FieldMap SourceField="Type" LimitValue="E" />
            <m:RelationshipMap Source="FK_Manager" Target="Manager"/>
        </m:Map>
        <m:Map Ref="PersonMap" Target="Manager">
            <m:FieldMap SourceField="Type" LimitValue="M" />
            <m:RelationshipMap Source="FK_Manager" Target="Employees"/>
        </m:Map>
    </m:Mappings>
```

Asymmetric Mapping and Other Common Mapping Patterns

Asymmetric mapping refers to mapping one table to multiple classes or one class to multiple tables, as shown in Figure 14-6. Mapping one table to multiple classes using the `Ref` attribute was shown in the previous example. A common example of mapping one class to multiple tables has to do with the way addresses are commonly represented in data models.

Let's look at the example of a `Customer` class that has a structure that corresponds to the customer's address. However, the relational database designers have decided to abstract the address information into a separate table, perhaps to enforce a standard address-validation routine. This can be represented as a special "composite" syntax in the `TargetField` value of the `FieldMap` for the composite class.

```
<! - Mappings section  ->
  <m:Map Source="Customer" Target="Cust">
  <m:FieldMap SourceField ="CustomerID" TargetField="customerId"/>
```

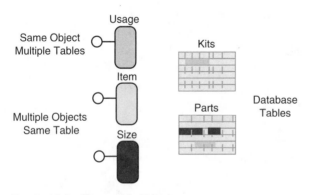

FIGURE 14-6: Asymmetric Mapping

```
  <m:FieldMap SourceField ="ContactName" TargetField="name"/>
  <m:FieldMap SourceField ="Street" TargetField ="Address.street" />
  <m:FieldMap SourceField ="City" TargetField ="Address.city" />
  <m:FieldMap SourceField ="State" TargetField ="Address.state" />
  <m:FieldMap SourceField ="Zip" TargetField ="Address.zip" />
</m:Map>
```

In addition to these two simple asymmetric relationships, ObjectSpaces also supports:

* Distinguishing between association and composition—Whether or not the lifetime of the inner object corresponds to the lifetime of the outer object and whether the inner is explicitly fetched when the outer object is.

* Mapping repeated database fields to an array—Address1, Address2, and Address3 in the database map to Address[3] in the object model.

* Using the same class in multiple persistence classes—The address class is used in the employee class and the shipping class.

* Read-only denormalized properties of child classes; for example, an `Order` class that contains a `Customer` class, but you are not allowed to change the `Customer` information through the `Order`.

* Nested classes.

* Mapping a UDT to a class or a portion of a class.

Management of Object IDs

Object identity is a central concept of object-oriented design. In memory, object identity is the memory address of the object—two reference variables, `cust1` and `cust2`, of type `Customer` are equal if they are references to the same instance of `Customer`. In object-oriented database systems, this has to be made concrete by assigning each object an object identifier (OID). Although this sounds like a natural mapping to a SQL Server identity column, identity columns aren't an option in multimaster replication scenarios. In this case, a GUID (`UNIQUEIDENTIFIER` in SQL Server) as a primary key could be used. In addition, some designers prefer user-specified primary key algorithms because of fear about `IDENTITY` or GUID locking them into a specific database product, or of the performance implications of using a GUID as a primary key in SQL Server.

ObjectSpaces mapping supports automatically managing `IDENTITY` and GUID columns by annotations on the column in the RSD portion of the schema (`AutoIncrement` and `GuidType`, respectively). In addition, a special set of attributes on the `<Member>` element allow you to specify that a .NET method can be used to generate a primary key according to a user-defined algorithm. This will then be used in persistence. Note that a synthetic key like a GUID does not have to be exposed. You can use the `hidden` attribute on the field in the OSD definition.

ObjectSpaces also supports key composition, in which, for example, the part key is actually made up of two keys from other tables. This is through mapping and a special interface for using "entity keys," in which an object can "find" its parent through a portion of the key.

Maintaining Object Identity and State

`ObjectManager` is the class that acts as a container for the state of type instances that will be persisted to the database. It also tracks object identity, allowing you to have two instance variables that represent the same instance in the database. The `ObjectSpace` class manages database interaction by using an `ObjectManager` class to keep track of the state of each instance managed by the `ObjectSpace`. The `ObjectManager` keeps track of the original values of each instance as well as tracking changes made to existing instances and instance deletions. A `Manager` property is associated with each `ObjectSpace` instance; `ObjectSpace` implements `IObject Tracking` and delegates those calls to its `ObjectManager` instance.

Type instances are associated with an `ObjectManager` by adding them to a collection managed by an `ObjectSpace`. An `ObjectSet` usually shares the `ObjectManager` with the `ObjectState` that created it, except in special cases. When using remoting or Web Services, it might have its own distinct `ObjectManager`. Adding an instance to an `ObjectManager` does nothing immediately with respect to the database, but simply tells the `Object Manager` to manage the instance. With new instances, a separate method, `StartTracking`, is used to add an instance. Instances obtained through `GetObjectSet` or `GetObject` are always added to the manager as they are processed; instances obtained with `GetObjectReader` and related classes are not added to the manager. The `ObjectManager` manages object identity by assigning each instance a unique identifier; this is not necessarily the same as the database's primary key. The `ObjectManager` also keeps track of the state of each instance with respect to the database. Each instance has an `ObjectState` that identifies whether the instance is known to the `ObjectManager` and whether the instance would be `Inserted`,

TABLE 14-1: ObjectState Enumeration

ObjectState	Meaning
Inserted	The object is a newly created object that does not exist at the data source. This is the default, if no ObjectState is specified when calling StartTracking.
Modified	The object is a persistent object that exists at the data source with the current property values of the added object. Because the ObjectManager has no information about the added object before the call to StartTracking, adding an object with ObjectState. Modified will result in the current and original versions of the object data being identical.
Deleted	The object is a persistent object that exists at the data source with the current property values of the added object. The object will be deleted from the data source when updates in the current ObjectManager are persisted.
Removed	The object has been removed with the set of instances tracked by ObjectManager. The object will not be deleted from the data source when updates in the current ObjectManager are persisted.
Unchanged	The object is a persistent object that exists at the data source with the current property values of the added object.
Unknown	The ObjectManager does not contain information regarding the specified object. You cannot add an object to a manager with ObjectState.Unknown.

Deleted, Modified, Removed, or remain Unchanged if the ObjectSpace were "told" to update the database. The ObjectState enumeration is shown in Table 14-1.

Here's an example of adding an object to an ObjectManager and querying for its ObjectState.

```
public static void Main()
{
  string connect_string = GetConnectStringFromConfigFile();
  SqlConnection conn = new SqlConnection(connect_string);

  ObjectSpace os = new ObjectSpace("mappings.msd", conn);
  ObjectManager mgr = os.Manager;

  Person p1 = new Person();
  Person p2 = new Person();
```

```
    os.StartTracking(p1, ObjectState.Inserted);

    // prints ObjectState.Inserted
    Console.WriteLine(mgr.GetObjectState(p1));

    // prints ObjectState.Unknown
    Console.WriteLine(mgr.GetObjectState(p2));

    // update the database
    os.PersistChanges(p1);

    // prints ObjectState.Unchanged
    Console.WriteLine(mgr.GetObjectState(p1));

    p1.Name = "Fred";
    // prints ObjectState.Modified
    Console.WriteLine(mgr.GetObjectState(p1));
}
```

In addition to adding an instance to an `ObjectManager` using `Start`
`Tracking` with an `ObjectState.Inserted`, you can use `ObjectState.`
`Modified`. This could be useful for optimizing deletion of existing instances,
although ObjectSpaces may have a better optimization for this in the future.
For example, suppose you knew that a `Person` with a unique identifier
of 42 existed in the data store, and you wanted to delete the `Person` without having to make a trip to the data store just to get the `Person` out. You
could accomplish this with the following code.

```
public static void Main()
{
    string connect_string = GetConnectStringFromConfigFile();
    SqlConnection conn = new SqlConnection(connect_string);
    ObjectSpace os = new ObjectSpace("mappings.msd", conn);

    Person p1 = new Person();
    p1.Id = 42;

    os.StartTracking(p1, ObjectState.Modified);
    os.MarkForDeletion(p1);

    // Delete person 42 from the database
    os.PersistChanges(p1);
}
```

`ObjectManagers` are cumulative with respect to instances. If we add
an instance to the `ObjectManager`, and use it to update the data store,
and then add more instances, the `ObjectManager` contains the original

instance that we added in addition to all the new instances. There is only one instance per identity, however.

When you are managing a collection of objects, you can remove an instance from the collection by using the collection's Remove method. Remove simply removes the instance from the ObjectManager; that is, the ObjectManager no longer controls its interoperation with the database. You can only cause any instance, whether or not it's a member of a collection, to be deleted in the database by calling MarkForDeletion on the ObjectSpace or ObjectManager, with the instance as a parameter. Finally, you can cause the ObjectManager to stop tracking any instance by calling EndTracking on the ObjectSpace or ObjectManager, with the instance as a parameter.

Notice that until this point, we have used the ObjectSpace.Persist Changes method on a single instance managed by an ObjectManager. If you define a collection of instances, it is possible to update the entire collection at the same time by calling an overload of PersistChanges or using the ObjectSpace's PersistAllChanges method. PersistChanges just goes through each member of the collection, checking the original and current state of the instance. This makes a single round-trip to the database. Notice that we've used an Array in this case, but any class that implements ICollection can be used. Here's an example.

```
public static void Main()
{
    string connect_string = GetConnectStringFromConfigFile();
    SqlConnection conn = new SqlConnection(connect_string);
    ObjectSpace os = new ObjectSpace("mappings.msd", conn);
    Author[] a = new Author[2];

    // create two Author instances and initialize
    a[0] = new Author();
    a[0].Id = "111-11-1111";
    // remainder of initialization elided for clarity


    a[1] = new Author();
    a[1].Id = "111-11-1112";
    // remainder of initialization elided for clarity

    // Add them to the ObjectManager
    os.StartTracking(a[0], ObjectState.Inserted);
    os.StartTracking(a[1], ObjectState.Inserted);

    // Use them to update the database
    os.PersistChanges(a);
}
```

`ObjectSpace.PersistChanges` uses optimistic concurrency semantics with respect to the database. You can also use an optional `Persistence Option` parameter to persist the entire graph at the same time, or persist all of the changes in any of the instances managed by an `ObjectSpace` using `PersistAllChanges`.

In order for you to handle exceptions that may occur during object persistence, it is instructive to understand how persistence works under the hood. The ObjectSpaces infrastructure issues parameterized UPDATE and DELETE commands to the database based on keeping track of multiple occurrences of the same instance. Special methods on the base `ObjectManager` class, `GetCurrentValueRecord` and `GetOriginalValueRecord`, allow you to get the values that will be used. `ObjectSpace.Resync` gets the current values from the database and replaces both the original and current values in its built-in `ObjectManager`. You can specify which fields are used in optimistic concurrency by specifying the attribute `UseForConcurrency` in a per-field basis in the mappings. Additional annotations in the mappings file allow you to use a timestamp or row version field for concurrency and additionally hide it from the class instance. This field would then be managed only by the `ObjectManager`.

Reading Objects with an ObjectReader

An `ObjectReader` is produced by a query against the database that returns a collection of instances. You create an `ObjectReader` (and execute the corresponding database query) by calling the `GetObjectReader` method on the `ObjectSpace`. The `ObjectReader` reads instances one instance at a time, using the `Read` method. The `Read` method returns `false` when there are no more instances to read. An `ObjectReader` must be closed by calling the `Close` method after reading all the instances, to free up the underlying database connection.

`GetObjectReader` is a generic method that takes an `ObjectQuery`, a `CompiledQuery`, or a simple OPath expression. To read all the instances from the database, specify an empty string as an OPath expression. Here's an example that reads all the `Customer` instances from the database.

```
public static void Main()
{
  string connect_string = GetConnectStringFromConfigFile();
  SqlConnection conn = new SqlConnection(connect_string);
  ObjectSpace os = new ObjectSpace("mappings.msd", conn);

  ObjectReader<Customer> ordr = os.GetObjectReader<Customer>("");
```

```
  foreach (Customer a in ordr)
    Console.WriteLine("customer {0} found", a.Id);
  // don't forget to close the reader
  ordr.Close();
}
```

Notice that in this simple example, we're just reading objects from the database and printing out one of the fields. An `ObjectReader` does not add instances that it fetches to the `ObjectSpace`. Here's a variation of the first program that updates each instance as it is read, and attempts `PersistChanges` to apply the updates to the database; this will not update any rows.

```
public static void Main()
{
  string connect_string = GetConnectStringFromConfigFile();
  SqlConnection conn = new SqlConnection(connect_string);

  ObjectSpace os = new ObjectSpace("mappings.msd", conn);

  ObjectReader<Customer> ordr = os.GetObjectReader<Customer>("");
  foreach (Customer c in ordr)
    {
    Console.WriteLine("customer {0} found", a.Id);
    a.Contract = true;
    }
  // don't forget to close the reader
  ordr.Close();

  // no rows are updated in the database
  os.PersistAllChanges();
}
```

Readers familiar with the ADO.NET `DataReader` may notice a lot of similarity between the `ObjectReader` and the `DataReader` with respect to instance navigation. As with the ADO.NET `DataReader`, `ObjectReader` implements `IEnumerable`, and it can be used as a `DataSource` with ASP. NET WebForms data binding. Here's an example of binding an `Object Reader` to a `ComboBox`.

```
public class MyASPNetPage : System.Web.UI.Page
{
  public ComboBox combo1;

  void Page_Load()
  {
  string connect_string = GetConnectStringFromConfigFile();
  SqlConnection conn = new SqlConnection(connect_string);
```

```
ObjectSpace os = new ObjectSpace("mappings.msd", conn);

ObjectReader<Order> ordr = os.GetObjectReader<Order>("");

combo1.DataSource = ordr;
combo1.DataTextField = "orderid";
combo1.DataBind();
ordr.Close();
}
```

Although an `ObjectReader` may encapsulate a `SqlDataReader`, there is currently no way to obtain the underlying `SqlDataReader` or `IData Reader` interface. There is, however, a low-level way to create a class called `DbObjectReader` on the fly from an existing `IDataReader` You would simply make a new `DbDataReader` generic class using the constructor that takes an `IDataReader`, a `MappingSchema`, and an optional `ObjectManager`.

ObjectSet

When you just want to add a collection of `Customer` instances to the database, it is wasteful to use a database connection and obtain an `Object Reader` with no objects, just to associate a collection of objects with an `ObjectManager`. You may also want to manage your object collections inside an `ObjectSpace` as a cache. You might use the cache with a Windows Forms graph interface and have the `ObjectManager` work in concert with the `BindingContext` in Windows Forms data binding. The `Object Set` provides an alternative to the `ObjectReader` for these purposes.

You can create an `ObjectSet` from the results of an `ObjectQuery` using a factory method on the `ObjectSpace` class.

```
// create an ObjectSpace only to parse the mappings
string connect_string = GetConnectStringFromConfigFile();
SqlConnection conn = new SqlConnection(connect_string);
ObjectSpace os = new ObjectSpace("mappings.msd", conn);

// create an ObjectSet filled with Customer instances
ObjectSet<Customer> oset = os.GetObjectSet<Customer>("");
```

You can also create an `ObjectSet` by using its constructor and using a `MappingSchema` and an optional `ObjectManager`, although this will usually only be used along with data obtained through remoting or Web Services. An `ObjectSet` is almost always managed by the `ObjectSpace` that is used to create it, although in remoting scenarios, it may have a separate `ObjectManager`.

```
// create an ObjectSchema to parse the mappings
// or acquire it through a remote method call
ObjectSchema oschema = new ObjectSchema("mappings.msd");

// create an ObjectSet of Customer instances
ObjectSet<Customer> oset = new ObjectSet<Customer>(oschema);
```

ObjectSet is a specialized collection class that implements an additional interface, IBindingList, to permit it to be managed by the Binding Context in Windows Forms. The IBindingList interface contains properties that allow the programmer to control whether members can be added, updated, or deleted. These properties are used by some of the Windows Forms controls like the DataGrid to control presentation features. For example, if IBindingList.AllowInsert is set to True, the DataGrid will contain a blank row for the user to enter new data.

IBindingList can be used to allow controls to sort the list and to be notified when the list changes. The ObjectSet supports both sorting and notifications through a related private class, ObjectSetView. ObjectSet is able to retrieve the ObjectSetView by implementing IListSource. IListSource is just a class that permits Windows Forms data binding to use the class that implements IListSource to retrieve a class that implements IList.

In addition to the functionality exposed by IBindingList and IList Source, the classes that you use with ObjectSpaces can support the IEditableObject interface to permit rich editing using Windows Forms controls. Supporting IEditableObject allows you to begin an edit operation on an instance of the class and commit or roll back the edit. In other words, IEditableObject makes changes to the instance "transactional." In order to support IEditableObject, you have to keep multiple copies of your instance state (to support rollback called IEditableObject. CancelEdit) and keep track of when an instance is deleted during an edit, so that you might "restore" it should the user call CancelEdit. You commit an IEditableObject by using EndEdit. The three methods of IEditableObject are shown next.

```
interface IEditableObject
{
    void BeginEdit();
    void CancelEdit();
    void EndEdit();
}
```

The ObjectSpaces Query Model

Whenever you query for an `ObjectReader` or an `ObjectSet`, you can specify an `ObjectQuery` to indicate which objects to retrieve and how much of the graph will be retrieved. Until now, when we've retrieved an `Object Reader` or an `ObjectSet`, we've either retrieved the entire set (`GetObject Reader` with an empty string and a generic type that indicates which class we wish to get) or retrieved a discrete subset of instances (`GetObject Reader` with an OPath predicate). We'll discuss the specifics of OPath in the next sections, but note that these are just shortcut methods that create an `ObjectQuery` behind the scenes. For example, these two queries, which retrieve `Customers` from Oregon, as shown in Figure 14-7, are identical and retrieve only the `Customers` in Oregon.

```
// convenience overload
ObjectSet<Customer> oset = os.GetObjectSet<Customer>("State = 'OR'");

// equivalent explicit query
ObjectQuery<Customer> oq = new ObjectQuery<Customer>("State = 'OR'");
ObjectSet<Customer> oset = os.GetObjectSet<Customer>(oq);
```

Much of the time, using the convenience overloads will be sufficient, but you would want to use a specific class that encapsulates query capabilities if you want to compile and query, and save it for later use. The members of the `ObjectQuery` are shown in Table 14-2; they are also members of the `BaseQuery` class.

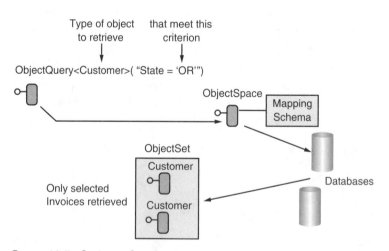

FIGURE 14-7: Customer Query

TABLE 14-2: Properties of the ObjectQuery Class

Property	Type	Meaning	In Base?
Aliases	QueryAliasList	Field aliases	Y
BaseTypeOnly	Boolean	Should derived types' properties be returned?	Y
CommandTimeout	int	Database command timeout	Y
IsolationLevel	IsolationLevel	Database transaction isolation level	Y
ObjectType	Type	Top-level object type	Y
Parameters	OPathParameters Collection	OPath parameters	Y
Query	OPathExpression	Complete OPath expression	N
QueryJoin	QueryJoin	Parameters for arbitrary joins	Y
QueryOrderBy	QueryOrderBy	Order by list	Y
QuerySelectList	SelectList	Fields to be selected	N
ResultAlias	QueryAlias	Name of the query result	Y
ReturnKeys	Boolean	Should keys be returned?	N
Span	Span	Span specification	Y
WhereExpression	WhereExpression	"Where" portion of OPath expression	Y

The second feature is accomplished by using the Compile method of the ObjectSpace class to produce an instance of the CompiledQuery class. You can execute a CompiledQuery (which contains the underlying SQL statement) multiple times with different parameters. In addition, a CompiledQuery can contain parameter defaults—the values set before compiling it. Instances of CompiledQuery can also be serialized to disk for later use. You specify parameters in an OPath expression using names beginning with an at sign, as SQL Server does.

Here's an example of building an `ObjectQuery` from scratch, compiling it, and executing it using parameters. Compile is a method on `Object Space` because the `ObjectSpace`'s underlying mappings are used to compile the query, in the step that creates the corresponding SQL statements.

```
// create the compiled query
ObjectQuery GetCityStateQuery(ObjectSpace os)
{
  // use the convenience method
  ObjectQuery<Customer> oq = new ObjectQuery<Customer>(
      "City=@City and State=@State");

  oq.QueryOrderBy.Add("Company", OrderByDirection.Descending);
  return (os.Compile(oq));
}

// use it to create an ObjectSet
void UseCityStateQuery(CompiledQuery cq, string city, string state)
{
  OPathParameterTable parms = cq.CreateParameterTable();
  parms["City"].Value = city;
  parms["State"].Value = state;

  ObjectSet<Customer> oset = os.GetObjectSet<Customer>(cq, parms);
}
```

OPath Language Essentials

OPath is a predicate language that specifies the equivalent of a "where clause" in SQL. It can be used in conjunction with an `ObjectQuery` or `CompiledQuery`, or standalone in instance-returning methods, although this actually creates an `ObjectQuery` under the covers. The following statement:

```
ObjectQuery<Customer> oq = new ObjectQuery<Customer>("State = 'OR'");
```

uses an OPath predicate that narrows the retrieval to customers in Oregon. You can use OPath operators to qualify predicates or group predicates to indicate their order of execution. OPath uses a simple but powerful set of operators, and provides alternate operators for programmers that are most familiar with C# or Visual Basic syntax. Table 14-3 lists the OPath operators in order of precedence.

Most of the operators are familiar from other query languages or programming languages, although some programmers might not be familiar with the difference between division (the result of a mathematic divide of

TABLE 14-3: OPath Operators

Operator	Symbol
Primary	., [ ], ( )
Unary	!, not
Multiplication, division, modulus	*, /, %
Addition	+, -
Comparison	<, >, <=, >=
Equality	=, !=, <>, ==
Conditional AND	and, &&
Conditional OR	or, ‖

two numbers) and modulus (also called the remainder of a division expression). The primary operators—dot, square brackets, and parentheses—however, allow you to use OPath to query graphs at different levels of the graph, and we'll explain these in detail now.

The dot is meant to separate parent-child portions of the graph. If, for example, we have a hierarchical graph containing Customers, Orders, and OrderDetails and want to find any customer that has orders with any detail item that costs over $50, we could phrase the OPath query like this:

```
Orders.OrderDetails[cost > 50]
```

using the dot notation to separate the levels of the object graph. Note that the entire ObjectQuery need not specify the "root type" as well—the type that is the root of the search. The ObjectQuery for this example, which returns (only) Customers instances, would be this.

```
ObjectQuery<Customer> oq = new ObjectQuery<Customer>(
    "Exists (Orders.OrderDetails[cost > 50])");
```

In addition to the dot operator, you can use the circumflex (^) operator to enable navigation from child to parent. This example:

```
ObjectQuery<Customer> oq = new ObjectQuery<Customer>(
    " Exists (Orders.OrderDetails[cost > 50]and ^.^.State = 'OR'])");
```

will use the `OrderDetails.cost` property and the `Customers.State` property inside the filter. Here the parent-child relationship is with respect to a navigation path—not the object model. The object model can be a graph instead of a tree, so there may be multiple parents—but a navigation path is guaranteed to have a unique parent for any element.

Another point to notice about the primary operators is that when the square brackets are used, as they are in XPath, the subset of the returned objects is based on a condition, as is the case when you use a SQL WHERE clause. Instead of the using the previous query to find the set of `Customer` with `Orders` where any detail item costs more than $50, we could have used the following query, which would have returned the same results.

```
ObjectQuery<Customer> oq = new ObjectQuery<Customer>(
    "Exists (Orders.OrderDetails.cost > 50");
```

Because `cost` is an attribute (field) of the `OrderDetails` object, you can either specify the "cost" as a predicate using the square brackets notation or as part of the operand that is being compared. However, if we wished to find `Customers` in Oregon that had orders with items over $50, the easiest way to do this would be to use the square brackets within the hierarchical query, like this.

```
ObjectQuery<Customer> oq = new ObjectQuery<Customer>(
    "Customers[State='OR'].Orders.OrderDetails.cost > 50");
```

You accomplish a string comparison by using single quotes and a numeric comparison by leaving the quotes out. This is similar to SQL. Parentheses can be used to change the precedence order in query evaluation, just as in other query languages.

OPath is case sensitive with respect to property names, but case insensitive with respect to language keywords, as shown in this query.

```
// base query
" Orders.OrderDetails.cost > 50 and Orders.OrderDetails.unitprice < 30"

// this produces identical results
" Orders.OrderDetails.cost > 50 AND Orders.OrderDetails.unitprice < 30"

// this is not the same
" Orders.OrderDetails.Cost > 50 AND Orders.OrderDetails.Unitprice < 30"
```

Although the OPath query syntax may look similar to program syntax, OPath queries, like SQL queries, are compiled and evaluated during program execution, not during program compilation. So the last query in the previous example would most likely produce an error (since `Order Details` does have a `cost` property but not a `Cost` property, the error will occur at execution time). However, instances of the `ObjectQuery` class can be used multiple times, saving the compilation step in subsequent uses. OPath uses the same query intermediate format as SQLXML; see Chapter 13 for a description of query compilation and execution. OPath queries can be parameterized, as we've seen earlier. Parameters can be used in predicates, filters, and functions (we'll define functions soon).

Data Types

The OPath language is used to query .NET types or to construct (through mapping) SQL queries. It therefore uses .NET types in its query evaluation, although the set of types in `System.Data.SqlTypes` (which add nullability; see Chapter 11) is also supported. The supported types include the following:

- `String`
- `DateTime`
- `TimeSpan`
- `Guid`
- Integral types (`Int16`, `Int32`, `Int64`)
- Decimal (`System.Decimal`)
- `Double`
- `System.Data.SqlTypes`

The format that you use to specify literals of these types is determined by the format accepted by the date type's `Parse` method. For example, one format that can be used for `DateTime` literals is #mm/dd/yyyy#. Note that all the supported date types, with the exception of `TimeSpan`, have corresponding equivalent types in SQL Server. Except for the numeric types, OPath does not attempt to do any type conversion or type promotion. There is, however, a `Convert` function that can be used to manually perform type conversions.

Functions and Predicates

The set of functions and predicates that OPath supports is similar to the set supported by ADO.NET Column Expression language (see the .NET

Framework documentation on `System.Data.DataColumn.Expression`, in the Class Library Reference, for details). Because these are also the functions supported by the `System.Data.DataTable.Select` method and the `System.Data.DataView.RowFilter` property, users of ADO.NET should be right at home. Tables 14-4 and 14-5 enumerate the predicates and functions supported.

As you've seen, OPath is a powerful predicate language that can be used to produce `ObjectSets` or `ObjectReaders`. You can use it to query `Objects` or, through mapping, the SQL Server database. It is most like SQL, but adds object graph inheritance navigation through the dot and circumflex operators, similar to OQL, and predicate filtering syntax through the square bracket construct, like XPath. There is also a set of functions and operators. OPath, like the XQuery, XPath, and XSLT compilers in .NET 2.0, uses the same common intermediate format as its underlying engine and shares optimization potential with these query languages by virtue of being based on the common query runtime. If OPath's functionality still isn't enough, or you'd like to use a totally different query language, Object Spaces provides hooks for this. We'll be mentioning these hooks shortly.

TABLE 14-4: OPath Supported Predicates

Predicate	Behavior
LIKE	Partial matching with wildcards like T-SQL
IN	List matching like T-SQL
IsNull	Allows checking for a NULL value (database) or a null property (object)

TABLE 14-5: OPath Supported Functions

Function	Behavior
Convert(expression, type)	Performs data type conversion
Trim(string)	Removes leading and trailing spaces
Len(string)	Gets the length of a string field
Substring(string, start) Substring(string, start, length)	Extracts a portion of a string
IIF(condition, true-result, false-result)	Handles if-else condtions

Manipulating Graphs of Related Objects — Optimizations

The major problem with object-relational mapping layers in past APIs is that they have a fixed granularity with respect to manipulating object graphs and that they are either too granular or not granular enough. In EJB 1.0 entities, for example, you could only access an entity instance through accessors at a column level; there was no way to marshal all the columns at a time. ObjectSpaces permits you to specify your object types having whatever methods you desire; getters and setters can be chunky or granular. In addition to this simple chance for optimization, ObjectSpaces offers a few ways to optimize reading and writing arrays of graphs of objects from the database to optimize performance. Some of them are part of the `Object Query`, others are refinements to the ObjectSpaces API. We'll look at them here, using the canonical `Customers-Orders-OrderDetails` graph as a demonstration vehicle.

Fetching Optimizations

The `ObjectReader` fetches a graph of objects specified by an OPath query. By default, only the type specified in the OPath query is fetched; so in the default case, the following query:

```
ObjectQuery<Customers> oq = new ObjectQuery<Customer>("");
```

retrieves only the `Customer` instances. No `Orders` or `OrderDetails` are retrieved. If we now go back to the database and retrieve `Orders` and `OrderDetails` separately, they will be added to the same `ObjectSpace` where the `Customers` live. The following code fetches the entire object graph in three server round-trips.

```
public static void Main()
{
    string connect_string = GetConnectStringFromConfigFile();
    SqlConnection conn = new SqlConnection(connect_string);

    ObjectSpace os = new ObjectSpace("mappings.msd", conn);

    ObjectSet<Customer> ordr = os.GetObjectSet<Customer>("");

    ObjectSet<Order> ordr2 = os.GetObjectSet<Order>("");

    ObjectSet<Details> ordr3 = os.GetObjectSet<Details>("");
}
```

By explicitly coding the types and instances of those types that you want, combined with the fact that the `ObjectManager` is additive (that is, adding `Order` instances to the `ObjectManager` does not disturb existing `Customer` instances), you can optimize round-trips to the database by fetching only the instances that you want.

But what if you would like to get the `Customers` that live in Oregon, their Orders and `OrderDetails` in a single database roundtrip? A common use case is for a programmer to walk the graph, fetching corresponding related instances as she goes. To minimize database round-trips if you know you're eventually going to fetch the instances, an `ObjectQuery` can specify a "span." This span indicates what specific related types should be fetched through the `ObjectSet`. An example of an `ObjectQuery` that fetches related `Order` instances, but not `OrderDetail` instances, would look like this.

```
ObjectQuery<Customer> oq = new ObjectQuery<Customer>(
                          "Customer.State = 'OR'",
                          "Orders");
```

The third parameter specifies the name of the property of the related instance that you wish to fetch. Using the property instead of the type name allows you to distinguish between two properties of the same type denoting different paths—for example, `HomeAddress` versus `WorkAddress`.

To fetch multiple related types, simply change the string to name all the types, separated by commas or dots. The following code fetches the entire graph in a single round-trip.

```
ObjectQuery<Customer> oq = new ObjectQuery<Customer>(
                          "Customer.State = 'OR'",
                          "Orders.Details");
```

Some problem domains lend themselves to delay loading of related types. Because you won't be using every instance on the client, you may only want to load related objects when an instance references them. An example of this would be a Windows Forms application that displays a large set of root instances in a grid and only needs to get the corresponding children when a user clicks on a particular row of the grid. The default behavior in ObjectSpaces, when the types are specified in an `ArrayList` like the following:

```
public class Customer
{
    public string Id;
```

```
      public string Name;
      public string Company;
      public ArrayList Orders = new ArrayList();
}

public class Order
{
  public string OrderId;
  public DateTime OrderDate;
}
public static void Main()
{
  string connect_string = GetConnectStringFromConfigFile();
  SqlConnection conn = new SqlConnection(connect_string);

  ObjectSpace os = new ObjectSpace("mappings.msd", conn);

  ObjectReader<Customer> ordr = os.GetObjectReader<Customer>("");
  foreach (Customer c in ordr)
  {
    //corresponding Orders fetched here
    Console.WriteLine("Customer {0} found", c.Id);
  }
  ordr.Close();
}
```

is to load all the Orders the first time the program references a Customer.

Sometimes, you might want to control exactly when the child instances are loaded. For this behavior, you would use an ObjectHolder for one-to-one relationships or an ObjectList for one-to-many relationships.

Types referenced through an ObjectHolder or ObjectList are only fetched when the Order is referenced through the ObjectHolder or Object List, like this.

```
public class Customer
{
    public string Id;

    public string Name;
    public string Company;
    public ObjectList<Order> Orders = new ObjectList<Order>;
}

public class Order
{
  public string OrderId;
  public DateTime OrderDate;
}

public static void Main()
{
```

```
string connect_string = GetConnectStringFromConfigFile();
SqlConnection conn = new SqlConnection(connect_string);

ObjectSpace os = new ObjectSpace("mappings.msd", conn);

ObjectReader<Customer> ordr = os.GetObjectReader<Customer>("");

bool printOrders;
foreach (Customer c in ordr)
{
  //corresponding Orders not fetched here
  Console.WriteLine("Customer {0} found", c.Id);
  // some client-side business logic here
  if (printOrders)
    // All Orders for this Customer fetched here
    foreach (Order o in c.Orders)
      Console.WriteLine("Order {0} found", o.OrderId);
}
ordr.Close();
}
```

You can also specifically refresh members of an `ObjectList` on demand by using `ObjectSpace.FetchRelatedObjects` and passing in the appropriate `Customer` instance.

Note that, in this case, it's not an optimization to use lazy loading, because ObjectSpaces makes a separate round-trip to the database per customer to fetch orders, and you may read all the orders eventually anyhow. If you don't need any of the `Orders`, you can control this with a span. When you are using an `ObjectSet` as a cache, lazy loading can be an optimization by only getting the data that you need, at the expense of possible round-trips later on.

An `ObjectHolder` or `ObjectList` is a generic container that hides delay loading. Because it is generic, the instances that it produces must be cast to the appropriate type. This can be hidden behind a public property that encapsulates the `ObjectHolder` or `ObjectList`. In the previous example, where an `Order` could also keep a reference to its corresponding `Customer` through an `ObjectHolder`, the `ObjectHolder` can be modified to use strong types. To accommodate this, the `ObjectHolder` has a member called `InnerObject`. It can be used like this.

```
public class Order
{
    public int OrderId;

    private ObjectHolder p_Customer = new ObjectHolder();
```

```
public Customer Customer
{
  get { return p_Customer.InnerObject as Customer; }
  set { p_Customer.InnerObject = value; }
}
}
```

The corresponding `Customer` instance can be accessed as `Order. Customer`, a strong type. The `ObjectList` has a corresponding property called `InnerList`.

Another fetching optimization is that the ObjectSpaces mappings file permits the use of stored procedures for fetching. This allows you to add complex business logic in the stored procedure, closer to the source of the data. This is a big performance gain when compared with fetching the entire set of objects from the database, only to eliminate some of them through business logic on the middle tier.

Updating Optimizations

We've just mentioned one of the big-win optimizations for updating: the use of stored procedures. Stored procedures can be associated with insert, update, and delete operations, just as they can with fetch operations. In addition, when we choose to update, we have the following four choices in the ObjectSpaces API:

- Using the `PersistAllChanges` method
- `PersistChanges` on a single instance, using the overload of `PersistChanges` that takes an instance
- `PersistChanges` using all the changes of an entire collection, using a different overload of `PersistChanges`
- Specifing `PersistenceOptions` when using `PersistChanges`

`PersistenceOptions` gives you two ways to control updating a graph. The `Depth` field allows you to specify whether you want a single root instance or a collection of root instances only to be updated, or you should update the entire object graph. This is an "all or root-only" enumeration; you are not allowed to specify which child should be updated in a granular fashion, as you can with a span through an `ObjectQuery`.

The second way that you control updating is to specify when an error should be thrown. ObjectSpaces uses optimistic concurrency to determine whether or not to update the database from the graph. If any of the fields in the database corresponding to an instance that you are trying to update have been changed by another user since you fetched them, the update will fail. `PersistenceOptions.ErrorBehavior` enables you to tell the ObjectSpaces engine whether, for a multiple instance update, it should throw an error when it encounters its first error, basically stopping the update in midstream, or it should throw an error after all the updates are complete, returning an `ArrayList` of errors for each instance that could not be updated. Which option you choose should be related to whether or not you are using transactions.

Transaction Optimizations

As we mentioned before, ObjectSpaces by default will not lock rows in the database when you retrieve the corresponding object instances through an `ObjectReader`. To accommodate composing multiple updates into a single atomic transaction, you can use local transactions bracketing `Persist Changes` as shown.

```
public class Customer
{
  public int Id;
  // remainder of implementation elided
}

public

public static void Main()
{
  string connect_string = GetConnectStringFromConfigFile();
  SqlConnection conn = new SqlConnection(connect_string);

  ObjectSpace os = new ObjectSpace("mappings.msd", conn);

  ObjectReader<Customer> ordr = os.GetObjectReader<Customer>("");
  ArrayList Customers = new ArrayList();
  while (ordr.Read())
  {
    Customers.Add(c);
  }
  ordr.Close();

  // make some changes to some customers
  // now update ...
  os.BeginTransaction();
  try
  {
    os.PersistAllChanges();
```

```
  }
  catch (PersistChangesException ue)
  {
    os.Rollback();
  }
}
```

Notice that this starts a local transaction and that this transaction is only "active" for the shortest possible time. In addition, ObjectSpaces has the ability to use `System.EnterpriseServices` distributed transactions using COM+. The way in which you accomplish this is to have the class that uses the `ObjectSpace` derive from the class `ServiceComponent`. To read more about using `EnterpriseServices` and how it works, refer to *Essential ADO.NET*, Chapter 3. Depending upon the transaction isolation level that is specified in the COM+ catalog, this could result in extended locking in the database and is not recommended.

Beyond the ObjectSpace Class— Customizations

At the beginning of this chapter, we mentioned that the `ObjectSpace` class is a façade class. Under the covers, it uses a class called the `ObjectEngine` to accomplish its work. Although the `ObjectSpace` and related classes will provide more than enough functionality for most users, not only can you use `ObjectEngine` directly, but you can customize other pieces of the ObjectSpaces environment as well. Customizing the API is an advanced topic, and we'll just mention the possibilities here.

`ObjectEngine` is a class that contains an instance of a parsed mapping. It is instantiated using the default `ObjectMapping`, which can be customized separately. It defines low-level interfaces and classes to permit user control for the following:

- Managing data sources and their locations
- Managing materialization and persistence of objects and graphs
- Managing and using keys
- Compiling queries and obtaining their properties
- Redirecting the sources of the objects to different locations at runtime
- Fetching related objects in a graph
- Maintaining object state

The exact details of the `ObjectEngine` class are in flux at the time of this writing, but the goal is to allow vendors of other databases or data sources to hook in to the model. In addition, `ObjectEngine` could be used to incorporate the persistence layer of an existing object model.

Mapping is customizable as well. You can split the mapping into multiple files (this is called *mapping segmentation*) and dynamically load pieces of the object model as needed at runtime by providing a class that implements `IMappingResolver`. In addition to the use in managing different applications that use different views or subsets of an enterprise-wide schema through multiple mapping files, you might use this interface to customize maps of objects to be resolved through XML schemas. Finally, mapping uses class names to load .NET types. You can customize how mapping maps the `Name` property in the OSD to the .NET type to load by implementing a custom class that implements the `ITypeLoader` interface.

Where Are We?

We've seen that, along with the extensions to the database itself for accommodating object data and XML data, ObjectSpaces provides a layer on the client or middle tier to accommodate interacting with relational data as objects, using object-relational mapping and some optimizations designed for performance. SQL Server 2005, combined with the .NET 2.0 version of the client libraries and additional paradigms for dealing with data models using client-side APIs, has given us free rein to expose and interact with our data using alternate models and alternate query languages.

We'll complete our tour with a discussion of how SQL Server 2005 includes some brand-new functionality to allow us to write certain variations of data-driven scalable applications. These are asynchronous queuing applications and notification applications.

15

SQL Server Service Broker

S QL SERVER SERVICE BROKER (SSB) is a new part of the database engine that is used to build reliable, asynchronous, message-based distributed database applications. Service Broker allows these applications to concentrate their development efforts on the issues of the problem domain in which they are going to be used. The system-level details of implementing a messaging application are delegated to Service Broker itself and can be managed independently by personnel who know the system issues.

Messaging Applications

Messaging applications are nothing new. Almost all large scalable enterprise applications use some sort of messaging infrastructure. Messaging applications take a different approach to providing a service than application based on functions. When you need a service from a message-based application, you send it a message and go on about your business. If you care, the service will some time later return to you a message concerning the status or completion of your request. Some of the compelling reasons for message-based applications are the following.

- *Deferred processing*—It may not be possible, or necessary, to perform all the work associated with a particular task at one time. For example, a stock trade to sell 100 shares cannot be completely processed when it is initially entered into a trading system; the person who enters the trade and the one who completes the processing of the trade by actually selling or buying the stock are different people separated in time. Service Broker can manage the trade from the time it is initially entered until it is completed at some later time so that an application can concentrate on implementing each phase of the processing of a trade. Service Broker is completely capable of managing deferred processing over indefinite spans of time, even months or years, and across database restarts.

- *Distributed processing*—The work associated with a task must be completed in a timely manner. However, it is often quite difficult to predict in advance how many tasks there will be and how many resources it will take to complete them. Distributed systems allow processing resources to be applied where there are needed and be incrementally expanded without changing the applications that make use of them. Service Broker allows system administrators to manage the resources in a distributed system so that the application can be developed as though all the resources it needs were always available to it.

These features are compelling because they allow an application to concentrate on its problem domain and leave tedious and difficult to implement system details to Service Broker. A number of details of system implementation for a messaging application will be unrelated to its problem domain and hard to properly implement. Improper implementation of these details results in an unreliable application. These details fall into three major areas.

- *Message order*—It is much easier to write a messaging application that receives messages in the order in which they were sent to it. In practice, messages cannot be depended on to arrive in the order in which they were sent, and may not arrive at all. Service Broker will ensure that messages are received, and received in the order in which they were sent.

- *Message correlation*—Messaging applications often require replies to the messages they send. The replies for these messages may be quite delayed in time and rarely arrive in the same order in which the messages that caused them were sent. Finding the message that caused the reply to be sent is called correlation. Service Broker can be used to manage the correlation of replies with the messages that caused them.

- *Multithreading*—A messaging application will often run on multiple threads in order to more effectively make use of system resources or more easily manage independent items of work. Resources—for example, queues and other states—are shared among all the threads in the application and, if not properly managed, will lead to two threads mutually corrupting the shared resource. This is sometimes called the "synchronizer problem" and is very difficult to prevent. Service Broker can be used to manage shared resources so that a messaging application can be written as though the synchronizer problem did not exist, but still take advantage of running on multiple threads.

SQL Server Service Broker Overview

The SQL Server Service Broker is a technology for building message-based, asynchronous, loosely coupled database applications. Service Broker makes it possible for applications to send and receive ordered, reliable, asynchronous messages. It is built into the SQL Server engine, and applications are developed using extensions to T-SQL. This allows an enterprise to leverage its existing database and/or CLR skills to build message-based applications.

Service Broker manages services that receive, process, and send messages. Multiple services may share an instance of SQL Server, use different instances of SQL Server, or do a combination of both.

Messages are sent to a service. When a message arrives at the service, it is put into a queue associated with the service. Once a message arrives in a queue, it may be processed by a program, called a service program. Any program that has access to the queue can do that processing. However, a standard way of processing these messages is to assign a stored procedure to a queue. When this is done, Service Broker will invoke that stored procedure when a message arrives in the queue.

The service may be configured to use a limited number of instances of the stored procedure so that more than one message at a time may be processed. If the service is very busy, a number of messages may build up in the queue, but eventually they are processed. Figure 15-1 shows a simple message-based system that illustrates how Service Broker invokes instances of a stored procedure so the stored procedure can process messages as they arrive in a queue.

The system in Figure 15-1 receives orders from applications and processes them. It only requires that the service program be implemented

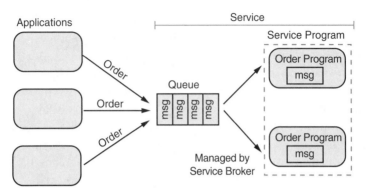

FIGURE 15-1: Simple Message-Based System

by someone who is familiar with the problem space of processing orders; everything else is configuration that can be done after the service program is written and even unit tested. The service in this example is configured to use the order service program to process the messages that arrive in its queue. The applications only need to be able to make a connection to SQL Server to be able to submit orders into the service. If there are messages in the queue, Service Broker will eventually invoke an instance of the service program. In this simple message-based system, the order service program would read the message from the queue and process it.

However, the service program is not required to process any messages in the queue at the time it is invoked; it can choose to do otherwise. In other words, Service Broker will invoke a service program when messages are available for processing, but it is up to the service program to decide whether or not to process messages in the queue.

Of course, the system illustrated in Figure 15-1 could have easily been implemented by having the applications directly call the service program itself, but this example is meant to show the basics of message processing as it is done by Service Broker. It is worth noting, however, that even this simple example limits the number of messages that will be simultaneously processed, which is a key problem in system design. Without Service Broker, this would require the implementer of the order stored procedure to have knowledge beyond the problem space of processing orders, to prevent an unexpected rush of orders from swamping the system by trying to make it process too many messages at once.

Queues are one of the two main features of Service Broker. They allow processing of messages to be deferred. A message stays in a queue until resources are available to process it. Resources may be unavailable because of the limited number of instances of a service program to process them. Most importantly, queues may be reconfigured while an application is running.

In almost all applications, there are some tasks that must be done immediately and others that can be deferred. For example, during peak load, one queue for a service processing deferrable messages might have the invocation of its service process turned off by the system administrator. And another that must process messages immediately might have the number of instances of its service process increased by the system administrator. This diverts resources to services that must process their messages immediately. When the peak passes, the system administrator can reconfigure again to allow deferred messages to again be processed. This ability to reconfigure Service Broker at runtime greatly aids in maintaining the scalability and performance of a system. Figure 15-2 shows a Service Broker application that has been configured for peak load.

In software, constructing a queue is very easy; in fact, the .NET Framework includes the `System.Collections.Queue` class to do this for you. However, the queue that can be made from this class is transient; it is meant to be used only as long as the program that created it is running.

You can't build a messaging system using the simple queues provided by `System.Collections.Queue` and similar classes, because they just are not reliable enough. Under the covers, in Service Broker a queue is implemented in a table, and messages can be removed or added to a queue using a transaction. This gives the queue in Service Broker the same features we expect of anything else that operates on data in a database—it is atomic, consistent, isolated, and durable. Basically, it is reliable.

In fact, not only does Service Broker use SQL Server to implement queues, it uses SQL Server to store and implement all aspects of a messaging

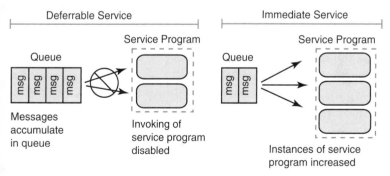

FIGURE 15-2: Service Broker Application Configured for Peak Load

application. This, then, is the second main feature of Service Broker: It provides a complete framework based on SQL Server for implementing reliable messaging applications.

It is hard to overemphasize the importance of this feature—without Service Broker or some similar framework, probably 80% of the code written for a messaging application would be for infrastructure, not the problem space of the application. The resulting framework would, of course, not be SQL Server and would require a completely different set of skills and utilities than those needed to maintain SQL Server. A Service Broker application is just a collection of SQL Server objects that can be maintained using the same skills and tools used to maintain anything else in SQL Server.

A note on terminology: Terms that refer to *type* and *instance* are often overloaded and depend on context, which is often not clear, to distinguish between which overload is being used. The term "message" might sometimes refer to the definition of the format of a message and at other times refer to an actual message. Anytime the term "message" is used in this chapter, it is referring to an actual message that complies with a message type definition; that is, it is an instance of some message type. The term "message type" will always be used to refer to a definition of a message format. This distinction is necessary because Service Broker not only manages messages, it also manages message types.

A service uses Service Broker to send a message to another service. Service Broker does this by putting the message into an output queue and then sending it, possibly at a later time, to the queue for the other service. A number of messages may build up in the output queue, waiting to be sent, but they will eventually be sent and sent in the order in which they were put into the queue.

The advantage of this extra layer of queuing is that the service sending the message never waits for anything. But the extra layer also introduces extra overhead. Service Broker will skip the output queue when both services are on the same instance of SQL Server. In this case, it will put the message directly into the queue from which the receiving service gets its messages. Figure 15-3 shows how Service Broker efficiently sends a message from one service to another.

So far we have seen a very general picture of how Service Broker is used to make messaging applications. Service Broker is a framework and extensions to T-SQL that are used to create and use the components used to build a message-based application. We have already used some of these

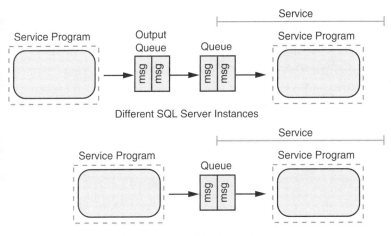

FIGURE 15-3: Sending Messages between Services

components: messages, queues, and services. Concise definitions of the components used in a Service Broker application follow.

- *Service program*—A service program is used to process messages. A service program may be a stored procedure written in T-SQL or a CLR-compliant language. A service program may also be a program written in any language that has access to SQL Server. As part of the processing of a message, the service program may send messages to other services.

- *Queue*—A queue is a component that has a name and can hold messages in the order in which they were received while the messages await processing. A queue may have a particular service program associated with it, but it is not required to.

- *Message type*—A message type is a definition of the format of a message. It is stored in SQL Server and has a name. One service communicates with another service by sending an instance of a message type. A service can only send a message for which a message type has been defined.

- *Contract*—A contract is a set of names of message types. It is stored in SQL Server and itself has a name. The contract defines nothing about the order in which the message types must occur, but each message type must be marked as being sent by an INITIATOR, a TARGET, or ANY, which determines how it may be used.

- *Service*—A service is a specification that is stored in SQL Sever and has a name. It must specify a queue that will be used to hold messages sent to it. Optionally, it may also list a set of contracts that specify the types of message that may be sent to it.

- *Conversation*—A conversation is a component that is used to correlate and order messages a service receives. It is created using the BEGIN DIALOG CONVERSATION T-SQL command and is the principal component an application uses to make use of Service Broker. Any program that has access to SQL Server, including a service program, can create a conversation.

Services communicate with each other using a conversation. When a service wants to communicate with another service, it creates a conversation.

The conversation includes a service contract, which will be used during the conversation. A conversation is between two services that are named in the BEGIN DIALOG CONVERSATION command, using the message types defined in the contract associated with the conversation.

These are some other Service Broker components used by conversations.

- *Conversation group*—A conversation group is created by Service Broker and assigned a unique identifier. A conversation group represents a user-defined set of conversations.

- *Routes*—Routes are used when conversations are created between different instances of SQL Server. They serve as a level of indirection so that the actual instance of SQL Server being used can be changed without changing any of the service programs when a target is moved.

- *Remote service bindings*—The remote service bindings associate a remote service with the user in the local database. They are used to handle authorization for the remote service and encryption of the messages exchanged with the remote service.

A trivial Service Broker application that makes use of some of these components is shown in Figure 15-4.

In this trivial Service Broker application, there is a validate service and a fulfill service. The validate service is used to validate an order. If the order is valid, the validate service sends the order to the fulfill service to have it shipped.

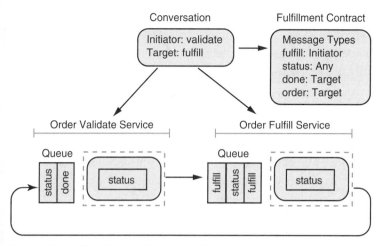

FIGURE 15-4: Trivial Service Broker Application

The fulfillment contract specifies four types of messages: fulfill, status, order, and done. The fulfill message may only be sent by the initiator. The validate service is the initiator because the dialog specifies it as the initiator. The order and done messages may only be sent by the target. The fulfill service is the target because it was specified as a target in the dialog.

The status message may be sent by either the validate or the fulfill service. In this trivial application, the status message would be sent whenever something of significance occurs in the processing of an order, to let the other service know about it. This relieves the other service of having to poll for status.

As shown in the trivial Service Broker application, the fulfill service is currently processing a message. When it is completed, it will send a done message to the validate service. It has a number of other messages in its queue waiting for processing.

The contract ensures that only messages specified can be sent only in the direction specified. An attempt by either service to send the wrong message will result in an error for that service. When the validate service receives a done message, it will use the correlation capabilities of Service Broker to figure out which fulfill message has been processed by the fulfill service.

This example shows the "big picture" of how Service Broker works and glosses over all the details. Conversations are central to understanding Service Broker. Let's take a closer look at the many facets of conversations now. We will not be looking at the details of the APIs yet; that comes later. Here we just want to present a model of how Service Broker uses conversations.

A conversation is created using BEGIN DIALOG CONVERSATION. It must list a FROM service and a TO service by name; a conversation always takes place between two services. The FROM service is, in effect, the reply-to address the TO service will use when it needs to reply to a message. Messages for the FROM service will go into the queue specified by the FROM service, and similarly for the TO service.

A conversation must also specify the contract from the set of contracts listed as being supported by the TO service. This limits the message types used in the conversation to those listed in the contract. It further limits the FROM service, in this conversation, to receiving in its queue only those message types marked as being sent by an INITIATOR or ANY. And likewise it limits the TO service to receiving in its queue only those message types marked as being sent by a TARGET or ANY.

Although you can think of "sending a message to a service," there is no way to do this directly. In fact, probably the biggest hurdle in understanding Service Broker is in understanding how it manages conversations. Messages are not sent to a service, they are sent ON a particular conversation. This is how messages are correlated and ordered; obviously, all messages sent ON the same conversation are correlated.

A service program reads a message from a queue by using the T-SQL command RECEIVE. A queue physically is a table, and in effect this selects a row from the table and then deletes it. The message includes a conversation handle, which identifies the conversation on which the message was sent.

If the service program needs to send a reply to that message, it sends the reply message on the conversation handle that was in the message it read out of the queue. This way, the service program does not need to specify the specific service as the recipient of the message. Sending messages on a conversation handle rather than to a specific service greatly simplifies creating distributed applications.

Hopefully, by this point you will be thinking, "OK, I can easily reply to any message I receive; how does the first message that starts things going get into the queue?" When a program, which could be a stored procedure or any program that has access to SQL Server, creates a conversation using BEGIN DIALOG CONVERSATION, it gets back a conversation handle. It can then send a message on that conversation handle, and the message will be sent to the queue of the TO service. From there what happens depends on the service program that reads that message out of that queue.

It is easy to see how sending messages on a conversation instead of to a service allows Service Broker to guarantee message order and correlation. However, in real-life messaging applications this is not enough. Only a trivial messaging application could depend on a single conversation between two services. A typical business process would involve many services, which means there would be many conversations. All these conversations must be coordinated for two reasons. One is to guarantee the processing order of messages across a group of conversations. The other is to allow state to be maintained for a group of conversations and used by any service program that processes messages from that group of conversations.

Service Broker calls a group of related conversations a *conversation group*. Every conversation belongs to a single conversation group, and every conversation group has a conversation group ID. Every message contains both a conversation handle and the conversation group ID of the conversation group to which the conversation belongs. An application decides if a conversation should be part of a new conversation group or added to an existing one when it creates the conversation using BEGIN DIALOG CONVERSATION.

In order to make the new conversation part of a particular conversation group, the application needs either a conversation handle or a conversation group ID to pass into BEGIN DIALOG CONVERSATION. If a conversation handle is passed in, the new conversation will be added to the conversation group of that conversation.

If a conversation group ID is passed in, it will be added to that conversation group. You might get this conversation group ID from a message you are processing, or you might just create a new conversation group with no conversations in it. You can do this by using the NEWID() function and passing the UNIQUEIDENTIFIER that it returns into BEGIN DIALOG CONVERSATION. This allows you to have the conversation group ID before you do BEGIN DIALOG CONVERSATION. Later when we look at shared state, you will see that this technique lets you set up shared state before any conversation begins.

If neither a conversation handle nor a conversation group ID is passed into BEGIN DIALOG CONVERSATION, a new conversation group is created for that conversation.

A conversation group has a lock associated with it. This lock is used to guarantee message order and manage state across all conversations in the conversation group.

The conversation group can be locked in two ways. Whenever a message is read from or sent to a queue, the conversation group associated with the message will be locked. Messages are read from a queue using the RECEIVE command and sent to a queue using the SEND command.

The second way to lock a conversation group is to use the GET CONVERSATION GROUP command. The GET CONVERSATION GROUP command is issued for a particular queue. The command locks the conversation group associated with the first message in the queue from a conversation group that is not locked. Note the logic here: The GET CONVERSATION GROUP command will skip over messages from conversation groups that are locked until it finds one from a conversation group that is not locked.

The lock associated with a conversation group has a lifetime. It remains locked until the transaction under which it was locked completes. In typical usage, a transaction will have been started before RECEIVE or GET CONVERSATION GROUP is called.

When a conversation group is locked, all threads except for the one that locked the conversation group are blocked when they try to use RECEIVE to get a message that is from the locked conversation group. A RECEIVE that attempts to get a message from a different conversation group that is not locked will not be blocked.

The RECEIVE command can be selective about which messages it will read from a queue. It can choose to receive all messages in a queue, only the messages associated with a particular conversation group, or the messages for a particular dialog.

In typical usage, a transaction is started, GET CONVERSATION GROUP is used, and then RECEIVE is used, followed by either a COMMIT TRANSACTION or a ROLLBACK TRANSACTION. If a ROLLBACK TRANSACTION is used, all messages that were read from the queue are placed back into it, and all the messages that were sent are removed from the queues that received them. Until the transaction is committed, of course, nothing that was sent is visible to the outside world.

Though it is not required, RECEIVE is typically used after a GET CONVERSATION GROUP command. Using GET CONVERSATION GROUP first will find a message from an unlocked conversation group, lock the conversation group, and then return the conversation group ID. The RECEIVE can then be used to get messages only for the conversation group that GET CONVERSATION GROUP locked, and thus is guaranteed not to block. If RECEIVE is used to indiscriminately read messages from a queue, it may become blocked if one of the messages it is trying to read from the queue is from a locked conversation group. Blocking on a RECEIVE command can lead to decreased scalability and performance.

This may seem to be a bit of a complicated way to manage a transaction. Since in fact the queue is implemented as a table with messages in it, why not just start a transaction, select out a row—that is, a message—and then delete that row, all under the transaction? Functionally, this would work but would be extremely inefficient. The problem is that the queue in most cases will be holding messages that come from many different conversation groups. Locking the entire queue, which is what a SELECT, DELETE under a transaction would be doing, prevents the queue from being read or written by anyone else. This means that all processing of messages in the queue would be stopped, not just the processing of messages for a single instance. In addition, it would prevent all new messages from being added to the queue. RECEIVE in effect does the SELECT and DELETE under a transaction in a more efficient way.

Both RECEIVE and GET CONVERSATION GROUP are each specially designed so that, in effect, you can wrap message processing for a single conversation group in a transaction without affecting the processing of messages in other conversation groups.

So, putting conversation group locks all together, in typical usage a service program would first do a BEGIN TRANSACTION, then a GET CONVERSATION GROUP, then a RECEIVE. It would obtain a message that came from some conversation group. It could then process the message, knowing that no other service process could be processing another message from the same conversation group until it either does a COMMIT TRANSACTION or ROLLBACK TRANSACTION, but still allow messages in other conversation groups to be freely processed.

To see why being able to lock a conversation group is important, let's look at an example of what might happen if we couldn't lock a conversation group. We will look at a simple service that inserts a work order into a database. A work order usually has a header that includes the location where the work is to be done and some line items that indicate the tasks to be completed. In the database there is a table for headers and another for line items that uses referential integrity to link back to the header table. This service is like the one shown in Figure 15-1 at the beginning of this chapter in that it is designed to process many messages at once.

An application starts sending messages to the queue for the work order service. First it sends a message that contains the work order header, followed by a number of messages containing line items for the work order. The header is put into the queue first, and processing is started on it first. However, as soon as processing starts on the header, another instance of the service process starts working on one of the line items. As luck would have it, the instance of the service process working on the line item finishes first and tries to insert the line item into the line item table, which fails because it violates referential integrity.

It turns out in the end, the work order would be properly inserted into the database because queues are transactional, and when the insert failed, the message would be put back into the queue and processed again later after the header had been inserted, but at the cost of a lot of overhead.

Now let's look at what happens with conversation group locks. The messages for the header and all the line items are in conversations that are in the same conversation group. The application always puts the message with the header into a queue first, followed by a message for each line item. One of the instances of the service process uses GET CONVERSATION GROUP, which, as it happens, locks the conversation group for a work order. It then uses RECEIVE to get all the messages in the queue associated with the conversation group it has just locked. This could include the header and a number of line items. It processes these in order by making INSERTs into the appropriate tables and then returns.

It may be that a second instance of the service process, running at the same time, also does a GET CONVERSATION GROUP. It may also lock a conversation group for a work order, but it will not be the same work order as the first instance locked. It will proceed to process this second work order in the same way the first instance is processing the first work order.

After the first instance of the conversation group finishes, it releases the lock on the conversation group. Then yet another instance of the service process does a GET CONVERSATION GROUP. It may end up locking the conversation group associated with the first work order and process subsequent line items that were put into queue after the first instance of the service processed completed.

There are many variations on this theme. For example, the service process might issue a second RECEIVE after it is done processing the first set of messages but before it completes the transaction, to see if any more messages have arrived for the conversation group it has locked.

There are two important things to note about this example. One is that every possible instance of a service process is running at the same time, each working on a different work order and doing so without ever blocking the others. The second is that a queue can continue receiving more messages for a conversation group even while that conversation group is locked. Neither of these things would be possible if a service process used the BEGIN TRANSACTION, SELECT, DELETE sequence to remove messages from a queue. Conversation groups and their locks are crucial to the efficient operation of Service Broker.

Another important use of a conversation group is to have a way to maintain state across the conversations in a conversation group. There is always state to be maintained in a messaging application. A trivial example of this is a messaging application that is used to process a purchase order and has to keep track of the purchase order number. It can do this in three ways. One is to keep track of the purchase order number in memory, like a local variable. The second is to put the purchase order number in every message. And the last is to put the purchase order number in a table in SQL Server. Of course, if the state involved was a just purchase order number, almost any solution would work, but in real applications there is a lot more state than that.

The first option is not scalable and is very hard to manage. The more service programs there are, the more memory required to hold onto their purchase order numbers. This means that the memory requirements would be growing at a rate greater than the number of purchase orders being processed.

The second solution is reasonably easy to manage and does use SQL Server for storage, but it also is not scalable. The problem is that the storage required for purchase order numbers goes up as the number of messages increases. This in effect multiplies the amount of storage required in SQL Server by the number of messages involved, not just the number of purchase orders involved.

Both of the first two solutions also suffer from the problem of data being duplicated in many places. Of course, in practice this would be an unreliable way to maintain state.

What you really want to do is to put all the state for a conversation group into some tables in SQL Server. That way, there is only one copy of the state and just one place to maintain it. For this to work, however, you will need two things. Both are easy to get. First of all you need something to key the state you will be storing in SQL Server. The conversation group ID is unique and is a UNIQUEIDENTIFIER, so it is ideal to use for a key.

The second thing you need is a lock, and you have that too. As long as your service program is accessing a queue under a transaction, you can be sure other service programs are not touching the shared state. In fact, this is another use of the GET CONVERSATION GROUP command. Using RECEIVE locks the conversation group, but it also reads the queue. Sometimes you need to access or manipulate the state you are sharing within a conversation group before you read the queue. GET CONVERSATION GROUP gets the conversation group associated with the next message in the queue and returns the conversation group ID, but it does not read the queue. In either case, you can then use the conversation group ID to look up the state and then decide whether or not the queue should be read.

Service Broker Application Guidelines

It is important to keep in mind what Service Broker does best when you are using it to develop an application. Service Broker works best when an application has a number of independent tasks to perform. If your application cannot be broken into a set of independent tasks, it is not a candidate for implementation with Service Broker.

The work order example in the previous section illustrates this. Service Broker can be configured to distribute the independent tasks over all the resources available when the load is light, and when the load is heavy, it can be configured to focus the resources on the critical tasks and defer others until the load lightens.

So the first thing you must do to use Service Broker is to break your application into independent tasks. Once you have done this, you must categorize each task as being critical or deferrable.

Critical means the task must be completed almost immediately when the application is invoked. One of the critical tasks might be to set up state so the overall progress of the application can be tracked.

A deferrable task is one that, of course, does not have to be completed immediately. In the work order example, you might decide that getting the header into the database right away is critical so that users would have some picture of where work was going to be done. However, the actual work order line items might be deferred because they would not be needed until work crews were assigned, which is done overnight.

If your application doesn't have any deferrable tasks, it is probably not a candidate for implementation in Service Broker.

Next you will have to define your services. There is no hard-and-fast rule for this, but you might start with a service, and its associated queue and stored procedure, for each kind of task in your application. Once your services are defined, you can implement the stored procedures, which in turn will create the conversations needed.

You will probably have one task that starts things off. Again, there is no hard-and-fast rule, but this should be a critical task that creates a conversation group and allocates the state that will be needed to track the progress of the application.

Service Broker Example

The sections that preceded this presented a conceptual overview of Service Broker and how it is used. What follows is an example of an application that uses Service Broker. It models a stock brokerage house, which offers to buy and sell stock to the public, and a stock trading house, which executes the actual trades on a stock exchange. A simple example designed to illustrate the use of Service Broker DDL and DML extensions in SQL Server 2005 follows.

Message Type

It is of vital importance that the sender and the receiver in a messaging application understand what messages will be sent. In Service Broker the description of the messages is defined in a message type object. The message type object defines the name of the message and the type of data the message contains. For each database that participates in a conversation, an identical message type is created.

Listing 15-1 shows the syntax for creating a message type.

LISTING 15-1: Syntax for Creating a Message Type

```
CREATE MESSAGE TYPE message_type_name
        [ AUTHORIZATION owner_name ]
    [ VALIDATION = {  NONE | EMPTY | WELL_FORMED_XML |
        VALID_XML WITH SCHEMA COLLECTION schema_collection_name } ]
```

The arguments and their definitions are as follows.

- message_type_name—The name of the message to create. It can be any valid SQL string. By convention, it has the form of //hostname/pathname/name. An example for a message type that deals with order entries could be //www.develop.com/orders/orderentry. Using this name in SQL Server would require square brackets around it—for example, [//www.develop.com/orders/orderentry]. Although using a URL format is not required, it's generally easier to ensure uniqueness if you use a URL.
- AUTHORIZATION owner_name—Defines which user or role owns the message type.
- VALIDATION—What kind of XML validation should be performed on received messages.

- NONE—The message isn't validated at all. This is done for non-XML messages or XML messages coming from a trusted source.
- WELL_FORMED_XML—The message is parsed to ensure the XML data is well formed.
- EMPTY—The message body is empty.
- VALID_XML WITH SCHEMA COLLECTION schema_collection_name— Specifies the XML schema collection to validate the message against. The schema collection must be registered in SQL Server before it can be used in the creation of the message type. (Chapter 8 covers how to register a schema collection in SQL server.) If WITH schema_collection_name is not used, the message will not be validated; however, the XML will still have to be well formed.

A broker must request that a brokerage make a trade, and that brokerage must acknowledge that request. Two messages will be required to do this:

- The message that is sent from the broker/trader to the brokerage containing the original order
- The acknowledgment message from the brokerage to the broker/trader

Listing 15-2 shows the two message types created in order to accomplish the order entry. Both use XML encoding, which means that any a message with valid XML will be processed.

LISTING 15-2: Example of Creating a Message Type with XML Encoding

```
-- first the message for the trade entry
CREATE MESSAGE TYPE
[//www.develop.com/DMBrokerage/TradeEntry]
VALIDATION = WELL_FORMED_XML

-- then the acknowledgment message
CREATE MESSAGE TYPE
[//www.develop.com/DMBrokerage/TradeAck]
VALIDATION = WELL_FORMED_XML
```

In Listing 15-2 the various endpoints that receive the messages with the TradeEntry and TradeAck message type don't care about the XML as such. They try to process it as long as it is well-formed XML. This may not be an ideal situation for an enterprise application. In an enterprise application, you may want to make sure that the endpoints always get valid messages. For that purpose, the `message type` can be created indicating that the message should be validated against an XML schema. This is shown in Listing 15-3. The code listing shows both the code to register the schemas and how to refer to the schemas from the creation of the `message type`.

LISTING 15-3: Example of Creating Message Types Whose Messages Will Be Validated against XML Schemas

```
-create the schema collection for the tradeEntry message
CREATE XML SCHEMA COLLECTION TradeEntrySchema AS
N'<?xml version="1.0" ?>
<xsd:schema xmlns:xsd="http://www.w3.org/2001/XMLSchema"
    targetNamespace=
      "http://www.develop.com/DMBrokerage/schemas/tradeEntry">

    <xsd:complexType name="tradeEntry">
      <xsd:sequence>
        <xsd:element name="RICCODE" type="xsd:string"/>
        <xsd:element name="CustomerID" type="xsd:int"/>
        <xsd:element name="OrderID" type="xsd:int"/>
        <xsd:element name="Date" type="xsd:date"/>
        <xsd:element name="BuySell" type="xsd:date"/>
        <xsd:element name="Volume" type="xsd:int"/>
        <xsd:element name="Price" type="xsd:decimal"/>
      </xsd:sequence>
    </xsd:complexType>
  </xsd:schema>'

 -create the message type based on the schema
CREATE MESSAGE TYPE
  [//www.develop.com/DMBrokerage/TradeEntry]
VALIDATION = VALID_XML WITH SCHEMA COLLECTION TradeEntrySchema

 -create the schema collection for the tradeAck message
CREATE XML SCHEMA COLLECTION
  N'<?xml version="1.0" ?>
  "http://www.w3.org/2001/XMLSchema"
    targetNamespace=
        "http://www.develop.com/DMBrokerage/schemas/tradeAck">

    <xsd:complexType name="tradeAck">
      <xsd:sequence>
        <xsd:element name="OrderID" type="xsd:int"/>
        <xsd:element name="AckId" type="xsd:int"/>
      </xsd:sequence>
    </xsd:complexType>
  </xsd:schema>'
```

```
-- create the message type for the trade ack
-- based on the schema collection
CREATE MESSAGE TYPE
[//www.develop.com/DMBrokerage/TradeAck]
VALIDATION = VALID_XML WITH SCHEMA COLLECTION TradeAckSchema
```

These `message types` need to be created in both the broker/trader database and the brokerage database. In a real-world application, there would be most likely be more `message types` to accomplish more tasks.

Apart from the message type the developer defines, there are some pre-defined message types in Service Broker. These three are the most common.

- `http://schemas.microsoft.com/SQL/ServiceBroker/ DialogTimer`—A dialog can have an explicit timer assigned. This message is received when the timer expires.

- `http://schemas.microsoft.com/SQL/ServiceBroker/Error`— Service Broker creates error messages based on this message type to report errors to the application. This message type can also be used by the application to report errors or violation of business rules.

- `http://schemas.microsoft.com/SQL/ServiceBroker/ EndDialog`—When a dialog ends, the broker sends the `EndDialog` message to the remote endpoint.

These message types are implicitly part of every contract, so any target can receive instances of them.

Changing Message Types

A `message type` can be altered or dropped using the normal T-SQL DDL syntax `ALTER` and `DROP`. The syntax to change a message type is shown in Listing 15-4.

LISTING 15-4: Syntax to Alter a Message Type

```
ALTER MESSAGE TYPE message_type_name
  [ VALIDATION = {  NONE | EMPTY | WELL_FORMED_XML |
        VALID_XML WITH SCHEMA COLLECTION schema_collection_name } ]
```

The `ALTER` syntax allows us to change the `VALIDATION`. To drop a message type, you use this syntax: `DROP MESSAGE  TYPE message_type_name [ ,...n ]`. Notice that the syntax permits dropping one or more `message types`. The only caveat with dropping a `message type` is that to be dropped, it cannot be referenced from a `contract`. If that is the case, an error is raised saying that the `message type` cannot be dropped because it is referenced by one or more `contracts`.

Now that we have mentioned contracts, it is time to see what a contract is and how it is created.

Contracts

Service Broker services need to know what messages to expect, the outline of the messages, and what messages they can send. As we saw earlier, a `message type` defines the message, and we use a `contract` to define what messages each service (endpoint) can send and receive. Contracts are created and persisted in each database that participates in a conversation.

As we will cover later, the endpoints can be defined to be either the initiator or the target of a conversation. Subsequently, `message types` can be defined by the `contract` to be sent either by the initiator, the target, or both. Listing 15-5 shows the syntax to create a `contract`.

LISTING 15-5: Syntax for Creating a Contract

```
CREATE CONTRACT contract_name
[ AUTHORIZATION owner_name ]
( message_type_name
SENT BY { INITIATOR | TARGET | ANY } [ ,...n] )
```

The arguments and their definitions are as follows.

- `contract_name`—The name of the contract to create. It can be any valid SQL string. As with a message type name, you would enter it in the form of `//hostname/pathname/name`.
- `message_type_name`—The `message type` (or `message types`) that this contract uses.
- `SENT BY`—Defines which endpoint can send the defined `message type`. The possible arguments are `INITIATOR`, `TARGET`, or `ANY`.
- `INITIATOR`—The initiator of the conversation can send the defined `message type`.
- `TARGET`—The target of the conversation can send the defined `message type`.
- `ANY`—The specified message type can be sent by either the `INITIATOR` or the `TARGET`.

- AUTHORIZATION owner_name—Defines which user or role owns the contract. If this isn't specified, the contract is owned by the user who created the contract.

For the stock trading application, we need to create contracts in both the broker/trader database and the brokerage database. The TradeEntry message type initiates in the broker/trader database, and the TradeAck message type initiates in the brokerage database. The code in Listing 15-6 shows how to create the contract in the broker/trader database.

LISTING 15-6: Create a Contract

```
--create the contract against the message types
CREATE CONTRACT
   [//www.develop.com/DMBrokerage/EnterTrade]
   ( [//www.develop.com/DMBrokerage/TradeEntry]
       SENT BY INITIATOR,
   [//www.develop.com/DMBrokerage/TradeAck]
       SENT BY TARGET
   )
```

When a contract is created, at least one message type needs to be marked as sent by the INITIATOR.

Contracts, like message types, can be dropped. The syntax to drop a contract is this: DROP CONTRACT contract_name [, . . . n]. Notice that several contracts can be dropped through one DROP statement.

At this stage, according to the outline of how to design a Service Broker application, we should create the outline of the service program. We would like to wait with that and instead create the queues the application uses.

Queues

The queue is used to store the messages the endpoints send. When the service at one end sends a message to the service at the other end, the message is placed in a queue at the receiving end. Later, when the application receives the message and commits the transaction, the broker deletes the messages from the queue. The service broker manages the queues and presents a database table-like view of the queues.

The syntax to create a queue is shown in Listing 15-7.

LISTING 15-7: Syntax to Create a Queue

```
CREATE QUEUE queue_name
[ WITH  [ STATUS = { ON | OFF } ]
   [ RETENTION = { ON | OFF } , ]
   [ ACTIVATION (
      [ STATUS = { ON | OFF } , ]
      PROCEDURE_NAME = stored_procedure_name ,
      MAX_QUEUE_READERS = max_readers ,
      EXECUTE AS { SELF |  'user_name' }) ] ]
```

There are quite a few options when you are creating a queue, and a short explanation of the various arguments follows. The queue is the only Service Broker object that can be named with a three-part name.

- queue_name—Is the name of the queue that is created. This must be a SQL Server identifier. Because the queue is never referred to outside the database it is created in, the URL-like syntax used for other Service Broker names isn't necessary for queue names.

- STATUS—Decides whether the queue is created in a disabled state or not. The choices are ON (active) and OFF (disabled). When a queue is disabled, it cannot receive messages, nor can messages be removed from the queue. If this clause isn't specified, the queue is created in the ON state.

- RETENTION—Specifies the retention setting for the service. If RETENTION = ON, all messages sent or received on conversations using this service are retained in the queue until the conversations have ended successfully. The RETENTION argument is useful if you do compensating transactions. With RETENTION = ON, you can do a compensation transaction if something goes wrong during the conversation (remember that the conversation can have a very long lifespan), since the messages are kept in the queue until the conversation ends.

- ACTIVATION—Specifies information about the stored procedure that will be activated to handle messages that arrive on this queue. If STATUS is set to OFF, the queue does not activate the stored procedure; the default is ON. We cover different aspects of activation of the service programs later in this chapter.

- PROCEDURE_NAME—Is the stored procedure to execute. This procedure is also the service program for the application. The procedure has to be in the same database as the queue or be fully qualified.

- MAX_QUEUE_READERS—When a message arrives on the queue, the procedure will be activated. As more messages build up in the queue, more instances of the procedure will be activated, up to MAX_QUEUE_READERS.

- EXECUTE_AS—Specifies what SQL Server login the activated procedure runs under. If this optional clause is set to SELF, the procedure runs under the user who created the queue.

In the stock trading application example, we need one queue in the brokerage database to handle the order entry messages coming from the broker/trader database. We also need a queue in the broker/trader database to handle the acknowledgment messages from the brokerage database. In a real-world application, we would probably have more queues to handle different messages. Feel free to create as many queues as you deem necessary for your application.

The code to create the queues for the stock trading application is shown in Listing 15-8. Notice that if you want to automatically activate a stored procedure (the service program) when a message arrives on the queue, you need to supply the PROCEDURE_NAME clause with the name of a valid procedure. The easiest approach is to create a procedure that is just an empty shell, as in the following code snippet, and catalog it in SQL Server.

```
--create in the broker/trader database
CREATE PROCEDURE tradeAckProc
AS

RETURN 0
GO

--create in the DMBrokerage database
CREATE PROCEDURE tradeEntryProc
AS

RETURN 0
```

LISTING 15-8: Creation of Queues

```
--create the queue in the broker/trader database
--this queue handles the acknowledgments from
--the brokerage
USE Trader1
GO

CREATE QUEUE tradeAckQueue
WITH STATUS = ON,
ACTIVATION (
```

```
  PROCEDURE_NAME = tradeAckProc,
  MAX_QUEUE_READERS = 5,
  EXECUTE AS SELF)

 -creation of the queue in DMBrokerage
 -this queue handles the new orders coming from
 -the broker
USE DMBrokerage
GO

CREATE QUEUE tradeEntryQueue
WITH STATUS = ON,
ACTIVATION (
  PROCEDURE_NAME = tradeEntryProc,
  MAX_QUEUE_READERS = 5,
  EXECUTE AS SELF)
```

The queues created in Listing 15-8 act as receive queues for replies and error messages.

When you create a queue, you create an object of the type Service Queue. This object maps to a SQL Server internal table with the same name as the queue. To view what queues exists in a database, you can do a SELECT against the sys.service_queues catalog view. You can view the content of a queue through a simple SELECT statement: SELECT * FROM queue_name. Issuing a SELECT against one of the created queues in Listing 15-8 results in an empty resultset, but at least you can see the columns. Table 15-1 shows the content of a queue.

In the process of developing a Service Broker application, we now have the "basic plumbing," which consists of the following:

- Message types
- Contracts
- Queues

These may exist in different databases on different servers. We now need to create the information about where the messages are sent. This is handled by the services. Table 15-1 shows some columns that hold information about services, and in the following section we cover how to create services.

TABLE 15-1: Columns in a Queue

Column Name	Data Type	Description
status	tinyint	Status of the message (0=Ready, 1=Dequeued, 2=Disabled).
priority	tinyint	Reserved for future use.
queuing_order	bigint	Message order number within the queue.
conversation_group_id	uniqueidentifier	Conversation group identifier for the message.
conversation_handle	uniqueidentifier	Conversation identifier for the message.
message_id	uniqueidentifier	Message identifier.
message_sequence_number	bigint	Sequence number of the message within the conversation.
service_name	nvarchar(512)	Name of the service that this message targets.
service_id	int	The object_id of the service that the message targets.
service_contract_name	nvarchar(256)	Name of the contract that the message follows.
service_contract_id	int	The object_id of the contract that the message follows.
message_type_name	nvarchar(256)	Name of the message type that describes the message.
message_type_id	int	The object_id of the message type that describes the message.
validation	nchar	What validation is done before the message is put on the queue; one of (N = None, X = XML, E = Empty).
message_body	varbinary(MAX)	Content of the message. Note that this is a binary column; you will have to cast it to a readable type to see what it contains: CAST(message_body as XML).

Services

A service is an endpoint for specific functionality in the Service Broker application. Based on the service name, Service Broker routes messages between databases and puts the messages on the queue for that particular service and message type. The specific functionality that the service is an endpoint for is defined by the contract. By specifying the contract, the service indicates it serves as a target for that particular functionality.

Having said this, we can see that a service:

* Defines which queue to receive messages on.
* Defines what contracts to support.

Therefore, when a service is created, we need to map it to an existing queue and, optionally, to one or more contracts. The syntax to create a service is shown in Listing 15-9.

LISTING 15-9: Syntax for Creating a Service

```
CREATE SERVICE service_name
[ AUTHORIZATION owner_name ]
ON QUEUE queue_name
[ ( contract_name [ ,...n ] ) ]
```

The arguments for CREATE SERVICE are as follows.

* service_name—Is the name of the service to create.
* queue_name—Specifies the queue that receives messages for the service.
* contract_name—Specifies a contract that this service exposes. Notice that when a contract is specified, it does not mean that the particular contract is exclusive to the service. Other services can also use the same contracts, and the service can send messages on contracts that are not specified here.
* owner_name—Sets the owner of the service to the name of a database user or role.

The syntax specifies both a queue name and a contract name. By defining those arguments, we make sure that any message(s) based on the defined contract(s) are delivered to that particular queue.

In the stock trading application, we now have two message types, one contract, and one queue in each participating database. Listing 15-10 shows the code to tie this together. The code creates a service in each database that maps to a queue and a contract.

LISTING 15-10: Code to Create Services

```
-create the service in the trader db
USE Trader1
GO


CREATE SERVICE enterTrade
ON QUEUE tradeAckQueue
([//www.develop.com/DMBrokerage/EnterTrade])

-create a service in the brokerage db
USE DMBrokerage
GO

CREATE SERVICE
    [//www.develop.com/DMBrokerage/TradeEntryService]
      ON QUEUE tradeEntryQueue
([//www.develop.com/DMBrokerage/EnterTrade])
```

Figure 15-5 illustrates the interaction between services, messages, and queues.

When you look at Figure 15-5, you can see how messages are sent between the services and queues. In the following section, we'll look at how to initiate the message exchange.

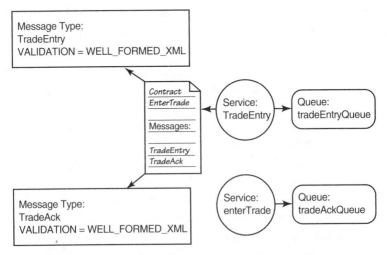

FIGURE 15-5: Interaction between Services, Messages, and Queues

Dialogs

Service Broker applications communicate through *conversations*. A conversation involves endpoints communicating with each other. Theoretically, the conversation can be one-to-one, one-to-many, or even many-to-many. However, at this time Service Broker only supports one-to-one conversation. This type of conversation is called a *dialog*. A dialog is communication between exactly two endpoints. It is a logical connection between service programs, which run on service brokers. The dialog ensures that any messages associated with a dialog are delivered exactly once and in the order in which they were sent throughout the lifetime of the dialog. This is an extremely important point because the lifetime of the dialog can span several transactions. Other messaging applications guarantee in-order delivery within a transaction but not spanning multiple transactions.

The dialog ensures in-order delivery by sequence numbering of the messages. The sending endpoint assigns a sequence number to the message. This sequence number is used by the receiving endpoint to order the messages correctly. If a message is received out of order, Service Broker holds on to the message until the missing messages have arrived. At that time, the out-of-order message is put on the queue.

In a messaging application, it may be of importance to correlate messages from endpoints if there are multiple dialogs. In other words, you want to tell which received messages correspond to which sent messages. The dialog handles correlation automatically for you. The correlation of messages is handled by a unique identifier of the conversation: the `conversation_handle`.

Another important part of dialogs is the message acknowledgment. Dialogs incorporate automatic message acknowledgment for all messages with a sequence number. When a message is sent, the sending broker keeps the message on the transmission queue until an acknowledgment has been received from the remote broker.

Before an application starts sending messages, it needs to establish a conversation. It creates a dialog. At this time it needs to indicate what endpoints are involved and what contract to use. Therefore, the syntax to start communication is shown in Listing 15-11.

LISTING 15-11: Syntax to Begin Communication

```
BEGIN DIALOG [ CONVERSATION ] dialog_handle_identifier
    FROM SERVICE service_name
    TO SERVICE 'service_name' [ , instance_identifier ]
    ON CONTRACT contract_name
```

```
[ WITH
[ { RELATED_CONVERSATION = conversation_handle
  | RELATED_CONVERSATION_GROUP = conversation_group_id } ]
[ [ , ] LIFETIME = dialog_lifetime ]
[ [ , ] ENCRYPTION = { ON | OFF } ] ]
```

The arguments for BEGIN DIALOG CONVERSATION are as follows.

- dialog_handle_identifier—When a dialog is created, the system assigns it a unique dialog handle. This is the variable to store that handle in.

- FROM SERVICE service_name—Specifies the service that is initiating the dialog. This is the service that will receive response and error messages from the target.

- TO SERVICE 'service_name'—Specifies the target service with which to initiate the dialog.

- instance_identifier—Specifies the database that hosts the target service.

- ON CONTRACT contract_name—Specifies the contract that defines messages used in this conversation.

- RELATED_CONVERSATION = conversation_handle—This dialog can be associated with the conversation group of an existing dialog through the conversation_handle variable.

- RELATED_CONVERSATION_GROUP = conversation_group_id— When starting a new conversation, Service Broker also creates a new conversation group (we cover conversation groups later). This argument allows us to associate the dialog with an existing conversation group instead of creating a new conversation group.

- LIFETIME = dialog_lifetime—Specifies the lifetime in seconds for the dialog. If this is not specified, the dialog remains open until it is explicitly closed.

- ENCRYPTION—Specifies whether messages sent and received on this dialog must be encrypted. The default for ENCRYPTION is ON. Having ENCRYPTION set to OFF does not necessarily mean that messages won't be encrypted. That depends on the existence of certificates, which are covered later in this chapter.

It is worth noting a couple of things about the TO SERVICE argument. The service name variable must be a string. The variable must be quoted and match the name of the remote service, including case.

You should also notice that the RELATED_CONVERSATION and RELATED_CONVERSATION_GROUP clauses do the same thing. They link the dialog created to an existing conversation group. You would use the RELATED_CONVERSATION_GROUP if you created your own UNIQUEIDENTIFIER for the conversation group ID. By using RELATED_CONVERSATION, you link the dialog to the conversation group ID of the specified conversation_handle.

We can also define what instance to target. This is important because we can have deployed the service to several databases in the same instance of SQL Server, or to databases in other instances/remote servers. The instance_identifier specifies which database we want to target. The instance_identifier is the service_broker_guid for the database. You retrieve the UNIQUEIDENTIFIER through the following syntax.

```
SELECT service_broker_guid
FROM sys.databases
WHERE database_id = db_id('<db_name>')
```

An interesting question is, what happens if we have deployed the service to several databases and we have not specified an instance_identifier? In this case, Service Broker picks randomly which service to target.

Let's now go back to the stock trading application and look at the syntax shown in Listing 15-12 to create a conversation between our services.

LISTING 15-12: Start a Conversation in the Stock Trading Application

```
--declare a variable for the conversation handle
DECLARE @dh uniqueidentifier;
--this starts the dialog from the
--broker/trader database
--and we get a dialog/conversation handle automatically
BEGIN DIALOG CONVERSATION @dh
  FROM SERVICE enterTrade
  TO SERVICE
     '//www.develop.com/DMBrokerage/TradeEntryService'
  ON CONTRACT
  [//www.develop.com/DMBrokerage/EnterTrade];
```

The code in Listing 15-12 is run from the broker/trader database and causes an entry in the conversation endpoints table to be made. This can be investigated by calling SELECT * FROM sys.conversation_endpoints. At this stage, nothing has happened in the brokerage database yet. Nothing will happen until we send a message. This can be verified by running SELECT far_broker_instance FROM sys.conversation_endpoints in the broker/trader database. `far_broker_instance` is a column that holds the ID for the remote server. The SELECT returns NULL; in other words, Service Broker has not yet decided which endpoint to talk to. The decision about the endpoint happens when the first message is sent for this particular dialog.

The code in Listing 15-12 does not explicitly set a lifetime for the dialog; the dialog is alive until it has been closed explicitly. The syntax to close a dialog follows.

```
END CONVERSATION conversation_handle
  [ [WITH ERROR = failure_code DESCRIPTION = failure_text]
  |[WITH CLEANUP]
  ]
```

The `conversation_handle` variable is obtained through the BEGIN DIALOG CONVERSATION call. You may want to end the dialog if there is an error during the dialog lifetime. To do this, call END CONVERSATION with an error number and an error description. When you end a conversation, a message will appear on the receiving service queue of the type `EndDialog`. The message type will be `Error` if you have ended the conversation through the WITH ERROR option.

You saw in the syntax for BEGIN DIALOG CONVERSATION (Listing 15-11) that you can set an explicit lifetime on the DIALOG. When you set the lifetime for the dialog and the timeout happens, the dialog ends and an error message is put on the target queue and the initiator queue. At this stage, you cannot use that particular dialog again. In other words, if you set lifetimes, the initiating service should know the expected lifetime of the dialog and be fairly certain that the dialog actually ends before the timeout.

However, sometimes the initiating service does not know the expected lifetime, or the initiator just wants to know that something takes longer than expected but does not want to end the dialog. The initiator wants to be notified when an expected timeout has been exceeded, but the dialog should not end. In this scenario, you can use a CONVERSATION TIMER. The CONVERSATION TIMER allows you to start a timer on a particular conversation handle. When the timer expires, you get a `Timeout` message on the local queue for that dialog, but the dialog does not end. When the timeout message arrives, the service will be activated to handle the timeout appropriately. The syntax for starting the timer follows.

```
BEGIN CONVERSATION TIMER (conversation_handle)
TIMEOUT = timeout
```

The `conversation_handle` variable is the unique identifier for the conversation, and the `TIMEOUT` is set in milliseconds.

In this section about dialogs, we have seen how we (and Service Broker) keep track of the various conversations through the `conversation_handle` identifier. The question is then how to keep track of several related conversations with different identifiers that belong to the same service. Enter the *conversation group.*

Conversation Group

You use the conversation group to group related conversations together. Imagine that when an order is entered in our application, we need to do more things than just notify the brokerage. We may have to check the client's credit, check against some authority that the client actually is allowed to trade, and so on. In this scenario, we would probably start several different dialogs. These dialogs would get different conversation handles, and it might be hard for us to keep track of the different conversations. Fortunately, Service Broker comes to help. When we start a new dialog, it creates a new conversation group identifier automatically. The identifier is a GUID (SQL server data type `UNIQUEIDENTIFIER`). The identifier is appended to the messages we receive. You can create the identifier yourself (in T-SQL you use `NEWID()`). Subsequently, when you do `BEGIN DIALOG CONVERSATION`, you relate the dialog to the identifier using the syntax in Listing 15-11. Relating the dialog to a conversation group identifier is the solution if you want to use an existing identifier for your dialog or associate your dialog with the conversation group of an existing dialog.

To obtain the identifier within a conversation, you do a `SELECT` against the `conversation_group_id` column in the message queue. The identifier can also be retrieved by the `GET CONVERSATION GROUP` call. Calling `GET CONVERSATION GROUP` gets the conversation group identifier for the next message to be retrieved. As we will see later, the conversation group identifier is useful if we want to keep state information. In addition, it puts a lock on the instance. See the SQL Server Books Online for the full syntax for `GET CONVERSATION GROUP`.

The biggest benefit of the conversation group is that of locking the dialogs. You may ask why it is important to lock dialogs. We have already stated that Service Broker guarantees the in-order delivery of messages. That is true, but the issue is that a queue can have multiple readers (this is discussed more in the Activation section later in the chapter). In other words, we have multithreaded queue readers.

The problem with this is that there is parallel processing of messages. If the messages are parent-child data (think orders with order lines), a situation can occur in which even if the messages appear on the queue in order, they can be processed out of order. Think about a scenario where it takes longer to process the parent data than the child data.

In this scenario a parent message arrives first, followed by child messages. Queue reader 1 (qr1) gets instantiated and starts processing the parent data. Shortly thereafter, a child message arrives, and because qr1 is still active, a second queue reader gets activated (qr2). Because the parent data takes so much longer to process than the child data, the child data may try to commit before the parent, and there will be a referential integrity constraint violation. Obviously, the transaction rolls back, and the message is put back on the queue and can be processed later, but this is not optimal.

In Service Broker, when a receive is done, a lock is put on the conversation group, and no other queue readers can receive messages on dialogs in that particular conversation group until the transaction is committed.

A conversation group is also beneficial when you want to keep application state. You can store any state data in the database based on the conversation group identifier and retrieve it when needed, because every message you receive will have the conversation group ID in the result. For those of you who are ASP developers, you can see the conversation group ID as a cookie. Naturally, the lifetime of a conversation group is important if you rely on it for state data. A conversation group is alive as long as it has conversations associated with it.

Service Programs

Figure 15-5 illustrates the process for a new trade in our application.

- A user enters a trade through a user interface.
- A stored procedure in the Trader database processes the trade entry and creates a message.
- The stored procedure sends the message, and Service Broker puts the message in the tradeEntryQueue in the DMBrokerage database.
- The tradeEntryProc procedure is activated and processes the message from the queue.
- When the message is processed, the TradeEntryService sends a reply to the enterTrade service on the tradeAckQueue.
- The procedure on the tradeAckQueue is activated and processes the message.

These steps are done through service programs, the part of the application that processes messages for the application. A service program is typically a stored procedure, which is activated when a message arrives on a queue. In this case, we say the service program is the *target*. So, if a service program acts as a target, then we also need something that starts a message exchange. Therefore, a service program can be an *initiator*, which sends the first message to a target. A service program can also be the initiator of one dialog and the target of another. A service program could theoretically also be the initiator and the target of the same dialog. This could be used when you're doing some time-critical processing and you may want to queue up some work to do later when you have time.

In our stock trading application, the initiating service program is the stored procedure that is invoked when a user places an order. The target is the stored procedure on the `tradeEntryQueue` in the `DMBrokerage` database. There is an additional target in our application. It is the stored procedure in the `Trader` database that accepts the acknowledgments of the trades on the `tradeAckQueue`.

We mentioned earlier that a stored procedure is *activated* when a message arrives on a queue. In the following section, we will look a little more closely at the activation features in Service Broker.

Activation

In a traditional messaging application, you have basically two options to find out that a message has arrived on a queue.

- You poll against the queue.
- The messaging infrastructure exposes some sort of event that an application listens for.

Service Broker differs in some respect from this—not so much for the polling scenario, because we can poll a queue through either T-SQL or some external program. However, for events, it looks different.

When you rely on events, you normally need to have a program running that is listening for events. In Service Broker you do not need to do this. Service Broker introduces an activation mechanism.

The activation in Service Broker is based on the CREATE queue syntax. Remember from Listing 15-7 how the syntax takes some optional ACTIVATION arguments. The interesting ones are PROCEDURE_NAME and MAX_QUEUE_READERS. As we mentioned in the section about queues, the PROCEDURE_NAME argument defines which stored procedure to activate when a message arrives on that particular queue. The MAX_QUEUE_READERS argument defines the maximum number of stored procedures that should be activated. The way it works is as follows.

When SQL Server starts, the internals of SQL Server know about the queues in the instance and what queues have activation procedures defined. SQL Server starts to monitor these queues. When the first message arrives on any of the monitored queues, the activation procedure is started to process the message. If messages are put on the queue faster than the procedure can process them, new procedures are started. This continues until the load is handled or the MAX_QUEUE_READERS number has been reached. When the MAX_QUEUE_READERS number has been reached, the messages are queued up on the queue until a service program is available to process the messages.

To make this work with the best performance possible, you need to bear in mind a couple of things when designing your service programs (stored procedures).

- Make sure the program reads messages from the correct queue. If it doesn't, the program will be killed and the messages will queue up.
- The activation monitor code has no way of knowing when a program has finished executing, apart from noticing that the program has terminated. Therefore, make sure the program exits soon after the queue is empty.
- There may be several message types on any given queue. Make sure the program can handle all message types.

In the last bullet item, we said that the service program should be able to handle all message types. You may ask what all message types are. "All message types" means the following:

- All message types marked TARGET or ANY in the contracts defined by the service or services that use the queue.
- All message types marked INITIATOR or ANY in the contracts for the conversations that the service program initiates.
- At least Error and EndDialog. If the program sets a conversation timer, the program should handle Timeout messages, too.

Activation happens when a message is received. Now it is time to look at how messages are exchanged.

Sending and Receiving Messages

When a dialog has been created, your only choices are to send a message, end it, or start a dialog timer. The Listing 15-13 shows the syntax for sending messages. Notice that if SEND is not the first statement in the batch or stored procedure, it has to be preceded with a semicolon (;).

LISTING 15-13: Syntax to Send a Message

```
SEND
    ON CONVERSATION conversation_handle
    MESSAGE TYPE message_type_name
    [ ( message_body_expression ) ]
```

The SEND command takes a conversation_handle variable, which is obtained either from the BEGIN DIALOG CONVERSATION statement or from the conversation_handle column in the message queue. The message_type_name variable must be of a message type that is included in the contract for the conversation. The third argument is the message body. SEND does an explicit cast of the message body to varbinary(MAX), so it will take any valid data type as an argument. If the encoding is EMPTY, the message has no body.

For the stock trading application, we have a stored procedure in the broker/trader database that processes the trade entries. This stored procedure also initiates a dialog and sends a message to the brokerage database. Listing 15-14 shows the part of the stored procedure that creates the dialog (according to Listing 15-12) and sends the message.

LISTING 15-14: BEGIN DIALOG CONVERSATION and Send the Message

```
--code to process the incoming trade omitted

--declare variable for the conversation handle
DECLARE @dh uniqueidentifier;
--variable to hold the message in XML format
DECLARE @msgBody XML

--set the message, in real world you'd create
--it from the in params in the proc
--here we just set it to something
SET @msgBody = '<id>Order1</id>'

--begin the dialog
BEGIN DIALOG CONVERSATION @dh
```

```
FROM SERVICE enterTrade
TO SERVICE '//www.develop.com/DMBrokerage/TradeEntryService'
ON CONTRACT [//www.develop.com/DMBrokerage/EnterTrade];

--send the message we use the conversation handle from
--BEGIN DIALOG CONVERSATION
SEND ON CONVERSATION @dh
  MESSAGE TYPE [//www.develop.com/DMBrokerage/TradeEntry]
  (@msgBody)
```

To test if it works, follow these steps.

1. Create two databases (it can be done in one, but it is more realistic in two). Name them, for example, Trader1 and DMBrokerage.

2. Create the message types and contracts from Listings 15-2 and 15-6 in both databases.

3. Create the tradeAckQueue in Trader1 and the tradeEntryQueue in DMBrokerage according to Listing 15-8. When you create the queues, do not set any ACTIVATION arguments just yet.

4. The last thing to do before you can test is to set up the services as in Listing 15-10.

5. When you finish the preceding steps, you can run the code in Listing 15-14 from the Trader1 database.

At this stage in the Trader1 database, there is an entry in both sys.conversation_groups and sys.conversation_endpoints catalog views. The record in sys.conversation_endpoints holds information about the conversation, the conversation group, and the endpoints. There are similar entries in the sys.conversation_groups and sys.conversation_endpoints catalog views in the DMBrokerage database. The actual message is in the tradeEntryQueue queue, and you can view it by doing SELECT * FROM tradeEntryQueue. Selecting against a queue does not affect the messages in the queue. To remove messages from a queue, you use the RECEIVE command.

The full syntax for RECEIVE is shown in Listing 15-15. Note that if RECEIVE is not the first statement in the batch or stored procedure, it has to be preceded with a semicolon.

LISTING 15-15: RECEIVE Syntax

```
[ WAITFOR ( ]
   RECEIVE [TOP (n)]
      < column_specifier > [ ,...n ]
      FROM queue_name
      [INTO table_variable ]
      [WHERE { conversation_handle = conversation_handle
      |conversation_group_id = conversation_group_id } ]
[ )
[ , TIMEOUT timeout ] ]
```

The syntax looks almost exactly like SELECT, and both SELECT and RECEIVE return a resultset. The difference, as we mentioned earlier, is that RECEIVE removes the message(s) from a queue, whereas SELECT leaves them on the queue.

The WAITFOR argument in the RECEIVE syntax indicates that the RECEIVE operation is to wait for a message to arrive on the queue if the queue is empty or the WHERE criteria doesn't return a result. TIMEOUT can only be used together with WAITFOR, and it indicates, in milliseconds, how long to wait for a message to arrive. If WAITFOR is specified and TIMEOUT is –1 or TIMEOUT is not specified, the wait is unlimited. If a timeout occurs, the RECEIVE statement returns an empty result.

Because WAITFOR is optional, you may ask yourself whether you should use it or not. In messaging applications in general, it is considered good practice to use WAITFOR (or equivalent statements). One scenario where you probably would not use WAITFOR is when your service program (where your receive code is) is activated by an incoming message, and you are certain that no other messages will be arriving within the time it takes to process a message plus the time it takes to activate a new instance of the stored procedure. If the volume is high, it is better use a TIMEOUT value (fairly short). The reason is that it probably does not make sense to start a new service program for each new message. On the other hand, if the service program is an external application and not activated by Service Broker, you should use a reasonably long TIMEOUT.

Since the RECEIVE command allows you to do a RECEIVE with a TOP clause, should you consider receiving message by message or multiple messages? In most cases, you need to process the messages on a message-by-message basis. Bearing this in mind, if you are using T-SQL, you are probably better off doing a RECEIVE TOP(1), especially since you cannot create a cursor of the result from a RECEIVE. You would have to retrieve the messages into a table variable and create the cursor over that variable. If you receive messages into an external service program, you are better off, from a performance perspective, receiving a resultset of multiple messages.

Listing 15-16 shows the code to receive the conversation handle and the message body from the first message in the tradeEntryQueue as a resultset.

LISTING 15-16: RECEIVE from the Queue

```
-receive the first message on the queue
RECEIVE  TOP(1) conversation_handle,
     message_body FROM tradeEntryQueue
```

When you run the code in Listing 15-16 from the DMBrokerage database, it retrieves the message you sent in Listing 15-14. If you do a SELECT against the tradeEntryQueue after the RECEIVE, no messages are there. Notice that the body of the message is output as VARBINARY. If you want to view it as readable text, you have to cast it to another type, like this.

```
RECEIVE CAST(message_body AS XML) FROM MyQueue
```

Listing 15-17 shows a code snippet that uses the WAITFOR and TIMEOUT arguments. The TIMEOUT is set to one minute (60,000 milliseconds).

LISTING 15-17: RECEIVE with WAITFOR and TIMEOUT

```
-declare a variable to hold the conversation handle
DECLARE @dh UNIQUEIDENTIFIER;

-declare a variable for the message body
DECLARE @msg VARBINARY(max)

WAITFOR(
-receive the first message on the queue
RECEIVE  TOP(1) @dh=conversation_handle,
     @msg=message_body FROM tradeEntryQueue),
TIMEOUT 60000

SELECT @dh, @msg
```

You can test the code in Listing 15-17 by first executing the code in the DMBrokerage database. The status bar in SQL Server Management Studio will say "Executing Query." Switch over to the broker/trader database and execute the code in Listing 15-14. Switch back to the DMBrokerage database again, and you can see that a message has been removed from the queue.

Flow in a Service Program

At this point, all code necessary for the stock trading application is done. It is time to tie it together and look at the work flow in a service program. We have discussed how service programs can have different roles when it comes to conversations: initiators, targets, or both. A pure initiator is not that interesting, because it only begins a conversation and goes away.[1] Look at Listing 15-14 for an example of an initiator program.

The interesting role is the target, and most service programs that act as a target follow a common process model. This model looks very much like Windows message loop programming. Listing 15-18 illustrates this through the code for the stored procedure that is activated in the DMBrokerage database when a message arrives on the tradeEntryQueue.

LISTING 15-18: Code for Service Program in DMBrokerage

```
CREATE PROCEDURE tradeEntryProc
AS

-declare variables
DECLARE @dh              UNIQUEIDENTIFIER
DECLARE @msg             XML
DECLARE @ack             XML
DECLARE @cg              UNIQUEIDENTIFIER

WHILE (1=1)
BEGIN

- 1. start a transaction
BEGIN TRAN;
SET @cg = NULL;


- 2. Lock the conversation group if
- dealing with state data
WAITFOR (
GET CONVERSATION GROUP @cg
FROM tradeEntryQueue
),
TIMEOUT 10000

-check that we have a message
IF @cg IS NULL
```

---

[1] Even though a pure initiator service doesn't expect actual data to return, it should be prepared to handle error messages and end-dialog messages. For this purpose, even a pure initiator should have an activation procedure attached to the initiator queue.

```
BEGIN
  ROLLBACK TRANSACTION
  BREAK
END;

- 3. Do what is necessary to deal with state

- 4. RECEIVE
- we need the conversation handle from the send
  ;RECEIVE TOP(1) @dh=conversation_handle,
         @msg=message_body
  FROM tradeEntryQueue
  WHERE conversation_group_id = @cg

- 5. process received data
- code omitted that deals with the received data
- here we probably create the message to send
- back as well

- in our case we just hardcode something
SET @ack='<id>1</id><ackid>1</ackid>'

- 6. send the message
;SEND ON CONVERSATION @dh
  MESSAGE TYPE [//www.develop.com/DMBrokerage/TradeAck]
  (@ack)

- 7. end the conversation
END CONVERSATION @dh

- 8. Update eventual state data
- do some stuff to deal with state

- 9. Commit or roll back
COMMIT TRAN
END
```

The reason we compare this flow with Windows message loops is that when the process is done, it starts all over again. Let's look at the various parts of the model.

- *Begin transaction*—The transactional model is one if the biggest benefits with Service Broker, compared with other messaging systems. In Service Broker the messaging and the database share the same transactional engine, which is very rare in other systems. Everything done against the database, which is associated with a message, should be part of a transaction. If the transaction rolls

back, the database changes are rolled back and the removed messages are put back on the queue. The outgoing messages are not sent, and we can start all over again.

- *Lock conversation group*—Applicable if we deal with application state. The conversation group will under all circumstances be locked when the RECEIVE happens.

- *Retrieve state data*—If applicable.

- *Retrieve messages*—For this application, we have decided to use a fairly short TIMEOUT and retrieve one message per RECEIVE. We need the conversation handle in order to send messages back to the initiator.

- *Process data*—In a real-world application, we would probably receive messages for different message types on the same queue. We need, therefore, to check what message type we receive and process the message accordingly. For this sample, we suggest that you just insert the message body in some table in the database.

- *Send data*—In our application, we need to process the incoming data before we can send. There is nothing that says, however, that a send has follow a receive. It can be anywhere in the model.

- *End conversation*—A conversation should always be ended at one stage. It does not need to be ended when the service program exits, if it makes sense to keep it alive. In our example, this is the last message for this particular task, so it makes sense to end.

- *Update state*—If applicable.

- *Commit transaction*—This is where it happens. Database updates are committed, messages are sent and received messages are taken off the queue.

To see this in action, you need to change the stored procedure in Listing 15-18 so it does something with the processed data. Then it needs to be cataloged in the DMBrokerage database. ACTIVATION arguments need to be added to the tradeEntryQueue with the following code snippet.

```
ALTER QUEUE tradeEntryQueue
WITH STATUS = on,
ACTIVATION (
   PROCEDURE_NAME = tradeEntryProc,
   MAX_QUEUE_READERS = 5,
   EXECUTE AS SELF)
```

Create a stored procedure in the broker/trader database that functions as the service program for messages on the `tradeAckQueue`. You can see an example of this in Listing 15-19. Note that you need to add some code to handle the received messages.

LISTING 15-19: Code for the Service Program in the Broker/Trader Database

```
CREATE PROCEDURE tradeAckProc
AS

 -declare variables
DECLARE @dh            UNIQUEIDENTIFIER
DECLARE @msg           VARBINARY(max)
DECLARE @cg            UNIQUEIDENTIFIER
DECLARE @mt            NVARCHAR(max)

WHILE (1=1)
BEGIN

BEGIN TRAN;
SET @cg = NULL;

WAITFOR (
GET CONVERSATION GROUP @cg
FROM tradeAckQueue
),
TIMEOUT 10000

IF @cg IS NULL
BEGIN
  ROLLBACK TRANSACTION
  BREAK
END;


  RECEIVE TOP(1) @dh=conversation_handle,
         @msg=message_body,
         @mt = message_type_name
  FROM tradeAckQueue
  WHERE conversation_group_id = @cg


 - process received data
 - code omitted that deals with the received data

END CONVERSATION @dh

COMMIT TRAN
END
```

Make sure that the queue in the broker/trader database (Listing 15-8) has its activation arguments set to use the stored procedure in Listing 15-19. Run the code in Listing 15-14 and notice how the stored procedures were activated and handled the messages.

At this stage, messages have been exchanged between different databases in the same server instance. What about message exchange between different instances or different machines altogether? In order to achieve message exchange between instances and/or machines, we need to discuss routes and remote service bindings.

Routes

In the Dialogs section earlier, we mentioned how entries are added in the `sys.conversation_endpoints` table when a dialog is started through the `BEGIN DIALOG CONVERSATION` syntax. We also mentioned that at that time the endpoint has not been resolved to a physical location; this happens when the first message is sent.

The way Service Broker resolves endpoints is by using routes, where a route is an entry in a routing table (`sys.routes`) in a specific database and/or in `MSDB` (`msdb.sys.routes`). When Service Broker tries to resolve an endpoint for a message originating in the local database, it first looks in the routing table in the local database and searches for a matching service name and a broker instance identifier (if an identifier is included in `BEGIN DIALOG CONVERSATION`). If no entry is found, Service Broker searches for a matching service in the local instance databases and picks the first that is found. When searching for a matching local service, Service Broker does not look through all the different databases on the local instance. It does instead a lookup against an in-memory mapping table. If the message Service Broker tries to resolve the endpoint for was received from outside the service (a forwarding scenario), Service Broker looks in the routing table in `MSDB`.

So, by this we can see that in order to exchange messages with remote servers, we need to create routes. A route is created with the following syntax.

```
CREATE ROUTE route_name
[ AUTHORIZATION owner_name ]
WITH
    [ SERVICE_NAME = 'service_name' , ]
    [ BROKER_INSTANCE = 'broker_instance' , ]
    [ LIFETIME = route_lifetime , ]
    ADDRESS =  'next_hop_address'
```

```
    [ , MIRROR_ADDRESS = 'next_hop_mirror_address' ]
[ ; ]
```

Some of the more interesting options are as follows.

* SERVICE_NAME—The name of the service this route points to.
  The name is case sensitive and collation independent. Notice that
  SERVICE_NAME is optional.

* BROKER_INSTANCE—The optional service_broker_guid (which
  we mentioned in the Dialogs section earlier) of the database that
  hosts the service.

* LIFETIME—The number of seconds the route is kept in the routing
  table. LIFETIME is optional, and the route never expires if this option
  is not defined.

* ADDRESS—The network address for the route. It is defined in the format of TCP://address :port_number, where address can be either
  DNS name, NetBIOS name or IP address. The port number is the
  port on which the Service Broker listens. By default, it is 4022. This
  can be changed by the CREATE/ALTER ENDPOINT syntax. At the time
  of writing this chapter, that syntax hadn't been fully specified, so we
  use an alternate syntax: sp_configure 'broker TCP listen port',
  port_number.[2] Notice that the service needs to be restarted after
  changing the port. We mentioned earlier that Service Broker searches
  through the routing tables for services, and if no service is found, it
  looks in local databases. In the case of a service residing in a local
  database, there would be a slight performance gain from explicitly
  pointing to the service in a routing table. For this purpose, Service
  Broker accepts an ADDRESS of LOCAL with no port number. In fact,
  whenever a broker application is created, Service Broker inserts a
  default LOCAL address in the routing table for that database.

* MIRROR_ADDRESS—If ADDRESS points to a principal database mirror
  service, MIRROR_ADDRESS should point to the mirror server for automatic failover to work.

To apply this to our example from earlier in this section, we first need
to imagine that our application runs on different machines on the same

---

[2] In order to run this sp_configure statement, you may need to enable advanced sp_
configure options first by calling sp_configure 'show advanced option', 1 followed by
RECONFIGURE.

network: `Trader` for the broker/trader database and `DMBroker` for the `DMBrokerage` database. The following code shows how to create the necessary routes (from `Trader` to `DMBroker` and vice versa).

```
-create the route in the trader db on the Trader machine
USE Trader1
CREATE ROUTE TradeEntry
WITH service_name =
            '//www.develop.com/DMBrokerage/TradeEntryService',
ADDRESS = 'TCP://DMBroker:4022'

-now on the DMBroker machine in the DMBrokerage db we need a
-route to the service on the Trader machine
USE DMBrokerage
GO

CREATE ROUTE EnterTrade
WITH service_name = 'enterTrade',
ADDRESS = 'TCP://Trader:4022'
```

Theoretically, we should now be able to exchange messages between services on these two machines (if the necessary message types, contracts, queues, and services are set up). However, at this stage, if we tried, no messages would be delivered. This is because Service Broker by default only allows messages to be exchanged between services on the same database server. In the following section, we cover some of Service Broker's security features and how to enable sending messages between services on different servers.

Security

Service Broker is designed to run enterprise applications in very secure environments. Service Broker obviously uses regular SQL Server security to assign permissions to users in order for the users to create and use the various Service Broker objects. However, Service Broker also has special security requirements because of the loosely coupled and asynchronous nature of its applications, where the involved services may be located in different trust domains and so on. In addition, because Service Broker supports routing of messages, it is not guaranteed that the initiator and the target are directly connected to each other. Because of this, Service Broker can not always use NTLM or Kerberos security but is based on public key certificates.[3]

---

[3] For an explanation of certificate usage in SQL Server, look under the Certificate topic in SQL Server Books Online.

The special security requirements we mentioned earlier apply to the following parts of the Service Broker architecture.

- Dialogs—Make sure the services that exchange messages are who they say they are.
- Messages—Make sure no one tampers with or reads the message in between the endpoints.
- Transport—Enable exchanging messages between instances, and optionally authenticate the different SQL Server instances on the transport level.

Transport Security

The last bullet item covers transport, and we mentioned earlier that Service Broker by default only allows the exchange of messages between services on the same database instance. The way Service Broker enforces this is by having the transport protocol disabled. It is controlled by this setting in the registry:

```
HKLM\Software\Microsoft\Microsoft SQL
Server\MSSQL.<instance_no>\SSB\TransportEnabled
```

By default this value is 0 (not enabled), and it needs to be set to 1 to enable the transport layer. After the change, SQL Server needs to be restarted.

When the transport is enabled, it is a question whether additional security is needed on the TCP/IP level. Transport security controls what instances can communicate with each other and has no impact on dialog and messages, which we cover later. If the instances run on the same network or between trusted networks, it may not be necessary. But if the communication goes over the Internet, it is definitely necessary. Service Broker decides whether to use transport security or not by using the CREATE or ALTER ENDPOINT DDL. There are three possible values, as follows:

- 1—Authentication not supported
- 2— Authentication supported
- 3—Authentication required (default)

In our example, because we run on a trusted network, we can change our setting to "not supported." If the application needs authentication, Service Broker supports the following two models:

- SSPI
- Certificate authentication

So the authentication depends on the setting on the endpoint and whether the instances contain certificates in the master database.

SSPI

For SSPI authentication, it is required that both instances be part of the same domain. It is also required that the master database of each instance have a login account for the remote SQL Server's startup service account.

Certificate Authentication

For certificate-based authentication, a certificate holding the credentials for each local instance is required. The certificate is created for the owner of the master database of each instance. Listing 15-20 shows the code that the dbo for the Trader instance runs to create the certificate. The dbo for the DMBroker instance runs similar code to create the DMBroker certificate.

LISTING 15-20: Create the Certificate

```
-create the local cert for the Trader instance
USE master
GO

CREATE CERTIFICATE TraderCert
AUTHORIZATION sa
FROM file = 'c:\Certs\Trader.cer'
WITH PRIVATE_KEY (FILE = 'c:\Certs\Trader.pvk',
DECRYPTION_PASSWORD = 'Tra5de@r')
GO
```

By setting the AUTHORIZATION to sa, we make sure that it is owned by master.dbo. The PRIVATE_KEY FILE argument points to the private key file you create together with the certificate (or that the certificate is created against). In a production environment, the certificate would be issued by a trusted issuer, such as VeriSign. For testing, the certificate can be created through the makecert tool in the .NET Framework, as the following code shows:

```
C:\>makecert -n "cn=Yukon1" -r -m 12 -sv c:\Certs\Yukon1.pvk
c:\Certs\Yukon1.cer
```

The argument `c:\Certs\Trader.pvk` sets the path and the name of the private key file created, and the last argument, `c:\certs\Trader.cer`, is the path and file name of the actual certificate.

When the instances in the application try to connect, they somehow need to authenticate each other based on credentials. The local credentials are the certificate we just created. The remote credentials are being authenticated against a certificate based on the public key from the remote instance, which means that the instances need to exchange public keys.

In our example, as Listing 15-21 shows, the `Trader` instance creates a specific login and creates a certificate with this login as owner, based on the `DMBroker` public key.

LISTING 15-21: Certificate for a Remote Public Key

```
--create the remote login which will hold the remote pk cert
USE master
CREATE LOGIN DMBrokersa
WITH PASSWORD = '5#C1yk4*'

--create the cert for the remote instance
CREATE CERTIFICATE RemoteDMBrokerCert
AUTHORIZATION DMBrokersa
FROM file = 'c:\Certs\DMBroker.cer'
GO
```

The `FROM FILE` argument is the path and name of the public key certificate that the `dbo` of the `Trader` instance has received somehow from the `dbo` of the `DMBroker` instance. The `dbo` of the `DMBroker` instance does the same with the public key certificate it has received from the `Trader` instance.

Now each master database in the two instances holds its own certificate plus the public key certificate from the other instance. When the two instances try to authenticate each other, the certificates will be used just because the certificates exist in the master database. Note that the authentication mode setting needs to be set to at least support authentication (value 2).

Dialogs and Messages

For dialogs and messages, Service Broker has the following types of security:

- Full security
- Anonymous security
- No security

The difference between these three types is the level of trust between the initiator and the target of the dialog and what user the connection on each side runs as.

In full security, both sides trust each other, and the two sides have designated user accounts in the respective databases. This is accomplished though certificates and REMOTE SERVICE BINDINGs, both of which we cover later.

For anonymous security, it is required that the initiating service trust the target but not vice versa. For this to work, the initiating service needs a REMOTE SERVICE BINDING in the database. The target database needs to enable the guest user and give the guest user SEND rights on the service.

With no security, no certificates and no REMOTE SERVICE BINDINGs exist, and the dialog is created with ENCRYPTION = OFF. In this case both databases need to enable the guest user and grant it SEND rights on the service.

By default, messages are encrypted and dialog security is used when you are using SSB between instances. For Service Broker dialogs and messages inside the same server instance, messages are never encrypted and dialog security is not used.

The type of security used is based on a combination of the following three things:

- How the dialog is created through the BEGIN DIALOG CONVERSATION syntax
- The existence of REMOTE SERVICE BINDINGs
- The existence of certificates in the initiating and target databases

Remember from the discussion about dialogs earlier in the chapter how the syntax of BEGIN DIALOG CONVERSATION allowed a last argument, which was ENCRYPTION = ON |OFF. This argument indicates to Service Broker whether to encrypt the messages or not. We say "indicates," because Service Broker may encrypt the message even if ENCRYPTION is set to OFF. This is dependent on the existence of REMOTE SERVICE BINDINGs and certificates.

Certificates

To accomplish full security, Service Broker uses certificate authentication. The certificate authentication for dialog security is mostly set up the same way as for transport security mentioned previously, and the syntax for creating a certificate is the same, except that the certificate is created against a user instead of a login. To accomplish full security, take the following steps for certificates.

1. Create a full certificate against a login in the respective database.
2. Create a user.
3. Create the public key certificate from the remote database against the user.
4. Grant the user CONNECT rights in the local database and SEND rights on the service.

The need for the user is because in full security, operations in the remote database run as that particular user. For this purpose, REMOTE SERVICE BINDINGs are used.

Remote Service Bindings

We mentioned earlier that operations in the remote database run in the context of the user for the remote login. The credentials that are exchanged are based on the certificates, as in transport security. Therefore, when Service Broker starts a dialog, it must determine which particular certificate to use for the public key for that service. To tell Service Broker which certificate to use, the developer creates a REMOTE SERVICE BINDING. The REMOTE SERVICE BINDING needs only to be created in the initiating database.

The syntax to create a REMOTE SERVICE BINDING follows.

```
CREATE REMOTE SERVICE BINDING binding_name
    [ AUTHORIZATION owner_name ]
    TO SERVICE 'service_name'
    [ ON CONTRACT  contract_name ]
    WITH  USER = user_name
    [ , ANONYMOUS = { ON | OFF } ]
[ ; ]
```

Notice that a contract can be defined in the case where different contracts on the same service should be used with different certificates. The last argument, ANONYMOUS, decides whether the credentials of the local user are transferred to the remote service or not. If it is ON, the credentials are not transferred, and the initiating service connects as guest. In this case, guest needs SEND rights on the remote service and CONNECT rights to the database. The default for ANONYMOUS is OFF.

Where Are We?

SQL Server Service Broker is a platform that deeply integrates messaging into the database architecture. By doing this, Service Broker delivers on both performance and reliability. At the same time, Service Broker solves some of the more common problems in message-based applications.

The Service Broker platform natively provides much of the plumbing required to build a distributed application, significantly reducing the application development time. Developers can now use the queuing and messaging functionality that Service Broker provides to develop powerful database applications.

Service Broker is not only for external applications, but those that are used extensively inside the SQL Server engine as well.

Service Broker is an example of how Microsoft moves SQL Server from being a pure database server to an application platform. In the next chapter, we will see another example of this, when we look at SQL Server Notification Services.

16

Notification Services

NOTIFICATION SERVICES is another example of how SQL Server becomes a more visible part of a multitier service-based application architecture. This chapter is a brief introduction to Notification Services.

What Is SQL Server Notification Services?

SQL Server Notification Services was originally released in the summer of 2002 as a licensed part of SQL Server 2000. It shipped as an MSI file that you downloaded from the Microsoft Web site, similar to the way improvements to SQLXML support were available as "Web releases." When installed, SQL Server Notification Services did not change the internals of `sqlservr.exe`, nor were the services loaded in SQL Server's process. It was not integrated in the SQL Server 2000 installation process, but provided its own install and a command-line utility called `NSControl` to deploy and administer the service on the target computers.

SQL Server Notification Services (we'll abbreviate this as SQLNS from now on, for brevity) is an executable process (`NSService.exe`) and a framework for building a specific type of applications, notification applications. Like SQL Server's Analysis Services and Service Broker, it extends your application coding reach and moves SQL Server and related services toward being an integrated platform for scalable application systems. Unlike with Service Broker, you do not code DDL for Notification Services or store its metadata inside SQL Server catalogs, though when you generate an SQLNS application, its metadata is stored in two separate SQL Server databases. SQLNS is, in SQL Server 2005, one of the series of application-enabling services that ship "in the box." When you install SQL Server 2005, one of the first installation screens provides a choice of installing one or more of the following:

- SQL Server Database
- Analysis Services
- Notification Services
- Reporting Services
- Data Transformation Services
- Documentation and Samples

That is because these services all work in concert to provide pieces of a service-oriented architecture for building data-centric applications. In SQL Server 2005, you can control and monitor SQLNS applications from SQL Server Management Studio (although this was not part of the beta 1 release), along with SQL Server itself. SQLNS application coding is not integrated in the SQL Server Management Studio environment, though you can use C++ makefile projects in Visual Studio to group the components in a Notification Services application and run the appropriate application generation utilities.

There are a few key enhancements to SQL Server Notification Services in SQL Server 2005, some of which we already alluded to.

- Notification Services install is integrated in SQL Server install.
- There is a new management interface for NSControl operations in SQL Server Management Studio.
- The application-dependent Notify() function has been replaced with SQL INSERT INTO . . . SELECT syntax to improve security.
- There is 64-bit support for scale-up.
- Business Intelligence (BI) integration is provided.
- Vacuuming performance improvements have been made.
- Object model reflection enhancements for subscription objects have been added.

Notification Applications

Almost everyone has been affected by notification applications in their daily lives. When you receive a daily weather forecast through your cell phone or PDA, when you're notified that your upgrade to first class has been granted on the way to the airport, and when you receive traffic reports over Instant Messenger at the office so you can more effectively plan your route home, you are interacting with notification applications. From a consumer point of view, notification applications consist of two pieces.

* You subscribe to receive notifications based on certain criteria through a subscription application, often over the Web.
* You receive notifications through the communication vehicle of your choice. Some popular choices are messaging products, cell phones, and e-mail.

Some examples of existing Notification Services applications and scenarios are the following:

* Financial services—Receiving and reacting to personal portfolio changes and current market conditions
* Travel and hospitality—Flight arrivals, schedule changes
* Electronic commerce—Search criteria, buying and selling
* Monitoring business data
* Alerting the appropriate person or system when action is required
* Defining the events that occur in the LOB application
* Tracking critical company data
* Numeric data reaching a threshold
* Focusing on key performance indicators
* Coexisting with and broadening existing monitoring—Going beyond the console to devices like cell phones
* Keeping employees informed—Updates to projects, timely research, alerts to actions that may be required

The SQL Server Notification Services architecture abstracts event, subscription, and notification data into classes using XML within two configuration files built by the application developer. The application generation process generates database tables and procedures based on application-specific data. It abstracts the mechanism for providing events, formatting notifications, and delivering notifications into a provider model. The SQLNS product comes with some providers built in, other providers come with related products, and if none of the providers meet your needs, you can build your own using managed code and optionally a COM wrapper API.

As an application developer, you must define the following:

- Incoming events that may provide the fodder for your notifications
- What types of notifications your users will be allowed to sign up for
- A subscription application, so users can sign up
- Pieces of information (data) that will make up your notification
- An algorithm for matching the existing subscriptions with incoming events (or other data to be queried) to produce notifications
- The format of the notification on different delivery vehicles (devices)

Through this short description, you can see that notification applications are publish-subscribe applications and that the SQLNS product gives you all the tools you need to build the applications and a service process that runs the applications. SQLNS uses SQL Server to store its metadata and state data (SQL Server is mandatory, although it can integrate with outside data in other DBMS products and with Analysis Services) and also uses SQL Server stored procedures and T-SQL statements to affect its matching rules. Figure 16-1 shows an overview of the SQLNS application architecture.

This diagram shows that some parts of Notification Services are provided for you, some follow an extensible provider-based architecture, and some you must code yourself. Subscriptions enter the system through a custom subscription management application (1), which can be written using a Notification Services subscription object model. This object model contains subscriber, subscription, and subscriber device classes (among others) and stores its data in the database (2). Events enter the system through event providers (3) and are stored in the database in batches. A Notification component known as the generator executes T-SQL match rules, which generate notifications from events and subscriptions (4). Another component, known as the distributor, formats the notifications (using formatters) and delivers them to the ultimate destination (5).

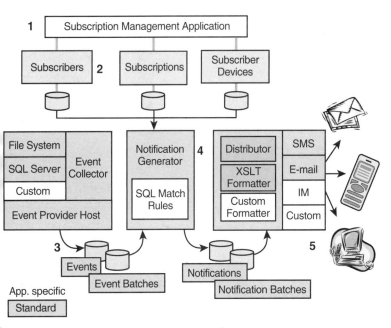

FIGURE 16-1: An Overview of SQL Server Notification Services

Components of SQL Server Notification Services

When you choose to install SQL Server Notification Services, all its components install in a separate subdirectory of the SQL Server installation directory. You can see that there are very few discrete components.

- NSService.exe—Instances of Notification Services run as Windows
  services, using this program as the executable to run. Notification
  Services instances should not be confused with SQL Server
  instances.

- Microsoft.SQLServer.NotificationServices.dll—
  NSService.exe loads this .NET assembly, which contains the
  code for SQLNS, the built-in providers, and components that you
  call to insert and retrieve data in the SQLNS tables when building
  subscription applications.

- NSControl.exe—This utility program generates the SQL Server
  databases and database objects that the Windows service program
  and your subscription application uses. The application also maintains metadata about Notification Services instances (instances of

NSService.exe) that is stored in the registry. You can also use NSControl.exe to enable and disable parts of your SQLNS application, provide status information, and detect the version(s) of Notification Services installed.

- *XML schemas*—When generating Notification Services applications, you specify the information in XML control files. NSControl.exe uses these schemas to validate your XML control files before it uses them to store metadata inside SQL Server database tables.

- *Sample applications*—SQLNS comes with a series of sample applications that you can use as a starting point to build your own applications or try out various SQLNS features. These applications come with C++ makefile projects and test data. Visual C++ must be installed for you to use these projects.

- *Providers*—As mentioned earlier in the chapter, what makes SQLNS extensible is the provider model for event providers, formatters, and delivery protocol providers.

Here's a list of built-in providers at the time of this writing, providers in development, and the interface you would implement to build your own. These are the **event providers**.

- *File Watcher event provider*—Built-in provider that watches for files to be dropped into a directory on the file system. Files must be in XML format, and you must write an XML schema that the SQLXML bulk loader (from SQLXML 3.0) will use to load the events into the event classes.

- *SQL Server event provider*—Built-in provider that runs the SQL statement of your choice at an interval you configure to determine whether rows in a SQL Server table have changed or merit that an event be submitted. Note that SQL Server linked server connections are used, this data could be in a non-SQL Server database.

- *Analysis Services event provider*—In development for SQL Server 2005, this will produce events based on Multidimensional Expressions (MDX), such as those used for key performance indicators.

- *SQLNS stored procedures*—You can use SQLNS-defined stored procedures, which are generated on a per–event class basis, to insert batches of events. This is not an event provider in itself but is an alternative way to generate event batches.

- `IEventProvider` *and* `IScheduledEventProvider`—You can write classes that implement one or the other of these interfaces to produce a custom provider.

These are the **content formatters**.

- *XML/XSLT formatter*—This built-in provider formats notifications into XML and then passes them through the XSLT transform that you specify.
- `IContentFormatter`—You can write classes that implement this interface to produce a custom provider.

These are the **delivery protocol providers**.

- *SMTP*—This built-in delivery provider delivers notifications using any SMTP-compliant mail server.
- *File*—This built-in delivery provider writes notifications to the file of your choice and is used mostly for debugging applications.
- `IDeliveryProtocol`—You can write classes that implement this interface to produce a custom provider.
- *HTTP*—You can write classes that implement `IHttpProtocol Provider`. SQLNS comes with a class, `HttpExtension`, that encapsulates sending through HTTP. It's simpler to implement this interface if your custom protocol provider uses HTTP.
- *Microsoft Alerts provider*—This provider comes with the .NET Alerts 6.0 toolkit and is used to send notifications to the Microsoft Alerts service. From there Microsoft Alerts can deliver them to Instant Messenger, e-mail, or SMS-compliant cell phones. Providers for older versions of the .NET Alerts toolkit are also available.
- *SMS providers*—There are providers to send notifications to cell phones through the major commercial SMS aggregators.
- *Third-party products*—There are third-party products, released or in development, for fax delivery, SMS, and the Blackberry Server.

When you start up a Notification Services application, the command that is run is `NSService.exe`. If your application is called DMTrade, for example, the whole command line actually looks like this:

```
[fullpath to NSService]\NSService.exe "DMTradeInstance"
```

When NSService.exe starts up, it reads that command-line parameter and looks for an application called DMTradeInstance in the registry (SQLNS keeps a list of all of its applications as registry subkeys of HKLM\Software\Microsoft\Notification Services). One parameter of this subkey holds the location of the SQL Server where the metadata for this instance is stored. It will connect to that instance of SQL Server, using integrated security or a SQL Server user ID and password, and read the metadata it needs to control the instance. This metadata includes information such as:

- What event, subscription, and notification classes are defined.
- Which providers should be loaded, including custom providers.
- Parameters for the service's generator and distributor subsystems. (We'll discuss the intricacies of these systems shortly.)

A couple of details should be mentioned before we go on. First, multiple instances of SQLNS can run on a single machine, much as multiple instances of SQL Server itself can run on a single machine. A single instance of NSService.exe can run a single Notification Services application or more than one application. We'll define applications in more detail later, but we'll mention here that each application has its own application database separate from the instance database. Usually, one instance means one set of subscribers, because subscribers and subscriber delivery vehicles (known as subscriber devices) are stored in tables in the instance database. Subscriptions (to an application), events, and notifications are stored in the application database. This is shown in Figure 16-2.

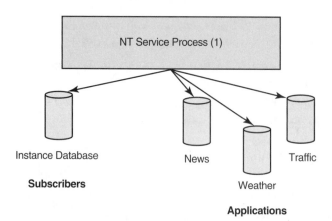

FIGURE 16-2: One Application per Instance versus Multiple Applications per Instance

Finally, the generator and distributor subsystems can be spread across multiple machines. Each machine would run its own instance of `NSService.exe`, and the SQLNS work would be split among multiple machines. This is similar in concept to running federated SQL Servers. This is an advanced deployment concept not explained in detail in this chapter.

Notification Applications Design Patterns

Notification applications follow a few common patterns. The first distinction between application types is the distinction between event-driven subscriptions and scheduled subscriptions. To use an application that reports weather information to a cell phone, as an example, if we are interested in receiving a Portland, Oregon, weather forecast each day at 8 AM, this is a scheduled notification. However, if we're interested in receiving notification when the temperature in Portland, Oregon, goes below 10 degrees, this is an event-driven notification. This difference demonstrates the different types of subscriptions and how the generator process handles event-based and schedule-based subscriptions in SQLNS.

With an event-driven notification pattern, events are written into event tables on a fairly continuous basis, as configured by the application administrator. Every so often the SQLNS generator wakes up and looks for batches of events to process. It will run the algorithm (written in T-SQL and known as a match rule) for each batch processed, matching current events against subscriptions to produce notifications. In addition, each time the generator wakes up, it will obtain all the scheduled subscriptions that are due at that time and match these subscriptions against data to produce notifications. The data used in generating event-driven notifications is typically the raw event batches themselves. The data used in generating scheduled subscriptions is kept in "history tables," known as chronicle tables. There are two flavors of chronicle tables: event chronicles and subscription chronicles.

A few refinements of these patterns are useful in making the notifications more meaningful to the consumer. Another variation of the scheduled subscription is the trend-based subscription. In this subscription type, we don't want to retrieve static information on a schedule (like the weather forecast at a certain time), but a historical trend, like the highest and lowest temperature of the day. This is accomplished by adding functionality to the T-SQL statement that updates the event chronicle table, known as the chronicle rule.

A second refinement might be based on the fact that we want to know when the temperature in Portland goes below 10 degrees at most once a day. Although temperature change events are reported every 5 minutes, we don't want to be reminded every 5 minutes once the temperature goes below 10 degrees! This is known as duplicate removal and is accomplished by keeping historical subscription data known as subscription chronicle files.

Notification Services Delivery Features

Digest delivery is an option that makes for a better consumer experience. Let's say we subscribe to a stock subscription service that notifies us by e-mail when the stocks of our choice reach a certain threshold. We're interested in ten different stocks. If four of them go over the threshold price that we've set at the same time, we don't want to get four individual messages, but a single message that has notifications about the four stocks. This is known as digest delivery.

One final feature is used not to enhance the consumer experience, but to make the notification formatting (and possibly delivery) more efficient. If 1,000 people each register to receive the weather forecast for Portland by cell phone, and the notification message is the same for each user, the formatter doesn't need to format the same message 1,000 times. In addition, a Microsoft Alerts–based application that delivers cell phone messages may accept a single message with 1,000 different destinations. Producing a single message for multiple users and delivering it through a list is known as multicast delivery.

Terms Used in Notification Services

Notification Services uses quite a few overloaded terms—that is, terms that you might be familiar with in a different context with a different meaning. Before we go any further, we should define the vocabulary we're using and what these terms mean in a SQL Server Notification Services environment.

- *Events*—Events are external items that trigger notifications. In our example, it is changes of stock prices. The events can come from a variety of sources: stock ticker feeds, changes of rows in database tables, news feeds, file directory changes, and so on. Event providers capture events and store them in the appropriate database tables. To improve scalability, SQLNS processes events in batches.

- *Subscribers*—Subscribers are the end users of the application. Subscribers are not exclusive to a specific SQLNS application but can be shared between applications. A subscriber can have a locale specified (language and possibly dialect) and a time zone.

- *Devices*—Devices are what the notifications are delivered to (e-mail, cell phones, Web Services). A subscriber can have several subscriber devices.

- *Subscriptions*—The subscriptions define what events a subscriber wants to be notified of. Depending on the events, a single application may use one or more subscription styles.

- *Chronicle tables*—Chronicle tables are used to store event history. The chronicle tables are useful for the different subscription styles mentioned earlier.

- *Generator*—The notification pipeline consists of the event processor, the generator, and the distributor. The generator runs T-SQL match rules to generate notifications.

- *Distributor*—The distributor's job is to format and distribute notifications.

- *Quantum*—Both the generator and the distributor fire every so often; that duration is defined in seconds. This is known as the quantum.

- *Formatters*—Formatters are used to shape the raw notification data into a format the subscriber and the device understand. This can be based on device, locale, or both.

- *Delivery channels*—The delivery channel is the logical delivery mechanism, and a delivery channel targets one or several devices. It is mapped to delivery parameters: server name, user ID, and so on. Delivery channels are also mapped to delivery protocols—however, not in a one-to-one relation. Several delivery channels can use the same protocol.

- *Delivery protocols*—The delivery protocol is the physical delivery mechanism. Typical protocols are SMTP and HTTP.

Designing, Coding, and Generating a Notification Services Application

Because much of the application infrastructure is provided in the box in SQLNS applications, planning the application will be much more involved than designing or coding the applications. Here are two lists of steps that outline the process.

Planning Steps

1. Decide which notifications to expose:
   - One or many notification classes
   - Scheduled or event-driven subscriptions
   - Digest (consolidated) or individual notifications
   - Whether many subscribers will get the same notification
2. Tie notifications to subscriptions:
   - Category of notifications versus categories of subscriptions
   - Locale-driven notifications
   - Items of subscriber information used to personalize
3. Decide how events cause notifications:
   - Which criteria must be specified (SQL `JOIN` rules)
   - Whether notifications are event-driven or scheduled
   - What history needs to be kept using chronicles or other supplemental data tables
4. Decide where subscribers and subscriptions come from:
   - Existing applications (for example, an existing line-of-business application or extracted from an Active Directory hierarchy)
   - Specially written Web application
5. Pick your providers:
   - Event provider(s)
   - Content formatter
   - Delivery protocol(s)—one per delivery channel

Coding Steps

1. Code your instance and application definition files.
   - Decide where you will store event schema files if using the File Watcher event provider.
   - Decide on a directory to watch for files of events to arrive if using the File Watcher event provider.
   - Decide where you will store XSLT transforms for formatting if using the XSLT formatter.
   - Code these locations into your application definition files.
   - Code event, subscription, and notification classes in the application definition files.
   - Code information needed for delivery formatting and locations.

- Code machine locations where the SQL Server holding the databases will live, along with locations for the generator and the distributor.
- Code generator quantum duration and other generator and distributor behavior parameters.
- Code a schedule for the vacuum utility, which will run every so often to dispose of stale data.

2. Code your subscription management application.
   - It may be written in ASP.NET or ASP.
   - It will use the subscription application object model in the SQLNS DLL.

3. Code your event XML schemas if using the File Watcher event provider.

4. Code your XSLT transforms, one for each combination of locale and device supported.

Application Generation Steps

1. Run `NSControl Create` to create the instance and application databases.

2. Run `NSControl Register` to create the registry entries and the Windows service process.

3. Run `NSControl` to start (or stop) the various services used for the Notification Services instance and applications.

Some of these steps may refer to terms that haven't been discussed in detail yet. We'll delve into the details in our sample application.

A Sample Notification Application

The rest of this chapter consists of a series of tutorials that show developing a sample Notification Services application step by step. We begin with the minimalist application to keep from printing many pages of large configuration files, and add functionality to the application incrementally, so you can see the changes to the minimalist configuration needed to implement different application functionality. On the way, we'll discuss the options available in an SQLNS application by looking at the options of the control file XML elements. The step-by-step application code, as well as the final application, is available as part of the book samples.

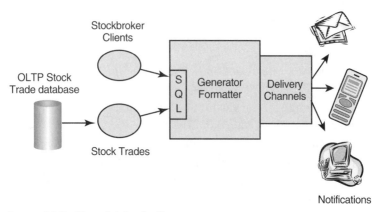

FIGURE 16-3: Financial Application

Imagine for a moment that you are a developer for a stock trading application. Apart from letting the clients enter trades over the Web, the clients should also be notified when certain stocks reaches a specified price (the client has specified the price). The stock prices come in through a feed from a vendor of financial information. The prices are fed into tables in a SQL Server. As soon as the prices change, the application should notify the client if the price matches the preset price. Figure 16-3 shows what it looks like.

This example is one pattern: an event-driven notification application matching stock code and price from the event feed, with the stock code and a trigger price specified in the subscription. In addition, the customer may want to be notified at a certain time of the highest or lowest price at which a particular stock has traded at during a trading day. The same application now contains two kinds of notification patterns: event-driven notifications and scheduled notifications.

Instance and Application Configuration Files

In Notification Services, one instance of the notification server service can consist of one or more applications. As we mentioned earlier, the instance database holds the subscriber information and control tables. The various application databases store the information specific to the application (stock, news, weather) and control tables. We mentioned earlier that the instance is responsible for collecting events and so on. You may be asking yourself how the instance knows about the applications. The answer to this is the configuration files, which exist for both the instance and the applications. These configuration files define the state and behavior of instances and applications. The configuration files are in XML format and are schema based. In SQL Server 2005, the schema for both the instance configuration file and the application configuration file can be located in the SQL Server directory under `\90\NotificationServices\<version>\ XML Schemas\`. The schema for the instance file is called `Configuration FileSchema.xsd` and the application schema is named `Application DefinitionFileSchema.xsd`.

The instance configuration file contains control information and lists the applications. The application configuration file lists the applications schema and the actions. Let's now focus more closely on these two files, starting with the instance file.

Instance Configuration File

The instance configuration file describes a single instance of Notification Services. It holds metadata information about the applications that the instance hosts. The metadata information for applications consists of the application name, base directory path, and name of the application configuration file. The configuration file also contains metadata about the instance, database server, delivery protocols, and delivery channels.

A sample instance configuration file is shown in Listing 16-1. The file contains only the required sections and elements for a valid instance configuration file.

LISTING 16-1: Instance Configuration File

```xml
<?xml version="1.0" encoding="utf-8" ?>
<NotificationServicesInstance
xmlns="http://www.microsoft.com/MicrosoftNotificationServices/
ConfigurationFileSchema">

<InstanceName>DM</InstanceName>
<SqlServerSystem>SERVNB02</SqlServerSystem>

<Applications>
     <Application>
          <ApplicationName>StockPrice</ApplicationName>
        <BaseDirectoryPath>
      C:\MyPath
    </BaseDirectoryPath>
          <ApplicationDefinitionFilePath>
      appADF.xml
    </ApplicationDefinitionFilePath>
     </Application>
</Applications>
```

```
<DeliveryChannels>
     <DeliveryChannel>
          <DeliveryChannelName>FileChannel</DeliveryChannelName>
          <ProtocolName>File</ProtocolName>
     </DeliveryChannel>
</DeliveryChannels>

</NotificationServicesInstance>
```

When you inspect the file in Listing 16-1, you can see the metadata entries for the instance, as follows:

- `InstanceName`—The logical name for the instance of the Notification Services
- `SqlServerSystem`—The name of a SQL Server instance that hosts the instance database and its application databases
- `DeliveryChannels`—Contains `<DeliveryChannel>` nodes that describe all the delivery channels used by all applications hosted by the instance (more about delivery channels later)

In the file, you can also see the metadata for one particular application. It is contained within an `<Application>` node under the `<Applications>` section.

- `ApplicationName`—Is the logical name of the application. It must be unique within the configuration file.
- `BaseDirectoryPath`—Is the application directory path. It is used to locate files specific to the application. These files are typically XML and XSLT files.
- `ApplicationDefinitionFilePath`—Is the name of, and optionally the path to, the application definition file (ADF).

As we mentioned before, the file in Listing 16-1 contains the bare minimum of information. You'll probably want to include more information in your configuration file, and SQL Server Books Online lists the complete set of elements and nodes available. For example, you may want to enter version information through the `<Version>` node. If you create custom delivery protocols, you register them with `<Protocol>` nodes in the `<Protocols>` section.

When you look at the configuration file in Listing 16-1, you may notice that all information is hardcoded into the file. For a production system, this is not ideal. For this reason, both the instance configuration file and the application configuration file have a `<ParameterDefaults>` node containing one or more `<Parameter>` nodes. The parameters are symbolic names appearing as name/value pairs. The application configuration file can inherit parameters from the instance file. Listing 16-2 shows an example of the configuration file in Listing 16-1 using parameters.

LISTING 16-2: Configuration File Using Parameters

```xml
<?xml version="1.0" encoding="utf-8" ?>
<NotificationServicesInstance
xmlns="http://www.microsoft.com/MicrosoftNotificationServices/
ConfigurationFileSchema">

<ParameterDefaults>
    <Parameter>
        <Name>Instance</Name>
        <Value>DM</Value>
    </Parameter>
    <Parameter>
        <Name>DBSystem</Name>
        <Value>%COMPUTERNAME%</Value>
    </Parameter>
    <Parameter>
        <Name>BasePath</Name>
        <Value>C:\MyPath</Value>
    </Parameter>
    <Parameter>
        <Name>AppName</Name>
        <Value>StockPrice</Value>
    </Parameter>
</ParameterDefaults>

<InstanceName>%Instance%</InstanceName>
<SqlServerSystem>%DBSystem%</SqlServerSystem>

<Applications>
    <Application>
        <ApplicationName>%AppName%</ApplicationName>
      <BaseDirectoryPath>
    %BasePath%
  </BaseDirectoryPath>
        <ApplicationDefinitionFilePath>
    appADF.xml
  </ApplicationDefinitionFilePath>
    <Parameters>
                <Parameter>
                    <Name>_App_</Name>
                    <Value>%AppName%</Value>
```

```
            </Parameter>
            <Parameter>
                  <Name>_NSHost_</Name>
                  <Value>%COMPUTERNAME%</Value>
            </Parameter>
      </Parameters>
   </Application>
</Applications>

<DeliveryChannels>
      <DeliveryChannel>
            <DeliveryChannelName>FileChannel</DeliveryChannelName>
            <ProtocolName>File</ProtocolName>
      </DeliveryChannel>
</DeliveryChannels>


</NotificationServicesInstance>
```

Compare the file in Listing 16-2 with the one in Listing 16-1, and you'l
see that we have a <ParameterDefaults> section, where we define differen
variables that are used farther down in the file. Within the <Application>
section, we have a <Parameters> section, where we redefine some o
the variables and give them new names. These names are inherited by the
application configuration file.

You should also notice that we use systemwide environment variables
In this case, it is %COMPUTERNAME%. We are not restricted to system environment variables, but we can set up our own variables in scripts and use the
scripts when we build the SQLNS applications. This is very useful if you
use Visual Studio .NET to build your applications.[1]

By now, you may be asking yourself how we go about building databases, tables, and stored procedures from the configuration files. In order
to build these items, you run the executable NSControl.exe and give it the
name of your instance configuration file. We'll cover this shortly; first we
need to look at the configuration file for the application: the application
definition file.

Application Definition File

The ADF stores all metadata about a particular SQLNS application. The file
must conform to the schema in the ApplicationDefinitionFileSchema.

---

[1] At the time of writing this book, native Visual Studio projects for Notification Services don'
exist. To build SQLNS applications, you use VC++ makefile projects. These projects allow you
to run predefined build scripts.

xsd schema. Also, the nodes and elements in the file must be provided in the same order as in the schema. Listing 16-3 shows a minimal ADF file.

LISTING 16-3: Minimal ADF File

```xml
<?xml version="1.0" encoding="utf-8" ?>
<Application xmlns="http://www.microsoft.com/
MicrosoftNotificationServices/ApplicationDefinitionFileSchema">

<SubscriptionClasses>
  <SubscriptionClass>
    <SubscriptionClassName></SubscriptionClassName>
    <Schema>
      <Field>
        <FieldName></FieldName>
        <FieldType></FieldType>
      </Field>
    </Schema>
  </SubscriptionClass>
</SubscriptionClasses>

<NotificationClasses>
  <NotificationClass>
    <NotificationClassName></NotificationClassName>
    <Schema>
    </Schema>
    <ContentFormatter>
      <ClassName></ClassName>
    </ContentFormatter>
  </NotificationClass>
</NotificationClasses>

<Generator>
  <SystemName></SystemName>
</Generator>

<Distributors>
  <Distributor>
    <SystemName></SystemName>
  </Distributor>
</Distributors>

</Application>
```

The ADF file has four required nodes.

- `SubscriptionClasses`—This is used to define the subscription classes you use in your application. The classes are defined by a name and a schema. The schema indicates what fields of data you store for the subscription and what the data type of each field is. You can optionally define attributes for the fields. These attributes are SQL Server field attributes, such as nullability and default values.

- `NotificationClasses`—This is used to define the classes your application uses for notifications. As with subscription classes, you enter a name and a schema. In addition to the subscription class, you need to define what formatter is used to format the content of a notification.

- `Generator`—The generator manages the rule processing for the application. This node holds information about what system runs the process. Optionally, you can set how many operating system threads the generator can use. Read more in Books Online about this.

- `Distributor`—The distributor manages formatting and delivery of notifications. The node allows you to specify what systems run the distributor, and optionally the thread pool size and how often the distributor fires.

We mentioned before that the file in Listing 16-3 contains the minimal requirements. Although you can write an SQLNS application without defining `EventClasses`, `EventClasses` are also part of most applications. Later in this chapter we will cover more about the required nodes as well as what more we need to create a fully functional application.

Listing 16-4 shows an ADF file for our stock price application meeting the minimum requirements. The file is based on the file in Listing 16-3 and the instance configuration file in Listing 16-2. Notice how the parameters defined in the file in Listing 16-2 are used in the ADF file.

LISTING 16-4: ADF File for the Stock Price Application

```
<?xml version="1.0" encoding="utf-8" ?>
<Application xmlns="http://www.microsoft.com/
MicrosoftNotificationServices/ApplicationDefinitionFileSchema">

<SubscriptionClasses>
  <SubscriptionClass>
    <SubscriptionClassName>
      %_App_%Subscriptions
    </SubscriptionClassName>
    <Schema>
      <Field>
        <FieldName>StockSymbol</FieldName>
```

```
        <FieldType>varchar(255)</FieldType>
      </Field>
    </Schema>
  </SubscriptionClass>
</SubscriptionClasses>

<NotificationClasses>
  <NotificationClass>
    <NotificationClassName>
      %_App_%Notifications
    </NotificationClassName>
    <Schema/>
    <ContentFormatter>
      <ClassName>XsltFormatter</ClassName>
    </ContentFormatter>
  </NotificationClass>
</NotificationClasses>

<Generator>
  <SystemName>%_NSHost_%</SystemName>
</Generator>

<Distributors>
  <Distributor>
    <SystemName>%_NSHost_%</SystemName>
  </Distributor>
</Distributors>

</Application>
```

We can read from the file in Listing 16-4 that we have one subscription class and we store only one field of data for the subscription. That field is called StockSymbol (although, technically, other helpful fields, like Device Name, should be stored). To format the notifications, we use the Xslt Formatter, which comes out of the box with the SQLNS framework. Finally, the local system generates and distributes the notifications.

Having the files in Listings 16-2 and 16-4, we can now build the stock price Notification Services application. The NSControl.exe tool is used for this.

NSControl

NSControl is a tool for administering SQLNS. You use it to deploy, configure, monitor, and control SQLNS instances and applications. It is run from the command prompt, and Table 16-1 presents the available commands. SQL Server Books Online covers these commands and their syntax in detail.

TABLE 16-1: Commands for NSControl

Command	Description
Create	Creates a new instance of Notification Services.
Delete	Deletes an existing instance of Notification Services.
Disable	Disables the specified Notification Services components.
DisplayArgumentKey	Displays the key used to encrypt delivery channel and event provider arguments.
Enable	Enables the specified Notification Services components.
ListVersions	Displays information about the installed versions and registered instances of Notification Services.
Register	Registers an instance of Notification Services.
Status	Displays the current enabled or disabled status of instances and applications.
Unregister	Unregisters an instance of Notification Services.
Update	Updates an existing instance of Notification Services.
Upgrade	Upgrades an instance from Standard Edition to Enterprise Edition, or to a newer version of Notification Services.

You use the Create command to create your new SQLNS instance. The syntax for NSControl Create follows.

```
nscontrol create
    [-help] |
    -in configuration_filename
    [-sqlusername login_ID  -sqlpassword password]
    [-argumentkey key]
    [parameter_name=value [,...n] ]
    [-nologo]
```

Here is a description of the arguments.

- -help—Displays the command syntax.
- -in configuration_filename—The path and file name of the instance configuration file. The path is not required if the file is in the current directory.

- `-sqlusername` *login_ID*—If you are using SQL Server authentication to log in to SQL Server, this is the SQL Server login ID. Best practice, however, is to use Microsoft Windows authentication to log in to SQL Server. In that case, do not use the `-sqlusername` and `-sqlpassword` arguments.

- `-sqlpassword` *password*—The password for the `-sqlusername` login ID.

- `-argumentkey` *key*—The value used to encrypt the delivery channel and event provider arguments that are stored in Notification Services databases.

- `parameter_name=value`—A name/value pair used to pass parameters to the configuration file from the command line.

- `-nologo`—Suppresses the product and version statement that appears when you run an `NSControl` command.

Now that you know the syntax for `NSControl Create`, it is time to compile the application. You need two XML files: `appConfig1.xml` and `appADF1.xml`. They represent the files in Listings 16-2 and 16-4, and you can use these two files to create your application. Copy them to a directory on your hard drive, and change the `BasePath` parameter in the `app Config1.xml` file to the directory you copied the files to. Before you can run the `NSControl Create` command, you need to make sure that `NSControl.exe` is on the path. Alternatively, you can run `NSControl Create` with a fully qualified path.

The following code creates an SQLNS instance together with the stock price application. It is run from the directory where the configuration files are. It assumes that the `NSControl` exists on the path, and it uses integrated security to log on to SQL Server.

```
NSControl Create -in appConfig1.xml
```

When you run this, you will see something like this in your Command window.

```
Microsoft Notification Services Control Utility (Enterprise) 9.0.242
Copyright (C) Microsoft Corporation 2004. All rights reserved.

Creating instance
DM

Creating application
Application name: StockPrice

Create successful.
```

If you now log on to the SQL Server that is defined in the DBSystem parameter, you can see two new databases: the instance database, named DMNSMain, and the application database, called DMStockPrice. You should *never* alter the data in these databases directly, but it's helpful to have a look at what's inside them at this point.

So far the databases do not contain that much application data. The instance database has a table called NSApplicationNames, which consists of one record: the StockPrice application. Notice, however, that in the instance database, there are tables for time zones. These tables make it really easy to create time zone–aware applications. The application database does not have that much more interesting information either. You can see the notification and subscription classes in the NSNotification Classes and NSSubscriptionClasses tables. Although EventClasses aren't technically required, most applications will use one or more event classes and event providers. We'll add them next.

Events

Events can come from a multitude of sources, and they are the occurrences that cause notifications. The events are processed by *event providers*, which send the event data to the application, where it is inserted in the event table.

We discussed the built-in providers and customization hooks available at the beginning of the chapter. Apart from standard and customized event providers, SQLNS also differentiates between hosted and nonhosted (independent) event providers. Hosted event providers run inside SQLNS, and they either run continuously or fire based on a schedule. The schedule for a hosted scheduled provider is defined in the ADF file for the application. The hosted providers are controlled by a component in Notification Services, the event provider host. An independent event provider runs as an external application, and it submits events according to its own schedule.

Events in SQLNS are handled in batches in order to improve performance. So, for example, let's assume that the event provider picks up three events since it last fired. The provider can create a batch with a batch ID and insert each event into the event table together with the batch ID. The events are processed by the generator the next time the generator fires. This allows the generator to compare multiple events with subscriptions at one time instead of doing it on an event-by-event basis. This is done because it gives good scalability for the trade-off of real-time processing. If a little latency is allowed, it scales to huge numbers.

Event Classes

In order to catch the events you are interested in, you have to define what events to accept. This is accomplished by using event classes and event class definitions in the ADF file. Listing 16-5 shows the required elements and nodes for one event class definition.

LISTING 16-5: Event Class Definition in the ADF File

```
<EventClasses>
  <EventClass>
    <EventClassName></EventClassName>
    <Schema>
      <Field>
        <FieldName></FieldName>
        <FieldType></FieldType>
      </Field>
    </Schema>
  </EventClass>
</EventClasses>
```

You can see that it looks very much like the definition for the subscription class and notification class in Listing 16-4. Both the EventClass node and the Schema node support quite a few optional nodes and elements, and they are listed in Books Online.

In our stock price example, we are interested in the stock code (like MSFT, IBM, and so on), the exchange the stock trades on, and the price.[2] Listing 16-6 shows how the event class definition looks in our stock price application. Notice that there are a couple of nonrequired elements in the file: the FieldTypeMods element, to set attributes on the fields in SQL Server, and the IndexSqlSchema node, where in the SqlStatement you create indexes on the table.

LISTING 16-6: Event Class Definition in the ADF File

```
<?xml version="1.0" encoding="utf-8" ?>
<Application xmlns="http://www.microsoft.com/
MicrosoftNotificationServices/ApplicationDefinitionFileSchema">

<EventClasses>
  <EventClass>
```

---

[2] A stock can trade on different exchanges and not necessarily for the same price. For simplicity, we assume that all exchanges trade in the same currency.

```
<EventClassName>StockEvt</EventClassName>
<Schema>
  <Field>
    <FieldName>StockCode</FieldName>
    <FieldType>varchar(10)</FieldType>
    <FieldTypeMods>not null</FieldTypeMods>
  </Field>
  <Field>
    <FieldName>ExchangeCode</FieldName>
    <FieldType>varchar(15)</FieldType>
    <FieldTypeMods>not null</FieldTypeMods>
  </Field>
  <Field>
    <FieldName>Price</FieldName>
    <FieldType>decimal(18,5)</FieldType>
    <FieldTypeMods>not null</FieldTypeMods>
  </Field>
</Schema>
<IndexSqlSchema>
  <SqlStatement>
    Create Index DMStockIndex on StockEvt
    (StockCode, ExchangeCode)
  </SqlStatement>
  <SqlStatement>
    Create Index DMStockIndex2 on StockEvt
    (ExchangeCode)</SqlStatement>
</IndexSqlSchema>
  </EventClass>
</EventClasses>

<SubscriptionClasses>
  <! -Rest of file omitted
  ...


</Application>
```

There is still something missing from the ADF file in Listing 16-6, and that is the information about what event provider to use. Remember that earlier we discussed hosted versus independent providers? Initially, we will use an independent provider to collect the events.

Event providers are entered and named in the ADF file. They are located under the `<Providers>` node. This node contains `<HostedProvider>` and `<NonHostedProvider>` nodes. First, as we mentioned, we'll use a nonhosted provider. Although some event providers need to be entered in the ADF to provide supporting information, others (like nonhosted providers) are entered mostly for internal documentation. We add to the ADF file in

Listing 16-6 the `<Providers>` node, as shown in Listing 16-7. Notice that the `<Providers>` node needs to be placed after the `<Notification Classes>` node but before the `<Generator>` node.

LISTING 16-7: Providers Node in the ADF File

```
</NotificationClasses>

<Providers>
     <NonHostedProvider>
          <ProviderName>SqlStockEvents</ProviderName>
     </NonHostedProvider>
</Providers>

<Generator>
```

With these updates to the ADF file, the SQLNS application can be updated. For updates, the NSControl Update command is used, according to the following syntax.

```
nscontrol update
    [-help] |
    -in configuration_filename
    [-verbose]
    [-force]
    [-sqlusername login_id -sqlpassword password]
    [-argumentkey key]
    [parameter_name=value [,...n] ]
    [-nologo]
```

The Update command looks almost like the Create command. The only differences are the verbose and force flags. The verbose flag displays the information that has changed in the configuration file and the ADF file as it is found. The force flag forces the update to proceed without prompting for approval after displaying the actions that will occur. To set up the event classes in the SQLNS application, you run NSControl Update against the configuration file and the changed ADF file.[3] Running NSControl Update -in appConfig2.xml causes some changes to the application database.

* Additional tables have been created: NSCurrentStockEvtEvent Batches, NSCurrentStockEvtEvents, NSStockEvtEventBatches,

---

[3] On the book Web site of samples, you will find the updated configuration file, appConfig2. xml, and the new ADF file, appADF2.xml, with the Notification Services samples.

NStockEvtEvents. As the names of the tables indicate, they are used to store event and event batch information.

- Data has been inserted in the NSEventClasses and NSEventFields tables.

- Among the new stored procedures are procedures for writing events and event batches.

In the ADF file, we indicated that we would use a nonhosted provider, and we gave it the name SqlStockEvents. With a nonhosted provider, the only element that needs to be defined is the name of the provider. We will see how the name is used when events are submitted through the SQLNS stored procedures.

Event Stored Procedures

These are the stored procedures that have been created to write events to the database.

- NSBeginEventBatch<EventClassName>—Creates a new event batch and returns an ID for the batch.

- NSEventWrite<EventClassName>—Submits one event to the events table for the event. The NSBeginEventBatch<EventClassName> must be run first to obtain the batch ID.

- NSEventFlushBatch<EventClassName>—Closes the batch and marks it complete. When the batch is marked complete, the generator can process the events.

- NsEventSubmitBatch<EventClassName>—The previous procedures in this list are mostly used to write to the event table when the event is a single event from an outside source. When the events to collect are multiple entries in a database, we use this procedure, which allows us to specify a query to retrieve a batch of events to collect.

In this stage of our application, we are only submitting single events, so we start the event collecting process by starting a batch. This is done using the NSBeginEventBatch<EventClassName> procedure. The syntax follows.

```
NSEventBeginBatchEventClassName
   [@ProviderName =] 'event_provider_name',
   [@EventBatchId =] event_batch_variable OUTPUT
```

The `EventClassName` is picked from the `EventClassName` element in the `EventClass` node. The procedure takes a provider name as the input parameter. This has to be the same name that appears in the `ProviderName` element. It returns a batch ID as the output parameter.

The batch ID is used in the `NSEventWrite<EventClassName>` stored procedure. This procedure also uses the event class name. The syntax looks like this.

```
NSEventWriteEventClassName
   [@EventBatchId =] event_batch_ID ,
   [@event_class_field_name =] event_class_field_value [, ...n]
```

The `@EventBatchId` parameter is the parameter received from the `NSEventBeginBatch` procedure. Name/value pairs follow the batch ID parameter. These name/value pairs correspond to the `FieldName` element in the `EventClass` node and its value. In the stock price database, the signature for the procedure looks like this.

```
NSEventWriteStockEvt
    @EventBatchId   bigint,
    @StockCode varchar(10) = NULL,
    @ExchangeCode varchar(15) = NULL,
    @Price decimal(18,5) = NULL
```

You close the batch with the `NSEventFlushBatch<EventClassName>` procedure when the event is submitted. This procedure takes the batch ID and optionally the number of events submitted as parameters.

```
NSEventFlushBatchEventClassName
   [@EventBatchId =] event_batch_ID
   [, [@EventCount =] number_of_events]
```

The code to create an event is shown in Listing 16-8. Because the application has just been created (and updated), it needs to be enabled and registered first. `NSControl` is used for this, and the syntax is as follows:

```
NSControl Enable -name instancename -server servername
```

where `-name` is the instance name and `-server` is the name of the server where the instance is installed.

LISTING 16-8: Code to Create an Event

```
DECLARE @ProviderName varchar(255)
DECLARE @EventBatchId bigint
DECLARE @EventCount bigint
DECLARE @RicCode varchar(6)
DECLARE @ExchangeCode varchar(6)
DECLARE @Price float(10)
DECLARE @EventClassName varchar(255)

SET @ProviderName = 'SqlStockEvents'
EXECUTE NSEventBeginBatchStockEvt @ProviderName,
                                  @EventBatchId OUTPUT

SET @RicCode = 'MSFT'
SET @ExchangeCode = 'NYSE'
SET @Price = 53.33
EXECUTE NSEventWriteStockEvt @EventBatchId,
                            @RicCode,
                            @ExchangeCode, @Price

SET @EventCount = 1
EXECUTE NSEventFlushBatchStockEvt @EventBatchId, @EventCount
```

To view information about the batch end the events in the batch, we can use a stored procedure named NSEventBatchDetails. The syntax for the procedure follows.

```
NSEventBatchDetails
    [@EventClassName =] 'event_class_name' ,
    [@EventBatchId =] event_batch_id
```

It takes the name of the event class and the ID of the batch you want the information about, and it produces two resultsets. The first resultset contains general information about the batch, such as the provider, how many events are in the batch, when the batch started, when it ended, and the total collection time in milliseconds. The second resultset contains information about the individual events in the batch: the event ID and the individual event fields of the event. Apart from getting information about batches and events, there are stored procedures for information about event providers and event classes.

- NSDiagnosticEventClass—This procedure produces information about event collection and processing of events by the application.
- NSDiagnosticEventProvider—This procedure contains information about the events collected through a specified event provider.

Event Providers

We started this whole section about events by discussing event providers. We also mentioned briefly the event providers that are part of the SQLNS framework: the File Watcher event provider and the SQL Server event provider. Let's now take a close look at them, starting with the File Watcher event provider (FS).

The File Watcher event provider monitors a directory. The provider fires when an XML file is added to the directory. It reads the content of the file into memory and writes the event data to the event table. Internally, the provider uses the `FileSystemWatcher` class from the .NET Framework. It is being run as a hosted nonscheduled provider, and it is set up in the ADF with these three mandatory arguments in addition to the provider name, class name, and system name:

- `WatchDirectory`—Full path and name of the directory that the event provider monitors
- `EventClassName`—Name of the event class that defines the events
- `SchemaFile`—Full path to a SQL-annotated schema file that describes the schema for the events

Listing 16-9 shows the provider part of the stock price application's ADF file when we have added the FS as a hosted provider.

LISTING 16-9: ADF File with Hosted File System Watcher Provider

```xml
<Providers>
  <HostedProvider>
  <ProviderName>StockEP</ProviderName>
  <ClassName>FileSystemWatcherProvider</ClassName>
  <SystemName>%_NSHost_%</SystemName>
  <Arguments>
    <Argument>
      <Name>WatchDirectory</Name>
      <Value>%_BasePath_%\Test\Events</Value>
    </Argument>
    <Argument>
      <Name>SchemaFile</Name>
      <Value>%_BasePath_%\EventsSchema.xsd</Value>
    </Argument>
    <Argument>
      <Name>EventClassName</Name>
      <Value>StockEvt</Value>
    </Argument>
```

```
      </Arguments>
    </HostedProvider>
    <NonHostedProvider>
      <ProviderName>SqlStockEvents</ProviderName>
    </NonHostedProvider>
</Providers>
```

The provider is named StockEP, the class name has to be FileSystem WatcherProvider, and the system name refers to the _NSHost_ parameter. In the arguments node, we point the directory to watch to the \Test\ Events directory underneath the base directory. The schema is located in the EventsSchema.xsd file in the base directory and is shown in Listing 16-10. Finally, we tell the provider that the event class to collect events for is the StockEvt class.

LISTING 16-10: Schema for the Stock Price Events

```
<xsd:schema xmlns:xsd="http://www.w3.org/2001/XMLSchema"
    xmlns:sql="urn:schemas-microsoft-com:mapping-schema">
  <xsd:element name="event" sql:relation="StockEvt">
    <xsd:complexType>
      <xsd:sequence>
        <xsd:element name="StockCode" type="xsd:string"/>
        <xsd:element name="ExchangeCode" type="xsd:string"/>
        <xsd:element name="Price" type="xsd:decimal" />
      </xsd:sequence>
    </xsd:complexType>
  </xsd:element>
</xsd:schema>
```

NSControl Update can now be run again against the configuration file. The configuration file's ApplicationDefinitionFilePath element needs to point to an ADF file containing the Providers section in Listing 16-9. Notice, however, that the _BasePath_ parameter is not defined at the application level. It needs to be defined first either in the configuration file or in the ADF file. We leave it up to the readers to figure out how to do it (or you can look in the appConfig3.xml and appADF3.xml files in the book's Web site samples). Before any updates can take place, the instance needs to be disabled. Use NSControl Disable to do this with a -name parameter and a -server parameter. These parameters are the same as those used for NSControl Enable. After the update has taken place, run NScontrol Enable again, as you did earlier before you submitted events to the application in Listing 16-8.

The FS provider is a hosted provider and as such runs under the SQLNS service. So far we haven't registered the service, but we have run SQLNS in nonservice mode. Unless we start the service, several parts of SQLNS won't run. Among them are the generator of events and notifications and the distributor of notifications.

To register the instance, we use `NSControl Register` with the name of the instance, the name of the server SQLNS runs on, and the `-service` argument, which registers this instance of SQLNS as a Windows service. It looks like this from the command line:

```
NSControl Register -name instance-name -server server-name -service
```

Notice that the previous command does not start the service explicitly. It needs to be started from Start | Administrative Tools | Services. The name of the service is `NS$` followed by the instance name. Therefore, if the instance name is `DM`, for example, the service name is `NS$DM`.

When the instance is registered and the service is started, the FS is ready to look for events in the watch directory. When a new file with an `.xml` extension placed into the watch directory, the FS loads the file into memory. It then uses an SQLNS `EventLoader` object to write the event information into the event table. When the batch has been processed and closed, the XML source file is renamed to indicate that it has been processed. The new file name is the original file name, to which is appended the date and time of its processing. A counter value is also appended to differentiate files processed at the same time, and a `.done` extension. If FS could not process the file, it will be renamed as described earlier, but with an `.err` extension. In the Notification Services sample code on the book's Web site is an XML file, `EventsData.xml`, that can be used to test the FS provider.

The second provider that is part of the SQLNS framework is the SQL Server event provider (SEP). This provider uses a user-defined query to query a database table for events. After retrieving the events, it uses the SQLNS event stored procedures to write the events to the event table. Queries can be defined to do pre- and postprocessing of the data. As opposed to the FS provider, the SEP runs as a scheduled provider, and the developer of the SQLNS application needs to define the schedule under which it should be run. Listing 16-11 shows an example of an entry for the SQL Server event provider in the ADF file. By now, you should be familiar with the schema of the file, so let's look at what is new in it. There is a `<Schedule>` node that has two children elements: the `<StartTime>` and the <Interval>. The <StartTime> element is optional and defines at what time the provider should start running after the application has been set up. The <Interval> defines at what interval it should run. The <Interval> in Listing 16-11 indicates that the provider runs every minute (60 seconds).

LISTING 16-11: ADF File with an Entry for a Scheduled SQL Server Event Provider

```
<Providers>
  <HostedProvider>
    <ProviderName>SQLStockPrice</ProviderName>
    <ClassName>SQLProvider</ClassName>
    <SystemName>%_NSHOST_%</SystemName>
    <Schedule>
      <StartTime>15:00:00</StartTime>
      <Interval>P0DT00H00M60S</Interval>
    </Schedule>
    <Arguments>
      <Argument>
        <Name>EventsQuery</Name>
        <Value>SELECT StockSymbol, StockPrice
              FROM StockPriceTable</Value>
      </Argument>
      <Argument>
        <Name>EventClassName</Name>
        <Value>StockEvents</Value>
      </Argument>
    </Arguments>
  </HostedProvider>
</Providers>
```

The format of the <Interval> entry is according to the XML duration data type. This data type is defined as P0DT00H00M00S, which specifies the interval as follows:

- P—Defines the duration data type
- 0D—Number of days
- T—Defines the time portion of the type
- 00H—Number of hours
- 00M—Number of minutes
- 00S—Number of seconds

The <Arguments> node has two children nodes. One defines the query to run, through the EventsQuery name; this is a required entry. The other argument is the EventClassName, which also is required. There is a possible third, optional argument, `PostQuery`,which defines a query to run after the events have been collected.

Chronicles

We have seen in this events section how events are collected. The model for events collection is based on the presumption that each event can cause a notification. They will not necessarily do that, but potentially they can. For a scenario where the user is only interested in being notified at a certain time regardless of whether an event occurred at that time or not, the model does not work that well. These are some possible scenarios.

- The user wants to get a traffic report at a certain time.
- The user wants to see the highest price of a particular stock during the day.
- The user wants to see historical event information.

To accomplish this, SQLNS uses chronicle tables and chronicle rules to store event data from event batches. Chronicle tables are defined in the `/EventClasses/EventClass/Chronicles` section of the ADF file, as Listing 16-12 shows.

LISTING 16-12: Chronicle Table Creation in the ADF File

```
<EventClass>
  <! -  other EventClass elements  ->
  <Chronicles>
    <Chronicle>
        <ChronicleName>StockEvtChron</ChronicleName>
        <SqlSchema>
            <SqlStatement>
                - drop table before creating it
                IF EXISTS(SELECT name FROM sys.tables
                WHERE name = 'StockEvtChron')
                 DROP TABLE dbo.StockEvtChron
                CREATE TABLE StockEvtChron (
                   [StockCode] nvarchar(6),
         [ExchangeCode] nvarchar(6),
                   [StockPrice]        decimal(18,5))
            </SqlStatement>
          </SqlSchema>
        </Chronicle>
  </Chronicles>
<! -  other EventClass elements  ->
</EventClass>
```

The chronicle tables are populated from the corresponding event class through chronicle rules. The rules are defined by SQL statements, and they can be defined in two places: either in the `<ChronicleRule>` node of an event class or in the `<EventRules>` node of a subscription class. The decision of where to place the rules depends on when the chronicle data should be affected. If the data is to be affected before notifications are generated, the rule should be defined in the `<ChronicleRule>`. If the chronicle data should be affected after the notifications have been generated, the rule should be placed in the `<EventRules>` node. The following code shows a chronicle rule that updates entries in the chronicle table if the price in the events table is greater than the price in the chronicle table. Notice that the developer of the ADF file has to use the entity references of the greater-than (>) and less-than (<) signs because those are reserved characters in XML.

```
<EventClass>
  <!-- other EventClass elements -->
  <ChronicleRule>
      <RuleName>StockEventsChronRule</RuleName>
        <Action>
          -- Update value in the chronicle
          UPDATE   StockEvtChron
            SET    StockPrice = e.StockPrice
            FROM   StockEvt e
      JOIN StockEventsChron c
            ON e.StockCode = c.StockCode
      AND e.ExchangeCode = c.ExchangeCode
      WHERE  e.StockPrice &gt; c.StockPrice
        </Action>
        </ChronicleRule>
  <Chronicles>...</Chronicles>
</EventClass>
```

Events and chronicles are not interesting in themselves; we need someone to be interested in the events. In other words, we need subscribers and subscriptions.

Subscribers and Subscriptions

In order to send subscriptions, the SQLNS needs information about the following:

- Who to send information to—The subscribers
- What information to send—The subscriptions
- What devices the information should be sent to—The devices

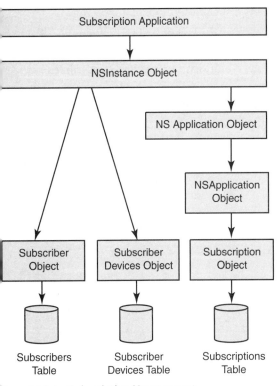

FIGURE 16-4: Subscription Management

The setup of this is done through using subscription management objects in SQLNS. Information about the subscribers and their devices is stored in the SQLNS instance database, whereas information about subscriptions is stored in the SQLNS application database. The developer of the SQLNS application also needs to define information about subscriptions in the ADF file by subscription classes and device information in the configuration file (see Listing 16-1 or 16-2, where there is an entry for a <DeliveryChannel>).

Figure 16-4 tries to give a graphical illustration of how subscription information is entered through a subscription management application. The subscription management application uses the management objects to create subscriber information in the instance database and subscription information in the application database.

In Figure 16-4 you can see references to various objects (subscriber, subscription, devices). These objects are part of the SQLNS management objects mentioned earlier, and for subscription management we specifically use the objects in the following list.

- `NSInstance`—Represents a specific SQLNS instance. Several Notification Services classes require a reference to this object in order to be initialized.

- `Subscriber`—Represents a Notification Services subscriber. Subscriptions and subscriber devices in the Notification Services system are associated with a subscriber by means of the subscriber ID.

- `SubscriberDevice`—Represents a device belonging to a subscriber that can be used to receive notifications.

- `NSApplication`—Represents a specific SQLNS application. As with the `NSInstance`, many SQLNS classes require a reference to this class.

- `Subscription`—Represents a single subscription within an SQLNS application.

All these classes live in the `Microsoft.SqlServer.Notification Services` namespace, and they are the main classes for developing subscription applications. However, these are not the only classes available for subscription management. There are classes for enumeration/information of subscribers, devices, subscriptions, and so on. The `Notification Services` namespace is not just for subscription management; it contains all the SQLNS classes and interfaces. All the classes in the `Notification Services` namespace are written in managed code, but they also have COM wrappers so they can be used from COM automation languages. In addition to the classes related to instances, applications, and subscription management in general, the namespace holds classes and interfaces related to the following:

- Submitting events to the Notification Services system
- Developing custom Notification Services components

Looking at Figure 16-4, we can see the steps to create subscription management applications: create subscribers, create devices, and finally create subscriptions. Before the subscriptions can be created, the subscriptions schema needs to be defined in the ADF file through `SubscriptionClasses`.

Subscription Classes

One or more subscription classes in the ADF file decide the types of subscriptions that the SQLNS application accepts. A subscription class generally holds information about the device, information about the event, and what constitutes an event. In addition to this, you can add further information, such as locale. SQLNS use some subscription fields automatically for formatting and delivery. Examples of such fields are the subscriber ID and the device name, which are used by the formatter and the delivery mechanism; and the formatter uses the locale field.

An example of an ADF file with a subscription class is shown in Listing 16-13. Perusing the code in the Listing 16-13, we see that there are subscription fields defined for the device, the locale, the event information, and at what point an event triggers. The subscription class has in addition a SQL statement for dropping and creating indexes on the subscription table.

LISTING 16-13: Subscription Class Information in the ADF File

```
<SubscriptionClasses>
  <SubscriptionClass>
    <SubscriptionClassName>
      %_App_%Subscriptions
    </SubscriptionClassName>
    <Schema>
      <Field>
        <FieldName>DeviceName</FieldName>
        <FieldType>varchar(255)</FieldType>
        <FieldTypeMods>not null</FieldTypeMods>
      </Field>
      <Field>
        <FieldName>SubLocale</FieldName>
        <FieldType>varchar(10)</FieldType>
        <FieldTypeMods>not null</FieldTypeMods>
      </Field>
      <Field>
        <FieldName>StockCode</FieldName>
        <FieldType>varchar(15)</FieldType>
        <FieldTypeMods>not null</FieldTypeMods>
      </Field>
      <Field>
        <FieldName>ExchangeCode</FieldName>
        <FieldType>varchar(15)</FieldType>
        <FieldTypeMods>not null</FieldTypeMods>
      </Field>
      <Field>
        <FieldName>TriggerVal</FieldName>
        <FieldType>decimal(18, 5)</FieldType>
        <FieldTypeMods>not null</FieldTypeMods>
      </Field>
    </Schema>
    <IndexSqlSchema>
      <SqlStatement>
        IF EXISTS (SELECT name FROM sys.indexes
        WHERE name = &apos;StockSubIndex&apos;)
```

```
      DROP INDEX %_App_%Subscriptions.StockSubIndex
    </SqlStatement>
    <SqlStatement>
      CREATE INDEX StockSubIndex
      ON %_App_%Subscriptions (SubscriberID)
    </SqlStatement>
  </IndexSqlSchema>
 </SubscriptionClass>
</SubscriptionClasses>
```

For event-driven subscriptions, the subscription class also needs to define event rules. The event rules define how notifications are generated for the subscriptions. These rules are executed each time a new event batch is processed. The event rules are entered in the EventRules node in the subscription class; we cover more about event rules in the section about notifications. For schedule-driven notifications, the rules are created in a ScheduledRules section in the ADF file.

The ADF file can now be updated with the section in Listing 16-13. To update the application database, disable the SQLNS instance, run NSControl Update, and then enable the instance again. Let's now look at the users of the subscription class: the subscribers and their subscriptions.

Subscribers

Subscribers are instance specific and are added to the instance database. The main class for subscribers is the Subscriber class mentioned earlier, which has methods for adding and deleting subscribers to the instance. From the Subscriber class you can also get information about what subscriptions a particular subscriber has.

Listing 16-14 shows an example of a managed console application used for adding subscribers to an instance. In a production application, it is doubtful that a console application would be used. Instead, the application would probably be an ASP.NET WebForms application. With the support for COM, it could also be an ASP application. Notice the using statement for the Microsoft.SqlServer.NotificationServices namespace. When compiling, the application needs a reference to the microsoft.sqlserver. notificationservices.dll file, which can be found in the .\Program Files\Microsoft SQL Server\90\NotificationServices\<version>\ bin directory. The code shows how we first create an instance of the NSInstance class. The NSInstance class has an overloaded constructor where one constructor method takes the instance name as a parameter and initializes the SQLNS instance. If the constructor method that does not take an instance name as a parameter is used, the instance can be set by a property. In that case, the SQLNS instance needs to be initialized separately by the Initialize method.

The instance is then used as constructor parameter for the initialization of the Subscriber class. The ID of the subscriber is set on the SubscriberId property and Add is called.

LISTING 16-14: Code to Add Subscriber

```
using System;
using Microsoft.SqlServer.NotificationServices;

class nssub {
    static void Main(string[] args) {
    string subId = "NielsB";
    string inst = "DM";
    AddSubscriber(inst, subId);
    }

static void AddSubscriber(string inst, string subId) {
    NSInstance nsInst = new NSInstance(inst);
    Subscriber sub = new Subscriber(nsInst);
    sub.SubscriberId = subId;
    try {
      sub.Add();
    }
    catch(Exception e) {
      Console.WriteLine(e.Message);
    }
  }
```

After successful completion of the methods, there will be an entry in the NSSubcribers table in the instance database. After subscribers have been added, devices need to be added, to define on what devices a subscriber can receive notifications. A device is tied to a delivery channel, which is tied to a delivery protocol. We haven't yet discussed delivery channels or protocols much; they are covered later in this chapter. For now, what we need to remember is that the SQLNS framework comes with a couple of predefined delivery protocols. You may remember that in the configuration file in Listing 16-2 we defined a delivery channel named FileChannel, which used the file protocol. The file protocol is one of the predefined protocols in the SQLNS framework. It is mainly used for debugging, and we will use it for the time being until we discuss delivery channels and protocols in greater detail later on.

The reason we go on about this is that when we define the devices, we also need to define the delivery channel to use, as the code in Listing 16-15 shows. Be aware that there is a FOREIGN KEY CONSTRAINT between the NSDeliveryChannels table and the NSSubscribersDevices table on the DeliveryChannelName columns. In other words, you need to make sure that the DeliveryChannelName property on the SubscriberDevice instance exists in the NSDeliveryChannels table. The records in the NSDeliveryChannels table depend on what has been entered in the configuration file under the <DeliveryChannels> node.

LISTING 16-15: Adding a Subscriber Device

```
static void AddSubscriberDevice(string inst, string subId) {
    NSInstance nsInst = new NSInstance(inst);
    SubscriberDevice dev = new SubscriberDevice(nsInst);
    dev.DeliveryChannelName = "FileChannel";
    dev.DeviceAddress = "";
    dev.DeviceName = "FileDevice";
    dev.DeviceTypeName = "File";
    dev.SubscriberId = subId;
    try {
        dev.Add();
    }
    catch(Exception e) {
        Console.WriteLine(e.Message);

    }
}
```

The code in Listing 16-15 shows the following properties on the SubscriberDevice class:

- DeliveryChannelName—The name of the delivery channel used by the device
- DeviceAddress—The address of the device
- DeviceName—The name of the device
- DeviceTypeName—The name of the device type that describes the subscriber device
- SubscriberId—The ID of the subscriber.

Subscriptions

The subscriptions node defines what information each subscriber gets and on what device he gets them. The class to use to add subscriptions is the

Subscription class. This class has methods to add and delete subscriptions for a specific subscriber as well as methods and properties to get and set information about the subscription record.

The code in Listing 16-16 shows how the Subscription class is used to add a subscription for an existing subscriber. The NSInstance class is instantiated first, followed by the NSApplication class. The constructor of the application class takes the instance and the name of the application we want to instantiate as constructor parameters. The Subscription class is created with the instance and the name of the subscription class. The subscription class name is needed because there can be several subscription classes in the application. The Subscription class can now be used, and we call the SetFieldValue on the class. SetFieldValue is a method that takes a name/value pair as separate parameters. The name parameter corresponds to a subscription field in the aforementioned subscription class, and the value part sets the value of that field. From the code, you can see how we set the device the subscriber wants the notifications on, what locale to format the notifications with, the event information (StockCode and ExchangeCode), and when to trigger a notification (TriggerVal). We set the SubscriberId property to indicate who this subscription is for, and finally we call Add.

LISTING 16-16: Adding a Subscription

```
static void AddSubScription(string inst, string appName, string subId) {
  NSInstance nsInst = new NSInstance(inst);

  //create an instance of the NSApplication class
  NSApplication app = new
            NSApplication(nsInst, appName);

  Subscription sub =
            new Subscription(app, "StockPriceSubscriptions");

  //set the value of the fields
  //in the subscription record
  sub.SetFieldValue("DeviceName", "FileDevice");
  sub.SetFieldValue("SubLocale", "en-US");
  sub.SetFieldValue("StockCode", "SUNW");
  sub.SetFieldValue("ExchangeCode", "NASDAQ");
  sub.SetFieldValue("TriggerVal", 7);
  sub.SubscriberId = subId;
  try {
    sub.Add();
  }
```

```
catch(Exception e){
  Console.WriteLine(e.Message);

}

}
```

The code in Listing 16-16 inserts the subscription information in the `NS<SubscriptionClassName>Subscriptions` table. The SQLNS framework, based on the schema in the subscription class, creates this table. The table is used when the framework generates notifications.

Notifications

Notifications are generated by finding matching information in event and subscription tables by joining those tables. The notification data is the event information that meets the subscription requirements, plus any additional information the developer wants to include. The data to include in a notification is defined in one or several notification classes in the ADF file. Information required in the notification class are the event data, what content formatter to use for the notifications, what delivery protocols this notification class uses, and how long notifications should be re-sent before being deemed out of date. In addition to this information, the notification class can define whether the notification class uses the following.

- Digest delivery—Digest delivery groups together all notifications to one subscriber during one notification generation and sends them as one notification.
- Notification batch size—Normally, the generator creates one batch per firing. This setting defines how many notifications should be included in one batch. If this is set, the generator breaks the batch into smaller sizes that meet the set size.
- Multicast delivery—Notifications that share identical data and are in the same distributor work item are formatted once and sent to all subscribers.

Listing 16-17 shows one `NotificationClass`, which defines the data in a notification. The class uses the XSLT formatter, and the file protocol is used to send the notifications. There is an expiration time of two hours. If a notification has not been successfully sent after two hours, the notification is considered out of date.

LISTING 16-17: Notification Class in the ADF File

```
<NotificationClasses>
  <NotificationClass>
    <NotificationClassName>%_App_%Notifications
</NotificationClassName>
    <Schema>
      <Fields>
        <Field>
          <FieldName>StockCode</FieldName>
          <FieldType>varchar(15)</FieldType>
        </Field>
        <Field>
          <FieldName>ExchangeCode</FieldName>
          <FieldType>varchar(15)</FieldType>
        </Field>
        <Field>
          <FieldName>Price</FieldName>
          <FieldType>decimal(18, 5)</FieldType>
        </Field>
      </Fields>
    </Schema>
    <ContentFormatter>
      <ClassName>XsltFormatter</ClassName>
    </ContentFormatter>
    <Protocols>
      <Protocol>
        <ProtocolName>File</ProtocolName>
      </Protocol>
    </Protocols>
    <ExpirationAge>PT2H</ExpirationAge>
  </NotificationClass>
</NotificationClasses>
```

Running NSControl Update updates the NS<NotificationClassName>
Notifications table with the fields from the notification class. In addition, it alters a SQL Server user-defined function (UDF), which was originally created when NSControl Create ran.

Notification Rules

Remember from the discussions about subscription classes, that we mentioned we needed event generation rules in order to generate notifications.
Event rules are SQL queries defining the contents of a notification and
what constitutes a notification. When a notification is created, the raw data
is inserted into the notifications table, and the only way that can happen in
an SQLNS application is through the notification function. In other words,
the SQL query for the event generation rule needs to use the function in
some way.

In pre–SQL Server 2005 versions of SQLNS, this was accomplished by executing an SQLNS-generated user-defined function in the SQL query sending in the necessary parameters. The parameters to the UDF were based on the fields defined in the notification class schema plus some generic parameters. The "notify function" looked somewhat like this.

```
StockPriceNotificationsNotify(@SubscriberId NVARCHAR(255),
    @DeviceName NVARCHAR(255), @SubscriberLocale NVARCHAR(10),
    @StockCode varchar(15), @ExchangeCode varchar(15),
    @Price decimal(18, 5))
```

The only change in SQLNS between pre–SQL Server 2005 versions and the SQL Server 2005 version is the replacement of the notify function with an INSERT INTO / SELECT statement. This is an optimization because in previous versions the notify function had to be executed for each notification; the new mechanism is executed only once and is an optimizable T-SQL JOIN. In addition, you can add information from tables other than the subscription table and the event and event chronicle tables. This makes the notification generation mechanism more extensible.

Notice that the first columns in the INSERT statement are subscriber ID, device, and locale. These always need to be included because the framework uses this information when generating and formatting the notifications. In addition to these fields, event data and other subscription data can be included.

Listing 16-18 shows the EventRules entry needed in the subscription class. In the event rule, we send in to the function the ID of the subscriber, the device, and the locale. This information is taken from the subscription table. The event information used is the stock code, the exchange code, and the price, all of which come from the event table. Finally, it is matched on the stock code and exchange code, and we only want data where the price is greater than the trigger value set in the subscription table. The Event Rule also indicates in the EventClassName element which event it is for.

LISTING 16-18: Event Rule

```
</Schema>
  <EventRules>
    <EventRule>
      <RuleName>EvtRule</RuleName>
      <Action>
      INSERT INTO %_App_%Notifications(
          SubscriberId, DeviceName,
          SubscriberLocale, RicCode,
```

```
        ExchangeCode, Price)
    SELECT s.SubscriberId, s.DeviceName, s.SubLocale,
        e.RicCode, e.ExchangeCode, e.Price
    FROM StockEvt e, %_App_%Subscriptions s
    WHERE e.RicCode = s.RicCode
        AND e.ExchangeCode = s.ExchangeCode
        AND e.Price &gt; s.TriggerVal
    </Action>
    <EventClassName>StockEvt</EventClassName>
  </EventRule>
 </EventRules>
<! - Index schema information follows  ->
<IndexSqlSchema/>
```

In addition to writing the notifications to the notifications table, the notification function participates in creating notification batches. When the function is called for the first time during firing of a rule, the system creates a new notification batch record. The notifications that the function creates are all part of this batch, unless a batch size has been defined, in which case multiple batches would be generated. When the batches are closed, the notifications are ready for formatting and distribution.

Distributor and Formatters

The part of the SQLNS framework that is responsible for both formatting and distributing notifications is the distributor. The distributor runs continuously and partitions the batches ready for distribution into smaller *work* items. This allows the system to take advantage of parallel processing, whereas multiple distributors can run in parallel and/or a single distributor can process multiple work items in parallel.

Part of the processing of the work items is formatting the notification data. The distributor is responsible for the formatting and routes the notifications to a content formatter.

Formatters

The content formatter is a managed class that implements the IContent Formatter interface. The developer of an SQLNS application does not have to develop a customized formatter but can use the XSLT formatter that is part of the SQLNS framework. The XSLT formatter allows you to specify an XSL transform to be applied to the raw notification data. This XSL transform makes all the formatting changes that are required to prepare the notification data for display. The XSL transform does not have to

be the same for a given notification class. The transform can be differen
depending on locale and device.

The XSLT formatter reads the transform from a directory and creates a
intermediate XML document in memory. This XML document contains the
notification data. It then applies the XSL transform to the document, and
the result is the final formatted notification. The directory that the format
ter reads the transform from is based upon whether the formatting i
dependent on locale or device. Each type of device and locale supported
should have an individual transform file placed in its own directory.

To define the XSLT formatter, an entry in the ADF file is needed in
the `NotificationClass` section under the `ContentFormatter` node. List
ing 16-19 shows the necessary entries in the ADF file for the XSLT format
ter. The name of the class that is used for formatting is defined in the `Class`
`Name` node. For a custom formatter, the assembly name needs to de defined
as well in an `AssemblyName` element. Following the `ClassName` comes the
`Arguments` section, with one or more `Argument` nodes. When the XSLT for
matter is used, the base directory needs to be defined as well as the name
of the transform file.

LISTING 16-19: Content Formatter Information in the ADF File

```
</Schema>
<! -Schema information above  ->
  <ContentFormatter>
    <ClassName>XsltFormatter</ClassName>
    <Arguments>
      <Argument>
        <Name>XsltBaseDirectoryPath</Name>
        <Value>%_BaseDirectoryPath_%</Value>
      </Argument>
      <Argument>
        <Name>XsltFileName</Name>
        <Value>NoOp.xslt</Value>
      </Argument>
    </Arguments>
  </ContentFormatter>
<! - Protocol information below  ->
<Protocols>
```

The `NoOp.xslt` transform file in Listing 16-19 is a transform that come
with the sample applications of the framework. It is mostly used fo
debugging, and it outputs the raw notification data XML format. A slightly
more functional transform is shown in the following code snippet.

```
<?xml version="1.0" encoding="UTF-8" ?>
<xsl:stylesheet version="1.0"
xmlns:xsl="http://www.w3.org/1999/XSL/Transform">

<xsl:template match="notifications">
     <html>
          <body>
               <xsl:apply-templates/>
               <i>Thank you for using DMTrade and
     SQL Server Notification Services.</i><br/><br/>
     </body>
     </html>
     </xsl:template>

     <xsl:template match="notification">
          <b><xsl:value-of select="StockCode" /></b>
          at
          <b><xsl:value-of select="ExchangeCode" /></b>
          is trading at: $
          <b><xsl:value-of select="Price" /></b>
          <br/><br/>
     </xsl:template>

</xsl:stylesheet>
```

The XSLT transform matches the notifications and the notifications' elements. The `<xsl:apply-templates/>` creates the header of the notification, and the `<xsl:value-of select=""/>` produces the body information. When the notifications are formatted, they are handed to the delivery channels and protocols for delivery to the subscribers.

Delivery

Formatted notifications are distributed through delivery channels to delivery services. Delivery channels are an abstraction, and they consist of two concrete parts: the delivery protocol and the configuring/addressing information necessary to identify an endpoint. It is the protocol's responsibility to assemble formatted notifications into protocol packets that are sent through an external delivery system such as Simple Mail Transfer Protocol (SMTP).

The configuring/addressing information allows interaction with the delivery channel by including non-application-specific information. This information can be what gateway to use, authentication information, and so on. It is the distributor's job to figure out what delivery channel should handle a notification, by looking at the device targeted for the notification

(remember that device information is part of a notification record). By look
ing at the device record in the subscriber devices table, the distributor deter
mines which delivery channel to use. From there, the distributor decide
on the protocol to use by looking up the channel in the delivery channel
table and matching the channel with the protocol.

Delivery Protocols

Delivery protocols are one concrete part of delivery channels, and sev
eral channels can use the same protocol. The protocols used can either b
custom-developed protocols or any of the two protocols that are part c
the framework:

- File—Writes text data to a file specified in the configuration file
- SMTP—Creates and routes messages through SMTP mail systems

Information about delivery channels and protocols is located in bot
the application configuration file and the ADF file. For the file protocol, th
only thing that needs to be added to the configuration file in Listing 16-2 i
an entry for what file the output should be written to. The following cod
shows the relevant part of the configuration file.

```
<DeliveryChannels>
  <DeliveryChannel>
    <DeliveryChannelName>FileChannel</DeliveryChannelName>
    <ProtocolName>File</ProtocolName>
    <Arguments>
      <Argument>
        <Name>FileName</Name>
        <Value>%BasePath%\Notif\StockNotification.txt</Value>
      </Argument>
    </Arguments>
  </DeliveryChannel>
</DeliveryChannels>
```

In the `Argument` node is an argument called `FileName`, which points t
the actual file that receives the output. That is the only required argumer
for the file protocol. An additional, optional argument, named `Encoding`
defines what encoding to use in the output file. By default, this is `utf-8`
Every protocol used needs an entry in the `Protocols` section in each of th
notification classes using that particular protocol. For the file protocol, th
only entry needed is the `ProtocolName`, and it must be `File`. Listing 16-1
shows an example of this. Other protocols may need specific informatio

in the header of a notification, and for this purpose, you use the `Fields` section with `Field` nodes (more about this later). Each protocol can also have different execution settings: the interval between retries for a failed delivery, how many times a delivery can fail before an error is reported in the event log, and so on. This information is recorded in the `Protocol\ProtocolExecutionSettings` node.

Arguably, the file protocol is a "bare minimum" protocol, mostly used for debugging. The developer uses the file protocol to make sure that notifications are generated, formatted, and distributed as expected. For a production application, another protocol would be used, such as the SMTP protocol, which sends notifications to any SMTP mail system for delivery.

For SQLNS to be set up to work with the SMTP protocol, the entry in the configuration file's `DeliveryChannel` section should point to the actual SMTP server used. As with the file protocol, the encoding style can also be specified, as the following code snippet from a configuration file shows.

```
<DeliveryChannels>
    <DeliveryChannel>
        <DeliveryChannelName>EmailChannel</DeliveryChannelName>
        <ProtocolName>SMTP</ProtocolName>
        <Arguments>
            <Argument>
                <Name>SmtpServer</Name>
                <Value>SERVNB01</Value>
            </Argument>
            <Argument>
                <Name>BodyEncoding</Name>
                <Value>utf-16</Value>
            </Argument>
        </Arguments>
    </DeliveryChannel>
</DeliveryChannels>
```

Notice that the argument name for the encoding type is different between the file protocol (`Encoding`) and the SMTP protocol (`BodyEncoding`). The `ProtocolName` element must be `SMTP` for the SMTP protocol.

Compared with the file protocol, the SMTP protocol needs some more entries in the `/NotificationClasses/NotificationClass/Protocols/Protocol` section of the ADF file. The additional entries are the protocol fields we mentioned previously. The use of protocol fields is to specify protocol-specific header information, like From and To for an e-mail message, for example. Protocol fields are named expressions that operate on raw notification data and subscriber information, and they are defined as `Field Reference` elements or `SqlExpression` elements in the ADF file's `Fields` node of the `/NotificationClasses/NotificationClass/Protocols/ Protocol` section. A `FieldReference` element references fields in the `NotificationClass/Schema/Fields`, whereas a `SqlExpression` refers to arbitrary T-SQL expressions. An example of `SqlExpression` fields is shown in Listing 16-20. It shows the fields that the SMTP protocol uses. There are three required fields: `Subject`, `From`, and `To`. It also has two optional fields: `Priority` and `BodyFormat`. Listing 16-20 shows also how arbitrary string constants can be used from the `SqlExpression` element, by enclosing the constant in apostrophes. The apostrophes are defined by their entity reference, `&apos;`.

LISTING 16-20: SMTP Protocol Defined in the ADF File

```
<Protocols>
 <Protocol>
    <ProtocolName>SMTP</ProtocolName>
    <Fields>
      <Field>
        <FieldName>Subject</FieldName>
        <SqlExpression>
          &apos;Stock Notification: &apos;+
          CONVERT(varchar(30), GetDate())
        </SqlExpression>
      </Field>
      <Field>
        <FieldName>From</FieldName>
        <SqlExpression>
          &apos;tradingroom@dmgs.com&apos;
        </SqlExpression>
      </Field>
      <Field>
        <FieldName>To</FieldName>
        <SqlExpression>DeviceAddress</SqlExpression>
      </Field>
      <Field>
        <FieldName>Priority</FieldName>
        <SqlExpression>&apos;Normal&apos;</SqlExpression>
      </Field>
      <Field>
        <FieldName>BodyFormat</FieldName>
        <SqlExpression>&apos;html&apos;</SqlExpression>
      </Field>
    </Fields>
  </Protocol>
</Protocols>
```

Customization

In the last part of this section about delivery, we want to mention briefly that when existing protocols do not meet the requirements for the application, customized delivery protocols can be developed and used. Examples of custom protocols are protocols for MSMQ and Microsoft Instant Messenger. To develop a custom delivery protocol, developers need to implement one of two interfaces from the `Microsoft.SqlServer.Notification Services` namespace.

- `IHttpProtocolProvider`—This interface makes it easy to create an HTTP-based protocol. All HTTP-related functionality already exists, so developers only have to provide the code for formatting the envelope and processing responses.
- `IDeliveryProtocol`—Developers can use this interface for non-HTTP-based protocols or where more flexibility is required from the `IHttpProtocolProvider`.

When a custom protocol is developed, it needs to be defined in the `Protocols` section of the configuration file, with information about the protocol name, the class name, and what assembly the class can be found in. Also, a delivery channel that uses the protocol needs to be defined in the `DeliveryChannels` node of the configuration file.

Customization is beyond the scope of this chapter; for more information, look in SQL Server Books Online.

Where Are We?

SQL Server Notification Services is a platform for developing and deploying applications that generate and send notifications to users. It uses Windows services and SQL Server as the foundation for the framework. A series of commercial applications that use .NET Alerts (most use it in conjunction with Notification Services) are available for subscribers at http://www.microsoft.com/alerts. In addition, the Notification Services framework will be used to implement notifications for file and directory changes in the revolutionary WinFS file system, available as part of the Windows code name "Longhorn" operating system in the near future.

17

Wrap-up: Relations, XML, Objects, and Services

S QL SERVER 2005 is more than just a new version of SQL Server. It is the integration of relational data, object data, and XML data in a way that makes it easier to build secure, reliable, and scalable applications that are easily maintained, regardless of data paradigm. In addition, the new features more tightly integrate the data to the kinds of Web-based applications we are building today and will be tomorrow.

Lots of New Features

SQL Server 2005 contains an amazing number of new features. We've covered most of them in previous chapters but haven't even touched on new administrative features, replication features, the Reporting Services, the new Analysis Services, and DTS features, including .NET-based libraries for everything. We've concentrated on developer topics.

SQL Server core functionality is enhanced with each release. There were a great number of enhancements based on making SQL Server more secure and reliable. These included not only features like the separation of database user and database schema, and SQL Server user password-handling enhancements, but also increasing reliability and security by providing an in-database programming model using a managed-code environment.

An entire new concurrency model that uses versioning instead of locking was introduced. For those developers that have had difficulty porting or converting their applications to SQL Server because of the differences between locking-based and versioning-based concurrency, the new model goes a long way toward removing this obstacle.

Transact-SQL has also been improved, not only with new system-defined functions and new SQL extensions, but also by adding exception handling. Whether you use client-side ADO.NET and the `SqlClient` data provider, the in-server `SqlServer` provider, a COM-based API-like OLE DB or ADO, or ODBC, the SQL-92 standard database API, you're still always using statements that are written in Transact-SQL to invoke data-related functionality. Transact-SQL *is* your way of getting data. Processing the data, however, is a different story.

Data Models, Programming, and SQL Server

The new functionality in SQL Server 2005 gives us many choices for storing, processing, programming, performing calculations on, and sharing data. In large part because of the ease of sharing data over a well-known protocol, HTTP, in a few well-known formats, the concept of the remote application server—historically used only in monolithic systems—has become a "commodity" way of programming. The application server (and middle tier in the ANSI-SPARC three-tier architecture) has been popularized as the Web server. In addition, over time three programming and data-related trends have become entrenched.

- Data is stored in databases based on the relational model.
- Application programmers design and program using object-oriented concepts.
- XML is used to communicate among unlike architectures and has its own data model.

SQL Server 2005 and the libraries in .NET version 2.0 give programmers a lot of choices for which paradigm (relational, object-oriented, or XML) can be used at any layer and how it can be programmed. Here are a few contrived examples, for purists of each paradigm.

Relational data can be stored in SQL Server—it's SQL Server's native format. It can be accessed through an object-oriented layer based loosely on the SQL-CLI (SQL Call-Level Interface) known as ADO.NET, through

OLE DB, or through ODBC (the most well-known implementation of SQL-CLI) directly through a proprietary protocol, TDS.

The ObjectSpaces API can consume user-defined types and/or relational data and expose a "pure object" view of the world to the programmer. As far as the application programmer is concerned, SQL Server is an object-oriented database, even though it completely maintains its relational model.

XML data can be stored in SQL Server directly. It can be validated on the server because XML schemas are stored in the server. It can be indexed based on efficiency of query with the XQuery language, or XML documents can be searched based on their text content with full-text search. Relational data can also be exposed as XML through Transact-SQL extensions, and XML messages can be marshaled either using HTTP and Web Services for interoperability or using SQL Server Service Broker for the asynchrony and reliability that HTTP lacks.

Any Functionality at Any Tier

The most interesting thing (and scary, for those of us who want homogeneous, cut-and-paste solutions) is that this functionality can be split across any tier. There are almost too many choices. Using SQL Server and .NET 2.0 library code names, here are some of the ways you can split things out, if you divide the world into client, middle tier, and database. Big caveat: Some of these are technically possible, but not supported (actually prohibited from working) or, in some cases, recommended.

Here's what you can accomplish on the database alone.

1. You can store XML data in SQL Server using the XML data type.
2. You can query relational data in SQL Server as XML using SELECT . . . FOR XML and store it using the xml.nodes method, OpenXml, or XML Bulk Insert in Transact-SQL.
3. You can write .NET programs that use System.Xml and System.Data.SqlXml inside SQL Server to query XML or convert relational data to XML.
4. You can produce XML in a stored procedure and transport it using HTTP instead of TDS.
5. You can transport text or XML through asynchronous messaging.
6. You can extend SQL Server's scalar type system with UDTs.

7. You can coerce relational data into objects using `System.Data.ObjectSpaces` inside SQL Server.

8. You can use ADO.NET either through `System.Data.SqlServer` or `System.Data.SqlClient` inside .NET programs that run on SQL Server.

9. If you don't use the managed environment, you can still use extended stored procedures written in any unmanaged (unsafe) language and access data using ODBC or OLE DB.

10. You can manipulate the data entirely with Transact-SQL stored procedures and user-defined functions.

Here's what you can accomplish on the middle tier or client.

1. You can fetch and program against any type of data from SQL Server with ADO.NET (`SqlClient`), OLE DB, or ADO.

2. You can fetch any type of data with ODBC.

3. You can transform relational data to objects with `System.Data.ObjectSpaces`, and operate on it and persist it without caring what the relational tables look like.

4. You can transform relational data to XML with `System.Data.SqlXml`, and operate on it and persist it without caring what the relational tables look like.

5. You can retrieve data through HTTP or TDS.

6. You can work with extended scalar types from SQL Server as though they are .NET types.

7. You can directly bind data, in relational form, as collections of objects, or as XML trees, to graphical user interface components for either Web-based, interoperable consumption (ASP.NET, middle tier) or rich window user-interface consumption (Windows Forms, client).

SQL Server 2005 and the .NET Framework base class library APIs have accomplished the integration of relational, object, and XML data.

So Which Tier and What Data Model?

With so many choices, the question that always arises next is, "What are best practices?" when the new technological functionality is factored into the equation. We've always had a hard time with the concept of best practices because of the underlying implication that domain problems can fit into neat categories. They can't. It's like saying to an architect, "It's only a building; just build one just like the one you built last year." Although certain pieces can be prefabricated, the overall structure and look-and-feel depend on the landscape and ascetics. We can't start to count the number of hours we've spent in meetings listening to software developers argue over "elegant" versus "ugly" designs, or technological politics. Any software project must balance the concepts of ease of construction, time constraints, maintainability, and user responsiveness. Our favorite software development story is about a manager who writes the following on the whiteboard at a user/programmer architecture meeting:

Choose Any Two:

- Good
- Fast
- Cheap

Having said that, we'll propose what would probably be the safest set of "best practices," taking into consideration that since we're writing about a series of products currently in beta and technologies that have appeared on the landscape rather recently, we haven't had a heck of a lot of time to practice.

Since the time that we went from monolithic mainframe computers to distributed systems, one of the main worries of software programmers revolves around locality of reference and speed of transport. That is, if all the software is not in one place and we don't have a direct wire to the user, not only does it matter how fast things go inside the computer, but also how long it takes to get the data from here to there and how many round-trips we make. If we have the world's fastest supercomputer that can do calculations at below light speed, but it takes five calls to it and one second per call, why use it, if our personal computer can calculate the same result in two seconds?

A lot of the choices we've shown earlier are locality-of-reference choices. Whether it's useful to transform columns and rows to objects on the server or middle tier depends on how many round-trips are made and how long they take—or how powerful the server hardware is on the machine that's running the database. Whether they should be transformed to objects at all is based on the premise that object-oriented design saves money in development and maintainability.

Another big consideration is interoperability. It's more a consideration for applications used for sales and marketing that must have the widest possible reach, although it certainly makes it easier to add new business partners if you're a company that's not large enough to dictate the terms of intercompany communication. XML is the technology used today to ease interoperability. Because of its structured nature and strong typing, it's a great improvement over the comma-separated text files, in any variety of flavors, of the past. The same features make it a choice for marshaling data to unlike platforms.

As an overly-simplistic generalization, we'd start with the following:

* Data stored in SQL Server in relational format
* Object-oriented concepts used on the middle tier and client
* XML used as a transport format and for interoperability

Relational databases have been around for over 20 years. They are a known quantity. Most programmers that we've run into know SQL; the rest at least know what it is. There are domains in which user-defined types are very useful, such as time sequence, spatial data, multimedia data, and others. In addition, it may be easier for programmers in some cases to store objects for synergy with the middle tier and client. In the current implementation of UDTs however, unless the UDT is binary ordered, any SELECT type of operation must materialize each instance, fetching it from disk, in turn to operate on it. That's the equivalent of a query that cannot use search arguments (a "non-SARGable" query). XML data storage and query are in their infancy. It is interesting that, except for full-text applications, the preferred/fastest way to store XML documents is to decompose the data. It sounds rather relational—data decomposition, that is. XQuery has a lot of promise, just as SQL had a lot of promise (but was slow) in 1980. It will be interesting to see what happens when vendors have a few years to optimize XQuery parsers after the spec is completed.

Inside the database, using a managed environment for procedures that must extend the capabilities of Transact-SQL in domain-specific ways is a big improvement over having every programmer use a low-level,

ype-unsafe language. The idea of .NET stored procedures replacing ex-
ended stored procedures—for the percentage of programmers that can't
vait for Microsoft to produce everything they want as extensions to
T-SQL or as system-defined functions—is an appealing one. Likewise,
intil T-SQL stored procedures can be compiled, processor-intensive calcu-
ations that should be done in the server should use compiled .NET code.
Data-intensive routines should probably still be done in T-SQL until access
hrough the `SqlServer` provider catches up, but the fact that there is an
optimized, in-database provider makes it a more difficult decision.

Object-oriented programming concepts are here to stay. Whether you
ike a thin veneer of object orientation over a traditional data API, à la
ADO.NET, or want to treat your data as objects ignoring the underlying
persistence format, you'll be programming with objects in your middle tier
and graphical user interface. Direct data binding, both to the `DataSet` and
to the `XPathDocument`, makes using just ADO.NET or `System.Xml` without having to change your data into domain-specific classes more viable.
After all, the two most ubiquitous user interface paradigms are the grid
(columns and rows) and the tree (data-centric XML). If you have a lot of
domain-specific logic, it makes sense to use a domain-specific object model.
ObjectSpaces used on the middle tier, combined with its optimizations,
and possibly used in conjunction with asynchronous client notifications
where real-time cache coherency is required, is a viable middle-tier model.
XML-relational mapping, combined with an XML-data-centric object-
oriented .NET programming language, is a possibility looming on the
horizon. Such an XML-data-centric language would make storing XML in
its native format more appealing as well.

Interoperability among computer hardware and software vendors has
been a problem since the second computer vendor appeared. Each vendor
used slightly different hardware, and software was built to take advantage of the byte-order and floating point number format for speed. In addition, these differences sifted up into network protocols. To transmit fewer
bytes in vendor-specific format using proprietary protocols was a laudable
goal. As computers and networks have gotten faster, the search for the
universal format and protocol (at the expense of speed and packet size)
has quickened. Distributed systems, including current distributed object
systems and remote procedure protocols, have always used binary.
DCOM/RPC and IIOP are both binary based. Agreement on a common
format beyond comma-separated text and a common communication protocol beyond TCP is starting to be more prevalent, based on XML. For

maximum interoperability, you can marshal data between unlike platforms in XML format. Even when XML is used as a format and protocol, however, there are still cases of "multiple standards" that are chances for mismatch. Two of the current examples are the competing ebXML and SOAP protocols and document-literal versus RPC-encoded Web Service message format.

For the best chance at interoperability today, you can expose your data through Web Services. Whether the XML packets are served out of the database directly (making the database a combined storage system and application server) or from a separate application server (such as IIS or COM+) depends on your network configuration. If you know your users all will have the SQL Server client libraries installed (they have been installed on every Windows-family OS machine for a while), TDS is still your best choice. All the APIs such as ADO.NET, ODBC, and ObjectSpaces use TDS.

The Database as Part of the Platform

With SQL Server 2005, there are some new features that integrate the database into the application development platform. SQL Server Notification Services, in addition to being an application framework, enables easier integration between the "home office" and mobile devices. SQL Server Service Broker brings asynchronous messaging, including reliable in-order delivery of complex domain-specific multimessage exchanges, client notifications, and messaging in XML format, into the database server. In addition, direct storage of XML and user-defined types mean that any processing can be moved closer to the server.

HTTP endpoints make SQL Server a Web server for database data and HTTP-based Web Services as well. Reporting Services allow you to store and generate reports directly inside the database. Support of user-defined types and the upcoming filestream data type enable SQL Server to become a multimedia server as well, and filestream support means that SQL Server is becoming more integrated with the Windows file system. Look for more integration of file system storage and database storage in the future. A future version of Microsoft Exchange Server will use SQL Server as its underlying data repository.

The Windows platform consists of operating systems for server, user, and mobile devices, with integrated graphical user interfaces; tools for consumers, office workers, and programmers; and an underlying development environment to permit building applications. Software vendors seem to be moving toward high-level, safe, intermediate language and execution engine–based APIs to permit adapting quickly to different hardware environments (like the plethora of mobile devices). In addition, there is a trend to ubiquitous information, available anywhere either through a central repository or sent to the appropriate user at her desk or mobile device, but secure, administered, backed up, and internally consistent at the same time. SQL Server 2005 is a central adapter and facilitator as the platform evolves.

Appendix A—.NET 101

.NET IS THE LATEST component platform from Microsoft and is probably one of the biggest changes for software developers since the move from the 16 bits MS-DOS platform to the 32 bits Windows NT platform.

This Appendix gives a brief introduction to .NET and the CLR for you that haven't done any development at all using .NET.

The Common Language Runtime

One of the biggest changes in .NET is that there is an execution engine, the CLR (Common Language Runtime), which handles a lot of the tasks you had to do previously. The runtime is responsible for among other things:

- memory management
- lifetime management (garbage collection),
- field layout
- thread management
- type safety
- IO management

These are things that you as a developer had to handle before the CLR and .NET, and if not handled correctly it often caused errors in the applications you wrote. You are giving up control in (hopefully) order to become more productive and less error prone.

This situation, where you as a developer give up control, is very much like when you went from MS-DOS to Windows NT. In MS-DOS you were used to handle physical memory and dealing with interrupts. You gave up control over this in favor of virtual memory and threads. Now you give up control over memory management among other things in favor of using types. A type is declared as a class and I cover later in this appendix how to create them. Figure A-1 shows a simplified picture of the new programming model, and as you see, your code now executes inside the CLR.

Having the code execute inside the CLR raises an interesting question: What do I do if I want to code against Windows, databases or anything else outside of the CLR? Because most of the resources we know and use in our applications are outside of the CLR.

Well, you can access the underlying platform features from your application, and Microsoft has put down a lot of work on making it possible to interoperate between managed and native code. However Microsoft discourages this and ships with the CLR a family of runtime libraries that provide a language-neutral way to write web programs, database access programs, XML programs and Windows programs. Most of these libraries/ routines reside in a DLL, MSCORLIB.DLL, which also contains the metadata for the CLR type system. The runtime is an environment that is being initialized by various host environments: It is being **hosted**. Windows in itself acts as a host, ASP.NET acts as a host and yes, SQL Server Yukon acts as a host.

What makes it possible to host the runtime from native code is a COM DLL, MSCOREE.DLL. This DLL exposes a number of API functions that

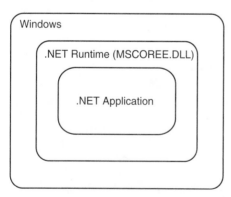

FIGURE A-1: The CLR Programming Model

are used to initialize and host the CLR. However, MSCOREE.DLL is just a thin layer over the runtime. As soon as it is initialized it loads either MSCORWKS.DLL or MSCORSVR.DLL dependent on certain rules. These two DLLs are the "real" runtime, and we discuss them in some more detail in Chapter 2. Because mscoree.dll is needed by every .NET application you do not need to explicitly link to it but the .NET compilers references it implicitly as well as Mscorlib.dll.

Development Languages

As opposed to other competing frameworks the CLR allows you to choose what development language you want to use. The only requirement is that the language has a compiler that produces CLR executables. This also means that the features of the CLR are available to all languages. For example; If the CLR allows implementation inheritance (which it does), then all languages can use that feature. Therefore, the choice of which development language to use can be based on what you feel comfortable with, not what restrictions the language puts on you. Microsoft ships compilers for five different languages together with the CLR:

* C# (C-Sharp)
* VB.NET (Viusal Basic.NET)
* MC++ (Managed C++)
* J Script
* MSIL (Microsoft Intermediate Language)

There are also compilers for other development languages available, ranging from Python to COBOL.

Looking at the list of languages above you may wonder what MSIL (IL) is. IL is the CLRs assembly language. It turns out that when you compile your code, the code is not compiled to machine code but as you can see in Figure A-2 to IL code, which can be seen as interpreted code.

Does this mean then that when your CLR application executes it executes interpreted code? No, because what happens when you run the application the IL code will be compiled into machine code as needed through the Just In Time Compiler (JITCompiler, also called JITter). After the application has been loaded it is the JITters responsibility to compile the IL code to machine code (native CPU instructions) when a function is first executed. The native code is saved, and for each subsequent time that particular function is called, the native code is executed without the JITter

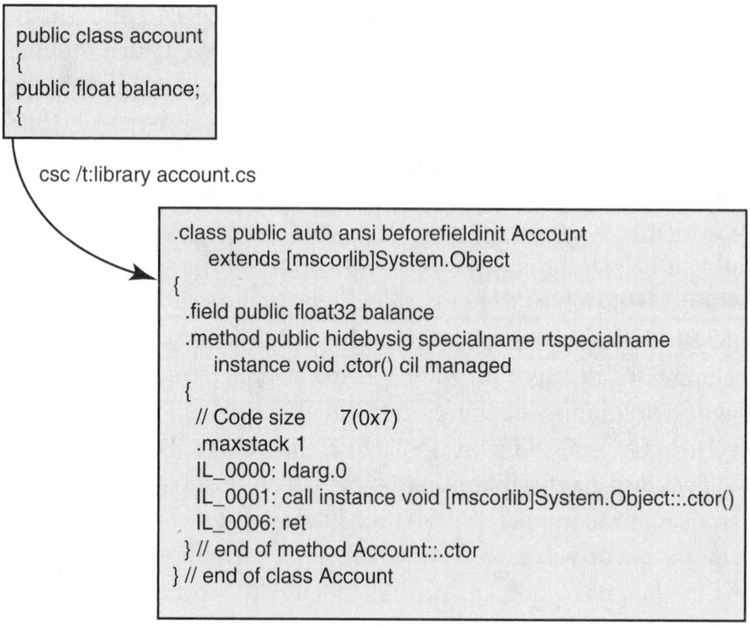

```
public class account
{
public float balance;
{
```

csc /t:library account.cs

```
.class public auto ansi beforefieldinit Account
      extends [mscorlib]System.Object
{
.field public float32 balance
.method public hidebysig specialname rtspecialname
      instance void .ctor() cil managed
{
  // Code size     7(0x7)
  .maxstack 1
  IL_0000: ldarg.0
  IL_0001: call instance void [mscorlib]System.Object::.ctor()
  IL_0006: ret
} // end of method Account::.ctor
} // end of class Account
```

FIGURE A-2: Compilation of Code into IL

being called. From a performance perspective there is a slight delay for the first call into a particular function, whereas subsequent calls are executed at optimal speed.

Because most applications execute the same methods repeatedly, the performance hit is not significant. However if you are worried over this you can use a specific tool in the .NET SDK, the NGen.exe, which compiles the IL code directly into native code.

Assemblies and modules

When you read about the .NET framework and the CLR, you are certain to come across the term Assembly. Before we can define what an assembly is we need to briefly discuss another term in the CLR; the Module.

Modules

Programs written for the CLR reside in modules. A CLR module is a byte-stream, typically stored as a file in the local file system or on a Web server. CLR modules contain code, metadata, and resources. The module's metadata describes the types defined in the module, including names, inheritance relationships, method signatures, and dependency information. The module's resources consist of static read-only data such as strings, bitmaps, and other aspects of the program that are not stored as executable code.

The compilers in .NET translate source code into CLR modules. The compilers accept a common set of command-line switches to control which kind of module to produce. You normally choose between producing an executable (EXE) or a library module (DLL). Listing A-1 shows how to use the C# compiler from the command line. The first un-commented line of code creates an EXE and the next un-commented code line creates a DLL. In both cases the source code file is called source.cs. It is the /target: switch that decides whether you want an EXE or a DLL. In Visual Studio .NET you make the same decision by choosing an executable or a class library as project type.

Listing A-1: Compiling from Command Line

```
//compiling an EXE
csc /target:exe source.cs

//compiling a dll
csc /target:library source.cs
```

Table A-1 shows what choices you have when deciding what you want to compile your C# application into.

Notice that you can not compile netmodules from Visual Studio .NET. You have to do it from command line.

In previous component model technologies, you had various ways of investigating the meta data of your component. In COM you used the

Table A-1: Target Switches

/Target: switch	Type of Module	Visual Studio Choice
exe	Console Application Executable	Console Application
winexe	Windows Forms Executable	Windows Forms
library	Class Library (DLL)	Class Library
module	netmodule[1]	N/A

Discussing netmodules is beyond the scope of what I cover here in this appendix. For a complete overview of assemblies versus modules, I recommend the book *Essential .NET* by Don Box.

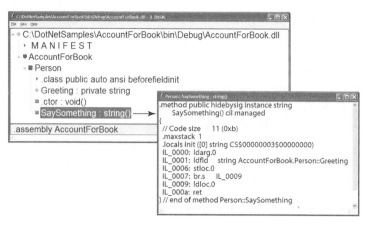

FIGURE A-3: Screenshot of ILDasm

OLEView.EXE to get type information and for non COM components you probably used DUMPBIN.EXE. In .NET you have various tools if you want to inspect a module or assembly.

One such tool is ILDasm.EXE which ships with the .NET Framework SDK. ILDasm stands for Intermediate Language Disassembler and you use ILDasm to view the metadata and disassembled code of your application in a hierarchical tree view.

Figure A-3 shows the metadata for a component, which consists of a class, called Person. Notice that you can see both private members as well as public members of the class. The figure also shows a method called SaySomething. As you can see, the method is fully disassembled and the code you see is the compiled IL code.

ILDasm is extremely useful, and I urge you to get to know it as it will help you when you develop applications as well as understanding what code from other developers do.

Assemblies

An assembly is the essential building block of your application and consists of a collection of modules and you can think of an assembly as the logical EXE or DLL. The assembly is also the fundamental unit for deployment and are used to package, load, distribute, and version CLR modules. The assembly consists of one or more modules, and the most common scenario is that your assembly has only one module. This is what you get when you compile a Visual Studio .NET project.

The main difference between a module and an assembly (between .net-module and EXE/DLL) is that in an assembly exactly one module holds not only the metadata for the particular module but also a manifest. The manifest is metadata with information about what types the assembly consists of, and in what files those types can be found. The module containing the assembly manifest will also have a list of externally referenced assemblies. This list consists of the dependencies of every module in the assembly, not just the dependencies of the current module.

In Listing A-2 you can see the manifest for the component which I showed the ILDasm for in Figure A-2. Notice that the only externally referenced assembly is MSCORLIB.DLL.

LISTING A-2: Manifest for Component

```
.assembly extern mscorlib
{
    .publickeytoken = (B7 7A 5C 56 19 34 E0 89 )
// .z\V.4..
    .ver 1:0:5000:0
}
.assembly account
{
    // -- The following custom attribute is added automatically, do not
uncomment  - - --
    //  .custom instance void
[mscorlib]System.Diagnostics.DebuggableAttribute::.ctor(bool,
    //
bool) = ( 01 00 00 01 00 00 )
    .hash algorithm 0x00008004
    .ver 0:0:0:0
}
.module account.dll
// MVID: {6802C533-1DBF-4E78-A61E-9B883723E40B}
.imagebase 0x00400000
.subsystem 0x00000003
.file alignment 512
.corflags 0x00000001
// Image base: 0x06cf0000
```

In Listing A-2 you can also see the version number for both the actual component as well as the version number for the referenced MSCORLIB. DLL. In the next section, I'll discuss Assembly names and versioning.

Assembly names and versions

If you have a COM background you probably remember that your components were uniquely identified by using a Globally Unique Identifier (GUID). In .NET, Microsoft has done away with the GUID's, and assemblies are identified by a four-part name. When the assembly is loaded by the runtime, this name is used to find the correct component. The nam consists of:

- friendly name
- locale
- developer
- version

The Name property of the assembly name corresponds to the under lying file name of the assembly manifest without any extension and thi is the only part of the assembly name that is not optional. The name i needed in simple scenarios to locate the correct component at load-time When building an assembly, this part of the assembly name is automati cally selected by your compiler based on the target file name. While strictl speaking, the Name of the assembly does not need to match the under lying file name, keeping the two in sync makes the job of the assembl resolver (and system administrators) much simpler.

Assembly names can contain a CultureInfo (locale) that identifies th spoken language and country code that the component has been devel oped for.

An assembly name can contain a public key (token) that identifies th developer of the component. An assembly reference may use either the ful 128 byte public key or the 8 byte public key token. The public key (token) i used to resolve file name collisions between organizations, allowing com ponents with the same name to coexist in memory and on disk. This is i each one originates from a different developer, each of whom is guaran teed to have a unique public key. When you give your components a pub lic key you give them a strong name.

All assembly names have a four-part version number (Version) o the form Major.Minor.Build.Revision. If you do not set this version num ber explicitly, its default value will be 0.0.0.0. The version number is se at build-time using a custom attribute in the source code or using a com mand line switch. The runtime is doing a version check during the loadin of the respective assemblies, which means you can differentiate betwee two assemblies with the same name and publisher based upon versio number. Notice that I said name and publisher. Publisher is the keywor here as the runtime only makes this version check for strongly name assemblies.

The CLR Type System

The CLR is all about types and some people go as far as saying that the CLR was developed to rectify previous models shortcomings in regards to type and type information. Be as that may be, types are essential in the CLR and there is a formal specification describing how to define types and how the types should behave. This formal specification is known as the Common Type System (CTS).

The CTS specifies among other things:

- what members a type can contain
- the visibility of types and members
- how types are inherited, virtual functions, and so on

The CTS also specifies that all types within the CLR have to derive from a predefined type, which acts as the root of the type system. This type is System.Object and because this type is the root, any member in the CLR can be assigned to variables of System.Object. This also means that every member in a class has a minimum set of behaviors (inherited from System.Object). Table A-2 shows the members of System.Object and what they do.

Because the CLR has a defined type system with System.Object as root, the runtime can make sure that the code we write is type-safe.

TABLE A-2: Members of System.Object

Member	Description
Equals	Checks if two instances of an object are equals
GetHashCode	Obtains the hash code for an object
GetType	Gets the type of the instance of an object
ReferenceEquals	Compares if the instrances of an object is the same instance
ToString	Gets a string representation of the current state of an object instance
Finalize	Allows an object to do cleanup before garbage collection
MemberwiseClone	Creates a bitwise copy of an instance

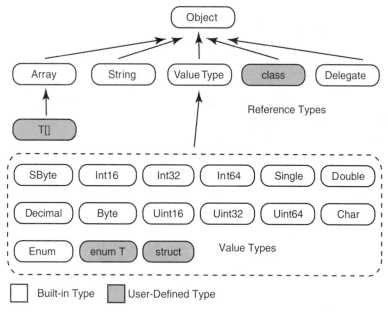

FIGURE A-4: The CLR Type System

Figure A-4 illustrates the CLR type system. Notice that the type system is logically divided into two subsystems; reference types and value types.

Programming languages in general has set of built-in types referred to as simple or primitive types. Normally they are `int`, `float`, `bool`, `char` and so on. You find in the CLR a rich set of these types, which Listing A-3 illustrates.

LISTING A-3: Types in the CLR Type System

```
struct Point
{
  bool outside;
  int X;
  int Y;
  float density;
}
```

In Figure A-4 you see some boxes which illustrates various user defined types based on the primitive types and in the following section will cover how to create these user defined types.

Classes and Types

When you create a type in the CLR, you ultimately derive from either `System.Object`, `System.ValueType` or `System.Enum`. Say for example that you want to create a new reference type called Person. The C# code for that would look something like in Listing A-4. However, because it is required that you ultimately derive from System.Object you can write your code as in Listing A-5.

LISTING A-4: Create Person class by Explicitly Derive from System.Object

```
class Person : System.Object {

}
```

LISTING A-5: Create Person class by Implicitly Derive from System.Object

```
class Person {

}
```

By this you can see that you indicate that you want to inherit from a type by using the colon after your class name followed by the type you want to derive from: `class YourType : TypeToDeriveFrom`.

Looking at the code Listing A-4 you may think that to create a value type you would write code something like: `class MyValueType : System.ValueType`. That is however not the case if you code in C# or Visual Basic.NET or some of the other programming languages in the CLR. The programming languages use their own concepts of types: such as class, interfaces, structures, enumerations, and so on. The runtime sees these ultimately as type definitions and it distinguishes between the various types based upon base class or attributes in the meta data.

When you use C #, you indicate what kind of type you want to create by using the syntax in Table A-3.

The keyword `struct` when creating a value type may be somewhat misleading and you may believe that the value type is only a data-structure and nothing more. That is not the case at all; a value type can have fields, methods, properties and so on, exactly like a class. The value type can also support interfaces.

TABLE A-3: Syntax for Type Definitions in C#

Syntax	Kind of Type
`public class MyClass { }`	Reference Type
`public struct MyValueType { }`	Value Type
`public interface MyInterface { }`	Interface
`public enum MyEnum { }`	Enumeration
`public delegate void MyDelegate { }`	Delegate

Visibility

When you create your types, you may want to decide how they should be accessible and if they should be visible to the outside world. For this reason (as I mentioned above) the CTS defines rules for visibility and access to types as well as members within a type. You decide what visibility and access you want by access modifiers. These access modifiers are keywords that you mark your type or member with. Table A-4 shows the

TABLE A-4: Access Modifiers

	C#	VB.NET	Visibility
Type	`public`	`Public`	Everywhere
	`internal` (default)	`Private` (default)	Inside of declaring assembly
Member	`public`	`Public` (default for methods)	Everywhere
	`internal`	`Friend`	Inside of declaring assembly
	`protected`	`Protected`	Inside of declaring type and subtypes
	`protected internal`	`Protected Friend`	Inside of declaring type and subtypes or other types inside of declaring assembly
	`private` (default)	`Private` (default for fields)	Inside of declaring type

access modifiers for both types as well as members. I will cover type members later in this appendix.

Listing A-6 shows some code that uses these access modifiers.

LISTING A-6: C# Code Making Use of Access Modifiers

```
public class Person {  //this class is visible to anyone

    private int    age;     //this is private
    string         name;    //this is also private
    public  string address; //this field is visible to anyone

    //this method is visible from anywhere inside the assembly
    internal void DoSomethingInternally() {}

    //this method is visible from anywhere
    public void DoSomethingPublically() {}

    //this method is visible only within the type
    //as the default is private
    void DoSomethingPrivately() {}
}
```

Instances

You access your types through instance variables. In Listing A-7 we could see how the type system were divided into reference types and value types.

A reference type variable contains the memory address of the particular object it refers to and is not the actual type instance. Before a reference type variable can be used, it must first be initialized to point to a valid object. Value types on the other hand are the instances themselves, not references. This means that a value type variable is useful immediately upon declaration.

In C# you initialize reference type by using the new keyword which will be translated into an IL newobj instruction. The corresponding keyword in VB.NET is New. The code in Listing A-6 shows how you initialize a reference type and a value type.

LISTING A-7: Initialization of Reference Types and Value Types

```
class RefPerson {
     public int age;
     public string name;
}
```

```
struct ValPerson {
  public int age;
  public string name;
}

class App {

 static void Main(string[] args) {
    //initilize the reference type
    RefPerson p = new RefPerson();
    p.age = 33;

    //initialize the value type
    ValPerson vp;
    vp.age = 33;

    //the following code will not compile as it is a reference type
    //there will be an error: 'Use of unassigned local variable 'p1''
    //RefPerson p1;
    //p1.age = 33;
  }
}
```

Notice that we get an error when we try to use an instance of the reference type without having initialized it with new. A value type can be initialized using new as well. The difference from a reference type is that the IL instruction will be initobj instead of newobj. Listing A-8 shows how a value type is initialized with the new keyword.

LISTING A-8: Initialize a Value Type with new

```
//the definition for RefPerson and ValPerson is the same as in
//   A-6
class App {

  static void Main(string[] args) {
    //initilize the reference type
    RefPerson rp = new RefPerson();
    rp.age = 33;

    //get a new variable for RefPerson
    RefPerson rp1 = rp;
    rp1.age = 35;

    //here you will see the same age (35) for both rp as well as rp1
    System.Console.WriteLine("Reference Types:\nrp's age is:
    {0}\nrp1's age is: {1}", rp.age, rp1.age);

    //initialize the value type
    ValPerson vp = new ValPerson();
    vp.age = 33;
```

```
   //get a new variable for ValPerson
   ValPerson vp1 = vp;
   vp1.age = 35;

   //vp's age is 33, vp1's age is 35
   System.Console.WriteLine("\nValue Types:\nvp's age is:
   {0}\nvp1's age is: {1}", vp.age, vp1.age);
  }
}
```

Listing A-8 also shows how assignment of variables works differently depending on the type. For reference types, the assignment results in a duplicate variable pointing to the same address space as the first. Subsequently when you change the state from one variable, that change is visible through the second variable as well.

The assignment for a value type results in copy of the instance, which is completely unrelated the first instance. Any change of state from one variable does not affect the other.

The main differences between reference and value types are:

- Reference types inherit from `System.Object` or a type that n its root of the inheritance chain has `System.Object`. A value type inherits from either `System.ValueType` or `System.Enum`[2] and those two types only. In other words, you can derive from a reference type but not a value type.

- A reference type is created on the garbage-collected heap whereas a value type normally is created on the stack. A value type can however be allocated on the heap. This happens for example when the value type is a member of a reference type.

- Another difference is that a reference type always is accessed via a strongly typed reference. A value type on the other hand can be accessed directly or via a reference.

From the perspective of the developer, there is not much difference between a reference type and a value type. A value type can have fields, methods, properties and so on, exactly like a reference type.

---

[2] `System.ValueType` derives from `System.Object` and `System.Enum` derives from `System.ValueType`.

Namespaces

When you develop your projects, the likelihood that you will have types related to each other is fairly big. These types may perhaps be located in different assemblies and you want to group them together. You accomplish this by using namespaces.

Namespaces provides a way to logically group types together. You use them both within your application to organize your types as well as an external organization system. When you look through the helper libraries in the CLR you find that namespaces are used everywhere. An example of this is the `System.Data` namespace. This namespace defines types that have to do with data access. It is further divided into namespaces for certain providers like the `System.Data.SqlClient` namespace or the `System.Data.OleDb` namespace.

The way you indicate that your type(s) belong to a namespace is by using the Namespace keyword as the code in Listing A-9 shows.

LISTING A-9: Creating a Namespace

```
namespace Developmentor {
  public class Person {

  }
  public class Instructor {

  }
}

public class Calculator {

}
```

In the code in Listing A-9 the Person and Instructor class both belongs to the `Developmentor` namespace. The `Calculator` class however does not belong to any namespace.

The CLR has no knowledge about namespaces and sees the `Person` type in Listing A-9 as being of the type `Developmentor.Person`. Subsequently when you want to create an instance of this type, you create an instance of `Developmentor.Person`.

With namespaces, the code to create an instance of a type can become pretty verbose as the code in Listing A-10 shows. Therefore, most compilers have mechanisms to make it easier for the programmer and reduce the

yping the programmer has to do. Listing A-11 shows how the C# developer can utilize the using directive.

ISTING A-10: Explicitly Typing Full Type Names

```
public class DataStuff {

  public void Main() {
    //from the compilers perspective as well as the CLR the type
    //is the full name including namespace
    System.Data.SqlClient.SqlConnection conn;
    conn = new System.Data.SqlClient.SqlConnection();
    //code to connect etc follows but not shown
  }
```

ISTING A-11: Use of the using Directive in C#

```
using System.Data.SqlClient;

public class DataStuff {

  public void Main() {

    SqlConnection conn;
    conn = new SqlConnection();
    //code to connect etc follows but not shown
  }
```

The directive for the VB.NET developer is Imports instead of using.

Members of Types

For a type to be useful, it has to contain something. This something is
member declarations which describes the state or behavior of the type. The
CLR supports six types of members and you can see them and their defini-
ions in Table A-5.

TABLE A-5: Type Members

Member	Definition
Fields	Data storage which can be read from or written to
Methods	Code that performs operations on the type. Also called functions.
Constructors	Special kind of method which is executed when the type is instantiated. A constructor can have parameters.
Properties	A special type of method which allows field-like syntax for setting or getting values of the state of the type.
Events	Allows a type to send notifications to a listening type or object
Types	A type can have nested types within it.

Listing A-12 shows code for a type containing the six members.

LISTING A-12: A Type with Members

```
using System;

class MyType {
  //field
  int _age;
  //field
  public string name;

  //constructor
  public MyType() {
    name = "Jim";
  }

  //method
  public void SayHello() {
    Console.WriteLine("hello");
  }

  //property
  public int Age {
    set { _age = value;}
    get {return _age;}
  }

  //this event doesn't do anything
  public event EventHandler MyEvent;
```

```
//nested type
class NestedType {
  //some members
}
}
```

Each member in a type is of a certain data-type. The data-type can be some of the built in types or a type that the developer has defined. Method and properties may not necessarily have a particular return type. You declare this in C# with the keyword void. In VB.NET you declare the method as a Sub.

Notice that the event MyEvent is not fully functional as it is not implemented through any methods. I do not intend to cover events in this appendix. I recommend the book Essential .NET by Don Box for a full coverage of events.

Fields and Properties

In the type in Listing A-12 I have declared two fields: _age and name. _age is private and name public. Declaring a field as public is not considered good coding practice as you should not allow direct access to the state of a type. Instead, fields should be accessed through properties. The property Age is an example of this.

Members can either be static members or instance members. The difference is that a static member is part of the type whereas an instance member is part of the object. A popular definition of static members is that they are global. Static members are accessed by the syntax: type.member, as opposed to the instance member, which is accessed through variable. member.

As I mentioned above in Table A-5, a property is a special type of method that allows field-like syntax to retrieve or set state values. To the CLR, a property is a binding of a name to one or two method declarations, one of which is the "getter," the other of which is the "setter." A property also has a type, which applies to the return type of the "getter" method and the last parameter to the "setter" method.

In C# you define a property as a special method which consists of a get part and a set part. Listing A-13 shows the code for a class with a property called Name. You make the property read only by omitting the set part. For a write only property, you omit the get part.

LISTING A-13: Property Declaration

```
public class Person {

  string _name;

  public string Name {
    set { _name = value;}
    get {return _name;}
  }
}
```

Note that when you assign a value to a property, the value is passed in through an intrinsic parameter called `value`. Listing A-14 shows how to access the `Name` property in `Person`.

LISTING A-14: Accessing a Property

```
public class App {

  string _name;

  static void Main() {
    Person p = new Person();

    //set the property this uses the value parameter
    p.Name = "Jim";

    //get the property
    System.Console.WriteLine(p.Name);
  }
}
```

Parameters and Methods

When you pass parameters to a method, the method's declaration determines whether the parameters will be passed by reference or by value. Passing parameters by value (the default) results in the method getting its own private copy of the parameter values. If the parameter is a value type, the method gets its own private copy of the instance. If the parameter is a reference type, it is the reference that is passed by value. The object the reference points to is not copied. Rather, both the caller and method wind up with private references to a shared object.

When the parameters are passed by reference the method gets a managed pointer pointing back to the caller's variables. Any changes the method makes to the value type or the reference type will be visible to the caller. Furthermore, if the method overwrites an object reference parameter to redirect it to another object in memory, this change affects the caller's variable as well. In C# you indicate you want to pass a parameter by reference by using the ref or out modifiers. Listing A-15 shows a method that takes three parameters, and how it is called. When you pass parameters by reference, you need to indicate that in the calling code by the ref or out modifiers.

LISTING A-15: Parameter Passing

```
public class Person {

  public int DoSomething(int x, ref string y, out int z) {
    //do something
    z = 100;
    //return a value
    return 99;
  }
}

public class App {
  static void Main() {
    int a = 99;
    string b = "Jim";
    int c;
    Person p = new Person();
    p.DoSomething(a, ref b, out c);
  }
}
```

The difference between the ref and out modifiers is that the out marked variable does not need to be initialized before calling. Subsequently it cannot be used in the method before it has been assigned a value from within the method.

Memory Management

Memory is allocated on the heap/stack by creating an instance of a type. The allocation is handled by the runtime and the developer does not need to explicitly care about memory management, field layout and so on. The same is true for reclaiming memory. The CLR is wholly responsible for reclaiming (deallocating) memory. The memory management is one of the primary benefits of the CLR's managed execution mode. So how does the CLR know when to reclaim memory?

When an object is created the CLR tracks the reference to this object (and all other objects references in the system). Because the CLR has this knowledge about the object references, it also knows when an object is no longer referenced. The memory allocated for the object can at this stage be reclaimed. The memory reclamation is done through garbage collection. Doing garbage collection affects performance. Because of this garbage collection does not necessarily happen as soon as the object is no longer referenced. Instead, the CLR performs garbage collection when certain resource thresholds are exceeded.

Normally the developer does not care about garbage collection, but if he wants explicit control, the System.GC class exposes the garbage collector programmatically. The Collect method tells the CLR to perform garbage collection as soon as the method is called. Be aware, however, that calling GC.Collect frequently can have a negative impact on performance.

Finalization and Destructors

Generally the objects do not need to know when they are garbage collected. Objects referenced by the one that is garbage collected will themselves be collected as part of the normal garbage collection run. Sometimes however there may be situations where an object holds references to resources that will not be garbage collected or scarce resources. Examples of this can be file handles, database connections, and so on. In a situation like that the object may wish to get a notification saying it is about to be collected.

This can be achieved by something called object finalization. System.Object exposes Finalize, which is a method that can be overridden in derived types. Finalization is however a technique which adds complexity. Because of this, you cannot implement Finalize directly in C#. Instead you implement a "destructor" which causes the compiler to emit your destructor code inside a Finalize method. Listing A-15 shows this. The compiler also makes sure that the Finalize method in your base class is called. As you see in Listing A-16 the destructor looks like a constructor but it is pre pended with "~".

LISTING A-16: Use of Destructor

```
public class Person {
  //other methods not shown

  ~Person() {
    //call your clean-up code
```

```
        `CleanUp();
    }

    void CleanUp() {
        //code to free scarce resources

    }
}
```

One thing to bear in mind about finalizers is that the finalize method may be called long after the object has been identified by the garbage collector. This is due to when the garbage collector tries to reclaim an object that has a finalizer, the reclamation is postponed until the finalizer can be called. Rather than reclaiming the memory, the garbage collector puts the object onto a specific finalization queue. A dedicated garbage collector thread will eventually call the object's finalizer and once the finalizer has completed execution, the object's memory is finally available for reclamation.

Disposing

If your objects have scarce resources, finalization may not be ideal based on the discussion in the preceding paragraph. Because of this Microsoft has introduced a standard idiom in the CLR, which provides an explicit method, which can be called when the user is done with the object. The method is `Dispose` and it is part of the `System.IDisposable` interface. In fact, it is the only method in that interface.

Implementing this interface indicates that the specific class requires explicit cleanup. It also indicates that it is the client programmers responsibility to invoke the `IDisposable.Dispose` method as soon as the referenced object is no longer needed. Listing A-17 shows a class that implements the IDisposable interface. Listing A-18 shows a client using the class in Listing A-16.

LISTING A-17: Implementing IDisposable

```
using System;
public class Person :IDisposable {
    //other methods not shown

    ~Person() {
        //call your clean-up code
        CleanUp();
    }
```

```
  void CleanUp() {
    //code to free scarce resources
  }

  public void Dispose() {
    GC.SuppressFinalize(this);
    CleanUp();
  }
}
```

You may wonder what the GC.SuppressFinalize(this) call does. As the Dispose method probably performs the same operations as your finalizer, you may not want the finalizer to run. The GC.SuppressFinalize (this) tells the runtime not to run the finalizer.

LISTING A-18: Using an IDisposable Class

```
class App {
  static void Main() {
    Person per = new Person();

    try {
      //do something with per
    }

    finally {
      per.Dispose();
    }
  }
}
```

As a C# developer you have the opportunity to let the compiler automatically call Dispose. The using statement (this is different from using for namespaces) does this. It allows the developer to declare one or more variables whose IDisposable.Dispose method will be called automatically. Listing A-19 shows client code utilizing using.

LISTING A-19: C# using

```
class App {
  static void Main() {
    using(Person per = new Person()) {
      //do something with per
    } //Dispose is called here
  }
}
```

Appendix B—
Tools Integration

THROUGHOUT THE BOOK, everything we have done can be accomplished with nothing more than the command line, a text editor, and the command-line compilers. However, most developers today are accustomed to using productivity-enhancing development tools—code editors with IntelliSense, tools to define database schemas, and so on. In fact, Microsoft is renowned for its development tools and Integrated Development Environments (IDEs).

In this appendix we will look at tool integration in SQL Server 2005 from a developer's perspective (as opposed to that of a DBA), and we will look at two tools specifically: SQL Server Management Studio (formerly known as SQL Server Workbench[1]) and Visual Studio 2005.

SQL Server Management Studio

If you have done any SQL Server development at all, prior to SQL Server 2005, you probably have come across SQL Server Enterprise Manager (EM) and SQL Server Query Analyzer (QA). You used EM to administer and manage SQL Servers and used QA to author queries, procedures, and

---

[1] The screenshots in this chapter were taken prior to the name change being complete. They read "SQL Server Workbench."

so on. Being used to this, you may be surprised the first time you open the Microsoft SQL Server program group and you cannot find either EM or QA. That's right, EM and QA have been replaced, and they have been replaced by one tool: SQL Server Management Studio.

One goal for SQL Server Management Studio is to give you one tool for managing and authoring SQL Servers. You should no longer need different tools for SQL Server, Analysis Services, SQL Server CE, and so forth. When you open SQL Server Management Studio the first time, you are greeted by an IDE looking like a mixture of EM, QA, and Visual Studio 2005, as Figure B-1 shows.

The similarities to Visual Studio 2005 are intended in order to make the development experience of SQL Server components and projects more like developing in Visual Studio 2005. By default, at the launch of SQL Server Management Studio, you are greeted with a dialog box to open the Object

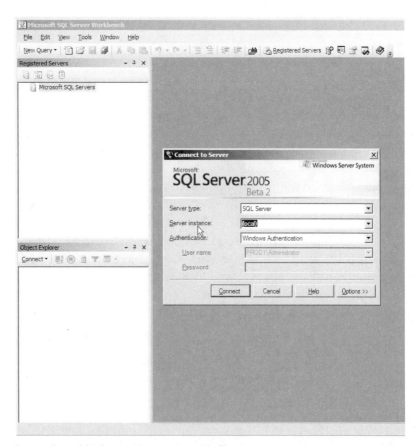

FIGURE B-1: SQL Server Management Studio

Explorer, as in Figure B-1. As with Visual Studio 2005, you have the option to customize the startup layout. This is accomplished from Tools | Options | Environment | SQL Environment Options.

On the left-hand side of Figure B-1, you can see two panes: Registered Servers and Object Explorer. The Registered Servers pane gives you the ability to register servers, as you did in EM.

Registering and Exploring Servers

When you register servers in SQL Server 2005, you can, as you could in SQL 2000, create server groups to more easily navigate between servers. You create a new server group or register a server by right-clicking in the Registered Servers pane and choosing New. This presents you with a dialog where you can choose to create a new group or register a new server. In Figure B-2, we have created two server groups, one for SQL 2005 Servers and one for SQL 2000 Servers, and registered one server in each group.

A difference from EM, as we mentioned earlier, is that in SQL Server Management Studio you can register all types of servers: SQL Server, Analysis Services, Report Server, and SQL Server CE. You choose what kind of server to register by using the icons at the top of the Registered Servers pane.

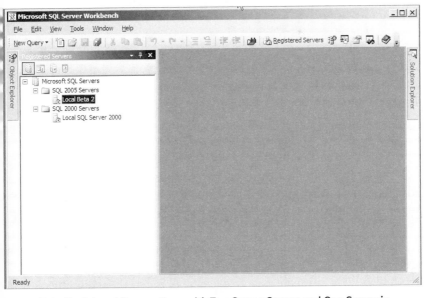

FIGURE B-2: Registered Servers Pane with Two Server Groups and One Server in Each Group

Notice in Figure B-2 that the Object Explorer pane is hidden and appears as a tab on the left-hand side of the screen. We have chosen to auto-hide the pane to gain more screen real estate. We accomplish this by clicking the pushpin icon in the top button bar of each window. When the icon points downward, the pane is docked, and when it points left, the pane auto-hides when the cursor is moved off the pane. Subsequently, it reappears when the cursor is moved back over the tab.

If you have used EM at all, you may expect that after registering a server, you can explore its objects and so on. Not so in SQL Server Management Studio. In SQL Server Management Studio the activities of registering a server are separate from those of connecting to a server and exploring the server's objects, and you need to explicitly connect to a server before you can do anything with it. In addition, you cannot explore a server's objects from the Registered Servers pane; you do it from the Object Explorer. Besides auto-connecting at startup, there are three ways to connect to a server in order to explore its objects.

- In Registered Servers, you right-click over the registered server and choose Connect. The connection appears in the Object Explorer.
- Also in Registered Servers, double-click the server name. The connection appears in the Object Explorer.
- Click the Object Explorer's Connect button and fill in the relevant information.

Figure B-3 shows a connected SQL 2005 Server. Notice the node for Notification Services, which lets you manage Notification Services. There is also a new Programmability node under a named database node. The Programmability node has further subnodes, depending on object type: Stored Procedures, Assemblies, and so forth.

Right-clicking an object in Object Explorer and choosing Properties opens a property dialog box, which enables you, as in EM, to manage and administer that particular object. One big difference, however, from EM is that the dialogs that open are nonmodal and resizable! Figure B-4 shows that we can have several dialogs open and do work both in Object Explorer and in the various dialogs.

The Object Explorer is based on the new SQL Server Management Object model (SMO), which can be seen as a superset of the old SQL-DMO model, and it is written in managed code. SMO is far beyond the scope of this appendix (and this book, for that matter), but if you are interested in

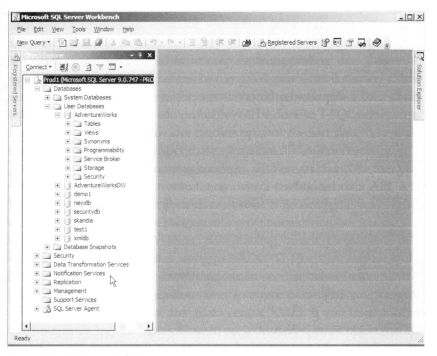

FIGURE B-3: A Connected Server

what you can do with SMO, we strongly recommend that you read about it in Books Online.

Authoring Queries

SQL Server Management Studio is not only a tool for management and administration of SQL Servers but also a tool for authoring all types of queries. To create an ad hoc query, from the File menu choose New | File (or use CTRL+N), and you are presented with the dialog in Figure B-5. As you can see, you are not limited to SQL Server queries; you can create, edit, and execute queries for SQL Server, Analysis Services, SQL CE, XML for Analysis (XMLA), and XQuery.

You achieve the same thing by clicking the New Query button on the toolbar, as in Figure B-6.

When you choose a query type, as in Figure B-5 or B-6, you launch a Query Editor window, which looks similar to what you would get using SQL Query Analyzer in previous versions of SQL Server. One big difference, however, is that by default you now can edit queries in disconnected

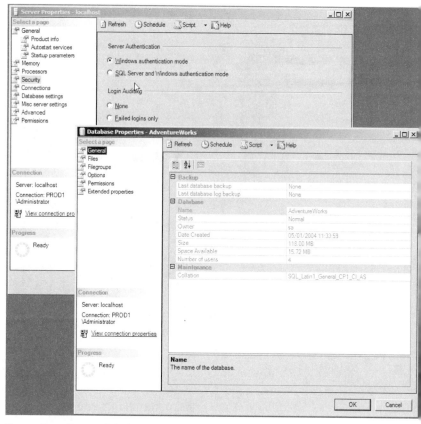

FIGURE B-4: Nonmodal Dialog Boxes

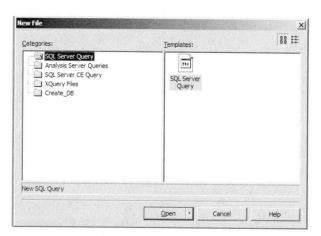

FIGURE B-5: New File Dialog

Figure B-6: New File from the New Query Button

mode. In other words, you can create or edit a query without having to choose a server and database. You can also disconnect a Query Editor window from one server and connect it to another. If you create or edit queries in disconnected mode, you will not be asked for a connection until you execute (CTRL+E or F5) or parse (CTRL+F5) the query. You can also explicitly connect to a server through the Connect option on the File menu.

Query Editor windows now appear as tabs within the SQL Server Management Studio IDE, just as in Visual Studio 2005, and the different Query Editor windows can be independently connected or disconnected. Figure B-7 illustrates this with two Query Editor windows. SQLQuery2 is disconnected, and the other Query Editor window, SQLQuery3, is connected, as we can see from the tab. The tab shows, in addition to the name of the Query Editor window, what server you are connected to as well as what user name you are connected as.

An improvement borrowed from Visual Studio 2005 is line revision marks. These are yellow and green lines appearing on the left-hand side of the Query Editor window while you write code, and they allow you to see changes you have made during a coding session. Code adjacent to a yellow line has been added since you last saved, and a green line indicates code unchanged since the last save.

Figure B-8 shows another feature of the IDE: line folding. When you are coding in a Query Editor window, the IDE automatically creates a block of code for each batch statement. This allows you to fold and unfold your individual batch statements. In Figure B-8 we have three batches, and the second batch is folded.

Notice also in Figure B-8 that you can view the folded code by hovering the cursor over the folded block (the bordered rectangle with three dots).

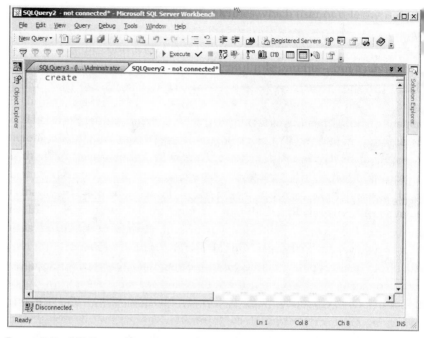

FIGURE B-7: SQL Server Management Studio with Two Query Editor Windows

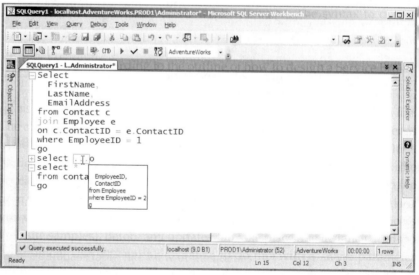

Figure B-8: Line Folding in a Query Editor Window

For more powerful query editing, SQL Server Management Studio introduces something called Assisted Editors. They can be seen as more powerful templates and are miniapplications living inside the Query Editor. You either invoke them from the Assisted Editor toolbar or drill down in your database of choice from the Object Explorer. Right-click under the Programmability node on the type of object you are interested in, and you are presented with a window looking something like Figure B-9 (we have already started editing the function within the editor). Figure B-9 shows the Assisted Editor for a scalar-valued function, and the upper part of the editor allows you to name the function, define parameters and the return type, and so on, whereas the lower part is used to edit the actual code for the function.

When you are done editing the object, you save it to the database by right-clicking the code canvas, as you can see from Figure B-9, and choosing Save. Assisted Editors are not only for T-SQL objects, you can use them for cataloging assemblies as well.

When editing queries, you can get help from templates. Templates are .tql files; several templates are delivered with SQL Server 2005, and you can create your own templates as well. To view templates, you choose Template Explorer from the View menu or use the keyboard shortcut

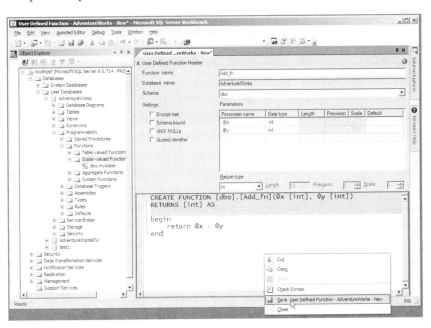

FIGURE B-9: Assisted Editor for a Scalar-Valued Function

CTRL+ALT+T. That brings up the Template Explorer pane, where you can choose the template you want to use.

Projects and Solutions

When you looked at some of the previous figures, you may have noticed a tab on the right-hand side of the IDE named Solution Explorer. That tab is there because editing queries in SQL Server Management Studio is solution based, and when you create a new query, you will also get a new solution. Each subsequent new query (Query Editor window) will then be added to that particular solution. Figure B-10 shows an example of this, where we have two Query Editor windows. When we view the Solution Explorer pane, we see that they are represented as two files under the Miscellaneous Files node.

If we were to close down SQL Server Management Studio without first having saved, we'd be asked if we wanted to save the files. In this scenario, the solution would not be saved. So in order to better organize files and development projects, we can associate a solution with one or more projects, exactly as you do in Visual Studio 2005. A project is a way of organizing files in a logical way, where you assign a name to the project and a location where the project should be stored on disk. To create a new project, you select New Project from the File menu, or use CTRL+SHIFT+N. Figure B-11 shows the dialog you are presented with.

FIGURE B-10: Solution Explorer Pane

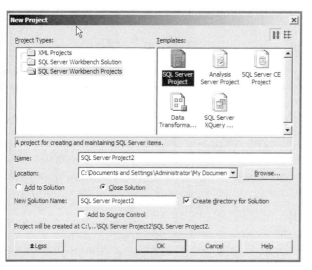

FIGURE B-11: SQL Server Projects

After you have created the project, there will be nodes in the Solution Explorer pane for Connections, Queries, and Miscellaneous Files. Right-click the project node in the Solution Explorer to add new items to the project (CTRL+SHIFT+A). By right-clicking any of the nodes in the Solution Explorer, you can add the files to a source control system.

Now that we have covered some aspects of SQL Server Management Studio, let's look at the new features for SQL Server 2005 developers in Visual Studio 2005.

Visual Studio 2005

With the release of Visual Studio 2005, Microsoft has as one of its goals making database development against SQL Server 2005 more transparent than it has been. In previous versions of Visual Studio, there was a specific project type for the database developer: the Database Project. It allowed the developer to connect to a database and create script files for stored procedures, triggers, and so on, and it had a graphical query designer. This project type still exists in the Visual Studio 2005 release, and it has been somewhat enhanced with predefined templates in the query designer for Common Table Expressions and Derived Tables.

What is more interesting, however, is the support in Visual Studio 2005 to develop, deploy, and debug SQL Server 2005 procedures, functions, triggers, and so on. Figure B-12 illustrates this by showing the new SQL Server Project project type in C#.

This project type is not limited to C# developers; it exists for all the different languages that Visual Studio 2005 supports. When choosing this project type, you have the ability to choose a database to connect to. This is done by choosing an existing database reference (connection) from the Add Database Reference dialog box or by adding a new reference. Figure B-13 illustrates how we add a new database reference by using the Connection Properties dialog box.

Now that we have chosen the database reference, the setup of the project is done, and the result is an empty workspace and, compared with a Class Library Project, two additional references:

- `Microsoft.VisualStudio.DataTools.SqlAttributes`
- `sqlaccess`

The reference to `sqlaccess.dll` should be familiar to you, since it is the in-process SQL Server provider. The `Microsoft.VisualStudio.DataTools.SqlAttributes` reference is a Visual Studio–specific reference,

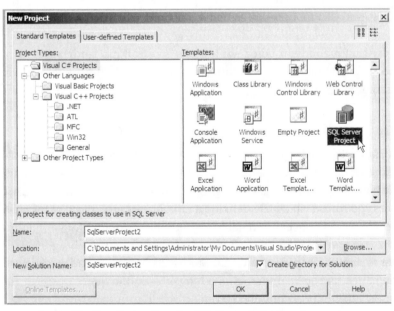

FIGURE B-12: The New Project Type for SQL Server 2005 Development: SQL Server Project

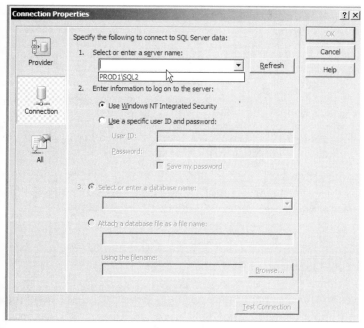

FIGURE B-13: Choosing or Creating a New Database Connection

and we cover the need for it later in this chapter. Another difference compared with a Class Library Project is the empty workspace. Before writing any code, you need to add a new item (Project | Add New Item or File | Add New Item or CTRL+SHIFT+A). Adding a new item presents a project-specific Add New Item dialog box, as in Figure B-14. As you can see from the figure, you have the choice of five SQL Server 2005 templates, depending on what kind of SQL Server 2005 object you want to create, and one Class template.

In Figure B-14 we chose the User-Defined Function template and gave it a name of Math. That produces a source file called Math.cs, containing a public partial class, UserDefinedFunctions, and a static public function, Math, as you can see in Figure B-15.

Deployment Attributes

Notice in Figure B-15 that the function is decorated with the SqlFunc attribute. You may remember from Chapter 3 that we discussed the Sql Function attribute and how you define through that attribute the behavior of the function. The SqlFunc attribute is applied by Visual Studio 2005 and has no relationship to the SqlFunction attribute. The SqlFunc

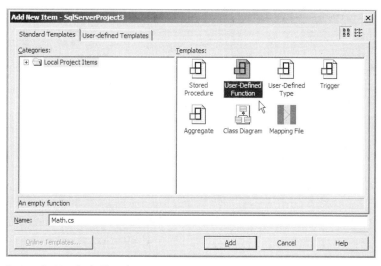

FIGURE B-14: Code Templates

attribute lives in the `Sql` namespace in the `System.Data.dll` assembl
together with other Visual Studio 2005–specific attributes (it used to b
in the `SqlAttributes` namespace in the `Microsoft.VisualStudio`
`DataTools.SqlAttributes.dll` assembly). Table B-1 lists the Visual Stu
dio 2005 attributes and their definitions.

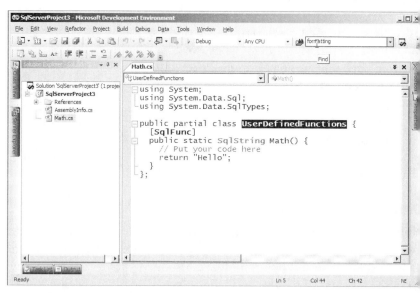

FIGURE B-15: Source File

TABLE B-1: Visual Studio 2005 Attributes

Attribute	Definition
SqlAssemblyAttribute	Definition of an assembly
SqlFuncAttribute	Definition of a function
SqlProcedureAttribute	Definition of a procedure
SqlTriggerAttribute	Definition of a trigger

These attributes define for Visual Studio 2005 at deployment time what type of object (procedure, function, trigger) the methods should be created as in SQL Server 2005. It is worth saying again that these attributes are Visual Studio 2005 specific and are ignored if you catalog the assembly through other means.

All the attributes in Table B-1 except for the SqlTriggerAttribute have a no-args default constructor plus a constructor that accepts a string. This string defines the name of the object created in SQL Server 2005 (the default is the name in the native method). The SqlAssemblyAttribute has a public Authorization property that allows the developer to set the owner role name of the assembly in SQL Server 2005.

The SqlTriggerAttribute, finally, has these two constructors.

- SqlTriggerAttribute(string target, string forClause)— Sets the name of the table or view for which the trigger is created and the type of trigger: INSERT/UPDATE/DELETE.

- SqlTriggerAttribute(string name, string target, string forClause)—The first argument is the name of the trigger, and the other two are the same as for the previous constructor.

Now that we have covered the various attributes, it is time to look at how to build and deploy the assembly.

Build and Deploy

The build part of the assembly is no different from any other Visual Studio 2005 assembly. You either use the Build menu or CTRL+SHIFT+B (note that in some pre-beta builds of Visual Studio 2005, CTRL+SHIFT+B is replaced by F2). After the assembly has been built, it is time to deploy it.

Of course, we can deploy the assembly in the same way we have done previously in this book: by running CREATE ASSEMBLY from SQL Server Management Studio. We mentioned, however, in the beginning of the Visual Studio section in this chapter that Microsoft has tried to make the development process for SQL Server 2005 more transparent. Part of the transparency is that the developer should not have to leave Visual Studio to deploy the assemblies.

Therefore, when you look at the build menu in Figure B-16, you can see that there are a couple of additional menu items: Deploy Solution and Deploy <ProjectName>. As the names imply, these are used for deploying the assembly to the database.

When the assembly is built and you choose Deploy Solution or Deploy <ProjectName>, Visual Studio 2005 creates the necessary SQL statements to catalog the assembly and create functions, procedures, and triggers in the database based on the source code. These statements are then executed against the database. You can verify this by running the SQL Profiler. The result of the deployment is shown in the Output window of Visual Studio 2005.

One major drawback in this version of Visual Studio 2005 is that the assemblies were created with the permission set EXTERNAL_ACCESS, and i

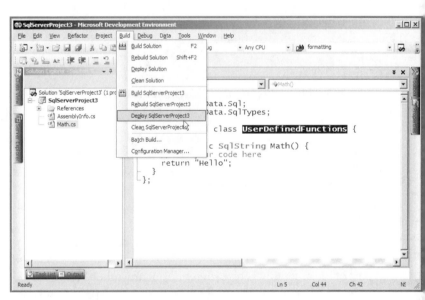

FIGURE B-16: Build and Deploy Menu

could not be changed from within Visual Studio 2005.[2] In later releases there will be a property setting to decide what permissions should be granted to the assembly. Finally, it is time to test the code.

Executing and Debugging the Code

To test the code, we can always execute the procedure or function created in the database from inside SQL Server Management Studio. However, it would be nice if this could also happen from inside Visual Studio 2005, and this is what happens when you choose Start from the Debug menu (or press F5).[3] At this stage, you can set breakpoints in your CLR code, and step through and debug the code as in any other .NET project.

It is not necessary to run the project from inside Visual Studio 2005 in order to debug the CLR code. If the debug symbols of the CLR assembly

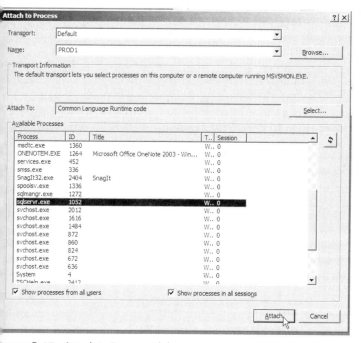

FIGURE B-17: Attach to Process Dialog

This appendix was written using an early pre-beta version of Visual Studio 2005.

In pre-beta versions of Visual Studio 2005, what made the execution of the code happen was file named debug.sql. At the time of the writing of this appendix, it is unclear whether the file will be in the released beta.

have been loaded into SQL Server, the procedure or function can be executed from inside SQL Server and stepped through in the Visual Studio 2005 debugger. To make this work, the debugger needs to be attached to the SQL Server process by following these steps.

1. From the Debug menu, choose Attach to Process.
2. In the Attach to Process dialog, choose the `sqlservr.exe` process, as in Figure B-17. Make sure the "Show processes from all users" and "Show processes in all sessions" check boxes are checked.
3. Set breakpoints in the CLR source file.
4. Execute the T-SQL code.

Bibliography

Ambler, Scott. "The Fundamentals of Mapping Objects to Relational Databases." http://www.agiledata.org/essays/mappingObjects.html, 2003–2004 (latest edition).

ANSI/ISO/IEC International Standard (IS). Database Language SQL. 1992, 1999, 2003.

Beauchemin, Bob. *Essential ADO.NET*. Boston: Addison-Wesley, 2002.

Brundage, Michael. *XQuery: The XML Query Language*. Boston: Addison-Wesley, 2004.

Date, C. J., and Hugh Darwin. *An Introduction to Database Systems, Sixth Edition*. Boston: Addison-Wesley, 2001.

Ewald, Tim. *Transactional COM+*. Boston: Addison-Wesley, 2001.

Gulutzan, Peter, and Trudy Pelzer. *SQL-99 Complete, Really*. Lawrence, Kansas: R&D Books, 1999.

Henderson, Ken. *The Guru's Guide to SQL Server Architecture and Internals*. Boston: Addison-Wesley, 2004.

Katz, Howard, ed. *XQuery from the Experts*. Boston: Addison-Wesley, 2003.

Melton, Jim. *Advanced SQL:1999: Understanding Object-Relational and Other Advanced Features*. San Francisco: Morgan Kaufmann, 2001.

Melton, Jim, and Alan Simon. *SQL:1999: Understanding Relational Language Components*. San Francisco: Morgan Kaufmann, 2001.

W3C XQuery Specifications. http://www.w3c.org/XML/Query#specs.

ndex

Platform Invoke (PInvoke) mechanism, 3, 31
Poet database, 460
Point class, 386–387, 390–391
Policies, password, 186–188
PORTS parameter, 352
Post-Schema-Validation InfoSet (PSVI), 17, 309
Power users, Web Services for, 362
Predicates
in OPath, 493–494
query, 315
Preemptive thread scheduling, 31
Prepare method, 108
Primary indexes, 282
Primary keys
in ObjectSpaces mapping, 476
in XML mapping, 444
Primary OPath operators, 491
principal_id column, 46
Principals in security, 179–183
Principle of least privilege, 175
priority column, 528
private access modifier, 632
PRIVATE_KEY FILE argument, 551
PROCEDURE_NAME argument, 525, 537
Procedures, 75–80
execution contexts in, 194–197
vs. functions, 81
stored. *See* Stored procedures
Process data component in SSB flow, 545
Processes for runtime hosts, 35–37
processing-instruction function, 288
Programmability node, 649, 653
Programming
models for, 95–99
new features in, 612–613
Prologs, query, 310
Promotable transactions, 428–429
PromptPassword method, 433
Properties
in CLR type system, 638–640
for UDTs, 153–155
protected access modifier, 632
Protection attributes, 38–39
ProtocolExecutionSettings node, 607
ProtocolName element, 607
ProviderBase namespace, 413
ProviderFactory class, 410

Providers
for events, 562, 580, 582–583, 587–591
in-process. *See* In-process data providers
.Net, 7
Providers node, 583
PSVI (Post-Schema-Validation InfoSet), 17, 309
public access modifier, 632
Public keys in assembly names, 628
PubsProc class, 111
PulleyDistance function, 56–58, 61

Q

QA (Query Analyzer), 21, 645, 649
QName data type, 274
Quantum in Notification Services, 567
Queries
in Common Query Abstraction, 439
nested, 292–293
ObjectSpaces models for, 488–490
optimizing, 451–453
parts of, 310
predicates for, 315
recursive, 243–249
XML, 17–19. *See also* XPath; XQuery engine
Query abstraction, 23
Query Analyzer (QA), 21, 645, 649
Query Editor window, 649–654
query method, 321, 325–329, 335
Query plans, 223
Query property, 489
QueryJoin property, 489
QueryOrderBy property, 489
QuerySelectList property, 489
Queue class, 507
queue_name argument
in CREATE QUEUE, 525
in CREATE SERVICE, 529
Queues in SSB, 506–509, 516, 524–528
queuing_order column, 528

R

RAISERROR command, 125, 264
RANK function, 259–260
Ranking functions in T-SQL, 258–263
RDS (remote data services) architecture, 20
READ COMMITTED transaction isolation, 213–217

T

Microsoft .NET Development Series

.NET Framework Standard Library Annotated Reference
Volume 1

Microsoft .NET Framework Class Libraries Team
Brad Abrams, Editor

0321154894

.NET Web Services
Architecture and Implementation

Keith Ballinger

0321113594

Essential .NET
Volume 1
The Common Language Runtime

Don Box
with Chris Sells

0201734117

Graphics Programming with GDI+

Mahesh Chand

0321160770

The C# Programming Language

Anders Hejlsberg
Scott Wiltamuth
Peter Golde

0321154916

A First Look at ADO.NET and System Xml v 2.0

Alex Homer
Dave Sussman
Mark Fussell

0321228391

A First Look at ASP.NET v.2.0

Alex Homer
Dave Sussman
Rob Howard

0321228960

The Common Language Infrastructure Annotated Standard

James S. Miller
Susann Ragsdale

0321154932

Essential ASP.NET with Examples in C#

Fritz Onion

0201760401

Essential ASP.NET with Examples in Visual Basic .NET

Fritz Onion

0201760398

Building Applications and Components with Visual Basic .NET

Ted Pattison
with Dr. Joe Hummel

0201734958

Windows Forms Programming in C#

Chris Sells

0321116208

Windows Forms Programming in Visual Basic .NET

Chris Sells
Justin Gehtland

0321125193

The Visual Basic .NET Programming Language

Paul Vick

0321169514

Programming in the .NET Environment

Damien Watkins
Mark Hammond
Brad Abrams

0201770180

Pragmatic ADO.NET
Data Access for the Internet World

Shawn Wildermuth

0201745682

For more information go to www.awprofessional.com/msdotnetseries/